GLOBAL HISTORY

GEOPOLITICAL PATTERNS
& CULTURAL DIFFUSION

Authors:

Sue Ann Kime

Paul Stich

Editor:

Wayne Garnsey

Illustrations, and Artwork:

Eugene B. Fairbanks

Cover Design:

Wayne Garnsey & Paul Stich

N & N Publishing Company, Inc.
18 Montgomery Street   Middletown, New York 10940

www.nandnpublishing.com   (800) NN4 TEXT   email: nn4text@warwick.net

Special Appreciation

Dedicated to our students, with the sincere hope that

GLOBAL HISTORY — GEOPOLITICAL PATTERNS & CULTURAL DIFFUSION

will further enhance their education and better prepare them
with an appreciation and understanding of the people
and historical events that have shaped our world.

Special Credits

Thanks to our many colleagues who have contributed their knowledge, skills, and years of experience to the making of our endeavor. To these educators, our sincere thanks
for their assistance in the preparation of this manuscript:

Kenneth Garnsey
Fran Harrison
Howard Van Ackooy
Maureen Van Ackooy

Reference

Top-rate references are most important to consistency in word and fact. We are grateful to the
authors, editors, contributors, and publishers of two of the finest resources:

The American Heritage Dictionary© – fundamental definitions and appropriate word usage
[available on CD-ROM through SoftKey Multimedia Inc, Cambridge, MA]

1999 Grolier Multimedia Encyclopedia© – date and information varifications
[available on CD-ROM through Grolier Interactive Inc, Danbury, CT]

© Copyright 1999, Revised 2000
N & N Publishing Company, Inc.
18 Montgomery Street   Middletown, New York 10940
www.nandnpublishing.com   (800) NN4 TEXT   email: NN4TEXT@aol.com

Soft Cover Edition: ISBN # 0-935487 66 2
2 3 4 5 6 7 8 9 0 BMP 2005 2004 2003 2001 2000

Printed in the United States of America, Book-mart Press, NJ

SAN # 216 - 4221

TABLE OF CONTENTS

THEMES & CONCEPTS

HISTORY
Change
Choice
Culture
Diversity
Empathy
Identity
Interdependence

POLITICAL SCIENCE
Citizenship
Civic Values
Decision-Making
Government
Human Rights

Values

GEOGRAPHY
Environment
Environment & Society
Human Systems
Physical Systems
Places & Regions
Uses of Geography
World in Spatial Terms

ECONOMICS
Economic Systems
Factors of Production
Needs & Wants
Scarcity
Technology

Unit 1

4 MILLION PLUS YEARS

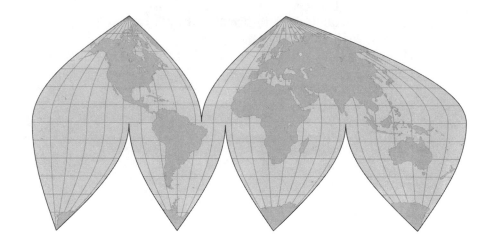

 Hominids in Africa (4 million BC)

 Neolitic Revolution (60,000 BC)

INTRODUCTION TO GLOBAL HISTORY

3000–

Ancient Civilizations & Religion (4000 BC – 500 AD)

2000–

1000–

BC
0–
AD

Expanding Zones of Exchange and Encounter (500 AD – 1200 AD)

1000–

Global Interactions (1200 – 1650)
First Global Age (1450 – 1770)
Age of Revolutions (1750 – 1914)
Half Century of Crisis & Achievement (1900 – 1945)
Homer's Illiad & Odyssey (the world since 1945)

2000–

Global Connections & Interactions
(Present to Future)

Writing and imagination can change your world.

PREFACE

Global history is not a romance of the past. It is reality. It makes sense of larger patterns of the past. It examines chains of events that have affected people of different cultures.

Understanding the human experience in a broad context helps us become more aware of ourselves. Understanding the human experience is vital to our way of life, too. As citizens, we are participants in a democracy. We must make thoughtful decisions to keep us free, to have dignity, and to achieve happiness. Simply put, democracy dies without our participation.

To keep democracy alive, citizens must realize that free societies evolved from struggles that people endured over many centuries. To appreciate that fact and act on it, we must be conscious of the problems people face and the sacrifices they must make.

Making rational choices flows from knowing alternatives. A grounding in the past allows us to analyze and select truth, recognize bias, and avoid delusion. Reflection on past experience is the only realistic guide to the present and the future. It gives us a point of reference from which we can make sound choices.

Achieving a global history point of reference requires mastering basic learning standards. Social studies learning standards are tools and methods that students need to analyze the vast amounts of detail. The standards include historical interpretation, geographic awareness, economic assessment, and political analysis.

STANDARDS OF THE SOCIAL SCIENCES

HISTORY

HISTORICAL SKILLS AND ANALYSIS

In the broadest sense, **history** is knowledge of the past. To reconstruct the past, historians analyze physical evidence including oral traditions, art, folklore, written records, and even climatic changes.

Key Terms
citizen participation
democracy
Divine Right
governance
history (knowledge of the past)
hypothesis (thesis)
interdependence
Market – Command – Tradition } Mixed
power
primary source
scarcity
secondary source
sovereignty
spatial relationships
trade-offs

History is also a perpetual dialog among historians. New sources from research or archeology may prove or disprove long-accepted interpretations. Also, they can lead scholars to new hypotheses. A **hypothesis** is a tentative explanation that accounts for a set of facts. For example, there is no evidence of a separate indigenous race in the Americas. All available evidence to date has led to the hypothesis that Amerindian ancestors crossed an extinct land bridge in the area of the Bering Strait from Asia. However, this and any other hypotheses can be tested by new evidence found by further investigations. Students of global history must observe how different historians use facts and interpretations to:

- support hypotheses
- identify issues, values, differences of opinion, and raise relevant questions
- formulate a position and explore its consequences

Historians look at **primary sources** (originated at the time being studied) and **secondary sources** (analyses written later by

Primary Sources	Secondary Sources
documents	histories
journals	epic poems based on oral
diaries	traditions
autobiographies	broad-based commentaries
eyewitness interviews	paintings, sculptures,
artifacts	monuments
quantitative data	songs, poems, operas
graphs	(all created after an event
photos	transpires)

historians). Examining primary sources develops skills in determining the value of solid evidence (tests of credibility). Looking at secondary sources develops a sense of perspective and recognition of patterns and trends. Secondary sources give a "big picture" to help see how others interpret primary evidence.

Students must learn to use a multiplicity of sources to:

• analyze the assumption(s) from which a narrative of events was constructed
• compare what authors include and exclude from a narrative
• distinguish fact from opinion
• understand the causes and consequences of people's actions

• understand the relationships that civilizations have to each other in shaping events
• see the dynamic interplay of differing interpretations

The availability, quality, and quantity of information gathered determine the scope and accuracy of the historian's investigation. No matter how painstaking the research, interpretation and presentations can be very subjective (personal). Certain data will impress one scholar more than another, resulting in a particular analysis (point of view). Often, conflicting interpretations arise and become controversial for years.

Skill Activity

Below is a list of materials reviewed by a student researching the sinking of the British White Star Line's luxury liner *Titanic*, 14-15 April 1912:

• Eaton, J. and Ballard, R., *The Discovery of the Titanic*, 1989 (documentary account of underwater exploration for the ship's remains)
• fragment of the *Titanic's* log 14 April 1912 recovered by search submarines in 1993
• Lord, Walter, *A Night To Remember*, 1955 City: NY, Holt (novel)
• "Titanic," *Encyclopedia Britannica*, Vol. 28, 1995 ed.
• "Titanic Hits Iceberg; 1,500 Drown in Icy North Atlantic - Survivors Say Ship Lacked Sufficient Lifeboats" *New York World*, 16 April 1912 (front page newspaper article)

Answer the following questions based on the information given above.

1 Which item is primary source?
   1 the novel
   2 the encyclopedia article
   3 the 1989 exploration documentary
   4 the fragment of the ship's log

2 Which item would give the student the broadest picture of the causes and effects of the sinking?

3 Why would the student bother to use the Walter Lord novel? Why use Eaton and Ballard's exploration book?

Note to Student: On global history exams, questions on specific factual data or graphics usually come in series. The first one is usually directly from the material presented. The next question(s) ask you to apply broader historical concepts and contexts to the material.

CONNECTIONS AND INTERACTIONS OF PEOPLE ACROSS TIME AND SPACE

Sometimes we think of the past as dead and we ignore the powerful influence it has had on modern life. The forces that moved Christopher Columbus to venture across the Atlantic created the world we live in just as much as Congress approving funds for space exploration.

Actions taken in isolated places often influence life beyond that time and place. For example in Switzerland in 1863, Jean Henri Dunant formed a volunteer society to help people beset by difficulties. Today, his movement (now officially called the International Movement of the Red Cross and Red Crescent) aids millions in wars and natural disasters and promotes cooperation throughout the world. Another example is the 3,000 year-old caste system of India. It still affects the modern nation's political, economic, and social life.

Across time and space, people have faced common issues and situations. Change is important in life, but continuity is a great force throughout the world. The more students read and learn about history, the more they appreciate that patterns of behavior are often remarkably predictable. Reacting to oppression, coping with geographic factors, tradition clashing with modern ways, leaders influencing events, and people migrating for economic improvement are all constant themes in history. Since they are common and very powerful forces, they are often the focus of historians' work.

TIME FRAMES AND PERIODIZATION

Developing a sense of time helps students grasp patterns of human interaction. Knowing the meaning of the BC/AD division, centuries, and decades creates a sense of order. For example, the earliest civilizations evolved over 7,000 years. As agriculture was adopted, human contact slowly spread among the clans. Awareness of the length of this evolution helps students to see it as a basis for more rapid change and development in later periods. Another example is viewing how long the Roman Catholic Church was entrenched as the center of Medieval European life (400-1500 AD). This creates a

Skill Activity

Below is a list of time periods in European history:

- The Enlightenment
- The Neolithic Revolution
- The Cold War

- The Renaissance
- The Industrial Revolution
- The Protestant Reformation

Answer the following questions based on the information given above.

1   Look up the dates for the periods in the list and rearrange in chronological order.

2   Which period is chronologically most distant from the others?

3   Knowing the Renaissance came before the Reformation and the Enlightenment helps to explain the
1   impact of its questioning spirit
2   breakdown of the Roman Empire
3   power of Soviet communism
4   economic need for a single currency

Note to Student: On global history exams, chronology questions usually involve cause and effect relationships as in question number 3 above. Knowing when an event took place helps to see how it is related to what is being asked in the question.

sense of its power. Knowing major time periods helps in making time connections in narrative essays.

Place is also an important category of knowledge. As with time, knowing where an event occurs helps students see how events in proximity can influence others nearby. (Spatial relationships are further discussed under the geography section below.)

CONCEPTUAL THEMES

Besides time and place, historians use other theme patterns based on certain ideas to clarify the past. Narrative essay questions on global history examinations often reflect these themes:

- **multiple causation**
- **change and its effects**
- **ends influence means**
- **role of individual and group actions**

- **comparing and contrasting differing sets of ideas** (religions, ideologies, philosophies) **and detecting linkages among them**
- **moral and / or practical consequences of decisions**

GEOGRAPHY

Geography is the study of the Earth and its features. It also studies the distribution of life on the Earth, including human life and the effects of human activity.

IDENTIFYING AND DEFINING WORLD REGIONS

A **region** is a large portion of the Earth's surface, encompassing many inhabitants. Being precise about what defines region is often difficult. Regions are usually unified by physical or human characteristics, such as proximity to an ocean (e.g., the "Pacific Rim") or language and culture (e.g., "Latin America") or a political system (e.g., the "Roman Empire").

Skill Activity

Below is a sample constructed-response question focused on comparing and contrasting differing ideologies.

A "... the power to make laws is given to the many rather than the few. While every citizen has an equal opportunity to serve the public, we reward our most distinguished citizens by asking them to make our political decisions. Nor do we discriminate against the poor. A man may serve his country no matter how low his position on the social scale."

– Pericles, *Funeral Oration*

B "Whoever undertakes to maintain the organizational structure of another political party or to form a new political party will be punished with penal servitude up to three years, if the deed is not subject to other regulations."

–Law against the establishment of parties, Germany, 14 July 1933

Answer the following questions based on the information given above.

1   Which of the two documents supports democracy?

2   Compare the two documents on participation in government by citizens.

Skill Activity

Using a classroom map or World Atlas, identify the 8 regions of the world. Label the map below with the names of the regions.

In the modern world, political geographers usually refer to eight broad-based regions that are loosely connected by culture and history:

- Middle East
- Europe & Russia
- Sub-Saharan Africa
- South & Southeast Asia
- Central & East Asia
- Oceania & Pacific Rim
- North America
- Latin America

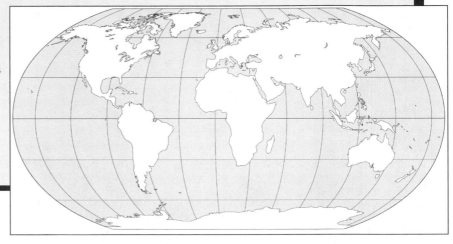

In history, perceptions of regions change often. Historians redefine them as circumstances change. For example, when civilization first developed in the Tigris-Euphrates-Nile area, historians called the region the "Fertile Crescent." Later in the Classical Greco-Roman Era, historians referred to it as the "Mediterranean World." A huge, sweeping region from North Africa to Pakistan and into Indonesia is religiously identified as the "Islamic World," although the followers of Islam can be found in every region on the globe. Thus, regions shift and overlap. Their definition depends on the times and the contexts in which they are being studied.

SPATIAL RELATIONSHIPS

Geographic features have a significant impact on where and how people live. When studying history, geography helps explain the relationship of the natural environment and the human environment. Relationships to climate, water, land forms, and mineral deposits shape how people live and act toward others.

Distances alter relationships, too. One of the greatest expeditions in modern history, Napoleon's 1812 invasion of Russia, failed in part because French commanders extended sup-ply lines over too vast a distance and underestimated the harshness of the climate.

A more modern instance of geographic factors altering relationships is environmental conditions. For example, nations have industries whose pollution becomes airborne (e.g., acid rain) and affects conditions in other countries. Less developed countries (**LDCs**) balk when pressed by others to cut down their industrial pollution. The LDCs cite the need for income to raise their nations' standard of living.

Studying the natural environment reveals much about how civilizations develop (e.g., river valleys as cradles of civilization). Relative location can indicate what motivates a nation (e.g., Russia's traditional desire for navigable Baltic and Black Sea ports).

People identify with a place's physical characteristics or have to adapt to them (e.g., mountaineers, islanders, forest dwellers). Their culture, music, and architecture can reflect such characteristics. An area's livelihood may spring from geographic factors. Examples include fishing – a chief industry for Norway, and sheep herding for the Australian Outback. The Phoenicians became ship builders and therefore, traders in the Ancient Mediterranean World.

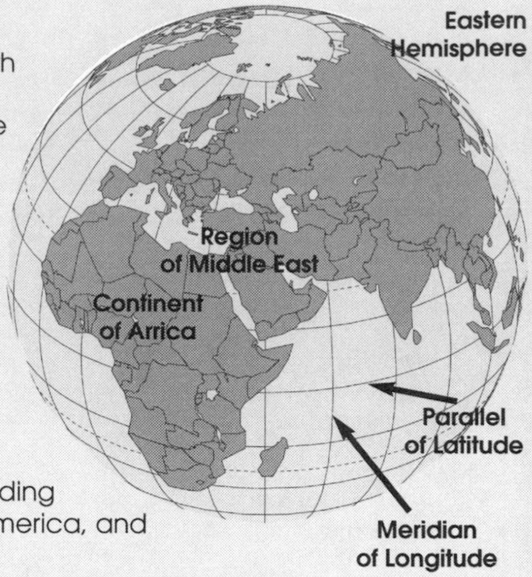

TERM	EXPLANATION
Meridian	an imaginary great circle passing through the North and South geographic poles; lines of **longitude** measuring East or West to 180 degrees of the Prime Meridian (0° – running through Greenwich, England)
Parallel	any of the imaginary lines representing degrees of **latitude** that encircle the Earth parallel to the plane of the Equator (0°) measuring North and South to 90 degrees (geographic poles)
Hemisphere	either the northern or southern half of the Earth as divided by the Equator, or the Eastern or Western half as divided by a meridian
Continent	one of the principal land masses of the Earth, including Africa, Antarctica, Asia, Australia, Europe, North America, and South America
Region	a large portion of the Earth's surface unified by physical or human characteristics such as language, culture, economic activity, or a political system
Ocean	any of the principal divisions of the Earth's salt water surface (71%), including the Atlantic, Pacific, and Indian Oceans, their southern extensions in Antarctica, and the Arctic Ocean
Sea	a relatively large body of salt water completely or partially enclosed by land
Strait	a narrow channel joining two larger bodies of water
Bay	a body of water partially enclosed by land with a mouth accessible to the sea
Gulf	a large area of a sea or ocean partially enclosed by land
Lakes	a large inland body of fresh water or salt water
River	a large natural stream of water emptying into an ocean, a lake, or another body of water
Mountains	a significant natural elevation of the Earth's surface having considerable mass, generally steep sides
Plateau	an elevated, level expanse of land; a tableland
Plain	an extensive, level, usually treeless area of land
Peninsula	a piece of land that projects into a body of water

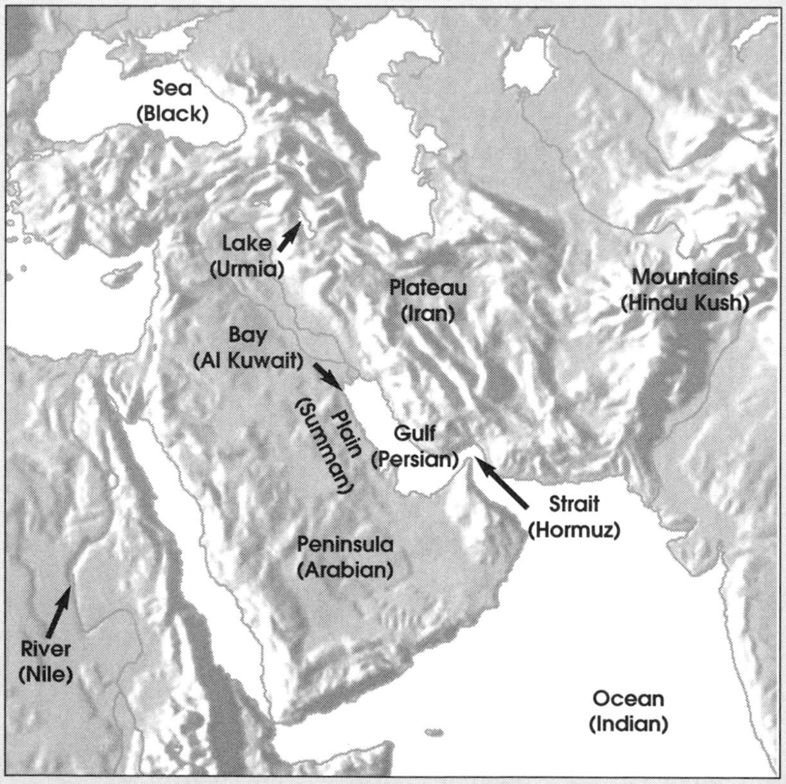

Eastern Hemisphere

Region of Middle East

Continent of Arrica

Parallel of Latitude

Meridian of Longitude

Sea (Black)

Lake (Urmia)

Plateau (Iran)

Mountains (Hindu Kush)

Bay (Al Kuwait)

Plain (Summan)

Gulf (Persian)

Strait (Hormuz)

Peninsula (Arabian)

River (Nile)

Ocean (Indian)

CLIMATE

As a geographic factor, climate has often played a key role in human development. It shapes culture (e.g., desert dwellers are usually nomadic; monsoons govern the agriculture of the Indian Subcontinent). In each world region, the general climatic conditions govern human progress. Knowing these conditions can often help explain why things have happened in the region throughout history. The chart (key) and map to the right is an adaptation of a climate classification system developed in the *Handbook of Climatology*, Wladimir Peter Koppen (German, 1846-1940).

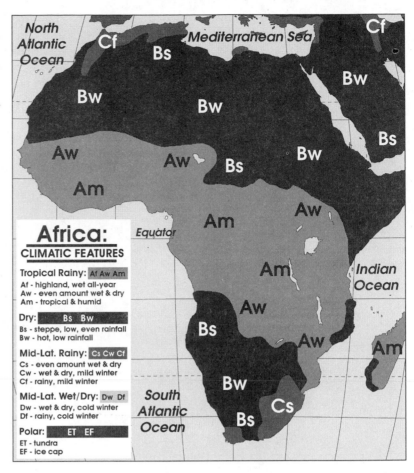

Africa: CLIMATIC FEATURES

Tropical Rainy: Af Aw Am
Af - highland, wet all-year
Aw - even amount wet & dry
Am - tropical & humid

Dry: Bs Bw
Bs - steppe, low, even rainfall
Bw - hot, low rainfall

Mid-Lat. Rainy: Cs Cw Cf
Cs - even amount wet & dry
Cw - wet & dry, mild winter
Cf - rainy, mild winter

Mid-Lat. Wet/Dry: Dw Df
Dw - wet & dry, cold winter
Df - rainy, cold winter

Polar: ET EF
ET - tundra
EF - ice cap

ORGANIZING, AND ANALYZING GEOGRAPHIC INFORMATION

Maps (including navigation charts) are a primary way to organize geographic data for use in human activities. Map projections transform the spherical surface to a flat surface while minimizing the distortion.

Maps attempt to represent three-dimensional features in a two-dimensional format. Actually, a globe is the only accurate representation of the Earth's surface. Unfortunately, globes are difficult to handle, can only show the world at a very small scale, and the entire surface of the Earth cannot be viewed at one time.

Ancient **cartographers** (mapmakers) relied on sketches and stories told by seafarers. Modern cartographers employ technological devices and get data from satellites orbiting the Earth and computers linked to the **Global Positioning System** (**GPS**).

Working with different kinds of maps helps visualize historical events and patterns. Some maps are very technical and help navigators, surveyors, and military commanders. On the other hand, the maps in a global history book are called **thematic maps**. Thematic maps may portray hemispheres, climates, landforms, settlement patterns, the extent of empires, war strategies, and invasion and migration routes.

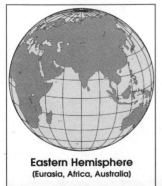

Eastern Hemisphere
(Eurasia, Africa, Australia)

Western Hemisphere
(North & South Americas)

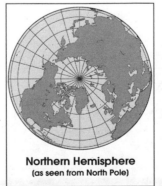

Northern Hemisphere
(as seen from North Pole)

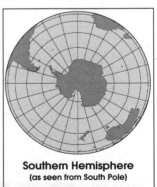

Southern Hemisphere
(as seen from South Pole)

Just as there are many types of maps to study the globe and its history, there are many dimensions of geography. In a global history course, the geographic emphasis is on human geography. **Human geography** studies the changing distributions of people, their activities, and their interaction with the natural environment. Human geography blends understandings about culture, population, politics, and economics to help comprehend historic patterns.

Skill Activity

Using a classroom map or World Atlas, identify (by letter) and describe what each map below portrays.

Representative Maps used to describe or illustrate Global History:

____   Physical (or Relief) Map

____   Climatic Feature Map

____   Population Distribution Map

____   Thematic (Historic) Event Map

____   Political Boundary Map

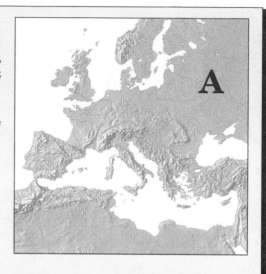

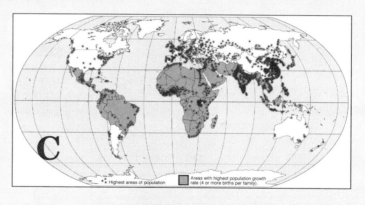

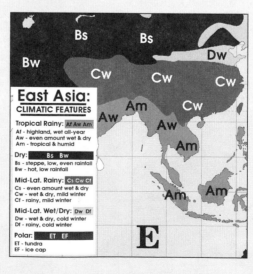

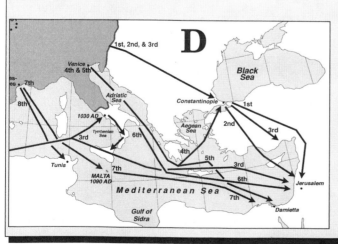

ECONOMICS

MAJOR ECONOMIC CONCEPTS

Students beginning a global history course require some grounding in economics, because it is a basic force underlying human activity. People need resources to produce the goods and services to sustain life and give comfort. The basic resources that humans use include:

- **Natural resources** – land, water, trees, minerals ...

- **Human resources** – labor, talent, organizational skills ...

- **Capital resources** – tools, computers, machinery, financial investment ...

- **Information resources** – research, ideas ...

These basic resources are vital to human existence. Yet, this is a finite world. While some resources are plentiful at certain times and in certain places, all resources have limits. This presents a very large, persistent problem in life: *all the resources listed above are limited in some way.* Economists call this the problem of **scarcity** – there are not enough resources to supply all the demands of humanity for all time.

Since there never has been enough of anything to meet everyone's needs and desires, scarcity is a basic fact of life. It is also an uneven condition. In reality, supply never equals demand. Of course, at certain times, some people, living in some places, have plenty. Yet, it does not take very much searching to discover that most people on the globe suffer from a lack of resources in some way.

Supply is the amount of a resource or service available for meeting a demand. **Demand** is the amount of a resource or service that people are ready and willing to consume. Simply put on a global scale, the supply of resources is finite and the demand for resources is infinite.

DECISION-MAKING: TRADE-OFFS AND SACRIFICES

Scarcity forces individuals, families, communities, and nations to look at the limited resources they have and make basic decisions (and sacrifices). **Economics** is the study of how humans decide:

- What to produce?
- How to produce it?
- Who gets the products?

These questions seem simple enough on a personal level. Individuals assess their resources and consider their needs and desires. They decide to exchange their resources for something. Most often, they want a substantial amount of things, but only have the money for one thing. As a result, they **sacrifice** (**trade-off**) the purchase of one thing for another. That is **real cost** – the expenditure of resources plus the sacrifice of other opportunities to use the resources.

However, when groups of people have to make decisions, the process becomes harder. People have different values and needs. Satisfying everyone is difficult. Evaluating the needs of the present versus the needs of the future, setting acceptable priorities, and using resources wisely becomes very complex.

For example, should a society use its natural, capital, and human resources to produce pasta, vacuum cleaners, mobile homes, schools, and health care, *or* should it use those resources for bread, forklifts, computers, railroad cars, airplanes, bridges, and office buildings? (Remember, some resources, such as petroleum, are **non-renewable**. Once used, they are gone forever.) Trying to make decisions on this level can lead to conflict within a society. Civil wars can erupt when groups feel "cut out" of the decision-making process. Conflicting desires can also lead to struggles among societies. Countries have gone to war with others over trade differences, water rights, and mineral deposits.

ECONOMIC SYSTEMS

Societies, nations, and civilizations have evolved different systems or ways to make economic choices about scarce resources. Economists see three general systems for how societies make decisions about scarce resources: **traditional**, **command**, **market**. The kind of system found in a particular society evolves from various elements. These include historic experience, values, culture, the leaders' political ideology, and current conditions.

Basic Economic Systems

Type	Decision-Making	Characteristics	Problems
Traditional	based on past experience, custom, religion	common to small, primitive, isolated societies; labor-intensive, static, subsistence level, no chance to produce surplus	not equipped to deal with major change in natural or social environment; with no past patterns or guidelines to follow in emergencies, chiefs or clan elders had to issue orders to deal with dislocations until people could go back to their old ways
Market	individual producers and consumers	flexible, rapid change	business activity fluctuates, makes long-term planning difficult; sometimes insecure and unstable
Command	government planners	slow-moving, often inflexible	personal initiative not rewarded; innovation is limited to government sponsored programs; lack of competition affects quality of products

Most modern economic systems blend governmental (**command**) and individual (**market**) decision-making. These **mixed** systems vary. Availability of critical resources, cultural values, political and religious beliefs, limitations of the natural environment, and historic experience are just some of the factors that shape a society's mixture of command and market structures.

INTERDEPENDENCE OF ECONOMIC SYSTEMS THROUGHOUT THE WORLD

In the modern world, especially in the age of the Internet, the choices being made every moment all over the globe mean resources are being shifted at a blistering pace. Making informed and well-reasoned economic decisions in a high-speed environment is not an easy task. Millions of individuals – producers and consumers – make resource choices daily. These decisions drive global markets. Public and private organizations or institutions – including various levels of government, corporations, unions, and political parties – make an unending array of decisions at every moment.

The availability (or lack of availability) of resources and the transfer of them on a worldwide basis is the foundation of modern existence. Just thinking about the array of products an individual uses in daily routines, shows the complexity of modern life. Where do these resources come from? How are they put together? How do they get to the place where they are to be used? It also shows that **interdependence** is the driving force on the globe today.

Necessity links humanity, and yet, different values and perspectives divide people. Different economic systems and national agendas cause friction and conflict. Making global interdependence work demands understanding and cooperation.

POLITICAL SCIENCE

Political science is the study of the structures, activities, and behavior of government. Global history students need to see that the political philosophies that have evolved with human existence vary greatly. Students must reach beyond their awareness of their own system to compare government and politics in other places and times and note the similarities and differences among them.

THE PURPOSES OF GOVERNMENT

Humans, acting in groups, devise systems to make decisions concerning their common goals. A **government** is an agency that exercises control and administration of a political unit. Governments – small and large – regulate people and speak for people to other governments.

ECONOMIC DECISION-MAKING CONTINUUM*

* continuous with no part distinguishable from another part

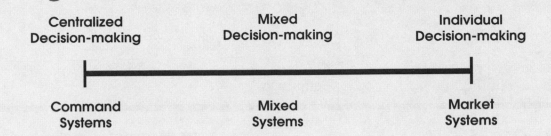

Centralized Decision-making	Mixed Decision-making	Individual Decision-making
Command Systems	Mixed Systems	Market Systems

Modern economic systems fall along a simple continuum based on who is answering the three basic questions about allocation of scarce resources (WHAT to produce?, HOW to produce. For WHOM is it produced?). Most systems mix government (centralized) decision-making with individualized decision-making. Traditional systems are not shown on the continuum because there is no conscious dynamic of decision-making – traditions dictate the activities and allocations. If a storm were to disrupt the normal flow of activities in a traditional system, a village leader or council would have to consider the situation and consciously reallocate resources. At that point, tradition fails, and a command structure has temporarily replaced tradition.

Skill Activity

Answer the following questions based on the information given above.

1   In the 1990s, China's communist government began to allow private ownership of small business. Which system change is taking place?
    1   tradition to command   3   market to tradition
    2   command to market   4   command to tradition

2   When the tsunamis (seismic sea wave) destroyed the boats and docks, the village council had to order all the pineapple growers to work with the fishermen with the rebuilding. Which system change is taking place?
    1   tradition to command   3   market to tradition
    2   command to market   4   command to tradition

3   Kelly's father orders her to give up a job at the mall and devote more time to building a grade-point average that will get her into college. Explain which system seems to be operating here.

4   What factors influence the type of system or mix of systems a society adopts?

Note to Student: On global history exams, questions on specific factual data or graphics usually come in series. The first one is usually directly from the material presented. The next question(s) ask you to apply broader historical concepts and contexts to the material.

Types of Government (Who holds power?)

General Type	Power held by	Example
Monarchy	one	Louis XIV in France (absolute)
Oligarchy	an enlightened few	Ancient Sparta's Ephors
Democracy	many	Ancient Athens (direct); Current U.S.A. (representative democracy)

POLITICAL CONCEPTS OF POWER, AUTHORITY, GOVERNANCE, AND LAW

Political science studies the principles on which governments rest, and whether they live up to those principles.

Historically, there have been many theories on where governments get their power and authority. The most common theories include:

- **Divine Right** – the belief that power comes to an individual or group from the authority of some supernatural force

- **Physical Power** – the strongest, or best armed, holds power and offers protection to the weaker

- **Consent of the Governed** – power is granted by the authority of the group being ruled

No matter what is deemed to be the source of authority, to keep control and order, governments need two essential powers – the sword and the purse. First, a government must be able to **enforce** the rules (sword) and order its desires. Second, a government must be able to **finance** (purse) its enforcement and provide services (usually through taxation). Even with these two essentials, a government's **sovereignty** (supreme independent authority) can be limited in many ways, internally and externally. Internally, constitutions outline the power of government. They often set limits on the government's scope and authority over the people within their authority. Externally, other governments could compromise sovereignty (e.g., a mother country exerting authority over a colony, or a federal government preempting some power of a state government).

Governments have come in all sizes and configurations – from the clan and tribal councils of primitive times to the superpowers and international governments of today. Some governments have established empires that ruled peoples across national, language, and ethnic boundaries. Modern nation-states have governments that operate at many different levels from villages to cities, counties, provinces, and states.

Governments usually reflect the values and needs of the power groups that run them. If security and order are high priorities, a **unitary system** may evolve where all authority is linked in a seamless chain of command from the national level through the local. Where freedom and diversity are prized, but order is still important, a loose **federal system** may form. It distributes power among a central government and subdivisions (e.g., states, provinces). Where individuality is essential, a fragile **league** or **confederation** may form. It has a weak central government with very limited power. The smaller units (states) in a confederation retain their sovereignty.

A key function of government is to control the society by setting the rules (laws) and enforcing them. **Law** is a system of standards of conduct, obligations, and rights. Laws include written statutes, administrative rules and regulations, and judicial precedents. There are five general types of law:

- **Constitutional Law** – outlines the body of rules by which the powers of government are exercised

- **Administrative Law** – governs the organization, operation, regulations, and procedures of government agencies

- **Private or Civil Law** – applies rules when one person claims that another has injured his or her person, property, or reputation

- **Criminal Law** – imposes penalties for anti-social behavior

- **International Law** – sets rules on boundary disputes, warfare limits, trade

Skill Activity

"True law is right reason in accord with nature; it is of universal application, unchanging and everlasting..."

– Marcus Tullius Cicero, *Commonwealth* (51 BC)

Answer the following questions based on the quotation above.

1   Identify and explain what the source of law is for Cicero.

2   In their historic correspondence, John Adams and Thomas Jefferson said the United States must have

"...a government of laws rather than men..."

Why would Cicero agree?

POLITICAL SYSTEMS AROUND THE WORLD

History shows many attempts of nations and empires to deal with others in rational ways. Yet, only in modern times have permanent organizations been created to promote peace, cooperation, and understanding. Founded as part of World War I's *Treaty of Versailles*, the **League** of Nations lasted from 1919 to 1946. It fell apart in the 1930s but some of its support systems lasted until the **United Nations** (1945) absorbed them. Both of these voluntary organizations became forums for debate and negotiations. The U.N. has gone beyond the League by sending international peacekeeping forces to trouble spots in the world. The United Nations is an international government in theory, but in reality, nations still cling to their sovereignty and do not always cooperate for peace.

Regional associations also have a long history. From the Peloponnesian League of ancient Greek city-states, to the North Atlantic Treaty Organization of modern times, governments have joined with others for defense and to promote trade. Yet, such associations have seldom exerted great control. In modern times, members of the **European Union** struggled to build a supranational government on the basis of the earlier Common Market's economic cooperation to make Europe stronger in trade and economic competition.

RIGHTS AND RESPONSIBILITIES OF CITIZENSHIP ACROSS TIME AND SPACE

Ancient societies and kingdoms did not always perceive individuals as citizens. Today, by virtue of either birth in a country or because of the citizenship of one or both parents, a person becomes a citizen. The citizen possesses certain rights and privileges and is expected to perform certain civic duties.

While various limits exist, in most countries a citizen has the right to:

- enjoy the country's protection and its laws
- hold and transfer all types of property
- vote
- seek elective office
- hold governmental positions
- receive welfare and social benefits

With limits, in most countries citizens have corresponding responsibilities to:

- pay taxes
- obey the laws of the nation
- defend their nation
- serve jury duty

DEFINING CULTURE AND CIVILIZATION

THE MEANING OF CULTURE

Anthropology studies the cultural development and differences among human beings. Anthropologists define **human culture** as the sum total of human knowledge and acquired behavior of humankind. Anthropologists record customs and collect artifacts in order to reconstruct the history of societies. Most human societies are organized groups of individuals which have a set of behavioral rules that are transmitted from one generation to another.

ELEMENTS OF CULTURE

There is great diversity among human cultures but in all societies, anthropologists identify certain **universals of culture** (general concepts).

The key universals include:

- primary means of subsistence — for example, hunting and gathering, agriculture, industrialized labor
- some form of the primary or nuclear family
- system of kinship (extended family)
- set of rules of social conduct
- religion
- material culture (tools, weapons, clothing)
- forms of art

CULTURAL DIFFUSION

Cultural diffusion occurs when elements of one society's culture spread to other geographical areas and change other societies in some significant way. Sometimes religious beliefs, habit, and caution cause rejection, but usually there is a blending and absorbing of the new culture by the older one. For example, the denim jeans once worn by American prospectors, farmers, and cowhands are worn globally.

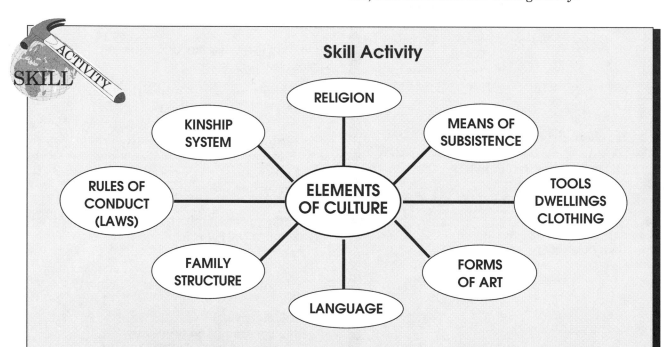

Skill Activity

ELEMENTS OF CULTURE
- RELIGION
- KINSHIP SYSTEM
- MEANS OF SUBSISTENCE
- RULES OF CONDUCT (LAWS)
- TOOLS DWELLINGS CLOTHING
- FAMILY STRUCTURE
- FORMS OF ART
- LANGUAGE

Answer the following question based on the information given above.

1 Give a specific example of how any one (1) of the elements could affect the same element of another culture.

In history, Korea was a cultural bridge that filtered Chinese culture into Japan as early as the Ch'in Dynasty, 220 BC. The Crusaders of the 10th century AD observed a blending of Southwest Asian, African, and European ideas.

Today, diffusion is accelerated by "high tech" communications and fast modes of travel. Innovations spread throughout the world with great rapidity.

Of course, cultural differences exist, even within modern nations. When the differences are great or when there is a history of conflict, strains can arise. The violent confrontations among ethnic and religious groups in the Balkans (Bosnia, Croatia, Serbia) are examples.

CONCLUSION

A knowledge of the world gives an individual a better perspective on life. Mastering global history requires meeting standards involving a broad range of social sciences.

Understanding how historians analyze facts and ideas is the beginning point. But, the sense of history must be strengthened by the basic analytical tools of political science, anthropology, economics, and geography. Success in studying global history begins by acquiring a basic knowledge of these fields. It is worth the study time and effort to see the interdependence of the fields.

Unit 2

4000 BC – 500 AD

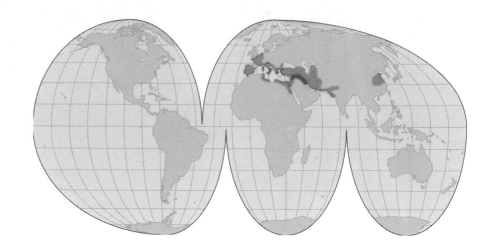

 Hominids in Africa (4 million BC)

Neolitic Revolution (60,000 BC)

ANCIENT WORLD: CIVILIZATIONS & RELIGION

3500–

Menes unites Egypt (3,100 BC)

3000–

Sumarian City-states emerge (2700 BC)

2500–

Great Pyramids built (2400 BC)

2000–

Hammurabi's Code (1792 BC)

1500– Aryans invade Indus Valley (1500 BC)

1000– Zhou overthrows Shang in China (1027 BC)

Homer's *Illiad & Odyssey* (800 BC)

500– Roman Republic begins (500 BC)
Alexander spreads Hellenistic culture (325 BC)
Asoka expands Maurya rule in India (272 BC)
AD
0– Octavian begins Pax Romana (31 BC)
BC

Fall of Han Empire (220 AD)

Constantine legalizes Christianity (313 AD)

500–

PEOPLE	PLACES	THINGS
Confucius	Fertile Crescent	aristocracy
Hammurabi	Harappa	bureaucracy
Julius Caesar	Hellas	caste system
Laozi	Huang He	cultural diffusion
Mohammed	Olduavi Gorge	cuneiform
Neanderthal	Peloponnesia	infrastructure
Pericles	Persia	Mandate of Heaven
Siddarta Gautama	Phoenicia	monotheism
Wudi	river valleys	oligarchy
	Rome	polytheism
	Silk Road	republic

EARLY PEOPLES
(PREHISTORY — 3000 BC)

Paleontology studies life in **prehistoric**[1] or geologic times through fossil remains of animals, plants, and other organisms. Using scientific techniques such as **radiometric dating**[2], paleontologists trace the evidence of ancestral species of the genus **Homo** or **hominid**[3] to 4.4 million years. Discoveries in Africa show species such as **Australopithecus** living in small family communities. Important sites include **Olduvai Gorge** (Tanzania) and others in Kenya and Ethiopia. Australopithecus were confined to the African **savanna**, but were **nomadic**[4].

Paleontologists have found evidence of a more advanced hominid, **homo habilis**, living in the **Paleolithic Era**[5], preceding the emergence of agriculture. Homo habilis showed the ability to make and use chipped stone implements. In the middle of that era, paleontologists have identified remains of an even more advanced hominid species – **homo erectus**.

Homo erectus lived in hunter-gatherer groups mastering fire, creating clothing, and using language while ranging over wide areas. The **Zhoukoudian** site near Beijing, China (first excavated in the 1920s) is evidence that homo erectus existed beyond Africa. Use of language enabled these groups to organize work and pass skills and culture to their young.

In addition to paleontologists' work, knowledge of ancient life comes from **archaeologists**. These scientists study **artifacts**[6] to gather knowledge of early human activity. Archaeological findings indicate that in the later part of the Paleolithic Era, approximately 100,000 – 26,000 BC, the modern hominid species emerged. This was **homo sapiens** or **Neanderthals**[7]. Homo sapiens increased rapidly in numbers and migrated to the other continents.

Dating to 50,000 BC, the remains of **Cro-Magnon** homo sapiens, discovered in Europe and Asia, show significant development. These prehistoric people were still nomadic hunter-gathers. However, they lived in more permanent shelters and caves. They domesticated dogs for hunting, practiced primitive forms of medicine, and depicted life in cave paintings and stone figures such as those found in **Lascaux** (France) and **Altimira** (Spain).

NEOLITHIC REVOLUTION
& EARLY RIVER CIVILIZATIONS

THE NEOLITHIC ERA (NEW STONE AGE)

Paleontologists and **anthropologists**[8] detected a gradual fundamental change in human behavior occurring between 65,000 and 30,000 BC. Because the change was so radical, scientists call it the **Neolithic Revolution**. It began at different sites over a long period, but it

---

1 prehistoric (before writing)
2 radiometric dating (measuring the age of materials by their radioactive contents)
3 Homo or hominid (human-like creatures)
4 nomadic (moved over large areas seeking food)
5 Paleolithic Era (Old Stone Age – 2 million to 12,000 BC)

6 artifacts (objects produced by human craft: tools, weapons, or ornaments)
7 homo sapiens or Neanderthals (early human-like remains found in Germany's Neander Valley)
8 anthropologists (social scientists who study the origins and the physical, social, and cultural development of human beings)

marked a shift away from hunting-gathering to agriculture. Scientists have unearthed many simple farming sites that date to Neolithic times. Discoveries have been made in Thailand (**Non Nok Tha** on the Mekong River), in Southwest Asia (the Fertile Crescent of Mesopotamia, Egypt, Greece, Turkey, the Caucasus Mountains), in China (**Yangshao** culture on the Yellow River), and in Mexico.

In the Orkney Islands off Scotland's northeast coast, are the remains of the **Skara Brae** settlement (c. 3000 BC). They indicate Neolithic peoples established remote villages devoted to herding, fishing, and primitive agriculture.

Agricultural life was more intense and organized than hunting and gathering. People had to work constantly to experience success. Yet, farming could provide a steady supply of food in one place, and that meant more people could survive and be secure. Families, clans, and communities grew. This led to a more settled form of civilization. Staying in one place, as opposed to nomadic movement, meant population increased, because better care could be offered infants. Staying in one place and waiting for crops to mature also allowed people to increase possessions and improve their lives. There was time to develop better techniques for making tools, utensils, pottery, and even jewelry. There is evidence in the ancient ruins of **Jericho** (Israel, c. 8000 BC) that more permanent dwellings multiplied into sizeable settlements with commercial activity, religious practices, writing, and central governments.

Technology developed rapidly in the settled agricultural communities. It accelerated the pace of change. The invention of the wheel and training animals to pull primitive wooden plows to till the soil made the lives of Neolithic farmers easier. These innovations also allowed time for developing other pursuits, such as weaving cloth, building strong, durable dwellings, and working with metals to make better tools and weapons.

Creating better weapons became important as villages clashed in wars over the land and the water needed to sustain their new agricultural way of life. Specialized talent, such as pottery and weapon making, led certain individuals to become **artisans**[1]. Such **specialization**[2] led to more technological progress such as making **alloys** by mixing metals (e.g., soft copper + soft tin = tougher bronze).

Cultural diffusion[3] increased as individuals and groups traveled outside the community to trade for scarce goods.

Although farming was an individual or family pursuit, small-scale governments emerged from the need to make decisions involving the whole community. Chiefs and consulting councils deliberated on issues such as water rights, public works (e.g., irrigation systems, community grain storage), natural disasters, penalties for anti-social behavior, and defense against other communities.

Spiritual beliefs and rituals predate the Paleolithic Era. Neolithic farmers sought spiritual assistance, as they struggled to deal with the natural environment. Storms, floods, droughts, landslides, and earthquakes disrupted the cycles of agricultural life. Neolithic farmers' desires to control the forces of nature led most groups to create **polytheistic**[4] worship systems for intercession and protection. Administering these worship systems gave rise to another new class – priests and shamen – that grew in power and prestige as the societies matured.

CAUSES OF RIVER VALLEY SETTLEMENT

Production of larger quantities of food drew Neolithic farmers to river valleys because of the availability of water and richer soils (silt or loess carried down river by currents and spread by floods). Rivers also made transportation and trade easier. It was natural for the early African and Asian cities and civilizations to emerge along the banks of major rivers such as the Nile, Tigris and Euphrates, Indus, and Huang He (Yellow).

The transformation of small agricultural communities into civilizations was complicated. Because of their location and management, some river villages grew into cities that evolved into commercial and administrative centers of

---

1 artisans (craftsmen)
2 specialization (focusing on a craft or skill)
3 cultural diffusion (mixing of ideas, technologies, and cultures)
4 polytheistic (many gods and goddesses)

civilization[1]. These levels of human society were marked by complex social and political development. This development included key elements such as concentration of population into cities, surplus agricultural production to support city population, the adoption of writing for communication and records, calendars for keeping planting schedules, religious systems, central government, and specialized labor.

With river valley cities growing, large concentrations of non-agricultural groups such as priests, artisans, merchants, government officials, and military units presented a problem. Cities had to offer farmers protection and public services (dams, irrigation projects). These groups performed such needed services, but they depended on farmers to raise and deliver enough surplus products to feed them.

As cities grew and exerted authority over the surrounding region, traditional systems could not change to provide answers to rapidly changing economic needs. A **barter system**[2] evolved with people trading goods and services for items they needed. However, bartering is cumbersome, and societies eventually developed **money**[3]. Coins and paper money were first used in ancient China and were in widespread use after 1000 BC in most areas of human activity. However, bartering remained as a useful exchange system in local communities.

As life in early civilizations became more complex, so did economic decision-making. Simple village cultures evolved **traditional economies**. In these structures, people looked to past practices plus cultural and religious beliefs to decide what to produce, how to produce it, how products would be distributed, and even when tasks should be performed. Focusing only on rituals and on the past, traditional economies were static (not flexible) and not open to change or growth.

At first, priests, as spokesmen of the gods, exercised enough spiritual authority to make city governments work. As cities expanded in wealth, stronger demands for defense and the need for collecting **revenue**[4] put warriors in positions of control. Enforcing the law, directing public works, and managing finances created a need for a **bureaucracy**[5].

When emergencies arose or conditions changed, the traditional societies had to temporarily convert into a **command economic structure** where basic decisions were made by a central authority. The rulers of the great cities sometimes issued commands that reallocated economic resources. For example, Egyptian **pharaohs** (rulers) ordered farmers and artisans to work on dikes, temples, pyramids, and other public works. This took people and raw material out of the normal flow and disrupted economic activity. In some cases, kings and their advisors began deciding what crops were to be produced, what supplies were needed, and in what quantities. However, these were never the comprehensively planned economic management systems one would find in modern command economies. After a special need was satisfied or an emergency was met, economic activity returned to being tradition-driven.

CIVILIZATIONS DRAW INVASIONS

When human populations settled into river valleys, reorganized into agricultural communities, built up cities, and engaged in commerce, they produced stability. Nomadic and semi-nomadic peoples on the edges of these civilizations were drawn to their better way of life. Because of the differences in behavior between the two groups, clashes often took place. Frequency of contact, coupled with the desire by the nomadic and semi-nomadic groups to acquire the advantages of the civilization, led to invasions. At times, the invaders destroyed the civilization. More often, they subdued the civilization and tried to confiscate wealth and live within them (sometimes enslaving them). Quite often, the stronger, better organized culture of the civilization would absorb the invaders, and they would become part of it. Scholars refer to this as the process of **assimilation**[6]. This process repeated itself over the thousands of years of these early river valley civilizations.

---

1 civilization (level of human society marked by complex social and political development)
2 barter (trading goods and services without money)
3 money (exchangeable equivalent of all other commodities used as a measure of their comparative values)

4 revenue (government income from taxes and fees)
5 bureaucracy (a corps of administrators, clerks, and officials that carry out the laws, policies, programs, and decrees of a government)
6 assimilation (to incorporate and absorb into the mind)

RESULTS OF RIVER VALLEY SETTLEMENT

The expansion of river valley civilizations accelerated the growth of social institutions. Religious, governmental, and educational systems grew larger and became more complex. The spread of authority brought civilizations into conflict and wars of conquest increased. The building of temples and water control and distribution systems increased architectural knowledge and engineering technology.

OVERVIEW: ANCIENT EGYPTIAN CIVILIZATION: 5000 - 1000 BC

GEOGRAPHY

A warm desert climate (Koppen classification: BW type) and annual flooding (as opposed to steady rainfall) created a narrow corridor of rich land irrigated by the Nile River that attracted Neolithic farmers to the lower Nile Valley. Nearly 700 miles of rich silt ran from the Nile's first cataract (falls) through the Nubian and Lybian Deserts and into the wide delta at the eastern edge of the Mediterranean Sea. This rich northern third of the Nile was a stable environment for agricultural development. In addition, the river – world's longest river at over 4,132 miles – provided transportation for regional traders.

GOVERNMENT

Upper Egypt and Lower Egypt were united around 3100 BC by the Nubian King Menes (the first pharaoh). Succeeding pharaohs and **dynasties**[1] created a strong absolute monarchy with the aid of **viziers**[2] who presided over large standing armies and a bureaucracy of tax collectors, scribes, and officials. Tradition supported the pharaohs' claim to rule by **divine right**[3]. Eventually, this concept elevated the pharaohs to the status of gods. Stability was also a key factor in the growth of Egyptian Civilization. For more than a thousand years, Egypt did not have to absorb large new populations with languages and ideas different from those already established.

Natural and financial disasters caused the decline of the pyramid-

---

Mini Assessment

MINI-ASSESSMENT

1 Neolithic agricultural societies paved the way for civilization by
 1 converting earliest farmers into hunter-gatherers
 2 fostering settled and secure communities
 3 depicting life in cave paintings and stone figures
 4 mastering fire and using language while traveling over wide areas

2 Early civilizations arose along the Nile, Tigris-Euphrates, Indus, and Huang He because
 1 easy access invited invasion
 2 rivers contributed to nomadic lifestyles
 3 building materials were easy to find
 4 climate and geography favored agriculture

3 As cities expanded in wealth, which factor put warriors in positions of control?
 1 organization of religion   3 demands for defense
 2 educational systems   4 cultural diffusion

Constructed Response:
"Between the planting and the harvest, the Pharaoh decreed that all able-bodied farmers and artisans leave their fields and assist in building of his great temple."
– An Egyptian Diary

1 Why is the above quotation characteristic of a command economy?

2 Why might the building of a temple be more important to a ruler than agriculture?

---

1   dynasties (family of hereditary rulers)
2   viziers (prime ministers)
3   divine right (god-given absolute right to rule with no responsibility to those ruled)

From 1550 to 1100 BC, pharaohs such as Queen **Hatshepsut** and **Ramses II** rebuilt power and extended the Egyptian Empire south into Nubia and northeastward into Palestine and Syria. After 1100 BC, Egyptian power declined again during waves of invasions from Assyria, Persia, Greece, and Rome.

building pharaohs' rule by 2000 BC. Widespread corruption left Egypt weak. An invasion of chariot driving **Hyksos** (people of Southwest Asia) in 1700 BC placed Egypt under outside dominance for nearly two centuries. The Hyksos conquerors gradually absorbed the Egyptian language but remained culturally separate. The Egyptians overthrew the Hyksos in the 1500s BC.

WRITING AND THE ARTS

At an early stage, Egyptians developed a writing system based on **hieroglyphics**[1] that flowed from "sacred carved letters" for holy scriptures. The writing was later streamlined into a cursive **demotic**[2] for commerce. Scribes recorded events and transactions on stone and wooden tablets and later on paper-like **papyrus** plant leaves. This aided in the expansion and maintenance of the far-flung empire. Scribes compiled the ***Book of the Dead*** containing prayers and advice on achieving the afterlife.

In the arts, the ancient Egyptians left paintings and statuary to depict momentous events, conquests, and scenes from everyday life that tell us much about their 3000 year-old culture.

ISIS – Egyptian goddess of fertility and nature

RELIGION

Egyptians were polytheistic. They worshiped deities such as **Ra Horakhty** – the sun-god (later Amon-Re), **Osiris** – the god of the afterlife, **Isis** – goddess of fertility and nature, and **Horus** – god of light and son of Amon-Re whom the pharaohs supposedly personified. In the 3000-1000 BC period, belief in an afterlife and

MEDITERRANEAN SEA

PHEONICIA

CANAAN

NATRUN VALLEY

AVARIS

QATAR DEPRESSION

SINAI

MEMPHIS
LISHT

Great Pyramids

THIS   **KARNAK**
              THEBES

RED SEA

NUBIA

NILE RIVER VALLEY CIVILIZATION 3000 BC – 1000 BC

1 hieroglyphics (pictorial symbols)
2 demotic (common language)

the early pharaohs' belief in their own divinity led them to build monumental pyramid tombs. In the tombs, their bodies were **mummified**[1] for the afterlife.

SOCIAL STRUCTURE

Egyptian society was stratified with the pharaohs at the pinnacle, followed by the priestly class, noble warriors, merchants and artisans, peasants, and slaves. Women in ancient Egypt had more freedom than in other ancient societies. They could own property, engage in commerce, and even be a priestess.

TECHNOLOGY

Egyptian scholars developed a 12-month calendar, geometric systems for land development and reclamation, elaborate irrigation and dike systems, and surgical procedures and pharmacology in the medical field.

ARCHITECTURE:

The great stone pyramid tombs and temples to various gods in places like Giza and Karnak are still considered monumental achievements in building technology.

LEGAL SYSTEMS:

Justice was administered tightly through provincial governors and magistrates who were controlled by the pharaohs' bureaucracy. Judgments were arbitrary and adhered to central bureaucratic codes.

---

1 mummified (process of maintaining the dead body of a human being or an animal that has been embalmed and prepared for burial, as according to the practices of the ancient Egyptians)

Mini Assessment

MINI-ASSESSMENT

1 In ancient Egypt, which item was a cause of the other three?
   1 stable agricultural development
   2 geometric systems for land development and reclamation
   3 warm desert climate and annual flooding of the Nile
   4 building elaborate irrigation and dike systems

2 Which factor contributed most to the growth and development of ancient Egypt for the thousand years after King Menes rule (c. 3100 BC)?
   1 polytheism and slavery
   2 flexible social structure
   3 widespread use of hieroglyphics
   4 unity and stability

3 The importance of religion in ancient Egypt is portrayed in the
   1 development of medical sciences
   2 divine right rule of the Pharaohs
   3 dominance of warriors over other groups
   4 courts following central bureaucracy codes

Constructed Response:

"If the Nile smiles, the Earth is joyous,
Every stomach is full of rejoicing
Every spine is happy
Every jawbone crushes its food."
– ancient Egyptian hymn

1 Why did Egyptians find joy in the annual flooding of the Nile?

2 In what ways did the Nile unify Egyptian society?

OVERVIEW: ANCIENT MESOPOTAMIAN CIVILIZATIONS: 5000 -1600 BC

GEOGRAPHY

Mesopotamia means "land between the rivers." It has the generally mild mid-latitude desert (Koppen classification Bw) and steppe (Koppen classification Bs) climates of Southwest Asia. The mild climate and dual river system created an environment for agriculture. The **Tigris and Euphrates** flow southeastward from the highlands of Turkey and empty into the Persian Gulf. This **Fertile Crescent** cradled a number of civilizations (see map below). The need for irrigation and flood control often brought groups together from which city-states eventually emerged.

Sumer/Akkad (3100-2000 BC) were the first of the major Mesopotamian civilizations. The ancient city-states of Erech, Kish, Lagash, Uruk, and Ur were first unified as a monarchy by the Akkad's leader **Sargon the Great** (c. 2300 BC). Akkad rule weakened, and Ebla and Ur briefly dominated the region until 2000 BC.

Babylon/Assyria (2000-500 BC) became strong after an invasion by the Amorite people of western Syria. The Babylonian's great leader, **Hammurabi** (c. 1792-1750 BC), unified the city-states into a kingdom. He oversaw a golden age of scientific, legal (see Code of Hammurabi), and literary achievement. Afterwards, the region was dominated by the Hittite Empire (modern Turkey) and Assyria.

Babylon reemerged for a brief period from 800-500 BC. The great king of this era, **Nebuchadnezzar** (c. 612 BC) built the famed Hanging Gardens and enslaved the Hebrews of Israel. The Babylonian Empire fell to two Persian conquerors, **Cyrus the Great** (c. 539 BC), and **Darius** (c. 500 BC).

GOVERNMENT

City-states had different forms of governments such as monarchies and oligarchies. The unified empires were monarchies ruled by priest-warriors such as Sargon and Hammurabi.

WRITING AND THE ARTS

Sumer originated **cuneiform**[1] (c. 3100 BC). It is believed to be the world's first writing system and slowly evolved into an easier-to-use script writing. Sumer set up schools for training scribes in cuneiform. Sumerian literature includes the epic tale of the heroic king, *Gilgamesh*. Stone carvings, jewelry, and pottery celebrated great military victories and were tributes to the gods of the various cities.

RELIGION

Although Mesopotamians had polytheistic beliefs, each city-state had its own special god as protector (e.g., Marduk, protector of Babylon) and a large **ziggurat**[2] to honor the god. After 600 BC, the Persian conquerors introduced the monotheistic teachings of **Zoroaster**. His sacred book, *Zend-Avesta*, taught devotion to the one god, **Ahura Mazda**, and the god's fight against evil. The religion spread rapidly throughout the areas under Persian rule.

---

1 cuneiform (wedge-style ideographs on wet clay tablets)
2 ziggurat (pyramidal temple to honor a god)

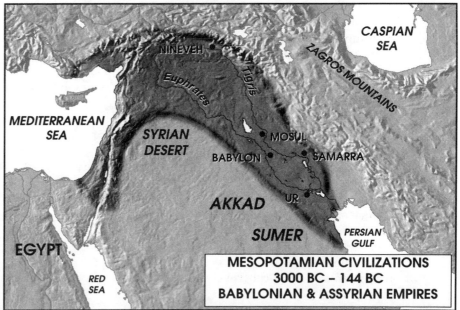

CASPIAN SEA

ZAGROS MOUNTAINS

NINEVEH

Euphrates

Tigris

MEDITERRANEAN SEA

SYRIAN DESERT

MOSUL

BABYLON

SAMARRA

AKKAD

UR

SUMER

PERSIAN GULF

EGYPT

RED SEA

**MESOPOTAMIAN CIVILIZATIONS
3000 BC – 144 BC
BABYLONIAN & ASSYRIAN EMPIRES**

SOCIAL STRUCTURE

The social hierarchy of the Mesopotamian civilizations varied little from that of Egypt. The rulers, priests, and nobles were at the top, the artisans and merchants made up a small middle class, and the vast majority were peasants. Slaves were conquered people taken as hostages in wars or debtors who sold themselves and their families into bondage. Mesopotamian women were more subject to the will of their husbands than those in Egypt. However, they could own possessions, operate businesses, and own and buy slaves.

Assyrian Chariot

TECHNOLOGY

Mesopotamian culture introduced bronze for use in tool and weapon making. The **Hittites** introduced iron during their invasions of the region (c. 1400 BC). Mesopotamian cultures developed a 12-month lunar calendar and the sundial. The feared Assyrians introduced wheeled chariots that made their mobile armies invincible. The Babylonians developed higher mathematics (algebra, geometry - 360 degree circle).

MINI-ASSESSMENT

Mini Assessment

1 In which way did ancient Egypt and ancient Mesopotamia differ?
  1 Mesopotamia enslaved conquered people. Egypt did not.
  2 In Mesopotamia, merchants exercised power. In Egypt, priests exercised power.
  3 Mesopotamia had competing city-states. Egypt had a unified kingdom.
  4 Mesopotamia had an independent court system. In Egypt, the Pharaoh dominated the courts.

2 In addition to being great warrior-kings, Babylonia's Hammurabi and Nebuchadnezzar were also
  1 lawgivers and builders
  2 businessmen and religious leaders
  3 farmers and scholars
  4 geographers and mathematicians

3 Which was the most common reason for the emergence of city-state societies in Mesopotamia?
  1 organization of religion
  2 educational systems
  3 irrigation and flood-control
  4 slave labor

Constructed response:

Sumerians developed cuneiform, using a wedge-shaped implement on clay tablets to represent syllables and sounds.

SUMERIAN CUNEIFORM

1 Cuneiform was an early system of _____.

2 Why did scribes hold such a special position in ancient civilizations?

ARCHITECTURE

The Sumerians introduced canal-building for transportation, flood relief, and irrigation to offset scarce rainfall. The canals unified the area via commerce and travel. Mesopotamian cultures also introduced the arch allowing more flexibility and strength in building design.

LEGAL SYSTEMS

Priests, sometimes acting as magistrates, enforced the king's laws such as the **Code of Hammurabi**. The Code was an ordered arrangement dealing with labor, personal property, and business. It sought to protect the state and the gods, promised harsh penalties, and held that the strong should not injure the weak.

OVERVIEW: ANCIENT INDUS VALLEY CIVILIZATION

The earliest ancient river valley civilization of the Indus Valley was the **Harappa** culture. It was a group of related, but widely dispersed, cities in northwestern India (modern Pakistan). Remains of the cities of Mohenjo-daro and Harappa show they were contemporary with civilizations of Egypt and Mesopotamia. These cities spread over a wide region. They were well developed with grid patterns, large blocks, and uniform housing. Surrounding farmers produced a wide variety of grains.

Floods and other ecological disasters weakened the civilization around 1700 BC, but some scholars believe there was a final massacre. It may have been done by conquering Aryan peoples whose epics refer to their conquest of walled cities.

From 1500-500 BC nomadic people, called **Aryans** from the Black and Caspian Sea region of central Asia, invaded the Indus Valley. They descended south and eastward through the Hindu Kush (western Himalayas) with horses, chariots, and cattle. Their **rajahs**[1] enjoyed war, chariot races, and festivals. As herdsmen, their wealth was measured in cattle, and they frequently raided each others' herds. Merging with the native people of the Indus Valley, they gradually changed to agriculturalists.

GEOGRAPHY

The Himalayas to the north and deserts to the west of the Indian **subcontinent**[2] cut off the people but did not completely isolate them. As with Egypt and Mesopotamia, mild climates (Koppen-type: Bs [steppe], Cw [mid-latitude mild) made the area hospitable. However, life in the subcontinent was (and still is) determined by the **monsoons**[3]. In summer, air rising over the hot land areas produces maximum precipitation. Inland mountain streams contribute to the Indus, Ganges, and Brahmaputra Rivers. During winter, cool winds from the interior of Asia dry the subcontinent. A late monsoon may bring drought, and a few more monsoon disturbances than normal may produce floods.

GOVERNMENT

The Indus Valley cities of the 4000-2000 BC era appear to have been well-organized. Yet, little is known about their governmental structures.

---

1 rajahs (warrior chiefs)
2 subcontinent (large landmass, such as India, that is part of a continent but is considered either geographically or politically as an independent entity)
3 monsoons (wind system that influences large climatic regions and reverses direction seasonally)

Map labels:
CASPIAN SEA
IRANIAN PLATEAU
MESOPOTAMIA
HARAPPA
HIMALAYAS
INDUS RIVER
PERSIAN GULF
INDO GANGETIC PLAIN
MOHENJO-DARO
GULF OF OMAN
KATHIAWAR
DECCAN PLATEAU
ARABIAN PENINSULA
ARABIAN SEA
BAY OF BENGAL
INDIAN OCEAN

**INDUS RIVER CIVILIZATIONS
2700 BC – 500 BC
HARAPPA & ARYAN CULTURES**

There are no known records of great kings or empires uniting these early settlements.

WRITING SYSTEM

Archaeological evidence shows that Harappans placed pictograms on commercial seals, but no other evidence of writing has been found, and the images remain a mystery. Later, under the Aryans, children attended school and learned the written language, **Sanskrit**, which has constructions similar to those found in English, Spanish, French and German. From Sanskrit evolved hymns and epics (the 100,000 verse *Mahabharata* and the 24,000 verse *Ramayana*).

Krishna god of love

RELIGION

Early religion involved polytheistic worship of gods connected to nature and an eternal spirit, **Brahman Nerugna**. The **Hindu** religion's holy books stemmed from centuries of oral traditions. The *Vedas* were written down between 1500 and 500 BC. The *Vedas* represented a cultural blend of Aryan religious ideas with those of original peoples of South Asia. Over many centuries, their religious customs flowing from the *Vedas* and other epics gradually merged into Hinduism.

Between 800 and 400 BC, Hindu beliefs were blended in the writings that became the *Upanishads*. The key idea was that all living things have souls under Brahman Nerugna (the one eternal spirit). Even animals became sacred, and killing them was forbidden. This moved Hinduism toward vegetarian practices. The *Upanishads* also taught the concept of **reincarnation**[1]. The object of life was to commit to the ideal way of life through

Rama – god of conquest

dharma[2] and ahimsa[3]. The soul had to move through several reincarnations. In each successive phase of existence, actions and conduct (**karma**[4]) had to be purer. Ultimately, this would lead to achieving **moksa**[5] with Brahman Nerugna.

SOCIAL STRUCTURE

The *Vedas* outlined the 5 basic **varnas**[6] from which grew subclasses called **jati**. This developed a very complex and rigid **caste system**. To some extent, the system remains in place today. The five classes, in order of importance or rank in Vedic/Aryan society were:

- **Brahmins** (priests) = ± 1% of population
- **Kshatriyas** (warriors) = ± 9% of population
- **Vaisyas** (herders, farmers, merchants, artisans) = ± 10% of population
- **Sudras** (servants, laborers) = ± 30% of population
- **Pariahs** (outcasts, slaves) = ± 50% of population (later called untouchables)

Aryan society was male-dominated, but women played active economic and social roles. In the earlier Harappan civilization, women had high status. In later Aryan society, women were more restricted.

TECHNOLOGY

Harappans were among the first people in the world known to have kept chickens. They also had dogs, buffalo, and cattle. They may also have had domesticated pigs, horses, camels, and possibly, elephants. The Harappans cultivated wheat, barley, and cotton. Their artifacts show varied pottery forms and designs along with spears, knives, and other objects of copper and bronze.

---

1 reincarnation (rebirth of the soul)
2 dharma (responsible action and conduct proper to the varna - social class)
3 ahimsa (non violence)
4 karma (the total effect of a person's actions and conduct)
5 moksa (liberation from the world and union with Brahman Nerugna)
6 varnas (social classes)

CLOSE LOOK

Literary Works of Ancient India

Mahabharata relates the turbulent history of the ancient kingdom of Kurukshetra and contains the teaching of the god Krishna. With the *Ramayana*, the *Mahabharata* is the principal source of Hindu social and religious doctrine.

Ramayana describes the efforts of Kosala's heir, Rama, to regain his throne and rescue his wife, Sita, from the demon King of Lanka, Ravana.

Bhagavad Gita is one of the most widely studied sacred writings of Hinduism. Taken from the *Mahabharata*, the *Bhagavad Gita*, written as a poem. It is Krishna's response to questions posed by Arjuna, a warrior prince, concerning his responsibility in good and evil as he is about to go into battle.

ARCHITECTURE

Harappan cities were remarkably similar. Each had baked brick construction with a **citadel** (fortress) at the center, silos for grain, baths, sophisticated dikes, and drainage systems against floods. Aryans were nomadic peoples and left few significant architectural remains in the Indus Valley.

OVERVIEW: ANCIENT CHINESE CIVILIZATION

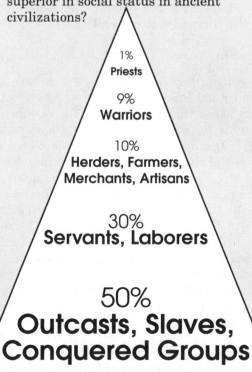

GEOGRAPHY

The **Huang He (Yellow) River Valley** is surrounded by mountains on three sides and bordered by the Pacific on the east. This environment gave protective isolation to the early Neolithic farmers who were drawn by fertile loess and

MINI-ASSESSMENT

Mini Assessment

1 Which frequent pattern characterizes the Aryan conquest of Harappan civilization of the Indus Valley?
   1 Warriors settled down to become hunter-gatherers.
   2 Conquerors blended into conquered civilizations.
   3 Technological progress was reversed.
   4 The values of the conquerors obliterated the religion of the conquered society.

2 A major determinant of life in the subcontinent of India is the monsoon, a
   1 wind system influencing large climatic regions
   2 ranking system of social classes
   3 process for domesticating animals
   4 Sanskrit writing system

3 Harappan cities were similar in construction and layout. What does this indicate about their political organization?
   1 Democracy allowed for diversity.
   2 Harrapans had highly centralized rule.
   3 Only the educated held high office.
   4 Harrapans had no political organization.

Constructed Response:

1 Which of the groups below make up the majority of the people in Aryan Society?

2 Why are priests and warriors considered superior in social status in ancient civilizations?

1%
Priests

9%
Warriors

10%
Herders, Farmers, Merchants, Artisans

30%
Servants, Laborers

50%
Outcasts, Slaves, Conquered Groups

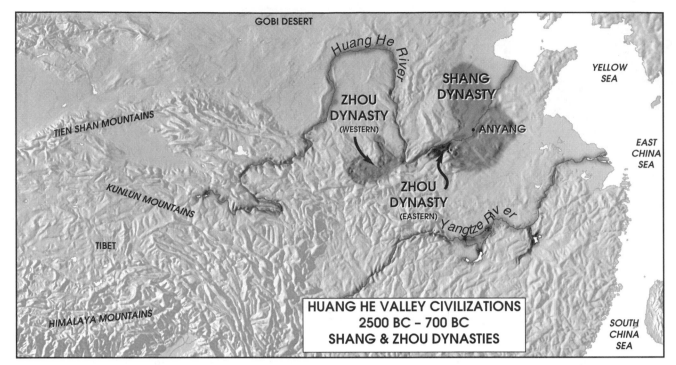

HUANG HE VALLEY CIVILIZATIONS
2500 BC – 700 BC
SHANG & ZHOU DYNASTIES

water resources. The rainy, mild winter and rainy cool winter climates (Koppen-types Cf and Df) made the area hospitable. Like those in other river valley civilizations, the early Huang He inhabitants had to deal with periodic flooding from winter snow melt and summer monsoons. Though not as intense a factor as in the Indus Valley, the summer monsoons blowing across China from the Pacific intensified flooding in the Huang He River Valley.

GOVERNMENT

As with other river valley civilizations, the common need for flood control and irrigation projects led to the organization of governments. Although myths and legends go back to before 5000 BC, the first documented Chinese civilization was the **Shang Dynasty** (1700 BC). Up to c. 1027 BC, Shang rulers gradually conquered a large area of the Huang He River Valley. From the walled capital **Anyang**, the Shangs controlled a loose confederation of settlement groups in the Henan region of Northern China. The kingdom was divided among loyal family members and followers. Control was in the form of a **feudal system**. It involved the exchange of military service by **vassals**[1] for a noble's grant of land, and it bound them together by complex codes of allegiance, honor, and duty. The right to govern was a modified divine right system called the **"Mandate of Heaven."** This meant the ruler's power depended on heaven's continued

favor of his personal behavior. If nobles or war lords sensed a dynasty was weakening and losing divine favor (or even because of severe natural disasters sent by the heavens), the dynasty could be replaced.

Around 1027 BC, King Wu, leader of the **Zhou** (Chou), a semi-nomadic people from the northwest (Xi'an), overthrew the weak Shang king, Zhouxin. The early Zhou rulers continued most practices of the Shangs. They reorganized a bureaucracy of aristocrats in the central region and put the outlying areas under the rule of vassals. After 770 BC, the Zhou kings presided over a period of great intellectual achievement – China's "Golden Age." It developed classical Chinese literature and the philosophies of **Confucianism**, **Taoism**, and **Legalism**.

WRITING SYSTEM

Shang civilization was characterized by an advanced system of ideographs that evolved into a complex universal writing system of 10,000 basic characters. **Calligraphy**[2] became an admired skill. The king's scribes recorded much ancient oral myth in works such as *I Ching* and *The Book of Songs* (c. 500 BC).

---

1 vassals (subordinate people who held land from a feudal lord and received protection in return for homage and allegiance)
2 calligraphy (creative and artistic manor and style of fine handwriting)

SOCIAL STRUCTURE

The classes in China were similar to those in other early river valley civilizations – warriors, artisans, merchants, peasants. The warriors' feudal code also had a parallel in civilian life in the form of complex rules of social etiquette and personal deportment called **li**.

TECHNOLOGY

Artisans of the Shang and Zhou civilizations practiced sophisticated skills with bronze and iron. These ancient civilizations also had a system of coinage, developed the first 365-day calendar, used chariots in war, and cultivated silk and soy bean crops.

RELIGION

As was the case in Mesopotamia, the Shang kings functioned as high priests of the supreme deity, **Shang-Di**. Aided by a priestly class, the Shang kings called on their powerful ancestral spirits to intercede on their behalf with the gods of nature. The people looked to the most powerful of the Shang gods to bring rain for good crops and other blessings.

Records of these priestly activities have survived in the form of **oracle bones**. Priests wrote questions about the future on animal bones, heated them until they cracked, and interpreted the cracks. One key spiritual belief for the ancient Chinese was that life revolved around maintaining a balance between the opposing forces in the universe – **yin**[1] (represented by the Earth/Moon) and **yang**[2] (represented by Heaven / Sun).

Chinese Symbol – *Yin Yang*

---

1 yin (passive, feminine, darkness, principle, represented by the Earth / Moon)
2 yang (active, masculine, light principle, represented by Heaven / Sun)

Mini Assessment

1   Scholars note that the earliest of China's dynasties, the Shang, exercised control through a feudal system. This involved the exchange of military service for a
  1   ceremony to pacify angry gods
  2   central bureaucracy
  3   contract to build great temples
  4   grant of land

2   Functioning as high priests of the supreme deity increased the Shang kings power because the people expected them to
  1   control the philosophy of Confucianism
  2   interpret the oracle bones
  3   maintain a balance between yin and yang
  4   intercede with the gods to bring rain for good crops

3   Shang and Zhou warriors had a technological advantage against enemies in using
  1   calligraphy
  2   oracle bones
  3   the mandate of heaven
  4   wheeled chariots

Constructed Response:

Use the relief map on the opposite page to assist in answering the following questions:

1   Which physical barriers surround China?

2   In what way did the environment of China differ from ancient Egypt, Mesopotamia, and India?

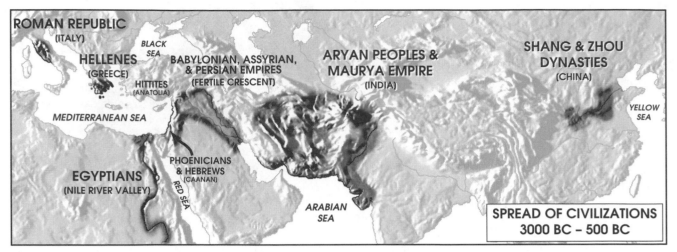

SPREAD OF CIVILIZATIONS 3000 BC – 500 BC

Map labels: ROMAN REPUBLIC (ITALY) · HELLENES (GREECE) · BLACK SEA · BABYLONIAN, ASSYRIAN, & PERSIAN EMPIRES (FERTILE CRESCENT) · HITTITES (ANATOLIA) · ARYAN PEOPLES & MAURYA EMPIRE (INDIA) · SHANG & ZHOU DYNASTIES (CHINA) · YELLOW SEA · MEDITERRANEAN SEA · EGYPTIANS (NILE RIVER VALLEY) · PHOENICIANS & HEBREWS (CAANAN) · RED SEA · ARABIAN SEA

CLASSICAL CIVILIZATIONS AND CONTRIBUTIONS

GEOGRAPHY OF CLASSICAL CIVILIZATIONS

In the period between 600 BC and 500 AD civilization expanded rapidly out of the river valley "cradles" and over the continents of the globe. The search for economic betterment, acquiring resources, and seeking trade caused civilizations to expand. That expansion spread the ideals and philosophies, religions and institutions, and laws and technologies born in the river valleys. In most cases the spread of civilization and economic enrichment set the scene for "golden ages" of intellectual and creative achievement

Despite a sometimes near paranoiac fear of outside influence and invasion, Q'in and Han rulers spread China's civilization from the Huang He Valley southward into the Yangtze and Si River Valleys. They influenced life to the north and east toward Manchuria, Korea, and Japan. Their merchants spread westward through the deserts and mountains of Central Asia toward Persia along the **Silk Route** (see pg. 51). In the process, China became an empire.

The Indus River Valley Civilization spread eastward into the Ganges Valley and across the northern plains of the subcontinent. With Maurya and Gupta rulers came the spread of Hinduism and Buddhism.

Out of Mesopotamia grew the Persian Empire of Darius and Cyrus who conquered lands east to the Indus and west around the Mediterranean Basin into Egypt, North Africa, Asia Minor, and the edge of Europe. They created tight-knit administrations by dividing their empires into provinces. They protected merchant caravans so that trade and commerce would strengthen the ties of their realms.

New empires arose in this classical period as older ones weakened. On the edges of ancient empires, seafaring traders built sophisticated societies that linked the older civilizations. The **Lydians**, **Minoans**, and **Phoenicians** traded with the **Egyptians**, **Assyrians**, and **Hittites** across the Eastern Mediterranean Sea. To broaden their commerce, they sailed westward and founded colonies that reached into less developed areas. They settled and traded from stations on Cyprus, Crete, Sicily, the islands of the Aegean and the Adriatic Seas, and the Greek mainland. The societies they contacted developed and grew into **Hellenistic**, **Carthaginian**, and **Roman civilizations**.

First, Greek city-states colonized the Mediterranean World. Then, Alexander spread Hellenistic culture from the Mediterranean to the Indus. Eventually, Rome wrenched control of the Mediterranean from Carthage and went on to build an empire that stretched from the British Isles to Egypt and Syria.

In the turmoil of this great economic and political expansion arose the great world religions. **Hinduism**, **Judaism**, **Buddhism**, and **Christianity** spread along the cultural highways of the great empires.

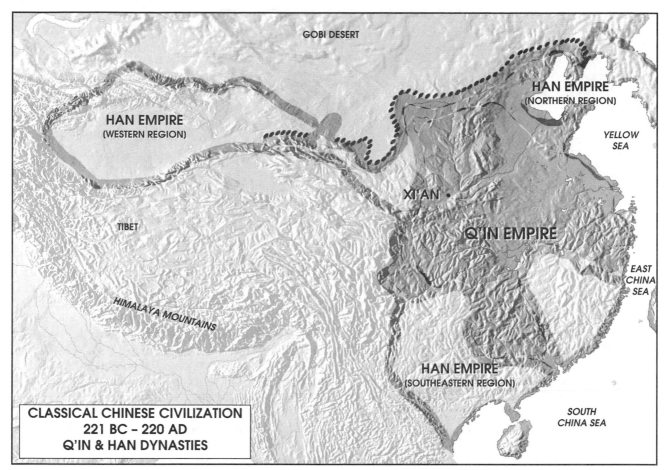

**CLASSICAL CHINESE CIVILIZATION
221 BC – 220 AD
Q'IN & HAN DYNASTIES**

CLASSICAL CHINESE CIVILIZATION

By 256 BC, the **Zhou** (Chou) **Dynasty** began to disintegrate as various vassal states warred with the Zhou kings. The fighting with local nobles destroyed the 800-year rule of the Zhou Dynasty.

A new dynasty emerged from the struggles that followed the downfall of the Zhou – the **Q'in** (or Ch'in). It lasted only a brief time (221-206 BC), but it united all the warring factions into China's first centralized empire. The young Q'in king adopted the title **Shi Huangdi** (First Emperor).

GREAT WALL OF CHINA
©PhotoDisc, Inc 1993

During eleven years, he and his chief minister, Li Si, replaced feudal states with military districts. They assigned military officials to govern them while requiring nobles to live in the capital. They standardized weights and measures, coinage, and the language. They built roads to move troops quickly throughout the empire. Shi Huangdi squashed opposition and began building the Great Wall for defense against nomadic invaders. Li Si made the Legalist school of philosophy the basis of the system. Shi Huangdi built irrigation systems as well as huge palaces and tombs. In the 1970s AD, excavation of the grave complex of Shi Huangdi in Xi'an (Sian) yielded a magnificent treasure of life-sized **terra cotta**[1] men and horses.

After Shi Huangdi's death in 210 BC, harsh policies and high taxes led to unrest among nobles. Conditions indicated the Q'in had lost the mandate of heaven and the dynasty was overthrown in 207 BC.

TERRA COTTA FIGURES
SHI HUANGDI GRAVE
Xi'an, China
©Sue Kime 1997

A new ruling family emerged under peasant military leader, **Liu Bang** (or Liu Qi, r. 210-195 BC), who founded the **Han Dynasty**. It ruled China for the next 400 years (210 BC-220 AD). China experienced another golden age of culture. Liu Bang created a central government system, trained a scholarly corps of Confucian administrators, and picked the most able among them to run his government. The dynasty grew stronger over the next 100 years.

The greatest of the Han emperors was Liu Qi (Liu Chi), later called **Wudi** (Han Wu Ti - martial emperor). He ruled for half a century (141-87 BC) and began China's classical golden age. Wudi developed a testing system for civil officials to avoid corruption. He pushed the Han borders northward into Manchuria and Korea, outward to the Pacific, and westward into Tibet. With expeditions to drive nomadic peoples away from China's borders, Han armies brought back knowledge of civilizations in the west such as Persia, Greece, and Rome. Ancient Central Asian trade routes were re-explored and China's silk found markets in the Middle East. At the same time, agricultural products such as figs, dates, and grapes found their way to China.

Confucianism became the Han official belief system. Scholars returned to studying Classic works of the Zhou era. Poets such as **Sima Xiangru** flourished, and *Shi Ji* (*Records of the Historian*, c. 100 BC), the first major history of China was written by **Sima Qian**. The growth of an educated class led to achievements in astronomy, chemistry, medicine, engineering,

and literature. Under the Han leadership, trade expanded marked by walled cities with magnificent wooden temples.

ANCIENT HEBREW CIVILIZATION

Around 2000 BC, a nomadic people of the Fertile Crescent settled on the eastern Mediterranean shore (Canaan) and founded the ancient civilization of the Hebrews. It became unique for its contribution of **monotheistic**[2] religion – **Judaism**. It remains the oldest living religion in the Western World. Its value system – concern for ethical behavior, justice, and the dignity of the individual – became the moral foundation for Western civilization.

The **Torah**, the first five books of the Hebrew Bible (called the "Old Testament" by Christians), became the basis for Judaism. According to the *Bible*, the one true God promised the Hebrew leader **Abraham** special protection for the twelve tribes (descendants of his grandson Jacob, or Israel). The ancient Hebrews developed a system of law (Halachah) encompassing personal, family, and social responsibilities, as well as civil and criminal procedures.

Famines caused the tribes to migrate from Canaan to Egypt (c. 1800 BC) where they became enslaved. Around 1200 BC, the Hebrew leader, **Moses**, led a mass exodus into the Sinai Desert. Following the exodus, Moses received the divine revelation resulting in basic laws called the **Ten Commandments**.

Several military campaigns resulted in the Israelite tribes resettling in southern Canaan or Palestine. By 1000 BC, **David** was able to unite the tribes into a Kingdom of Israel. His son, **Solomon**, turned Jerusalem into a major urban settlement and erected a great temple for worship.

---

1 terra cotta (hard, semifired, waterproof ceramic clay used in pottery and building construction)
2 monotheistic religion (belief in one God)

After King Solomon's death (c. 930 BC), dissension and revolts split the kingdom and weakened it. In the 8th century, Assyria conquered Israel and Judea. In 586 BC, Jerusalem was destroyed and the Hebrews were enslaved and exiled to Babylon (**Diaspora**[1]).

In 539 BC, the Persian King **Cyrus the Great** allowed the Hebrew exiles to return and resettle in Palestine – the southern area of their former kingdom, near the Dead Sea – living as a subject people of the Persians. After Persia fell to **Alexander the Great** (c. 330 BC), their country of Judea was dominated by Egypt and Syria, and Jews resettled throughout the Middle East. There was a brief period of independence for Judea under the Maccabees (139-63 BC) before Judea came under the rule of Rome in 63 BC. Later, many of the teachings of Judaism became the basis for two other great monotheistic belief systems, Christianity and Islam.

---

1 Diaspora (the dispersion of Jews outside of Israel from the sixth century BC, when the Jews were exiled to Babylonia, until the present time)
2 Hellenic culture (the Greeks called their region "Hellas")

ANCIENT GREEK CIVILIZATION

Unlike early civilizations, Greek civilization did not arise from river valleys, but from migrations and trading ventures of other peoples on the edges of the older civilizations. Archaeologists theorize that the first Greek speaking peoples, the **Mycenaeans**, migrated from Central Asia into the Balkans around 2000 BC. They conquered the Greek mainland, Peloponnesus and finally settled Crete.

In the mild, rainy climate (Koppen-type Cs) of the Mediterranean and Aegean Seas, the Mycenaeans set up a trading empire that lasted until 1200 BC. From their chief fortified cities at **Mycenae** (Peloponnesus) and **Knossos** (Crete) warrior-kings had commercial connections to most of the civilizations of the Eastern Mediterranean. There was great cultural diffusion as the trade contacts blended elements of Egyptian, Mesopotamian, and other cultures into early Greek or **Hellenic**[2] culture. The Mycenaeans amassed huge fortunes in their citadels and kept tight control through palace

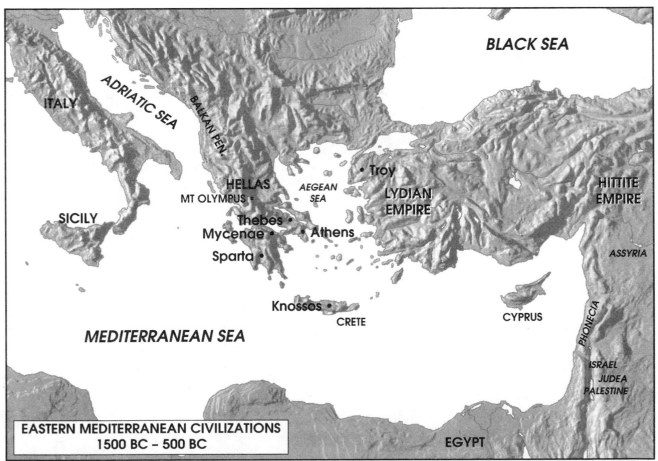

EASTERN MEDITERRANEAN CIVILIZATIONS
1500 BC – 500 BC

bureaucracies. Mycenae declined because of a combination of natural disasters and wars with surrounding peoples, such as the fabled Trojan War (c. 1300 BC), described by **Homer** in the *Iliad*.

Other regional people launched conquests. By 1100 BC, the invasions by a northern warlike people, the **Dorians,** began an era when civilization faded amid constant warfare from 1200 to 800 BC. Each small **polis** (city-state) grew in strength, but remained as isolated outposts of civilization. in the rugged terrain of the Balkan peninsula. The poet Homer's *Iliad* and *Odyssey* are epic poems of life in this chaotic era.

Two factors kept communication alive among the Greek **poleis**[1] (plural of polis): the sea and religion. The rocky coasts and islands forced Greeks to look to the sea for survival. They became fishermen and traders for food and resources, which brought them into rivalries with each other, but also brought them into alliances. Sailing farther for goods also brought them into contact with other civilizations. As they traveled, they absorbed others' ideas and customs. The Hellenic alphabet evolved from contacts with the Phoenicians of the Eastern Mediterranean coast.

The ancient Greeks were also unified by worshiping a similar **pantheon**[2]. They celebrated common festivals of the gods, whom they believed resided on Mount Olympus. **Delphi** was a sacred city where the temple of the god Apollo became a religious center that drew Greeks from most of the poleis. The prophecies of the **oracle**[3] that resided at Delphi were used to help rulers make key decisions. This common religious contact led to a sharing of values that supported rules among the poleis on basic conduct in war.

---

1 poleis (city-states of ancient Greece)
2 pantheon (all the gods of a people)
3 oracle (an authoritative religious counselor)

MAJOR DEITIES IN ANCIENT GREECE'S OLYMPIAN PANTHEON

God	Associated With
Zeus	King of the gods; most prominent deity of Greek mythology; god of the sky, lightning, rain; a ruler-father, sovereign, and controller
Hera	goddess of the original inhabitants of Greece; of marriage, virtue, women, and childbirth
Athena	patron goddess of Athens; wisdom and good sense; a major warrior figure; creator of the olive tree and handicrafts
Hermes	protector of flocks and shepherds; guide and protector of travelers; conductor of souls to the underworld; messenger of Zeus; bringer of good luck; patron of orators, writers, athletes, merchants, and thieves
Aphrodite	goddess of love and beauty
Apollo	god of prophecy, medicine, the fine arts, archery, beauty, flocks and herds, law, courage, and wisdom; god of the sun, light, truth, and music
Artemis	goddess of the hunt; mistress of wild things; the protectress of youth and women
Poseidon	producer of thunder; also the earth-shaker; god of the sea
Dionysus	god of fertility, ritual dance, and mysticism; supposedly invented wine making and was considered the patron of poetry, song, and drama

Mini Assessment

1 The spread of civilization beyond the "cradles" of the river valleys
   1 strengthened the original river valley civilizations
   2 set the scene for great "golden ages" of cultural achievement
   3 had a negative effect on global communications
   4 led to equality among all ancient peoples

2 The Q'in Dynasty (221-206 BC)
   1 created the first democracy in the ancient world
   2 conquered India, Persia, and Egypt
   3 relaxed strict laws and lowered taxes
   4 united factions into China's first centralized empire

3 The Mycenaeans established the base for the first Greek civilizations that developed into
   1 poleis   3 pantheons
   2 oracles   4 monotheists

Constructed Response:

"And God spoke these words, saying: I am the Lord your God, which [who] has brought you out of Egypt, out of the house of bondage. You shall have no other gods before me ..."

– Exodus

1 According to the quotation, why did the Hebrews leave Egypt?

2 In what way did the ancient Hebrew belief system differ from those of surrounding cultures?

GREEK INFLUENCE IN THE MEDITERRANEAN WORLD

Between 750 and 500 BC, the Greek city-states prospered and their populations grew. They colonized other areas of the Mediterranean (see chart below). Colonies supplied their "mother city" with agricultural products. As Hellenic civilization spread across the Mediterranean, trade expanded. Markets grew for Greek oil, wine, and other products in return for precious metals, timber, and grain.

GREEK CITY-STATE COLONIAL EXPANSION: 8TH – 6TH CENTURY BC	
Note: Neither Sparta nor Athens were colonial powers.	
Mother City	**Colony**
Corinth	Epidamnus, Corcyra, Syracuse, (greatest Greek city in the west)
Chalcis (modern Khalkis)	Naxus, Scione, Methone
Miletus, Samos, Phocaea,	Side, Appolonia, Istros, Odesseus, Olbia, Theodosia, Sinope, Siris, Elea, Nicaea, Agatha, Hemeroscorpian, Molaca
Thera, Samos, and Rhodes	Gela, Lipari, founded kingdom of Cyrene in northeast Libya
Megara	Byzantium, Megara Hyblaea

Persian Wars

In 546 BC, **Cyrus the Great** of Persia (599-530 BC) conquered Lydia near the Ionian coast (today = Anatolia or western Turkey). Ionia revolted in 499 BC, and Persia's King **Darius I** (522-480 BC) put down the revolt. Darius then tried to punish Athens for aiding the rebels. Athens surprised the Persians and defeated them at Marathon (490 BC). Darius' son, **Xerxes** (486-465 BC), attacked Athens again in 480 BC. Sparta aided Athens and a sea attack

RIVAL CITY-STATES – ATHENS AND SPARTA

SPARTA	ATHENS
Location: Peloponnesus	**Location:** Attica Peninsula
Founders: Dorians	**Founders:** Mycenaeans
Economy: agricultural (non-colonial)	**Economy:** seafaring traders and some (non-colonial) agriculture
Labor: helots (farm slaves or serfs) and foreign artisans provided most labor	**Labor:** common people were artisans, and farmers; middle and upper class were merchants and traders; conquered people, used as slaves, did mining, farm work, and tutoring
Social Order: military society; boys went into military training at age 7; from ages 20-30 men did frontier military service; at age 30 they married but lived in barracks until age 60; women given physical training to increase strength to marry at 14-19 to breed sons for the military; women were not citizens but could own property and interact socially	**Social Order:** private education for males 7-18 (studies included math, literature, music, and rhetoric, as training for citizenship); 2-year military service, ages 18-20; no formal education for females, trained at home in domestic skills
Government: oligarchy evolved slowly; dual kings had military role, but did not govern; the assembly (all male citizens over 20) had general law-making role; main power was in Council of 5 **Ephors** (veto power over actions of the Assembly); a **Council of** (28) **Elders** formed the judiciary and counseled the Assembly and the Ephors	**Government:** democracy evolved slowly; at first, just natural born landholders could be citizens; later, all males could be citizens regardless of class and participate in the Assembly; later, foreigners could become citizens; from 621-508 BC there were periods of rule by **tyrants** (benevolent dictators supported by the Assembly): • **Draco** (621 BC) encoded laws; severe punishments • **Solon** (594 BC) abolished debt-slavery; bicameral legislature (Council of 400 = aristocrats plus Assembly=commoners) • **Peisistratus** (561 BC) reformer; redistributed land • **Cleisthenes** (510 BC) expanded democracy; Assembly chose military high command and a lottery chose **Council of 500** (= bureaucracy); developed a large scale jury system
Achievement: strong military role in Greek conflicts (Persian and Peloponnesian Wars); strict military rule and tight social control stifled intellectual development, creativity, and technical advancement	**Achievement:** prosperity led to an expansive creativity, especially in drama, and allowed the city to adorn itself with magnificent public buildings such as the Parthenon (c. 447)

Prosperity meant homes and public buildings reflected more care in design. The 5th century design of the Parthenon, the great temple to Athena, manifests the Athenians' love of beauty and simplicity. The simple rectangular building is surrounded by slim, yet substantial Doric order columns. They give the building a sense of depth, height, and strength that pay tribute to the beloved goddess. The low, triangular pediment (roof gable) and columns are a design that has been used for centuries.

PARTHENON
©PhotoDisc, Inc 1994

cut off Xerxes' supply ships and destroyed his fleet at Salamis.

The clashes with Persia raised the Greek city-states' consciousness of their wealth and power but did not unite them. Athens became the central polis of a naval alliance – the **Delian League**. Athens came to dominate the League and drew tribute from other members. Sparta, because of pride in its different social and political order, resisted Athens' leadership. Sparta formed a military alliance of its own – the **Peloponnesian League**. Eventually, the two city-state alliances clashed.

GOVERNMENT IN THE GREEK CITY-STATES

At first mostly **monarchies**[1], the Greek poleis gradually changed into many different forms of government. As wealth grew, kings (monarchs) were challenged for power. Eventually, power in most city-states shifted to a small number of individuals. The general name for rule by a small group is **oligarchy**[2]. There are various types of oligarchies, depending on the nature of the decision-makers. For example, as the growth of trade increased the wealth of landholders, merchants, and artisans, these wealthy groups sought more decision-making power. They formed the type of oligarchy called an **aristocracy**[3].

As Hellenic education, knowledge, and military service broadened to encompass more mem-

bers of the community, some city-states sought to bring larger numbers of citizens into the process of decision-making. Rule by a broad-based citizenry is **democracy**[4]. While only a few city-states like Athens ever offered participation to the majority of inhabitants, establishing limited democracy had a great influence on civilization. Opening government decisions to debate and opinions of a large number of people (but not all) set an enduring example in human affairs. The ideal of a true, universal participation became a goal still sought by people.

RIVAL CITY-STATES – ATHENS & SPARTA

In the 5th century BC, the rivalry between Athens and Sparta spawned a great conflict. While not colonial powers, their leadership in the Persian wars elevated them to the strongest powers in Greece – Athens through trade and a strong navy and Sparta through its stringent military discipline. They symbolized differing social and governmental systems of the ancient Greek poleis.

ATHENS V. SPARTA: PELOPONNESIAN WAR

Pericles

Athens rebuilt itself with great energy after the destruction of the Persian Wars, and its culture reached a peak during the golden **Age of Pericles** (461-429 BC). The Athenians created beautiful temples (including the Parthenon) on the Acropolis (high hill). Pericles' skill as a statesman elevated

1 monarchies (single person rule)
2 oligarchy (rule by the few)
3 aristocracy (rule by a small group of rich individuals)
4 democracy (government by the people, exercised either directly or through elected representatives)

Athens to supreme power over other city-states in the Delian League (Aegean Sea area) and created an Athenian Empire. Pericles once boasted, "Athens is the school of Hellas."

Sparta faced internal problems (slave revolts) after the Persian Wars, but began to oppose Athens' power by forming a rival alliance (Peloponnesian League) and helping Megara (c. 457 BC) when attacked by Athens. In 431 BC, both city-states began military campaigns against the other's allies and colonies. The plague (typhus) killed off one-third of Athens population in 429 BC. Each power tried to unsettle the other's government. Sparta built Persia a navy in exchange for a pledge not to attack Ionia. Sparta then laid a successful siege against Athens which surrendered in 404 BC. The thirty years of warfare divided, weakened, and impoverished the Greek cities. Sparta's harsh leadership led to continuous challenges in the next sixty years. The poleis clashed and skirmished constantly in the 4th century BC. The continual conflicts weakened them until Macedonia conquered Greece in 338 BC.

GREEK CONTRIBUTIONS

The Greek poleis contributed greatly to government structures in the world. Because they were small, the city-states created models of different types of government (monarchy, oligarchy, democracy). In each polis, a basic type of government emerged and was then modified as the centuries ensued. Some were strict, some benevolent, but all had characteristics that have been studied and emulated, even in the modern world. None is a better example than Athens. Its evolution into a participatory democracy created a model for later generations.

As Hellenic civilization prospered, it entered what historians call its **classical period** – the most artistically developed stage of a civilization. Like all people, the Greeks dealt with processions of difficult problems (inter-city competition, foreign invasions, civil wars, class wars, slave revolts, natural disasters, plagues, and famines). Yet in the 5th century BC, their

civilization produced a level of expression in the arts, literature, philosophy, and science that became a lasting legacy.

As with other civilizations that prospered, artisans and craftsmen had time to perfect their skills and aspired to make them pleasing to their clients. First, potters experimented with different shapes and designs. Then, they embellished their **urns**[1] and other vessels with scenes from life or myths. From the earth or from shipwrecks have come painted urns that show scenes from everyday life as well as lyrical scenes depicting the exploits of heroes from the *Iliad* and the *Odyssey*.

Statue/Columns on South Porch of the Erechtheum on Athens' Acropolis near the Parthenon　©PhotoDisc, Inc 1994

The Greeks cherished beauty and order. They admired perfection of the human form. The sculptures of athletes, warriors, gods, and goddesses by **Myron**, **Phidias**, and **Praxiteles** realistically celebrate the power and strength of a great people.

The Greeks not only revered the human spirit and form, but the perfection of the human mind. Before the Age of Pericles, groups of Greek thinkers abandoned the idea that life was controlled by the gods. These **philosophers**[2] observed and analyzed the world around them, questioning the causes of what they saw. In science, figures such as **Democritis**[3], and **Hippocrates**[4] began to work in fields such as

1　urns (vase with footed base)
2　philosophers (scholars who analyze the processes of reason)
3　Democritis (studied composition of matter, the atom)
4　Hippocrates (studied medicine, plant composition)

physics, biology, and chemistry. **Pythagoras** expanded knowledge of geometry, music theory, and astronomy.

In the 5th century BC, as Athens entered the Age of Pericles, the **Sophists** emerged. They were a group of teachers who turned their attention from science and philosophy skills to practical studies – politics, law, and **rhetoric**[1].

Many Greek scholars rejected the approach of the Sophists as too narrow and materialistic. These anti-sophists devoted themselves to pure thought, universal truths, and seeking answers to questions about justice, **ethics**[2], and beauty. Three leaders who opposed the Sophists gradually helped Greek philosophy become the enduring basis for the intellectual life of Western civilization – Socrates, Plato, and Aristotle.

Socrates' (c. 469-399 BC) work marked a turning point in Western philosophy. Through the **Socratic method**[3], he moved philosophy toward consideration of **virtue**[4] and principle. His beliefs, especially the use of reason, became known through the work of his student, Plato.

Plato's (c. 428-347 BC) work presented the great concepts of philosophy, psychology, logic, and politics. In 387 BC, he founded the Academy and spent most of his life there teaching philosophy and the sciences. Plato's writings are nearly all written as his version of dialogues between his hero, Socrates, and others. His greatest work was *The Republic*, in which he presents an ideal political community and the education needed by its rulers. Plato distrusted democracy and wanted an orderly society run by **philosopher-kings**[5]. Plato's philosophy strongly influenced Islamic, Byzantine, Roman, and Mediaeval European thinkers for centuries.

Aristotle's (384-322 BC) work strongly influenced the fields of logic (*On Interpretation*), ethics (*Metaphysics*), physics (*Meteorologica*), biology (*History of Animals, Parts of Animals*), and literary criticism (*Poetics*). In government, Aristotle leaned toward a benevolent form of monarchy. In 335 BC, he founded his own school, the Lyceum. One of his students was Alexander the Great. Learning focused particularly on the detailed study of nature. Historically, Aristotelian philosophy dominated Western thought. It is the foundation for many modern intellectual disciplines.

Once Socrates, Plato, and Aristotle redirected philosophy toward the search for truth, a variety of sects emerged. Examples include:

- **Cynics** (Diogenes, Antisthenes) believed happiness is achieved by cultivating virtue and self-control.

- **Epicureans** (Epicurus) believed knowledge is based on sense perception.

- **Stoics** (Zeno) believed virtue is achieved by seeking a reasonable outlook and not giving way to emotion.

The ideals of beauty and order show themselves in the Classical Greek style of literature. The poetry of **Sappho**, **Pindar**, and **Aeschylus** influenced the themes and metrical pattern of poets for centuries. Greek drama reflected not only myths and legends but also the great debates of philosophers. The comedies and tragedies of the Age of Pericles are still performed today. The Greeks also applied their literary skills to writing accurate history.

---

1 rhetoric (effective public speaking)
2 ethics (moral behavior)
3 Socratic method (teaching by asking questions)
4 virtue (moral excellence, right behavior, goodness)
5 philosopher-kings (an educated elite group of citizens)

CLASSICAL AGE GREEK DRAMA	
DRAMATIST	**Work**
Aeschylus	*Oresteia* (tragedy) law should guide the community
Sophocles	*Antigone* (tragedy) – Individual moral duty; *Oedipus Rex* (tragedy) suffering is part of life
Euripides	*The Trojan Women* (tragedy) tragic flaws of the human character
Aristophanes	*The Clouds* (comedy-satire); *Lysistrata* (comedy-satire)

Mini Assessment

1 Most of the poleis of ancient Greece were controlled by
1 oligarchs   3 philosophers
2 oracles   4 foreign kings

2 Athens and Sparta headed rival alliances of Greek city-states which clashed in the
1 Poleis Wars
2 Persian Wars
3 Pantheon Wars
4 Peloponnesian Wars

3 The combined work of Socrates, Plato, and Aristotle in Greece's classical period created
1 widespread support for the Sophist philosophy
2 an intellectual basis for Western thought
3 the basis for democracy in all the poleis
4 new theories on the origin of the universe

Constructed Response:

"... Until philosophers are kings, ...cities will get no rest from troubles and neither will mankind. Then only will this State of ours see the light of day with a good chance of survival."

– Socrates speaking in Plato's *The Republic*

1 According to the quotation, on what does the survival of the State depend?

2 Why is having education an important quality for a ruler?

Herodotus (the father of history) and **Thucydides** focused on sifting fact from the stories and legends of the past.

SPREAD OF HELLENISTIC CIVILIZATION

By the middle of the 4th century BC, the Greek poleis weakened due to their continual infighting. To their north on the Balkan Peninsula, a new kingdom arose to dominate them – **Macedonia**. In 356 BC, **Philip II**, a skillful leader became king of Macedonia. Methodically using force and diplomacy, Philip won control of Delphi and its allied cities in central Greece. Then, in 338 BC, he conquered Thebes and Athens. Philip had dreams of leading his new Hellenistic kingdom against its traditional enemy, Persia. However, he was murdered in 336 BC.

Philip's son, the brilliant **Alexander the Great** was a student of Aristotle's and only 20 years old when he succeeded to Macedonia's throne. The young warrior carried out Philip's dream of a magnificent new

empire. Historians refer to this as the **Hellenistic Age** (c. 324 to 27 BC). To avoid confusion of two similar terms, *Hellenic* refers to the culture developed during the classical age of the Greek poleis. The *Hellenistic* culture is post-classical; it developed after the Greek poleis faded in power. Hellenistic culture emerged as a blend of the cultures of the vast region conquered by Alexander the Great and extended to the beginning of the Roman Empire under Augustus.

ALEXANDER'S CONQUESTS & HELLENISTIC WORLD   c. 323 BC

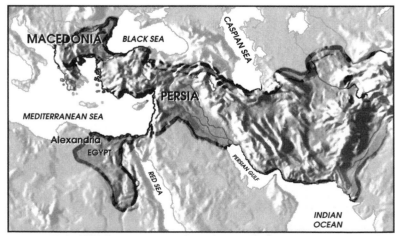

Alexander began his conquests by crushing revolts in the Greek cities (336 BC). In the next two years, he threw the powerful Macedonian cavalry and **phalanx**[1] into an onslaught of campaigns that overpowered the Persians in Palestine and Egypt. In the next ten years (334-324 BC), he moved his forces steadily eastward, overpowering strong resistance from local Persian administrators. The result was a grand empire that stretched from Greece to the Indus River Valley.

PARALLEL GRECO-ROMAN DEITIES		
GREEK	**ASSOCIATION**	**ROMAN**
Zeus	ruler-father, sovereign, controller	Jupiter
Hera	marriage	Juno
Hermes	athletics, poetry, travelers	Mercury
Aphrodite	love	Venus
Ares	war	Mars
Apollo	medicine, fine art, wisdom	Apollo
Artemis	the hunt, protector of women	Diana
Poseidon	earth and sea mover	Neptune
Dionysus	fertility, dance, song, drama	Bacchus

Alexander ordered the building of libraries and centers of learning such as that of Alexandria, Egypt. There, the knowledge of classical Greece fused with that of the East. Alexander's empire was short lived. In 323 BC, he died in Babylon as he was returning home from the Indus Valley. The Greek traders and artisans that supplied his armies diffused their culture, blending it with the cultures of Egypt, Palestine, and Persia. Intermarriage of his soldiers with inhabitants of conquered territories intermixed the cultures even more.

The result was a new Hellenistic civilization that carried learning and the arts to new heights. Hellenistic scholars looked at nature and studied patterns and laws. They organized bodies of knowledge in science and mathematics. **Pythagoras** and **Euclid** blended knowledge of three continents into the basis of geometry. In science, **Aristarchus** (Earth orbits the Sun) and **Archimedes** (water displacement, principles of simple machines) began to work in fields such as astronomy and physics.

After Alexander's sudden death, his generals broke the empire into Asian, Egyptian, and Macedonian dynasties. The Greek city-states once more fell into struggles for power.

ROME: CITY OF CONQUEST

According to tradition, members of the **Latin** tribe founded **Rome** in 753 BC. From the 7th to the 1st centuries BC, Rome's citizen warriors (lifetime military service was required as it had been in Sparta) conquered all of the Italian Peninsula, Sicily, and Carthage. In the process, Rome's government moved from monarchy, to **republic**[2], to dictatorship. The Etruscan kings of the 7th century BC drained marshes around the Tiber and built the Circus Maximus and the **Forum**[3], but they were hated by the Latins.

By 200 BC, Rome's new strength was rising in the central Mediterranean. By the 2nd century BC, it was growing into a major power. Before it fell 600 years later, it conquered Greece, much of Alexander's former holdings in the Eastern Mediterranean, and eventually, most of North Africa and Europe.

Rome conquered Macedonia and made it an imperial province in 148 BC. Rome's rulers allowed Greek poleis **autonomy**[4] and preserved and protected the more important ones, such as Athens, as centers of learning. The Romans' admiration of Greek civilization led them to take for their own much of the Greek culture – art, architecture, technology, education, and religion (see chart above).

As imperial army legions moved through the Eastern Mediterranean, Roman leaders replaced monarchs and reorganized kingdoms. Some areas overthrew their traditional rulers in places such as Pergamum and Palestine.

THE ROMAN REPUBLIC

The Roman Republic evolved over a long period. In 509 BC, the Roman **Senate**, an advisory body to the Etruscan kings, overthrew the monarchy. The **Roman republic** (*res publica* – "the peoples' thing") began as an oligarchy of

---

1 phalanx (blocks of infantry carrying overlapping shields and long spears)
2 republic (representative democracy)
3 Forum (public square)
4 autonomy (home rule)

patricians[1]. The patricians of the Senate created the laws of Rome and elected two **consuls**[2]. To limit power, consuls were elected annually and served for only one term. As the city grew, other officials were selected to serve under the consuls, and a bureaucracy emerged.

Not all Romans participated in the patrician government. Women, slaves, and foreigners were excluded. The **plebeians**[3] were second class citizens. They paid taxes, did military service, but had no voice in the government. By the 5th century BC, the plebeians began campaigning for more rights. They demanded the laws be written and made public. In 450 BC, plebeian agitation led the patricians to place the **Laws of the Twelve Tablets** in the Forum. They became the basis for the Roman legal system. The plebeians' **Assembly of Tribes** gained the right to have **tribunes**[4] address their concerns in the Senate, and some plebeians were appointed to administrative positions. In 366 BC, plebeians could be chosen consuls. Finally, in 287 BC, the plebeian Assembly of Tribes earned the right to make the laws for the republic.

MOVING TOWARD EMPIRE

During the era of the Republic, Rome's military organization and tightly disciplined citizen-army conquered the Italian Peninsula. The Romans copied the battle tactics of the Greeks and Macedonians, but split their legions into smaller, highly mobile forces of 100 men (**centuries**). Part of the Romans' success was the management of conquered peoples. They created military colonies (permanent occupation forces) within the conquered territories. They conscripted conquered soldiers into their legions. They allowed some people to govern themselves, while giving others limited Roman citizenship.

In 264 BC, Rome came into conflict with another great Mediterranean power – the Phoenician city of **Carthage** in North Africa. In the three Punic Wars, Rome and Carthage struggled for control of the Western Mediterranean. In the **First Punic War** (264-241 BC), Rome took the grain producing island of Sicily, becoming a sea power in the process, but Rome also lost nearly one-fifth of its citizens

in the war. In 238 BC, the Romans took Sardinia and Corsica and threatened Carthage's colonial settlements in Spain.

In the **Second Punic War** (218-201 BC), Carthage's great general, **Hannibal**, launched an invasion from Spain, crossing the Pyrenees and the Alps and swooping down on Rome from the north. The Romans suffered heavy losses and lost control of the Gauls in the north. For the next six years, Hannibal won battles on the Italian Peninsula, but was unable to conquer Rome itself. In 210 BC, the Roman general **Scipio** cut Hannibal's supply lines in Spain, and in 204 BC, Scipio crossed the Mediterranean and invaded Carthage itself. Hannibal had to transfer his efforts to defend Carthage. The Romans decisively defeated Carthage in 202 BC.

Over the next fifty years, Carthage rebuilt its economy, but did not break the peace of 202 BC. Still, Rome saw Carthage's recovery as a threat to its power and allies in the Mediterranean. In the **Third Punic War** (149-146 BC), Rome attacked to protect its North African ally, Numidia. Rome destroyed the city of Carthage, ruined its land, and sold the Carthaginians into slavery.

THE END OF THE ROMAN REPUBLIC

Constant warfare in the 2nd century BC against Carthage and subduing the peoples of the Eastern Mediterranean, Spain, and Gaul took an economic toll on the republic. Some individuals became wealthy using slave labor to work **latifundias**[5] to supply the city and the Roman legions. The average Roman citizen did not share in this wealth but had to pay increasingly burdensome taxes for imperial conquests.

The political unrest that festered at the end of the 2nd century BC broke into civil war in the 1st century BC. Between 130 and 100 BC, reformers such as tribunes **Tiberius** and **Gaius Graccus** offered hope of land reform, but mob violence tragically ended their efforts. Consul **Gaius Marius** (r. 104-100 BC) began to pay army volunteers from the poorer classes, creating a professional army. Marius was overthrown by aristocratic General **Lucius Sulla** in a civil

---

1 patricians (aristocrats)
2 consuls (administrators / army commanders)
3 plebeians (common people - farmers, merchants, artisans)
4 tribunes (representatives)
5 latifundias (large farms)

The Colosseum is one of Rome's most famous landmarks. Begun in 69 AD by the Roman Emperor Vespasian, this massive amphitheater has survived although greatly damaged in many wars. Today, the Colosseum faces its greatest challenge from corrosive air pollution.

ROMAN COLOSSEUM
©PhotoDisc, Inc 1994

war in 88 BC. Sulla became dictator and purged the plebeians from the leadership, restoring patrician rule. In 70 BC, consuls **Gnaeus Pompey** and **Marcus Crassus** joined with Senator **Julius Caesar** to form a **triumvirate**[1] and restored stability to Rome.

The internal disruptions of the early 1st century led outlying provinces to rebel against Roman rule. Once the triumvirate settled problems in Rome, the ambitious Caesar and Crassus took armies to quell the outlying areas. Crassus died in battle in Persia in 53 BC. Caesar was successful in subduing Gaul (Gallic Wars) and spreading Roman control into northern Europe.

Pompey and the Senate feared Caesar's legions were too powerful and would overthrow the government. In 49 BC, Pompey and the Senate ordered Caesar to leave his army and return to Rome. Caesar marched his legions on Rome and began a civil war (49-45 BC). He pursued Pompey's forces through Eastern Mediterranean, North Africa. In Egypt, Caesar made Cleopatra his mistress and then queen. Finally, he ended up in Spain. After eliminating this opposition, the Senate appointed Caesar dictator-for-life.

Caesar changed the tax structure, reordered the land holding system, expanded Roman citizenship to all Italy and many provinces, and reformed the calendar. He was popular and, as his power grew, so did the fear he would change Rome into a monarchy. In 44 BC, Brutus and Cassius, leaders of Caesar's enemies in the Senate, assassinated him.

Another civil war ensued. Caesar's followers, **Marc Antony**, **Marcus Lepidus**, and his nephew **Octavian**, defeated his enemies and formed a new triumvirate. In the next twelve years, the harsh, three-way dictatorship disintegrated. Lepidus was removed from power and Octavian and Anthony quarreled. Anthony fled to Egypt and allied himself with Cleopatra. Octavian defeated Anthony and Cleopatra in a great naval battle (Actium, 31 BC) and became sole ruler of Rome. This was how the Roman Republic met its end.

THE ROMAN EMPERORS

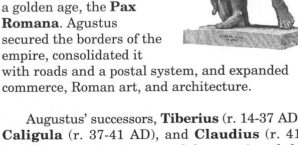

Augustus

Octavian established himself as **princeps** (first citizen) and chief army commander but turned the Republic into a monarchy. In 27 BC, he took the title **Imperator Caesar Augustus** (exalted emperor). The Emperor Augustus (r. 27 BC-14 AD) continued Julius Caesar's reforms, and oversaw a golden age, the **Pax Romana**. Agustus secured the borders of the empire, consolidated it with roads and a postal system, and expanded commerce, Roman art, and architecture.

Augustus' successors, **Tiberius** (r. 14-37 AD), **Caligula** (r. 37-41 AD), and **Claudius** (r. 41-54 AD) were sometimes cruel, but continued the imperial development. The last of Augustus' relatives, Nero (r. 54-68 AD), began the persecutions of the Christians. Nero's successor,

1 triumvirate (3 person oligarchy)

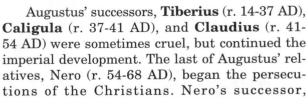

Vespasian (69-79 AD), restored order and had the Colosseum built. Other significant Roman Emperors included:

- **Trajan** (98-117 AD) pushed the Empire northeastward and created a series of aqueducts.

- **Marcus Aurelius** (161-180 AD) expanded the Empire in Europe and reformed taxes.

- **Diocletian** (284-305 AD) transformed the Empire into a true monarchy, created a royal court and a civil service, employed forced labor, raised taxes, and divided the Empire into eastern and western regions.

- **Constantine the Great** (306-337 AD) reorganized the empire and provinces, created an occupational caste system to stabilize the economy, moved the capital to Byzantium (Constantinople), and legalized Christianity.

THE DECLINE OF THE ROMAN EMPIRE

The Pax Romana began to disintegrate in the 3rd century AD. The Roman Senate lost all of its power and the military deposed and installed a constant procession of mediocre emperors. During this period of internal chaos, support for the legions defending the borders and frontiers also declined. **Teutonic invaders** (Germanic tribes – Vandals, Goths, Saxons, Alemanni, Franks) assailed the Roman forces in northern Europe and Spain. These "barbarian attacks" disrupted commerce. Supply lines for food and raw materials were interrupted. Shortages plagued the cities of the empire and prices of scarce goods rose. Without raw materials, artisans cut production. Workers were laid off, incomes were reduced, and tax revenues declined. The entire economic system fell into chaos.

CONTRIBUTIONS OF THE ROMAN EMPIRE

The Romans became blenders and adapters of many cultures over the centuries that they ruled their vast Empire. Roman law, flowing from the Twelve Tables (c. 450 BC), was precise in logic and organization. However, Roman law was not a law of equality. It was applied differently to different classifications of citizens and non-citizens. Roman law did create a consistent basis for the laws of the Empire.

Latin became the common tongue of the Empire, and helped to unify a vast region. Latin

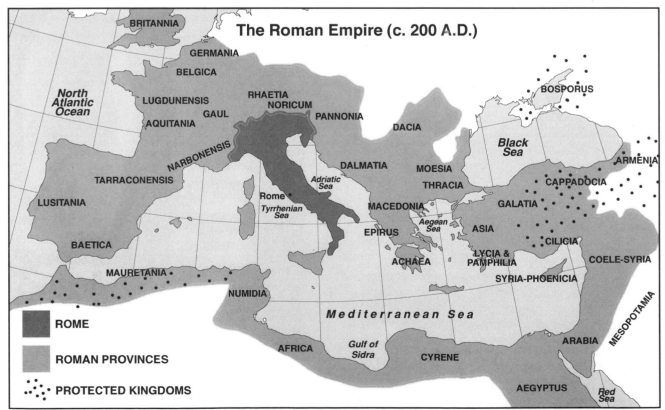

The Roman Empire (c. 200 A.D.)

BRITANNIA
GERMANIA
BELGICA
North Atlantic Ocean
LUGDUNENSIS
GAUL
AQUITANIA
NARBONENSIS
RHAETIA
NORICUM
PANNONIA
DACIA
BOSPORUS
Black Sea
ARMENIA
TARRACONENSIS
DALMATIA
MOESIA
THRACIA
CAPPADOCIA
Rome
Adriatic Sea
Tyrrhenian Sea
MACEDONIA
GALATIA
LUSITANIA
EPIRUS
Aegean Sea
ASIA
CILICIA
BAETICA
ACHAEA
LYCIA & PAMPHILIA
COELE-SYRIA
SYRIA-PHOENICIA
MAURETANIA
NUMIDIA
Mediterranean Sea
MESOPOTAMIA
ARABIA
AFRICA
Gulf of Sidra
CYRENE
AEGYPTUS
Red Sea

■ ROME
ROMAN PROVINCES
∴ PROTECTED KINGDOMS

also became the language of the Christian Church and continued to be the intellectual language of Europe for more than 1000 years.

The cultural impact of Rome was great. Roman legions and administrators brought the diverse culture of the Empire to remote provinces, villages, and towns on far flung frontiers. Roman engineers and architects adapted the columns and stonemasonry of the Greeks and other great civilizations to build an **infrastructure**[1]. Roman builders combined the columns, triumphal arches, and domes into magnificent palaces, temples, forums, fortifications, bridges, aqueduct systems, and road networks. In a large sense, the Romans were not original thinkers in philosophy and the pure sciences like the Greeks. Instead, Romans were appliers of other cultures' theories. They studied and modified others' ideas and applied them to practical needs.

In literature, Roman poets such as **Virgil** (*Aeneid*, c. 19 BC) and **Ovid** (*Metamorphoses*, c. 8 AD) provided lyrical tales connected to the past glories of Rome and Greece.

Others, such as **Horace** and **Juvenal** wrote to amuse and entertain. Roman historians (Livy, Tacitus) were precise, but still sang their country's praises.

The power of the Roman legions and navy created a vast, protected region in which trade and exchange of ideas flourished. Food and raw materials for artisans came from the provinces to Rome. Traders took manufactured articles to the world beyond. Their commerce flowed over Roman roads to all points of the Empire and beyond, via the Silk Route and other caravan routes to Persia, China, and elsewhere in Asia.

The Romans revered Greek and Hellenistic art and philosophy and saw themselves as preservers of ancient culture. Yet, after the chaos of the 3rd century AD, the Greek connection faded in the west. After Constantine made Byzantium his capital in 324 AD (and renamed it Constantinople), Greek civilization gave strength and cultural grounding to the Byzantine Empire.

---

1 infrastructure (basic installations needed for the running of society such as transportation and communications systems)

Mini Assessment

MINI-
ASSESSMENT

1 A similarity between Alexander the Great's empire and the Roman Empire is that both
   1 started as small republics
   2 were undermined by new religions
   3 adapted and spread Greek civilization
   4 disintegrated after initial conquests

2 In the century after the Punic Wars against Carthage, the Roman Republic experienced
   1 a golden age of intellectual achievement
   2 a strengthening of the role of the Senate
   3 devastating invasions by barbarians
   4 political unrest and economic problems

3 Rome's cultural contributions to Western civilization rested on
   1 adaptation and preservation of Greek and other cultures
   2 conquest of Teutonic tribes and outlying peoples
   3 suppression of religious movements
   4 a long succession of brilliant emperors

Constructed Response:
The events listed below occurred between the 4th and 5th centuries AD. Use these events to construct an outline on the lines below.

Loss of a central government
Weak emperors
Fall of Rome
High taxes and rising prices
Decline of unified language and culture

Title: _____

A. Causes:

_____

_____

B. Effects:

_____

THE MAURYA EMPIRE IN INDIA

In the centuries after the ancient Harrapan culture succumbed to the invasons of Aryans (c. 1500-500 BC), civilizations in the Indus Valley remained divided into small kingdoms. There was a great deal of commercial contact with the Persians to the west. Alexander the Great conquered the western area of the Indus around 327 BC.

At about the same time, farther eastward, in the Ganges Valley in the Himalayan foothills, the Kingdom of Magadha expanded. Its king, **Chandragupta Maurya** (r. 321-297 BC), conquered neighboring kingdoms. Chandragupta built an impressive armed force, and he created a bureaucracy to administer his conquests. The roads he built to carry troops and messengers encouraged caravan commerce. By 303 BC, The Maurya Kingdom stretched from the plains of the Ganges across northern India.

Chandragupta's kingdom eroded after he turned power over to his son. His grandson, **Asoka** (r. 272-232 BC), reconquered lost territories and had extended Maurya control across the subcontinent to the Indus Valley by 250 BC. Guilt over the terrible toll of human life taken by his armies at **Kalinga** (c. 268 BC) led Asoka to renounce war and convert to Buddhism. His philosophy of non-violence led him to send Buddhist missionaries to all parts of his realm and beyond. He installed pillars on which laws were inscribed (the so-called **"Rock Edicts"**), and his administration of justice followed the moral guidance of *dharma*. He built public works, dredged harbors, and made travel and commerce easier.

The Mauryas ruled for another sixty years, but weaker successors changed to harsher policies and the kingdom declined. Various groups from Persia and central Asia invaded and set up kingdoms in the Indus and Ganges and the central portions of the subcontinent for the next 500 years before the new Gupta Dynasty could rise and consolidate rule.

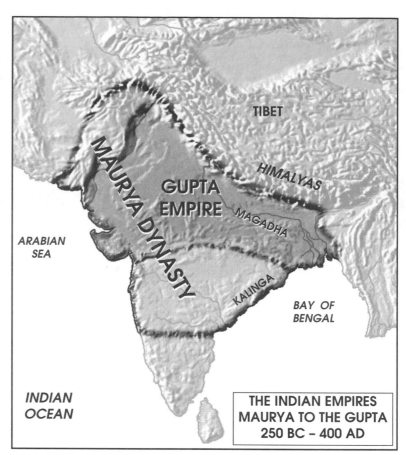

THE INDIAN EMPIRES
MAURYA TO THE GUPTA
250 BC – 400 AD

CLASSICAL CIVILIZATIONS AND GLOBAL TRADE

MARITIME TRADERS: PHOENICIA

Classical civilizations were often linked by smaller groups of people that lived on their edges and carried trade and culture among the great empires of the ancient world. **Phoenicia** was a small, loosely united group of city-states (Sidon, Tyre, Ugarit) clustered along the eastern Mediterranean coast. Related to the Canaanites, the Phoenicians were traders and manufacturers (cedar wood, purple dyes, glass, wine, weapons, and metal and ivory) who appeared in Egyptian and Mesopotamian history as early as 3000 BC. Location and trade even made the Phoenicians influential in Israel's development. The Phoenicians of Tyre supplied materials for King Solomon's legendary temple at Jerusalem in the 10th century BC.

Because of their location and economic drive, the Phoenicians never became politically powerful. They were dominated by the great powers of the

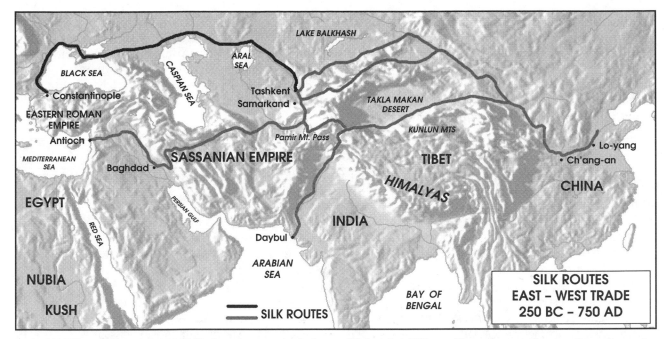

**SILK ROUTES
EAST – WEST TRADE
250 BC – 750 AD**

region (Egyptians to 1200 BC, then successively by the Assyrians, the Babylonians, the Persians, Alexander, and finally the Romans after 64 BC).

As traders, the Phoenicians ranged far and wide in the Mediterranean World. After 1000 BC, they established trading stations (small colonies) on Cyprus and Sicily. By 800 BC, they were sailing their ships toward the Atlantic, and establishing colonies on the North African coast at Carthage, Sicily, and in Spain (Cadiz).

The interaction of trade created a Phoenician culture that mixed Egyptian, Greek, and Mesopotamian characteristics. The Phoenician alphabet, which emerged in the 1500s BC was adapted by the Greeks about 800 BC and became the basis for the languages of Western Europe.

OVERLAND TRADERS: THE SILK ROUTE

Besides the connections made by seafaring peoples, there were other groups that provided overland links among classical civilizations. In western Asia, various groups established trade between civilizations of the Eastern Mediterranean and Mesopotamian regions and China. As early as 2500 BC, merchants created a trade route that became known as the **Silk Route** (or Silk Road). It was a series of caravan paths that ran from the Caspian Sea, through treacherous Pamir Mountain passes, around the Takla Maken Desert in Central Asia, and into western

China's Xi'an Province. Samarkand and Tashkent became important commercial centers along the way.

The Silk Route was also a cultural link between East and West. For example, over its pathways, caravans spread ideas of a variety of cultures, such as Buddhist beliefs from India. Companies of travelers spread and intermixed (cultural diffusion) the arts, customs, and ideas of Hellenistic, Roman, Egyptian, and Persian civilizations with those of China and hundreds of others along the way. It was a dangerous trip and took up to three years to make. There were physical hardships, natural perils, and harassment by nomadic tribes and bandit clans. Rarely did a single group traverse the entire route. Specialized trade groups emerged, equipped with their own small armies. Goods changed hands many times over short spans. The Silk Route remained a main line of East-West contact until the 15th century AD.

MARITIME AND OVERLAND TRADE ROUTES LINKED AFRICA AND EURASIA

Ancient and classical civilizations stretched across North Africa from earliest times and had constant contact with Southwest Asia by land and sea. As Egyptian civilization spread along the Nile Valley, it acted as a bridge between Mediterranean peoples and southern empires such as Nubia (Kush). Nubian kings even conquered and ruled Egypt (c. 750 BC). Nubia bridged trade between Egypt and African peoples to the south and west, trading ivory, gold, and slaves with Mediterranean people.

Africans of the interior also traded with Carthage and came into contact with Greco-Roman civilization through commerce with Numidia. The introduction of camels from Asia in the 3rd century AD increased trade from the Mediterranean coast across the Sahara Desert and into the more southerly kingdoms of Equatorial Africa.

SUMMARY: RISE AND FALL OF TWO GREAT EMPIRES

HAN EMPIRE (202 BC – 220 AD)	Roman Empire (27 BC – 476 AD)
Growth:	*Growth:*
• Early Han rulers Liu Bang and Han Wudi defeated rival power groups and brought a large region under control through treaties and intermarriage	• Octavian defeated rival power groups and brought region under control through conquest and domination of Senate
• Defended against nomadic invaders (Great Wall) such as the Hsiung-nu	• Defended against nomadic (Germanic) invaders
• Cultivated relations with new class of merchants and land holders	• Economic growth redistributed land among land holding elite (eques)
• Kept taxes reasonable	• Cultivated relations with new class of merchants and land holders
	• Kept taxes reasonable
Organization:	• Granted Roman citizenship to some conquered peoples
• Distance and mountains isolated China's civilization on the west and south	
• Unified learning and behavior under Confucian principles	*Organization:*
• Created qualified civil service (bureaucracy) by examinations	• Mediterranean became the great connecting tissue for Roman conquest
• Created peasant army loyal to emperor	• Ousted uncooperative local rulers and set up military provinces
• Built infrastructure (road and messenger system) to improve communications	• Required military and provincial administrators to coordinate efforts with capital
• Abolished older kingdoms and created military provinces	• Military command of professional army by emperor key factor in demoting the Senate into an advisory body
• Required military and provincial administrators to coordinate efforts with capital	• Appointed bureaucratic officials were loyal to emperor
• Set up an intelligence corps (spies) spread Chinese as imperial language	• Spread Latin as imperial language
• Redistributed nobles' land among peasants	*Decline:*
• Made nobles and families live in capital, Ch'ang-an	• Court intrigues and frequent military coups
• Cultivated relations with new class of merchants; kept taxes reasonable	• Rising power of local warlords
	• Infrastructure fell into disrepair
Decline:	• Dissent caused by heavy taxes burdening peasants, merchants, and landholders
• Court intrigues	• Inability to defend against foreign invaders (e.g., Goths, Vandals).
• Rising power of local warlords	• Division of Empire into Eastern (Byzantine) and Western (Latin) sections (c. 395 AD)
• Infrastructure fell into disrepair	
• Revolts caused by heavy taxes burdened peasants, merchants, and landholders	
• Inability to defend northern provinces from nomadic foreign invaders	

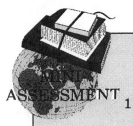

EMERGENCE AND SPREAD OF BELIEF SYSTEMS

Scientific studies show that primitive hominids had spiritual rituals, and early river civilizations had organized worship of common gods. After 2000 BC, major religions and philosophical systems took many centuries to develop. Their followers spread their beliefs over vast geographic areas. From primitive **Animism**[1] to Islam, major belief systems became an important aspect of culture and cultural diffusion.

Early societies believed different gods controlled natural circumstances and certain human behaviors. Interpretation of natural events (floods, storms, earthquakes) or humans' dreams, fantasies, and death led early people to sense unexplainable forces at work. They assigned names and characteristics to these forces. These forces evolved into general conceptions and myths of gods. As civilizations grew, shamen and priests developed ideas into organized beliefs, rituals, and ethical practices connected with certain gods.

The search for order led some polytheistic societies to elevate certain gods into roles of control and supremacy such as that of Zeus for the ancient Greeks and Jupiter for the Romans. Other societies rejected polytheism in favor of **monotheism** – the conception of a single God. As travel became more common and civilizations grew and made both friendly and hostile contacts with others, isolated, localized religions blended and became more universal. **Hinduism**, **Buddhism**, **Judaism**, **Christianity**, and **Islam** grew into great cultural forces. As they spread, they became vehicles for cross-cultural progress for humankind.

---

1 Animism (holds there is a conscious life within every object. A spirit directs the object's being and affects conditions in the world)

JUDAISM

Origins Canaan (Palestine / Israel, Judah) c. 1500-1000 BC; (Abraham) Moses, Solomon, David, prophets, and judges

Sacred Texts Torah (*Mishna* and *Talmud*), Hebrew Bible

Organization autonomous local synagogues led by rabbi

Beliefs Judaism was the first organized religion to teach monotheism; God had special covenant with the ancient Israelites to bring God's message to humanity by their example; seeks a just and peaceful world order; prohibition of images

Practices strict discipline through daily prayer, family relationships, ethical behavior (*Ten Commandments*), ritual practices, dietary laws, individual prayer, and public observances (Passover, Rosh Hashana, Yom Kippur)

Divisions wide variations of individual adherence to dietary and Sabbath behavior

ISLAM

Origins Arabia (570-632 AD), Prophet Muhammad

Sacred Texts *Qur'an* (English: Koran); *Shari'a* ("the way") – the laws and regulations for Muslim life and conduct

Organization community structure (once an empire headed by a caliph, now some entire countries are Islamic states – Iran, Afghanistan, Pakistan); in others local communities in separate mosques

Beliefs monotheist (commitment in faith, obedience, and trust to the one and only God – Allah); "Five Pillars": *shahada* (profession of faith in God); *salat* (ritual prayer, performed five times a day facing Mecca); *zakat* (alms giving); *sawm* (fasting); *hajj* (pilgrimage to Mecca); sometimes *jihad* (literally, "striving in the way of God" – varies from sacred war to striving to fulfill the ethical principles of the *Qur'an*)

Practices The Shari'a is the creed and worship of the community (*umma*), as well as a code of ethics, a culture, a system of laws, an understanding of the function of the state; main festivals: Id al-Fitr (breaking of the fast at the end of Ramadan) and Id al-Adha (sacrifice)

Divisions Sunnis (majority) follow Rightly Guided Caliphs (a kind of "mandate of heaven" authority) and Shi'ite (minority) contend leadership flows from descendants of Ali (Prophet Muhammad's son-in-law)

CHRISTIANITY

Origins Palestine, 1st century BC, founder Jesus of Nazareth

Sacred Texts Christian Bible (Old and New Testaments)

Organization Roman and Orthodox churches have hierarchal rule by chief bishop (Pope or Patriarch), archbishops, bishops, pastors; in Protestant sects, congregations tend to be more autonomous

Beliefs monotheist; Jesus was and is the Messiah or Christ promised by God in the prophecies of the Old Testament; freed believers from sin and offered resurrection and salvation in an afterlife; Trinity (one God in essence is viewed as 3 personifications: Creator (Father), Redeemer (Son), and Sustainer (Holy Spirit))

Practices Two principal rites (sacraments): Baptism, initiated converts; and the Eucharist, a sacred meal with prayers, chants, and scripture readings (Mass)

Divisions Western European (Latin Church) branch and a Byzantine (or Orthodox Church) branch. The Western church was in turn divided by the 16th century Reformation into the Roman Catholic Church and a large number of smaller Protestant churches : Lutheran, Calvinist (Reformed), Anglican, and sectarian

HINDUISM

Origins Indus Valley c. 1500-500 BC - based on Aryan invaders practices

Sacred Texts *Veda* (including *Upanishads*) and epics (*Bhagavad Gita, Mahabharata, Ramayana*)

Organization individual temple rituals assisted by members of Brahmin class (priests)

Beliefs polytheistic; commitment to an ideal way of life (*dharma*) and notion of action, especially religious or ritual action (*karma*) to purify human acts during rebirths of the soul so as to leave the material world (*moksha*) and become part of the eternal universal spirit of life (Brahman Nerguna)

Practices self-denial, fasting to purify the soul, individual rituals (initiations, marriages, funerals) assisted by members of Brahmin class (priests)

Divisions variety of sects devoted to Vishnu, Shiva, Shakti

BUDDHISM

Origins India (c. 566-486 BC), founded by noble Siddarta Gautama ("Buddha"– the Enlightened One)

Sacred Texts *Tripitaka* - narrative scriptural text Buddha's teaching (*sutras*)

Organization independent sanghas – monastic orders

Beliefs Four Noble Truths: (*duhkha*) all beings suffer in a cycle of rebirth (*samsara*) in which their actions (*Karma*) keep them wandering; suffering itself has a cause (*pratity asamut pada*); suffering and rebirth can cease (*nirvana*)

Practices Eightfold Path – combines ethical practices and disciplinary training in meditation to achieve enlightened wisdom (*panna*).

Divisions numerous sects based on schools of meditation such as Theravada (South & S. E. Asia) and Mahayana (China, Korea, Japan)

CHINESE PHILOSOPHIES: CONFUCIANISM

Origins Ancient China, teacher / political advisor Confucius or Kongzi (c. 551-479 BC)

Sacred Texts *Analects* - guide to ethical principles of correct behavior, moral judgment, and social order

Organization The Confucian school functioned as a recruiting ground for government positions, which were filled by those scoring highest on examinations in the Confucian classics

Beliefs Social order stems from benevolence (kindly acts, generosity), traditional rituals, filial piety (child's respect for parents), loyalty, respect for superiors and for the aged, social interaction is shaped by convention; correct behavior follows a natural pattern (li)

Practices maintain domestic order, preserve tradition, and maintain a constant standard of living for the taxpaying peasants

Divisions (none)

CHINESE PHILOSOPHIES: DAOISM (TAOISM)

Origins China, Laozi (Lao-tzu c. 6th century BC) and Zhuangzi (Chuang-tzu, c. 369-286 BC)

Sacred Texts the *Daode Jing* , and the *Zuangzi*

Organization independent monastic orders

Beliefs Seek tranquil life by excluding desire, impulse, and aggression; act in harmony with nature and accept life's inevitable changes; create action (wei) by shaping desires (yu); yin and yang - balance and harmony in life

Practices monasticism and the ritual of community renewal, and study revealed scriptures; Taoist writings reflect some Buddhist influences

Divisions numerous sects (faith healing through the confession of sin; spiritualism; visionary communication with divinities)

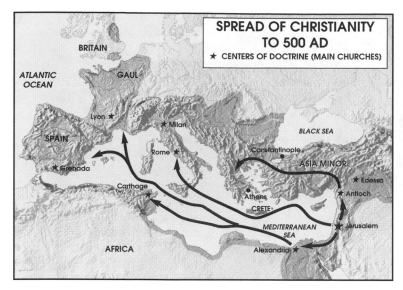

SPREAD OF CHRISTIANITY TO 500 AD
★ CENTERS OF DOCTRINE (MAIN CHURCHES)

early Christian Churches. Some disputes alienated the churches of Egypt, Syria, Mesopotamia, and Armenia. This created a **schism**[1] in the Eastern Roman (Byzantine) Empire. Later, the lack of unity hurt Christians' chances of holding back the Islamic invasion in the 7th century.

In the West, Roman rule was ended by the Germanic invasions of the 5th century. The Church was strengthened by the guidance of leaders as St. Augustine (354-430) and Pope Gregory I (590-604). The Roman Church survived to become the main civilizing influence in Europe during the Middle Ages.

EXPANSION OF CHRISTIANITY, ISLAM, AND BUDDHISM THROUGH CONQUEST AND TRADE

CHRISTIANITY EXPANDS

Christianity emerged in the Jewish culture during the 1st century AD. It spread from Palestine through the Mediterranean world dominated by Rome. In the 4th century, it became the official religion of the Roman Empire.

During its early history, the Christian Church remained independent of any government. From the 4th century to the 18th century, however, it accepted the protection of emperors, kings, and princes and became closely allied with secular governments.

By the middle of the 1st century AD, missionaries were spreading the new religion among the peoples of Egypt, Syria, Anatolia, Greece, and Italy. Christianity was transformed from a Jewish sect to a world religion and organized itself as a permanent institution under the leadership of its bishops. Early Christian theological development was the interpretation of the faith in terms of concepts drawn from Greek philosophical thought. Many theological disputes upset the

BUDDHISM EXPANDS

Buddha (Siddartha Gautama, c. 566-486 BC) lived during great social and religious change in India. Aryans continued to settle the Ganges. Commerce and cities were developing rapidly. Differences later arose over the Buddha's teaching (dharma) and the rules of the order (vinaya).

Around 250 BC, the Asoka tried to make Buddhism the state religion of the Maurya Empire and spread it throughout Asia. Asoka sent missionaries to Sri Lanka, Burma (Myanmar), Thailand, Southeast Asia, and

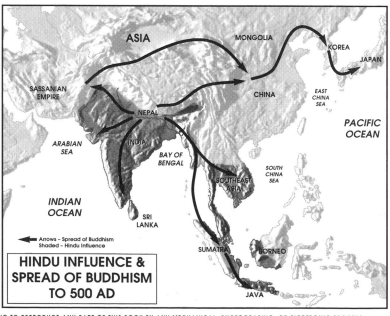

HINDU INFLUENCE & SPREAD OF BUDDHISM TO 500 AD

Arrows – Spread of Buddhism
Shaded – Hindu Influence

1 schism (serious breakup)

Indonesia. Buddhism carried Indian culture into these areas and northward into Central Asia, a crossroads of creeds from all parts of Asia and the Near East.

Between the 7th and 13th centuries AD, Buddhism declined in India. Muslim invaders persecuted Buddhists. Gradually, it blended back toward Hindu tradition.

Buddhist monks moved into China in the 1st century AD and became very influential at the Chinese court. They blended their texts with Daoist (Taoist) terminology and adopted Chinese stress on the importance of the family. In the 9th century, Chinese emperors persecuted Buddhists, destroying many temples and confiscating monastery lands. Buddhism never regained its influential position in Chinese life.

Buddhism was introduced to Japan from Korea about the 6th century, and it became the state religion from 710-784. During the 9th century, there was a mixing of Buddhism with various Japanese Shinto (animist) practices.

ISLAM EXPANDS

In 610 AD, the Prophet **Muhammad** (b. 570) received revelations convincing him he was God's messenger. From that time, Islamic civilization spread rapidly through the Arabian Peninsula, the Middle East and North Africa, the Fertile Crescent, and eastward toward India.

Through the *Qur'an* and the *sunna*[1], and his military leadership, Muhammad left ideas for the foundations of an Islamic community that eventually became a great empire.

After his death (632 AD), the Prophet's followers chose his father-in-law, **Abu Bakr** (r. 632-34), as successor (**caliph**[2]). He and the next two caliphs continued to expand Islam's boundaries. By 656, their conquests stretched from Persia to Lybia and from Armenia to Egypt. When Muhammad's son-in-law, Ali, became the fourth caliph, Islam's followers split

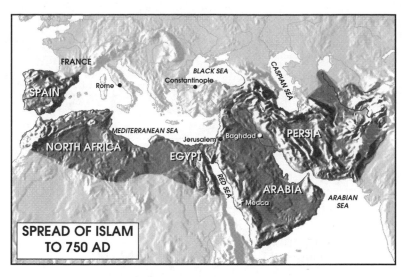

SPREAD OF ISLAM TO 750 AD

into two groups. Ali was murdered in 661, and his **Shi'ite** followers rejected the **Sunni** Caliph **Muawiya**, who founded the **Umayyad Dynasty** (661-750 AD). Umayyad rulers continued expansion and consolidation of Islam into India, China, North Africa, and Spain. They made Arabic the official language, built roads, used a common currency, and set up a provincial government system.

TIME CAPSULE

During the Neolithic Revolution 10,000 years ago, bands of hunter-gatherers began to form agricultural villages. In river valleys, certain villages grew, prospered, and produced broader cultures. The need for trade, protection, and irrigation moved groups to interact and pool resources into formative civilizations with cities and social institutions. As civilizations developed resources, they formed economic interdependencies, built great public works of architecture, organized spiritual beliefs into religions, and created bodies of literature and scientific and technical knowledge. By the Roman and Han Eras, civilizations interacted steadily and changed as they progressed. As new nomadic groups entered them – peaceably and forcibly – societies absorbed, remade, and diffused global cultures into great imperial systems.

GLOBAL HISTORY ARCHIVE

---

1 sunna also sunnah (the way of life prescribed as normative in Islam, based on the teachings and practices of Mohammed and on analysis of the Koran)
2 caliph also calif or khalif (male leader of the nation of Islam, example – successor to Mohammed)

MULTI-CHOICE QUESTIONS

1   Which best characterizes the difference between hunter-gatherer societies and Neolithic agricultural societies?
1   agricultural life was more organized but promised a steady supply of food in one place
2   hunter-gatherer societies provided a more secure and leisurely way of life
3   hunter-gatherer societies were small, simple, and more politically stable
4   agricultural societies lacked time for making tools, utensils, and pottery

2   Production of larger quantities of food drew Neolithic farmers to the Tigris and Euphrates, Nile, Indus, and Huang He River Valleys because of the
1   ease of defense
2   availability of water and richer soils
3   rich deposits of minerals for iron production
4   freedom from oppressive governments

3   In Ancient Egypt, the early pharaohs' belief in their own divinity led them to
1   be mummified for their afterlife
2   conquer surrounding peoples
3   rule with the aid of viziers
4   maintain large standing armies

4   How did Mesopotamian civilization differ from that in ancient Egypt?
1   Slavery was forbidden.
2   No written language emerged.
3   Organized religion was lacking.
4   Power changed hands among city-states.

5   As societies became more complex, economic decision-making based on tradition gave way to other systems because of the need for
1   change and flexibility
2   consistency
3   cultural diffusion
4   religious observances

6   Which was a result of the other three?
1   increased invasions by Teutonic tribes
2   the decline of the Roman Empire
3   loss of power by the Roman Senate
4   high taxes and economic chaos

Base your answers to questions 7 and 8 on the diagram below and your knowledge of global history.

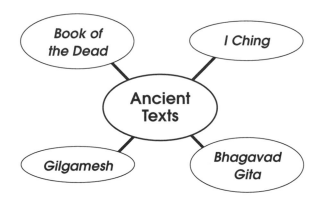

7   Which is a common theme among these texts of ancient civilizations?
1   the interplay of good and evil
2   the high status enjoyed by women in ancient societies
3   the problems created by caste systems
4   the process of assimilation

8   Anthropologists theorize that early farmers developed polytheistic worship systems reflective of their
1   strong belief in universal human rights
2   devotion to kings and emperors
3   advances in learning and technology
4   struggle to deal with the natural environment

Base your answers to questions 9 and 10 on the
diagram below and your knowledge of global history.

A HINDU PANTHEON

Including the gods of early sacred literature, the deities reach into the millions. They included defied mortals as well as animals, birds, mountains, rivers, and trees.

God or Avitar (Incarnation)	Association
Brahma	The Creator – set the universe in motion
Shiva	The Destroyer – powerful demon slayer; symbol of male fertility; composite of older gods
Vishnu	The Preserver – helper of mankind; appears periodically as reincarnation
Parvati	Shiva's wife; daughter of Himalayas; unity of man and woman
Rama	avatar of Vishnu; kindly ruler; valiant leader against oppression; gentle husband
Sita	wife of Rama; represents ideal wife
Krishna	avatar of Vishnu; lover of humanity; hero in battle; god of love and joy

9 Which term would help to define the ancient Hindu belief system?
1 neolithic
2 feudalistic
3 monotheistic
4 polytheistic

10 "Among Hinduism's achievements is a blending of countless cults, gods, and totems into a vast mythology ..." This quotation refers to Hinduism's cultural
1 diversity
2 unity
3 clarity
4 security

THEMATIC ESSAY

Theme: Cultural Diffusion

Historically, contacts among people have spread and intermixed ideas and cultures.

Task:
- Define culture:

- Select one ancient civilization which you have studied and explain the circumstances that brought it into contact with another civilization.

- Explain how the contact between the two civilizations changed them.

Suggestions:
You may use any ancient civilization that was impacted by another. Some groups you might wish to include: Egypt / Hittites; Persia / Macedonia; Greece /Rome. **You are not limited to these suggestions.**

DOCUMENT BASED QUESTION

Directions:

The following question is based on the accompanying documents (1-4). Some of the documents have been edited for the purposes of this exercise. The question is designed to test your ability to work with historical documents. As you analyze the documents, take into account both the source of the document and the author's point of view.

- Write a well-organized essay that includes an introduction with a thesis statement, several paragraphs explaining the thesis, and a conclusion.
- Analyze the documents.
- Use all the documents.
- Use evidence from the documents to support your thesis position.
- Do not simply repeat the contents of the documents.
- Include specific related outside information.

Historical Context:

The relationship between children and parents can be a basis for a civil society. The documents below present views of law from ancient times.

Task:

Decide how important the social role of the family was in ancient societies and support your opinion with the documents below and **your** knowledge of global history.

Part A - Short Answer

The documents below relate to ancient systems of law and morality. Examine each document carefully, then answer the question that follows it.

Document 1:

"The superior man while his parents are alive, reverently nourishes them; and when they are dead, reverently sacrifices to them. His chief thought is how, to the end of life, not to disgrace them.

"There are three degrees of filial piety. The highest is being a credit to our parents; the next is not disgracing them; the lowest is merely being able to support them."

– *Confucius*

Document 1 Question:

How can everyone acting so as not to disgrace their parents help a society run smoother?

Document 2:

"Honor your father and your mother: that your days may be long upon the land which the Lord your God gives you."

– *Book of Exodus* (Hebrews)

Document 2 Question:

Explain what "honor" means in this quotation.

Document 3:

"If a man has struck his father, his hand shall be cut off."

– *Code of Hammurabi*

Document 3 Question:

Why would this punishment be so severe?

Document 4:

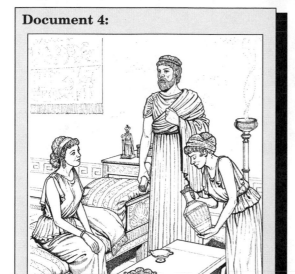

Document 4 Question:

How would this kind of portrayal of an ideal family help keep order in a society?

Part B - Essay Response

Discuss the role of filial piety in ancient societies.

Your essay should be well organized with an introductory paragraph that states your thesis as to the social role of the family in ancient civilizations. Develop and support the reasons for your thesis in the next paragraphs and then write a conclusion. In your essay, include specific historical details and refer to the specific documents you analyzed in Part A. You may include additional information from your knowledge of global history.

Unit 3

500 AD – 1200 AD

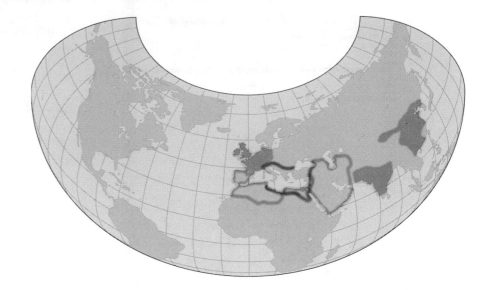

500– Byzantine Emperor Justinian codifies Roman Law (528 AD)

600– Li Yuan founds T'ang Dynasty (618)
Abu Bakr becomes first Muslim Caliph (632)

700– Muslims conquer Spain (718)
Umayyads overthrown by Abbasids (750)

800– Charlemagne crowned Holy Roman Emperor (800)

900–

Zhao Guangyn founds Song Dynasty (960)

1000– Grand Duke Valdimir I of Kiev converted to Orthodox Christianity (988)

1100– Pope Urban II launches the First Crusade (1095)

Ibn Rushd (Averroes) preserves work of Aristotle (1180)

1200–

EXPANDING ZONES OF EXCHANGE & ENCOUNTER

INTRODUCTION

This was an age that built new civilizations on the foundations of ancient ones. Growing trade, commerce, military conquests, improved medicine, and better living conditions of the ancient world expanded contacts among people. In the first **millennium**[1] AD, as civilizations grew and intermixed, cultures merged and awareness of the world expanded.

From 500 to 1200 AD, great changes occurred to cause more cultural diffusion. Awareness of civilizations in India and China broadened as merchants carried their observations – as well as goods – to civilizations in the west. As Buddhism, Christianity, and Islam expanded, they unified large groupings of people. Invading tribes from Asia pressed provincial peoples of ancient empires into protected kingdoms and intermixed groups even more. The facades of the new civilizations appeared unique, but inside they housed thousands of years of cultural assimilation and prepared humanity for even greater progress.

INDIA: GUPTA EMPIRE (320-550 AD)

GROWTH AND ORGANIZATION

By 184 BC, the glory of India's mighty Mauryan Dynasty faded. The expansive empire of Chandragupta Maurya and Asoka splintered into tiny, hostile states. Five hundred years passed before a prince could unite the northern and central region of India into a realm. In 310 AD, a new dynasty radiated from the place the Mauryas had started – Magadha, in the Ganges Valley. The armies of **Chandragupta I** (r. c. 320-330) swept westward across the sub-

1 millennium (thousand year period of time)

continent to the Arabian Sea. From the conquests, he built a union of locally autonomous villages and provinces that controlled central India until 550 AD.

Under the Gupta Dynasty's peace and security, trade with the surrounding regions created an economic underpinning for the empire. Merchants traveled to the Mons and Funan kingdoms of Southeast Asia, to the Persian Sassanid Empire of Middle East, and to Axum and coastal cities of East Africa.

ARTISTIC AND SCIENTIFIC ACHIEVEMENTS

For more than two centuries, the Gupta dynasty presided over a splendid golden age of India. **Chandragupta II** (r. 375-415) oversaw a magnificent renewal of traditional Indian music, dance, painting, and architecture. Hindu

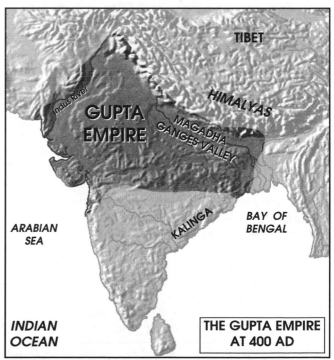

THE GUPTA EMPIRE AT 400 AD

and Buddhist masters unified and organized religious philosophy at centers such as Nalanda. In mathematics, Gupta scholars introduced the concept of zero, the decimal system, and numerical symbols that Arab traders carried home and made the basis of the "Arabic numbers" for Western civilization. They developed medical practices such as bone surgery and smallpox vaccination that, over centuries, traders brought to the Arab kingdoms and eventually, to Europe.

The Gupta Period's architects created great palaces, Buddhist stupas[1] and monasteries, and Hindu temples with elaborately carved statues and murals of gods and ancient life. Eminent writers and poets composed Sanskrit works such as *Shakuntala* and *Meghaduta* (**Kalidasa**, c. 400 AD). Like architects, they built on Hindu traditions flowing from the classics (*Upanishads*, *Mahabharata*, *Ramayana*).

As happened with Rome in the 5th century, the Gupta Dynasty declined in the 6th century as a result of Hun invasions from Central Asia and civil wars. These forces split India into many weak kingdoms once again.

CHINA: T'ANG DYNASTY (618-902 AD)

ORGANIZATION / GEOGRAPHY

The greatest of the first millennium empires in size, wealth, and population was China's **T'ang** Dynasty. From the collapse of the Hans in 220 AD, China experienced infighting among warlords and constant invasions by Central Asian groups.

In 589, Yang Jian united the north once more and tried to return to the Han culture. His cruel treatment of peasants led to rebellions against his successor until rebel leader **Li Yuan** (r. 618-626) consolidated power and founded the T'ang Dynasty. Claiming the "mandate of heaven," he resumed the civil service examination structure of the Han Era.

Li used the system to obtain obedient, Confucian-trained, loyal administrators for the vast empire that his efficient, disciplined cavalries conquered in Eastern and Central Asia. Li Yuan relinquished power to his son

T'aizong (r. 627-649), who expanded the Empire into Tibet and westward into Central Asia.

T'ang emperors built canals for internal trade, organized the legal system, and redistributed land among the peasants (undercutting the power of landlords). Early in the 10th century, the T'angs fell from power amid the growing independence of military commanders that led to rebellions and civil wars. China split into ten independent warlords' provinces. It was not reunited until 960 AD when General **Zhao Guangyin** (also K'uang-yin) founded the **Song** (also Sung) Dynasty (960-1279).

The Song Dynasty revived China. Song rulers expanded and regulated trade, issued paper currency, revitalized the central bureaucracy, controlled the military, and oversaw a rebirth of Chinese culture. Landscape painting (Mi Fei, Xia Gui), moveable type, and a Confucian and a poetic revival all flourished under the Songs until 1279. In that year the Mongols, under Genghis Kahn's grandson, **Kublai Kahn**, established the **Yuan** Dynasty.

ACHIEVEMENTS

The T'ang rulers – one was China's first woman ruler, Empress **Wu Zhao** (690-705) – presided over a golden age. The T'ang Era saw technical advances in printing, weaving, porcelain making, time keeping, and inventing gunpowder. T'ang poets such as **Li Bo** and **Du Fu** (c. 750) wrote of nature and moral dilemmas.

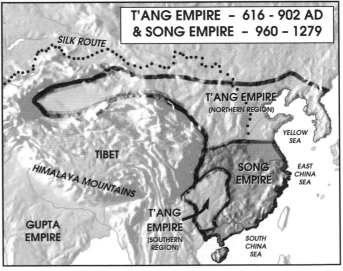

T'ANG EMPIRE - 616 - 902 AD & SONG EMPIRE - 960 - 1279

SILK ROUTE

T'ANG EMPIRE (NORTHERN REGION)

YELLOW SEA

TIBET

HIMALAYA MOUNTAINS

SONG EMPIRE

EAST CHINA SEA

GUPTA EMPIRE

T'ANG EMPIRE (SOUTHERN REGION)

SOUTH CHINA SEA

1 stupas (domed shrines)

Artist **Wu Daozi** (c.689-760) painted both figures and landscapes with Buddhist and Daoist themes. Builders created great wooden palaces and temples characterized by tower-like **pagodas**[1].

T'aizong's western conquests allowed a reopening of trade with India and along the Silk Route to the Middle East. In return for protection, he made tributary states out of Japan, Korea, and Vietnam. Students from these areas journeyed to the capital of Chang-an and brought Chinese culture back to their homes. By allowing foreign travelers and scholars to live among their subjects and study in their learning centers, T'ang rulers opened China to new ideas, technologies, and religions, such as Christianity.

CHINESE INFLUENCE ON JAPAN

In Japan, in the southern part of Honshu, a ruling **uji** (clan) arose from a blend of early peoples – the **Yamato**. Their chiefs claimed descent from Amaterasu – the sun goddess. The Yamato formed alliances among the clans and unified

the country by the 4th century AD. In the next century, the Yamato launched military expeditions into Korea and established a colony in Mimana, on the southern tip of the peninsula. An era of scholarly pilgrimages brought contact with China. Japan adapted Chinese script, and in 538, Buddhism was introduced and began intermixing with the native Shinto practices.

MEDITERRANEAN: THE BYZANTINE EMPIRE

ORGANIZATION / GEOGRAPHY

In 286 AD, pressed by **Teutonic invaders** (Germanic tribes) and unable to support a defensive army on all fronts, the Emperor Diocletian split the Roman Empire into two great provinces. The provincial trading town of **Byzantium** on the Bosporus Strait became the center of the Eastern Zone. After the fall of the Western Section in 476 AD, Byzantium became the center of the Roman world for the next thousand years. Modern historians refer to it as the Byzantine Empire, but those that lived within it always viewed it as the Roman Empire and thought of themselves as Romans.

By 330 AD, the Roman Emperor Constantine had reorganized the government, adopted Greek as the official language, recognized Christianity as an official religion (**Edict of Milan**, 313), and renamed Byzantium "New Rome" – his successors renamed it **Constantinople**. The Emperor modeled his new city in the likeness of Rome with a forum, imperial palaces, theaters, baths, and a refurbished Hippodrome – a 60,000-seat amphitheater. He also began the construction of 14 churches including the **Hagia Sophia** (Church

---

1 pagoda (religious building of the Far East, especially a many-storied Buddhist tower, erected as a memorial or shrine)

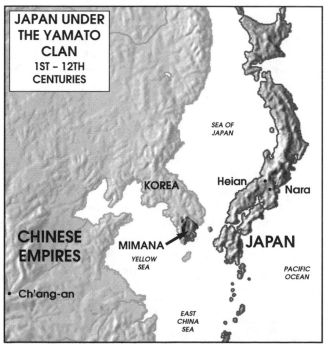

JAPAN UNDER THE YAMATO CLAN
1ST – 12TH CENTURIES

SEA OF JAPAN

KOREA

Heian
Nara

CHINESE EMPIRES

MIMANA
YELLOW SEA

JAPAN

PACIFIC OCEAN

Ch'ang-an

EAST CHINA SEA

Hagia Sophia – Church of the Holy Wisdom

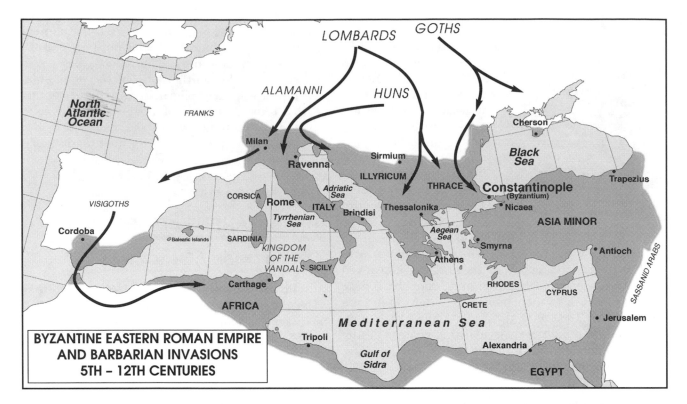

BYZANTINE EASTERN ROMAN EMPIRE AND BARBARIAN INVASIONS 5TH – 12TH CENTURIES

of the Holy Wisdom) which became the great central church of Orthodox Christianity. Riots and a great fire destroyed most of Constantinople in 532, but it was meticulously rebuilt by the Emperor Justinian.

Constantinople became a great Mediterranean center of trade, especially in luxury goods – furs, corn, and salt from Russia; grains from Egypt; gold and slaves from Africa; sugar, honey, and wax from the Middle East; and, silk, damask, porcelain, and amber from India and China. Yet, far more important was the Byzantine Roman preservation and nurturing of Hellenistic culture. Blending it with Christian liturgy created a new identity among citizens of the Empire.

POLITICAL STRUCTURE

Byzantine emperors were **autocrats**[2] with a senate (and to a lesser extent, the Church) to "rubber-stamp" their decisions. The emperors' survival depended on knowing their court and unearthing conspiracies against them. Hereditary succession was not guaranteed, and many emperors met violent deaths. As with the old Roman Empire, many emperors were overthrown by the military, and many generals

ascended to the throne. Byzantine Romans developed an elaborate and expensive bureaucracy to administer and control the provinces whose borders were constantly challenged by invaders.

A rigid social structure bound peasants to the land and artisans to their jobs. However, merchant classes had freedom and accumulated the wealth and power to influence imperial decisions. Military service was rewarded with grants of land. Because of this, army commanders became rich landlords and taxpayers. This landed aristocracy gained enormous political influence by the 10th century.

As time progressed, the emperors could not control the aristocrats and were forced to give them tax exemptions and expand their estates. To make up for lost land tax **revenues**[3], import taxes fell heavily on the small merchant class. The free peasants (ex-soldiers) saw taxes rise on their small plots, too. This weakened the imperial economy and made it difficult to defend against outside forces such as the Normans, the Serbs, the Seljuk Turks, and even the European Crusaders. The Empire disintegrated in the 13th century.

---

1 liturgy (prescribed form or set of forms for public Christian ceremonies)
2 autocrats (dictators with unlimited power)
3 revenues (income)

Eastern Orthodox Catholic churches are easily identified by their "onion" shaped (often gold) domes.

EASTERN ORTHODOX CATHOLIC CHURCH
©PhotoDisc, Inc 1994

THE ORTHODOX CHRISTIAN CHURCH

The **Orthodox Christian Church** (sometimes called the Eastern, the Greek Orthodox, or the Orthodox Catholic Church) played a major role in the affairs of the Byzantine Empire. Church affairs and doctrines affected everyday life. The emperors and empresses appointed patriarchs and other **clergy**[1] and used the wealth and power of the Church to influence the public.

When Constantine moved the Roman capital to Byzantium and recognized the early Christian movement (313 AD), the Church's leadership generally emanated from Rome. As Rome declined and the Byzantines preserved the Empire in the East, most Church councils and intellectual and cultural developments took place in the Eastern region. Byzantine Church leaders, with their differing Greek translations of the Gospels, often disagreed with Roman authorities.

The Orthodox Christian Church evolved as the Byzantine Empire strengthened. At first, there was no formal distinction, and Eastern Christians still recognized the leaders in Rome as foremost in the Church. However, the Eastern Christians were more conservative about interpreting **dogma**[2] and preserving the traditions of Jesus' twelve apostles who spread the Gospels in their lands. Over several centuries, differing theological interpretations led to an increasing number of disputes between Byzantine and Roman authorities. Eventually, the division moved beyond basic doctrine to questions of Church government, especially concerning the Pope's doctrinal supremacy among the bishops and patriarchs. Still, a **schism**[3] did not come until 1054. There were attempts at reconciliation, but they ended when Western Crusaders attacked Constantinople in 1204.

Culturally, the Orthodox Church's special place in Byzantine life influenced a vast region far beyond the imperial borders. From

1 clergy (church officials)
2 dogma (doctrine relating to matters such as morality and faith, set forth in an authoritative manner by a church)
3 schism (formal break)

RUSSIAN ORTHODOX CATHOLIC CHURCH
©Wildside Press, 1995

East Europe:
PHYSICAL FEATURES

Mediterranean
Temperate Grasslands
Temperate Forests
Taiga (Northern Forests)
Tundra (Permafrost)
Mountains

250 Km
250 Mi.

STEPPES

In the 9th century AD, most of these people fell under the influence of the Scandinavian-Norse-Vikings who were called **Varangians** by the Byzantines. From fortified strongholds, they dominated the inland trade routes from Central and Eastern Europe to Constantinople. In the late 800s, the Varangian leader **Rurik** captured the Slavic trading centers of Novogorod and Kiev.

In the early 10th century, Rurik's successor, **Oleg**, made **Kiev** (on the Dnieper River in modern Ukraine) the center of a loose alliance of settlements controlled by Varangian warriors. They adopted Slavic language and culture.

In 988, Grand Duke **Vladimir I** of Kiev converted to Orthodox (Byzantine) Christianity. Kiev became a cultural center that spread Byzantine civilization throughout Eastern Europe. Between 980 and 1054, the **Kievan Rus'** (city-state) was under

Constantinople, Orthodox Christian missionaries spread the faith into Russia, Persia, and Africa, bringing the Hellenistic culture with them to these far-flung regions.

BYZANTINE IMPACT ON RUSSIA AND EASTERN EUROPE

In 832 AD, Byzantine Emperor Michael III sent an Orthodox monk named **Cyril** to teach in Moravia (Central Europe). Cyril laid the basis for the Slavic alphabet (Cyrillic) and Byzantine culture that evolved into Slavic and Russian culture in the centuries that followed.

Byzantine culture strongly influenced the Indo-European peoples that had settled the **steppes**[1] of Eastern and Central Europe after 2000 BC (Cimmerians, Scythians, Sarmatians) as well as those who invaded in the early centuries AD (Goths, Huns, Avars, Khazars, Bulgars, and Slavs). They were nomads who became farmers and traders along a north-south route from the Baltic Sea to the Black Sea and Constantinople.

1 steppes (semi-arid grass-covered plains)

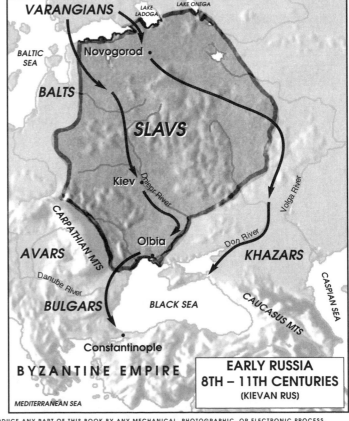

EARLY RUSSIA 8TH – 11TH CENTURIES (KIEVAN RUS)

the rule of Grand Duke **Yaroslav the Wise** and was at its height of power and achievement. Yaroslav defeated his brother for the throne in a bloody civil war and later staved off invasions by the Poles, but failed in his attempt to conquer Constantinople in 1043.

Under Yaroslav's rule, Byzantine civilization and Orthodox Christianity strengthened. Afterwards, constant feuding among nobles led to the Kievan Rus' collapse. East-west trade began to bypass the northern Black Sea river routes in the 11th century. The area was in disarray in the 13th century when the Mongol Golden Horde of Genghis Kahn's grandson, **Batu**, conquered it (1240).

BYZANTINE ACHIEVEMENTS

In 528 AD, the Byzantine Roman emperor **Justinian** (r. 527-565) appointed a commission that classified and organized a great mass of Roman edicts, legal decisions, and imperial proclamations into a code of 4,652 civil and stern criminal laws. The **Justinian Code** (*Corpus Juris Civilis*) included discussions of religious crimes such as heresy. It trans-ferred the wisdom of Roman law in such clear fashion that it became the basis for most modern legal systems in Europe.

The Byzantine Romans preserved and innovated in the arts and engineering. Building on the Hellenistic tradition, they constructed churches, palaces, and public buildings that incorporated the domes and arches of classic Greco-Roman design. To these same structures, they added murals and mosaics with Christian themes.

In the Byzantine Roman Empire, the applied arts held great importance. Byzantine artists and monks produced illuminated manuscripts, **icons**[1], **frescoes**[2], **carved ivory**, and **cloisonne**[3] for churches and the emperor's palaces. The style was **Romanesque**[4] because of the Empire's connection to the artistic heritage of Greek and Roman art and architecture, and it spread throughout the Balkans, Eastern Europe, and Russia.

---

1 icons (sacred paintings)
2 frescoes (murals done in wet plaster)
3 cloisonne (colored enamels enclosed in burnished gold)
4 Romanesque (European architecture containing both Roman and Byzantine elements, prevalent especially in the 11th and 12th centuries and characterized by thick walls, barrel vaults, and rounded arches)

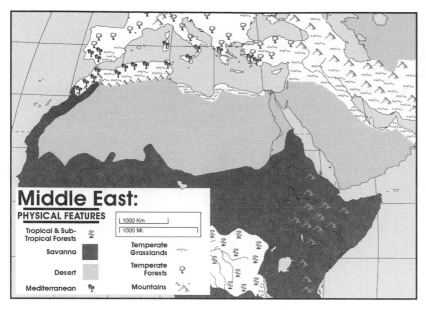

Middle East:
PHYSICAL FEATURES

1000 Km
1000 Mi.

- Tropical & Sub-Tropical Forests
- Savanna
- Desert
- Mediterranean
- Temperate Grasslands
- Temperate Forests
- Mountains

MIDDLE EAST: FROM ARAB CONQUEST TO ISLAMIC EMPIRE

GEOGRAPHIC SCOPE

Arabia is a one million square mile area of arid plains and deserts on the Indian Ocean between the Red Sea and the Persian Gulf. It is sparsely settled because of its dry Desert (Koppen-type Bw) and Steppe (Koppen-type Bs) climates. In the 7th century AD, Arabia was geographically remote from the great empires of the Middle East. The conquest launched by Muhammad and his followers resulted in a vast new empire that eventually stretched from Spain in the West to the Indus River Valley in the East.

After the death of Muhammad, his followers chose his father-in-law, **Abu Bakr** (r. 632-34) as **caliph**[1]. In a series of *jihads*[2], Abu Bakr and the next three caliphs expanded Muslim rule beyond the Arabian Peninsula, conquering lands held by the Byzantines and Sassanids (Persia) in Southwest Asia and North Africa. The old empires were weak and the Arab

camel and horse cavalries were victorious, because of their unified faith and common goal of spreading Islam.

UMAYYAD AND ABBASID DYNASTIES

During the reign of the fourth Caliph, **Ali** (the Prophet's son-in-law), a feud arose between his followers (**Shi'ites**[3]) and the **Sunn'ites**[4]. Ali's murder in 661 led to a schism. The Sunn'ite majority recognized **Muawiya I** of the **Umayyad** clan as caliph. The Shi'ites supported Ali's sons as successors, but they were killed shortly afterward.

The Umayyad rulers decreed Arabic as the official language, and set up new provinces along military lines with governors reporting to the caliphs. However, the rulers' inexperience in dealing with civilians led them to lean on a corps of local officials, some of whom worked under the Persian and Byzantine structures.

Under the Umayyad Dynasty, Shi'ite strength built among lower classes and higher taxed non-Arabs of Persia and Iraq. Opponents rallied behind Abu al-Abbas who began a revolt that overthrew the Umayyads in 750. (The Umayyads were killed and only one escaped to

---

1 caliph (khalifa, successor)
2 jihads (crusades to spread the faith)
3 Shi'ite (member of the branch of Islam that regards Ali and his descendants as the legitimate successors to Mohammed and rejects the first three caliphs)
4 Sunn'ites (members of Islamic majority, Sunni – branch of Islam that accepts the first four caliphs as rightful successors of Mohammed)

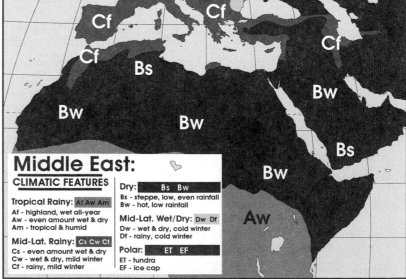

Middle East:
CLIMATIC FEATURES

Tropical Rainy: Af Aw Am
Af - highland, wet all-year
Aw - even amount wet & dry
Am - tropical & humid

Mid-Lat. Rainy: Cs Cw Cf
Cs - even amount wet & dry
Cw - wet & dry, mild winter
Cf - rainy, mild winter

Dry: Bs Bw
Bs - steppe, low, even rainfall
Bw - hot, low rainfall

Mid-Lat. Wet/Dry: Dw Df
Dw - wet & dry, cold winter
Df - rainy, cold winter

Polar: ET EF
ET - tundra
EF - ice cap

The Development of Islamic Law and Its Impact

In addition to being the pathway of religious belief and ritual, the *Shari'a* is the basis for a universal Islamic law. As such, it outlines rules of conduct and rights, and it distinguishes between what is permitted and what is prohibited. It prescribes the rules governing marriage, divorce, inheritance, contractual relations, and commerce. Thus, it shows the pathway of Islamic law.

The *fiqh* is the human effort to translate the will of God into specific rules. Basically, *fiqh* is Islamic jurisprudence – the practice of law. Islamic law classifies duty as twofold: *Ibadat* – duty to God and *Muamalat* – duty to people. In the two centuries after Muhammad's death, scholars struggled to reconcile these two concepts and to codify the *fiqh*. In the late 8th and early 9th centuries, **al-Shafii** prioritized the sources of the law (*usul al-fiqh*) as: 1) *Qur'an*; 2) *sunnah* – Muhammad's pronouncements on the *Qur'an*; 3) *ijma* - the consensus of the community (judicial precedents); 4) *qiyas* - cautious use of analytical reasoning. *Qiyas* was to be used only in the rare case when proper guidance was not available from the three primary sources.

This basic set of priorities guided the fair and equal jurisprudence in all parts of the Islamic World – from Spain to Africa to the Middle East, India, and Indonesia down to the present day. Only in the realm of international laws of commerce, when Islamic practice meets other legal systems, has there been some modification. In the realm of personal law, the basic universality of *fiqh* has been a unifying factor in the Islamic World for centuries.

set up a rival province in Spain.) The **Abbasid Dynasty** established a new, centralized capital at Baghdad. Abbasid rulers were more tolerant and shared power among the Arabs (religion), Persians (government), and Turks (military).

After 850, the strains of governing such a large empire eventually weakened Abbasid power. An Umayyad caliph retained control of the southern tip of Spain, and Shi'ite challengers ruled in Tunis and Egypt. Other rivals arose. The Seljuk Turks of Central Asia moved into Asia Minor and the Fertile Crescent around 1000. The European Christians began a series of Crusades in 1095. In 1258, an invasion by the Mongols of Central Asia took Baghdad and ended Abbasid rule.

ISLAMIC SOCIETY

Despite the great urban centers of power and culture, the larger part of the Islamic society was rural. As a whole, the *ummah*[1] was more fluid than societies of the past. It was based on the fundamental principles of justice and unity. There were rich and poor, but nothing like the rigid castes elsewhere. Individuals could rise in social status through their own actions. Military service was a common way to gain status.

Education, especially reading and writing for religious learning, was open to boys of all classes. The sons of the rich often went beyond basic skills and entered places of higher learning such as theological schools.

Men were allowed more than one wife (polygamy), and women's roles were traditional (wife, mother, caregiver, household manager). A woman could own and inherit property, attend services in the mosque, and many were allowed to learn to read and write.

Slavery[2] was common in the Islamic Empire. It was common in the Middle East long before Muhammad, but Islam did not change this. The *Qur'an* did not disapprove of slavery, but it did speak of humane treatment. Muslims could not be taken as slaves, but the 7th and 8th century wars produced many slaves from conquest of non-Muslim realms.

Slaves were used for personal and domestic service. Some became skilled artisans and some were even used as soldiers. In the Islamic Empire, however, they were not often used in large commercial farms, as they were later in history. Children of slaves who converted to Islam were given freedom. If an owner married a female slave, she was freed.

---

1 ummah (religious community living in accordance with the *Shari'a*)
2 Slavery, a social system in which one individual is owned and exploited by another

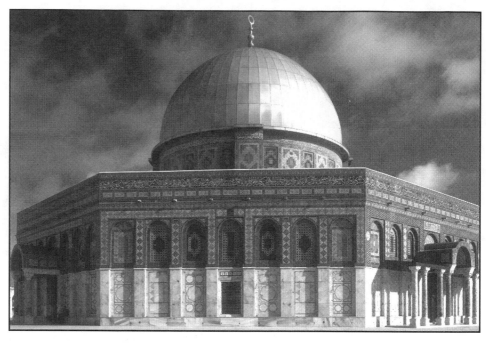

Islamic rulers were tolerant of conquered peoples. However, those who retained other religions had to pay a special tax, but they were treated well and allowed to live in peace.

The general unity of language and security under the Abbasid Dynasty meant that **commerce**[1] could extend over a vast and varied area. Trade within the Empire was brisk and profitable. Fruits and vegetables from Spain were sold at bazaars in Baghdad and Kufa while intermixing with the silks and spices of the Orient.

---

1 commerce (buying and selling of goods, especially on a large scale, as between cities or nations)

ISLAM'S GOLDEN AGE

Islam's "golden age" emerged under the Abbasids between 850 and 950. The Empire's great urban centers – Baghdad, Damascus, Alexandria, Kufa – became centers of commerce and learning. In the countryside, food was pro-

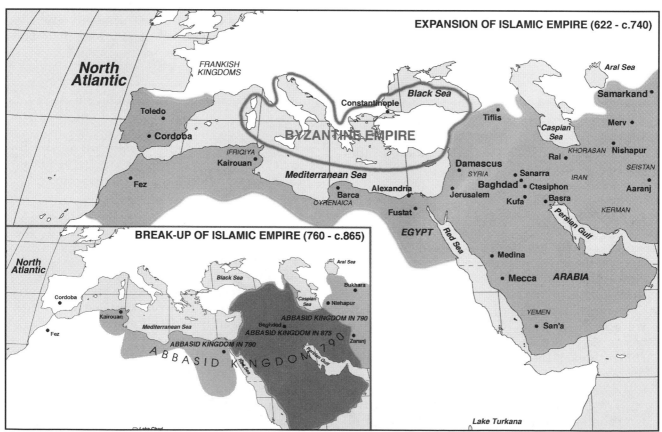

EXPANSION OF ISLAMIC EMPIRE (622 - c.740)

BREAK-UP OF ISLAMIC EMPIRE (760 - c.865)

ALHAMBRA PALACE
Grenada, Spain
10th Century

ing and a golden age of intellectual achievement. In philosophy, **Ibn Rushd** (known to the West as "Averroes," 1126-1198) preserved and developed Aristotle's works, using them as a basis for analysis of Islamic and Christian approaches to reason, ethics, and logic. Mathematicians translated the ancient Gupta concepts to communicate what became known as "Arabic numerals," the concept of zero, and the digital place-value system. Scholars such as Al-Khwarizmi organized and developed the discipline of algebra. Astronomy and navigation reached new heights. This included research on eclipses and celestial and tidal charts along with improvements on instruments such as the astrolabe. Chemists created a classification system that is still in use. **Ibn Sina** (known to the West as "Avicenna") wrote the *Canon of Medicine* around 900 AD. The work became the basis for medical education for Western civilization.

duced for the cities using irrigation methods on large landed estates.

The conquest of Byzantine lands in the Middle East and Africa presented the opportunity to study, translate, and adapt the classical learning of Greece, Rome, and Egypt. Muslim scholars preserved and intermixed such learning with Islamic culture.

In art and architecture, Islamic tradition blended Greco-Roman and Christian Byzantine art with that of Persia and influences from Central Asia and India. Islamic art flowed from daily life. Fortresses and palaces with magnificent courtyards such as the **Alhambra** (Grenada, Spain) reflected people's love of beauty. Domed mosques and minarets (slender towers) reflected the Islamic faith. Decorative arts produced abstract patterns through rich color glazes in ceramics, carved wood wall panels, and woven textiles and rugs. Islamic artists illuminated books to explain ideas and deepen knowledge. Literature included legendary stories of Aladdin and Sinbad as well as poetry such as the *Rubaiyat* (Omar Khayyam, c. 1000 AD).

The urban centers produced great learning. They drew together ideas from many civilizations. They produced Arabic translations from which Islamic scholars built a scientific awaken-

ISLAMIC SPAIN

As the Roman Empire declined, Spain fell to the Germanic Visigoth people. They drove out the Roman authorities, but slowly accepted Christianity and absorbed Greco-Roman culture. Their monarchy was weak and the kings had little control over the aristocracy. In 711, amid a civil war, the Muslims crossed over to Gibraltar and conquered much of Spain by 718.

Many Christians converted to Islam, and Arab settlers moved into Spain from the deserts of North Africa. The Muslims (or **Moors** as the Christians called them) clustered along the southern coast, calling the area al-Andalus. After the Umayyads were overthrown (c. 750), the survivors moved from their North African kingdom and became rulers of Muslim areas in Spain, becoming the **emirs** (rulers) of Cordoba.

The al-Andalus region carried on a prosperous trade in glass, paper, leather, metalwork, and silk. Science, medicine, and philosophy flourished. In 1002, the area broke up into small quarreling states. The Almohads (North African Muslim invaders) reunited the provinces, but the Spanish European kingdoms were growing strong by the 13th century, and the Moors were gradually driven out (Reconquista).

THE RISE OF MEDIEVAL EUROPE (500-1300)

Western historians refer to the period in Europe between the 6th and 14th centuries as the **Medieval Era** (also the **Middle Ages**). It is the period between the end of the Roman Empire and the Renaissance.

GEOGRAPHIC ORGANIZATION

The continent of Europe comprises the western portion of the Eurasian land mass, extending roughly from the Ural Mountains (Russia) in the east, to the Atlantic Ocean on the west, from the Arctic Ocean in the north, to the Mediterranean Sea on the south. Except in the northern extremes, climates are generally cool to mild, rainy mid-latitude (Koppen-types C and D) with abundant rainfall (27" annual average).

The good climates and fertile plains of the northern section and the more rugged, but mild climates of the southern sections attracted groups from earliest times. Europe experienced centuries of successive invasions by Central Asian people drawn to the productive, open lands. Partially, the invasions were successful because of the sheer numbers of newcomers, but the openness of the northern plains was also a factor. The plains offer inhabitants few natural defenses. The relatively low mountain ranges across the central region – the Alps of Switzerland and Austria, the Carpathians of Hungary, Poland, and Romania, and the rugged ranges of the Balkan Peninsula – offered Mediterranean civilizations some protection, but did not stop the westward flow of invaders from Central Asia.

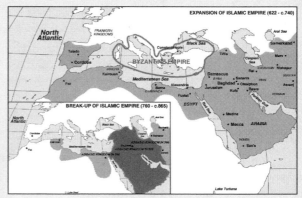

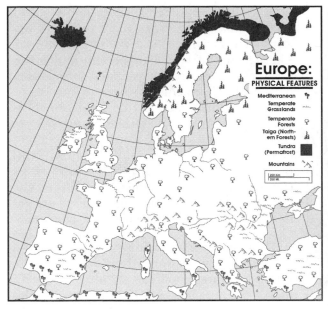

Europe: PHYSICAL FEATURES

Mediterranean
Temperate Grasslands
Temperate Forests
Taiga (Northern Forests)
Tundra (Permafrost)
Mountains

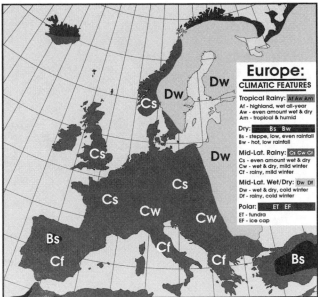

Europe: CLIMATIC FEATURES

Tropical Rainy: Af Aw Am
Af - highland, wet all-year
Aw - even amount wet & dry
Am - tropical & humid

Dry: Bs Bw
Bs - steppe, low, even rainfall
Bw - hot, low rainfall

Mid-Lat. Rainy: Cs Cw Cf
Cs - even amount wet & dry
Cw - wet & dry, mild winter
Cf - rainy, mild winter

Mid-Lat. Wet/Dry: Dw Df
Dw - wet & dry, cold winter
Df - rainy, cold winter

Polar: ET EF
ET - tundra
EF - ice cap

FRANKISH EMPIRE

The Romans subdued most of the western half of Europe and dominated the clans and tribes living there into the 4th century AD. Rome weakened as a result of civil wars, declining population, economic problems, and a bloated bureaucracy. Nomadic invasions from Eastern Europe and Central Asia increased. Imperial authority faded, and roads, bridges, and aqueducts decayed. Education and trade declined. Early historians referred to the era as "The Dark Ages."

As Huns, Vandals, and other invaders pushed westward and southward in the 400s, older, more settled Germanic peoples pressed against the Roman and Byzantine perimeters. For their own defenses, the Germanic peoples began to form small, often poor, kingdoms along the imperial borders (400-700 AD).

- **Goths** occupied Italy and Spain (5th century)
- **Franks** established themselves in Gaul (France) (5th century)
- **Anglo-Saxons** conquered Britain (5th century)
- **Lombards** replaced the Goths in Italy (6th century)
- **Avars and Slavs** occupied the Balkan Region (6th century)

As Rome was collapsing between the 4th and 5th centuries, there was a great intermixing of the Mediterranean (Phoenician-Greco-Roman), Celtic, and Germanic cultures into a new European culture. Amid this diversity, the Christian faith and its clergy emerged as the single strongest cultural element. The Church grew very slowly in status and power from a number of centers. Irish monks helped convert the Britons and Franks; missionaries from Rome and Constantinople converted northern Germans and Slavs.

In the 7th century, the Christianized kingdoms of Western Europe were also pressured from the south. Arab-Muslim invaders crossed the Mediterranean into Spain and pushed northward through the Visigoth lands and into the territories controlled by the Franks.

BARBARIAN KINGDOMS 5TH – 8TH CENTURIES

ANGLO-SAXONS
SLAVS
ATLANTIC OCEAN
FRANKS
ALEMANNI
AVARS
VISIGOTHS
LOMBARDS
BYZANTINE EMPIRE
MEDITERRANEAN SEA

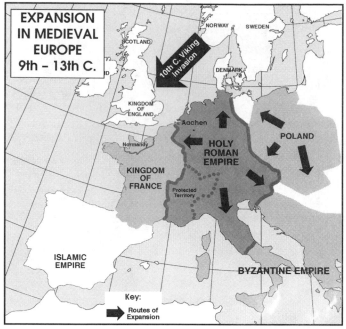

EXPANSION IN MEDIEVAL EUROPE 9th – 13th C.

NORWAY SWEDEN
SCOTLAND
10th C. Viking Invasion
DENMARK
KINGDOM OF ENGLAND
Aachen
Normandy
HOLY ROMAN EMPIRE
POLAND
KINGDOM OF FRANCE
Protected Territory
ISLAMIC EMPIRE
BYZANTINE EMPIRE

Key:
Routes of Expansion

pope's authority over secular politics, but tried to make his Western European kingdom into a workable Christian empire. Through military campaigns and diplomacy, he created a secure environment for missionaries to work among the Saxons and Slavs. He appointed nobles to rule local provinces and sent his personal **missi dominici**[1] to report on conditions. He also set up a bureaucracy to codify laws and keep imperial records. He promoted learning centers at his court and in monasteries throughout the kingdom. Charlemagne's building of irrigation ditches boosted agricultural production.

While Charlemagne's efforts united Western Europe for a few decades, the Empire disintegrated shortly after his death in 814. Yet, the idea of a Holy Roman Empire continued. Popes continued to bestow the title of Holy Roman Emperor on German rulers until the 19th century, but it was never a strong state again. Charlemagne's son Louis let the Empire crumble. It was divided among Charlemagne's grandsons in 843.

Europe fell prey to more destructive invasions after the decline of Charlemagne's heirs. The **Magyars** moved in from the east, the Muslims continued attacks in the south, and from the north came the **Vikings**. From the 8th to the 12th centuries, these Scandinavians moved beyond their homelands to trade with Byzantium, the Muslim Middle East, and Western European Christian kingdoms, and even to explore areas of North America.

In 732, **Charles Martel**, founder of the **Carolingian** Dynasty, led the Franks in successfully defending against the Muslims at Tours. In 752, the pope anointed Martel's son, **Pepin**, as king of the Franks. Pepin then warred against the Lombards in Italy, regaining papal lands. Pepin's son, **Charlemagne** ("Charles the Great," r. 771-814), battled against the Saxons in the west, the Muslims in Spain, the Lombards in Italy, and the Avars and Slavs in the east. The result was a Western European kingdom that stretched from the North Sea to the Mediterranean.

In 800, Pope Leo crowned Charlemagne as "Roman Emperor of the West." The idea was to restore a two-part Roman Empire with a Byzantine emperor in the east and a Germanic king as emperor in the west. The Byzantines were angered and never agreed, viewing Charlemagne's **Holy Roman Empire** as illegitimate scheming by the pope. The crowning of Charlemagne contributed to the eventual schism between the Eastern Orthodox and Roman Catholic Christian Churches.

Charlemagne had doubts as to the

Mostly in small bands, but sometimes in combined forces, Viking warriors fiercely attacked and pillaged the British Isles, France, and the Mediterranean. Other groups went east and then southward down the Volga and set up the Russian state of Kiev. Viking chiefs set up enclaves (small armed settlements) and extorted **tribute**[2]

1 missi dominici (traveling inspectors)
2 tribute (protection payments)

from English and Frankish towns such as London and Paris. For almost a century, Danish Vikings controlled large parts of eastern and northern England, called the **Danelaw**, where Danish laws and customs persisted for several centuries. The Byzantines called the Vikings "Varangians," and the Byzantine emperor employed a mercenary Varangian Guard.

In Western Europe, the Vikings absorbed Anglo-Saxon culture. They became Christians and the kingdoms they forged out of their many clans became Denmark, Norway, and Sweden.

MANORIALISM

After the disintegration of Charlemagne's Carolingian-Frankish Empire, Western Europe had no strong central authority. Trade declined, and the region disintegrated into isolated communities organized around the manorial land-holding system. **Manorialism** was the relationship between those who held the land (lords) and the peasants or serfs who worked on it. The system actually surfaced as Rome declined in the 4th century when small farmers found themselves in need of protection from more powerful neighbors. It evolved into a system where the strong dominated the weak.

Parts of the lord's (**manor**[1]) were assigned to individual peasants. They paid the lord in crops and services for protection and the privilege of farming. Under attack, the people of the manor – peasants/serfs, artisans, and their families – gathered in the lord's home and strong-

ARUNDEL CASTLE – Arundel, England
Built in the 11th century by Norman Richard Fizalan overlooking the Arun river. ©PhotoDisc, Inc 1994

hold. At first, these were basic, wooden walls with various earth works, ramparts, parapets, and bulwarks. As time passed and the lords' wealth increased and quarried stone became more available, the fortified homes evolved into great castle citadels with protective berms, moats, drawbridges, and portcullis (armored gate).

In a few places, some tenants were free peasants. In most others, tenants gave up rights and became **serfs**[2], binding themselves, their families, and their descendents to the land. Basically, it was the duty of the peasant / serf to support the ruling classes.

Manors were self-sufficient farm communities. Trade and outside contacts were minimal because travel was dangerous. The manor land was divided into the lords' fields (**demesne**[3]), the arable land for the peasants / serfs, common meadows for grazing, and land for support of the Church. On each manor, good land was limited and a three-field system developed to preserve its fertility. Each year,

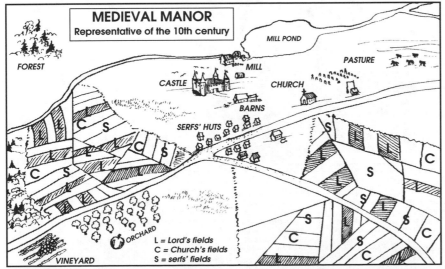

MEDIEVAL MANOR
Representative of the 10th century

FOREST
MILL POND
MILL
PASTURE
CASTLE
CHURCH
BARNS
SERFS' HUTS
ORCHARD
VINEYARD

L = Lord's fields
C = Church's fields
S = serfs' fields

1 manor (district over which a lord had rule and could exercise certain rights and privileges in Medieval Western Europe)
2 serf (member of a class of people in Europe bound to the land and owned by a lord)
3 demesne (Manorial land retained for the private use of a feudal lord)

MANORIAL RELATIONSHIPS

Peasant Serf Provided	Landlord Provided
• payments in kind for use of arable land • labor to the lord for tasks such as building roads, bridges, and dams. • help defending the castle in attacks • labor on the lord's demesne	• land for the tenants • military protection • economic security against crop failures • justice in a local court

one field was Spring-planted, a second was Fall-planted, and a third left **fallow**[1] to regenerate naturally. The most common crops were peas and beans along with hay, rye, barley, oats, wheat, and flax (for linen cloth).

Justice in the lord's court was swift and arbitrary. Punishments were cruel. Peasant trials were often by **ordeal**[2]. Executions were by drowning and hanging; other punishments included branding, mutilations, amputations, and eye gouging for lesser offenses.

Although it varied from place to place, the manorial structure was common in Europe by the 10th century. As it developed, certain lords' power grew, and the size of their manors increased.

FEUDALISM

Manorialism was Medieval Europe's economic land system that involved inherited relations between peasants and their lords. **Feudalism**[3] was the often contractual structure that governed political and legal relations among the nobility.

The overlord, as the largest landholder in a region, gave a **fief**[4] to a **vassal**[5]. Vassals pledged an oath of **fealty**[6] and **homage**[7] to the overlord. The oath bound the vassal to provide the overlord with financial, civil, and military service along with perpetual loyalty. Vassals could subdivide their estates and have vassals of their own. In this way, overlords created intricate networks of vassals with estates who would gather to defend the overlord's domain in time of peril. Overlords exercised political, economic, and social control over vassals.

Vassals were the overlord's loyal **knights**[8] — mounted warriors specifically trained from boyhood in military skills at the overlord's direction. At age 15, a trainee became a squire to an existing knight. After a period of trial, the overlord promoted him to a full-fledged knight, usually making him a vassal and granting him a fief. In the later Middle Ages, knights adopted a code of behavior called **chivalry**[9]. Knights were supposed to be guided by accepted ethics and honor in battle, by loyalty to God and their lords (and the overlord's lady), and by vows to defend the sick and disadvantaged.

---

1 fallow (plowed but left unseeded during a growing season)
2 ordeal (accused had to endure physically painful or dangerous tests, the result being regarded as a divine judgment of guilt or innocence)
3 feudalism (political and economic system of Europe from the 9th to about the 15th century, based on the holding of all land in fief or fee and the resulting relation of lord to vassal and characterized by homage, legal and military service of tenants, and forfeiture)
4 fief also called feud (an estate in land granted by a lord to his vassal on condition of homage and service)

5 vassal (lesser noble holding land from a feudal lord and received protection in return for homage and allegiance)
6 fealty (allegiance, loyalty, faithfulness to obligations, duties)
7 homage (publicly showing obeisance, honor, and respect)
8 knights (medieval gentleman-soldier-tenant giving service as a mounted man-at-arms to a feudal landholder)
9 chivalry (principles, and customs idealized by knighthood, such as bravery, courtesy, honor, and gallantry toward women)

FEUDAL RELATIONSHIPS

Vassal Provided	Overlord Provided
• allegiance, homage, fealty • tributary money or goods • military service when summoned • ceremonial duty • 3 feudal dues: ransom, dowry, knighthood • hospitality and entertainment for lord's visits	• landed estates (fief) • armed forces • roads, bridges, and dams • justice in disputes among vassals (trials by combat)

THE ROLE OF THE CHURCH

The Romans persecuted the Christian Church for nearly 300 years until 313 when the Emperor Constantine ordered toleration of all religions. In 392, the Emperor Theodosius proclaimed Christianity the official religion of the Empire. Theodosius was the last emperor to rule over the Eastern and Western sections of the Empire. In the next 200 years, the Church in the west grew strong enough to fill the power vacuum in Europe as Rome weakened and decayed.

As the state religion, the Christian Church was exempt from taxes. This allowed its wealth to grow.

Llandalf Cathedral, England

The building of churches by the emperors enhanced the power of the clergy in major communities throughout Europe. One example of the power of Christian Church officials is that it was not the emperor who rode out to meet Attila and dissuade him and his Huns from sacking Rome in 452, but Pope Leo I.

The new barbarian leaders who set up kingdoms after the fall of Rome preferred conquest to desk work. They depended on Church leaders and clerics to help them organize and govern their conquests. Because of their learning, clerics became the bureaucracy for Europe. They codified laws, kept track of judicial precedents, oversaw taxation, and managed public works. Often, clerics took advantage of this status by using Church teachings to restrain worldly excesses of barbarians. Church leaders wanted an ideal Christian community or "commonweal" as described in St. Augustine's 5th century work, *The City of God*. In this process, the clerics' service to rulers blurred the separation of power between Church and state.

These complex entanglements led to struggles between rulers and Church officials throughout the Middle Ages. To compound the problem, lords had land grant power over many abbots (heads of monasteries) and bishops. They received lands from lords to set up monasteries and Church facilities, and they pledged fealty in return. Abbots and bishops sometimes subdivided their land grants among lesser lords, thus setting up their own fighting forces. Because these churchmen had both spiritual and political

CLOSE LOOK

Medieval Economic Structure

The manorial and feudal relationship became the basis for a **barter economy** (direct exchange of goods and services of equal value without use of money). It became the system of distributing and allocating resources in the Middle Ages.

As the threat of invasions slowed in the 10th century, long-distance trade was renewed by groups such as the Italians. They imported spices and silks from the East. In return, they took amber, furs, and timber products from Europe to the Orient. Eventually, a money system emerged that was easier and less clumsy than the barter system.

CLOSE LOOK

Monastic Centers of Learning

In organized religion, monasteries are religious communities bound by vows and often living in partial or complete seclusion. After the 6th century, Medieval Christian monasteries followed the Rule of Saint Benedict of Nursia (**Benedictine Rule**). It governed the monks and transformed their communities to serve areas as combination hospitals, schools, research libraries, and travel shelters.

The monks' selfless focus on efficient work made monasteries centers from which came ideas on improving agriculture, animal husbandry, cloth making, building techniques, medical treatment, and other useful arts. They also wrote chronicles on everyday life. The monks' command of Latin obligated them to labor intensely at preserving sacred texts and secular works such as the writings of Caesar, Cicero, Virgil, and Ovid to make translations into Latin of the Greek classics such as Aristotle's writings.

Some monasteries remained focused on serving their local region, while some became repositories of learning for kingdoms or, in some cases, the Continent at large. Later in the Middle Ages, new orders of monks became missionaries, spreading Christianity and its unifying culture to Britain, Germany, and Poland.

power, emperors and rulers wanted control over them. On the other hand, archbishops and popes often crowned kings and emperors, and therefore claimed that the Church was the primary universal authority.

In the later Medieval Period, popes increased their power during the **investiture controversy**. The dispute was over who should appoint (invest) Church officials. In 1122, a Church council forbade all lay (non-Church) investiture of clergy. In the **Concordat of Worms**, the Holy Roman Emperor compromised and agreed to the selection of bishops and abbots by the clergy.

In the economic arena, the Church collected large amounts through the **tithe**[1] obligation. Much of this wealth was used for others' benefit, especially financing the work of monasteries. Church regulations forbade **usury**[2]. Because loans were sinful, many lords were impoverished. Often, they sought funds from outside the Christian community turning to the Jews for loans. These arrangements later led to the establishing of banking houses. Accumulation of wealth among Jews led to prejudice, jealousy, and periodic persecution. Sometimes, defaulting lords expelled Jewish lenders rather than repay them.

ART, ARCHITECTURE AND LITERATURE

Under Charlemagne, scholars and artists focused on classic works of ancient Greece and Rome. At his capital at Aachen, Charlemagne had his palace chapel reflect a Greek-Byzantine design. In the early Middle Ages, the Romanesque styles dominated churches. It evolved into the lighter, refined, and soaring spires of the **Gothic style**[3] found in the cathedrals and castles of the later Medieval Period.

The monks' **illumination**[4] of manuscripts reflected classical art. Gospel books and psalters (books of the psalms) for the 8th and 9th centuries have illustrations copied from earlier Greek and Roman texts combined with stylized portraits of the saints.

Carvings, jewelry, painting, and sculpture depicted religious themes, but there were some efforts to preserve the history of the era. For example, the 11th century **Bayeux Tapestry**, portrays the Norman conquest of England by William the Conqueror (1066). It is a 230 foot

---

1 tithe (tenth part of one's annual income contributed voluntarily or due as a tax, especially for the support of the clergy or church)
2 usury (in Medieval times, lending money at interest – in modern times, charging interest at an exorbitant or illegally high rate)
3 Gothic style (architecture prevalent in Western Europe from the 12th through the 15th century and characterized by stained glass windows, pointed arches, rib vaulting, and flying buttresses)
4 illuminations (decorating text pages with ornamental designs or lettering)

long, linen and wool embroidery with words describing scenes celebrating the events of the conquest.

The Church was the source of most Medieval literature. The Crusades' contacts with the Muslim world spawned cross cultural awareness (see next section). Latin translations of classical philosophers such as Plato and Aristotle from Greek and Arabic became the focus of **Scholasticism** – reconciling the classical works with the teaching of the Church. Scholastic philosphers followed the 5th century Church Father Augustine's famous phrase, "Understand so that you may believe, believe so that you may understand."

The works of **Peter Abelard** (French, 1079-1142) and **Thomas Aquinas** (Italian, 1224-1274) are the most significant of the scholastics. Abelard's teachings launched great debates on theology in the 12th century.

Thomas Aquinas' magnificent *Summa Theologiae* reconciled Christian teachings with Aristotelian philosophy. Aquinas' work also examined the Muslim analysts of Plato and Aristotle (Avicenna, Averroes). From the 13th century to the present, it became the basis for much Church doctrine and dogma.

CRUSADES AND THEIR IMPACT

During the centuries after the Fall of Rome (476), Western Europe was splintered into many kingdoms and feudal holdings. Charlemagne's Holy Roman Empire was strong for only a few decades, and the Church was the only unifying institution. Yet Western Europe was not isolated. There was constant contact between the West and the Byzantine Empire. Waves of barbarian invaders pounded Europe before and after Charlemagne, changing and blending the cultures. The Muslim conquests expanded into

Mini Assessment

1 In the Medieval Era, the relationship between the lord and those who lived and worked his lands was called
   1 feudalism
   2 illumination
   3 manorialism
   4 investiture

2 The Scholasticism of the Medieval Era
   1 reconciled ancient classics with church teaching
   2 limited the Church's power over kings
   3 governed the rules for feudal relationships
   4 rallied military forces to defeat the Vikings

3 Which statement best describes the role of the Christian Church in Medieval Europe?
   1 The Church set the rules for the manorial system.
   2 The Church provided moral and social leadership for the era.
   3 Popes exercised political power through their role as Holy Roman Emperors.
   4 All kings had to follow the Rule of St. Benedict.

Constructed Response:

"The baron and all vassals of the king are bound to appear before him when he shall summon them, and to serve him at their own expense for forty days and forty nights, with as many knights as each one owes. ... And if the king wishes to keep them more than forty days at their own expense, they are not bound to remain if they do not wish it. And if the king wishes to keep them at his expense for the defense of the realm, they are bound to remain."

– *Legal Rules for Military Service*, 1072

1 How long must vassals give military service to the king at their own expense?

2 Under what circumstances would they be bound to serve longer?

3 What did vassals receive in exchange for military service to their overlord?

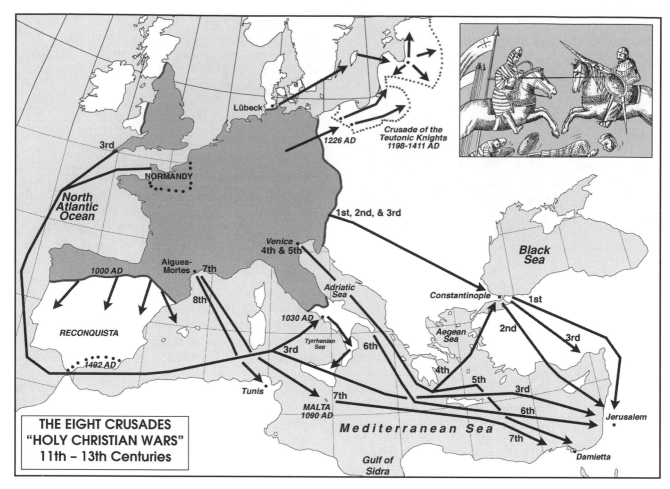

THE EIGHT CRUSADES "HOLY CHRISTIAN WARS" 11th – 13th Centuries

Spain, challenging Christian kings and exchanging and renewing knowledge and ideas.

By 1000 AD, the kingdoms of Western and Central Europe, while lacking unity, were growing in wealth and strength. The Byzantine Empire, on the other hand, was declining in size and strength and was threatened by Muslim invaders from Central Asia – the **Seljuk Turks**. By the end of the 11th century, the Seljuk Turks had conquered Asia Minor (Turkey) and most of the eastern Mediterranean coastal states and cities.

In 1095, Byzantine Emperor Alexius I begged Pope Urban II to send him military aid to stop the Seljuk Turks and rescue the Holy Land. The Pope rallied support for the First Crusade - a military expedition to stop Muslim expansion and restore access to the holy places in Palestine.

Between the 11th and the 14th centuries, European Crusaders launched eight expeditions.

Crusaders assumed they were soldiers of Christ and wore a red cloth cross sewn on their tunics. Leaders such as Godfrey of Bouillon, Baldwin of Flanders, England's Richard the Lion Hearted, France's Philip II, and Germany's Frederick II established a number of short-lived Latin Kingdoms in the Middle East. In 1204, Crusaders sacked Constantinople itself and

THE DAMASCUS GATE GATE OF JERUSALEM
A major objective of the Crusaders – c.1200

THE CRUSADES: CAUSES AND RESULTS

Categories	Causes	Results
Religious	• To restore the right of Christians to make pilgrimages to the holy shrines in Jerusalem • To reunifiy the Orthodox and Latin branches of the Church under the Pope	• Hardened Muslim attitudes toward Christians • Stimulated broad religious spirit
Political	• To aid the Byzantine Empire against the Seljuk Turks	• Led directly to the Turkish wars and expansion of the Ottoman Empire into the Balkans
Economic	• To gain some of the fabulous riches of the East • To acquire new feudal lands at a time of crop failures • To gain access to trade routes by rising Italian cities (Genoa, Pisa, and Venice)	• Drained European resources • Expanded use of a money economy • Stimulated trade, architecture, and the growing urban culture
Cultural	• (see religions)	• Broadened contacts with the Muslim world • Prepared Europe for the discoveries of the modern age • Transmitted Islamic science, philosophy, and medicine to the West

later temporarily overthrew the Byzantine Empire (restored in 1261). Also, there were minor crusades against against Slavic pagans in Germany (1147), Prussian and Lithuanian pagans near the Baltic Sea (1198-1411), heretics in southern France (1209-29), and against the Moors in Spain until 1492 (Reconquista).

TIME CAPSULE

GLOBAL HISTORY ARCHIVE

This was an era of change. Some societies and civilizations were divided, some were destroyed, and others were unified. Older, classical civilizations lost influence, but new social institutions, such as the great religions, brought cultural unity as well as cultural diffusion. Buddhism, Christianity, and Islam reached new heights of influence over vast areas.

The rise of the Gupta and T'ang Dynasties brought new brilliance to civilization in Asia, while the fall of Rome left a political, social, and cultural void in Europe. The division of the Christian Church into a Western Latin (Roman) branch and Eastern Orthodox (Byzantine) branch further broke down cultural unity.

As the Byzantine Empire struggled to preserve classical culture, Islam arose. In its struggle to spread its beliefs, it reorganized, revitalized, and spread Arab culture from India to Spain.

Teutonic, Viking, and Central Asian invasions of Western Europe created a time of turmoil. The Christian Church slowly became the preserver and unifier of European culture. Manorialism created an isolated economic order, while feudalism created a stratified social and political order and stability.

Amid all the danger and divisive forces, cultures intermingled. Intellectual and scientific discoveries crossed cultures with the journeys of religious missionaries, diplomats, and scholars. Trade junkets and military expeditions, such as the Christian Crusades and the Islamic Jihads, also caused civilization to widen in scope. The stage was set for changes that ushered in a new global age.

MULTI-CHOICE QUESTIONS

1   In the Gupta Empire of India (320-550 AD), classics such as *Shakuntala* and *Meghaduta* were based on
    1   the teachings of Buddha
    2   Hindu tradition
    3   Confucian morality
    4   Islamic law

2   After subduing local warlords and ending invasions from Central Asia in the 7th century, T'ang rulers claimed authority through
    1   Benedictine rule
    2   Missi Domenici
    3   The Edict of Milan
    4   The Mandate of Heaven

Base your answers to questions 3 and 4 on the map below and your knowledge of global history.

3   Geography influenced the economic life of the Byzantine Empire because of its nearness to
    1   monsoon wind systems
    2   protective mountain systems
    3   fertile river valleys
    4   major bodies of water

4   Although it controlled much of the Mediterranean Basin after the fall of the Roman Empire, the Byzantine Empire was
    1   purely Greek in culture
    2   ruled democratically
    3   frequently under foreign attack
    4   conquered by the Roman legions

5   Byzantine culture preserved and blended
    1   Christian liturgy and Hellenistic culture
    2   Sunn'i and Shi'ite schisms
    3   Sanskrit and Chinese technology
    4   Carolingian bureaucracy and Viking culture

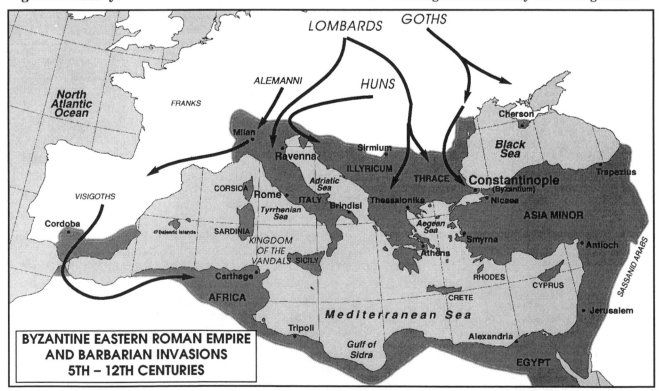

BYZANTINE EASTERN ROMAN EMPIRE AND BARBARIAN INVASIONS 5TH – 12TH CENTURIES

6 Unlike contemporary Indian and Byzantine civilizations, which element was not prevalent in early Islamic society?
1 slavery　　3 social castes
2 taxation　　4 golden ages

7 Seventh century Islamic art and architecture
1 remained isolated from foreign styles
2 blended styles of many cultures
3 banned all Christian influences
4 was available only to merchant classes

8 Under manorialism, tenants agreed to work the lord's demesne in exchange for
1 military protection
2 religious salvation
3 collection of the tithe
4 cultural diffusion

9 In the late Middle Ages, popes increased their political power as a result of the
1 work of merchants
2 investiture controversy
3 mandate of heaven
4 monastic rules

10 Pope Leo's crowning of Charlemagne in the 9th century united
1 Empires of the Gupta and T'ang
2 Western and Central Europe for a few decades
3 Orthodox and Roman Christian Churches
4 peoples of the Byzantine and Roman cultures

11 Under feudalism, vassals and lords observed chivalry, a code which guided
1 agricultural production cycles
2 theological learning
3 marriage rites
4 ethical behavior and loyalties

12 "And so, between the 11th and 15th centuries, a long series of campaigns channeled surplus manpower and energy into a Western counteroffensive. ..."
The "series of campaigns" refers to the
1 Golden Ages
2 Varangian Wars
3 Christian Crusades
4 Islamic Jihads

THEMATIC ESSAY

Theme:　Political and economic systems

Political, economic, and social conditions often alter human existence.

Task:
- Define self-sufficiency.
- Explain how the medieval manor was self-sufficient.
- Why was it necessary for the Medieval manor to be self-sufficient?

DOCUMENT BASED QUESTION

Directions:
The following question is based on the accompanying documents (1-5). Some of the documents have been edited for the purposes of this exercise. The question is designed to test your ability to work with historical documents. As you analyze the documents, take into account both the source of the document and the author's point of view.

- Write a well-organized essay that includes an introduction with a thesis statement, several paragraphs explaining the thesis, and a conclusion.
- Analyze the documents.
- Use all the documents.
- Use evidence from the documents to support your thesis position.
- Do not simply repeat the contents of the documents.
- Include specific related outside information.

Historical Context:

Some scholars hold that the Christian Church of Rome exerted significant influence in Medieval European society. The documents below present some aspects of Church activity.

Task:

Decide whether the role played by the Christian Church of Rome was a positive or a negative force in Medieval European society and support your opinion with the documents below and your knowledge of global history.

Part A - Short Answer

The documents below relate aspects of the Christian Church of Rome influence in Medieval European society. Examine each document carefully, then answer the question that follows it.

Document 1:

"[In the Dark Ages] throughout Europe, whenever the turmoil subsided and barbarian rule took root, the new masters came to rely more and more on the civilizing counsel of men of the Church. As experienced administrators and as custodians of the knowledge and learning of the past, these men started Europe on its slow, upward climb out of chaos."

– The Age of Faith

Document 1 Question:

Why did barbarian kings use clergy as advisors and to organize their realms?

Document 2:

"Thus concerning the Church and her power, is the prophecy of Jerimiah fulfilled, 'See, I have this day set thee over the nations and the kingdoms,' ...Furthermore we declare, state, define and pronounce that it is altogether necessary to salvation for every human creature to be subject to the Roman pontiff."

– Pope Boniface VIII, Unam Sanctam (1302)

Document 2 Question:

How might kings and lords view this statement?

Document 3:

Document 3 Question:

How did the cultural activity depicted in this scene influence Medieval society?

Document 4:

Translation:

"The Lord be with you. And with thy spirit. Lift up your hearts. We lift them up to the lord."

Aside from orally transmitted folk songs, Gregorian Chant was the main music form preserved, written down, and practiced universally in Medieval Europe. It blended Greek, Roman, and Hebrew sources. It was simple in range for most voices, had free flowing rhythm, and was sung in unison.

– *The Age of Faith*

Document 4 Question:

How did the Church's music influence Medieval society?

Document 5:

"From the confines of Jerusalem and the city of Constantinople a horrible tale has gone forth ...that a race of the Persians, an accursed race, a race utterly alienated from God has invaded the lands of those Christians and has depopulated them by the sword, pillage, and fire ... it has entirely destroyed the churches of God or appropriated them for the rites of its own religion.

"On whom therefore is the labor of avenging this territory incumbent, if not upon you?... Let this one cry be raised by all the soldiers of God: It is the Will of God! It is the Will of God!"

– Pope Urban II *Speech at the Council of Clermont* (1095)

Document 5 Question:

On what basis is Urban trying to rally support for a crusade in the Holy Land?

Part B – Essay Response

Discuss the Church as a force in Medieval society.

Your essay should be well organized with an introductory paragraph that states your thesis as to the role of the Medieval Church. Develop and support the reasons for your thesis in the next paragraphs and then write a conclusion. In your essay, include specific historical details and refer to the specific documents you analyzed in Part A. You may include additional information from your knowledge of global history.

Unit 4

1100 AD – 1650 AD

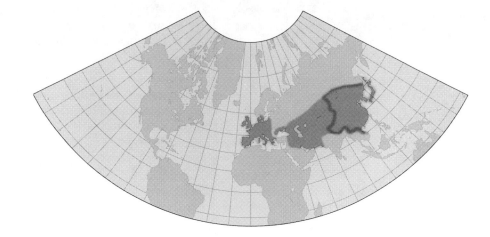

BC	
3000–	Yayoi people move into Japan from Asia (3000 BC)

AD	
600–	Japan's Classical Heian Period (604 AD)

AD	
1100–	
1200–	Minamoto Yoritomo becomes Shogun (1180 AD)
	Genghis Khan launches the Mongol invasions (1206 AD)
1300–	
	Black Death sweeps through Europe (1348 AD)
1400–	Renaissance takes hold in Europe (1400 AD)
	Zheng He's expeditions to South Asian and Africa (1405 AD)
	Turks capture Constantinople (1453 AD)
1500–	Vasco DaGama arrives in India (1498 AD)
	Protestant Reformation begins – Luther posts 95 Theses (1517 AD)
1600–	British East India Company founded (1600 AD)

PEOPLE	PLACES	THINGS
burghers	cloth towns	absolutism
Elizabeth I	ghettoes	bartering
Genghis Khan	Middle East	Black Death
Henry VIII	Mongol Empire	Bushido
Kublai Khan	Northern Italian cities	bureaucracy
Leonardo DaVinci	seasonal trade fairs	capitalism
Martin Luther	Venetian Republic	domestic system
Nicolo Machiavelli	Wittenberg Cathedral	guild
Prince Henry the Navigator		humanism
Tokugawa Shogun		magnetic compass
Zheng He		Thirty Years' War

INTRODUCTION

Around 1000 AD, civilizations in East Asia and Europe went through political and social changes that led to interactions that paved the way for the modern age. Japan emerged as a unique civilization. China regrouped into a formidable power. Mongol conquerors from Central Asia swept through India, the Middle East, and into Eastern Europe. They then brought a peace that allowed trade to revive between Europe and Asia. Europe revived after the Crusades. Its commercial interactions caused upheavals of feudal life that began challenging all its institutions.

EARLY JAPANESE HISTORY AND FEUDALISM

SPATIAL ORGANIZATION / GEOGRAPHY

Japanese society emerged as a unique island culture nearly 10,000 years ago. The formidable natural environment of the **archipelago** (island group) made settlement difficult. The southern three of its major islands (Honshu, Shikoku, Kyushu) have a mild climate (Koppen-type Am) tempered by warm ocean currents and monsoons. The northern islands, such as Hokkaido, have a rainy, cold winter climate (Koppen-type Df) intensified by cold ocean currents from the Arctic. Earthquakes, volcanic eruptions, landslides, and **tsunami**[1] afflict the islands. The land (142,000 sq. mi.) is mostly rugged mountains and **arable land**[2] limited to small river valleys. Early on, the Japanese turned to the seas for food.

1 tsunamis (very large ocean wave caused by an underwater earthquake, underwater landslide, or volcanic eruption)
2 arable land (agriculturally suitable to be cultivated and plowed)
3 Shinto (religion native to Japan, characterized by veneration of nature spirits and ancestors and by a lack of formal dogma)

EARLY TRADITIONS

Anthropologists theorize that the influence of the natural environment partially accounts for the evolution of **Shinto**[3]. It is a form of animism. Shinto means the "way of the kami." **Kami** are spiritual entities. They include natural elements (winds, trees, rivers, rocks, the sea). Kami also include clan gods, souls of ancestors and great heroes, and gods such as the sun-goddess Amaterasu, from whom the imperial family claimed descent.

Throughout its early history, the seas sheltered the Japanese archipelago from conquest. Yet, they separated the people from other cultures, too. The island location also allowed the Japanese a freedom to accept or reject outside influences. Often, Japan was subject to powerful cultural influences from China.

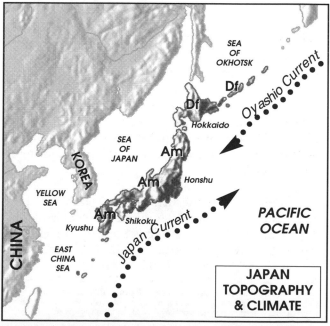

JAPAN TOPOGRAPHY & CLIMATE

Mt. Fuji, a massive dormant volcano is a symbol of Japanese culture's respect for the forces of nature that shaped ancient Shinto beliefs. ©PhotoDisc, Inc 1994

rituals to the Japanese imperial court. Buddhist influence became particularly strong in this era.

In 604, **Shotoku Taishi** created central authority based on laws related to China's Confucian social order. In 646, the rulers redistributed land to break the power of a rising aristocracy. Japan's first permanent capital was built at **Nara** in 710. The aristocrats' power was transferred to a nobility-controlled, Chinese-style bureaucracy (without a merit examination system). Nara became the center of Buddhist activity, and priests influenced the government until a new capital was founded at **Heian** in 794.

Early anthropological data show the Jomon culture intermixed with northern Ainu peoples around 8000 BC. In the 3rd century BC, the **Yayoi** people migrated from continental Asia and intermixed with the Jomon. They began rice cultivation, weaving, pottery, and domesticated horses and cows.

TIES WITH CHINA AND KOREA: CULTURAL DIFFUSION - BUDDHISM AND CONFUCIANISM

From this blend of early people, a ruling **uji** (clan) arose in the southern part of Honshu – the **Yamato**. The Yamato chiefs claimed descent from the goddess Amaterasu. They formed alliances among the clans and unified the country by the 4th century AD. In the next century, military expeditions into Korea and scholarly pilgrimages brought contact with China. The Yamato even had a colony in Mimana, on the southern tip of the Korean Peninsula. Japan gradually adapted Chinese script. In 538, **Buddhism**[1] was introduced and began intermixing with Shinto.

Beginning in the 6th century, and for the next 200 years, many Japanese travelers and diplomats visited the T'ang capital in Chang-an. Returning visitors and scholars introduced Chinese language, writing, cuisine, dress, and

Although contact with China lessened, the Japanese court at Heian oversaw a great cultural period from the 9th through the 11th centuries. Poet **Sei Shonagon** (c. 966-1013) produced *The Pillow-Book*, a diary describing court life. **Murasaki Shikibu** (c. 978-1026), wrote the classic *Tale of Genji*, an early novel of life among the court nobles. However, Heian was a world to itself. The emperor ruled the city, but in the country beyond, the great uji retained power.

By the 11th century, the imperial land reforms of the 7th century had crumbled. Families such as the **Fujiwara** controlled the country and founded feudal estates. At Heian,

---

1 Buddhism (doctrine, attributed to Buddha, that suffering is inseparable from existence but that inward extinction of the self and of worldly desire culminates in a state of spiritual enlightenment beyond both suffering and existence)

the Fujiwara intermarried with the emperor's family. In the 11th century, they became the ruling group. Power shifted to the independent land-holding warriors and their **samurai**[1] (vassal knights). The samurai gave their loyalty to the **shogun**[2] – the chief military commander. The shoguns eventually moved Japan into a feudal culture that lasted until modern times.

JAPANESE FEUDAL SOCIETY

As in Medieval Europe, the political and social structure of Japan was land-based. Although the feudal systems were different, historians note significant similarities between the two regions.

As land fell into private hands in the provinces, new feudal lords arose – the **daimyo**[3]. Gradually, the daimyo replaced the imperial court nobles in power. They formed alliances and sometimes warred among themselves. They created private armies staffed by samurai. The daimyo guaranteed the samurai land holdings in return for military service.

The daimyo and their samurai became the bureaucracy at the head of Japan's class system. Next came the peasants, artisans, and merchants.

As in Europe, samurai vassals lived in strongholds. Unlike Europe, peasants were not bound to the land as were serfs, but they did pay high taxes. Around 1000 AD, towns gradually became market centers, and a new style of urban life began to develop.

In the 12th century, the Minamoto family emerged as the strongest daimyo group. As a result of a civil war in 1180, **Minamoto Yoritomo** (r. 1192-1199) became shogun. He set up a military alliance of daimyo that ruled Japan until 1868. In these years, the emperors became figurehead rulers, with no power. The shogun oversaw a system of samurai military governors. In the later stages of the shogunate, the daimyo followed the code of **bushido**[4] – a combination of chivalry, Confucian-military discipline, and Zen Buddhism. From time to time, emperors tried to overthrow shoguns and gain control through civil wars, but they were largely unsuccessful.

The power of the shogun was demonstrated in the 13th century, when China's Mongol ruler, Kublai Khan, attempted to invade Japan. Twice the daimyo defeated the Mongol fleets. They were aided by violent storms that legend refers to as **kamikaze** (divine winds).

TOKUGAWA SHOGUNATE

From 1603 to 1867, a long line of shoguns descended from **Tokugawa Ieyasu** ruled Japan. After moving the capital to Edo (now Tokyo), the Tokugawa Shoguns became obsessed with discipline and order. They blocked social and political change.

To avoid the conspiracies which plagued other shogunates, they made all daimyo live in the capital. If a lord left Edo, family members had to be left at Edo as hostages.

After 1639, the Tokugawa Shoguns began a **seclusion policy**. It isolated the country from the outside world. They restricted trade to one tightly guarded port – Nagasaki. Only ships from China and the Netherlands were allowed to enter. They expelled Christian missionaries and persecuted Japanese Christians.

---

1 samurai or samurais (Japanese feudal military - professional warrior belonging to the aristocracy)
2 shoguns (hereditary commanders of the Japanese army who until 1867 exercised absolute rule under the nominal leadership of the emperor)
3 daimyo or daimio (feudal lord of Japan who was a large landowner)
4 bushido (traditional code of the Japanese samurai, stressing honor, self-discipline, bravery, and simple living)

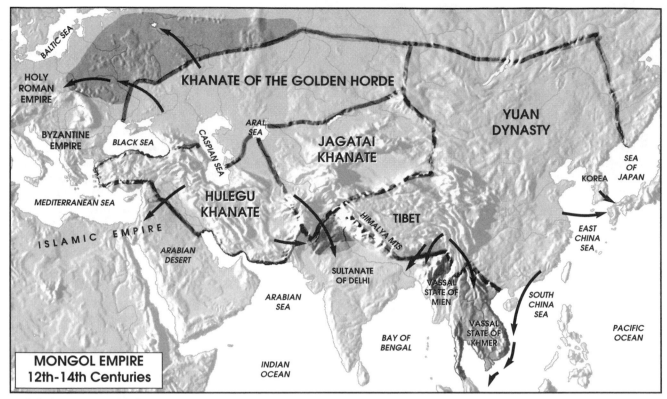

MONGOL EMPIRE
12th-14th Centuries

SOCIETY AND CULTURE UNDER THE SHOGUNS

Peace brought prosperity. Internal trade in textiles and food blossomed, but Japanese society became static. By law, a strict, hereditary social order was imposed. Classes descended from warriors to farmers to artisans to merchants. Farmers became bound to the land just as the serfs had in Europe. There were peasant rebellions in the countryside in the 1400s. They reduced the shoguns' power and enhanced the prestige of local warlords and clans. However, the rebellions never improved the peasants' lot. The only class to expand were the merchants who provided goods for the daimyo while lending money to them.

Still, the arts flowered in the general prosperity of the shogunate. Dramatic classics emerged from the **Noh** theater (Zen Buddhist themes), and later, the **kabuki** theater offered more free-wheeling comedy and drama. A national literature burgeoned with works such as *Heike Monogatari* (*The Tale of Heike*, 1240) and *Tsurezure Gusa* (*Idle Jottings*, 1320). Short stories, essays, and poetry such as the simple, three-line **haiku**[1] flourished. Architects created

masterpieces such as the Golden Pavilion (1395) and the Moss Garden of Kyoto (15th century).

RISE AND FALL OF THE MONGOLS AND THEIR IMPACT ON EURASIA

ORIGINS

The Mongols were descendants of a variety of nomadic people of the Central Asian Plateau including the Huns, Turks, and Uighurs. In 1206, a fierce warrior, Temujin (1167-1227), united the Mongols. They proclaimed him the "universal ruler," **Genghis Khan**. He launched a highly organized, disciplined cavalry against China. In 1215, the Mongols conquered Beijing laying the groundwork for the Yuan Dynasty.

In 1219, Genghis Khan sent the Mongols westward and took the Central Asian trading cities of Tashkent, Samarkand, and Bukhara. The Mongols moved into the steppes of Russia and through Himalaya passes into India.

---

1 haiku (Japanese lyric verse form having three unrhymed lines of five, seven, and five syllables, traditionally invoking an aspect of nature or the seasons)

MONGOL IMPACT

Area	Impact
China	• 1st foreigners to rule all of China. Yuan Dynasty (1279-1368) • Created capital at Beijing • Retained the Chinese bureaucracy • Opened China to foreign contacts
India	• Mughal Dynasty (1526) by Babur, a Muslim descendant of both Genghis Khan and Timur • Ruled Indian subcontinent until the mid-18th century • Policy of tolerance toward Hindu subjects • Great rulers: Akbar (r. 1556-1605), Jahngir (r. 1605-1627), Shah Jahan (r. 1627-1658) • Became mere puppets of the British in 19th century • Magnificent Mogul art and architecture (Taj Mahal) influence Indian styles
Southwest Asia	• Hulegu (Persia – Iran, Iraq, Syria), became assimilated into Islamic culture • Jagatai Khanate (Central Asia) became Turkish in language and custom; adopted Islamic faith • Law codes based on loyalty • Influenced culture of Afghanistan, Turkmenistan, Uzbekistan, Kazakistan • Briefly regenerated by Tamerlane (c. 1400)
Russia	• Destroyed Kievan Rus' urban life • Depleted the population • Exploited Russians with tribute payments in silver • Indirect rule through local Russian princes • Orthodox Church exempted from tribute (allowed it a cultural leadership role) • Isolated area from Byzantium and Western Europe • Moscow princes defied Mongols and offered peasants protection • Overthrown by Ivan III in 15th century

THE MONGOL EMPIRE

Genghis Khan created the largest empire in human history. The Mongol domain eventually stretched from the Pacific Ocean to the Black Sea. When the "universal ruler" died in 1227, his descendants divided his empire into four **khanates**[1]:

• China – empire of Kublai Khan (Yuan Dynasty 1279-1368)
• Persia – Hulegu Khanate
• Turkestan – Jagatai Khanate
• Russia – Khanate of the Golden Horde

By the 14th century, Mongol drives brought them into Central Europe, India, and Southeast Asia. They were destructive as conquerors, but more benevolent as rulers. Rarely did they impose a social or political order on conquered peoples, nor did they enslave large groups. Except in Russia, the Mongols absorbed and assimilated local cultures. However, they did extort heavy **tribute**[2]. Their tight discipline and military control over a vast area ensured peace and security.

Because of this regional stability, some historians even refer to the brief era of Mongol rule as the "**Pax Mongolia**," and compare it to the *Pax Romana* (31 BC - 167 AD). As a result of the stability, trade among societies in Asia, the Middle East, and Europe strengthened. Travel and wealth increased in the region. In the 14th century, the Mongol khanates disintegrated. **Timur Lenk** ("Tamerlane"), a Turk-Mongol, briefly revitalized the Persian and Turkestan khanates. He challenged the Ottomans for Asia Minor, but his empire collapsed after his death in 1405.

---

1 khanates (realm of khans or kingdoms)
2 tribute (payment in money or other valuables made by a feudal vassal to an overlord to show submission or as the price of protection or security)

THE YUAN DYNASTY: RULE BY NON-CHINESE

The Mongol conquest marked the first time foreigners had ruled over all of China. Genghis Khan's grandson, **Kublai Khan**, set up the Yuan Dynasty (1279-1368). At his capital at Beijing, high officials were Mongols. Yet, he retained the Confucian Chinese bureaucracy. He did not make great changes in Chinese governmental structure. However, he opened China to contacts with the world at large. Frequent Middle Eastern and European visitors included Christian missionaries and traders.

Economic problems and resentment of the foreign dominance of Kublai Khan's successors led to a rebellion in 1368. The Chinese overthrew the Yuan Dynasty and set up the Ming Dynasty (1368-1644).

MONGOL INTERACTION WITH THE WEST

The Mongols' discipline and control over a vast area strengthened trade between Asia and the Middle East and Europe. It reestablished the Silk Route, and brought more travel and wealth. Two famous traveler-explorers in the region were the Italian **Marco Polo** (1254-1324) and the Arab **Ibn Battuta** (1304-1368).

Marco Polo of Venice wrote of his adventures as a merchant in Asia with his father and uncle. In 1271, they crossed the Mongol khanates of Central Asia along the old Silk Route. For 17 years, they served at Kublai Khan's court. Marco Polo's tales aroused Western interest in trade with the Orient.

The security of Mongol rule also allowed Ibn Battuta to travel through Central and South Asia. Between 1325 and 1354, he is said to have traveled a remarkable 75,000 miles. He also journied to North and East Africa, India, and the Middle East. His tales expanded knowledge of the world beyond Europe and the Middle East.

GLOBAL TRADE INTERACTIONS

When the era of the Crusades dawned, Constantinople was the main connection between the West and Asia. Later, new global trading centers arose with the demand for goods. Commercial interests and adventurers in

GLOBAL TRADING CENTERS		
City	**Connections**	**Background**
Canton, China (now Guangzhou)	Asian goods traded for Indian, Persian, Arab, and European goods	Settled in 9th century BC, it became earliest Chinese international port. European traders came during the T'ang dynasty (618-907). Foreign merchants were confined to a small area outside the city wall.
Cairo, Egypt	Middle Eastern goods traded for East and Sub-Saharan African, Central Asian, Indian, European goods	This old Roman town was made military camp by Arabs in 640. Its real growth began under Fatimid dynasty after 969 and expanded under Saladin in late 12th century. It declined after plagues, a Mongol attack (c.1400), and the Turkish conquest (1517).
Venice, Italy	European goods exchanged for Middle Eastern, African, Central Asian, Chinese, and Indian goods	Venice controlled Adriatic Sea (9th century AD) and became a chief staging area for the Crusades. After the 4th Crusade devastated Constantinople (1204) and Venice defeated rival Genoa in 1380, it was unchallenged in Mediterranean. Venice led a coalition against Turks at the Battle of Lepanto (1571).

Mini Assessment

1 Which is an example of cultural diffusion?
   1 Shinto was partially derived from animism.
   2 12th century wars elevated the shoguns to power.
   3 Tokugawa shoguns enforced a seclusion policy.
   4 Nara became a center for Chinese Buddhist missionaries.

2 Which resulted from Mongol rule over a vast area of Eurasia?
   1 Mongols enslaved large numbers of conquered people.
   2 Japan's rulers copied the Chinese-style bureaucracy.
   3 It allowed the travels of Ibn Battuta and Marco Polo.
   4 Bushido became the Samurai code of behavior.

3 In which area did Mongol rule last longest?
   1 China   3 Russia
   2 India   4 Southwest Asia

Constructed Response:

1 Which two factors in the diagram are the basis for Mongol rule?

2 Why do historians compare the Pax Mongolia to the Pax Romana?

---

contact with Asian centers led Westerners to seek new routes and arrangements.

EXPANSION OF CHINESE TRADE

In the mid-14th century, the Ming Dynasty emerged from years of rebellion against the Mongol Yuan Dynasty. The Ming rulers restored traditional customs and order to China. With new farming techniques came increased food and agricultural surpluses that broadened trade. The Ming rulers devoted efforts to public works (canals, irrigation). Prosperity led to a flowering of the arts and compiling of great historical volumes.

The early Ming emperors launched a series of large-scale maritime expeditions. In 1405, the adventurous admiral **Zheng He** (or Cheng Ho) left Ming shores with an expeditionary fleet of hundreds of ships. In seven great expeditions over the next thirty years, **Zheng He's** fleets ventured to the East Indies, India, Persia, and along the East African coast. Chinese merchants followed in his wake, spreading Chinese culture throughout the Eastern Hemisphere. However, later Ming emperors felt the expeditions were too expensive and curtailed them. They also felt that China was superior to all other civilizations. With the attitude of "let others come to us," they allowed a six thousand ship navy to fall into ruin. The Ming emperors' Confucian officials held merchants in low esteem. Disregarding the sea, they turned their attention to strengthening China's northern borders.

PORTUGUESE TRADE EXPANSION

At the western end of the Silk Routes, the hostile Turks blocked European traders from crossing to the Middle East and Central Asia. Traders received little help from China. Because it was rich and self-sufficient, China did not have the same economic energy as the West. With land routes blocked, Westerners sought water routes to lower trading costs.

In the early 1400s, Portugal was driving the Muslims from the Iberian Peninsula. Also, it launched military expeditions against Muslim

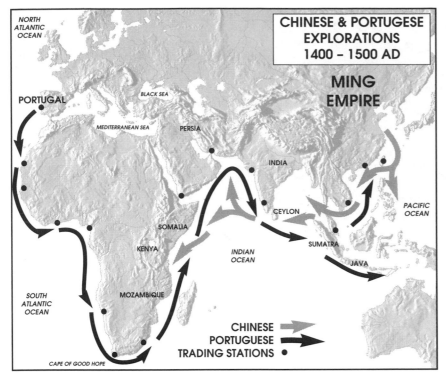

CHINESE & PORTUGESE EXPLORATIONS 1400 – 1500 AD

CHINESE ⟹
PORTUGUESE ➜
TRADING STATIONS ●

Portuguese exploits drew mariners from Spain and the Netherlands into longer oceanic ventures. The **Age of Exploration** aroused European interest in the 16th and 17th centuries.

RESURGENCE OF EUROPE

EUROPE REVIVES

Many changes affected Europe in the late Middle Ages. The Crusades accelerated consciousness of other cultures. They also brought awareness of new products. At the same time, forces were breaking down the static life of manorialism. As drier, cooler climatic conditions developed, cereal production increased. Slow, but steady advances in agricultural technology led to surpluses. From 1000-1300, economic change was spurred by new technology:

- marsh drainage
- iron plows and harrows
- collar harnesses (allowed use of horses in plowing rather than slower oxen)
- water-mills and wind-mills (process grain)

rulers in North Africa. These ventures expanded knowledge and wealth. They supported the urge to find southerly water routes around Africa. Portugal's **Henry the Navigator** (1394-1460) founded a center at Cape St. Vincent for navigational studies and expedition planning. Prince Henry's center educated captains and trained crews for long voyages. They worked with new **charts**[1], **magnetic compasses**[2], and the Arabic **astrolabe**[3].

Knowledge accumulated at Cape St. Vincent helped mariners overcome fears of open-water sailing. From these beginnings, the Portuguese became the European leaders in African coastal exploration. Bartolomeu Dias reached Africa's Cape of Good Hope in the late 1480s. Vasco DaGama reached India by rounding the Cape in 1497. The Portuguese adventurers built a trading empire along the seacoasts of East Africa, Arabia, India, the East Indies, Indochina, and China. The

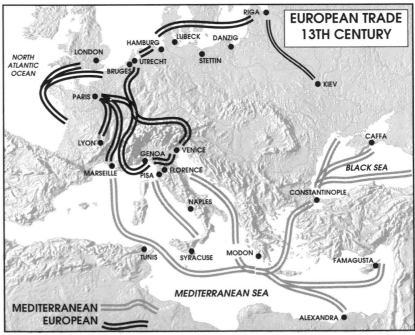

EUROPEAN TRADE 13TH CENTURY

MEDITERRANEAN ═══
EUROPEAN ───

1 chart (map showing coastlines, water depths, or other information of use to navigators)
2 magnetic compass (instrument that uses a magnetized steel bar to indicate direction relative to the Earth's magnetic poles)
3 astrolabe (Medieval instrument, now replaced by the sextant, that was once used to determine the altitude of the Sun or other celestial bodies)

All of these simple innovations made farms larger and more productive. The surpluses led to trade, more plentiful food, and greater material comfort. These factors brought population increases. Between the 10th and 13th centuries, Europe's population doubled to 60 million.

FAIRS, TOWNS, AND GUILDS

As population increased, demand for goods rose. General peace made travel safer. Merchants ventured out among settlements to meet demand. This increased interaction among people at **seasonal trade fairs**, such as the famous one in Champagne in eastern France. Later, permanent trading centers appeared along well-traveled routes near larger castles and universities. Centers for the linen and wool trade (Flanders) and Eastern spices (northern Italy) grew into significant Medieval towns. Artisans in these centers began distributing their goods through traveling merchants.

As the early towns formed, kings and local feudal lords charged fees to merchants and artisans in exchange for protection and operating space. The kings and lords formalized the arrangements by granting official contracts to merchant councils. Gradually, these **charters**[1] became the bases for town government.

Town dwellers who made their money through trade or industry (as opposed to peasants who worked the land) came to be called **burghers**[2] in Germany. In France they were-*bourgeoisie*; in England, they were *burgesses*. As the land-bound feudal system broke down, these burghers became the "middle class" between the lords and the peasants. As burghers grew wealthier, they formed councils to regulate trade, levy taxes, and administer justice. The councils were oligarchies that governed towns and rendered protection. They built walls, fortifications, and port facilities.

Very slowly, towns became independent of the local lords. In Italy, some towns grew into city-states (Venice, Milan, Florence) and emerged as small, independent republics. Self-government, sanctuary, and freedoms increased.

The towns grew rapidly with little planning. There were no building codes. Houses were constructed of thatch and wood and heated by open fires. Houses and whole towns burned frequently. There was no sanitary processing of wastes; diseases such as cholera and typhus spread rapidly.

Between the 12th and 15th centuries, merchants and artisans tried to control trade by forming monopolies called **guilds**[3]. These were alliances among the members of an occupation. Only members of the guild could practice that trade in the town.

Master craftsmen[4] made arrangements with parents to take their sons and teach them as **apprentices**[5]. Guilds regulated apprentices for 2 to 15 years, then certified them as **journeymen**[6]. Journeymen worked for pay until the guild certified them as masters. The guilds had many important activities:

- contributed to the defense of the town and provided leaders to keep order
- regulated trade and industry (quality, just prices)
- provided technical training
- organized social welfare for members
- promoted building of cathedrals and universities
- developed artistic crafts

Famous main door of Brewers' Guild, London

---

1 charter (written grant from the sovereign power conferring certain rights and privileges on a person or group)
2 burgher (member of the mercantile class of a Medieval European city)
3 guilds also gilds (associations of persons of the same trade or pursuits, formed to protect mutual interests and maintain standards, as of merchants or artisans)
4 master craftsmen (highly skilled workers such as blacksmiths, weavers, armorers)
5 apprentices (beginner learning a trade or occupation, especially as a member of a guild)
6 journeymen (qualified worker in another's employ who has fully served an apprenticeship in a trade or craft and is experienced and competent)

BLACK DEATH - Bubonic Plague

In the late Middle Ages, poor sanitation in rapidly growing, tightly packed towns led to frequent plagues and epidemics. Between 1348-1353, bubonic plague wiped out nearly one-third of Europe's population. Known among the Mongols, it appears to have been carried by rats on ships traveling from Black Sea ports into the Mediterranean. In six years, it swept across Europe like a tidal wave, killing millions from Sicily to Scotland.

Death toll estimates in 14th century Europe, Asia, and Africa exceed 100 million. It took two centuries to bring the population back to 1347 levels.
Bubonic plague is caused by a bacterium transmitted by fleas that have fed on the blood of infected rats, It is commonly transmitted by breathing air exhaled by infected persons. It spreads through the bloodstream and the lymphatic system. In untreated cases, death occurs within a few days – and unlike today, there was no cure in the 1300s.

The Black Death disrupted Asian trade routes and brought Europe's revival to a standstill. It triggered crop shortages and famines since few were left to tend the farms. Guilds and crafts suffered as master craftsmen were lost. Knowledge of the law declined as jurists perished, and universities closed for lack of staff. Serfs and peasants rebelled or ran off when lords demanded pre-plague payments they could not make. In some areas, loss of serfs meant lords had to begin paying wages to laborers.

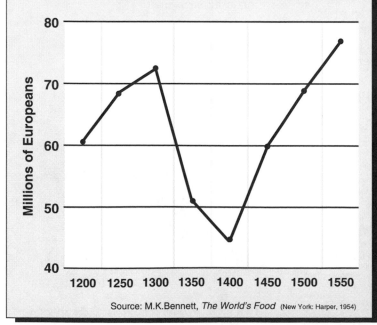

Source: M.K.Bennett, *The World's Food* (New York: Harper, 1954)

THE HUNDRED YEARS WAR

The Black Death took a terrible toll on the revival of Europe, but so did ongoing warfare. In the **Hundred Years' War** (1337-1453), France and England battled sporadically over dynastic claims in France. The conflicts symbolized the change in loyalties in Europe as power shifted from local feudal lords to national monarchs.

England's feudal claims in France were contested by French monarchs. The English registered several convincing victories in the long string of clashes (Crécy, Agincourt, Poitiers). However, the French, led by **Joan of Arc**, won a decisive battle at Orleans in 1429. The English were expelled and the French nation's modern borders were established.

COMMERCIAL REVIVAL

By 1000 AD, the broadening of contact among people in Europe caused a need for better ways of transacting business than **bartering**[1]. As town life grew complex, the need to simplify and speed up trade became important. The use of **money**[2] as a common medium of exchange revived. (Most ancient civilizations had coinage, but its use fell off under manorialism.) Traveling merchants began to carry many different kinds of money.

This led to the need for agents (bankers) to change one kind of money into another. These early bankers began to store money for customers and issue credit certificates. The certificates began to function as a form of paper money. These early bankers also began lending money. At certain times, merchants and artisans needed

1 bartering (to trade goods or services without the exchange of money)
2 money (commodity, such as gold, or an officially issued coin or paper note that is legally established as an exchangeable equivalent of all other commodities, such as goods and services)

THE RESURRECTION OF MONEY

Coinage was invented in ancient China. Coins were common in the Roman Empire, but went out of use as the isolated manorial life patterns emerged on the manors of Medieval Europe. Peasants cultivated large estates in return for services and dues paid to their lords. Transactions were simple, localized barter arrangements.

As trading towns redeveloped after 1000 AD, commercial transactions became too complex for barter to work. Money reemerged as the basic medium (tool) of exchange.

Some individuals were long acquainted with trading gold and became experts at valuing the large variety of currencies that began to appear as the scope of trade broadened. Being outside the Church's authority and rules on usury, Jews were traditionally in positions to act as money changers and lenders. The independence of the Italian city states also allowed families such as the Medici of Florence to become bankers.

The accelerated use of money to finance commercial activities signaled the onset of capitalism. **Capitalism**[1] is an economic system that flows from private ownership of productive resources. Although the modern economic system of capitalism evolved slowly, its basic components were present in the late medieval period.

Expansion depends on individuals acquiring and reinvesting profits. As businesses borrow large sums of money (**capital**) to expand production, more goods become available (supply) to meet consumer wants (demand). The development of capitalist structures such as money and banking allowed the growth of global trade.

Gradually, new forms of business organization emerged. To finance broad trading ventures, businessmen formed **joint stock companies** such as the British and Dutch East India Companies (c. 1600). These companies sold **stocks**[2] to raise large amounts of money from many small investors. Later, in the Age of Exploration, joint stock companies became the main way to finance colonial ventures.

larger quantities of money to make exchanges when traveling traders came to town. At other times, they needed to buy materials in advance so that goods would be ready when a busy season began (e.g., harvest, feasts, or holidays).

Sometimes merchants and bankers pooled their wealth in local partnerships to buy very large quantities of raw material. Some formed leagues among neighboring towns for convoys, caravans, and trading expeditions.

---

1 capitalism (economic system in which the means of production and distribution are privately or corporately owned and development is proportionate to the accumulation and reinvestment of profits gained in a free market)
2 stocks (ownership shares in a company giving the stockholder dividends)

EUROPEAN TRADING STRUCTURES

Group	Profile
Hanseatic League	The League grew out of Medieval merchants traveling together for safety. It was an association of Medieval north European cities formed in the 13th century. It grew to 200 towns in the 14th century and lasted until the 17th century. The League had a central **diet** (assembly) that met to make rules on common commercial interests, provide defense against piracy on the Baltic and North Seas, and prepare charts and navigational aids, and negotiate trade treaties.
Italian City-states	In the 11th century, wealthy merchants, bankers, and trades people in Northern Italy broke away from feudal nobles to form independent city-states. Genoa, Florence, Pisa, Milan, and Venice fought to remain free and manage their own affairs and defenses. In the later Medieval Era, their wealth and **cosmopolitanism** (worldly sophistication, awareness of many spheres of interest) launched the European cultural Renaissance.

Another early form of business organization was the **domestic system**. Businessmen acted as agents, coordinating people doing piecework in their homes. The businessmen organized the labor and provided the materials. They then collected and marketed the goods. Centuries later, the factory system would put all workers and managers under one roof.

WESTERN EUROPE'S TRADE CORRIDOR

The revival of Western Europe's economy arose out of the merging of two areas – the Italian ports and the northern "cloth towns." The woolens and linens of Ypres, Lille, and Ghent moved southward to Milan, Venice, and Genoa. Cotton, spices, luxury fabrics, and gold of Africa and Asia found its way from the eastern Mediterranean's

Levant to the Italian ports. It then moved northward along the Rhone, Rhine, and Seine Rivers into the interior of Europe and outward to the Atlantic Coast. The broad corridor that connected these two zones became the avenue of revitalized trade. As the key cities grew, other trade structures and alliances formed to accelerate the interaction of commerce.

RENAISSANCE AND HUMANISM

Economic and political shifts can lead to cultural change. In the late Medieval Era, production of surpluses spurred trade and the rise of town life. This triggered new cultural interactions. Struggles for power between the Church and temporal rulers led to re-examination of views on power. From the early 14th to the late 16th century, a revival of interest in the values

Mini Assessment

1 Which combination led to Portugal's leadership in exploration of sea routes to Asia?
1 technological change and navigational studies
2 Medieval trade fairs and the bubonic plague
3 Baltic trade alliances and guilds
4 the Hundred Years War and the domestic system

2 Under the early Ming rulers, Admiral Zeng He's expeditions spread awareness of
1 capitalism into Mongolia
2 manorialism into Western Europe
3 China's culture in the Eastern Hemisphere
4 Buddhism throughout Africa

3 Which accelerated the growth of towns and trade in Europe in the late Middle Ages?
1 agricultural technology yielded marketable surpluses
2 Ming Confucian officials' low esteem for merchants
3 lack of construction codes in early towns
4 guild regulation of apprentices for 2-15 years

Constructed Response:

1 What did Northern and Western Europe supply to Venice for global trade?

2 Why did Venice become a world trading capital in the 11th century?

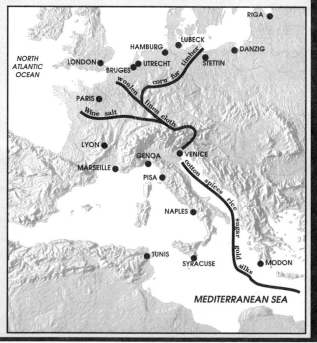

RENAISSANCE ACHIEVEMENTS

LITERATURE

Person	Work	Key Ideas
Petrarch (Francesco Petrarca Milan, Padua, Venice, 1304-1374)	*Africanus*; sonnets	sonnets and love songs in Italian and classical Latin
Giovanni Boccaccio (Florence, 1313-1375)	*Decameron*	100 traditional tales of Medieval life in vernacular Italian
Dante Alighieri (Florence, 1265-1321)	*The Divine Comedy*	epic allegory in Italian vernacular describes a journey through hell, purgatory and paradise
Geoffery Chaucer (England, 1340-1400)	*Canterbury Tales*	pilgrims tell tales of Medieval life in vernacular English
Desiderius Erasmus (Netherlands, 1466-1536)	*Praise of Folly*	used teachings of the Bible, early Christianity, and ancient pagan thinkers to ridicule the corruption of officials and the clergy
Thomas More (England, c. 1478-1535)	*Utopia*	lashed into the unjust social and economic corruption in England; describes an ideal state based on humanist reason
Francois Rabelais (France, 1483-1553)	*Gargantua and Pantagruel*	humanist attack on older Medieval values; call for Church reform
Miguel de Cervantes (Spain, 1547-1616)	*Don Quixote*	intended to poke fun at the Spanish romances of chivalry and to analyze the value of idealism

ITALIAN ART AND ARCHITECTURE

Person	Work	Key Ideas
Leonardo DaVinci (1452-1519)	*Mona Lisa, Last Supper*	model "Renaissance Man" – experimented in the arts, mechanics, science; constructed fountains, fortifications, churches; experimented in manned flight, war machines
Michelangelo Buonarotti (1475-1564)	*Moses, David,* Sistine Chapel ceiling, dome of St. Peter's	Biblical and classical figures of athletic prowess and dynamic action; painting, sculpture, and architecture
Raphael (Rafaello Sanzio – 1483-1520)	*Disputa, Sistine Madonna*	classical forms, allegories, madonnas, and subjects from antiquity

POLITICAL SCIENCE

Person	Work	Key Ideas
Nicolo Machiavelli (Florence, 1469-1527)	*The Prince, Discourses*	advice on increasing and holding power; recommended that absolute monarchs preserve power pragmatically (use violence carefully, respecting subjects and their property and preserve prosperity); claimed political actions have consequences that cannot be fully controlled, and the ruler must sometimes accept that "the end justifies the means;" called for Italian unity and an end to foreign intervention

TECHNICAL INNOVATION

Person	Work	Key Ideas
Johann Gutenberg (Germany, 1398-1468)	movable type, printing ink, letter press process	invented printing from movable type in Europe (already being done in China from the 8th century); supplied the needs for more and cheaper reading matter and expanded learning and communication

Florence, Italy
Center of
Renaissance Art

RELIGIOUS REFORMATION

For nearly 200 years problems divided the Roman Catholic Church. From 1309 to 1377, French popes ruled from Avignon under the influence of the French monarchs. After the papal court returned to Rome, mobs forced the College of Cardinals to elect an Italian pope. Simultaneously, another French cardinal claimed the papacy and set up court again in Avignon. During this **Great Schism** (1377-1414), two popes (and at one point, three) tried to rule Christendom. The Church Council of Constance (1414-1418) finally resolved the issue. The papal schism seriously undermined Church authority. During this same period, the Black Death decimated Church leadership. Scattered reformers protested the clergy's corruption. They began questioning its authority. Another result of the chaos was that political influence shifted toward monarchs.

and arts of Greece and Rome led to a golden age of cultural blending and innovation. Later scholars called the era a period of "rebirth." This **Renaissance**[1] transformed Western European life.

During the Renaissance, the Western Europeans' world image shifted from a strictly religious view to a more secular (worldly) outlook. Unlike the religious scholastics of the late Medieval Period (Aquinas, Abelard), Renaissance intellectuals had a growing confidence in individual human spirit and abilities (e.g., "...humans as masters of their own fate"). This new outlook came to be called **Humanism**[2]. It focused on the personal worth of the individual and human values, as opposed to religious belief. Renaissance humanists were influenced by the study of ancient Greek and Latin literature and philosophy. They tried to show that ancient values were consistent with Christian teachings and could help people toward better lives. Humanists were present-centered. They focused on life now, rather than the spiritual hereafter.

It was natural that Northern Italy became a cradle of humanism in the 14th century. The independence and wealth of the Northern Italian city-states allowed artists and scholars to explore ideas and learning of the ancient world and civilizations of the Eastern Mediterranean. They had little interference or official censorship.

In addition to these forces, the economic and social changes of the Renaissance altered the Medieval **status quo**[3] in Western Europe. These sweeping changes of the 14th and 15th centuries made life closer to what we know today. In the spirit of Renaissance humanism, people questioned tradition. Economic individualism and early capitalism made people more self-reliant and innovative. The printing press enabled writers to circulate new ideas and pose new questions. In the mid-1400s, there were 100,000 manuscripts circulating in Europe, although only about ten percent of the population could read. By 1500, there were an estimated 9 million books in print. (Most of them were religious in nature.)

Eventually, this new, questioning attitude changed social behavior and institutions. It affected the most powerful institution – the Roman Catholic Church. The result was a turbulent religious reform movement – the **Protestant Reformation**.

---

1 Renaissance (humanistic classical art, architecture, literature, and learning that originated in Italy in the 14th through the 16th century spreading throughout Europe, marking the transition from medieval to modern times)

2 Humanism (cultural and intellectual movement of the Renaissance that emphasized secular concerns as a result of the rediscovery and study of the literature, art, and civilization of ancient Greece and Rome)

3 status quo (existing condition or state of affairs)

In the 16th century, reformers protested the corrupt practices of the Church – thus, they became known as **Protestants**[1]. Corruption included **simony**[2], bribery of Church officials, and selling of **indulgences**[3]. Protestant reformers wanted to restore the Church to its early Christian roots. Although there were vast differences among the reformers, they promoted several key ideas:

- acceptance of the Bible as the key source of revelation
- salvation by faith alone
- the universal priesthood of all believers.
- self interpretation of the Bible
- questioning rituals and some of the sacraments

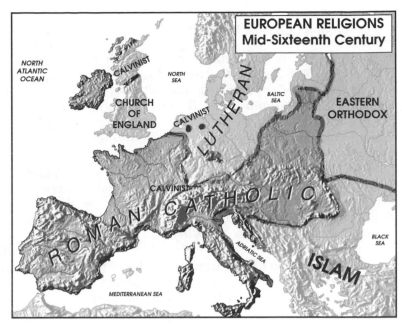

More than religious problems plagued the Church. The Pope and Holy Roman Emperor were distant authorities, too removed from local and regional problems. The monarchies in France, England, and Spain developed strength and unity, and they clashed with the Church over land, taxes, and judicial authority.

LUTHER AND THE NINETY-FIVE THESES

During the Renaissance, humanists such as Erasmus and theological critics such as John Wycliffe (1328-1384) denounced the Church's

Martin Luther protesting Church practices by posting his grievances on the door of the Wittenberg Cathedral.

corruption. They wanted reform to come from Church leaders and they avoided the disruption of a general "grass roots rebellion." After the changes of the Renaissance Era, the rebellion began.

In 1519, **Martin Luther**, a German cleric and Wittenberg University professor, posted his *Ninety-five Theses*. Luther condemned Church abuses. He translated the New Testament into the **vernacular**[4]. This enabled ordinary individuals to seek salvation through self-interpretation. Church authorities branded Luther as a dissenter (rebel). Yet, his actions opened the floodgates of protest against the Church all over Europe. Pope Leo X eventually condemned Luther as a **heretic**[5].

The Pope **excommunicated**[6] Luther in 1521. However, some strong German princes backed Luther, exerting their power against the Church. They were opposed to outside influences, had nationalistic feelings, were anti-tax, and wanted to keep their money at home. This defiance of Church authority helped the Protestant movement spread to Scandinavia, Poland, and Eastern Europe.

---

1 Protestant (member of a Western Christian church whose faith and practice are founded on the principles of the Protestant Reformation, especially in the acceptance of the Bible as the sole source of revelation)
2 simony (buying or selling of ecclesiastical pardons, offices, or monies)
3 indulgences (remission of often physical punishment still due for a sin that has been forgiven - sacramentally absolved)
4 vernacular (everyday language spoken by a people)
5 heretic (person who holds controversial opinions, especially one who publicly dissents from the officially accepted dogma of the Roman Catholic Church)
6 excommunicated (deprived of the right of church membership by ecclesiastical authority)

CALVIN AND OTHER REFORMERS

Self-interpretation of the Bible took other reformers in different directions. **John Calvin** (French, 1509-1564) published the *Institutes of the Christian Religion* and **Ulrich Zwingli** (Swiss, 1481-1531) wrote *Sixty-Seven Articles*. These writings spread the Reformation spirit into Switzerland, France, and the Netherlands. In Geneva, Calvin set up a **theocracy**[1]. It became a model for groups such as the Calvinist English Puritans who later settled in America. In Scotland, **John Knox** (1514-1572) used Calvin's ideas to found the Presbyterian Church.

As the religious reform movement swept Europe, other Protestant **sects** (groups) formed that were more radical in their approach than the Lutherans or Calvinists. They wished to purge the Church by rejecting elaborate rituals and sacraments. For example, the **Anabaptists**[2] rejected infant baptism and focused only on adults. They also rejected local governmental authority. Sects that derive from the Anabaptists include the Amish, Baptists, Mennonites, and Quakers.

The Reformation took a different turn in England. While religious reformers were active in the early 1500s, it was **King Henry VIII**'s desire for a male heir that led him to break with Rome. The Pope refused to annul (declare invalid) his marriage and allowed him to take a new wife (actually, Henry took 5 more). In 1534, Henry pressured Parliament into passing the *Act of Supremacy*. The Act broke relations with Rome setting up a new Church of England (**Anglican Church**), with the king as head. As a result, religious struggles lasted in England for several generations.

COUNTER REFORMATION

Once the Reformation was under way, the Church retained its strength in France, Southern Germany, Ireland, Eastern Europe, Spain, Portugal, and Italy. Northern Europe, Scandinavia, and Scotland slipped away.

For nearly 17 years, there was no active program within the Church to answer the Protestant criticisms. Slowly, the **Counter-Reformation** became an active reform movement inside the Church. It agitated for a general council to eliminate abuses. In 1536, a commission reported to Pope Paul III, but it took another six years before decisive action occurred. He tried to "clean up" the corruption that had led to the Church's credibility problem. He approved new religious orders such as the **Jesuits**[3]. They dedicated themselves to missionary work to reclaim souls for the Church. Paul III also convened the bishops at the **Council of Trent** (1545-1563). The reforms set by the Council have lasted into modern times. The Council's decrees redefined the Church's mission through the following actions:

- forbidding the sale of indulgences
- ordering each diocese to have a seminary to properly train clergy
- defining vague doctrines challenged by Protestants
- requiring the Mass and other rituals be said in Latin
- declaring the only acceptable version of the Bible was the Latin Vulgate (St. Jerome's 4th century translation of the Bible)
- reaffirming the importance of the seven sacraments

The Counter-Reformation energized and even hardened the resolve of the Roman Catholic Church. Missionaries such as Jesuit founder **Ignatius Loyola** (1491-1556) rekindled the faith in Europe and spread it into Asia and the Americas. Papal resources funded military activity against Protestant areas in Europe. The popes reinforced the **Inquisition**[4]. The Counter Reformation strengthened the Catholic faith in Southern Europe and spread it into new global regions. Although these actions slowed the Counter-Reformation, Protestantism was not eliminated as its founders had hoped.

IMPACT OF RELIGIOUS WARS IN EUROPE

In northern Europe, national Protestant churches developed that aligned themselves to national monarchs. The kings used the new churches to become independent of the Pope and the Holy Roman Emperor. Although Protestant

1 theocracy (community, state, or government ruled by religious principles)
2 Anabaptist (member of a radical movement of the 16th-century Reformation which believed in the primacy of the Bible, in baptism as an external witness of the believer's personal covenant of inner faith, and in separation of church from state and of believers from nonbelievers)
3 Jesuit (Roman Catholic Church - member of the Society of Jesus, an order founded by Saint Ignatius of Loyola in 1534)
4 Inquisition (court formerly held in the Roman Catholic Church and directed at the suppression of heresy)

Chateau of King Henry IV – Nantes, France

religious reformers argued doctrine and Church practice, secular princes used the Reformation to strengthen their political power.

The result was a century of wars fought in the name of religion. In the German states, nearly 100,000 were killed in the **Peasants' War** (1524-1526). Peasants, small-town artisans, and laborers sacked castles and monasteries before the authorities quelled the rebels. Later, **The Peace of Augsburg** (1555) ended twenty years of fighting between the Catholic Holy Roman Emperor Charles V and German Lutheran princes. The compromise allowed each ruler to decide the local religion. The result was a Germany so deeply fragmented that it was not united until the 19th century.

In France, Protestant groups such as the Calvinist Huguenots fought for survival in the **Wars of Religion** (1562-1598). Massacres, royal conspiracies, and assassinations continued for a generation. In 1598, King Henry IV issued the **Edict of Nantes**. It declared Protestants could:

- have limited freedom of worship and religious educational rights
- hold government office
- expect special courts would settle disputes between the faiths
- control certain crown fortress towns, such as La Rochelle
- conduct public worship in certain towns
- hold councils with royal permission

In the Low Countries (Netherlands and Belgium), Catholic Holy Roman Emperor Charles V struggled against Protestant princes as he had in Germany. His son, Philip II of Spain, escalated this conflict into a sporatic war that lasted eighty years (1568-1648). It resulted in the independence of the United Provinces of the Netherlands (northern section) being recognized as an independent state.

The **Thirty Years' War** (1618-1648) was the last major religious struggle in Europe. It was a series of wars fought mainly on German soil. It became part of a larger conflict over the European balance of power. A general revolt of Protestant nobles in Prague widened into a drawn-out European war with Catholic and Protestant countries shifting alliances for political power. The **Peace of Westphalia** (1648) ended the war and

- gave stronger authority and economic power to Catholic France and Lutheran Sweden
- took power and territory from Catholic Spain and Austria and Lutheran Denmark
- fragmented Germany into over 300 states
- began the long decline of the Holy Roman Empire

ANTI-SEMITISM IN EUROPE

Controversies swirling around the central role of the Christian Church led to tension and frustrations. Sometimes, this resulted in lashing out against others. Jews were often the subject of such venting (**anti-semitism**[1]). In the 13th century, Spain passed *Las Siete Partidas*, a code of laws that barred Jews from holding public office. In the same century, Pope Nicholas III called for efforts to convert Jews to Catholicism. During the Counter-Reformation, Spain expelled all Jews who refused to convert.

---

1 anti-semitism (discrimination, prejudice, and hostility against Jews or Judaism)

The Inquisition in Spain relentlessly investigated and tried Jews and Muslims who had converted to Christianity in order to retain their homes and wealth. England, France, and Germany launched similar waves of anti-Semitic oppression. Fear of alternative religious views and economic competition for merchants and guilds led to policies that forced Jews to live in segregated, walled-off neighborhoods (**ghettoes**[1]). In some cases, Jews who traveled outside the ghettoes were forced to wear identifying badges. Some of these restrictions remained for centuries.

RISE OF EUROPEAN NATION-STATES

In the 16th and 17th centuries, European monarchs overcame the power of the Church, the independence of cities, and feudal nobles. Under their leadership, their kingdoms grew into the nations of Europe. **Nations**[2] are more than just political boundaries and wide-ranging governments. They signify people joined by common backgrounds, cultures, and languages. By force of will and absolutist attitudes, monarchs of this age consolidated conflicting interests.

Absolutism[3] is a concentration of power in the hands of one person or a group of persons. In religious countries, the monarchs based their absolute power on **divine right**[4]. They claimed their right to rule came from God. Therefore, total, unquestioned authority could be applied; such as, if a subject "sinned against the king," it was the same as a "sin against God." This meant that kings were not responsible to their subjects or any representative bodies. They broadened their power through bypassing the older nobles and constructing their own bureaucracies and centrally commanded military forces.

---

1 ghettoes (section or quarter in a European city to which Jews were formerly restricted because of social, economic, or legal pressure)
2 nation (relatively large group of people who share common customs, origins, history, and frequently language, organized under a single, usually independent government)
3 absolutism (political theory holding that all power should be vested in one ruler or other authority)
4 divine right (doctrine that monarchs derive their right to rule directly from God and are accountable only to God)

MINI-ASSESSMENT

Mini Assessment

1 The Italian city-states led Europe into the Renaissance because they
   1 were the first to expel Jews and Muslims
   2 used absolutism and divine right
   3 created a power base for the Pope
   4 traded with Byzantine and Muslim Empires

2 The Renaissance paved the way for the Protestant Reformation through
   1 promoting a questioning of the status quo
   2 limiting economic resources
   3 denouncing classic Greek philosophy
   4 accepting the Medieval religious traditions

3 Which was a Church reform recommended by Martin Luther?
   1 require Mass and other rituals be said in Latin
   2 establish walled-off ghettoes for Jews
   3 allow self-interpretation of the Bible
   4 limit freedom of worship

Constructed Response:

1 What is one of the Renaissance values reflected in this work?

Early Wood Carving Printer's Plate of da Vinci's *Mona Lisa*

2 How did Renaissance art differ from Medieval art?

CASE STUDY: FRANCE

At the end of the Hundred Years' War (1337-1453), the French expelled the English. French monarchs such as Louis XI (r. 1461-1483) worked at unifying the kingdom. The kings also broadened their power beyond the boundaries of France. They launched a long rivalry with the Hapsburgs of Austria and Spain.

In the 16th century, two strong rulers, Francis I (r. 1515 to 1547) and Henry II (r. 1547-1559) solidified the nation. However, the Wars of Religion (1562-1598) involving the Calvinist Huguenots threatened the new national unity. Finally, **Henry IV** (r. 1598-1610), a Huguenot leader became the first king of the Bourbon Dynasty. Amid the carnage and massacres of the Wars, he converted to Catholicism. This kept the nation in tact, and allowed him to assume the throne. Henry then granted religious toleration to communities where Protestants were in a majority (Edict of Nantes).

fleur d'lis
emblem of the Bourbon
Kings of France

Henry IV set absolutist **precedents**[1] (examples for the future). He ignored the **Estates-General** (the national assembly). He surrounded himself with shrewd, talented ministers who rebuilt the national treasury, stimulated commerce, and strengthened the royal power of the monarchy. The chief minister of Henry's weak son, Louis XIII (r. 1610-1643), was **Cardinal Armand Richelieu** (1585-1642). The king gave this cardinal-minister full authority, and the Cardinal laid the foundation for the absolute power of the Bourbon monarchy.

Richelieu was a Machiavellian pragmatist. At home, he centralized control, deprived France's nobles of their power and began to regulate trade (see mercantilism). Abroad, his policies followed the idea of "raison d'état" (reason of state or national security, in the modern sense). During the Thirty Years War, he even used France's Catholic armies to defeat the Catholic forces of Austrian and Spanish Hapsburgs to make France the most powerful state in Europe.

CASE STUDY: ENGLAND

In England, power struggles between the monarchs and nobles led to a long process of change. **William the Conqueror** (William I, 1028-1087) led the Norman (French) conquest of England in 1066. He established a strongly personal monarchy. He reformed, and then he dominated the court system. William altered the relationship of the English monarchy to the nobility. He replaced English lords with French nobles loyal to him and set up a European feudal system. King William ordered the general **census**[2] recorded in the *Domesday Book* (1086). It listed the land holdings of the feudal nobility to accurately tax the land holders.

Many historians claim **Henry II** (r. 1154-1189) was England's greatest ruler. Henry set up an impressive administrative framework. Henry's justice system became the basis of the legal systems of most English-speaking peoples. His legal system included the common law, the jury, legal advocates, and basic due process rights (individual protection from abusive government). (See Unit V for charts on growth of individual rights.)

From the late 15th to the early 17th centuries, the Tudor Dynasty strengthened the monarchy in England. The Tudors did not achieve the absolute rule that monarchs did in Spain and France, but they became popular and greatly enhanced England's status as a world power.

Henry VII – first Tudor monarch – won the throne when he defeated (1485) King Richard III – of the Lancaster family – in the Wars of the Roses. Tudor monarchs included Henry VIII who established the Anglican Church, Edward VI, Mary I, and Elizabeth I. There was much religious strife under the Tudors, but they strengthened the monarchy.

The Tudor rulers were not absolutists. They had to share power with a strong **parliament**[3]. The English Parliament was originally a council of landholders, nobles, and Church leaders. Monarchs expanded it in the 1200s to include

---

1 precedent (act, legal decision, or instance that used as an example or standard in dealing with similar instances)
2 census (count of the citizens and an evaluation of their property for taxation purposes)
3 parliament (national representative body having supreme legislative powers within the state)

knights and wealthy burgesses. In the **Model Parliament** under Edward I in 1295, Parliament gained control over grants of **revenue**[1] allotted to the monarch. Later, the knights and burgesses evolved into the **bicameral** (two-chamber) House of Lords and the House of Commons. For centuries, Parliament competed for power with the monarchy.

Tudors rulers Henry VII and Henry VIII were skillful manipulators of Parliament, but **Elizabeth I** (r. 1558-1603) was probably the most adept. For fear of compromising her power, she did not call the Parliament into session or ask for money often. However, members of Parliament became deeply devoted to her.

As in Spain under Philip II, England's nationalism also grew. Elizabeth strengthened the Royal Navy and encouraged commercial development of trade. She supported "Sea Dogs" such as Sir **Francis Drake** (1541-1596) and other privateers. The Sea Dogs' raids on Spain's treasure-filled ships from the New World brought great damage. Elizabeth commissioned courtiers such as Sir **Walter Raleigh** to begin joint stock companies. Later, the companies set up permanent American colonies as business enterprises.

Queen Elizabeth I – Tudor Monarch of England

During Elizabeth's long reign, a national literature emerged in the works of William Shakespeare, Edmund Spenser, and Christopher Marlowe. The Queen was also skillful in war and diplomacy. She became popular by sending English forces to fight on the Protestant side in France's Wars of Religion and in the revolt of the Dutch against Spanish rule (c. 1568).

Perhaps Elizabeth's greatest achievement came in defeating Catholic King Philip II of Spain – the same King Philip II who had been married to her late half-sister, Queen Mary I, called "Bloody Mary" for her executions of Protestants. In 1588, Philip sent his great 130-ship armada to invade England with the intent of restoring Catholicism in England. The small, but fast English Navy, under skillful mariners like Drake, devastated the Spanish flotilla in the stormy waters of the English Channel.

Elizabeth I's Sea Dogs defeat the Spanish armada in the English Channel.

TIME CAPSULE

GLOBAL HISTORY ARCHIVE

The global interactions of the 13th to 17th centuries resulted in bringing different civilizations into closer contact. The interactions also intensified changes in the way people lived, worked, and thought. Population began to increase rapidly as a result of better food production and health practices. In Europe, capitalism emerged and accelerated commercial

---

1 revenue (treasury funds - "the power of the purse" - income of a government from all sources appropriated for the payment of the public expenses)

relationships. It changed the way production and labor were organized.

The great stimulus for change was trade. It led to a commercial revolution. The rulers of China and Japan strengthened traditional culture and struggled with the impact of increasing commercial contacts with other global regions.

In Europe, trade caused an opening of societies. The merchants of Italian city-states and Portuguese navigators unleashed a drive for sea routes to obtain the spices and luxuries of the Orient. That drive eventually led to the discovery of new continents.

Revitalized trade was a powerful force in Europe. It undermined manorialism and gave rise to towns. The towns grew into cities. Expanded commerce demanded broader education. The innovation of printing and books published in everyday languages caused learning to blossom. Urban cultural interactions produced the Renaissance –

the rebirth of interest in the classics. Renaissance humanism created a new culture.

These cultural forces homogenized life and changed social relationships. As manorialism and feudalism decayed, strong rulers increased their power and began to forge new nations. Monarchs centralized power with strong militaries to expand and protect national borders. Their bureaucracies circumvented both Church and nobility.

Religion played a significant role in global affairs. In Asia and the Middle East, the Mongols' rule created stability. Their successors, the Turks, strengthened the Muslim world. In Europe, amidst a great purging and revival of spirit, the Reformation focused new interest in spreading Christianity. The Reformation also fragmented European society. The key forces that forged the "modern world" emerged from all this change and interaction and led to the global interdependence of today.

MULTI-CHOICE QUESTIONS

1 Scholars attribute the power of the Tokugawa shoguns to their
   1 accumulation of immense wealth
   2 obsession with discipline and order
   3 claims of divine right
   4 focus on technological advancement

2 Increased economic activity among towns and merchants in Europe resurrected the use of
   1 money   3 tribute
   2 bartering   4 censorship

3 China's Ming rulers advanced
   1 technology and artistic pursuits
   2 military conquest of India
   3 Shinto missionary work
   4 seasonal trade fairs

4 In England, the Tudors strengthened the monarchy, but did not achieve
   1 popularity
   2 bicameral legislation
   3 religious unity
   4 absolute power

5 Catholics fought Protestants in the
   1 Thirty Years' War
   2 Hundred Years' War
   3 Pax Espania
   4 Domestic System

6 The British Parliament's bicameral structure is reflected in
   1 theocracy and seclusion policies
   2 absolutism and reliance on precedent
   3 diets and pragmatic administration
   4 the houses of Lords and Commons

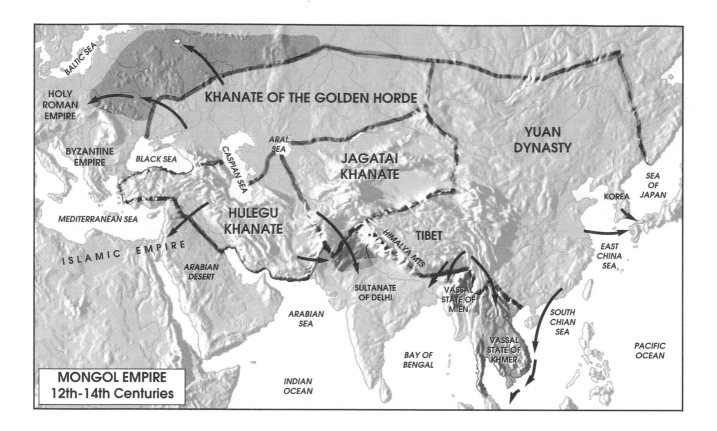

MONGOL EMPIRE
12th-14th Centuries

Base your answer to questions 7 and 8 on the map above and your knowledge of global history.

7   The "Pax Mongolia" in the 13th century khanates (kingdoms) increased
   1   commerce between Europe and Asia
   2   acceptance of divine right rule
   3   application of seclusion policies
   4   schisms among global religions

8   Like those of Alexander the Great, the conquests of Genghis Khan were
   1   centers of cultural enlightenment
   2   divided among his military chiefs
   3   appropriated by the Byzantine Church
   4   known for agricultural productivity

9   In the 15th century, the Turks' blocking of overland trade through the Eastern Mediterranean region led to
   1   military campaigns by the Japanese shoguns
   2   isolation policies by the Italian city-states
   3   water route explorations by the Portuguese
   4   the cosmopolitanism of the Mongols

Base your answer to question 10 on the following passage and your knowledge of global history.

"Man is the mediator of all creatures, the servant of superior beings, the lord of inferior ones, that he is the interpreter of nature by the keenness of his senses, the intermediary between time and eternity ... the nexus of the world."

– Pico della Mirandala
Oration on the Dignity of Man, 1486

10   This passage portrays (the)
   1   Way of the Kami
   2   Protestant Theology
   3   Renaissance Humanism
   4   Tokugawa Seclusion

11   Which individual promoted the growth of absolute power of the monarchy?
   1   John Knox
   2   Francis Drake
   3   Armand Richelieu
   4   Johann Gutenberg

THEMATIC ESSAY

Theme: Change

The global interactions of the 13th through the 17th centuries changed many civilizations.

Task:

- Select **one** major civilization which you have studied and describe its contact with another civilization.
- Explain how this cross-cultural contact changed the two civilizations.

Suggestions:

You may use any 13th-17th century cross-cultural contact. Some contacts you might consider: China and Japan; Mongols and Russia; Mughals and India; Europeans and China, Muslims and East Asia. **You are not limited to these suggestions.**

DOCUMENT BASED QUESTIONS

Directions:

The following question is based on the accompanying documents (1-5). Some of the documents have been edited for the purposes of this exercise. The question is designed to test your ability to work with historical documents. As you analyze the documents, take into account both the source of the document and the author's point of view.

- Write a well-organized essay that includes an introduction with a thesis statement, several paragraphs explaining the thesis, and a conclusion.
- Analyze the documents.
- Use all the documents.
- Use evidence from the documents to support your thesis position.
- Do not simply repeat the contents of the documents.
- Include specific related outside information.

Historical Context:

Revitalized trade unleashed a significant change in European society. The documents below present some aspects of the change.

Task:

Analyze the impact of revitalized trade on Europe between the 12th and 15th centuries and support your opinion with the documents below and your knowledge of global history.

Part A – Short Answer

The documents below show elements of change in Medieval European society. Examine each document carefully, then answer the question that follows it.

Document 1:

"The mobility and awareness triggered by the Crusades, ...Europe's long, indented coast with its two inland seas ... made foreign commerce possible for all its regions and ignited economic energy in independent centers first in Italy, then in Spain, Portugal, France, Holland, and England."

— *The Epic of Modern Man*

Document 1 Question:

How did geography influence the changes in Europe?

Document 2:

"The contrast [in technology] is essentially between standards of living and of labor productivity of the peasantry ... the ox is slow but eats less expensive hay; the horse is faster but consumes more expensive grain ... better harnesses allowed Northern Europeans to increase their surpluses and freed humans for other activities in the towns."

– Technology in the Middle Ages

Document 2 Question:

Why did surplus production lead to the growth of towns and revitalization of commerce?

Document 3:

"As feudalism gave way before the rise of city-states or centralized territorial states under princes who were learning to use the power of money, kings allied themselves with burghers against unruly and obstreperous nobles."

– Reinterpretation of the Renaissance

Document 3 Question:

In the later Middle Ages, why did kings often align themselves with burghers (citizens) against nobles?

Document 4:

TRADE, TRAVEL, COMMUNICATIONS

EXCHANGE OF IDEAS

Document 4 Question:

How did broader trade and travel affect the Roman Catholic Church in Europe?

Document 5:

"We wish to inform you of the action taken in support of all merchants who are governed by the law of Lubeck.

1) "Each city shall ... keep the sea clear of pirates ...

2) "Whoever is expelled from one city because of crime shall not be received in another ...

5) "If there are pirates on the sea, all the cities must contribute their share to the work of destroying them ...

6) "If a lord besieges a city, no one shall aid him in any way to the detriment of the besieged city, unless the besieger is his lord ...

7) "If there is a war in the country, no city shall on that account injure a citizen from the other cities either in his person or goods, but shall give him protection ..."

– *Decrees of the Hanseatic League,* 1260-1265

Document 5 Question:

How could rules such as these help the development of trade?

Part B – Essay Response

Discuss the impact of trade and travel on Western Europe in the 12th-15th centuries.

Your essay should be well organized with an introductory paragraph that states your thesis on the impact of revitalized trade in Europe between the 12th and 15th centuries. Develop and support the reasons for your thesis in the next paragraphs and then write a conclusion. In your essay, include specific historical details and refer to the specific documents you analyzed in Part A. You may include additional information from your knowledge of global history.

Unit 5

1450 AD – 1770 AD

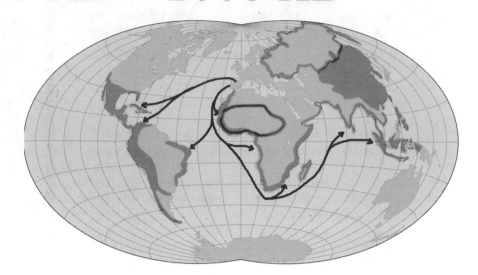

THE FIRST GLOBAL AGE

AD

1400–

Zeng He explores Indian Ocean for the Mings (1425)

Mehemed II conquers Constantinople (1453)

1500–

Islamic Songhai Kingdom in West Africa (1500)

Cortés conquers the Aztecs (1521)

Ottoman westward expansion blocked at Battle of Lepanto (1571)

English fleet defeats Spain's Armada (1588)
Akbar unites Northern India (1590)

1600–

Romanov Dynasty begins in Russia (1613)

Spain conquers Peru (1632)

Puritans dethrone Charles I (1646)

England's Glorious Revolution (1688)

1700–

Peter the Great begins constructing St. Petersburg (1703)

PEOPLE	PLACES	THINGS
Akbar the Great	Asia Minor	absolutism
Christopher Columbus	Aztec Empire	constitutional monarchy
conquistadores	Ghana	encomiendas
Hong Wu	Inca Empire	ethnocentrism
Louis XIV	Lepanto	Glorious Revolution
Mansa Musa	Mali Empire	imperialism
Oliver Cromwell	savanna	mercantilism
Peter the Great	Spanish Empire	vertical climates
Philip II		westernization
Sulieman I		
Yong Le		

INTRODUCTION

In this first Global Age, the people of Asia and Europe actively engaged civilizations in Africa, the Americas, and the Pacific Rim. European encounters and exploration of the Western Hemisphere grew out of the quest for trade, wealth, and knowledge begun in the Commercial Revolution and Renaissance of the 13th, 14th, and 15th centuries.

AMERICAN CIVILIZATIONS (1400 BC - 1570 AD)

SPATIAL ORGANIZATION AND GEOGRAPHY

The two great land masses of the Western Hemisphere stretch 12,500 miles from the Arctic in the north almost to Antarctica in the south. Combined, North and South America and associated islands encompass nearly 16.2 million square miles. With such vast range, the two continents' climatic structures reflect nearly every major Koppen climate type.

The natural regions of the Western Hemisphere are broad based. The entire western margin (Pacific) of the two continents is paralleled by the Rocky–Sierra Madre–Andes **cordillera**[1] with intervening basins and plateaus. The eastern (Atlantic) sides of the continents have low mountains and coastal plains. The central eastern coasts have almost flat topography.

Both continents have great central basins drained by two of the three longest river systems in the world – North America's Missouri-Ohio-Mississippi River system and South America's Amazon. The vast interior of the con-

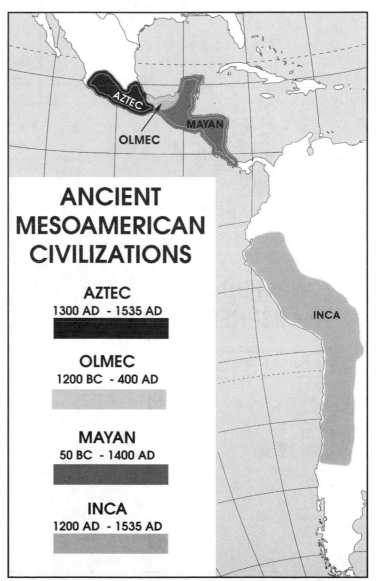

ANCIENT MESOAMERICAN CIVILIZATIONS

AZTEC
1300 AD - 1535 AD

OLMEC
1200 BC - 400 AD

MAYAN
50 BC - 1400 AD

INCA
1200 AD - 1535 AD

---

1 Cordillera (extensive chain of mountains or mountain ranges)

tinents is dominated by rolling plains in the north and rain forests in the south. In North America, the open plains and gently flowing rivers allowed early inhabitants ease of migration eastward. In South America, the rapid rivers and thick vegetation of the Amazon rain forest and the imposing heights of the Andes were barriers to settlement of the interior.

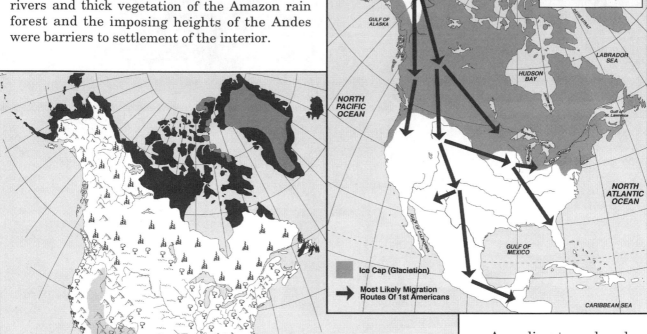

WESTERN HEMISPHERE

PHYSICAL FEATURES

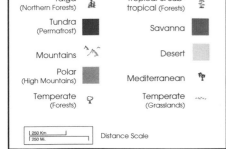

Taiga (Northern Forests)	Tropical & Sub-tropical (Forests)
Tundra (Permafrost)	Savanna
Mountains	Desert
Polar (High Mountains)	Mediterranean
Temperate (Forests)	Temperate (Grasslands)

250 Km
250 Mi.   Distance Scale

According to archaeologists' current assessments, the first humans entered North America between 30,000 and 10,000 years ago. They crossed the Bering Land Bridge from northeast Asia. Around 10,000 BC, global warming submerged that narrow bridge of land beneath the Bering Sea.

The early people were ancestors of the **Amerindians**[1]. The early people drew sufficient food supplies from the dry grasslands (steppes), tundra, marshes, and forests. The natural environment allowed for grazing ani-

---

1 Amerindians, also Native Americans, (members of any of the aboriginal peoples of the Western Hemisphere; the term Indian has always been a misnomer for the earliest inhabitants of the Americas. Many people now prefer Native American as a corrective to Columbus's mistaken claim)

mals (horses, reindeer). Wild game and fish provided additional food sources for early hunters. Early Amerindians lived in small groups and made spears, knives, scrapers, and other instruments from stone.

As in other global regions, Neolithic Era Americans eventually developed agricultural techniques, religious beliefs, trading networks, and even military tactics. Yet, current evidence indicates that highly developed civilizations with cities and imperial political structures developed much later in the Americas than in other global regions.

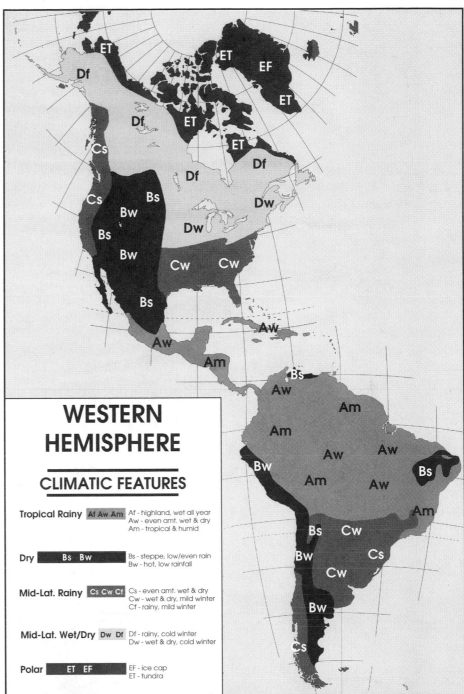

WESTERN HEMISPHERE

CLIMATIC FEATURES

Tropical Rainy	Af Aw Am	Af - highland, wet all year Aw - even amt. wet & dry Am - tropical & humid
Dry	Bs Bw	Bs - steppe, low/even rain Bw - hot, low rainfall
Mid-Lat. Rainy	Cs Cw Cf	Cs - even amt. wet & dry Cw - wet & dry, mild winter Cf - rainy, mild winter
Mid-Lat. Wet/Dry	Dw Df	Df - rainy, cold winter Dw - wet & dry, cold winter
Polar	ET EF	EF - ice cap ET - tundra

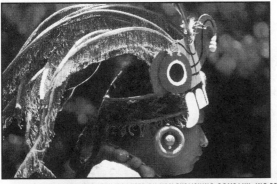

at left:

Ceremonial Mayan Headdress Mexico

at right:

Teotihuacan Aztec Figure Mexico

MESOAMERICAN EMPIRES: Organization & Contributions

OLMEC EMPIRE **1200 BC – 400 BC** **Southern Mexico** **El Salvador**	• formed the first truly complex Mesoamerican culture • established civic-ceremonial centers at San Lorenzo and La Venta, with temples, palaces • built towns with clay building platforms and stone pavements and drainage systems • traded in raw materials such as jade • created large stone jade sculptures of human heads • developed rudimentary hieroglyphic writing
MAYAN EMPIRE **50 BC – 1400 AD** Southern Mexico Yucatan Guatemala Central America	• invented writing system which mixed script with ideographs and phonetics • wrote historic records on pots, stone stele (upright inscribed slabs), and palace walls • cultivated corn as staple crop • produced a complex astronomical calendar • established religious rituals which included human sacrifice, mythology, and ancestral worship • created a monarchy that united small settlements into larger states • built flat-topped pyramids as temples and rulers' tombs • built palaces, shrines, large ball courts for ceremonial sport and astronomical observatories • invented math system, including zero base
AZTEC EMPIRE **1300 AD – 1535 AD** Central Mexico	• founded island capital Tenochtitlan (modern Mexico City) • created a highly specialized, strictly hierarchal society • conquered and dominated neighbors for tribute (protection payments), not for territory • elected by nobility, ruler-emperor (tlatoani) had near god status and supreme authority • formed a powerful priestly hierarchy to administer government • produced a severe legal code of laws with judgments based on generally accepted ideas of reasonable behavior • developed a sophisticated agricultural economy, carefully adjusted to the land with crop rotation and extensive aqueduct and irrigation systems • adopted Nahuatl as a language of learning that accompanied a hieroglyphic writing system • created a 365-day solar calendar system divided into 19 months of 20 days each
INCA EMPIRE **1200 AD – 1535 AD** Andes Mountains (Peru, Ecuador parts of Chile, Bolivia, and Argentina)	• established largest empire of the Americas – at its height in the 16th century, the Inca Empire controlled 12 million people, over 100 cultures with 20 different languages • formed a strong monarchy ruled from Cuzco by using strategic resettlement of loyal "colonists" among rebellious groups • believed emperors descended from the Sun god and worshiped them as divine beings • adapted an intricate 12,000 mile road system for traveling messengers and services for traveling bureaucratic officials • created agricultural terracing and irrigation systems • adapted various "vertical climates" of the Andes' elevations for a variety of crops • built elaborate fortress cities such as Machu Picchu • developed refined spoken language (Quechua) • instituted quipu (knot-cord) record keeping system • developed a religion centered on the worship of the Sun • mined gold for use by the elite for decorative and ritual purposes

CHICHEN ITZA

The Maya of the Yucatan created a great capital at Chichen Itza. Its architecture was advanced. The palaces had great colonnades that opened onto private patios. There are large paintings preserved that show hundreds of warriors celebrating feasts and battle victories.

©PhotoDisc, 1994

In the 13th century, the Maya built a new capital to the west of Chichen Itza. Mayapan, with a population estimated at 15,000, had great walls to protect against the increasing power of other warring states.

Fighting and competition among the Mayan city-states broke down their strength, and they succumbed to the Europeans – and the diseases they brought– in the 16th century. The Spanish took advantage of division and took control in 1542.

Conquistadors overpower Aztecs.

THE AZTEC PANTHEON

Huitzilopochtli – ancestral warrior-hero god

Huehueteotl – fire deity, identified with the renewal of time itself

Quetzalcoatl – "feather serpent," symbolic of the earth

Tezcatlipoca – the most powerful, supreme deity, associated with destiny

Tlaloc – rain deity, identified with life-giving rain

Tonantzin – the female earth-deity

Tonatiuh – sun deity, primary source of life associated with warriors

The term **Mesoamerica** refers to a cultural region occupied by the native people extending south and east from central Mexico to include parts of Guatemala, Belize, Honduras, and Nicaragua. Pre-Columbian ancient cultural groups included the Aztec, Maya, Mixtec, Olmec, Toltec, and Zapotec.

FALL OF MESOAMERICAN EMPIRES

The Aztec and Inca Empires came to an abrupt end with the Spanish conquests in the 1520s and 1530s. Gradual colonization and Christianizing undermined the cultural bases of the civilizations. Conquistador **Hernán Cortés'** (1485-1547) alliances with rival groups, the killing of the **Tlatoanis**[1] Montezuma II and Cuauhtemoc, and the Spanish soldiers' introduction of diseases destroyed the Aztec realm.

Conquistador **Francisco Pizarro** (1475-1541) and a small force of 180 Spanish troops arrived in Peru amidst a civil war among the Incas. In 1532, he captured Emperor Atahualpa and his army near Cuzco. Pizarro had the Emperor executed, and set up a puppet ruler. Inca leaders went into exile and continued to resist the Europeans for another 50 years, but they could not hold their diverse people together.

1 Tlatoanis (supreme rulers/commanders of the Aztec Empire, see chart p.118)

Mini Assessment

1 Knowledge of early Mesoamerican civilizations is limited because their
   1 religious rituals were closely guarded secrets
   2 remains were destroyed by rain forest growth
   3 ideographs cannot be translated
   4 European colonizers destroyed cultural remains

2 The Inca diet was enhanced by extensive crop varieties supplied through
   1 vertical climate agriculture
   2 the quipu processing system
   3 rebellious conquered peoples
   4 an accurate solar calendar

3 What does Aztec rule in Mesoamerica have in common with Mongol rule in Central Asia?
   1 building ceremonial pyramids
   2 collection of tribute from conquered peoples
   3 extensive astronomical research programs
   4 knot-and-cord record keeping systems

Constructed Response:

1 How can you tell the European from the Mesoamerican figures in the engraving above?

2 What military advantages did the Europeans have over Mesoamerican cultures?

RISE AND FALL OF AFRICAN CIVILIZATIONS: MALI AND SONGHAI EMPIRES

SPATIAL ORGANIZATION / GEOGRAPHY

Africa is the second largest continent after Asia. With more than 11.7 million square miles, Africa is more than three times the size of the United States.

When viewed as bisected by the Equator, Africa's natural and climatic regions almost mirror each other to the north and south. The largest natural area is the **savanna**[1]. These regions stretch in great bands to the north and south of the Equatorial rain forests. The northern savanna is shrinking because of relentless **desertification**[2]. The fragile Sahel region ("coast of the desert") along the southern edge of the Sahara Desert barely supports sparse vegetation because of uneven annual rainfall and over grazing. Beyond the savannas are two large desert regions – the 3.5 million square mile Sahara and the 100,000 square mile Kalahari. Fertile strips of farmlands with mild Mediterranean climate (Koppen type Cf) hug the southern Cape of Good Hope and the northern Mediterranean coast. The low mountains along the north (Atlas) and south (Drakensburgs) coasts have had little climatic and settlement influences.

Ninety percent of Africa's land is plateaus higher than 500 feet above sea level, and a substantial portion is not arable. The five major

---

1 savanna (flat grassland of tropical or subtropical regions)
2 desertification (transformation of arable or habitable land to desert, caused by a change in climate or destructive land use)

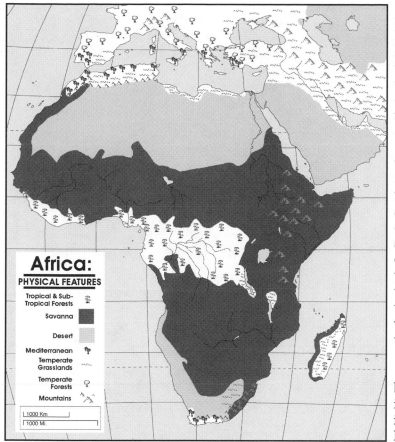

Africa:
PHYSICAL FEATURES

⚘ Tropical & Sub-Tropical Forests

▓ Savanna

░ Desert

Mediterranean

Temperate Grasslands

Temperate Forests

Mountains

1000 Km
1000 Mi.

regions. Historically, Egypt, Nubia, and North Africa interacted with Middle Eastern and Mediterranean civilizations and institutions. Christianity, and then Islam, spread across this area, but did not influence sub-Saharan Africa for centuries.

Awareness of civilizations south of the Sahara was sparse until after 1000 AD. Anthropologists estimate that the use of iron tools emerged for the sub Saharan groups between 500 BC-500 AD. As with other regions, the food surpluses that the tools helped to produce led to trade and land hunger. As these human contacts expanded, cultural diffusion occurred. For example, the Bantu root language spread, but written records did not emerge until the Muslim Era (10th-12th centuries).

Knowledge of early civilization is based on archaeology, radio-carbon dating, and oral traditions. Oral traditions include tales and genealogies, myths, legends, and proverbs. Mali's famed

rivers (Congo or Zaire, Niger, Nile, Chad, Zambezi) have cataracts (falls) down to the coasts, making inland navigation difficult. Africa has remarkably smooth seacoasts which offer few good natural harbors. The density of the rain forest makes travel very difficult, and diseases such as malaria are added deterrents. These factors made penetration of the interior of the continent difficult. As a result, Africa long remained a mystery to outsiders.

Areas of Africa are rich in natural resources such as petroleum and strategic minerals such as copper and cobalt. Mineral wealth also includes salt, iron, gold, and diamonds.

ORGANIZATIONAL STRUCTURES

The difficulties of penetrating the deserts and the uplands of the interior of sub-Saharan Africa limited interaction with people of other

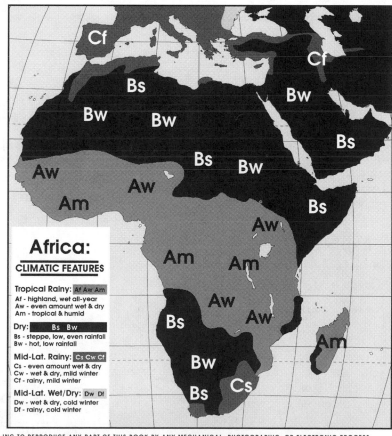

Africa:
CLIMATIC FEATURES

Tropical Rainy: Af Aw Am
Af - highland, wet all-year
Aw - even amount wet & dry
Am - tropical & humid

Dry: Bs Bw
Bs - steppe, low, even rainfall
Bw - hot, low rainfall

Mid-Lat. Rainy: Cs Cw Cf
Cs - even amount wet & dry
Cw - wet & dry, mild winter
Cf - rainy, mild winter

Mid-Lat. Wet/Dry: Dw Df
Dw - wet & dry, cold winter
Df - rainy, cold winter

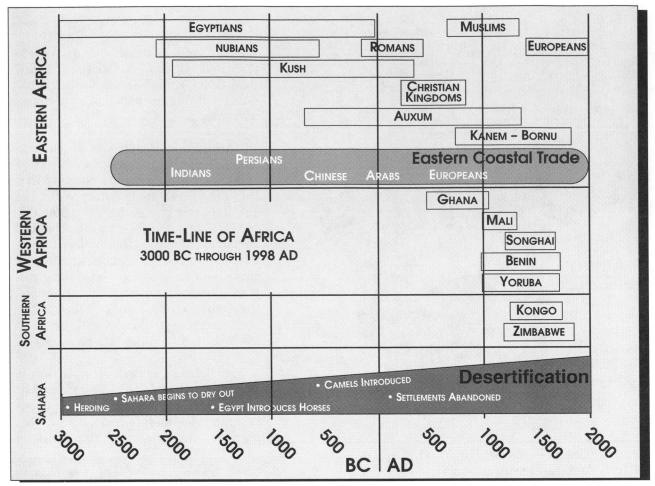

TIME-LINE OF AFRICA
3000 BC THROUGH 1998 AD

oral tradition produced the epic ***Sundiata***, the story of a young prince's quest to restore his father's kingdom.

Traditional religion intertwined with social and political order. As in many areas of the globe, early rulers and chiefs were credited with religious powers or divine status. Ancestor worship was common, and charms were valued as supernatural objects and passed through generations.

TRADING EMPIRES AND ISLAMIC INFLUENCE

The Sahara and the seas were formidable natural barriers. Not until the 9th and 10th centuries did Arab traders cross the Sahara. They founded prosperous cities with organized governments and artisans. One such city was the West African city of **Timbuktu** on the Niger River. In these prosperous communities, there was a lively exchange of coastal gold for inland salt.

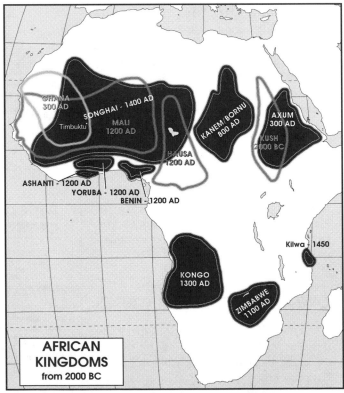

AFRICAN KINGDOMS
from 2000 BC

The gold attracted increasing numbers of Arab traders. As they crossed the Sahara, cultural diffusion occurred. The diversity of Islam allowed it to merge with traditional religious practices. Although there was some conflict with divine powers claimed by traditional leaders, Islam spread rapidly through the southern Saharan region. It created a common cultural bond and the disciplined life that helped leaders form empires.

After 1000 AD, Islamic trading states emerged in West Africa. **Ghana** grew from exchange centers for leather, kola nuts, cotton cloth, and slaves that moved north to the Mediterranean. Successor states included **Songhai** and **Mali**. Mali's great **Mansa** (Emperor) **Kankan Musa** (r. 1312-1332) raised Timbuktu to the level of a great university city and created one of the most renowned Islamic states of history.

From the 12th to the 15th centuries, East African city-states such as **Kilwa**, off the coast of Tanzania, traded with Arabs, Indians, and Chinese. Kilwa traded inland goods from kingdoms such as Zimbabwe. Great cultural diffusion took place in the cosmopolitan environment, but the cities also supplied slaves from inland communities to traders from Persia and India.

ACHIEVEMENTS

Although East and West African civilizations were developed and diverse before 1000 AD, Islamic traders and scholars brought knowledge and technology. Traditional African art varied widely. Common themes in sculptures, masks, and figures depict religious symbols, ancestor veneration, and chieftains' divine powers. Carved wood, ivory, and metal ceremonial objects were used in singing and dancing rituals. Artisans from the West African kingdom of Benin created unique sculptures in brass and bronze, many dating from the 13th century.

13th Century
Benin Bronze
Sculpture

Traditional African art reflects beliefs. A blending of wild, chaotic forces of nature with the controlled social life of the village is common. Artisans created figurines, charms, and amulets to help people guide natural and supernatural forces to make life better.

SLAVERY

A large combination of factors led to the decline of trading states and empires in Africa. The kingdoms of West Africa and the Sudan region were loose unions of trading centers forged through alliances of military strongmen. Competition for trade led to shifting of alliances and civil wars. When Arab and European traders introduced new products, especially weapons, it caused disruption. Later, the dynamic introduction of Christianity by Europeans caused more strains and shifts in loyalties. Most disruptive was the increase in the slave trade in 16th

Islamic influence is seen across Africa. The Mosque above is in the city of Mombasa, Kenya.   © David Johnson, 1992

century which led to communities warring against each other.

From earliest times, Africa was the source of a slave trade. Slavery had been common for centuries among African tribes. Persian traders had a lively slave trade with East African cities for centuries. In West Africa, the colonization of the Americas increased Europe's demand for slaves. The trade from West Africa grew gradually until the last decades of the 16th century. Portuguese and Spanish colonists demanded great numbers. The slaves were taken from all along the coast of Africa, but especially from Senegal, Ghana, Nigeria, and Angola. Later, the Dutch entered African slave commerce and were joined by Swedish, Danish, German, French, and English companies.

CHINA: THE MING DYNASTY RESTORES ETHNIC CHINESE RULE

In 1368, a peasant rebel (Zhu Yuanzhang, 1328-1398) overthrew Mongol authority and launched the Ming Dynasty (1368-1644). Zhu took the name **Hong Wu** and established a new government at Nanjing. He purged Mongols from the civil service and returned Confucian teaching to prominence. Later, absolutist Ming rulers built a strong central government in Beijing, created strict law codes, and oversaw a long period of stability and economic growth. The era of Ming rule was also a period of cultural expansion.

CHINA'S RELATIONSHIP WITH THE WEST

Ming rulers launched public works, restored roads and canals, and resettled Chinese farmers into the northern provinces. These moves improved food production. Soon, agricultural surpluses freed labor for undertaking of new industries such as silk, tea, and porcelain production. Seeking imperial glory in the early 1400s, Emperor **Yong Le** (r. 1403 to 1424) launched trade expeditions to central Asia, reestablishing the Silk Route. It was Yong Le who sent Admiral Zheng He to explore the seas as far as Africa. These contacts aroused the interest of Western traders.

Later Ming emperors restrained Chinese traders, fearing an undermining of Confucian

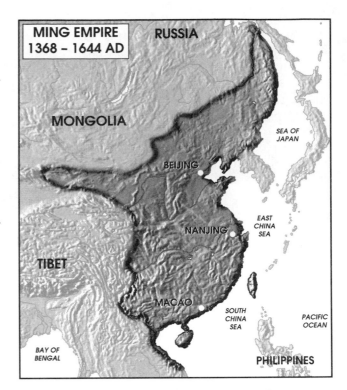

order by lowly merchants. Western traders continued to call at Chinese ports, but the emperors deemed their goods inferior and restricted access to only a few ports such as Canton. In the 16th century, Portuguese traders established a permanent outpost in Macao. Under strict, limited guidelines, the emperors allowed Jesuit missionaries to study and make Christian conversions at the court in Beijing. Unable to make much progress, the Jesuits eventually gave up and were recalled by the Pope.

Ming power declined in the 17th century. A rebellion by local chieftains united the Manchurian tribes of the north and brought the Q'ing (Manchu, or Ch'ing) Dynasty to power.

CHINA'S IMPACT ON SOUTHEAST ASIA

The ousting of the foreign ("barbarian") Mongol Yuan dynasty and reestablishment of ethnic Chinese rulers rekindled an ancient sense of cultural superiority. The experience of securing borders and consolidating rule had an emotional effect akin to what was later to be called nationalism. Scholars refer to this exaggerated sense of cultural superiority as **ethnocentrism**[1]. Sea expeditions and military excursions under the early Ming emperors con-

---

1 ethnocentrism (belief in the superiority of one's own ethnic group and an over-riding concern with race)

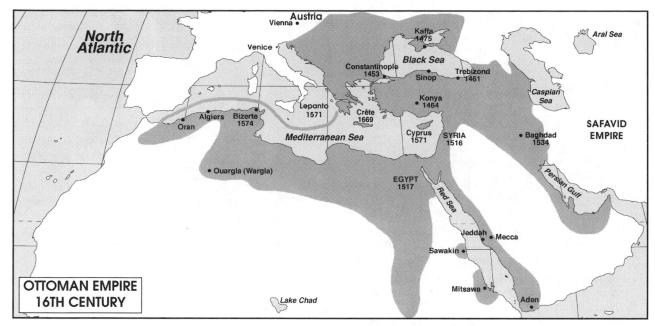

OTTOMAN EMPIRE
16TH CENTURY

firmed the feeling of moral and cultural superiority among China's elite.

Threats of conquest by Emperor Yong Le led to **tributary arrangements**[1] with Japan, Korea, Vietnam, and other Southeast Asian kingdoms. The culture of the northern rim of Southeast Asia had long been influenced by its proximity to China. The civilizations of Vietnam were especially under constant threat of conquest from the north. Vietnamese kings were the vassals of the Chinese emperor for over 1000 years. This led to a gradual blending of cultures with the Vietnamese assimilating Chinese writing forms and Confucian philosophy.

ACHIEVEMENTS

Intellectual and cultural flowering accompanied the peace and economic expansion under the Mings. Philosophy, painting, and drama (*The Peony Pavilion*) blossomed. Even Jesuit missionary **Matteo Ricci** (1552-1610) became involved in the expansion of astronomy under Ming scholars in Beijing. The painted porcelain of the Ming period is regarded as a high point in Chinese ceramics.

IMPACT OF THE OTTOMAN EMPIRE

ORGANIZATION

Turkic peoples are descendants of large bands of nomads from northern Mongolia and the steppes of Central Asia. In the 6th and 7th centuries, these accomplished cavalrymen conquered an empire (Gok Turk) that stretched from Central Asia to the Pacific. By the 11th century, the western Turks, or Turkmen, were assimilated into the Islamic culture and served as mercenaries under the Seljuk Turks. From the 12th through 14th centuries, the Mongols pushed them into Anatolia (Asia Minor or modern Turkey).

In the 15th century, the Turkmen of northeastern Anatolia, called the Ottomans, built a new empire under Sultans Mehmed I and Murad II. In 1453, **Mehmed II** conquered Constantinople. The Ottomans built a strong navy and dominated the Eastern Mediterranean. By the middle of the 16th century, they ruled most of the Middle East from Iran to Algeria, and pressed into southeastern Europe as far as the Danube. The Ottomans settled in Serbia, Albania, and Bosnia, where they intermarried with Slavic groups.

The Ottoman sultans were absolute rulers who also usurped the role of caliph (Islamic religious leader). They emerged from a ruling elite and accepted advice from a **divan**[2]. The sultans focused much attention on maintaining a well-trained military. The Ottomans allowed Muslims and Christians to retain their religious and national traditions in exchange for a special tax. Under the **devshirme system**, Christians

---

1 tributary arrangements (protection payments in place of conquest)
2 divan (council of religious advisors)

who converted to Islam were offered positions in the military and bureaucracy.

DISRUPTION OF ESTABLISHED TRADE ROUTES

The large and powerful empire the Ottomans created in the eastern Mediterranean replaced the decaying Byzantine and the splintered Mongol and Islamic realms. For Western Europe, just entering its first era of global commerce, the disruption of trade routes to the Orient was disastrous. The Ottoman presence in the Eastern Mediterranean interrupted the growing trade connections between the Orient and emerging Western European cities. Venice, along with the other Italian states and Spain, challenged the sultan's fleets. They blocked Ottoman westward expansion at the **Battle of Lepanto** in 1571. Still, the Ottoman presence triggered the Europeans' search for alternative trade routes. The Christians had a tremendous fear of the Ottomans. This fear persuaded the Portuguese (Prince Henry) and Spanish (Columbus) to launch

MOSQUE OF SULTAN SELIM II 16TH CENTURY

sea expeditions which ushered in the European Age of Exploration.

ACHIEVEMENTS

The Ottoman Empire peaked under Sultan **Suleiman I** ("the Magnificent," r. 1520-1566). Suleiman was a great codifier of laws for the diverse empire and oversaw a golden age. His conquest of Persia inspired an arts movement, especially in building and decorating mosques

Mini Assessment

MINI-ASSESSMENT

1 Early Ming rulers such as Yong Le encouraged
   1 integration of Buddhism and Islam
   2 special taxes on Christians
   3 trade with other global regions
   4 conquests of European countries

2 Africa's largest natural area is
   1 savanna   3 rain forest
   2 desert   4 mountain plateau

3 As a result of cross-Saharan contacts, the great trading kingdoms of West Africa converted to (the)
   1 military powers   3 ethnocentrism
   2 Islamic religion 4 tributary states

4 Ottoman sultans such as Suleiman I oversaw
   1 a revival of Persian culture
   2 extensive conquests of West African Empires
   3 conversion to Christian legal codes
   4 abandonment of ethnocentrism

Constructed Response:

"In fact, the news of the wealth and splendor of Mali had spread far and wide, mainly as a result of the pilgrimage to Mecca in 1324 of Mansa Musa, the greatest of all the Mali emperors. Musa was accompanied, it was said by a retinue of 60,000 men, including 500 slaves, each of whom bore a bar of gold weighing 500 mitqals, the equivalent of four pounds."

"Musa's domains stretched from the waters of the Atlantic along the northern coast of modern Senegal to the boundaries of modern Nigeria, and from the fringe of the rain forests to the oasis markets of the central Sahara. After the Mongol Empire in Asia, it was the biggest imperial system of its day."

– Basil Davidson, *African Kingdoms*

1 Why did Musa journey all the way to Mecca?

2 What helped keep the large Mali Empire united?

and libraries. Poets of the era, such as Baki and Fuzuli, converted Persian-inspired styles into the Turkish language.

As a military leader, Suleiman expanded the Ottoman Empire, conquering Tunisia and Algeria. He then challenged the Hapsburgs in Hungary and besieged Vienna. Finally, he campaigned against the Safavids in Iran and Mesopotamia. As a lawgiver, he reorganized the laws, aligned them with the Islamic *Shari'a*, and reinforced them with strict decrees.

15th Century Spanish Caravel

EUROPEANS ENCOUNTER ASIANS, AFRICANS, AND AMERICANS

In the 15th century, Portugal and Spain launched exploratory expeditions that began an interaction of the people of Europe, Asia, Africa, and the Americas. The interactive process resulted in a diffusion of ideas and cultural forces that reshaped the global environment.

SPAIN FOSTERS EXPLORATION

When two married royals ascended their respective thrones (**Isabella of Castile** [1472] and **Ferdinand of Aragon** [1479]), they ruled the two major kingdoms of Spain. They completed the seven-century *Reconquista* by driving the **Moors** (Muslims) from Grenada. Isabella and Ferdinand then brought the Catholic Inquisition to Spain. This led to the expulsion of Jews and strengthened Spain's Catholicism. However, these religious crusades drained the royal treasuries. Seeking new sources of wealth, Queen Isabella invested in an expedition of Italian mariner **Christopher Columbus** (1451-1506) to find an ocean route to the East.

EXPLORATION AND OVERSEAS EXPANSION

Columbus proposed finding a western water route to Asia. The Portuguese were already seeking water routes to India by sailing south around Africa. Columbus never reached the Orient. Instead, he discovered the Western Hemisphere. His four expeditions for Spain (1492-1502) began an era of competitive voyages of discovery.

For better and worse, the "**Columbian Exchange**" altered the course of global history in many ways:

- Native American civilizations (Inca, Aztec) destroyed
- European diseases killed millions of Native Americans
- European powers built extensive overseas empires
- Large numbers of Europeans migrated to the Americas
- Native American flora and fauna (maize, potato, tomato) were brought to Europe
- European plant diseases and rats infested the New World
- New World plantations required millions of African slaves
- Capitalism (private enterprise) expanded with the growth of trade
- Cultural exchanges occurred (language, arts, technology)

Columbus and other European explorers profited from vast changes in technology that emerged in the post-Renaissance era. New skills that developed from using the magnetic compass, the astrolabe, and primitive sextants were widely published in texts thanks to the new Gutenberg printing presses. Publication of new world maps, navigation charts, and engineering designs for better ships changed the guesswork of open ocean navigation into a science. Conquest in the newly encountered lands was made easier and more effective by the development of lighter weight muskets and artillery emerging from the European wars of 14th, 15th, and 16th centuries.

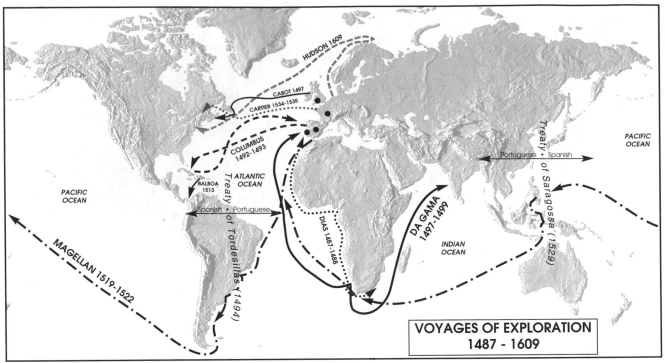

VOYAGES OF EXPLORATION
1487 - 1609

GLOBAL COMPETITION FOR COLONIES AMONG EUROPEAN POWERS

The knowledge gained from Columbus' voyages quickly led to a conflict between Spain and Portugal. The two rivals negotiated the ***Treaty of Tordesillas*** (1494) which set a Western Hemisphere dividing line (approximately 45°W Longitude). Portugal could make claims to the east of the line (Brazil, Africa, Indian Ocean) and Spain to the west (Western Hemisphere and the Pacific). Later, the two agreed on a similar line for the Eastern Hemisphere at approximately 135°E. Longitude (***Treaty of Saragossa***, 1529).

Of course, these treaties ignored the fact that other European powers' explorers laid claims in these regions. In the 16th century, the United Provinces of the Netherlands, England, and France joined the quest for "Gold, God, and Glory" and a northwest passage to the riches of Asia.

In the 16th century, Portugal developed a foothold in the New World by colonizing Brazil (1521). The Portuguese moved vigorously to build a trading empire along the coasts of Africa (Angola, 1574), Arabia, India (Goa, Madras), Ceylon, Southeast Asia, the East Indies (Malacca, 1505). They established a permanent

EARLY VOYAGES OF DISCOVERY

Year	Explorer (Country)	Area
1487-1488	Dias (Portugal)	west coast of Africa, Cape of Good Hope
1492-1493	Columbus (Spain)	West Indies, Caribbean
1497-1499	Da Gama (Portugal)	east coast of Africa, India
1497	Cabot (England)	Canada, North America
1513	Balboa (Spain)	Central America, Pacific
1519-1522	Magellan (Spain)	Circumnavigates globe
1534-1535	Cartier (France)	Canada - St. Lawrence R.
1608	Champlain (France)	Eastern Canada, northern U.S.
1609	Hudson (Netherlands)	Arctic Ocean, North America

trading and missionary outpost along the south China coast at Macao in 1557.

Spain's conquistadores subdued the Caribbean (Velazquez, 1511), Aztec Mexico (Cortés, 1521), and Peru (Pizarro, 1534). In the late 16th century, the Spanish moved into the Pacific, overpowering the Philippines in 1571.

In the second half of the 16th century the rising nation-states of northern Europe challenged the imperial monopoly of Spain and Portugal. Their competition shaped the future of colonialism. The Dutch (United Provinces of the Netherlands) gained a small toehold in North America's Hudson Valley and fought the Portuguese in nearly every other place from Brazil, to West Africa, to the East Indies.

The French moved into the St. Lawrence and Mississippi Valleys and Great Lakes of North America and probed opportunities in the Caribbean and India. Last into the contest was England. At first, England seemed satisfied with privateer raids on Spain's treasure ships and New World colonies. However, the British later claimed areas of North America's Atlantic Coast. In the next century, England ousted the Dutch and began a long contest with the French for North American supremacy.

HUMAN TOLLS OF IMPERIALISM: SLAVERY AND MERCANTILISM

In the 1600s, European **imperialism**[1] had broad effects on the global population. Spanish conquests brought disease and forced labor exploitation that nearly exterminated the Native American population. The exploits of Pizarro and Cortés killed nearly 100,000 Incas and Aztecs. Yet, the European diseases they brought (smallpox, influenza) killed millions.

With the Native American population decimated, the Spanish began importing African slaves to work plantations and mines of their New World empire. The slave trade burgeoned and continued for nearly 400 years.

A "triangle trade" pattern emerged for Africa, the New World, and Europe. Europeans traded goods for African slaves, then transported them under wretched conditions to the **encomiendas**[2] and plantations of the New World. Once in America, the empty slave ships loaded ores, hides, tobacco, sugar, and spices for return to European ports.

In the 16th, 17th, and 18th centuries, European governments tried to centralize power through a command economic system called **mercantilism**[3]. Mercantilists felt that to succeed, governments had to accumulate gold. Gold and silver were needed to purchase military supplies and conduct wars of conquest. Mercantilists desired a "favorable balance of trade" by assuring that the nation exported more than it imported. They wanted goods to flow outward, and gold to flow inward. Mercantilist governments:

- regulated production
- controlled trading companies
- restricted imports from other countries using tariffs and quotas
- controlled raw materials and markets through colonialism

Imperialism offered a means of keeping trade balances favorable. Colonies provided cheap sources of raw materials with little need to drain wealth by purchasing from other nations. Mercantilist governments could control colonies' production and colonies providing exclusive markets for the "mother country." A strong merchant marine linked colonies with the mother country, and a strong navy protected the trade from competing powers, privateers, and pirates. As a command system, mercantilism had a dampening effect on burgeoning capitalism. Some colonial merchants, smugglers, and privateers became rich by ignoring mercantilist rules.

1 imperialism (policy of extending a nation's authority by territorial acquisition or by the establishment of economic and political supremacy over other peoples)
2 encomienda (feudal grant of power over a territory and the people in it to a noble colonist)
3 mercantilism (theory and system of political economy prevailing in Europe after the decline of feudalism, based on national policies of accumulating gold and silver, establishing colonies and a merchant marine, and developing industry and mining to attain a favorable balance of trade)

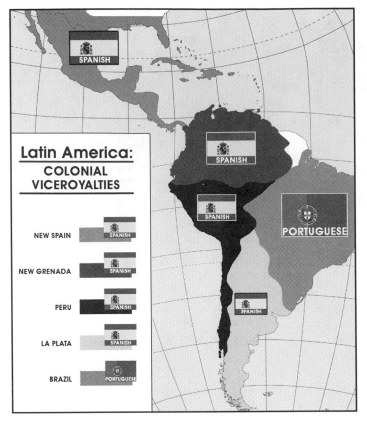

Latin America:
COLONIAL VICEROYALTIES

NEW SPAIN — SPANISH

NEW GRENADA — SPANISH

PERU — SPANISH

LA PLATA — SPANISH

BRAZIL — PORTUGUESE

SPANISH IMPERIALISM: THE ENCOMINENDA SYSTEM

After the Spanish captured and killed the the Aztec and Inca leaders, the decline of the empires was swift. There was some resistance to the invaders, but native rule ceased, and the societies quickly disintegrated. Spain imposed its rule on an area that extended from California to Tierra del Fuego.

The Spanish king named **viceroys**[1] with near-absolute power to administer vast regions of the Americas. The king's mercantilist advisors lured unwitting volunteers to set up encomiendas. The huge encomiendas became cash-crop plantations and mining operations using native labor as serfs. Later, the encomienda holders imported slave labor from Africa. Life on the encomiendas was brutal. Church clergy were largely silent about the abuses. In 1542, a lone Spanish missionary, Father **Bartolomé de las Casas**, broke the silence and reported on the inhumane treatment of natives and slaves. The crown ordered some weak reforms. The loss of life in the brutal encomienda existence continued and led to calls for more African slaves.

The migration of people to New Spain and New Grenada resulted in an intermixing of three races and a new social structure emerged (see diagram below). Spanish nobles, or **peninsulares**, remained the ruling elite. Their American-born children, or **criollos**, intermarried with Native Americans, producing **meztisos**, who gradually created the middle class of the colonies.

POLITICAL IDEOLOGIES: ABSOLUTISM

The nation-states and empires that arose at the close of the Medieval Era evolved into absolute monarchies. **Absolutism**[2] is a concentration of power in the hands of one person or a group of persons. For example, in 16th and 17th century Europe, monarchs overcame the power of the Church, the nobility, and city burghers. The monarchs claimed **divine right**[3] and held themselves responsible only to God, ignoring their subjects and representative bodies. They set up their own bureaucracies and commanded their own military forces.

PENINSULARES
Iberian Aristocrats

CRIOLLOS
Decendents of Peninsulares

MESTIZOS
Caucasian & Amerindian

MULATTOS
Caucasian & African

AFRICAN SLAVES

AMERINDIANS

LATIN AMERICAN COLONIAL CLASS STRUCTURE

---

1 viceroy (governor of a region or people, ruling as the representative of a king)
2 absolutism (form of government in which all power is vested in a single ruler or other authority)
3 divine right (doctrine that monarchs derive their right to rule directly from God and are accountable only to God)

Mini Assessment

1 The European colonial empires of the 15th through the 17th centuries negatively impacted population through
   1 reconquistas and missionaries
   2 cordilleras and cartography
   3 slavery and disease
   4 tribute and desertification

2 Which of the following was the cause of the other three?
   1 encomienda system
   2 mercantilist policies
   3 increased slave trade
   4 trade favoring the mother country

3 Which group dominated society in New Grenada and New Spain?
   1 Meztisos   3 Peninsulares
   2 Aztecs   4 Criollos

Constructed Response:

The events listed below relate to European overseas expansion in the 15th through 17th centuries. Use the list to construct an outline.

- Division into viceroyalties
- Christian missionary zeal
- Early imperialism
- Encomienda system
- Build national wealth
- Growth of slave trade
- Desire for national prestige

Title: _____

Causes:

Effects:

Some of these absolutist ideas were examined by Machiavelli (*The Prince*, see Unit IV). English philosopher and political theorist **Thomas Hobbes** (1588-1679) defended absolutism as part of "natural law." In *Leviathan* (1651), he claimed people willfully gave up freedom (the "nasty, brutish" chaos of nature) for the order and security provided by strong monarchs.

Although absolutism was widely practiced in this era, its applications varied greatly. The following selection of profiles are examples.

INDIA – AKBAR THE GREAT

Akbar the Great (1542-1605) united all northern India and Afghanistan under Mogul (Mughal) rule. He consolidated power by annexing Malwa, Bengal, Kabul, and Kashmir. Akbar ensured absolute control by setting up a paid bureaucracy. He stopped rewarding service with land grants to break up the aristocracy. He brought Hindu chiefs into his administration but limited their power. Although he ruled strictly and crushed opposition, he kept subjects in line by setting up a fair tax system and a uniform system of weights and measures, promoted

trade, and allowed religious tolerance. He adopted and promoted European technology (printing, gunpowder). Akbar set up a new state religion (a blend of Islam, Hinduism) and encouraged scholarship and the arts.

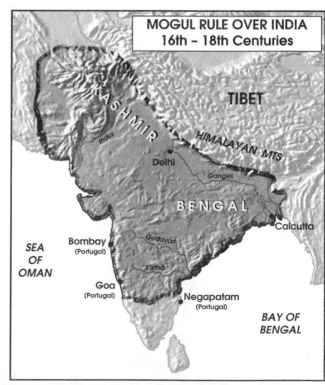

MOGUL RULE OVER INDIA
16th – 18th Centuries

SPAIN - CHARLES V AND PHILIP II

The grandson of Ferdinand II of Aragon, Charles (r. 1516-1556) became king of a united Spain and shortly thereafter was elected **Charles V, Holy Roman Emperor**. Charles' reign focused on Germany's problems during the Reformation and blocking the spread of the Ottoman Empire into Europe. Yet, his staunch defense of Catholicism, his building of an empire in the New World, and his use of Spaniards in imperial power positions allowed him to keep Spain united as a nation.

Charles' son, **Philip II**, became the absolutist king of Spain in 1556. He strengthened his control by centralizing the bureaucracy, annexing Portugal, warring against the Turks (Battle of Lepanto, 1571), and campaigning against Protestantism in the Netherlands. Philip's early reign was the high point of Spain's monarchy and a golden age for the nation. Philip patronized the arts and academic pursuits including the paintings of El Greco (1541-1614) and the writings of Cervantes. However, Philip engaged in expensive wars and intrigues against France. His armada suffered defeat by England in 1588. His loss of the northern provinces of the Netherlands combined with other problems to weaken Spain. The country began a long decline in power.

Palace of King Louis XIV – Versailles – France
© Sue Ann Kime 1997

FRANCE - LOUIS XIV

Louis XIV became the most famous of the absolute monarchs. Historians claim Louis declared that he himself was the state ("L'etat, c'est moi."). France's "Sun King," had the longest reign in European history (1643-1715). By the middle of his reign, he established a glittering court at Versailles. Nobles drawn by the dazzling life at Louis' "gilded cage" neglected their estates. This reduced their income and diminished their power to oppose the king.

Louis' early reign (1643-1661) was as a **regency**[1] As he was a minor, Louis' mother Anne was chosen to govern in place of the monarch. Actually, the chief minister, **Cardinal Mazarin**, dominated the government. Mazarin continued the harsh policies and taxes of Louis XIII and Cardinal Richelieu. A series of major revolts by merchants, peasants, and nobles (The Fronde, 1648-1653), temporarily ousted Mazarin. Later, he returned and assisted Louis as he began his personal rule.

After Mazarin's death in 1661, Louis proved to be a true Machiavellian. He took personal control and did not share power with a chief minister. Louis never convened the Estates General for advice. He used middle class officials to replace any nobles who challenged him.

Louis fought the Netherlands for commercial supremacy and invaded Germany to gain the Rhine as a boundary. His four major wars were expensive and revenue was partially raised through the mercantilist financial policies of **Jean Baptiste Colbert** (1619-1683). Colbert

King Louis XIV

1 regency (person or group selected to govern in place of a monarch or other ruler who is absent, disabled, or still in minority)

RUSSIAN EXPANSION
From the Late 15th Century

→ Expansion

Varangian Kiev–State
1000 A.D.

Early Tsarist State
c. 1500s A.D.

From Peter the Great & Catherine
the Great into the 19th century

codified France's laws, effectively restructured taxes, built an impressive navy, started a colonial empire, and oversaw state cultural and scientific undertakings.

After Colbert's death, Louis' last years (1685-1715) were beset by problems. He revoked the Edict of Nantes in 1685, and he expelled the Protestant Huguenots. Because the Huguenots were a key group in generating the mercantilist revenues, the country's economy suffered.

Louis' policies brought little to France. He lost colonial territories to England and gained little against rivals Spain and the Netherlands. However, French national pride was enhanced, and French culture came to dominate Western European society.

RUSSIA - PETER THE GREAT

From the late 15th century on, the grand dukes of Muscovy created a class of military vassals and placed towns under their direct rule. Building on this power, **Ivan IV** ("Ivan the Terrible," r. 1533-1584) assumed the title of **tsar** (ruler). He appointed an advisory council, drew

up a new law code, and enacted reforms, but also began binding peasants to the land. Ivan's conquests of the Central Asia and Siberia put a vast empire under tsarist rule. Toward the end of his reign, Ivan took absolute control of the state. He turned against his council and created a secret police to purge and exile nobles and

Ivan IV

officials. Ivan's wars against Poland-Lithuania, Livonia, and Sweden nearly bankrupted Russia. Internal revolts, outside invasions, and weak tsars plagued Russia until the founding of the Romanov Dynasty in 1613.

When Peter I, known as **Peter the Great** (r. 1682-1725), became tsar of Russia, he decreed sweeping changes based on the models of European absolute monarchs. All classes of Russian society felt the brutally strong influence of his **Westernization** reforms and military campaigns against the Ottomans, Persia, and Sweden. Peter developed a civil service system that allowed officials to achieve noble rank, while diluting older nobles' power. He placed the Orthodox Church under his control and appointed his own Church leaders. His construction of a new capital at **St. Petersburg** removed his government from the influence of older aristocrats.

In the economic realm, Peter structured a mercantilist approach, opening trade with Western Europe. He built a modernized naval force, and founded new industries. Still, he kept the peasantry bound in near-medieval serfdom. While Peter's absolutist reforms and military conquests changed Russian society, the weakness of his successors left historians to debate whether he laid the foundation for the modern Russian state.

Large cannon built during Peter the Great's reorganization of the Russian military resulting from his study of Western technology. © Sue Ann Kime 1997

ENGLAND - JAMES I

After building a new national consciousness and stronger monarchy, Elizabeth I left no children when she died in 1603. Her cousins, the Stuarts of Scotland, inherited England's throne. King James I ascended the throne recognizing Parliament's power. James soon began to declare his notion of divine right of monarchy. Conflicts with Parliament over money became frequent. He alienated the House of Commons over religious issues. As a Scots Presbyterian, James was aware of the kind of Calvinist

Mini Assessment

1 Peter the Great's westernization of Russia included
   1 abolition of serfdom
   2 independence for the Orthodox Church
   3 colonial possessions in the New World
   4 creation of a civil service

2 Akbar the Great, Philip II, and James I were
   1 ethnocentrists 3 absolutists
   2 viceroys   4 bureaucrats

3 James I's clashes with the English Parliament revolved around
   1 culture and creativity
   2 reform and regency
   3 revenue and religion
   4 serfdom and security

Constructed Response:

"...the King is the overlord of the whole land, so he is master over every person that inhabiteth the same, having power over life and death of every one of them. For although a just prince will not take the life of any of his subjects, without a clear law, yet the same laws whereby he taketh them are made by himself or his predecessors."

– James I, *True Law of Free Monarchs*, 1598

1 In King James' opinion, what is the source of law?

2 How does this quotation reflect absolutism?

Oliver Cromwell

King Charles I

reforms the Anglican "Puritan" group wanted. Yet, as head of the Church of England, he angered the Puritans in Parliament by rejecting their requests for change. James' conclusion of a peace with Spain in 1604 made Parliament suspect he was pro-Catholic. His advisors constantly clashed with Parliament on financial matters.

RESPONSE TO ABSOLUTISM: THE PURITAN REVOLUTION AND THE ENGLISH BILL OF RIGHTS

Parliament's struggles with the Stuart monarchs came to a head under James' son, **Charles I** (r. 1625-1649). The friction between the English monarchs and nobles, middle class townspeople, and commoners had a long history.

Charles I tried to rule without Parliament and viciously persecuted his enemies, especially Puritans and the Scots. By 1640, Charles faced a war with Scotland and Ireland. He called the Puritan-controlled Parliament into session to get money.

Beginning in 1642, the Puritan Revolution pitted Parliament's Puritans ("roundheads") against royalist supporters ("cavaliers"). Charles rejected Parliament's "Nineteen Propositions" limiting royal power and tried to arrest Puritan leaders. Both sides raised armies, and in 1642, the English Civil War began. Puritan commander **Oliver Cromwell** defeated Charles' forces in 1646. The Puritans purged Parliament of cav-

aliers, and executed Charles in 1649. After they abolished the monarchy, Cromwell dismissed Parliament. A group of army officers drew up a **constitution**[1] (the ***Instrument of Government***) setting up a commonwealth, and naming Cromwell "Lord Protector." While Parliament was reinstated, Cromwell ruled as a dictator for 7 years, enforcing strict Puritan rules on social behavior. This was the only time in England's modern history when the country had a written constitution but did not have a monarch.

Cromwell died in 1658. In 1660, the army overthrew his son Richard and reconvened Parliament. During the **Restoration**, the government invited Charles I's son to assume the throne with permanent restrictions on the monarch's power. During Charles II's reign, Parliament settled religious toleration controversies and passed the **Habeas Corpus Act**[2]. During this "Restoration Period," English society reacted against the strict Puritan values and embraced a flamboyant lifestyle.

Charles II died in 1685 and was succeeded by his Catholic brother, James. As king, James II tried to regain absolute power and reopened the Protestant v. Catholic controversy. In the **Glorious Revolution** (1688), Parliament deposed James. It then established its supremacy by inviting new Protestant monarchs (**William and Mary of Orange**) to take the

---

1 constitution (system of fundamental laws and principles that prescribes the nature, functions, and limits of a government or another institution)
2 Habeas Corpus Act (arrested individuals were guaranteed a statement of charges against them, opportunity for bail, and a speedy trial)

DOCUMENTS OF ENGLISH RIGHTS

Document	Ideas
Magna Carta (1215)	English barons rebelled against King John's high taxes and military failures and forced him to sign the *Magna Carta*. It strengthened due process by requiring both a proper trial and lawful judgment in royal courts before levying a sentence.
Petition of Right (1628)	Charles I's extravagances and foreign wars required a Parliamentary session and a clash forced an important compromise. The *Petition of Right* restricted the monarch's power to collect taxes, quarter troops in private homes, declare martial law, and imprison individuals without just cause (habeas corpus concept) and insured jury trials.
Habeas Corpus Act (1670)	During Charles II's reign, Parliament settled religious toleration controversies and passed the **Habeas Corpus Act** – arrested individuals were guaranteed a statement of charges against them, opportunity for bail, and a speedy trial.
Bill of Rights (1689)	Under William and Mary, Parliament forbade taxation without its consent, and broadened due process rights to include protection from cruel and unusual punishments and excessive bail and fines.

throne. Parliament required them to sign the **Bill of Rights** (1689). The Bill secured Parliament's sovereignty over the crown, forbade taxation without its consent, and broadened due process rights.

From this series of confrontations, sometimes violent, but mostly bloodless, England evolved into a **constitutional monarchy**[1]. The accumulation of restrictions on the absolute power of monarchs laid a foundation for the concept of representative democracy in the modern world. The principles of individual freedom and rights of citizens in the face of governmental power slowly evolved from these confrontations between would-be absolute monarchs and nobles and churchmen in the 17th century.

TIME CAPSULE

This was an age of transition. Major forces that are the focus of human interest in our own times emerged in this age. Beginning in the 15th century and into the 18th century, this First Global Age saw a new and influential interaction of the civilizations of Asia and Europe with civilizations in Africa, the Americas, and the Pacific Rim.

By force of arms, the Ming, Ottoman, and Mughal Empires dominated Asia and North Africa. They unified diverse populations politically, culturally, and economically. In Europe, the rise of absolute monarchs employing the divine right theory attempted to eliminate opposition and unify their kingdoms. European encounters and exploration of the Western Hemisphere grew out of the quest for trade, wealth, and knowledge that intensified in the Renaissance and gained momentum as national monarchies developed.

The expansion of enterprises motivated the Chinese in the early Ming Era as well as the Portuguese and Spanish in the 15th century. Desire for tropical products – cotton, sugar, coffee, indigo, spices – led to the launching of extensive voyages of exploration that intensified intercontinental maritime trade. Bitter rivalries among the Portuguese and Dutch, Dutch and English, English and Spanish, and later, French and English promoted the growth of imperialism. Each nation sought naval supremacy and fought for overseas commercial stations and colonies.

GLOBAL HISTORY ARCHIVE

1   constitutional monarchy (monarchy in which the powers of the ruler are restricted to those granted under the constitution and laws of the nation)

MULTI-CHOICE QUESTIONS

1   In South America, the rapid rivers and thick vegetation of the Amazon rain forest and the imposing heights of the Andes
    1   improved communications among native peoples
    2   accelerated Spanish conquest and control of a large colonial empire
    3   hindered settlement of the continent's interior
    4   encouraged cultural diffusion

2   Which of these situations was the result of the other three?
    1   Aztec and Inca rule was based on forced tribute relationships.
    2   Mesoamerican empires fell to European conquerors.
    3   Frequent rebellions and civil wars occurred in and among Maya, Aztec, and Inca city-states.
    4   Europeans formed alliances with rival city-states and Mesoamerican people.

3   Which presented the greatest challenge to Spain's imperial supremacy in the New World?
    1   treaties with Portugal denoting zones of exploration and colonization
    2   introduction of slaves from Africa
    3   founding of missions by Catholic priests
    4   the activities of Cartier, Hudson, Champlain, and Cabot

4   Philip II of Spain, Louis XIV of France, and Peter I of Russia were all absolute monarchs. Which characteristic was common to their reigns?
    1   They conducted extensive foreign wars.
    2   They exerted power through national legislatures.
    3   They allowed toleration of various religions.
    4   They created strong alliances with Asian emperors.

Base your answer to question 5 on the sketch above and your knowledge of global history.

5   This view of a section of the Aztec city of Tenochtitlan resembles a
    1   tributary of Ming China
    2   savanna of Mali
    3   forum in an ancient Roman city
    4   manor of Medieval Europe

6   In the eyes of mercantilist policy makers, colonies helped to achieve wealth for the nation by
    1   providing cheap sources of raw materials and markets for the nation's goods
    2   increasing the imports the mother country needed from other nations
    3   trading directly with the colonies of other empires
    4   increasing the number of religious conversions

7   In the southern Saharan region, Islam's diversity allowed it to merge with traditional religious practices and spread rapidly. This made it easier for leaders in Songhai and Mali to form trading empires because it
    1   enhanced the power of local chiefs
    2   created a common cultural bond
    3   opposed ancestor worship
    4   promoted ethnocentrism

8 Which geographic factor had the greatest effect on interaction between sub-Saharan African and Mediterranean societies?
1 presence of desert areas
2 monsoon winds bearing moisture
3 lack of north-south rivers in sub-Saharan Africa
4 impassable mountain barriers

9 Which resulted from the presence of the Ottoman Empire as a military power in the Eastern Mediterranean in the 12th - 16th centuries?
1 decrease in the slave trade
2 breakdown of manorialism in Europe
3 rise of absolute monarchy in Europe
4 blockage of Asian-European trade

10 In England, the *Magna Carta*, the *Petition of Right*, and the *Bill of Rights* show an evolution of
1 mercantile policies
2 religious toleration
3 limiting the power of the monarch
4 scientific and technological achievement

THEMATIC ESSAY

Theme: Culture and Intellectual Life

Leaders can promote cultural development.

Task:
- Select a leader from the First Global Age (1450-1770) and explain how the leader's actions promoted cultural and intellectual development.
- Describe how the leader's actions altered his/her society.

Suggestions:
You may use any leader from the era. Some individuals you might consider: Mansa Kankan Musa, Yong Le, Suleiman, Peter the Great. **You are not limited to these suggestions.**

DOCUMENT BASED QUESTION

Directions:
The following question is based on the accompanying documents (1-4). Some of the documents have been edited for the purposes of this exercise. The question is designed to test your ability to work with historical documents. As you analyze the documents, take into account both the source of the document and the author's point of view.

- Write a well-organized essay that includes an introduction with a thesis statement, several paragraphs explaining the thesis, and a conclusion.
- Analyze the documents.
- Use all the documents.
- Use evidence from the documents to support your thesis position.
- Do not simply repeat the contents of the documents.
- Include specific related outside information.

Historical Context:
Contacts among people are never simple. A mix of motives propelled expansion of European contacts with Asia, Africa, and the Americas in the First Global Age. The documents below present some aspects of the contact.

Task:
Evaluate the reasons for the expansion of European influence in Asia, Africa, and the Americas in the First Global Age. Support your opinion with the documents below and your knowledge of global history.

Part A - Short Answer

The documents below relate aspects of the expansion of European influence Asia, Africa, and the Americas in the First Global Age. Examine each document carefully, then answer the question that follows it.

Document 1:

"Presently many of the inhabitants of the island assembled ... thus your highnesses should resolve to make them Christians, for I believe if the work was begun, in a little time the multitude would be converted to our faith, with the acquisition of great lordships, people, and riches for Spain."

– Christopher Columbus to King Ferdinand and Queen Isabella (1493)

Document 1 Question:

Why did the Church support voyages of discovery?

Document 2:

"The Dutch East India Company, organized in 1602, was a highly successful enterprise until the close of the 17th c. ... the average dividend from 1602 to 1796 was over 18 percent. The earnings of the English East India Company were stupendous. On some of the early voyages profits of 195, 221, 311, 318, and 334 percent were realized. During the 17th c. dividends averaged about 100:21 percent."

– E.J. Hamilton "American Treasure & the Rise of Capitalism (1500-1700)" Econnomica, November 1929

Document 2 Question:

Who benefitted from the wealth of the New World?

Document 3: Slave Trade Across the Atlantic

From the 1520s through 1867, an estimated 10 to 15 million Africans were transported to the New World.

WHERE SLAVES WERE DELIVERED

4 figures = 1 million slaves

Dutch West Indies (including Surinam)
French West Indies
Spanish Empire (including Cuba)
British West Indies, British North America, & United States
Brazil

Document 3 Question:

In what ways did the importation of African slaves affect the New World?

Document 4:

"In the 17th century northern Europeans rushed to colonize the remaining unsettled islands and turned aggressively on the Spaniards. ... As the nations battled, law and order broke down entirely; the pirates grew bolder than ever; ...After 1700 the Caribbean became a battleground for European navies and a magnet for the most dangerous outlaws of the sea. ... the Caribbean islands had grown rich satisfying Europe's appetite for sugar and tobacco."

– J.A. Hayes, *Medieval and Early Modern Times* (1963)

Document 4 Question:

Why did national governments in England, Holland, and France become so interested in the New World?

Part B - Essay Response

Your essay should be well organized with an introductory paragraph that states your thesis as to the reasons for European expansion during the first Global Age. Develop and support the reasons for your thesis in the next paragraphs and then write a conclusion. In your essay, include specific historical details and refer to the specific documents you analyzed in Part A. You may include additional information from your knowledge of global history.

Unit 6

1750 AD – 1914 AD

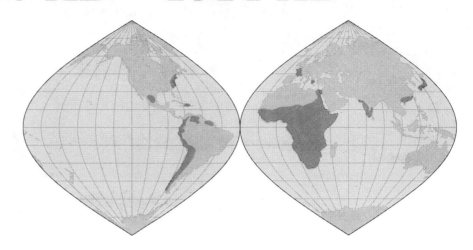

AN AGE OF REVOLUTIONS

Napoleon

Nelson

AD	
1750–	
	Wealth of Nations published (1776)
	French Revolution begins (1789)
	L'Overture begins Haitian revolt (1791)
1800–	
	Congress of Vienna meets (1814)
	Great Reform Bill in Britain (1832)
	Communist Manifesto published (1848)
1850–	Opening of Japan (1853)
	Sepoy Mutiny (1857)
	Emancipation Edict in Russia (1861)
	Berlin Conference (1885)
1900–	Boxer Rebellion (1899)

PEOPLE	PLACES	THINGS
Catherine the Great	Asia Minor	Boxer Rebellion
Cecil Rhodes	First French Empire	Congress of Vienna
Guiseppe Garibaldi	Trafalgar	coup d'etat
John Locke	Waterloo	*Declaration of the Rights of Man*
Karl Marx	Gran Colombia	enlightened despot
Kemal Ataturk	Chinese Republic	Enlightenment
Montesquieu	Transvaal	Guomindang
Maria Theresa	savanna	industrialization
Napoleon Bonaparte	Spanish Empire	laissez-faire
Otto von Bismarck		New Imperialism
philosophes		nationalism and revolution
Simon Bolivar		scientific socialism
Sun Yixian		Sepoy Mutiny

INTRODUCTION

Revolutions[1] are movements which bring about complete or drastic altering of economic, political, and/or social life change. The better known revolutions, in places such as the Britain's Atlantic Coast colonies in North America, France, Russia, Iran, and China, were political. However, many revolutions do not involve violence or political change. Revolutions have occurred in fields such as science, philosophy, and methods of production. Political revolutions are more likely to involve violence, but some political change has been brought about by **coup d'etats**[2]. Napoleon Bonaparte of France achieved power through a coup d'état in 1799.

1 revolution (overthrow of one government and its replacement with another)
2 coup d'etats (sudden, often bloodless overthrow of a government by a usually small group of persons in or previously in positions of authority)
3 Nicolaus Copernicus (1473-1543, Polish astronomer who advanced the theory that the Earth and other planets revolve around the Sun, disrupting the Ptolemaic system of astronomy)

THE SCIENTIFIC REVOLUTION

DEVELOPMENT OF SCIENTIFIC METHODS

Beginning as early as the age of **Copernicus**[3], some Western scientists began to question the ideas of the ancient Greeks and Romans. They began to observe and experiment and to base their conclusions on their findings. These procedures became known as the scientific method. Many scientists also adopted the inductive approach – working from many specific examples to develop more generalized conclusions. For example, they would examine many different varieties of leaves to come to a conclusion about what a leaf was. Not surprisingly, many scientific developments occurred during the Renaissance when the prevailing outlook favored questioning and progress.

Changes in thinking that occurred during the Scientific Revolution led to changes in other

SCIENTISTS OF THE ENLIGHTENMENT

Scientist	Work	Main Contributions
Nicolaus Copernicus	*On the Revolutions of Heavenly Orbs* (1543)	Heliocentric Theory – believed that the Earth and other planets revolved around the Sun – used mathematical calculations, not observation
Galileo Galilei	*Dialogues on the Two New Sciences* (1632)	Used telescope to prove planets revolved around Sun; laws of motion on Earth; observed sunspots; mountains on Moon
Isaac Newton	*Principia (The Mathematical Principles of Natural Philosophy* (1687))	Universal Law of Gravitation – explained movement on Earth and in solar system; co-developed calculus
Rene Descartes	*Discourse on Method* (1637)	Used reason ("I think, therefore I am") to arrive at truth; invented coordinate geometry; believed science should be applied to practical arts

fields. French philosopher-mathematician **Rene Descartes** (1596-1650) held the belief that science could have practical application. This is seen in the inventions of the Agricultural and Industrial Revolutions. In addition, changes developed in philosophy. Thinkers sought natural laws that governed the actions of people, just as England's Sir **Isaac Newton** (1643-1727) and others sought the laws that governed nature. Scientific groups such as England's Royal Society and France's Academy of Science circulated new ideas and made change and progress easier.

INTELLECTUAL REVOLUTION: THE ENLIGHTENMENT IN EUROPE

THE WRITINGS OF LOCKE, VOLTAIRE, ROUSSEAU AND MONTESQUIEU

The **Enlightenment** (also called the Age of Reason or the Intellectual Revolution) began in the 17th century in England and reached its peak in the 18th century in France and America. Most of the "**philosophes**[1]" were not original thinkers, but popularizers of the ideas of others. For example, the writings of Newton were difficult for men to understand and apply to their

1   philosophes (leading philosophical, political, and social writers of the 18th century French Enlightenment)

lives, but Voltaire's work on Newton changed that. The philosophes tried to use reasoning and a scientific approach to arrive at the characteristics of society and government intended by nature. They believed in progress and humanity's ability to bring about positive change. They often met informally in salons (parlors of private homes) to exchange ideas. In absolutist France, their criticisms led to them being censored and occasionally imprisoned.

THE IMPACT OF ENLIGHTENMENT ON NATIONALISM AND DEMOCRACY

Enlightenment writers used nature or natural laws to justify their ideas of how people should live together and what their form of government should be. Most liberal Enlightenment thinkers believed that nature grouped people together in nations which had different characteristics. People became more conscious of themselves as a national group, and this led to national pride and often to reactionary feelings against those regarded as foreign.

The philosophes were not a unified group, and often disagreed. Voltaire believed that rulers should have the power which would be used to benefit the people; Rousseau and Locke believed that power should rest with the people.

WRITERS OF THE ENLIGHTENMENT

Author & Work	Main Ideas	Impact
John Locke (1632-1704) *Two Treatises of Government* (1690)	Locke believed all men have natural rights of life, liberty, property; men have a right of revolution if government fails to protect rights	Influenced ideas of Jefferson and *Declaration of Independence*; used many times to justify revolution against unjust governments
Voltaire (Francois Marie Arouet, 1694-1778) *Letters on the English* (1728)	Voltaire admired relative freedom of religion and press in England; believed enlightened despots should use power to benefit people	Increased English pride in freedoms resulted in rise of enlightened despots
Jean Jacques Rousseau (1712-1778) *Social Contract* (1761)	Rousseau believed "man is born free, yet everywhere he is in chains"; wanted men to give power to government (General Will) which would act for common good with consent of people	Influenced development of democracy – government "of the people, by the people, for the people"
Montesquieu (Charles Louis de Secondat, 1689-1755) *The Spirit of the Laws* (1748)	Baron de Montesquieu believed in separation of powers (legislative / executive / judicial); wanted balance of power among various elements in government	Influenced structure of the *U.S. Constitution* and other constitutions based on it

As a consequence, very different forms of government could be justified using the ideas of the philosophes.

ENLIGHTENED DESPOTS

Enlightened despotism is a term associated with 18th century monarchs who, while denying democratic rights, used their absolute power to reform legal, social, and educational institutions and improve conditions for their subjects. Enlightened despotism owes much to the writings of Voltaire. He spent time at the court of Frederick the Great of Prussia and corresponded with Catherine the Great of Russia. Voltaire believed that a ruler could justify his/her power by improving society. Common actions taken by enlightened despots included: codification of laws, limitation of church power, construction of hospitals and elementary schools, development of a centralized bureaucracy, and modification of serfdom. They took similar actions, yet tailored their actions to conditions within their particular realms.

Maria Theresa of Austria (1740-1780)
- established paid bureaucracy of civil servants
- eased burdens of serfdom
- established tariff union for various parts of empire

Frederick the Great of Prussia (1740-1786)
- codified laws
- established a measure of religious freedom
- established some elementary schools

Catherine the Great of Russia (1762-1796)
- reorganized local government and established a civil service
- decreased use of torture
- codified laws

The efforts of the enlightened despots were not completely successful. Maria Theresa was succeeded by her son, **Joseph II**, who tried to bring about more extensive reforms. However, he and his successors were caught in a tide of reaction that undid most of the accomplishments. Frederick the Great neglected to train his successor, and conditions in Prussia deterio-

Mini Assessment

MINI-ASSESSMENT

1 Voltaire believed that complete power should be given to an enlightened despot and Locke believed that power should rest with the people. Which is a correct conclusion based on these statements and your knowledge of the Intellectual Revolution?
1 All philosophes believed in democracy.
2 Philosophes had widely differing views on government.
3 French philosophes believed only in absolutism while English philosophes supported democracy.
4 The nature of government was the only concern of philosophes.

2 A major contribution of the Scientific Revolution was the
1 emphasis it placed on practical application of scientific theory
2 increased reluctance to employ the inductive method
3 refusal to question ideas of the ancient Greeks
4 continued reliance on the geocentric theory

3 Which were likely actions of enlightened despots?
1 sharing power with an elected legislature and increasing rights for women
2 abolishing censorship and rights of assembly
3 codifying laws and establishing a government bureaucracy
4 establishing a state religion and church control of education

Constructed Response:

"When any number of men have so consented to make one community or government, they are thereby presently incorporated and ... the majority have a right to act and conclude [include] the rest."

– John Locke, *Second Treatise of Civil Government* (1690)

1 Which form of government does Locke support in this quotation?

2 How might Locke's ideas (this one and others), be applied in the French Revolution?

rated. In Russia, the revolution of a serf (Pugachev) threatened the reign of Catherine the Great and resulted in a slowing of the reform process. Nevertheless, conditions for the common people in countries ruled by enlightened despots were better than those in nearby countries.

POLITICAL REVOLUTIONS

THE AMERICAN REVOLUTION

The **Enlightenment**[1] had considerable impact on the decade of turmoil that swept Britain's Atlantic Coast colonies from 1764-1775 and resulted in the American Revolution (1776-1783). Such revolutionary leaders as **Benjamin Franklin** (1706-1790), **Thomas Paine** (1737-1809), and **Thomas Jefferson** (1743-1826) were influenced by the philosophes.

Benjamin Franklin was the main author of the *Albany Plan of Union* (1754) which urged the colonies to unite against the threat of French power in Canada. Later, he favored a system of Parliamentary representation for the colonists. After the Revolution, he lobbied for giving the U.S. Congress the power to tax. From 1775 to 1783, while serving as the Americans' representative in France, Franklin wore the common man's homespun clothing and tied his hair back in a simple queue (pigtail). To many Frenchmen, he seemed to be reflecting Rousseau's idea that man should return to as near the state of nature as possible.

Thomas Paine's *Common Sense* (1776) held the injustice of the British monarchy to blame for American dissatisfaction. Paine also found it unnatural for a small nation such as Britain to rule a large area such as America.

Thomas Jefferson's ideas in the *Declaration of Independence* (1776) blamed the British monarchy for violation of Americans' natural rights to life, liberty, and the pursuit of happiness. Jefferson also indicated that these violations gave Americans the right of revolution. Thus, his ideas clearly include those of John Locke and some of the other Enlightenment writers. The *United States Constitution* (1789) includes the ideas of Montesquieu on the separation of powers and a check and balance system.

The first ten amendments to the *U.S. Constitution*, the *Bill of Rights* (1791), enumerate the rights of American citizens to such privileges as freedom of speech, press, religion, private property, and trial by jury. Again they reflect the ideals of the Enlightenment thinkers.

The American Revolution of 1776 clearly inspired the **French Revolution** of 1789 and most of the other world revolutions which followed. The reforms of the French Revolution included the idea that a constitution was necessary to limit the power of the government. The French *Declaration of the Rights of Man and of the Citizen* (1789) included many of the ideas of the philosophes and the American revolutionaries. Later phases of the French Revolution led to the adoption of a republic. The American example had shown such a government system could work in a modern nation.

The revolutions in Latin America in the early 19th century were clearly inspired by those in the United States and France. Latin American revolutionary leader, Simon Bolivar, modeled his union of Gran Colombia on the United States experience. Worldwide, other revolutionaries took up the cries of natural rights and government by the consent of the governed. Such cries continue to be heard in modern times.

THE FRENCH REVOLUTION

The French Revolution was caused by a variety of economic, social, and political factors. Economically, the French government was virtually bankrupt. The early 18th century wars of Louis XIV and Louis XV were costly. The monarchs found it difficult to increase taxation. Within the **Estates**[2] in France – the clergy and the nobility – were largely tax exempt. They refused to accept taxation without an increase in power. The **Third Estate**[3] paid most of the taxes. With the exception of some of the bourgeoisie, the Third Estate was least able to pay. In addition, poor harvests plagued the nation in the latter half of the 18th century. The government was unable to provide much relief.

---

1 Enlightenment (philosophical movement of the 17th-18th centuries that emphasized the use of reason to scrutinize previously accepted doctrines and traditions and that brought about many humanitarian reforms)
2 Estates (social position or rank, especially of high order: 1st estate – major social class, such as the nobility, the commons; 2nd estate – clergy, formerly possessing distinct political rights; 3rd estate – common people)
3 Third Estate (the common people – bourgeoisie, proletariat, and peasantry)

The social and political structures of France were rigid and blocked advancement to a better life. The first two Estates had special privileges. The **First Estate**, the Roman Catholic Church, controlled education. Top Church officials often held high government positions. The **Second Estate**, the nobility, also held high positions in the government and the military. They also had the right to wear certain expensive fabrics and be driven in larger carriages with more horses. Both these Estates were able to tax the common people of the Third Estate.

Politically, the clergy and nobility controlled and profited from their hold on the government administration and revenues. From the days of Louis XIV, the **old regime** (ancien régime) structure allowed the king to wield absolute power over a tight-knit social hierarchy. A generation later, **King Louis XVI** thought that he could restore control by exerting the old regime's style of absolute power. He was encouraged in this idea by his wife, **Marie Antoinette**. The royal couple failed to see the times had changed.

Prior to 1789, the **Estates General** (the French legislative body), had not met for 175 years. The imminent bankruptcy of the nation forced Louis XVI to call the Estates General into session. The ensuing election campaign further spread the ideas of the philosophes. Their ideas were popularized by the writing of Abbe Sieyes

Wife of French King Louis XVI, Marie Antoinette with her children - painted by Mme. Lebrun - *Art & Artists*, (1888)

in *What is the Third Estate?* Many other pamphlets were published amid the turmoil of the era. In the spring of 1789, the Third Estate declared the right of the people to alter the government – Locke's idea – and demanded the Estates General meet as a unified group. When

EVENTS OF THE FRENCH REVOLUTION

Key Event or Reform	Significance
Tennis Court Oath (1789)	Delegates to Estates General formed a National Assembly and pledged to meet until France had a constitution
Storming of the Bastille (1789)	Proletariat led an attack on the Bastille prison, a symbol of the Old Regime; found few weapons for defense of Paris, but did kill 6 and freed a few prisoners
Abolition of special privileges (1789)	In a night session, nobles agreed to give up feudal dues, tax exemption, and hunting rights
Declaration of the Rights of Man and of the Citizen (1789)	Document reflecting ideas of philosophes; included rights of life, liberty, property, security, and resistance of oppression; taxation only by consent of people and equality of all before law
Civil Constitution of the Clergy (1790)	Placed Church under government control; Church officials to be elected by all and paid by the State; caused a major split in support for the Revolution
Reign of Terror (1793-1794)	Led by radicals such as Danton, Marat, and Robespierre, it resulted from concerns about traitors after war began; the Terror led to executions of Louis XVI, Marie Antoinette, and about 40,000 others on the guillotine
Thermidorian Reaction (1794)	Reaction against excesses of Reign of Terror; led to formation of the Directory, a more conservative, but corrupt, oligarchy

the other two estates refused, the Third Estate declared itself a **National Assembly**. The Estates General disintegrated. This unleashed peasant uprisings and the French Revolution began.

The course of the French Revolution is very complicated. Control of the Revolution passed from the moderate bourgeoisie to the more radical proletariat only to return to a moderate stance in its later phases. The country moved from an absolute monarchy, to a constitutional monarchy, and finally to a republic before succumbing to Napoleon. However, all groups were involved in the key events and the reforms that determined the impact of the French Revolution on history.

Confiscation of the Church's and the nobles' property led many nobles to become **émigrés**[1]. Nobles fled to various courts in other areas of Europe. They worked to encourage foreign countries to intervene on behalf of the **Old Regime**[2]. After the attempted flight of Louis XVI and Marie Antoinette and their capture at Varennes (June 1791), Austria and Prussia threatened to act to protect the monarchy.

Despite France's institution of **levee en masse** (drafting civilians into the military), the foreign armies were early victors. The loss of noble officers (many were émigrés) made possible the rise of young generals such as **Napoleon Bonaparte** (1769-1821) from Corsica. Napoleon's victories in Italy led to command in Egypt. He won on land, but lost on the seas to British Admiral Nelson in the Battle of the Nile (1798). With resources strained, Napoleon pushed an exhausted army to continue military actions in the Middle East for a year. He returned to France in 1799 to seize power in a coup d'état from the corrupt Directory (oligarchy). The National Convention sent Louis XVI and Marie Antonette to the guillotine on 21 January 1793.

Napoleon viewed himself as a "son of the revolution." He believed himself to be a liberal reformer and spread many of the ideals of the Revolution to areas he conquered. However, oth-

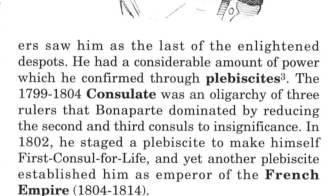
Napoleon
Bonaparte
(1769-1821)

ers saw him as the last of the enlightened despots. He had a considerable amount of power which he confirmed through **plebiscites**[3]. The 1799-1804 **Consulate** was an oligarchy of three rulers that Bonaparte dominated by reducing the second and third consuls to insignificance. In 1802, he staged a plebiscite to make himself First-Consul-for-Life, and yet another plebiscite established him as emperor of the **French Empire** (1804-1814).

Autocratic as he seemed, Napoleon carried out a number of reforms for the benefit of the French people, many of which are still in effect in France today.

- **Napoleonic Code of Laws** (1807) – established equality before law, supremacy of male head of household, religious freedom, and business laws

- **Concordat of 1801** – agreed with Roman Catholic Church to recognize Catholicism as the religion of the majority, Church gave up right to tithes, Pope regained some control over Church officials

- **University of France** (1802) – established a national system of education in France

- **Legion of Honor** (1802) – established to honor those who served France, civilian or military

1 émigré (one who has left a native country, especially for political reasons)
2 Old Regeme (government dominated by an absolute ruler and privileged nobles and clergy)
3 plebiscites (allowing voters to express their will on an issue directly at the polls, instead of through elected representatives)

Initially, Napoleon won numerous land battles against Austria, Prussia, and Russia and extended the French Empire. Many areas such as modern Belgium, the Netherlands, and parts of Italy were incorporated in the French Empire. Other areas were forced to ally themselves with France. However, Napoleon could not defeat Britain. When Admiral Nelson won the **Battle of Trafalgar** (off the southern coast of Spain, 1805) and destroyed most of the French navy, Napoleon could not invade Britain. In an

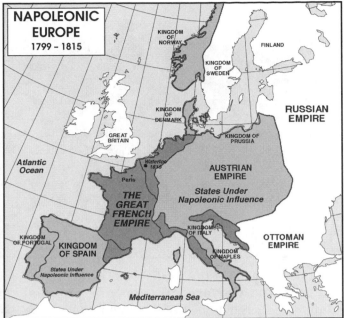

attempt to destroy Britain's economy, Napoleon enacted the **Continental System** (1806), a broad boycott of British trade. This backfired when the British countered with the **Orders in Council** (1807), a naval blockade of the European coast which effectively cut off trade to the Continent. Disenchantment with the Continental System and its hardships were factors in revolutions against Napoleon which broke out in 1808 on the Iberian Peninsula (Spain and Portugal) and in Russia in 1812.

Admiral Nelson (left) defeats Napoleon's French navy at the Battle of Trafalgar off the southern coast of Spain in 1805.

Napoleon's Retreat From Moscow

With the aid of the English, peasants turned to **guerrilla warfare**[1]. The Spanish peasants launched a rebellion in 1808. They harassed large French armies of Joseph Bonaparte (who had been established as King of Spain by his brother) and made it impossible to consolidate French control.

After Tsar Alexander I of Russia withdrew his country from the Continental System, Napoleon undertook an invasion of Russia. In 1812, he assembled the Grand Army of about 600,000 soldiers from France and its allied countries. Expecting a quick victory, Napoleon sent in his army with only summer clothing and supply lines stretching across hostile countries back to France. The Russians successfully employed a **"scorched earth tactic"** (burning and destroying anything of use to the enemy). They withdrew into the interior, destroying everything behind them. When Napoleon reached Moscow in September, he found the city in flames. An early arrival of winter convinced Napoleon to withdraw. Only about 100,000 soldiers survived the Russian Campaign and the rigors of the retreat.

Napoleon's defeat in Russia re-energized his opposition. A coalition defeated him at the **Battle of Nations** (Leipzig, 1814). He was sent into exile to the island of Elba.

The victorious powers met at the **Congress of Vienna** (1814-1815) and attempted to reestablish a balance of power and restore pre-Napoleonic dynasties where possible. While the Congress was meeting, Napoleon escaped from Elba and made one more attempt to achieve victory. However, he was defeated by the allies under the leadership of the English Duke of Wellington at the **Battle of Waterloo** (near Brussels, Belgium, June 1815). Napoleon was sent to his final place of exile, the island of St. Helena in the South Atlantic where he died in 1821.

The era of the French Revolution and Napoleon had a profound effect on France and the other areas of the world. Democratic reforms and a republic as a form of government achieved new popularity. Although the democratic republic in the United States of America was already achieving success, France was an old European country and seemed to be a better model for countries seeking to change from monarchy.

---

1 guerrilla warfare (small, mobile, irregular armed force that takes limited surprise actions as part of a larger political and military strategy)

Duke of Wellington

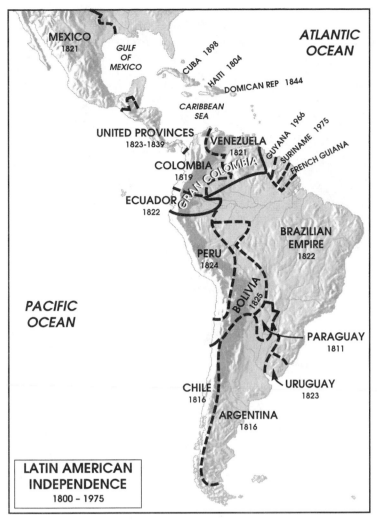

MEXICO
1821

GULF
OF
MEXICO

CUBA 1898

HAITI 1804

DOMICAN REP 1844

CARIBBEAN
SEA

ATLANTIC
OCEAN

UNITED PROVINCES
1823-1839

VENEZUELA
1821

GUYANA 1966

SURINAME 1975

FRENCH GUIANA

COLOMBIA
1819

GRAN COLOMBIA

ECUADOR
1822

BRAZILIAN
EMPIRE
1822

PERU
1824

BOLIVIA
1825

PACIFIC
OCEAN

PARAGUAY
1811

CHILE
1816

URUGUAY
1823

ARGENTINA
1816

**LATIN AMERICAN
INDEPENDENCE
1800 - 1975**

France was unable to control Spain's colonial empire in America because of English control of the seas. After Napoleon's forces seized Lisbon, the Portuguese royal family fled to Brazil to escape capture. This move eventually led to the colony's independence.

Revolutionaries, inspired by the successful movements in France and the United States launched campaigns for independence. The revolutionary movements in Latin America were typically led by **Creoles** (Criollos – Spanish subjects born in the American colonies) who were inspired with the ideas of the Enlightenment. Creole leaders such as **Simon Bolivar** (Colombia), **Jose de San Martin** (Argentina), and **Bernardo O'Higgins** (Chile) all had some military experience a well as direct contact with the United States or Europe.

However, **Toussaint L'Overture**, the leader of the Haitian revolution (1743-1803) was an exception. He was a former slave who had educated himself. In the 1790s, France was distracted by revolution. At the same time, Haitian sugar planters wanted independence but found themselves faced by a slave revolt. In the confusion, L'Overture was able to organize the slaves into a fighting force, and by 1800 the foreigners were ousted. L'Overture then tried to bring the various groups together and start a reform program. However, during a break in the European wars in 1802, Napoleon sent a French army to regain control of the valuable island.

L'Overture was captured and died in a French prison. However, the deaths of many French soldiers from yellow fever convinced Napoleon to abandon Haiti and his dream of re-establishing French power in America. The following year, he sold the sprawling Louisiana Territory to the United States. Haiti declared its independence in 1804, but squabbles among Haitian leaders limited progress for many years.

In 1807, while Spain was under Bonaparte's rule, **Simon Bolivar** (1783-1830) began the fifteen years of the Latin American wars for independence against the royalists. His early attempts were unsuccessful and resulted in his

During the 19th century, revolutions broke out in France, other European states, and other parts of the world as people tried to gain a voice in the government and democratic rights. Napoleon's leadership also promoted tremendous national pride in France. The French Empire became enormous in size, and the military victories intensified nationalism. However, the imperial expansion also led to nationalistic reactions against France's dominance in countries it controlled. Determination to end foreign domination grew. In effect, France's expansion planted the seeds of its own downfall.

REVOLUTIONARY MOVEMENTS IN LATIN AMERICA

The French Revolution and Napoleon's rule gave the people of Latin America an opportunity to end foreign domination and colonialism. From 1805, while the European wars were going on,

flight to Jamaica and Haiti. However, he won a major victory over Spain at the Battle of Boyacain (Colombia) in 1819. By 1821, **Jose de San Martin** (1778-1850) had defeated royalist forces in Argentina, Chile, Ecuador, and Peru with the help of **Bernardo O'Higgins** (1778-1842).

Between 1824 and 1830, Bolivar attempted to unify an area encompassing modern Venezuela, Colombia, Ecuador, and Peru into **Gran Colombia**. Although he was hailed as the "Liberator" and the "George Washington" of South America, Bolivar was unable to overcome the regional differences and saw Gran Colombia split apart by the 1830s.

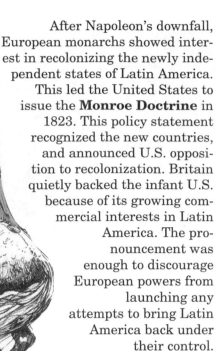
Simon Bolivar

After Napoleon's downfall, European monarchs showed interest in recolonizing the newly independent states of Latin America. This led the United States to issue the **Monroe Doctrine** in 1823. This policy statement recognized the new countries, and announced U.S. opposition to recolonization. Britain quietly backed the infant U.S. because of its growing commercial interests in Latin America. The pronouncement was enough to discourage European powers from launching any attempts to bring Latin America back under their control.

MINI-ASSESSMENT

Mini Assessment

1 Which is an economic cause of the French Revolution?
   1 the Catholic Church's control of education
   2 nobles' exclusive right to wear certain fabrics
   3 existence of an hereditary succession to the throne
   4 tax exemptions for the nobility and clergy

2 Napoleon might be considered the last of the enlightened despots because he
   1 ordered the codification of French law
   2 restored the power of the French Catholic Church
   3 used a democratic plebicite to establish himself as emperor
   4 transmitted French revolutionary ideas throughout Europe

3 Which included the ideas of John Locke?
   1 *The First Estate*
   2 *The Orders in Council*
   3 *The Continental System*
   4 *The Declaration of Independence*

Constructed Response:
Refer to the "Napoleonic Europe" map to answer the following:

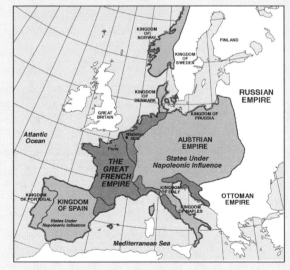

1 Describe the extent to which Napoleon controlled the continent of Europe.

2 Why did Napoleon extend the Great French Empire to control so many coastal areas?

THE REACTION AGAINST REVOLUTIONARY IDEAS

BALANCE OF POWER POLITICS: THE CONGRESS OF VIENNA

A **balance of power**[1] among nations is a stable atmosphere in which no nation or group of nations is able to dominate others. From the time of the Renaissance and the rise of nation-states, European diplomats often sought it by forming alliances.

After the defeat of Napoleon, restoring the balance of power to what it was before the French Revolution became a primary goal of the great powers. In 1814-1815, representatives attended an international meeting convened to reconstruct Europe – the **Congress of Vienna**. The major countries sought a balance of power to prevent any resurgence of French power, to limit Russian influence on the Continent, and to choke off the ideas of the French Revolution.

The ideas of nationalism and democracy were spread throughout Europe by the Napoleonic armies. **Nationalism**[2] is a strong feeling of unity among people who wish to control their own destiny. A nationalist might say, "My nation is as good as any other." However, a **chauvinist**[3] (an extreme nationalist) might say, "My nation is better than any other." In order to stop any further spread of revolutionary ideas, such as democracy and nationalism, most of the Congress' participants favored restoring the pre-1789 rulers or their heirs under what they termed the **principle of legitimacy**.

Each of the major participants at the Congress had specific goals. The actions taken represented compromises by all involved, but Minister Talleyrand skillfully negotiated so that little harm was done to France. The key players at the Congress included:

- Austria's **Prince Metternich** (1773-1859) – wanted to restore the pre-revolution system of government and rulers and limit Prussian power within the German States

- Russia's **Tsar Alexander I** (1777-1825) – wanted to gain control of Poland and establish a system of collective security

- England's **Lord Castlereagh** (1769-1822) – wanted to maintain British control of the seas and increase British colonial holdings

- France's **Foreign Minister Talleyrand** (1754-1838) – wanted to prevent French territorial loss and restore French prestige and position in Europe

The **Quadruple Alliance** (1815) of Austria, Prussia, Russia, and England included a pledge to provide troops to preserve the Congress of Vienna settlements. England eventually dropped out, disturbed by some of the anti-democratic actions taken. France took England's place in the alliance. The **Holy Alliance** (1815), proposed by Alexander I, was also signed by the major powers except for England. It pledged the monarchs to rule by the Christian principles of charity, peace, and justice. Faced with revolutions and challenges to their power, monarchs ignored their idealistic pledges. Since there was no way to enforce such an unrealistic proposal, the alliance never worked.

The Congress of Vienna settlement helped to prevent an outbreak of an all-European war for about 100 years. However, there were many revolutions within that time period. The Congress

---

1 balance of power (distribution of power in which no single nation is able to dominate or interfere with others)
2 nationalism (belief that nations will benefit from acting independently rather than collectively, emphasizing national rather than international goals; individual nationalism – feeling good about loyalty and patriotism)
3 chauvinist (militant devotion to and glorification of one's country; fanatical patriotism)

KEY ACTIONS OF CONGRESS OF VIENNA

- Establishment of the "Rhine Barrier" – a group of strong nations along the eastern border of France – designed to prevent French invasion of Central and Eastern Europe

- Confirmation of British acquisition of areas such as Malta, Cape Colony, and Ceylon

- Restoration of the monarchs in France (Louis XVIII) and Spain (Ferdinand VII)

- Acquisition of part of Poland by Alexander I and part of Saxony by Prussia

- Imposition of minor territorial losses on France along with an indemnity (payment for war damages)

- Establishment of a German Confederation under Austrian control

of Vienna settlement moved people from one government to another without their consent. For example, the Congress gave Belgium to the Netherlands, but its people were given no voice in the decision. Also, the Congress failed to unify either the German or the Italian states despite the wishes of many of the people. The Quadruple Alliance was designed to prevent revolution by stifling democracy and nationalism. Initially, the Alliance stopped some revolutions. However, the national self-interest of the major powers sometimes promoted nationalism and democracy, and some revolutions succeeded.

THE REVOLUTIONS OF 1848

In the 1820s, in 1830, and again in 1848, revolutions broke out in Europe. Many of them protested the Congress of Vienna settlement and reflected the strength of nationalism and democracy. Liberals demanded written constitutions, government protection of citizen rights, and the establishment of republics.

However, only in Greece, Belgium, and Latin America did such revolutions succeed. In 1830, a major revolution broke out in France. As a consequence, Charles X (successor to Louis XVIII) was replaced by Louis Philippe, Duke of Orleans. He was also known as the "Bourgeois Monarch" because of his support of the middle class.

In 1848, the French again revolted against their government to establish a new one that would protect the interests of all groups. According to Metternich, "when France sneezes,

all Europe catches cold" – and once again the spirit of revolution spread throughout the continent (see chart below).

Reactionary governments were able to re-establish their power after the revolutions. However, in many cases they began a series of economic reforms, fought corruption, and ended serfdom to justify their power. Still, little was done to improve individual freedoms or provide unity for national groups.

RUSSIAN ABSOLUTISM: REFORMS AND EXPANSION

During the Napoleonic Wars, French revolutionary ideas spread to Russian troops through their contact with the people of other nations. One result was the **Decembrist Revolution** (1825) – the first Russian revolution for democracy.

There was a dispute over inheritance of the throne after the death of Tsar Alexander I. Inspired by democratic ideals, some military officers demanded the throne for Alexander's older brother with the cry of "Constantine and Constitution." However, the succession was already decided in favor of the reactionary **Nicholas I** (1825-1855), a younger brother.

Nicholas established a government which stressed "orthodoxy, autocracy, and nationalism." This translated into domination by the Russian Orthodox Church, the Tsar, and the Great Russians – the dominant nationality group in Russia. Nicholas harshly suppressed his opposition. In fact, his conservative rule

KEY REVOLUTIONS OF 1848		
Country & Revolutionaries	**Causes**	**Results**
France workers and lower bourgeoisie	corruption, limited representation in legislature, government attempts to suppress opposition	Louis Philippe abdicated; republic formed with universal male suffrage; Louis Napoleon Bonaparte elected president
Austria national groups (Poles, Magyars, Italians)	desire for independence and/or self government	Metternich fled; nationalism suppressed by using one group against another
Germany Liberals	civil rights; desire for unity among the 39 German states	Frankfort Assembly failed to resolve promptly the question of Austrian inclusion; conservatives regained control; many German liberals fled to the U.S.

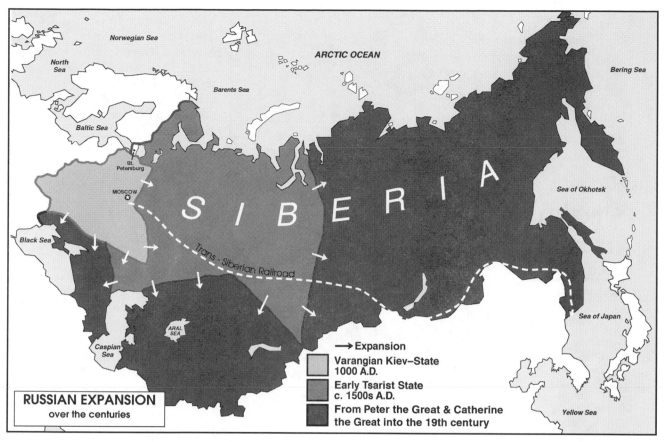

RUSSIAN EXPANSION
over the centuries

→ Expansion

Varangian Kiev–State
1000 A.D.

Early Tsarist State
c. 1500s A.D.

From Peter the Great & Catherine
the Great into the 19th century

resisted the outbreak of revolutions that swept Europe in 1848. He even aided in suppressing some in other countries.

While most serfs in Europe received their freedom after the 1848 revolutions, most Russian serfs remained the property of nobles or the government. In the 1770s, during Catherine the Great's reign, a serf rebellion led to a tightening of restrictions on serfs and placed more power in the hands of the land owners.

However, the devastating loss of the **Crimean War** (1854-1856) led Russia to a re-examination of serfdom. The government of **Alexander II** (1855-1881) accepted the idea that serfs made poor soldiers and moved to free them. The **Emancipation Edict** (1861) legally freed the peasants and made loans available for them to purchase about 50 per cent of the nobles' land. However, a noble could decide which land to sell and ownership was given to the *mir* (community or village), not the individual peasant.

The settlement of Siberia began during the early years of Romanov rule (17th century). Often, the first settlements east of the Urals were established by escaped serfs. Later, adventurers, traders, and trappers moved farther into the interior. Most settlements were along waterways, but Cossacks reached the Pacific Ocean in 1639. Eventually, Russian adventurers crossed the Bering Straits, entered Alaska, and moved down the coast of North America. Others penetrated the Amur River Valley where they encountered resistance from the Chinese. The harsh climate made it difficult to obtain permanent settlers.

Exiles being forced marched in Siberia

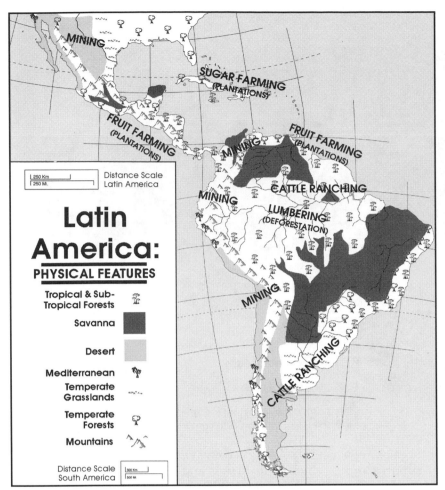

Latin America: PHYSICAL FEATURES

MINING

SUGAR FARMING (PLANTATIONS)

FRUIT FARMING (PLANTATIONS)

FRUIT FARMING (PLANTATIONS)

MINING

CATTLE RANCHING

MINING

LUMBERING (DEFORESTATION)

MINING

CATTLE RANCHING

Distance Scale Latin America
250 Km
250 Mi.

Distance Scale South America
300 Km
500 Mi.

Tropical & Sub-Tropical Forests

Savanna

Desert

Mediterranean

Temperate Grasslands

Temperate Forests

Mountains

The Atacama Desert in Chile and the rain forest of the Amazon River further complicated this problem. Difficult terrain made drawing boundaries a problem. The result has been continuing bitter border disputes.

Geography also contributed to differing economic interests among the people. Some influential criollos had sugar plantations; others were involved in mining, cattle ranching, or commerce. The different sources of wealth led to disagreement on government policies and an inability to unite.

Class differences, dating from the colonial period, also contributed to disunity. By the 19th century, Peninsulares, the Spanish-born elite, were disappearing. However, important class differences remained.

Eventually, the tsarist government used Siberia for internal political exile. This was the fate of those found guilty in the 1825 Decembrist uprising. People found guilty of opposing the government were sentenced to work on government farms or projects in Siberia. The real opening of the area came with the construction of the Trans-Siberian Railroad which began in 1891. The government wanted to utilize the forests, fur-bearing animals, and mineral wealth of the area. The government offered settlement incentives and higher wages, but large areas remained uninhabited.

LATIN AMERICA: THE FAILURE OF DEMOCRACY AND THE SEARCH FOR STABILITY

Geography is a major reason South America failed to unite after the revolutions led by Simon Bolivar (1808-1824). The Andes Mountains separated people and made communication difficult.

CRIOLLOS
Spanish born in America, wealthy and educated, had top positions

MESTIZOS
mixed Native American and European, lower middle class, merchants, managers, farmers

NATIVE AMERICANS
worked for others on haciendas, in mines

FREED BLACKS
laborers, some in skilled trades

SLAVES
property of owners, had some rights, could purchase freedom

CLASSES IN LATIN AMERICA IN THE EARLY 19TH CENTURY

In addition to problems of geography and class differences, Latin Americans had little governmental experience. This was a factor in the emergence of oligarchies controlled by the educated landholding elite, the Roman Catholic Church, and the military. Often, the leadership was drawn from the same families. This triangular leadership pattern reflected conservative policies. To retain power, these leaders placed limits on freedoms and ignored needed land reform. Power struggles within such ruling groups usually led to the emergence of a **caudillo** (strong man). With the aid of the military, directly or indirectly, caudillos dominated their countries over long periods of time.

Economic policies highlighted class differences. Spanish colonial mercantilism was followed by similar policies after independence. Areas became dependent on raw materials for export in the global market. Often an area would be dependent on one crop or product such as coffee, sugar, wheat, or beef. Working for plantation owners left peasants with little time or land to produce necessary subsistence crops.

One crop economies are fragile. A changeable climate or a change in world market conditions often led to economic disaster. Also, raw materials bring in less income than manufacturing finished products. This led to an ongoing trade deficit. These economic conditions increased demands for reform.

Nineteenth century Mexico also saw periods of foreign interference. In the 1830s caudillo General Santa Anna (1795-1876), became angry when the United States supported the Texans' drive for independence against him. The battle for Texas is capsuled in the 13 day siege of a Spanish mission, The Alamo, by Santa Anna's army of more than 5,000. After 12 days of continual cannonades, The Alamo fell and all 185-190 defenders were killed. Ultimately, Santa Anna was defeated by General Sam Houston and forced to acknowledge the independence of Texas (1836). Later, Santa Anna was removed from power by Mexican opponents after losing almost half of Mexico's territory to the United States in the Mexican War (1846-1848). This led to a nationalistic reaction in Mexico, resentment against the United States, and another struggle between liberals and conservatives.

In 1861, **Benito Juarez** (1806-1872), a liberal, and the first Indian to be elected President of Mexico took office. Shortly afterward, Emperor Napoleon III of France intervened in Mexico because of unpaid debts. He tried to take over the country by placing Austrian Archduke Maximilian on the Mexican throne. The scheme failed when Napoleon III withdrew French forces reacting to American threats at the end of its Civil War. Juarez was reelected in 1867 and tried to implement a reform program to decrease the power of the Roman Catholic Church and the landlords. He was successful in separating Church and state, but was not able to carry out all of his reforms.

After an interlude of representative government, a revolt broke out in 1876. Another caudillo, **Porfirio Diaz** (1830-1915), was in power for most of the 1877-1910 period. He strengthened the central government and carried out some economic reforms. However, Native Americans saw their lands seized and sold. Many

CLOSE LOOK

MEXICAN REVOLUTIONS

The **Mexican Revolution** of 1910-1930 shows the impact of class differences. The Revolution had its origins in the 1810 struggle for independence against Spain led by Father **Miguel Hidalgo** (1753-1811) whose protests on the part of peasants led to an uprising of the Mestizos and Native Americans. Hidalgo was captured by the Spanish and executed in 1811, but his demands for land reform alienated the Criollos. In the next 100 years, the land-owning Criollos, the Church, and the military were on one side; on the other side were the liberals who were concerned about the rights of the Mestizos and Native Americans.

were forced to become **peons** (laborers heavily in debt to landowners). Diaz was forced to resign in 1911. A liberal government was elected, but revolution soon broke out. A number of leaders with different agendas emerged during the revolution:

- **Pancho Villa** (1877-1923) – a colorful figure with a strong peasant following whom the U.S. refused to support because of alleged brutalities; retaliated against the U.S. by stopping trains and shooting Americans

- **Emiliano Zapata** (1880-1918) – a Native American with understanding of peasants' problems; supported freeing peons from debts and giving them land

- **Venistiano Carranza** (1859-1920) – a liberal who wanted a new constitution with government control over education, farms, and oil reserves; seizure of Church land; and limits on foreign ownership of land

Carranza was elected president in 1917. He created a new constitution before he was killed in a revolt in 1920. Implementation was delayed, but government stability increased and some reforms were carried out.

In 1929, the Institutional Revolutionary Party (PRI) was formed. Its one party approach limited opposition for many years, but it did support some social reform and diminished foreign involvement in the economy. Rising opposition, a number of scandals, assassinations, and economic problems plagued the PRI with instability into the late 20th century.

Mini Assessment

MINI-ASSESSMENT

1 In launching the Mexican Revolution in 1810, Father Manuel Hidalgo differed from other South American revolutionary leaders because he
1 lacked military experience
2 had no sympathy for Native Americans
3 opposed land reform
4 sided with the Church, the Criollos, and the military

2 The Russian *Emancipation Edict of 1861* provided the serfs with
1 private ownership of land
2 loans to help purchase land from nobles
3 freedom from military service
4 education and training in agricultural technology

3 The actions of the Congress of Vienna could be described as
1 victories for the concepts of nationalism and democracy
2 eliminating the causes of European Revolutions during the 19th century
3 successful in avoiding major European wars for about 100 years
4 making few changes in the boundaries of European countries

Constructed Response:

Using the map on page 154 as your information source, answer both of the following:

1 List three sources of 19th century wealth in Latin America.

2 Why did the natural environment make Latin American unity difficult?

Distance Scale
Latin America

Latin America:
PHYSICAL FEATURES

Tropical & Sub-Tropical Forests

Savanna

Desert

Mediterranean

Temperate Grasslands

Temperate Forests

Mountains

Distance Scale
South America

GLOBAL NATIONALISM

NATIONALISM'S ROLE IN POLITICAL REVOLUTIONS

Nationalism is an unusual force, because it acts in a variety of ways. It can work to bring people together as it did in the case of the Italian and German States. However, it can also work to pull apart existing countries. After World War I (1914-1918), national groups within Austria-Hungary revolted and the empire disintegrated into a number of small nation-states such as Poland, Hungary, and Czechoslovakia. In recent times, the world witnessed the breakup of Yugoslavia and Czechoslovakia, and nationalism continually threatens the unity of Canada and the Balkan countries. Also, it was certainly a factor in the breakup of the Soviet Union.

A number of different factors contribute to the development of national feeling – common goals, purpose, language, religion, history, government, culture, and tradition. Not all these factors need to be present for nationalism to exist. For example, there is nationalism in the United States, but there is no religious unity.

NATIONALISM'S ROLE IN THE UNIFICATION OF ITALY AND GERMANY

During the 19th century, Germany and Italy were unified as nation-states after struggles that date back to the late Middle Ages. The Italian Peninsula was the site of frequent wars among countries such as Austria, France, and Spain. Each wanted to prevent the others from controlling the area's wealth. The issue was further complicated by the Papal States. They stretched across the center of the Peninsula.

To unify Italy, territory had to be taken from the Papacy. However, during the reign of Napoleon I of France, a number of Italian states became part of his Kingdom of Italy and experienced a sense of unity. The Congress of Vienna ignored the desire of the Italians for their own nation and restored the Papal States and Austrian control over much of the area.

UNIFICATION OF THE GERMAN AND ITALIAN STATES
19th Century

The early history of the German States is similar. The Holy Roman Empire, a loose union of German states under Austrian control, dominated the area for centuries. Napoleon abolished some of the German States and placed the others under his control in the Confederation of the Rhine.

In 1815, the Congress of Vienna reduced the number of German states and established a German Confederation under Austrian control. This arrangement ignored the Germans' desires for a national state. Both Italy and Germany were fortunate to have nationalist leaders emerge who performed similar functions (see charts on the following page).

NATIONAL UNIFICATION LEADERS – ITALY

Leader	Leadership Role	Main Idea
Joseph Mazzini (1805-1872)	provided inspiration with pamphlets; organized Young Italy movement; he was called "the soul of Risorgimento" (Italian unification process)	duty to nation fits between duty to family and God
Camillo di Cavour (1810-1861)	provided political leadership; as prime minister of Sardinia-Piedmont, did much diplomatic work for unification	sought to create a constitutional monarchy
Guiseppe Garibaldi (1807-1882)	provided military leadership; Red Shirt campaigns helped free the Two Sicilies; he was called "the sword of Italian unification"	sought to create a republic, but accepted Cavour's ideas to achieve unification

NATIONAL UNIFICATION LEADERS – GERMANY

Leader	Leadership Role	Main Idea
Johann Fichte (1762-1814)	provided inspiration in his *Addresses to the German Nation* and his chauvinistic opposition to France	believed German people were better than others, urged them to keep race pure and to unify
Otto von Bismarck (1815-1898)	provided political leadership as chancellor of Prussia	believed in *realpolitik* – that governments should follow their own best interests, used diplomacy and military force ("Blood and Iron") to affect unification
Helmuth von Moltke (1800-1891)	provided successful military leadership against opponents	combined discipline and technology to create modern fighting force to achieve unification

After Austria's defeat in the Austro-Prussian War (1866), Prussia gained leadership of the German states. Prussia established a union of the German states called the **North German Confederation**. Also as a result of the Austro-Prussian War, Sardinia-Piedmont gained control of key Italian territories (Venetia and Lombardy). This led other Austrian dominated states in northern Italy to conduct **plebiscites**[1] and vote to join Sardinia-Piedmont.

When Prussia won the **Franco-Prussian War** (1870-1871), France was occupied by German troops. As part of the settlement, France turned over Alsace-Lorraine and was forced to pay a large **indemnity**[2] to Prussia. In the same war, Italy gained control of most of the Papal States when the French withdrew their protective forces

to fight Prussia. The war contributed greatly to the unification of both Germany and Italy.

---

1 plebiscite (vote in which a population exercises the right of national self-determination)
2 indemnity (financial compensation for damage)

Franco–Prussian War – French soldiers in retreat toward Paris

The wars that surrounded German unification had important consequences for the balance of power in Europe. For example, the Franco-Prussian War demonstrated the weakness of France. It raised other powers' concern about possible German control of Europe. German Chancellor Bismarck realized that nationalism might drive France to seek revenge. To guard against this, he created alliances which played a significant role in the outbreak of World War I.

NATIONALISM'S ROLE IN INDIA, PALESTINE, AND TURKEY

Nationalism became a factor in political life beyond Europe. In the late 19th century, it played a key role in opposition to foreign control and intervention. Indian nationalism arose out of opposition to British imperialism. Vietnamese nationalism opposed French imperialism. Turkish nationalism arose out of opposition to European intervention.

In general, nationalism in the developing areas involved fewer common elements than it did in the Western World. Consequently, when foreign control or intervention eventually ended, different language, religious, and tribal groups often fought each other and tore new nations apart.

In the early 19th century, Britain made several decisions that influenced Indian nationalism. At the urging of **Thomas Babington Macaulay** (1800-1859), a prominent British historian, Britain instructed Indians in English. Educated Indians were admitted to the civil service and the Governor's Council. Also, many wealthy Indians traveled to Britain for their higher education. There, they learned of basic individual rights in parliamentary democracies. When the students returned home, they demanded an increased role in the government.

To maintain control, the British played the Hindus against the Muslims ("divide and control"). This led to the formation of the **Hindu Indian National Congress** in 1885 and the **All-India Moslem League** in 1906. These orga-

nizations fostered nationalism, but religion was a factor in membership. The drive for independence remained divided. Yet, the British responded to some of their demands for more governmental power after World War I.

In the Middle East, nationalism played a role in drawing together diverse people seeking a homeland. The **Zionist Movement's** goal was to secure a Jewish homeland in Palestine. It sought to create a nation where Jews from all over the world could seek refuge and find a national identity. In 1897, **Theodor Herzl** (1860-1904) organized the first Zionist Congress in Basel, Switzerland. It led to the founding of the World Zionist Organization.

The roots of **Zionism**[1] go back to the 6th century BC Diaspora – the dispersion of the Hebrews after their captivity in Babylon. Hebrew prophets such as Jeremiah said that they would return to Jerusalem, and many believed that this was their destiny.

Modern Zionism developed out of a reaction against the anti-semitism that existed in Europe. The **pogroms**[2] against Jews in Russia and other countries led many of them to migrate to the West. A small number also went to Palestine. As a consequence, the dispersion of Jews became even more widespread. (Jews had been scattered into many areas of the world since the Roman Sack of Palestine in 70 AD.) However, the Zionist dream of a resurrected homeland remained strong.

Turkish nationalism developed in part as opposition to foreign intervention. The location of the Ottoman Empire on both sides of the straits of the Dardanelles and Bosporus put it in conflict with the interests of Russia, Austria-Hungary, Britain, and France.

The Ottomans suffered further humiliation due to **capitulations**[3] that foreign powers forced on them. The loss of parts of their North African and Middle Eastern Empire to European imperialists deepened their resentment. After the **Crimean War** (1854-1856), the Ottoman Empire failed to modernize and to separate church and state. The government of Abdul Hamid (1876-1909) established absolute power and forced exile on reformers such as the **Young Turks**.

---

1 Zionism (organized movement of world Jewry that arose in Europe in the late 19th century with the aim of reestablishing a Jewish state in Palestine)
2 pogrom (organized, often officially encouraged massacre or persecution of a minority group, especially one conducted against Jews)
3 capitulations (terms of surrender giving special privileges to the conqueror)

The Ottoman government's attempts to control its Balkan peninsula territory led to massacres in Bulgaria (1876) and in Armenia (1894). An 1870s revolt by the Ottoman's Slavic subjects provided Russia with an excuse for the **Russo-Turkish War** (1877-1878). The resulting Congress of Berlin led to a further dismemberment of the Ottoman Empire. The Young Turks gained power in 1908 and began a series of reforms.

INTERNAL REFORMS OF THE YOUNG TURKS

* A separation of church and state
* Adoption of Western dress
* More freedom for women
* Adoption of Western-style law codes

Kemal Ataturk

World War I interfered with implementation of the Young Turks' reforms. Not until after the Turkish republic was proclaimed in 1923, under the leadership of **Kemal Ataturk** (1923-1938), did the revolutionary changes take effect.

self-government. These factors created tensions that resulted in the area being called the "powder keg" or the "tinderbox." It was no surprise that World War I originated in the Balkans.

European involvement in the Ottoman Empire triggered nationalism in the Balkans – a key cause of World War I. Three large, multinational empires – the Austria-Hungarian, Ottoman, and Russian – also had interests in the peninsula. Each empire was weakening and became concerned about holding its territory and areas of interest. Each wanted to expand while preventing the others from seizing land.

Some parts of the Balkans received independence as a result of the Crimean and Russo-Turkish Wars. Still, the relationships remained complex. For example, while Bosnia-Herzegovina was technically owned by the Ottomans, it was governed by the Austrians.

At the same time, the Slavic inhabitants looked to Russia for leadership. The people of the area resented foreign control and wanted

BALKAN EMPIRES
19th Century

Mini Assessment

1 Which of the following headlines reflects strong feelings of nationalism?
    1 *GERMANS WIN GLORIOUS VICTORY OVER FRENCH*
    2 *U.N. PEACEKEEPERS SUCCESSFUL IN CONGO*
    3 *IRISH "TROUBLES" END IN ACCORD*
    4 *ARABS AND ISRAELIS SIGN TRUCE*

2 The Ottoman Empire (modern Turkey) has long been an area of interest to international powers because it
    1 has vast oil reserves
    2 commands the approach to the Suez Canal
    3 contains archaeological sites relevant to the first humans
    4 controls the Straits of the Dardanelles and Bosporus

3 Immediately after gaining independence, violence often occurs in an area as ethnic or religious groups struggle for control. A country whose history illustrates this idea is
    1 Turkey   3 India
    2 Germany   4 Italy

Constructed Response:

Use the diagram below to answer the following:

1 What non-war factors provided a basis for German nationalism?

2 Why do wars often lead to an increase in nationalism in countries involved in them?

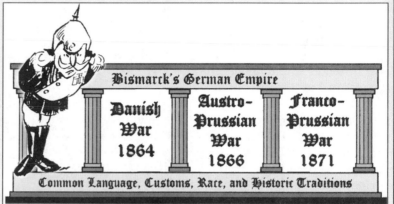

ECONOMIC AND SOCIAL REVOLUTIONS

AGRARIAN REVOLUTION – BRITAIN AND FRANCE

Revolutions involve major change, but they are not always political nor are they necessarily violent. This was true of the Agricultural and Industrial Revolutions of the 18th and 19th centuries. For agricultural changes to occur, it was necessary to move from the Medieval three-field system and strip farming to a situation where larger plots could be farmed to accommodate new methods and feed a growing population.

In the 16th century, world-wide demand for woolen textiles increased. The domestic system blossomed. In England, the wool market developed as England built up its navy, expanded its influence, and acquired colonies. Throughout Europe, demand prompted landlords to fence their open lands into enclosed pastures for sheep. The English Parliament passed a series of **Enclosure Acts** (16th-19th centuries). These acts allowed rich landlords to pay for surveys that forced small farmers off lands they had farmed since Medieval times. As time passed, these displaced agricultural workers migrated to towns and became factory and mine workers.

At the same time, the Agrarian Revolution was accelerating. New methods of production allowed cultivation of larger areas. Larger farms increased per capita production. Also, members of the nobility involved themselves in production and commerce, because it did not lead to loss of

INNOVATIONS OF THE AGRARIAN REVOLUTION

Researcher	Technology	Importance
Jethro Tull (1674-1741)	Seed Drill	Enabled large-scale planting of seeds in rows and at even depth
Charles "Turnip" Townshend (1674-1738)	Crop Rotation	Devised a sophisticated system of crop rotation to enhance natural fertility of soils (turnips were included)
Robert Bakewell (1725-1795)	Scientific Breeding	Increased weight and availability of beef

status. For example, one of the most prominent of the British agricultural innovators was Secretary of State Viscount Charles Townshend (1674-1738).

The Agricultural Revolution progressed less rapidly on the European Continent. France is an example. Key elements of the Medieval system were still present at the time of the French Revolution (1789). Serfdom was abolished by revolutionary action, but the Napoleonic Code of Laws provided for equality of inheritance for all heirs. France became a country of small farms, less suited to the changes found in large-scale agricultural production methods.

The changes in methods and the new inventions tremendously increased agricultural output in Britain. The efforts of three men were particularly significant in the early stages of the Agricultural Revolution - Jethro Tull, Charles Townshend, and Robert Bakewell (see chart).

During the 18th century, such innovators' work resulted in grain yields that increased from 6 to 20 bushels per acre and doubled the weight of mature cattle.

THE INDUSTRIAL REVOLUTION

The Industrial Revolution began in Britain about 1750. There are a number of reasons why Britain was the first country to experience this change. These included their:

- Domestic system
- Access to seas and good harbors
- Availability of labor
- Coal and iron resources
- Capital availability and willingness to risk it
- Supportive government policies
- Patent system

As expected, the first industry to be affected was textiles. Earlier, this industry had been

TECHNOLOGICAL MILESTONES OF THE INDUSTRIAL REVOLUTION

	Inventor	Invention	Effect
TEXTILES	John Kay (1704-1764)	Flying Shuttle	Doubled speed of weavers
	James Hargreaves (1730-1778)	Spinning Jenny	Could spin 8-20 threads at once
	Richard Arkwright (1732-1792)	Water Frame	Used water power; factories developed; could spin 48-300 threads at once
	Samuel Crompton (1753-1827)	Spinning Mule	Combined jenny and water frame; could spin fine thread
	Edmund Cartwright (1743-1823)	Power Loom	1st application of power to weaving
TRANSPORTATION	James Watt (1736-1819)	Steam Engine	New source of power allowed many applications and the location of factories in many different places
	George Stephenson (1781-1848)	Steam Locomotive	Faster land transportation
	Thomas Telford (1757-1783) and John MacAdam (1756-1836)	Hard Surfaced Roads	Faster land transportation in all kinds of weather

part of the **domestic system**[1]. Inability to meet the demand for wool cloth led men involved in production to invent new ways to increase output. The **factory system**[2] is an advanced method of industrial organization. Through discipline and supervision, a large number of laborers work in a centralized place and process materials through coordinated steps into manufactured goods.

Domestic transportation underwent a similar change. The need to move large quantities of goods around England made it necessary to improve roads and develop new methods of transportation.

Continental Europe was a little slower than Britain to embrace the changes. Many countries were distracted by domestic problems, new political systems, revolutions, and wars in the early part of the 19th century. After 1870, the Industrial Revolution spread quickly. The Low Countries were already industrializing, and France and a newly unified Germany moved forward rapidly.

An abundance of coal and iron resources were a major factor in Germany's industrial growth. By 1900, Germany was producing more steel than Britain. By 1914, Britain, France, and Germany produced over 80 per cent of Europe's coal, steel, and machinery. Germany also developed a substantial chemical industry prior to World War I. Two German inventors, **Gottlieb Daimler** (1834-1900) and **Rudolf Diesel** (1858-1913), played major roles in the development of automobile engines.

The tremendous jumps in production led to increased demand for raw materials to feed the machines. Demand for markets in which to sell surplus products also arose. These demands were primary causes of the new era of imperialism which began about 1870 (see next section).

Despite adverse conditions in the mines and factories, people eventually improved the quality of their lives. The Industrial Revolution led to an increase in size and importance of the middle class. The new **entrepreneurial system**[3] was open to men of talent.

CLOSE LOOK

THE FACTORY SYSTEM

The factory system brought many changes to the lifestyles of the people. Very rapidly, people moved from the rural green countryside to urban areas. They found themselves in the slums of areas such as Manchester, England. The cities were unprepared for rapid industrial growth. Unpaved streets, polluted rivers and streams, and crowded housing were common problems. Men, women, and children worked long hours under often dangerous conditions. It was not unusual for children 5 to 6 years old to work 14 to 16 hours per day. Factory owners took few voluntary safety precautions, and serious injuries occurred. Often, a parent could not obtain a job unless he/she had a child who could also work in the factory. There were no social welfare laws to protect children. Small hands, lower pay, and fewer discipline problems made child labor desirable for the factory owner. Women and children also worked beside men in mines. The dangers of explosions, black lung disease, and back injuries made the mines dangerous places.

Factory managers, merchants, and shopkeepers shared in the increased prosperity. British inventor Sir **Richard Arkwright** (1732-1792) was originally a barber who made a fortune with his water frame.

Non-Anglican Protestant dissenters, denied university educations and jobs in the government or military turned to manufacturing. Wealth joined birth as a criteria for status.

1 domestic system (work was done in the home or in small workshops)
2 factory system (coordinates a large number of laborers and power-driven machines in a centralized place)
3 entrepreneurial system (individuals organize, operate, and assume the risk for business ventures)

CONFLICTING ECONOMIC PHILOSOPHIES

Mercantilism	Laissez-faire
• Government should control the economy	• Government should minimize its involvement in the economy ("keep its hands off")
• Colonial economies should be controlled to benefit the mother country	• Attempts to control colonial economies violate natural rights
• Wealth is accumulation of gold and silver	• Wealth is productive resources
• Low wages and long hours are necessary to meet competition	• Higher wages and shorter hours lead to increased demand for goods

During the 19th century, many nations abandoned the tightly controlled protective trade policies of mercantilism and supported Adam Smith's doctrine of **laissez-faire**[1]. In 1776, Smith published his views in *The Wealth of Nations*. However, it was not until the mid-19th century that the British government came to accept his ideas. Smith's followers also formed a free trade movement to allow goods to flow more freely across national boundaries. When the British dropped major trade restrictions in 1846, France quickly did the same. However, the Depression of 1873 demonstrated how vulnerable markets were in the new global economy. At that point, many countries restored tariffs and government regulation of industry.

While many people supported laissez-faire capitalism, others blamed it for the abuses found in the factories and mines. Smith's opponents felt that the long hours, low wages, along with poor working and living conditions were a result of a failure of society and the government. As a consequence, a number of ideologies emerged that offered solutions to the problems (see chart).

Beyond the mainstream ideologies, another group of reformers called themselves **utopian socialists**[2]. Utopias are ideal societies in which the state functions for the good and happiness of all. **Count de Saint Simon** (Claude Henri de Rouvroy, 1760-1825) favored planned societies with public ownership of the means of production. **Charles Fourier** (1772-1837) favored ideal communities where all shared in the work and received the benefits of joint labor according to need.

The most famous utopian socialist was **Robert Owen** (1771-1858) of Britain. He became manager of a cotton mill at age nineteen. With the help of investors, he later purchased the entire town of New Lanark, Scotland. He provided decent housing, basic education, and an inexpensive company store for the workers. He also forbade work for the youngest children, decreased working hours for all, and increased wages, but still made a profit. Many famous people came to see his experiment, but few followed the example. Later, he founded a community at New Harmony, Indiana in the United States where people worked together for their joint improvement. The New Harmony experiment failed, and Owen returned to England and worked with consumer coopera-

---

1 laissez-faire (opposes governmental regulation or interference in commerce beyond the minimum)
2 utopia (ideally perfect place, especially in its social, political, and moral aspects) socialists (members of a system in which the means of producing and distributing goods are owned collectively)

POLITICAL IDEOLOGIES

Ideology	Ideas
Liberalism	supports parliamentary / representative government; for laissez-faire; against universal male suffrage
Conservatism	favors absolute monarchy, aristocracy, church; supports government control of economy; slow change, if at all
Socialism	favors parliamentary government, universal male suffrage; against laissez-faire and competition in market place; wants more even distribution of wealth

MARX'S IDEAS

Ideas	Explanation	Weaknesses
Economic Interpretation of History	Economic factors determine the course of history and those who control the means of production will control the society.	Does not account for other major causes of historical events (Crusades, religious wars, and nationalist wars).
Class Struggle	Throughout history, there have been struggles between the "haves" and "have-nots." In the Industrial Era, Marx claimed the struggles were between capitalists and proletariat.	Does not consider the cooperation between the proletariat and capitalists to increase production or profit-sharing arrangements.
Surplus Value Theory	"Price of product minus cost of labor equals surplus value." – here, Marx says the surplus value goes to the capitalists, but should go to the workers who produce the product.	Does not consider the need to provide a return for the capitalist who risks his resources and provides managerial services.
Inevitability of Socialism	Over the long period of time, overproduction will result in bankruptcies, and depressions will occur. Conditions will get so bad that the proletariat will revolt and establish a dictatorship of the proletariat.	This has not come true. Communism has not gained control in countries already significantly industrialized. Its greatest inroads have come in agrarian economies.

tives and the labor movement.

Very different ideas about solving the problems of the Industrial Revolution came from **Karl Marx** (1818-1883) and **Friedrich Engles** (1820-1895). In 1848, they joined together to produce the ***Communist Manifesto***, a pamphlet intended for workers. Later, Marx wrote a multi-volume work, ***Das Kapital*** (1st vol. published in 1867), which further explained his ideas. In it, he used past history and the existing problems of the Industrial Revolution as the basis for predicting the future (see chart above).

Marx rejected utopian ideas and considered himself to be a "scientific socialist." He claimed that his ideas were based on fact and that history inevitably led to their fulfillment. He felt they were based on the hope that world economic justice would increase and that the upper class would become sympathetic to the lower class. Marx also believed that a detailed description of his communist society would make it appear to be utopian. Therefore, he left little description of his society or how long it would take to achieve. He did state, however, that the government would own the means of production with a "**dictatorship of the proletariat**" (workers). Marx believed that only after class differences disappeared could the government "wither away."

While Marx's ideas seemed extreme, they did receive support from some of the proletariat. Ironically, his writings may have helped to pre-

vent the proletarian revolution he expected. In some of his later essays and letters, Marx admitted that democratic countries, such as Britain and the U.S., might be able to bring about change peacefully.

To address some of the problems of the Industrial Revolution, Britain's Parliament established two commissions. In 1832, the Sadler Report led to debates on factory conditions that resulted in the **Factory Act** (1833). It prohibited the labor of children under nine in textile factories. The Ashley Report (1842) triggered debates on mining and led to the **Mines Act**. It prohibited the underground labor of women and children under ten. Later, the **Ten Hours Act** (1847) limited the work day for women and children to ten hours.

Concern about revolution did lead some governments to modify their laissez-faire stance in the late 19th and early 20th centuries. In Europe and America, governments instituted reforms to improve conditions for the workers:

• Labor unions were legalized
• Restrictions were placed on big business
• Governments tried to limit the drastic "boom and bust" swings of the business cycle.

The Industrial Era triggered political reforms, too. The increasing demand by the middle class for a voice in the government was a major factor

PARLIAMENT BROADENS VOTING RIGHTS	
Reform Bill of	**Group Affected**
1832	middle class males
1867	urban workers (males)
1884	farm workers (males)
1918	universal male suffrage and women over 30
1928	universal suffrage
1969	lowered voting age to 18

in the passage of the **Great Reform Bill of 1832.** It gave middle class males the right to vote. The Bill abolished most **rotten boroughs**[1] and gave the seats to the new or growing industrial areas. Still, the working class felt left out. Workers started the **Chartist Movement** to gain the **franchise** (right to vote) and other governmental reforms. Gradually, most of their demands were met. The government reduced property qualifications for voting and extended franchise to include others (see chart above).

After limiting child labor and expanding voting rights, Parliament broadened educational opportunities. Although most areas failed to keep up with Britain, Europe began similar reforms. By 1900, literacy rates approached one hundred per cent in most countries of Northwestern Europe. The Industrial Revolution improved living standards in other ways.

In the early years of industrialization, many critics expected that the change would lead to problems of overpopulation and an inability to feed the growing numbers. **Thomas Malthus**, in his *Essay on the Principles of Population* (1798), predicted that the population would increase geometrically while the ability to provide food would increase only arithmetically. Malthus forecasted that industrialization would bring great famines in the 19th century.

While Malthus had persuasive evidence to make this dire forecast, the situation did not occur. The population did increase in the 19th century, but it was not because of a rise in birth rates. Average family size shrank in most countries in the 19th and 20th centuries. Most of the population increase resulted from declining death rates brought about by better nutrition and medical care. Life expectancy showed a considerable rise. In England, it was about 40 years in the 1840s. By 1933, life expectancy had increased to 59 years and to 76 years-old by 1993.

With the restriction of child labor and the establishment of compulsory education, each child cost parents an increasing amount to support. Combined with an increased agricultural output per capita, smaller families made it possible for Western nations to feed their populations under normal circumstances.

A major crisis developed in Ireland in the 19th century when a potato blight seriously damaged the crop that was the mainstay of the Irish diet. The result was a famine called "**The Great Hunger**" (also called the "Potato Famine") which began in the 1840s. Despite the famine, absentee British landlords demanded their rents and continued to export other agricultural crops. The British government was slow to enact legislation to relieve the situation.

Between 1841 and 1851, Ireland's population fell from 8.2 million to 6.6 million through starvation, disease, and emigration – especially to the United States.

---

1 rotten boroughs (places with little or no population, but represented in Parliament)

Eventually, the **Corn Laws**[1] were repealed in 1846, and food was imported to ease the situation. However, more than 750,000 Irish died from starvation and famine-related diseases and hundreds of thousands more left Ireland, many emigrating to the United States.

Immigration soared during the Industrial Revolution. Besides the United States, other popular destinations were Latin America, Canada, Australia, New Zealand, and South Africa. Between 1846 and 1932 in excess of 58 million people left Europe. Many countries welcomed immigrants because of their labor needs. With the end of serfdom in the 18th and 19th centuries, people were legally free to move. They saw potential for advancement elsewhere. In addition, many liberals wished to leave the Continent for political reasons after the Revolutions of 1848; others left to escape compulsory military service.

JAPAN AND THE MEIJI RESTORATION

Beginning in 1640, no Japanese could leave and no foreigners, except for a few Dutch and Chinese, could enter Japan. Concerns about the spread of Christianity and foreign involvement in internal politics led the Tokugawa Shogun to close their borders. However, a few Western

---

1 Corn Laws, (limited imports when domestic prices were below a fixed level)

Mini Assessment

1 • Governmental interference in economic affairs should be minimal.
   • Trade should flow unencumbered across national boundaries.
   • Wealth is the productive resources available to a nation.

   Of which economic philosophy are these statements characteristic?
   1   mercantilism   3   utopian socialism
   2   laissez-faire   4   scientific socialism

2 What did Karl Marx, Robert Owen, and Charles Fourier have in common?
   1   opposition to economic change
   2   proposals to solve some of the evils of the Industrial Revolution
   3   support for laissez-faire economics
   4   belief that individual effort was the key to success

3 "With respect to the age at which children are worked in mines and collieries in South Staffordshire, it is common to begin at seven years old. ... Black-damp very much abounds – the ventilation in general is exceedingly imperfect. ... Hence fatal explosions frequently take place. ... People have to work all day over their shoes in water. ... The regular hours of a full day's labour are 14 and occasionally 16."
   – *Hansard's Parliamentary Debates*, Vol. 63, 1842

This quotation describes conditions which led to
1   the ideas of Adam Smith
2   adoption of mercantilist ideas
3   *Great Reform Bill of 1832*
4   *Mines Act of 1842*

Constructed Response:

The conditions or events listed below were apparent or occurred in England between the 17th and 20th centuries. In the space provided, place each condition or event in the correct category to complete the outline.

The Agricultural Revolution
Good harbors and access to the seas
Extension of the right to vote
The Industrial Revolution in England
Increase in child labor abuses
"New" Imperialism (1870)
Availability of coal and iron

Title: _____

Causes:

Results:

ideas penetrated the closed society. Desire for Western medicine and technology increased, especially among the emerging merchant class.

In 1853, Commodore **Matthew Perry** of the U.S. Navy disrupted two centuries of virtual isolation when his steam frigates entered Tokyo harbor. The United States was concerned about the fate of sailors shipwrecked on Japanese shores and was also anxious to obtain refueling rights for the steamships that crossed the Pacific. Through his show of Western technology, military force, and diplomatic skill, Perry reopened Japan to the outside world – the "Open Door Policy."

By the **Treaty of Kanagawa** (1854), two ports were opened to American ships. Later, diplomats won additional rights such as **extraterritoriality**[1]. These treaties created a sense of humiliation among the Japanese who were determined to develop sufficiently to meet the Western challenge. In 1867, the last shogun was forced to **abdicate**[2] and accept blame for the unpopular treaties and being unable to protect Japan from the West.

The new Japanese government restored power to the emperor. A new emperor, Mutsuhito, inherited the throne in 1868 and took the name **Meiji** for his reign. The **Diet** (national legislature) had strictly limited powers. The civil service, however, was modeled on Western lines with different departments for the basic functions of government.

Once Japan made the decision to modernize its society, samurai were sent abroad to study the industrial, military, and financial institutions in the West. Based on their reports, the new Japanese government modeled its army on Prussia's and its navy on Britain's. The government also established a postal system and a national system of education. The government actively supported Shintoism, because it backed national sentiment and emperor worship.

The Japanese created a mixed system of free enterprise with intense government involvement. By studying foreign countries, the Japanese modernized their industrial and financial systems rapidly. In part because the Japanese used foreign models, they avoided

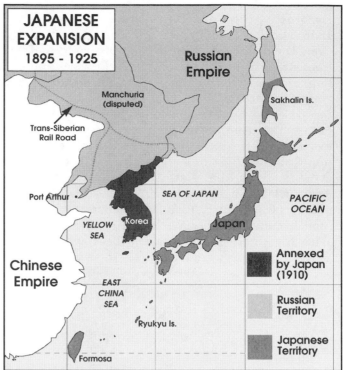

JAPANESE EXPANSION 1895 - 1925

Russian Empire

Manchuria (disputed)

Trans-Siberian Rail Road

Sakhalin Is.

Port Arthur

SEA OF JAPAN

PACIFIC OCEAN

YELLOW SEA

Korea

Japan

Chinese Empire

EAST CHINA SEA

Ryukyu Is.

Formosa

■ Annexed by Japan (1910)

□ Russian Territory

▨ Japanese Territory

problems such as child labor and horrible working conditions that others had encountered. Foreign trade, almost non-existent at the time of the Meiji Restoration, rose to about $200 million annually by 1900. The government provided financial support to begin industries, and many **zaibatsus**[3] quickly emerged. They received government support for their raw material and market needs.

The need for industrial resources played a strong role in Japan's actions toward other nations. Economic needs triggered the outbreak of the **Sino-Japanese War** (1894-1895) and the **Russo-Japanese War** (1904-1905). The Russo-Japanese War is worthy of special note. When the Japanese destroyed the Russian Navy, it marked the first defeat of a European nation by an Asian one. The **Treaty of Portsmouth** (1905), negotiated with the help of U.S. President Theodore Roosevelt, gave Japan ports on the mainland of China, control of Manchuria, a protectorate in Korea, and part of the island of Sakhalin (annexed to Japan in 1905). These acquisitions opened more areas for Japanese economic development.

---

1 extraterritoriality (right of foreigners accused of crimes to be tried in courts of their own country)
2 abdicate (give up power or responsibility)
3 zaibatsus (powerful family-controlled commercial combines of Japan)

CAUSES OF NEW IMPERIALIST EXPANSION

Type	Group Affected
Economic	• Need for raw materials and markets created by Industrial Revolution • Desire for place to invest excess capital at a high rate of return
Social	• Drive to spread Christianity ("White Man's Burden" – Kipling) • Rule by strongest and fittest and need to spread superior Western culture (Social Darwinism)
Political	• Desire for great power status (colonies meant power and prestige) • Competitive drive to gain control of an area and obtain bases and outposts for military before a rival could do so

The modernization of Japan is remarkable. Its astounding speed was partially the result of Japan's ability to adapt the achievements of others. The Japanese government provided incentives for the use of western technology and constructed new factories that were later purchased by wealthy businessmen.

Nationalism was also a factor. Japanese national pride helped the modernization effort. It drove them to achieve Western levels of development. Yet the infusion of Western technology had little effect on Japanese culture. Religion, the value system, and family life remained much the same. Some changes occurred in social class structure with the emergence of a wealthy and educated middle class, but this had begun prior to modernization.

Many emerging nations of the 20th century liked the Japanese model and hoped to obtain the desired technology without the loss of their valued cultural attributes.

IMPERIALISM

Imperialism is the control by a stronger, more powerful country over a weaker area or region. It has a long history going back to ancient times. However, the European Age of Exploration and Discovery (c. 15th century) led to a period of colonization and competition. After the Congress of Vienna settlement (1814-1815), only Britain maintained a strong colonial presence. The period between 1815 and 1870 was a quiet interlude in expansion. The revolutions of the first half of the 19th century and the stirrings of industrialism distracted Europeans.

Around 1870, new factors triggered tremendous expansion and competition among countries during the New Imperialism (c. 1870-1945). During the New Imperialism, the countries involved developed new methods of controlling less developed areas (see charts). The imperialists recognized that different areas required different approaches. Some areas that were seized had existing governments which could be used by imperialist powers, others required total control by the mother country.

THE BRITISH IN INDIA

The history of the British involvement in India goes back to the 17th and 18th centuries and continued into the period of New Imperialism. During the 1700s, the British and French were the main rivals for control of India.

IMPERIALIST CONTROL

Type	Arrangement
Colony	Direct total control by the mother country
Protectorate	Native ruler remains in place, but with foreign power's advisers
Sphere of Influence	Foreign power has exclusive rights to development
Concession	Foreign power has right to develop one specific aspect of economy
Lease	Foreign power leases (rents) an area from a less developed country

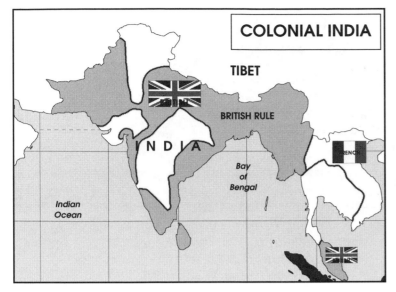

COLONIAL INDIA

TIBET

BRITISH RULE

INDIA

Bay of Bengal

Indian Ocean

The **Seven Years War** (1756-1763) was fought not only in Europe and North America but also in India. **Robert Clive** (1725-1774), an employee of the British East India Co., defeated the French with the help of British naval mobility.

The **British East India Co.** was a joint stock company chartered by Elizabeth I and privately owned. Its main responsibility was to its stockholders. The large Indian market, with its abundant natural resources, made it an ideal investment. The Company worked tirelessly to increase its power by winning support from native rulers. Religious divisions between Hindus and Muslims made it easy to increase areas of control by "divide and conquer" tactics.

However, by 1857 Indians were developing a sense of national identity. They resented the loss of property to the British, the dethroning of native rulers, and the insensibility of the British to their religious practices. One indignity involved the **Sepoys**[1]. The British cartridges used by the Sepoys had to be bitten to remove a covering before insertion into their guns. The coverings were said to be greased with pork and beef fat. The British action managed to anger the Hindus (no beef) and the Muslims (no pork) at the same time. The resulting

1 sepoy (regular soldier in some Middle Eastern countries, especially an Indian soldier formerly serving under British command)

Sepoy Mutiny (or Sepoy Rebellion) was put down, but the British government forced the East India Co. to relinquish control. The British government then began educating and training Indians for a role in their own Indian government. Eventually, this too led to demands for independence.

THE SCRAMBLE FOR AFRICA

The New Imperialism triggered the opening of Africa. European interest and claims in the area go back to the Age of Exploration and Discovery, but few had ventured into the interior. The Portuguese (Diaz, DaGama) had inched their way down the west coast of Africa in search of an all-water route to the East in the 15th and 16th centuries. They had claimed areas of interest that included the tip of Africa.

Later, other Europeans, including the Dutch, British, and French, began to explore the continent itself. Still, rain forests, deserts, climate, and the lack of river access to the interior discouraged penetration of inland areas. With the spread of the Industrial Revolution, the

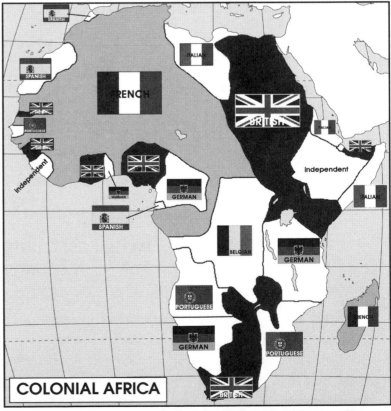

COLONIAL AFRICA

increased demand for raw materials and markets – along with the national prestige of having an empire – intensified the imperialist drive for Africa.

In 1885, German Chancellor Bismarck invited the European nations involved in Africa to the **Berlin Conference**. Bismarck opposed German involvement in Africa and thought that he could help to settle the differences. The Conference placed the Congo Free State under the personal control of Leopold II of Belgium. However, provisions were included that opened that area to trade with all nations. The Conference also established rules for claiming colonies. In order to claim an area, the nation involved must occupy and notify other nations of its claim. This led to a "scramble for Africa" as nations tried to establish their claims before others could.

The British were interested in a "Cape to Cairo" expanse running along the east coast of Africa. This clashed with the German goal of an east-west expanse from German East Africa to German Southwest Africa. The British dream also conflicted with French hopes. The French wanted an east-west expanse (Dakar to the Gulf of Aden) to protect their North African colonies from penetration from the south. This led to a confrontation between the British and the French at Fashoda in the Sudan in 1898. The French backed down after they gained a promise of British support for French control of Morocco.

This struggle for African lands led to a situation where by 1900 only Liberia and Ethiopia remained independent. By 1900, imperialism also was a contributing cause for World War I as the simmering rivalries continued to poison international relations.

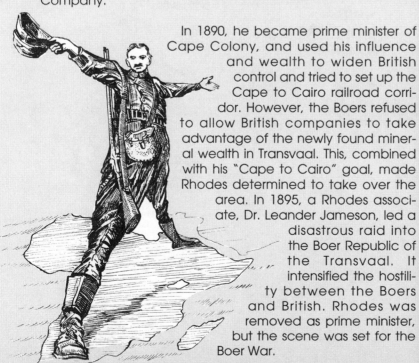

CLOSE LOOK

COLLOSUS OF RHODES

Cecil Rhodes (1853-1902) became a major figure in the British imperial dominance of Southern Africa. As a young adventurer in the 1870s, Rhodes became a rich man forming the De Beers Mining Company. It eventually controlled 90 percent of the world's diamond production). He also obtained interests in the gold fields of the Transvaal and formed the British South Africa Company.

In 1890, he became prime minister of Cape Colony, and used his influence and wealth to widen British control and tried to set up the Cape to Cairo railroad corridor. However, the Boers refused to allow British companies to take advantage of the newly found mineral wealth in Transvaal. This, combined with his "Cape to Cairo" goal, made Rhodes determined to take over the area. In 1895, a Rhodes associate, Dr. Leander Jameson, led a disastrous raid into the Boer Republic of the Transvaal. It intensified the hostility between the Boers and British. Rhodes was removed as prime minister, but the scene was set for the Boer War.

The people of Africa opposed the European takeovers. The **Boers** (Dutch farmers of Cape Town, also called Afrikaners) began to move into the interior in the 1700s. They faced the opposition of the Zulu people. In the first part of the 19th century, the Zulu leader **Shaka** emerged to organize his people into an effective fighting force.

The British obtained Cape Town at the end of the Napoleonic Wars (1815). In the 1830s, the Boers began their **Great Trek** into the interior to escape British control. The half-brother of Shaka opposed their advance, but the Zulus were no match for the modern weapons of the Boers. Still, the Zulus continued their struggle into the 20th century when they were finally defeated by the British.

British advance on the Boers in South Africa

The Boers of the Transvaal and Orange Free State fought against Britain in the **Boer War** (1899-1902). The superb Boer horsemen used their knowledge of the terrain and employed guerrilla tactics. Britain eventually used a force of 450,000 against the Boers. After their victory, the British united their South African colonies into the Union of South Africa (1910). It became a dominion with self-governing status within the British Empire.

EUROPEAN IMPERIALISM IN CHINA

Imperialism in China was somewhat different from that found in Africa. Most African areas south of the Sahara were divided into colonies and ruled directly by European nations. In China, imperialists used spheres of influence, leases, and concessions. Still, markets and raw materials remained the primary motives.

By the 1840s, when European interest in China was on the rise, the Q'ing Dynasty (1644-1912) was weakening. Corruption and a series of natural disasters convinced many that the Dynasty had lost the Mandate of Heaven. At the same time, Europeans wanted Chinese products such as tea, porcelain, and silk.

However, the Chinese had little interest in the products of Europe.

This led to an unfavorable balance of trade for the Europeans, until it was discovered that there was a Chinese market for opium. The Chinese government tried to stop this trade and actually destroyed many chests of opium owned by the British East India Company. This led to the first **Opium War** (1839-1841). The Chinese were no match for Britain's modern weapons and were easily defeated.

The War resulted in the unequal treaty, the **Treaty of Nanking** (1842). It opened more Chinese ports for trade, ceded Hong Kong to Britain, granted the British extraterritoriality, and required the Chinese payment of an indemnity. The Second Opium War was fought by Britain and France against China in 1857. The War ended with the **Treaty of Tientsin**. It opened even more ports and provided for protection of Christian missionaries and their converts in the interior of China. Other countries, such as Russia, the Netherlands, Germany, and the United States, soon sought and received similar privileges.

CHINA FOREIGN INFLUENCE 19TH CENTURY

RUSSIAN EMPIRE

Rail Road

RUSSIANS

HUI

BEIJING

SEA OF JAPAN

JAPANESE

BOXER REBELLION 1900

HUI

GERMANS

NANKING

SHANGHAI (BR)

TAIPING REBELLION 1850-1864

TAIPING

EAST CHINA SEA

JAPANESE

HUI HUI

MACAO (PORTUGAL)

HONG KONG (BR)

FRENCH

SOUTH CHINA SEA

Traditionally, the Chinese had regarded foreigners as inferiors and referred to them as "barbarians." The defeats in the Opium Wars were humiliating for the Chinese. Nationalist reformers denounced the Q'ing Dynasty and launched the **Taiping Rebellion** (1850-1864). A combination of regional armies and foreign mercenaries subdued the revolutionaries. Because they wanted a government that they could manipulate, the European imperialists aided the Q'ing Dynasty.

Sun Yixian

There was a "scramble for China" after the weaknesses of the country were further exposed in the **Sino-Japanese War** (1894-1895). The imperialists divided China into spheres of influence, and negotiated leases and concessions. Nationalists organized anti-imperialist resistance movements.

In 1899, resistance groups launched another uprising. The **Boxer Rebellion** began with a series of attacks on Chinese Christians, then on foreigners in the interior, and finally on the foreign diplomats in Peking (Beijing). The Europeans, joined by Japan and the United States, sent in an international force which ended the siege of the diplomatic missions and defeated the Boxers. As a consequence, China was forced to pay a large indemnity and to accept even more restrictions.

As the 20th century dawned, revolutionaries continued to agitate against both the Q'ing Dynasty and the foreigners. As their discontent spread, revolutionaries came under the leadership of Doctor **Sun Yixian** (also Sun Yat-sen, 1866-1925). Sun was educated in Hawaii and received a medical degree in Hong Kong. He felt that traditional China would have to adopt to more modern ways to face the West on equal footing.

Sun Yixian traveled extensively in the West and studied Western thought. He raised money for the revolutionaries and returned to China in 1911 after a new revolution broke out. With the support of the Chinese Army, the Q'ing Dynasty was overthrown and the Chinese Republic was proclaimed in 1911. Sun's associates organized the **Guomindang** (Kuomintang or Nationalist Party). In the turmoil of the early years of the republic, Sun was in and out of the presidency. It was not until after his death that a government came close to controlling China.

Sun is regarded as the founder of modern China by many. Just before his death, he published *The Three Principles of the People*, based on an earlier manifesto of his political beliefs:

- Democracy – the people were sovereign, but the elite should govern

- Nationalism – the Chinese people needed to think of themselves as members of a nation as well as a clan and family; they should be free of foreign influence

- Livelihood – equal distribution of wealth was necessary

POSSIBLE EFFECTS OF IMPERIALISM

Positive Effects	Negative Effects
Infrastructure improved	Peoples with common backgrounds separated
Education improved	Natural resources exploited
Access to medical care increased	Native cultures damaged
Food supply increased	Economic self-sufficiency lost
Economic development stimulated	Cash crops overemphasized
Decreased internal conflicts	Family life disrupted

Imperialism had both positive and negative effects on the areas controlled, but they varied from area to area. Many of them still impact the areas involved today.

European nations were also affected by their own drives for overseas empires. They clashed frequently with each other. Examples include the 19th century dispute between Britain and Russia over spheres of influence in Iran, the Fashoda Crisis (1898), and the Moroccan Crises (1905, 1911). These disagreements helped pave the road to World War I. Later, different imperialist disputes also contributed to World War II.

Many Europeans lost their lives in wars to control indigenous people in India, Africa, and China. A feeling of superiority developed among the Europeans. It was stimulated by the writings of Social Darwinists and authors such as Rudyard Kipling. This attitude

prevented the imperialists from seeing the value of other cultures and learning from them.

Economically, the Europeans became dependent on their empires as sources of cheap raw materials for their industries and markets for their finished products. The greed began during the Age of Exploration and Discovery expanded and intensified as new products reached European markets. Also, cultural diffusion occurred as colonial areas and imperialists each influenced the other's languages, art, sculpture, and clothes design.

Even today, the effects of imperialism are evident. The impact of the "boom and bust" of the industrialized business cycle is very apparent. Western technology has also spread and made the developing nations more competitive, both economically and militarily. In many respects, a homogenized global culture is emerg-

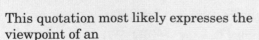

Mini Assessment

1 The Sepoy Mutiny, Boer War, and Boxer Rebellion are examples of
   1 challenges to rule of foreign powers
   2 colonial people's desire for economic status
   3 attempts by religious minorities to establish theocracies
   4 revolts to end the restrictions of mercantilism

2 "We [English] have to educate a people [Indians] who can not at present be educated by means of their mother tongue. We must teach them some foreign language. The claims of our own language it is hardly necessary to recapitulate. It stands preeminent even among the languages of the West."

This quotation most likely expresses the viewpoint of an
   1 anthropologist
   2 Indian nationalist
   3 American linguist
   4 English imperialist

3 The Berlin Conference of 1885 established
   1 Germany as the major colonial power in Africa
   2 rules for the division of Africa among European nations
   3 the Congo as a French colony
   4 Boer rule in South Africa

Constructed Response:

Use the cartoon below to answer the following questions.

1 What is Perry's ship preparing to do in the cartoon?

2 Why might this event be regarded as a major turning point in Japanese History?

ing despite the attempts of the developing nations to retain their own identities. The Western nations also exported their ideas of nationalism. Ironically, these became the very ideas that encouraged the developing nations to revolt against foreign control. In many ways imperialism spread the seeds of its own destruction – a destruction that occurred in the post World War II period.

TIME CAPSULE: 1750-1914

The Age of Revolutions saw dramatic political, economic, and social changes. These changes began with the Scientific and Intellectual Revolutions that changed basic institutions and the way of life for people all over the world. They contributed mightily to the later political revolutions. The French Revolution not only made major changes in France, but also helped to spread the forces of nationalism and democracy throughout the globe. As a consequence, European people struggled to establish nation-states and self-government. The later revolutions of the 19th century helped to achieve these goals. They also brought an end to serfdom and the feudal system in Europe. As European powers became imperialistic and seized less developed areas, they brought with them Western ideas. These very ideas eventually undermined and brought the colonial empires to an end.

Economically, the Agricultural and Industrial Revolutions made major changes in the methods of production. As per capita production increased on the farms, it freed many to move to the cities to work in factories. The jump in productivity increased the availability of goods and services, and led to improvements in the standard of living. However, the competition for raw materials and markets among the major powers fueled the fires of imperialism and helped to contribute to the tensions that brought on World War I.

Socially, the middle class began its rise to power and influence. Its dissatisfaction with political and economic conditions was a major factor in bringing about change. It was active in the struggle for nation-states and the establishment of democratic governments. The expansion of the right to vote to include the middle class also led to changes in governments. During the latter part of the 19th century, European governments began to place restrictions on business and institute free public education. In general, they became more concerned about the welfare of their citizens.

The 1750-1914 era provided the framework for the developments of the 20th century. Many of the events and decisions that were made during that time affected the global community for generations.

MULTI-CHOICE QUESTIONS

1 "When those who possess like myself, fields and houses, assemble for their common interests, I have a voice in this assembly. I am a part of the whole, a part of the community, a part of the sovereign. Here is my fatherland." – Voltaire

The main point of this quotation is to
1 list the author's sources of wealth
2 explain why the author feels a part of his country
3 justify the author's belief in democracy
4 maintain the importance of farming in the economy

2 The history of Mexico in the late 19th and early 20th centuries might best be described as
1 a period of revolutions and changing governments
2 a time of increasing democracy and protection of human rights
3 an era of rapid industrialization and economic progress
4 a time when class differences decreased significantly

3 Which is a likely result of the other three?
1 one crop economy
2 economic disaster
3 drought or excessive rain
4 drop in agricultural prices

4 The work of enlightened despots might best be described as
1 resulting in some improvements in the lives of their people
2 ending in a return to previous living conditions
3 succeeding politically, but failing economically and socially
4 resulting in failure because religious interest received protection

5 "_____ was above all a revolutionary, and his great aim in life was to cooperate in this or that fashion in the overthrow of capitalist society and the State institutions which it has created."

Which of the following names can be correctly placed on the blank line in the quotation?
1 Adam Smith
2 Robert Owen
3 Karl Marx
4 John Locke

Base your answer to question 6 on the map below and your knowledge of global history.

6 Which of the following forces was most instrumental in the unification movement shown in the map?
1 imperialism
2 capitulations
3 revolution
4 nationalism

7   The Revolutions of 1848 in Europe ended with the
    1   successful establishment of democratic governments
    2   re-establishment of prior governments which instituted some reforms
    3   organization of several new nation-states
    4   end of French domination of the Continent

Base your answer to question 8 on the cartoon below and your knowledge of global history.

8   The cartoon above refers to
    1   aiding the French victory in Russia
    2   Russia's use of "scorched earth" against Napoleon
    3   Napoleon's decision to destroy Moscow by fire
    4   Napoleon's view of life in the Russia of Alexander I

9   The real opening of Siberia occurred when
    1   fur traders and trappers established settlements
    2   tsarist political opponents were sentenced to internal exile
    3   the Trans-Siberian Railroad was constructed
    4   the Chinese were defeated and left the area

10 Which is the correct chronological order for the systems of production?
    1   guild system, domestic system, factory system
    2   domestic system, guild system, factory system
    3   factory system, domestic system, guild system
    4   guild system, factory system, domestic system

11 Declining birth rates and increased agricultural output per capita during the 19th century help to explain why
    1   the predictions of Malthus did not come true
    2   Robert Owen's New Lanark experiment succeeded
    3   Marx's proletarian revolutions did not occur
    4   Fourier's ideal communities consistently failed

12 Much of Japanese expansion may be explained in terms of the desire to
    1   prove its independence of Chinese influence
    2   acquire sources of raw materials and markets
    3   spread a superior culture
    4   end its isolation from world affairs

13 The "scramble for Africa" did not occur until the late 19th century. The reason for this delay in European division of Africa might best be explained by
    1   Africa's lack of valuable resources
    2   fears that slavery might be rekindled
    3   European concerns about Islamic opposition
    4   geographic obstacles to penetration of the interior

14 Extraterritoriality (China) and capitulations (Turkey) are results of Europeans'
    1   desire to protect their citizens from "inferior" legal and political systems
    2   demands for large grants of land
    3   provisions for exploitation of natural resources
    4   acquisition of sites for military bases

15 Sun Yixian differed from Mohandus Gandhi because he
    1   was unconcerned about the poorest people in the population
    2   wished to rid his country of Western imperialist control
    3   believed that Western ways were necessary to his country's development
    4   was opposed to the use of violence to bring about change.

THEMATIC ESSAY

Theme: Change

Throughout global history, revolutions – violent and non-violent –have brought about major changes in society.

Task:

- Select a revolution you have studied [**except the American Revolution**] and explain the factors which caused the revolution.

- Describe the changes made by the revolution in the area where it occurred *or* in global history.

Suggestions:

You may use any revolution from your study of global history – **except the American Revolution**. You might wish to consider the Scientific Revolution (16th-19th centuries), the Intellectual Revolution (17th-18th centuries), the Agricultural Revolution (18th-19th centuries), the Industrial Revolution (18th-19th centuries), the French Revolution (18th century), the Latin American Revolutions (1800-1821),the Mexican Revolution (1910-1930). **You are not limited to these suggestions.**

DOCUMENT BASED QUESTIONS

Directions:

The following question is based on the accompanying documents (1-7). Some of the documents have been edited for the purposes of this exercise. The question is designed to test your ability to work with historical documents. As you analyze the documents, take into account both the source of the document and the author's point of view.

- Write a well-organized essay that includes an introduction with a thesis statement, several paragraphs explaining the thesis, and a conclusion.
- Analyze the documents.
- Use all the documents.
- Use evidence from the documents to support your thesis position.
- Do not simply repeat the contents of the documents.
- Include specific related outside information.

Historical Context:

The "New" Imperialism (c. 1870) was caused by a variety of factors. The documents below express different reasons for expansion.

Task:

Identify and explain the various causes of the "New" Imperialism.

Part A - Short Answer

The documents below relate to the various causes of imperialism. Examine *each* document carefully, then answer the question that follows it.

Document 1:

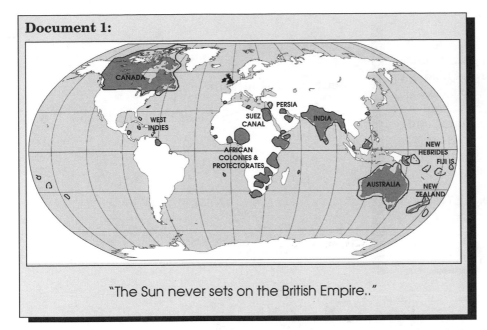

"The Sun never sets on the British Empire.."

Document 1 Question:

What feelings would British citizens have about this map?

Document 2:

"Take up the White Man's Burden –
Send forth the best ye breed –
Go bind your sons to exile
To serve your captives' need;
To wait in heavy harness,
Your new-caught, sullen peoples
Half devil and half child."

– Rudyard Kipling (1899)

Document 2 Question:

What attitude does Kipling express toward the colonial people?

Document 3:

PERCENTAGE OF TERRITORIES BELONGING TO THE EUROPEANS			
Area	1876	1900	Increase/ Decrease
Africa	10.8%	90.4%	+79.6%
Polynesia	56.8%	98.9%	+42.1%
Asia	51.5%	56.6%	+5.1%
Australia	100.0%	100.0%	– –
America	27.5%	27.2%	-0.3%

– Lenin, *The Highest Stage of Capitalism*

Document 3 Question:

Where did the greatest European expansion occur between 1876 and 1900? Why?

Document 4:

"...For as the nations grow to have wider and wider interests, and are brought into closer and closer contact, if we (U.S.) are to hold our own in the struggle for naval and commercial supremacy, we must build up our power without (outside) our own borders."

–U. S. President Theodore Roosevlt, Chicago, 1899

Document 4 Question:

What reasons does President Roosevelt give for U.S. imperialism?

Document 5:

EXPORTS FROM GREAT BRITAIN TO BRITISH POSSESSIONS	
Years	As a percent of total value of exports
1855-1859	31.5
1875-1879	33.0
1890-1894	33.5
1900-1904	37.0

– J.A. Hobson, *Imperialism: A Study*

Document 5 Question:

What do these statistics indicate about why Britain would want to keep and increase its colonial holdings?

Document 6:

"...I believe in the British Empire - and, in the second place, I believe in the British race. I believe that the British race is the greatest governing race that the world has ever seen. ...I say that ... as proved and evidenced by the success which we have had in administering the vast dominions which are connected with these small islands."

– Joseph Chamberlain, London, 1895

Document 6 Question:

How does Chamberlain justify British colonial control?

Document 7:

"...The people have found out that England is small, and her trade is large, and they have also found out that other people are taking their share of the world, and enforcing hostile tariffs. The people of England are finding out that 'trade follows the flag,' and they have all become Imperialists."

– Cecil Rhodes, in F. Verschoyle, *Cecil Rhodes: His Political Life and Speeches, 1881-1900*

Document 7

What reasons does Rhodes think caused the "New" Imperialism?

Part B - Essay Response

Discuss the reasons for the "New" Imperialism (c. 1870).

Your essay should be well organized with an introductory paragraph that states your thesis as to the reasons for the "New" Imperialism. Develop and support the reasons in the next paragraphs and then write a conclusion. In your essay, include specific historical details and refer to the specific documents you analyzed in Part A. You may include additional information from your knowledge of global history.

Unit 7

1900 AD – 1945 AD

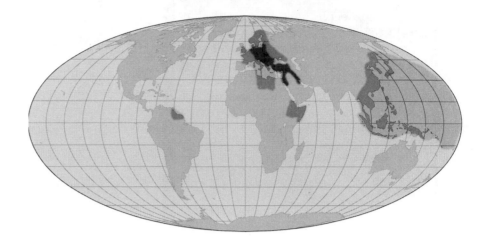

A HALF CENTURY OF CRISIS & ACHIEVEMENT

AD	
1900–	
	Triple Entente completed (1907)
1910–	
	Archduke Franz Ferdinand assassinated (1914)
	Russian Revolutions (1917)
	Treaty of Versailles signed (1919)
1920–	
	Republic of Turkey established (1923)
	Universal suffrage in Britain (1928)
	Great Depression begins (1929)
1930–	
	Hitler becomes German Chancellor (1933)
	Long March begins in China (1934)
	Nazi-Soviet Nonaggression Pact (1939)
1940–	
	Yalta Summit Conference (1945)

PEOPLE	PLACES	THINGS
Adolf Hitler	Amritsar	abdication
Albert Einstein	Potsdam	Axis Pact
Franz Ferdinand	The Hague	blitzkreig
Josef Stalin	Ukraine	coalition
Mao Zedong	Versailles	communism
Marie & Pierre Curie	Weimar Republic	ethnic
Mohandas Gandhi	Yalta	fascism
Nicholas II		Great Depression
Sigmund Freud		Holocaust
V.I. Lenin		totalitarian
Winston Churchill		

INTRODUCTION

Great advances in science, technology, the arts and women's rights marked the half century between 1900 and 1945. While the achievements in science and technology improved health care and the quality of human life, they also made killing easier. The important role of Western women in World War I paved the way for their achievement of voting equality.

In this short span of time, the globe was torn by two world wars and the emergence of totalitarian governments of the right and left. World War I was instrumental in bringing about the rise of communism in Russia and fascism in countries such as Italy and Germany. The dislocations of World War I were instrumental in causing World War II. World War II brought about the decline of colonial empires and the emergence of the Cold War between the United States and the Soviet Union. Many of the events and decisions of this tumultuous 50-year period had long-term repercussions.

SCIENTIFIC AND TECHNOLOGICAL ADVANCES

Beginning about the mid-point of the 19th century, rapid changes occurred in the fields of science and technology. The contributors often based their work on the achievements of earlier innovators. In some cases, they made corrections or adjustments to earlier theories. The fields of biology[1], physics[2], and psychoanalysis[3] saw major developments.

French physicists **Pierre Curie** (1859-1906) and **Marie Curie** (1867-1934) discovered that atoms were complex and unstable. As the atoms disintegrated, energy was released. The Curies' proof that atoms could be split corrected earlier ideas. For their work, they received the Nobel Prize for Physics in 1903. **Albert Einstein** (German, 1879-1955), expressed the Curies' concept in the formula, $E=MC^2$ (Theory of Relativity). Later, he published his famous *Theory of Relativity*. It stated that time, space, and motion were relative to an observer and his movement in space. He also developed a **unified field theory** to explain subatomic behavior, gravitation, and electromagnetism. This replaced some of Newton's ideas. Tragically, Einstein's brilliant discoveries in theoretical physics made possible the development of weapons of mass destruction.

Sigmund Freud (Austrian, 1856-1939) founded the field of psychoanalysis. He believed that some emotional upsets could be traced to early, forgotten experiences through the use of free association. In 1900, Freud published *The Interpretation of Dreams* in which he stressed the role of the unconscious and the use of dreams as a way to unlock it. His ideas and terminology became part of every day culture and language. This led to the conclusion that humans were not always rational.

---

1 biology (science of life and of living organisms, including their structure, function, growth, origin, evolution, and distribution. It includes botany and zoology and all their subdivisions)
2 physics (science of matter and energy and of interactions between the two, grouped in traditional fields such as acoustics, optics, mechanics, thermodynamics, and electromagnetism, as well as in modern extensions including atomic and nuclear physics, cryogenics, solid-state physics, particle physics, and plasma physics)
3 psychoanalysis (method of psychiatric therapy originated by Sigmund Freud in which free association, dream interpretation, and analysis of resistance and transference are used to explore repressed or unconscious impulses, anxieties, and internal conflicts)

MEDICAL ADVANCES

Contributor	Contribution	Significance
Louis Pasteur (French, 1822-1895)	Discovered diseases are caused by bacteria; developed vaccine for rabies	Led to the use of heat in pasteurization process to destroy bacteria; many lives saved through the use of rabies vaccine
Robert Koch (German, 1843-1910)	Established bacteriology as a separate science; discovered germ that causes tuberculosis; developed methods of diagnosing diseases	Structure laid the groundwork for later cures for many diseases
William Morton (American, 1819-1868)	Discovered the use of ether as an anesthetic	Paved the way for pain-free surgery and dentistry
Joseph Lister (British, 1827-1912)	Discovered the use of antiseptics to destroy bacteria	Decreased number of deaths from infection during surgery
Florence Nightingale (British, 1820-1910)	Founder of modern nursing; organized nursing care for wounded during the Crimean War	Recognized authority on caring for sick; advice led to improvement of nursing care

One of the most outstanding achievements of the pre-World War I era was the increase in life expectancy in developed areas. In 1850, the average life expectancy for males was about 40 years and for females about 42 years. By 1910, these figures had risen to about 52 years and 56 years, respectively. A number of factors were responsible for these changes. Civil order, improvements in agriculture and transportation, and improved health care were all important. Contributing factors also included uncovering the causes of disease and developing new ways of treatment (see chart above).

WORLD WAR I (1914-1917)

EUROPE: POLITICAL SETTING

In 1914, Eastern and Western Europe were organized in quite different physical and political ways. Eastern Europe was dominated by three large, multi-national empires: the Russian, the German, and the Austro-Hungarian. Each of these empires had an **autocratic**[1] government and large, **ethnic**[2] minority populations. Nationalism

was strong among some of the minorities, and some demanded independence. Also in Eastern Europe, there were some small, independent nation-states such as Serbia, Bulgaria, and Greece. These small nations acted as role

EUROPE AT THE START OF WORLD WAR 1 1914

ALLIED POWERS

CENTRAL POWERS

1 autocratic (unlimited power, authority; despotic)
2 ethnic (people sharing a common and distinctive racial, national, religious, linguistic, or cultural heritage)

models for minority peoples seeking self-government. The situation in Eastern Europe was very unstable. The Russian and Austro-Hungarian Empires were rivals for power in the Balkan Peninsula, and the weak Ottoman Empire wanted to restore its earlier power in the region.

The situation in Western Europe was entirely different. Most of the people were grouped into nation-states with some elements of democracy. Most of the Western European nations had largely **homogeneous**[1] populations.

BACKGROUND CAUSES

The causes of World War I are numerous and often overlapping: international disorder, alliances, economic competition, and the three "isms" – nationalism, militarism, imperialism. All of these played roles in bringing about the War.

INTERNATIONAL DISQUIET

At the turn of the century, there was no international organization capable of settling major disputes among the nations. Responding to the peace movement of the 19th century, Tsar Nicholas II headed two international conferences at The Hague in the Netherlands. The Hague Conferences (1899, 1907) established **The Hague International Tribunal** to solve disputes voluntarily submitted to its jurisdiction. The Conferences also established "humane rules of warfare" and provided rules for the treatment of the Red Cross. Regrettably, the Conferences did little to solve the major problems confronting the nations of Europe.

ENTANGLING ALLIANCES

An intricate, competing alliance system developed out of German Chancellor Bismarck's concern about French desire for revenge for its Franco-Prussian War losses in 1871. He formed an alliance with the Austro-Hungarian Empire (1879) and one with Italy (1882). This three-way agreement became the **Triple Alliance**. Also, Bismarck attempted to strengthen Germany's position through a secret agreement with Russia – the **Reinsurance Treaty** (1887).

Bismarck's alliance system was not strong. Tensions between Russia and Austria-Hungary in the Balkans made their cooperation in time of war questionable. Italy's commitment was doubtful because Austria-Hungary controlled territories its nationalists desired. Finally, after Bismarck's removal from office, German Emperor **William II** (r. 1888-1918) abandoned the Reinsurance Treaty with Russia in 1890.

Germany abandonment of the Reinsurance Treaty opened the door for a Russian-French alliance in 1894. Germany and Austria-Hungary then faced the possibility of a two-front war with France on the one side and Russia on the other. In 1904, France concluded an "Entente Cordiale" (friendly understanding) with Britain. In 1907, Britain came to an understanding with Russia which completed the **Triple Entente**. However, questions remained about the depth of British commitment. The British Parliament retained its right to declare war. Until the actual declaration of war in 1914, Germany hoped that Britain would remain neutral.

ECONOMIC COMPETITION

The German Empire's rise as an industrial rival for Britain heightened tensions between the two nations. Germany's later industrialization meant it had a newer **technological base**[2], and it could offer lower prices on world markets. By 1900, Germany was producing more steel than Britain, and was surpassed only by the U.S. From 1870 to 1913, the annual industrial

---

1 homogeneous (of the same or similar nature or kind)
2 technological base (machines and methods of production)

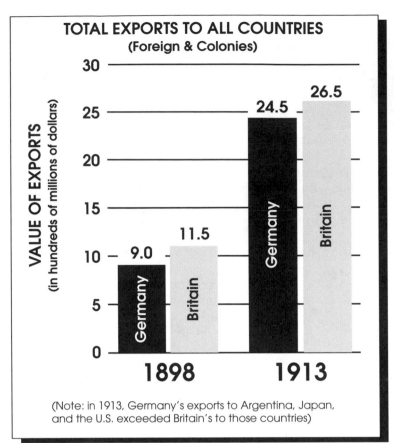

TOTAL EXPORTS TO ALL COUNTRIES
(Foreign & Colonies)

VALUE OF EXPORTS
(in hundreds of millions of dollars)

1898
- Germany: 9.0
- Britain: 11.5

1913
- Germany: 24.5
- Britain: 26.5

(Note: in 1913, Germany's exports to Argentina, Japan, and the U.S. exceeded Britain's to those countries)

growth rate in Britain was 2.2%, while Germany's rate was 2.9%. Britain's century-old economic advantage was being challenged.

MILITARISM[1] / ARMS RACES

As tensions deepened, most continental countries developed large standing armies with huge reserves. Many countries set up **conscription**[2] in peacetime. They used a system of **rotation in service**[3]. This system allowed countries to create extensive, trained reserves at low cost compared to maintaining large standing armies.

Britain and Germany began a naval race. The British wanted a navy larger than the next two largest navies combined. Kaiser William followed American naval strategist Alfred Mahan's view that naval power's ability to blockade and cut off supplies and reinforcements was the key to modern warfare. After 1898, the German naval expansion led to a similar increase in Britain's Royal Navy.

IMPERIALISM

Imperialist tensions went back to the 19th century. In general terms, countries that were able to settle these rivalries ended up on the same side in World War I. For example, Britain and France settled their differences over the Sudan (Fashoda Incident, 1898). Britain retained its influence in the Sudan, but France received a promise of British support for its control of Morocco. When Germany challenged the French in the Moroccan Crises (1905, 1911), Britain backed its ally. German acquisition of German East Africa thwarted Britain's desire for a Cape to Cairo expanse. This was not settled until after the War, when Britain acquired control of the area through the Paris Peace Conference.

NATIONALISM

Nationalism played a significant role in the outbreak of war. The French wanted revenge for their Franco-Prussian War losses. The British resented the German economic and naval challenge.

However, it was in the "tinderbox" or "powder keg" of the Balkans that nationalism became explosive. Serbia wanted to be the center of a South Slav state. Its **Pan[4]-Slavism** movement sought to unite minorities controlled by others. Russia supported the movement hoping to gain a sphere of influence in the area. In 1912-1913, the **Balkan Wars** broke out. Serbia, Bulgaria, Montenegro, and Greece joined against the Ottoman Empire but then fought over the spoils of war. With the Ottomans pushed aside, the Austro-Hungarian Empire remained the major obstacle to Pan-Slavism.

SARAJEVO: THE IMMEDIATE CAUSE

Not surprisingly, the incident which led directly to war occurred in the Balkan "powder keg." Bosnia, ruled by Austria, wanted more self government. Bosnian Serb radicals wanted union with Serbia. On 28 June 1914, a radical Serb group ("the Black Hand") assassinated the

1 militarism (glorification of the ideals of a professional military; a policy in which military preparedness is of primary importance to a state)
2 conscription or draft (compulsory enrollment in the armed forces)
3 rotation in service (trained soldiers were returned to civilian life for the workforce and new groups took their place for training)
4 Pan- (involving all of or the union of a specified group)

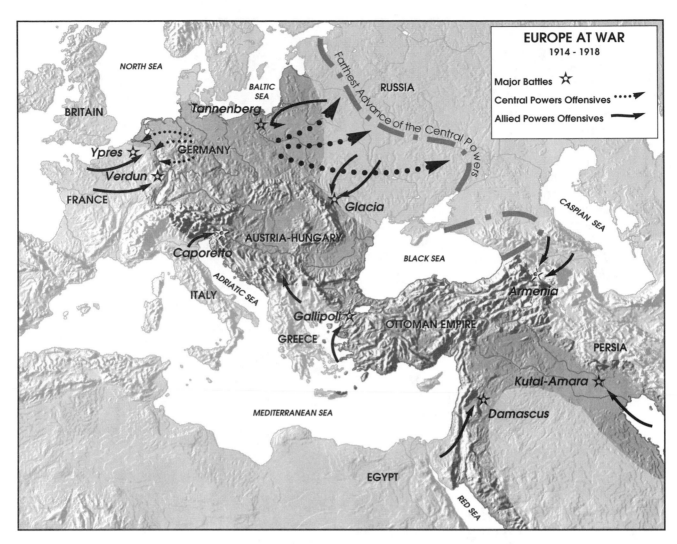

heir to the Austrian throne, Archduke **Franz Ferdinand** and his wife, Sophie, as they visited Sarajevo, Bosnia.

Austria blamed Serbia for the killings and threatened war. As Austria's ally, Kaiser William promised "carte blanche" (unqualified support) for any Austrian action. The Austrians issued an **ultimatum**[1] to Serbia. The Serbs rejected one provision that allowed Austrian authorities to hunt down Bosnian Serb nationalists, because it violated their sovereignty.

On 28 July 1914, Austria declared war on Serbia. Russia began mobilizing its army in support of Serbia and refused to stop in response to German demands. On 1 August, Germany declared war on Russia. This led to a flurry of war declarations in accord with the alliance commitments. Only Italy remained neutral.

---

1   ultimatum (a threatening final statement of terms)

MILITARY ACTION

World War I was largely a defensive war. The **Central Powers** included Germany, Austria-Hungary, Bulgaria, and the Ottoman Empire. Italy remained neutral until May 1915, when it joined the Allies. The Central Powers had the advantage of a central position and shorter internal lines of transportation and communication. The major Allied Powers included Britain, France, and Russia. The Allies had better access to the seas, but the German submarines made traveling the seas risky.

Systems of trenches separated by a "no man's land," machine guns, and heavy artillery barrages made it difficult for armies to advance. It became a stalemated war of attrition in which thousands died on each side for less than a mile of territory. For example, in the six-month battle of Verdun, each side had 330,000 to 350,000 casualties.

Large losses and no gains on the Eastern Front, plus scanty food and supplies were factors in bringing about the Tsar Nicholas II's abdication (March 1917), the Russian Revolutions, and the country's withdrawal from the War (December 1917). The loss of Russia hurt the Allies, but Germany's policy of unrestricted submarine warfare caused the United States' entrance into the War in April 1917. In particular, the sinking of the *Lusitania*, a British passenger ship with Americans on board, outraged the public.

America's entry brought fresh war supplies and much needed convoys to get them across the Atlantic. Within a year, Americans were fighting along side the Allies. The infusion of American assistance helped to turn the tide.

EUROPE AFTER WORLD WAR 1
1918 - 1922

New States (Results of WWI Peace Treaties)

Russia (U.S.S.R. after 1922)

CLOSE LOOK — THE FIRST MODERN GENOCIDE

Civilian populations suffered. Many children were orphaned or left without fathers. Particularly tragic were the **Armenian Massacres**. Most Armenians were Christians living in the Caucasus region near the Ottoman Empire's border with Russia. Their desire for independence resulted in massacres by the Muslim Ottomans in 1894. In 1915, the Ottoman government became fearful that the remaining Armenians might be traitors, conspiring with the Russians. The government deported them all. Massacres and deaths from the journey resulted in the deaths of up to 1,000,000 Armenians. Some historians refer to it as the "first genocide of modern times." By the end of the War, almost no Armenians lived within the new Turkish Republic. The few survivors scattered and had no homeland except for a small area within the Soviet Union.

IMPACTS OF THE WAR

The impact of the War was tremendous. Approximately 10 million died and another 20 million were injured. World War I ushered in many global changes. The role of European and American women was markedly changed by the War. For the first time, large numbers of women worked outside of the home. Some were military nurses and many others worked in factories to produce war materials. After the War, the contribution of women was recognized as country after country extended women the right to vote.

GOVERNMENTAL POWER INCREASED

To conduct the war effort efficiently, governments took command of industries, transportation, trade, and agriculture. This type of "planned" or **command economy**[1] provided an example that totalitarian governments later followed.

1 command system (economy in which central authority attempts to control resources and decision-making)

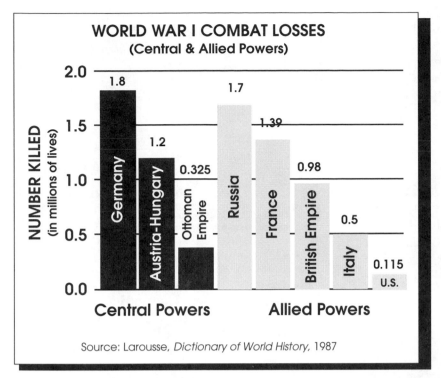

WORLD WAR I COMBAT LOSSES
(Central & Allied Powers)

NUMBER KILLED (in millions of lives)

Germany — 1.8
Austria-Hungary — 1.2
Ottoman Empire — 0.325
Russia — 1.7
France — 1.39
British Empire — 0.98
Italy — 0.5
U.S. — 0.115

Central Powers — Allied Powers

Source: Larousse, *Dictionary of World History*, 1987

Propaganda[1] and **censorship**[2] were widely used by both sides. Prior to the United States' entry, both sides tried to influence American public opinion. This use of the media also provided a model for later totalitarian regimes.

COLLAPSE OF EMPIRES

World War I marked the end of the Austro-Hungarian, German, Ottoman, and Russian Empires as they existed prior to 1914. The map of Europe was redrawn by the Paris Peace Conference and many small, new nations emerged.

The Ottoman Empire lost its possessions in the Middle East. During the War, British agent Colonel **T. E. Lawrence** (known as "Lawrence of Arabia," 1888-1935) served as a guerrilla organizer in the Arab Revolt of 1916-1918. The Revolt expelled the Turks from western Arabia and Syria and encouraged Arab hopes for an independent Arab nation.

As a result of the Arab-British correspondence, **Husayn ibn Ali** (1854-1931) established an Arab kingdom. When this action was opposed by the Zionists, the British issued the **Balfour Declaration** (1917). It vaguely promised the Jews a homeland in the same area of Palestine claimed by the Arabs while promising to preserve the rights of Palestinian Arabs. These conflicting promises were an attempt by the British to win support from the Arabs and the Zionists, but they continue to have repercussions today.

EMERGENCE OF NEW GLOBAL FORCES

The U.S. changed from a debtor nation to a creditor nation. Over $10 billion was owed to America by European nations at the end of the War. European nations also faced additional industrial competition. Cut off from their supply of European industrial products by the War, countries such as India, Brazil, and Argentina took steps to develop their industries.

SCIENTIFIC AND TECHNOLOGICAL ADVANCES

Weapons and communications technology developed during World War I were perfected and later played a major role in World War II. The use of radio, field telephones, aircraft, long range artillery, and tanks made possible the offensive war experienced from 1939 to 1945. Also, the settlements made at the Paris Peace Conference were contributing factors to the rise of Fascism in Europe. In many ways, World War I was a major factor in causing World War II.

LITERATURE AND ART

The war effort and its tragedies were commemorated in works such as: George M. Cohan's popular song, *Over There*, Leon Gellert's *Songs of a Campaign* – poems written about his experiences during the Gallipoli Campaign, T.S. Elliot's *The Hollow Men*, and Erich Remarque's *All Quiet on the Western Front*. Perhaps the most touching literary piece to come out of the War was John McCrae's *In Flanders Fields*:

"We are the Dead, Short days ago
We lived, felt dawn, saw sunset glow,
Loved and were loved, and now we lie
In Flanders Fields."

---

1 propaganda (use of the media to promote or oppose a cause or of information reflecting the interests of those people supporting such a doctrine or cause)
2 censorship (examination of books, films, or other material and removal or suppression of what is considered morally, politically, or otherwise objectionable)

McCrae died from pneumonia shortly after the poem was published. Art reflected the uncertainty of the times after the War as well as the psychology of Freud. It rejected realism and representational art. Artists like Salvador Dali in *The Persistence of Memory*, turned to subjectivism and the unconscious. This movement was called **surrealism**[1].

REVOLUTION AND CHANGE IN RUSSIA - CAUSES AND IMPACTS

After the assassination of Alexander II (r. 1855-1881), Tsar **Alexander III** (r. 1881-1894) began a period of reaction and authoritarianism. He felt that the assassination of his father and other acts of terrorism were encouraged by policies that were too **liberal**[2].

The Tsar's imperial two headed eagle looks both East and West, suggesting that he wanted to hold on to the old (Eastern culture) while trying to deal with the challenges of the new future (Western Society).

However, the Tsar's policies conflicted with modernization which accompanied industrialization and his subjects' increasing awareness of Western ideas. Also, issues of long hours, low wages, and poor living conditions concerned Russia's small, emerging **proletariat**[3]. Feeling oppressed, this class was willing to listen to the ideas of new socialists including the young V. I. Ulyanov (1870-1924), who later adopted the pseudonym **Lenin**.

---

1 surrealism (20th century literary and artistic movement that attempts to express the workings of the subconscious and is characterized by fantastic imagery and incongruous juxtaposition of subject matter)
2 liberal (favoring proposals for reform, open to new ideas for progress, and tolerant of the ideas and behavior of others; broad-minded)
3 proletariat (poorest class composed of industrial wage earners who, possessing neither capital nor production means, must earn their living by selling their labor)

MINI-ASSESSMENT

Mini Assessment

1 The work of people such as Louis Pasteur, Robert Koch, and Florence Nightingale is evident in
   1 improved farming techniques
   2 increased governmental stability
   3 improved life expectancy
   4 sophisticated military weaponry

2 A primary cause of the Armenian Massacres of 1915 was
   1 Turkish fears that Armenians might be conspiring with Russians
   2 Armenian aid to the Germans during World War I
   3 the refusal of the Armenians to sell oil to the Central Powers
   4 centuries long Russian animosity to the Armenians

3 The Balkans were often referred to as the "tinderbox" or the "powder keg" prior to World War I. Justification for this label can be seen in the
   1 formation of the Triple Entente
   2 British-German naval race
   3 nature of Pan-Slavism
   4 disputes over the water of the Danube River

Constructed Response:
Use the diagram on page 185 to answer the following questions:

1 What does the diagram indicate about the the causes of World War I?

2 Select two of the causes and briefly explain how they played a role in an event leading to World War I.

REVOLUTION OF 1905

Just as the defeat in the Crimean War (1854-1856) led to demands for reform, the defeat in the Russo-Japanese War (1904-1905) led to demands for change that erupted in the **Russian Revolution of 1905**. On 22 January, a Ukrainian priest, Father Georgi Gapon, organized a workers march in St. Petersburg to present a petition to Tsar **Nicholas II** (r. 1894-1917). The petition expressed respect for the Tsar, but also asked for worker reforms. Someone ordered soldiers protecting the Winter Palace to fire on the marchers.

The deaths on **Bloody Sunday** helped to destroy the feeling of the Russian people that the Tsar was the nation's "Little Father." Across the country, the incident triggered a series of strikes, peasant uprisings, mutinies, and terrorist acts. They culminated with a general strike in October, encouraged by the Petrograd Soviet (a group of radical socialists).

To restore order, Tsar Nicholas agreed to issue the **October Manifesto**. The imperial proclamation met some of the people's demands: a constitution, a **Duma** (national legislature), and basic civil liberties. However, it became apparent that the Tsar had no intention of following the spirit of the document. He repeatedly dismissed the elected Dumas until he ensured the election of a conservative legislature. Tsarist minister **Peter Stolypin** (1863-1911) came up with a program to turn peasants into private landowners. He believed that the normally conservative peasants would support the Tsar, if he met their desire for land.

The government cancelled the land payments in effect since Alexander II's emancipation of the serfs (1861). Peasants gained the right to leave the *mir* (village community), and some left to work in city factories. Other peasants purchased their land, and the number of **kulaks** (richer peasants) increased. However, land hunger continued in areas of fertile soil and large landed estates.

The continuation of 19th century problems, the limited success of the Revolution of 1905, and the authoritarian policies of the Tsar were signs of impending problems. The outbreak of World War I in 1914 placed the creaking government and economy under stresses that it could not solve. Reports of numerous casualties, of soldiers in front lines without guns, limited ammunition, and of high desertion rates reached the home front. Nicholas II decided to go to the front lines himself and left Tsarina **Alexandra** to run the government.

Unfortunately, the Tsarina's chief advisor was a dissolute monk, **Grigory Rasputin** (1865-1916). He gained influence with the imperial family, because he seemed to have the ability to ease the hemophilia attacks of the heir to the throne, Alexis. The Tsarina consulted Rasputin on major decisions involving the war effort and appointments to high offices. The Russian nobility greatly resented him. Finally, in December 1916, a group of nobles assassinated him. Some historians think that this was the beginning of the Revolution, because it undermined the imperial family's prestige.

MARCH 1917 REVOLUTION AND THE PROVISIONAL GOVERNMENT

The 1917 Revolution began in an unexpected fashion. On 8 March, a group of Petrograd (St. Petersburg) women began a protest against factory conditions. They were joined by a group of men who were locked out of their factories for striking. The two groups began to demand bread which was in short supply. Soldiers were called out to control the demonstrators, but they refused to fire. This led a Duma committee to form a **Provisional Government** which forced Nicholas II's **abdication** (give up power). The Romanov family were placed under house arrest. Later, the family members were sent to Siberia and were executed by the Bolsheviks.

The Provisional Government was based on Western principles of constitutional liberalism. At first, a moderate coalition of bourgeoisie-liberals controlled the provisional government. They envisioned a Western style democracy for Russia, but they could not meet the demands of the people for "Peace, Land and Bread."

In March 1917, **V. I. Lenin** (Vladimir Ilyich Ulyanov), a key leader of the radical **Bolshevik** socialist faction, returned from exile. Lenin was a student of Marxist ideas. However, Marx was vague about the post-revolutionary society. This allowed Lenin to develop his own beliefs. While

KEY IDEAS OF MARX AND LENIN

Marx	Lenin
• Large, open party	• Small party, led by a revolutionary elite
• Proletariat were revolutionary class	• Peasants and proletariat were revolutionary classes
• Long period of bourgeois, democratic government necessary before revolution of proletariat	• Revolution of proletariat possible without long period of bourgeois, democratic government

LENIN'S RULE: 1917-1924

Almost immediately, a Civil War also broke out in different areas of the country. The **Whites**[3], along with some of Russia's former World War I allies, tried to take control from the **Reds** (Bolsheviks). The charismatic socialist, **Leon Trotsky** (1879-1940), organized and trained the Bolsheviks' Red Army into an effective fighting force. Even though both sides committed atrocities, the Whites were unable to win the support of the peasantry. The Whites fought on the fringes of Russia. But, the Bolsheviks controlled the shorter, interior lines of communication.

pragmatic about molding Marx's ideas to fit the Russian situation, Lenin resented criticism of his own ideas. Anyone who disputed his approach was labeled a "revisionist." The **Bolsheviks** played to the Russians' desire for social and economic change.

At almost the same time that Lenin returned, **soviets**[1] were organized throughout the country. The **Bolsheviks**[2] joined other left-wing factions to form the **Petrograd Soviet of Workers' and Soldiers' Deputies** as a rival government to the provisional government.

NOVEMBER 1917: BOLSHEVIK REVOLUTION

In the summer and fall, Lenin's supporters gained majorities in the Petrograd and Moscow Soviets and in the Moscow city government. Lenin armed his followers for an uprising. On the night of 6 November 1917, the Bolsheviks and their allies captured key points in Petrograd. A week later, the Bolsheviks overcame resistance in Moscow.

Early in 1918, Lenin ended Russian involvement in World War I by signing the **Treaty of Brest Litovsk** with Germany. Russia lost control of large areas including Finland, Estonia, Latvia, Lithuania, and Poland that eventually became independent.

Lenin promotes his New Economic Policy before a gathering of proletariat, 5 May 1920.
Soviet Government Photo

CLASH OF GOALS

Demands	Provisional Leadership	Soviet Leadership
Peace	Continue the War	Withdraw from the War
Land	Eventual land reform	Immediate land reform
Bread	No plan to solve food shortages	Rationing food

1 soviets (councils of workers, peasants, and soldiers)
2 Bolsheviks (members of the left-wing majority group of the Russian Social Democratic Workers' Party that adopted Lenin's theses on party organization in 1903)
3 Whites (a disorganized group of tsarist army officers, nobles, and some members of the middle class)

During the Civil War, the Bolsheviks became known as **communists**[1] and implemented a policy known as **War Communism**. It called for seizure of "surplus" food from peasants, forced labor or military service for many, and some **nationalization**[2] of key industries. Lenin created the **Cheka**, a new secret police force, to deal with opposition, and he suppressed the Russian Orthodox Church. The Bolsheviks also seized some peasant land. By 1921 when the Red Army appeared victorious in most areas, Russian production was less that 50% of that in 1914.

In their 1922 Constitution, the communists established the **Union of Soviet Socialist Republics** (U.S.S.R.). While it appeared to be a democratic state, only "toilers" (workers) were given the right to vote. The 1922 Constitution gave the nationalities some voice in local government, but most of the power remained with the central government.

NEW ECONOMIC POLICY

- Major industries ("commanding heights") – natural resources and financial institutions were kept under government control
- Small private enterprise was permitted (light industry and retail operations).
- Farmers could sell surpluses for a profit.
- Foreign capitalists were given economic concessions to encourage trade.

By the end of the Civil War, the Russian economy was in shambles. A widespread peasant and workers uprising was brewing. To rebuild, Lenin compromised his Marxist proletarian economic plan and adopted the **New Economic Policy** (NEP, 1921-1927). The policy bore some fruit (see chart above). By 1928, the pre-World War I levels of production had been reached.

STALIN AND THE MODERN TOTALITARIAN STATE

Lenin's death in 1924 led to a power struggle in which **Josef Stalin** defeated his rival **Leon Trotsky**. One of the first things that Stalin did after consolidating his power was to institute the first **Five Year Plan** (1928). His goal was to increase heavy industry (steel, mining, and products necessary to make more goods, plus military hardware). The plan largely ignored light or consumer industry and called for government ownership of all the means of production. It also created **GOSPLAN**, a central planning agency that made economic decisions and allocated resources to achieve goals. This was a command economy.

The Plan demanded high levels of agricultural production while trying to free farm workers to work in factories. Agricultural exports were to pay for imports of needed machinery and materials for industrial development.

CLOSE LOOK

SUCCEEDING LENIN

Lenin's death in 1924 led to a power struggle between Leon Trotsky and Josef Stalin (1879-1953). Trotsky's base of power was the Red Army and his friendship with Lenin. He was a powerful orator and an intellectual. He was known internationally and favored immediate spread of revolution world wide.

In many ways, Stalin was his opposite. He was ruthless and a Machiavellian. He was willing to use his position as General Secretary of the Communist Party to intimidate and force others to do his will. He wanted to build up the Soviet Union as a base before attempting to spread global revolution. Despite Lenin's view of him as "rude," Stalin was able to win enough support to force the exile of Trotsky. Eventually, Trotsky was assassinated in Mexico in 1940, probably by agents sent by Stalin.

---

1   communism (system of government and economics in which the state plans and controls the economy and a single, often authoritarian party holds power, claiming to make progress toward a higher social order in which all goods are equally shared by the people; Marxist-Leninist version of communist doctrine advocates the overthrow of capitalism by the revolution of the proletariat)
2   nationalization (to convert from private to governmental ownership [takeover] and control)

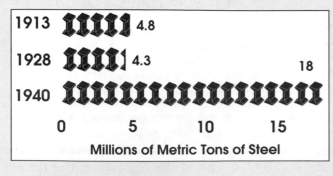

1913 **ⅠⅠⅠⅠⅠ** 4.8
1928 **ⅠⅠⅠⅠⅠ** 4.3
1940 **ⅠⅠⅠⅠⅠⅠⅠⅠⅠⅠⅠⅠⅠⅠⅠⅠⅠⅠ** 18

0   5   10   15

Millions of Metric Tons of Steel

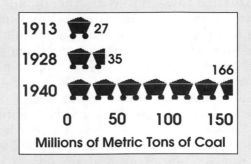

1913 🛒 27
1928 🛒🛒 35
1940 🛒🛒🛒🛒🛒🛒 166

0   50   100   150

Millions of Metric Tons of Coal

Ⅰ = 2,000,000 metric tons

🛒 = 25,000,000 metric tons

⬚ = 30,000,000 Barrels

⟁ = 5,000,000,000 kilowatt hours

SOVIET v. TSARIST PRODUCTION

1913 – Tsarist Russia
1928 – New Economic Plan
1940 – After Stalin's 5-yr Plans Began

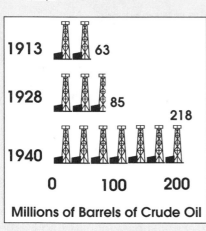

1913 🛢🛢 63
1928 🛢🛢 85
1940 🛢🛢🛢🛢🛢🛢 218

0   100   200

Millions of Barrels of Crude Oil

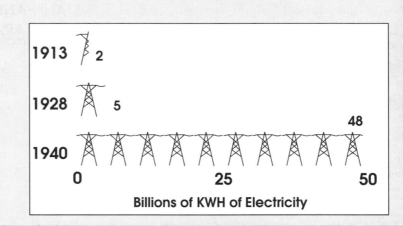

1913 ⟁ 2
1928 ⟁ 5
1940 ⟁⟁⟁⟁⟁⟁⟁⟁⟁⟁ 48

0   25   50

Billions of KWH of Electricity

To accomplish this, Stalin ordered the **collectivization**[1] of farms. The government seized privately owned farms, machinery, produce, and livestock. Theoretically, larger farms could be more easily mechanized and would be more readily controlled by the government.

The government took most of the production, but the farmers could share in the remaining profits. Farmers were given one acre plots which they could farm for themselves and their families. As time went on, the yield per acre from the small plots was much higher than that found on collective land. The private plots (2-3% of the acreage), produced about one-third of the dairy products, vegetables, and meat.

1 collectivization (principles or system of ownership and control of the means of production and distribution by the people collectively)

OPPOSITION: STARVATION IN UKRAINE

The dislocations caused by Stalin's Five Year Plan generated opposition, especially in Ukraine. Its black chernozem soil was singularly fertile, and kulaks had developed this into Russia's "breadbasket." Opponents of Stalin's collectivization fought back by destroying crops, equipment, and livestock. (It took 20 years to restore livestock levels to those found before Stalin's Plan went into effect).

Stalin ruthlessly suppressed this peasant resistance. While many kulaks were sent to Siberia, Stalin also used "terror famine" or "war by starvation" to rid himself of others. When a drought led to famine, he refused to decrease exports to alleviate the hunger. Estimates indicate that at least five million perished in the famines inflicted by nature and the government between 1929 and 1935.

Still, Stalin's Five Year Plans were successful in increasing heavy industry and Russian self-sufficiency. By 1939, only the U.S. and Germany had higher gross industrial outputs. Much of the new development was in the area east of the Ural Mountains to make it less vulnerable to attack in case of war. However, the cost of development was high. The government forced thousands to move to Siberia and work in the new factories. Some of the opposition were sentenced to the **gulags**[1] and required to work in unspeakable conditions. Few consumer products were available, and everyone was expected to make sacrifices for later generations. There was constant pressure to exceed production goals, and bonuses to individuals and factories were based on production.

TOTALITARIAN CONTROL

Along with this centralization of economic control came overwhelming political control. Stalin built a **totalitarian**[2] state. The government exercised absolute, centralized control over all aspects of life and suppressed opposing political and cultural expression. The ethnic groups lost much of the power granted to them in the 1922 constitution.

Stalin's constitution of 1936 appeared to be democratic, but its operation revealed a dictatorship. Elections were held, and people were required to vote or face stiff penalties. However, the Communist Party permitted only its list of candidates. The legislature was the bicameral[3] **Supreme Soviet**. The people were represented in the *Soviet of the Union*. The republics or regions were represented in the *Soviet of the Nationalities*. These two chambers were "**rubber stamp**[4]" bodies. When the *Soviet of the Union* was not in session, the **Presidium**, a smaller group, acted for it. The chairman of the Presidium was President of the Soviet Union, a largely honorary position. The Council of People's Commissars or Council of Ministers was similar to a Western cabinet and headed by the Premier – the most powerful figure in the government.

However, the key to power in the U.S.S.R. was not the government, but the Communist Party. Membership in the Party was restricted to the elite and probably included only about five percent of the population. These people helped to elect representatives to the Party Congress which met once every few years. Most power rested with two smaller groups, the **Politburo** and the **Secretariat**. The Politburo determined policies. The Secretariat made appointments to government and Party positions and kept records on Party members. The **General Secretary of the Party** was the head of the Secretariat and actually, the most powerful person in the Soviet Union.

Often the same people held comparable positions in the Party and the government. For example, Stalin was both Premier and General Secretary of the Party. Most of his successors also held both positions.

RUSSIFICATION AND A REIGN OF TERROR

During the 1930s, Stalin became obsessive about traitors and the possibility of threats to his power. This led to a reign of terror. Party leaders whose views varied from Stalin's were arrested and placed on trial as enemies of the state. The purges forced many officials to make confessions in open court, leading to their imprisonment or execution. Not until years later was it revealed that these confessions were obtained through psychological torture.

One of Stalin's most notorious purges occurred in 1937. Eight top-ranking army generals were convicted of conspiracy. Ultimately, about 50% of the army officers were arrested. Many were shot; others were sent to the gulags. This loss of experienced military leadership had serious consequences in World War II.

During the early years, the communists attempted to accommodate various cultures by providing for some local control. During the

---

1 gulags (forced labor camps of great suffering and hardship, especially for political dissidents, likened to the atmosphere in a prison)
2 totalitarian (form of government in which the political authority exercises absolute and centralized control over all aspects of life, the individual is subordinated to the state, and opposing political and cultural expression is suppressed)
3 bicameral (composed of or based on two legislative chambers or branches)
4 "rubber stamp" body (automatically approves laws proposed by the leadership)

1930s, Stalin felt the country needed a greater unity, as he was concerned about the loyalty of ethnic groups. Stalin returned to the practice of **Russification**[1], a common policy in tsarist Russia. The government required all schools to conduct classes in the Russian language and to teach Russian culture exclusively. Many leaders of ethnic groups were killed. There was also a large-scale transfer of Great Russians into ethnic republics and regions. They were given key positions and the best jobs. Stalin's version of Russification led to interesting consequences. After the breakup of the U.S.S.R. in 1991, many of the newly independent republics began returning to their native culture and forcing the Great Russians to leave.

BETWEEN THE WARS

Defeats in early 1918 forced the German Army to retreat back across France and Belgium. Although Allied armies were not on German soil, German generals advised Kaiser William II that Germany could not win and urged him to abdicate. William waited until after the armistice to abdicate. On 28 November 1918, the last King of Prussia and Emperor of Germany stepped down and went into exile in the Netherlands. At about the same time, the Austro-Hungarian Empire collapsed, and its ethnic groups began to form individual nation-states. The **armistice**[2] ending the fighting was signed on 11 November 1918.

When the Germans signed the armistice, they assumed that the final peace would be based on the *Fourteen Points* proposed by U.S. President **Woodrow Wilson** (1856-1924). Issued before the end of the War, the *Fourteen Points* were aimed at settling key causes of wars and avoiding future wars.

---

1 Russification (forcing Great Russian culture on other ethnic groups)
2 armistice (temporary cessation of fighting by mutual consent; a truce)

Mini Assessment

MINI-ASSESSMENT

1 The long term causes of the Russian Revolution in March 1917 might be best described as
   1 a result of German agitation during World War I
   2 having roots in 19th century events and conditions
   3 coming from the appeal of Marxism to the peasants
   4 a result of the assassination of Rasputin

2 The French Revolution (1789) and Russian Revolution (1917) are similar in that both
   1 resulted in a non-democratic government
   2 experienced no foreign involvement
   3 began during a war
   4 involved little violence

3 Which statement accurately describes Stalin's Soviet Union during the 1930s?
   1 A multi-party system was allowed.
   2 A free market system was established.
   3 Ethnic groups were given more freedom.
   4 There was tremendous growth in heavy industry.

Constructed Response:

Use the cartoon at the right to answer the following questions:

1 Identify two of the Tsarist Russian symbols shown in the cartoon.

2 For the two symbols identified, briefly explain the nature of the communist replacement.

THE FOURTEEN POINTS
KEY PROVISIONS

- A league of nations to settle disputes among nations
- Self-determination for peoples of Ottoman and Austro-Hungarian Empires
- A general decrease in arms
- Freedom to ship safely on the seas
- Jjust settlement of colonial problems
- End to secret agreements (alliances)

Wilson was viewed as a great world leader because the *Fourteen Points* appealed to the people of many countries as a means to preserving a stable peace. Admirable as they were, the *Fourteen Points* were not fully accepted by the major Allied leaders as the basis for the peace. At the **Paris Peace Conference** (January 1919-January 1920) at the Versailles Palace, the major decisions were made by the "Big Three" – U.S., Britain, and France. However, the leader of each of these countries had specific goals for the peace settlement.

WHO WAS WHO
AT THE CONFERENCE

- **President Woodrow Wilson** (U.S.) sought implementation of the **Fourteen Points**, especially a league of nations
- **Prime Minister David Lloyd George** (Britain, 1863-1945) – reparations, colonies
- **Premier George Clemenceau** (France, 1841-1929) – French security against German aggression, reparations

THE TREATY OF VERSAILLES

The Peace Conference resulted in five treaties, the Treaty of Versailles with Germany being the most important. Separate treaties were signed with other members of the Central Powers. Germany was not allowed to participate in the negotiations and was forced to sign the Treaty or resume fighting. The Germans were very resentful about what they regarded as unfair provisions.

TREATY OF VERSAILLES
KEY PROVISIONS

- League of Nations established
- New or re-established nations: Poland, Hungary, Czechoslovakia, Austria, Yugoslavia, Estonia, Latvia, Lithuania
- German territorial losses: Alsace-Lorraine, Polish Corridor, Danzig, Upper Silesia, Saar (later returned), all colonies which became mandates (governed by other countries under League supervision)
- War guilt clause: blamed Germany and its allies for causing the War
- Reparations: required Germany to pay reparations (compensation or remuneration for damage or injury during the war) for Allied losses (later set at between $30 and $35 billion)
- Limits on German military
- Occupation of German Rhineland (mining and industrial center)

The 1919 peace settlement at Paris created many problems. The Germans blamed it for their postwar problems and Hitler was able to use their resentment to win support. Mussolini was also able to use Italian dissatisfaction to help his fascist cause in Italy. The Senate of the United States refused to ratify the Treaty, and the U.S. never joined the League of Nations. In colonial areas, nationalism blossomed, and agitation for independence increased. The economic problems resulting from the Settlement were contributing causes of the Great Depression (1929). Most importantly, the agreements reached in Paris must be regarded as a major cause of World War II.

THE LEAGUE OF NATIONS

The League of Nations began operations in Geneva, Switzerland on January 20, 1920. Wilson was hopeful that any inequities in the Paris Settlement could be remedied by the League. However, the failure of the United States to join, and the limited German and Soviet involvement, weakened the organization right from the start. Although over forty nations joined the League, the Great Powers dominated.

The League's Central Council included the Great Powers as permanent members with other nations elected on a rotating basis. The Council had the power to impose diplomatic, economic, and military sanctions to enforce its decisions. However, decisions required unanimous votes which were difficult to achieve. The Assembly included all League members, but it had relatively little power. Most of the best work done by the League was in the economic and social fields. It supervised mandates, aided displaced persons, fought international narcotics traffic, and settled minor border disputes.

MODERNIZATION AND WESTERNIZATION FOR TURKEY

World War I also brought an end to the Ottoman Empire. The **Treaty of Sevres** (1920) resulted in major territorial losses, including control of the Straits of the Dardanelles and Bosporus. However, Turkish General Mustafa Kemal (1881-1938, later called **Ataturk**), led an uprising against the settlement. He pushed the Greeks and Allied support out of Anatolia, deposed the Sultan, and became the first president of the new republic (1923-1938). Ultimately, the new republic negotiated the **Treaty of Lausanne** (1923) cancelling the Sevres treaty and defining Turkey's boundaries and and restoring Turkish control of Istanbul and the Straits. However, much of the former Ottoman Empire became independent or mandates of Britain and France.

Ataturk had two goals for Turkey: **westernization**[1] and **secularization**[2] (separation of religion and government). His **Six Principles** were called Kemalism or Ataturkism. They included: republicanism, nationalism, populism, statism, secularism, and revolutionism. The new republic adopted a constitution based on Western models. It included an elected parliament with women's suffrage. However, it was a single party government, and Ataturk retained most of the power.

In 1928, Islam was removed as the state religion, and Islamic law was dropped in favor of a code of laws based on western examples. Other changes included: adoption of Western dress, use of the Latin alphabet, removal of women from the harem, and use of the Western calendar.

Steps were also taken to improve the literacy rate, and public works were started to improve the **infrastructure**[3]. Under Ataturk, Turkey made much progress, but was not a true democracy. Today, the struggle between the secularists and the Islamic fundamentalists continues.

WOMEN'S SUFFRAGE

The struggle for women's rights achieved some success in the period after World War I. **Women's suffrage**[4] became an issue after large groups of men obtained the right to vote in the 18th and 19th century in the Western world.

The women's suffrage movement in Britain was similar to that in the United States, but more violent. A key British leader was **Mary Wollstonecraft** who wrote A Vindication of the Rights of Women (1792). The Chartists also supported the demands of women in the 1830s and 1840s. However, the opposition remained strong and included Queen Victoria (r. 1837-1909) and two prominent Prime Ministers, Gladstone (1809-1898) and Disraeli (1804-1881).

By the 20th century, leadership of the British women's movement was in the hands of **Emmeline Pankhurst** (1858-1928). To achieve their goals, the British women broke windows, picketed, and used bombs. Suffragettes were frequently fined and jailed. However, World War I brought about a change in sentiment. The efforts of women in the military and the factories were rewarded with the right to vote for those over thirty in 1918. In 1928, universal suffrage was adopted for persons all over twenty-one.

Countries such as New Zealand (1893) and Australia (1902) were ahead of the European nations in extending the right to vote to women. Most European nations did so after World War I. However, Italy, Japan, China, and India did not grant women suffrage until after World War II. By the 1980s, women had the right to vote in most nations except for a few Muslim countries. Women political leaders also emerged including Prime Minister **Golda Meir** (Israel), Prime Minister **Indira Gandhi** (India), Prime

---

1 westernization (convert to the customs of Western civilization)
2 secularization (to draw away from religious orientation and to transfer from ecclesiastical or religious to civil or lay use or ownership)
3 infrastructure (basic facilities, services, and installations needed for the functioning of a community or society)
4 women's suffrage (right or privilege of women to vote)

Mini Assessment

1 Which statement best describes the position of the League of Nations in inter national affairs between 1936-1939?
1 It suppressed and minimized conflicts between nations.
2 It successfully applied sanctions against aggressor nations.
3 It was unable to deal with aggression by major powers.
4 It used military means to enforce its decisions.

2 "We have tried every means – processions and meetings – which were of no avail. We have tried demonstrations, and now at least we have to break windows... You only have one point of view and that is the men's, and while men have done the best they could, they cannot go far without the women..."

This statement was most likely made by a supporter of the ideas of the
1 suffragettes
2 Zionists
3 chauvinists
4 Moslem League

3 Many Germans thought that the Treaty of Versailles was unfair because
1 Germany was not involved in the crises which led to the War
2 bases for peace in the 14 Points were ignored in the Treaty of Versailles
3 the U.S. claimed many of Germany's former colonies
4 they resented the loss of Alsace-Lorraine to Britain

Constructed Response:
Use the maps below (also found on pages 184 and 188) to answer the following questions.

1 What happened to the Austria-Hungarian, Russian, and Ottoman Empires after WWI?

2 What do the new states resulting from the World War I peace treaties indicate about the priorities of the participants in the Paris Peace Conference?

Minister **Margaret Thatcher** (Britain), President **Corazon Aquino** (Philippines), and President **Violeta Chamorro** (Nicaragua).

RISE OF FASCISM

As a political philosophy, **fascism**[1] varied from country to country. Generally, its supporters believed that democracy was a sign of weak ness. They sought centralization of authority, strict obedience to the state, the use of violence, suppression of the opposition through terror and censorship, and chauvinism (extreme, belligerent nationalism). Many members of fascist groups were from the industrial and land hold-

---

1 fascism (system of government marked by centralization of authority under a dictator, stringent socioeconomic controls, suppression of the opposition through terror and censorship, and typically a policy of belligerent nationalism and racism)

ing classes or the lower middle class. In some countries, their rivals for power were the communists whose support came from the working class. The fascists and communists used similar tactics. However, the fascists eventually supported private ownership of property under strict state control while the communists wanted government ownership of the means of production.

MUSSOLINI AND ITALIAN FASCISM

In Italy, there were postwar problems with war debts, unemployment, peasant seizures of land, sit-down strikes by workers, and weak coalition governments. Many of these problems were blamed on the failure of Italy to gain what it expected from the Paris peace settlement.

Benito Mussolini (1883-1945), son of a school teacher and a blacksmith, was able to use these problems to rise to power. Originally, his Fascist Party (*Fàci di Combattimento*) supported worker demands, but later it became the defender of law and order and private ownership of property. The Italian fascists formed a paramilitary group, the "Blackshirts," to protect their meetings and harass their opponents. Beatings, murder, and arson were used against others. In 1922, Mussolini and the Blackshirts organized a March on Rome. King Victor Emmanuel III named Mussolini premier, and the first fascist government came to power legally.

GERMAN FASCISM: NAZISM

In Germany, the weak **Weimar Republic** (1919-1933) was plagued by forces from the left (communists) and from the right (fascists). Long used to strong, autocratic regimes, the German people lacked respect for the Republic's democratic government. It treated the opposition mercifully even when its activities seemed treasonable. Conservatives and elitists who lacked respect for the government dominated the courts, the educational system, and the military. A host of small political parties led to changing coalition governments. At times, Presidents Ebert and von Hindenberg resorted to using emergency powers. The German people also blamed this government for signing the hated Treaty of Versailles.

Economic hardship plagued Germany in the postwar period. The loss of its colonies and overseas investments, plus the trade restrictions imposed by other nations made it impossible to pay the reparations ($35 billion in compensation or remuneration for damages to the Allies) required by the Treaty of Versailles. In addition, Germany had its own war debts in excess of 47 billion dollars.

In the 1923, **Ruhr Crisis**, France declared Germany in default and sent in troops to occupy the mining and industrial center of the Ruhr. The Weimar government urged workers to refuse to work for the French and promised to pay their wages. The government increased printing of paper money and created runaway **inflation**[1]. At its peak, four trillion German marks equaled one U.S. dollar in purchasing power. The United States came up with the **Dawes Plan** (1923) to ease the crisis. It lowered the yearly reparations payments and provided loans to Germany. The Weimar government then recalled the existing currency and issued new money. It was during the Ruhr Crisis that Adolph Hitler made his first attempt to seize power.

After the Ruhr Crisis, the period from 1924-1929 was relatively good for Germany. The economy stabilized and some prosperity returned. Germany also regained some status internationally. The **Locarno Pact** (1926) was a series of treaties involving Germany, France, and Belgium guaranteeing existing borders. Germany also accepted the concept of boundary **arbitration**[2] with Czechoslovakia and Poland. As a result, Germany was admitted to the League of Nations. In 1928, it also signed the **Kellogg-Briand Pact** (Pact of Paris), pledging signatories not to resort to war as an instrument of national policy.

However, the Great Depression of the 1930s changed the picture dramatically for Germany. Based on their experience during the Ruhr Crisis, the middle class doubted the ability of the Weimar Republic to deal with the economic problems. Emotions ran high. Resentment of the

---

1   inflation (persistent increase in the level of consumer prices or a persistent decline in the purchasing power of money)
2   arbitration (process by which the parties to a dispute submit their differences to the judgment of an impartial person or group appointed by mutual consent or statutory provision)

harsh terms of the Treaty of Versailles continued. Many Germans began to support organized groups such as the communists or the fascists in hopes of reviving the economy. President von Hindenburgh began ruling by decree. In the 1932 elections, no party received a majority. The fascist National Socialist German Workers Party (Nazis) received the largest number of votes, and von Hindenburgh appointed Nazi leader Adolph Hitler as chancellor in 1933.

Post War Depression Bread Line

By 1938, only ten of twenty-seven governments in Europe were democratic. Often, the non-democratic governments were fascist. The lack of democratic tradition, low literacy rates, economic problems, desire for stability, fear of communism, and dissatisfied ethnic groups were factors in the decline of democracy.

WORLDWIDE DEPRESSION

In 1919 and the early 1920s, most countries experienced a **postwar conversion depression**[1]. Unemployment increased as factories closed and others converted from wartime to peacetime production. Soldiers released from the military worsened the unemployment situation. Formerly strong European economies found themselves competing not only among themselves, but with a strengthened United States and other developing areas. During the War, countries in Latin America and Asia industrialized to meet the product demands formerly filled with imports from Europe.

By 1924, the global economy began to improve, and prosperity appeared to be slowly returning to war devastated countries. Yet the the appearance of renewed prosperity hid a number of underlying problems:

• Overproduction in agriculture and industry led to lower prices, lower wages, lessened demand, and increasing unemployment.

• High tariffs (import taxes) diminished world trade.

• An unprecedented rise in the stock market led investors to buy on margin (with borrowed money).

When business profits declined, investors began selling stock to pay their margin loans. The rash of selling led to "Black Friday," the stock market crash in October 1929, when New York Stock Exchange prices plummeted. The crash uncovered a variety of global weaknesses that caused the Great Depression. It spread worldwide with serious results around the globe.

From 1929 to 1932, there was a 38% decrease in world production. In 1932, at the depth of the Depression, 30 million were unemployed worldwide. Governments responded to this economic disaster in a variety of ways. Economic nationalism arose as governments tried to protect their markets from foreign competition. Some nations devalued their currencies. Nations abandoned the gold standard and increased tariffs.

In the United States, President **Franklin Roosevelt** (1882-1945) instituted the "New Deal" program. It called for increased government spending on a variety of programs to ease the economic pain of American citizens. Roosevelt put into practice some ideas developed by English economist **John Maynard Keynes** (1883-1946). Keynes called for **deficit spending**[2] in order to "prime the pump" (get the economy moving upward). Other governments, however, were very concerned about balancing the budget.

---

1 economic depression (period of drastic decline in a national or international economy, characterized by decreasing business activity, falling prices, and unemployment)

2 deficit spending (spending of public funds obtained by borrowing rather than by taxation)

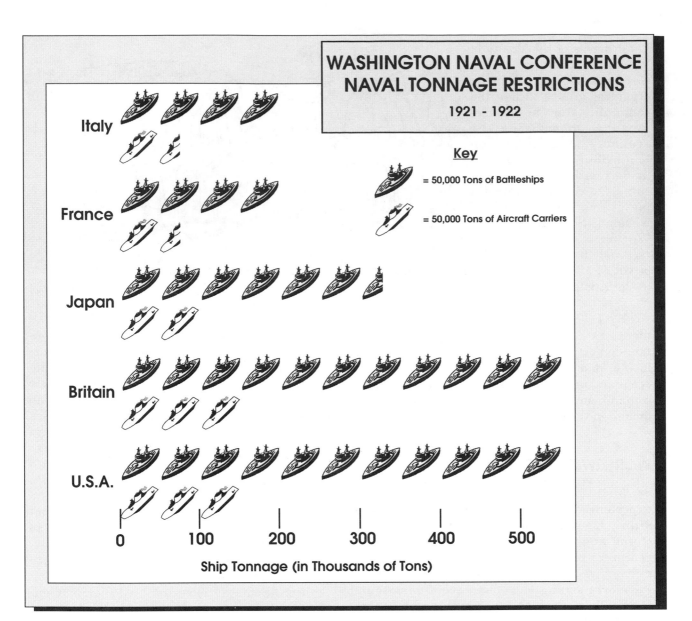

WASHINGTON NAVAL CONFERENCE NAVAL TONNAGE RESTRICTIONS
1921 - 1922

Key

= 50,000 Tons of Battleships

= 50,000 Tons of Aircraft Carriers

Italy

France

Japan

Britain

U.S.A.

0   100   200   300   400   500

Ship Tonnage (in Thousands of Tons)

In Britain, a **coalition government**[1] took steps to increase welfare, but was not prepared to spend its way out of the Depression. In Germany, there were 6 million unemployed at the peak of the Depression. Foreign loans stopped, and Germany was unable to meet its World War I reparations payments. Of the major economic powers in the 1930s, France suffered the least. Its balance between agriculture and industry left it less vulnerable to world market forces.

JAPANESE EXPANSION AND MILITARISM

In World War I, Japan was on the Allied side. It signed a treaty with Britain in 1902 and honored the commitment. However, it used the opportunity to seize German-controlled areas in China and the Pacific. It also forced China to accept the **Twenty-one Demands** granting Japan special privileges in Manchuria and on the Shantung Peninsula making Japan a colonial power in China. The 1919 Paris Peace Conference gave Japan mandates for German colonies north of the Equator and more rights on the Shantung Peninsula.

The War increased Japanese power and prestige. During the War, Japan expanded industrial production and acquired markets from war-beleaguered European producers. Japan also became a creditor nation and a rival for the United States in the Pacific region.

1 coalition government (combination of parties in order to obtain a voting majority)

The **Washington Conference** (1921-1922) attempted to deal with post-war naval arms race among the great powers. It also focused on some Far Eastern issues, attempting to stabilize East Asia and to provide for an independent Republic of China. Several agreements emerged from diplomatic efforts in Washington:

- The **Four Power Treaty** – (Britain, U.S., France, Japan) December 1921 agreement to respect possessions in the Far East

- The **Five Power Naval Armaments Treaty** – (Britain, France, U.S., Japan, Italy) February 1922 agreement arranged a 10 year cessation (break) in building major warships; the naval agreement established a battleship tonnage ratio in an attempt to stop a naval race (see graph); Japan resented its lack of equality with the other powers in this agreement

- The **Nine-Power Treaty** – pledged the signatories to respect the independence and territorial integrity of China and the **Open Door Policy** (a U.S. policy designed to keep Chinese trade open to all nations)

During the interwar years, the power and influence of the **zaibatsu**[1] and the military increased in Japan. The zaibatsu needed new sources of raw materials and markets. Manchuria's coal and iron mines and markets became a main target. In 1931, the Japanese used the excuse of a small bomb exploding near a Japanese-owned railroad to invade Manchuria. The League of Nations reacted by establishing the Lytton Commission to investigate. The Commission found the Japanese guilty of aggression, and their actions were condemned by the League. However, no further action was taken because of the reluctance of the other great powers to act. Japan established a puppet government in its new Chinese state of "Manchukuo." In 1937, Japan invaded China proper in a prelude to World War II. The Japanese assault on Nanking was accompanied by so many **atrocities**[2] that it was called the "rape of Nanking." In the same year, Japan joined Germany and Italy in the **Rome/ Berlin/ Tokyo Axis**, a mutual non-aggression pact.

---

1   zaibatsu (powerful family-controlled commercial combine of Japan; Japanese conglomerate or cartel)
2   atrocities (acts of extreme cruelty and violence inflicted by an enemy armed force on civilians)
3   mandate (commission from the League of Nations authorizing a member nation to administer a territory)

COLONIAL UNREST

Colonial people were also dissatisfied with the results of the Paris Peace Conference. Many of them had given troops and supplies to the Allies' war effort hoping to receive more self-government or independence at the end of the War. The victors did not end colonial rule. Instead, they established a **mandate system**[3] under League of Nations supervision. It was a renewal of colonialism in overseas territories of the former Central Powers. The British and French obtained mandates in Africa and parts of the Ottoman Empire. Japan and Australia took former German areas in the Pacific. As a consequence, the interwar period was marked by an increase in colonial nationalism and intensified demands for independence.

IRAN EMERGES

In Persia (name changed to **Iran** in 1935), **Reza Khan** (r. 1925-1941), expelled Soviet troops, overthrew the Shah, and established the Pahlavi Dynasty. His goals were to decrease or remove foreign influence, modernize, and secularize his country. He was able to win concessions from British oil interests. He obtained a greater share of the profits and promises to hire more local workers. Khan pursued a domestic program that was similar to Ataturk's. He adopted Western clothing and alphabet, established an educational system based on that of France, and built industries and railroads. He changed the Islamic code of laws to one based on European laws and increased the rights of women, particularly in regard to marriage. Khan's changes provoked the opposition of Islamic religious leaders. However, he held most of the power and had the support of the large landowners. The struggle between the forces of modernization and secularism still battle with tradition and religion in Iran today.

INDIA SMOLDERS

In 1906, **Muhammad Ali Jinnah** (1876-1948) founded the Muslim League, a religiously based nationalist group. Originally, Jinnah supported the idea of an independent India with a coalition government of Hindus and Moslems and protection of Muslim rights. However, fear of Hindu domination led the Muslim League to demand an independent Muslim state. At least some of the heightened feelings between Hindus

"THE HOLY ONE"

During the 1920s, **Mohandas K. Gandhi** (1869-1948) emerged as the leader of the Congress Party. He was a Hindu from a comfortable middle class background. He was educated as a lawyer in London and went to live in South Africa where he encountered prejudice against Indians and advocated passive resistance.

After he returned to India in 1914, he encouraged Indians to use passive resistance, civil disobedience, and non-violence against the British. Gandhi also supported boycotts against British goods and encouraged Indian production of home spun textiles to counter India's dependence on British imports. When his followers used violence or when he was imprisoned, he would often fast and pray for the violence to end. He opposed the caste system and the treatment of untouchables and women and also worked to help the poor.

In his **Salt March** (1930), Gandhi opposed the British monopoly on the production and sale of salt, a vital commodity for India. Thousands marched to the sea where Gandhi and others gathered salt. This defiance of British law led to his arrest and imprisonment. It is one of the most famous examples of Gandhi's methods.

and Moslems can be attributed to the British policy of "divide and rule" which played one group off against the other.

Indians fought on the side of Britain in World War I and received promises of self-government after the War. However, the British took few steps in that direction. The **Amritsar Massacre** (1919) further disillusioned Indians. British soldiers fired on a group that gathered peacefully to protest British rule in violation of a ban on meetings. Over three hundred people were killed and a thousand wounded. This led the Congress Party to agitate for independence.

CHINA – TORN BY CIVIL STRIFE

During World War I, China dissolved into chaos and civil war between warlords. Sun Yixian (Sun Yat-sen) resigned as President of the Chinese Republic in 1912 in favor of General **Yuan Shikai** in hopes of a restoration of law and order. After Yuan's death in 1916, civil war resumed. China also faced pressure from Japan for political and economic concessions during World War I. These concessions were largely approved by the Paris Peace Conference and continued China's humiliation at the hands of foreigners. This led to the student-generated May 4th Movement, a protest against Chinese weakness. After the suppression of this movement, some of the students turned to communism as an answer to China's problems.

Sun Yixian again emerged as a leader of a government in South China. He sought aid from the West, but was denied. He then turned to Russia which not only extended aid, but also gave up some of the territorial gains obtained under the tsars. As a result, Russia was perceived as a friend and the Chinese Communist Party allied with the Guomindang (Nationalist) Party of Sun in 1923.

Jiang Jieshu (Chiang Kai-skek)

After Sun's death in 1925, **Jiang Jieshu** (Chiang Kai-shek, 1887-1975) emerged as the new leader of China and the Guomindang. He opposed the communists, and in 1927, his forces carried out a massacre in Shanghai that led to civil war. **Mao Zedong** (1893-1976), a communist leader, escaped the massacre and fled to the mountains of the south where he joined others and founded the Chinese Red Army. The Guomindang forced the communists to leave this area. They went on the Long March (1934-1935) to the borders with Russia. Of the approximately 90,000 people who undertook this March, about 50% died. Once the communists arrived, they established a government and began to win peasant support.

Mao Zedong

However, Jiang persuaded the Western powers to give up most of their gains from the old, unequal treaties of the 19th century. He won support of landowners and business groups but was unable to make the reforms necessary to win the support of the peasants. In 1931, he had to face Japanese aggression in Manchuria.

Between the world wars, nationalism and the desire for independence strengthened among Arab nationalists and Zionists. The **Pan-Arab Movement** stressed the common ties among Arabs, pushed for an end to foreign control, and expressed anger at the post-war settlement.

Both the Arabs and the Jews aided the British war effort and received apparently conflicting promises for Palestine. At the Paris Peace Conference, much of the Middle East was divided between the French and the British under League mandates. Both countries wanted control of the area because of its important oil resources. Egypt (1922), Saudi Arabia (1927), and Iraq (1930) received independence and served as role models for others.

However, the main problem in the Middle East was Palestine. Zionists pushed for the creation of a Jewish state. Jewish immigration increased markedly during the 1920s and 1930s as a result of a rise in European anti-Semitism and fascism. Many immigrant Jews were prosperous and purchased factories and land from Arabs. This led to displacement of Arab tenant farmers, and their poverty levels increased. The Arabs demanded that the British limit Jewish immigration, because the land could not support a larger population. The British issued the **White Paper of 1939** which limited the immigration, but World War II prevented implementation of the plan. The problem of Palestine continues to plague Middle Eastern peace today.

WORLD WAR II : CAUSES AND IMPACT

THE NAZI STATE

Germany faced many problems in the interwar period. The Weimar Republic was burdened with the responsibility of signing the Treaty of Versailles, a postwar depression, hostility from the right and left, very unpopular reparation payments, and a lack of support from the population. The Ruhr Crisis of 1923 and currency

Mini Assessment

MINI-ASSESSMENT

1 The rise of Soviet communism and Italian and German fascism indicate that
   1 wars played no role in the rise of totalitarian governments
   2 revolutionary leadership was provided by the poorest class
   3 economic conditions often lead people to turn to extremist groups
   4 the three groups had identical economic ideas

2 A key cause of the Great Depression that began in 1929 was
   1 overvalued stocks and buying on margin
   2 government spending in excess of income
   3 constantly changing government economic policies
   4 failure of Germany to make any reparation payments after 1924

3 Reza Khan and Kemal Ataturk were similar in their
   1 unwillingness to use violence
   2 opposition to modernization
   3 creation of republics in their countries
   4 desire to secularize their countries

Constructed Response:

Use the Washington Naval Conference graph on page 202 to answer the following questions:

1 Which two countries had the largest battleship tonnage numbers?

2 What arguments could be used to justify the large tonnage numbers for Britain?

---

inflation eroded the support of the middle class. The Great Depression created a major crisis from which the **Nazis** (National Socialist German Workers Party) gained power, and Adolph Hitler became Germany's chancellor.

Chancellor Hitler called for new elections to try to win a majority in the **Reichstag** (lower house of the German parliament). The Nazis staged tremendous outdoor rallies and whipped the crowds into frenzies with cheers, songs, and speeches preceding dramatic entrances by Hitler. His speeches blamed Jews for the Depression and repeated key themes that he discussed in *Mein Kampf* (see Close Look, pg. 207).

Concerned that they might not win the desired majority, the Nazis apparently ordered the burning of the Reichstag building. They blamed the destruction on the rival Communist Party and cost them some support. The election results gave the Nazis 44%. With their Nationalist Party allies, they held 52% of the vote – again not a majority for the Nazis alone. The Nazi Storm Troopers (elite soldiers) denied the communist delegates access to the Reichstag.

Hitler began establishing a totalitarian state that would control all aspects of people's lives. The Ministry of Propaganda and Enlightenment, led by **Paul Joseph Goebbels** (1897-1945), censored newspapers and radio broadcasts and carried out book burnings. The Reich Culture Chambers controlled the work of artists, musicians, and writers. Young people were enrolled in the propaganda-oriented Nazi Youth Movement, and their education stressed physical fitness and obedience to the state. The local German states disappeared, and dedicated Nazis staffed the central government agencies – the civil service, courts, and universities. Opposition to **der Fuhrer** (the leader) was dangerous. Opposition parties and free labor unions were abolished, and religion was placed under government supervision. The **Gestapo** (secret police) struck terror into the hearts of all.

One of the Nazis' biggest challenges was the economic problems caused by the Great Depression. Industry remained in private hands but under the control of the government. It regulated production and controlled wages and working hours. The government launched an extensive public works program that included

---

ADOLPH HITLER

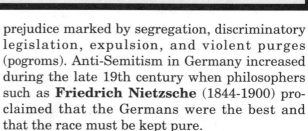

Austrian born **Adolph Hitler** (1889-1945) made his first attempt to seize power at the height of the Ruhr Crisis. As leader of the small NSDAP (National Socialist German Workers' Party), Hitler planned the Munich "Beer Hall" Putsch (8 November 1923) to seize control of the state government of Bavaria. The coup attempt was quickly put down. Hitler was arrested, tried, and convicted, but served only nine months of a five-year sentence.

While in prison, he wrote **Mein Kampf** ("My Struggle"). It described a vision of Germany flowing from his key ideas (anti-Semitism, anti-Communism, Aryan racial superiority, nationalism, the state's superiority over the individual, and hostility to democracy). His "master race" theories evolved to proclaim that the Germans were the superior race made up of light skinned, blue eyed, blond-haired people. All other peoples were ranked according to their closeness to the Aryans.

After his release from prison, Hitler decided to take the legal way to power. During the calmer period of relative prosperity in Germany (1924-1929), he built up the Nazi Party and practiced his political skills. The Great Depression gave him his opportunity. In the election of 1932, the Nazis won the largest number of votes, but not a majority. Conservative politicians persuaded the ailing General von Hindenburgh to appoint Hitler as chancellor in 1933. Thus, as was true of Mussolini, Hitler rose to power legally.

the famous autobahns (high speed highways). The Nazis also began a secret rearmament program, in violation of the Treaty of Versailles. Nazi military spending created jobs and acted to stimulate the economy.

The government removed women from most jobs. The role of women was to stay home and raise children for the Nazi Reich (empire). To achieve **autarchy**[1], a number of substitutes for products such as rubber, textiles, and plastics were developed. Outside trade, when essential, was based on barter or bilateral trade agreements and designed to benefit Germany. Many Germans sensed an improvement in the standard of living and were willing to exchange their civil and political rights for it.

ANTI-SEMITISM AND THE HOLOCAUST

Anti-Semitism reached new levels in Hitler's Third Reich. Jews experienced periods of intense prejudice marked by segregation, discriminatory legislation, expulsion, and violent purges (pogroms). Anti-Semitism in Germany increased during the late 19th century when philosophers such as **Friedrich Nietzsche** (1844-1900) proclaimed that the Germans were the best and that the race must be kept pure.

Under the Nazis, the **Nuremberg Laws** (1935) cost the Jews their German citizenship, forbid them to marry non-Jews, and largely eliminated them from the economy. Those who wished to leave Germany had to give up their wealth and possessions. After the murder of a German diplomat in France and accusations were made against a Jew, the Nazis embarked on **Kristallnacht** (Night of Broken Glass, November 1938). Jewish homes, shops, and synagogues were attacked. Insurance payments for

---

1 autarchy (policy of national self-sufficiency and nonreliance on imports or economic aid)

the damage done were confiscated by the state.

After World War II started, the Nazis forced the Jews to work in defense industries and sent them to **concentration camps**[1]. The Third Reich adopted the "Final Solution" in 1941. It called for the systematic elimination of the Jewish people. In concentration camps such as Dachau and Auschwitz, the Nazis forced Jews to work as slave laborers, subjected them to medical experimentation, or exterminated them in gas chambers.

The Nazis used **genocide**[2] against Jews in all countries that fell under their control. By the end of World War II, 83-90% of the Jews living in the Baltic States, Poland, Germany, Austria, and Czechoslovakia were killed. In what became known as the **Holocaust**[3], two-thirds of European Jews died – an estimated 6 million human beings. Other groups suffered severe losses, too. Poles, gypsies, the disabled, political opponents, "undesirables," and Jehovah's Witnesses died – approximately 3 to 6 million individuals.

MILITARISM, AGGRESSION, APPEASEMENT

The causes of World War II (1939-1945) were similar to those of World War I. Nationalism, imperialism, and militarism all played roles. The Italians desired **mare nostrum** ("our sea") – the lands around the Mediterranean; the Germans wanted **lebensraum** – lands in Eastern Europe; and the Japanese wanted **Asia for Asiatics**. All three countries wanted to change the conditions of the 1919 Paris Peace Settlement. Militarism reemerged in the early 1930s.

With the onset of the Great Depression, nations struggling to survive limited the diplomatic efforts that began in the 1920s to decrease the arms buildup. While the democracies tried to relieve Depression problems through social welfare and public works programs, fascist countries stimulated their economies by rebuilding their military armaments.

One difference from the prelude to World War I was that competing alliance systems were absent prior to World War II. Only the loose **Rome-Berlin Axis** emerged in 1936 (formalized in 1939, with other allies added later in WWII). There was no offsetting alliance to balance it.

The League of Nations provided a forum for discussing international problems and solved a few minor ones, but it was ineffective when the interests of the Great Powers were involved. Japan withdrew from the League in 1931 and Germany did the same in 1933.

In the 1930s the militarist states began a pattern of aggression that tested the resolve of the democracies to maintain the world order set at Versailles. In response, the League of Nations failed to take decisive action, and the Western powers employed neutrality and **appeasement**[4].

---

1 concentration camp (camp where prisoners of war, enemy aliens, and political prisoners are detained and confined, typically under harsh conditions)
2 genocide (systematic extermination of an entire ethnic group)
3 Holocaust (genocide of European Jews and others by the Nazis during World War II)
4 appeasement (policy of granting concessions to potential enemies to maintain peace)

ROAD TO GLOBAL WAR

Aggressors / Crisis	Results
Japan Manchurian Crisis (1931)	A suspicious minor bombing of Japan's South Manchurian Railroad created an excuse to spread forces throughout Manchuria and create the puppet state of Manchukuo. The League of Nations condemned Japan's actions. Japan then withdrew from the League.
Italy Ethiopian Invasion (1935)	Italy attacked from its colonies in Eritrea and Somaliland. Conquest created a large Italian East Africa province and heightened Italian nationalism for Mussolini's fascism. League imposed weak sanctions and later cancelled them.
Italy and Germany Spanish Civil War (1936-1939)	German and Italian armies tested their weapons and tactics. Fascist victory brought Generalissimo Francisco Franco (1892-1975) to power. Destruction in Spain kept it out of World War II.
Germany Austrian *Anschluss* (1938)	Hitler forced the Austrian leaders to accept Nazis in the government, then invaded, and forced it into union (*Anschluss*) with Germany.
Germany Sudeten Appeasement (Czechoslovakia, 1938)	Hitler demanded the predominantly German-speaking Sudetenland in western Czechoslovakia. At the international **Munich Conference**, France and Britain **appeased** Hitler (gave in to avoid war).

The final step prior to the outbreak of war was the signing of the **Nazi-Soviet Non-Aggression Pact** in August, 1939. Stalin signed this agreement with Hitler to avoid war at least temporarily. The purges of the Red Army leadership in the late 1930s left the U.S.S.R. weak. Hitler wished to avoid a two-front war. They also agreed to divide Eastern Europe between them. A week after the document was signed, the Germans began their **blitzkrieg** (lightning war) attack on Poland. Britain and France honored their commitments to protect Poland and declared war on Germany.

THE WORLD AT WAR

World War II was largely an offensive war. Weapons that first saw service in World War I (airplanes, tanks, motorized vehicles) swiftly changed attack strategies and battle tactics. The German blitzkrieg defeated Poland in about one month. Of course, the belligerents developed many new weapons during the course of World War II. In the air, **radar** made it possible for the Royal Air Force of Britain to win the Battle of Britain against the German Luftwaffe. At sea, **sonar** helped to detect the presence of German U-boats. It made it possible for U.S. convoys in the Atlantic to supply the Allies. Magnetic sea mines and the Schnorchel underwater breathing device also revolutionized naval warfare. Toward the end of the War, the Germans began to use V-1 and V-2 jet-propelled bombs – the forerunners of modern guided missiles.

However, the most devastating development by Allied scientists (including some refugees from Nazi Germany) was the atomic bomb. The decision to use the atomic bomb created much controversy. U.S. President **Harry S Truman (1884-1972)** hoped that lives might be saved if an invasion of the Japanese main islands could be avoided. The intense fighting by Japanese soldiers on Iwo Jima and the mass suicides by soldiers and civilians on Okinawa influenced his thinking. However, the tremendous loss of life that occurred and the subsequent health effects on those still alive and on future generations led many to question the correctness of the decision.

WARTIME CONFERENCES

During World War II, allied leaders met at several conferences to discuss strategy and the nature of the postwar world. President Franklin D. Roosevelt (1882-1945) and Prime Minister **Winston Churchill** (1874-1965) met at sea off Newfoundland and drew up the Atlantic Charter in August 1941.

Key Points of the Atlantic Charter:
- restoration of self-government for those who had lost it

- access to world trade and resources for all

- freedom from fear and want

STRATEGIC EVENTS OF WORLD WAR II: EUROPE AND NORTH AFRICA

Event	Significance
Invasion of Poland, 1939	German blitzkrieg (fast-moving, air-and-land strategy) conquered Poland in about one month with use of dive bombers, 6 panzer-tank and 4 motorized divisions
Battle of Britain 1940	German Luftwaffe's attempt (August 1940 - May 1941) to destroy Britain's defenses prior to a cross-Channel invasion; Royal Air Force use of radar made daylight raids too dangerous; Luftwaffe resorted to night attacks
North Africa 1940-1943	British defeat of Italian forces in E. Africa by February 1941 led Germans to send "Desert Fox" Erwin Rommel's crack tank divisions (Afrika Korps) to push British back to Egypt and threaten Suez; British Gen. Montgomery defeated Rommel at El-Alamein (November 1942); opened way for Allied invasion of the western part of North Africa; forced Axis troops into Tunis where they surrendered May 1943
Invasion of the U.S.S.R. 1942-1943	German invasion began June 1942 with victory expected in 10 weeks; 3-pronged attack against Leningrad (St. Petersburg), Moscow, and Stalingrad (Volgograd) failed – Russian winter and German supply difficulties were major factors; Russia launched counterattack in winter of 1942-1943; at Stalingrad, 300,000 Germans surrendered and rest of the German army slowly began retreating from the U.S.S.R.
Invasion of Normandy "D-Day," 1944	U.S. Gen. Eisenhower led Allies' cross Channel invasion of German-held France (Operation Overlord, June 1944); DeGaulle's Free French and Resistance forces liberated Paris; drive of Allies for Germany interrupted by vicious German counterattack at Battle of the Bulge (December 1944 - January 1945); Eastern and Western Allied advances into Germany ended in final surrender 8 May 1945

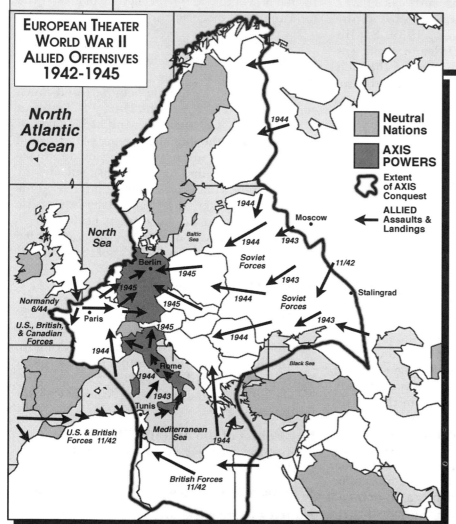

EUROPEAN THEATER
WORLD WAR II
ALLIED OFFENSIVES
1942-1945

At the **Teheran Conference** (Iran, late 1943), Churchill and Roosevelt met with Stalin. The Normandy invasion was confirmed and Stalin agreed to launch a simultaneous attack on Germany's eastern front. The occupation and demilitarization of postwar Germany were discussed, and plans were made for a new international organization to replace the League of Nations.

The "Big Three" met again at the **Yalta Conference** in early 1945. Decisions were made regarding Poland and Eastern Europe, disarmament and division of Germany into occupation zones, the organization and voting arrangements for the

STRATEGIC EVENTS OF WORLD WAR II: ASIA

Event	Significance
Pearl Harbor Attack 1941	Japanese surprise attack 7 December 1941 on U.S. naval base in Hawaii used carrier-based planes; crippled the U.S. Pacific fleet destroying and damaging 18 major ships and 200 aircraft, and killing 3,600; U.S. declared war on Japan and subsequently entered WWII against Axis Powers
Invasion of the Philippines 1942	Right after Pearl Harbor, Japan attacked Wake Island, Guam, British Malaya, Singapore, the Dutch East Indies, Burma, and Thailand; in the Philippines, Bataan fell (January 1942) after heavy fighting; U.S. Gen. MacArthur evacuated to Australia (February 1942); survivors of Bataan held out at Corregidor until May 1942 and suffered a grueling "death march" to Japanese prison camps
Battles of the Coral Sea and Midway 1942	Battles fought by carrier based aircraft: Allied Coral Sea victory discouraged Japanese invasion of Australia; loss of 4 Japanese carriers and 5 other ships at Midway (June 1942) blocked invasion of Hawaii and put Japan's grand strategy on hold
Island Hopping 1942-1945	Strategy of invading selected islands to avoid high casualties; gave Allies staging areas for attacks on Japanese home islands
Use of Atomic Bombs 1945	U.S. warned Japan of its possession of a new weapon of mass destruction; refusal to surrender led to (August 1945) decision to drop 1st A-bomb on Hiroshima, killing 78,000; 2nd bomb dropped on Nagasaki, killing 40,000, led to formal surrender 2 September 1945

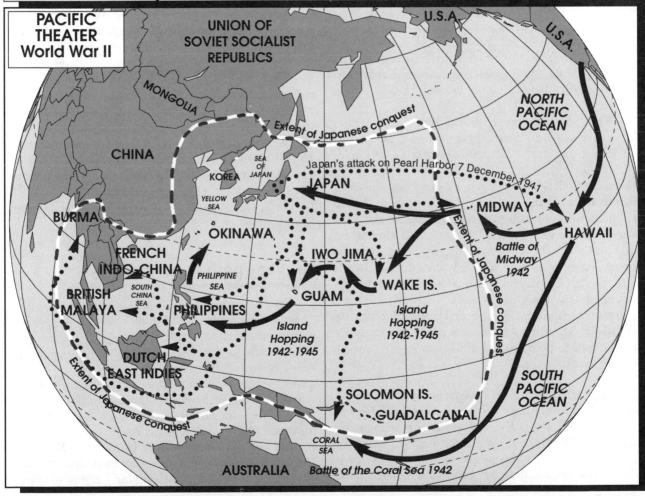

PACIFIC THEATER World War II

United Nations, and conditions for Russian entrance into the War against Japan.

By the **Potsdam Conference** in the summer of 1945, Roosevelt had died and Clement Atlee had replaced Churchill as British Prime Minister. Germany was to be disarmed, demilitarized, denazified. Plans were made to try war criminals (Nuremberg Trials, 1945-1946). The conferees agreed that the Soviet Union would take reparations from its occupation zone as compensation for war damages suffered. Also, they made changes in the boundaries in Eastern Europe.

WORLD WAR II: OUTCOMES

The second global war in less than a generation resulted in 40 million deaths and cost over one trillion, 100 billion dollars, excluding civilian property. It devastated the powers of Western Europe. Their weakness encouraged colonial peoples to demand independence. In some cases, independence came without violence, but in others, violence erupted. Two superpowers emerged from the war – the United States and the Soviet Union. Competition between these two giants dominated international politics for over forty years.

The period between World War I and World War II itself had tremendous impact on literature and art. In totalitarian countries, the arts reflected the tastes and goals of the dictators. In Germany, Hitler approved of pictures showing laborers working for the Reich, nationalistic themes, and sentimental nudes. Heroic Art featured the Aryan Theme. Art exhibits had to be approved by the government, and the government censored artists whose works did not fulfill the requirements of the state. Hitler also favored the musical works of 19th century German nationalist composer **Richard Wagner** (1813-1883), and at least one piece of Wagner's music had to be included in almost every concert in Germany.

Literature was also restricted by the government. Book burnings included works by Jewish authors and even Erich Remarque whose *All Quiet on the Western Front*, condemned war and sympathized with the plight of the common soldier. Remarque opposed the Nazi government

and left Germany in 1932. Stalin favored "social realism" in art. It often included workers or soldiers whose activities benefitted the state. Modern art was banned from most museums and art shows under his dictatorship.

Outside of the dictatorships, the ideas of Freud, the unconscious, and surrealism continued to influence art. Perhaps the most famous picture of the period was **Pablo Picasso**'s "Guernica" (1937). It displayed his outrage at the bombing of a Spanish town during the Spanish Civil War. The German Luftwaffe used the town to test civilian reaction to saturation bombing. The picture involves complex symbolism, but Picasso's horror of war was evident. **Wassily Kandinski**'s work became increasingly geometric after World War I. He refined his geometric style using lines, circles, and arcs. One of his best known works was "Circle and Square" (1943). **Paul Klee** turned to brooding and gloomy subjects as was evident in "Death and Fire" (1940).

American writer **Ernest Hemingway**'s works reflected reaction to World War I and the crises leading to World War II. *The Sun Also Rises* (1926) told of people who lost their belief in moral values because of World War I. It reflected the thinking of the "lost generation." In *For Whom the Bell Tolls* (1940), a work about the Spanish Civil War, he warned that the loss of liberty in one place endangered it everywhere. **Elie Wiesel**'s entire family and other Jews were deported from Sighet, Romania to Auschwitz in 1944 as a part of the "Final Solution." His work, *La Nuit*, (1958), told of his concentration camp experiences.

TIME CAPSULE: 1900-1945

The first half of the 20th century was marked by tremendous achievements, especially in science and technology, the emergence of totalitarian governments, and two global wars. Many improvements were made in medicine and methods of treating the ill. As a result, life expectancy was improved. Many of the improvements in science and technology also came in methods of fighting wars. Some of these

Mini Assessment

1 Hitler believed that
   1 power rested with the people
   2 all people were equal before law
   3 Germans were the greatest race
   4 religious toleration was important

2 The Manchurian Crisis, the Ethiopian Crisis, and the Spanish Civil War illustrate the idea that
   1 appeasement helps to avoid war
   2 years of tension often result in war
   3 only German and Japanese actions led to World War II
   4 international agreements are often effective in settling problems

3 "Germany, the United Kingdom, France, and Italy, taking into consideration the agreement, which has been already readied...for the cession to Germany of the Sudeten German territory, have agreed on the following terms and conditions..."

   This statement is part of the
   1 *Treaty of Versailles*
   2 *Locarno Agreements*
   3 *Nine Power Treaty*
   4 *Munich Agreement*

Jewish Losses in World War II			
Nation	Jewish Population Sept. 1939	Jewish Losses	Percentage of Jewish Losses
Poland	3,300,000	2,800,000	85.0
U.S.S.R. (Nazi occupied)	2,100,000	1,500,000	71.4
Czechoslovakia	315,000	260,000	82.5
France	300,000	90,000	30.0
Austria	60,000	40,000	66.6
Italy	57,000	15,000	26.3

Constructed Response:

Using the chart above, answer the following questions

1 Which nation suffered the greatest percentage of loss of its Jewish population?

2 Explain the lower percentage of loss in Italy and France.

changes, such as the development of airplanes and radar, ultimately improved civilian life, but others simply made the taking of human life easier and cheaper.

The Russian Revolution marked the emergence of the modern totalitarian government and the command economic system. The initial progress made in the Soviet Union sparked the interest of many in other areas. Often, rulers seemed willing to sacrifice civil and human rights in the name of economic advancement. This was especially true after the start of the Great Depression. At least in part, Mussolini and Hitler were able to rise to power because of the economic hardships their countries faced. Totalitarian governments exercised tremendous control over the lives of their people. The ultimate control was exercised by Hitler in the "Final Solution" in which he took the lives of millions.

Both world wars were expensive in terms of human life and the resources involved in fighting. Both also led to enormous changes. World War I sparked colonial nationalism which was then ignored when the victors retained their colonies and expanded their areas of control through the mandate system. However, after World War II there was an explosion of independence among the colonies. Some achieved this status peacefully, but others fought prolonged wars. Both wars resulted in the establishment of international organizations in hopes of preserving the peace. The League of Nations' limited success in the political field led to differences in the structure and organization of the United Nations in an attempt to achieve better results.

MULTI-CHOICE QUESTIONS

1 The first stage of the Russian Revolution of 1917 (Provisional Government) was similar to the first stage of the French Revolution of 1789 (National Assembly) because in both
1 major democratic documents became law
2 moderate, bourgeoisie leaders were in control
3 a reign of terror occurred to remove opposition
4 execution of the deposed royal families occurred

2 The New Economic Policy (1921-1927) in the U.S.S.R. (Russia) most resembled a
1 free market economy
2 traditional economy
3 command economy
4 mixed economy

3 The Bolsheviks were able to win support in Russia in 1917 because they
1 promised to establish a Western style democracy
2 pledged to carry out immediate land reform
3 controlled the Tsarist army officers
4 had the support of Russia's war allies

4 Under Stalin, Russification was designed to
1 promote increased economic production
2 increase the loyalty of ethnic groups
3 spread Russian culture beyond the U.S.S.R.
4 encourage support of the Russian Orthodox Church

5 The Manchurian Crisis (1931) indicated that Japan
1 wished to continue its close friendship with China
2 would obey the provisions of the *Nine Power Treaty*
3 used aggression to acquire markets and raw materials
4 needed a military victory before joining the Axis

Base your answer to question 6 on the graph below and your knowledge of global history.

TSARIST V. SOVIET PRODUCTION
1913 – Tsarist Russia
1928 – New Economic Plan
1940 – After Stalin's 5-yr Plans

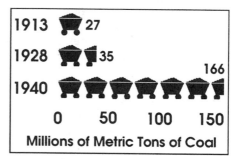

= 25,000,000 metric tons

6 Which conclusion is correct based on the graph above and your knowledge of global history?
1 Soviet 5-Year Plans always emphasized the production of consumer goods.
2 Command economies provide the best approach to economic development.
3 World War I and the Russian Revolution had no impact on industrial production.
4 Initial Soviet 5-Year plans increased production of goods necessary for heavy industry.

7 Which statement about culture in the period between the two World Wars is most accurate?
1 In totalitarian countries, writers and artists had to serve the purposes of the state.
2 Art and literature rarely reflected the problems of the time.
3 Realism was the major artistic influence in Western Europe.
4 Writers and artists rarely had their work censored.

8 The battles of El Alamein, Stalingrad, and the Coral Sea were
   1 defeats for German forces
   2 significant turning points in World War II
   3 steps toward allied control of Europe
   4 major naval victories for Britain

9 The apparently conflicting promises made to the Jews in the *Balfour Declaration* and the Arabs in the *Arab-British Correspondence* occurred during World War I because Britain
   1 was concerned about French influence in the Middle East
   2 needed to defeat the forces of T.E. Lawrence
   3 wished to win approval of U.S. public opinion
   4 desired the help of Jews and Arabs in winning the War

10 Which correctly describes the setting of Eastern Europe prior to World War I?
    1 The population was homogenous with few minority groups.
    2 It was dominated by three large multi-national empires.
    3 Expansive plains dominated the entire area.
    4 The Danube River was no longer an avenue of trade and commerce.

11 The Russian Revolution of 1905 was significant because it
    1 allowed the communists to seize power
    2 led to the establishment of democracy in Russia
    3 destroyed the paternalistic relationship between the people and the Tsar
    4 resulted in freedom for the serfs

12 The occurrence of World War I demonstrates the idea that
    1 alliance systems often lead to war
    2 a single incident can be the only cause of war
    3 nationalism rarely leads to war
    4 military strength helps to avoid war

13 Critics of British and French polices in the 1930s might argue that
    1 democratic nations fail to recognize danger
    2 neutrality helps to prevent wars
    3 appeasement often leads to further aggression
    4 collective security agreements are the only way to prevent war

14 A condition common to the periods prior to World War I and World War II was
    1 the lack of an international organization to deal with disputes
    2 the existence of competing alliance systems
    3 communist expansion into Eastern Europe
    4 a series of crises among the major powers

15 Which of these statements about the nature of World War II is accurate?
    1 It was a war fought primarily with atomic weapons and missiles.
    2 It was a defensive war in which front lines hardly changed.
    3 Sea power played almost no role in the outcome.
    4 It was a highly mobile, fast moving war.

———————————————

THEMATIC ESSAY

Theme: Diversity

Throughout history, many peoples have had difficulty accepting and treating other ethnic groups fairly and justly.

Task:
- Define ethnic group.
- Select one ethnic group which you have studied and explain how it was unfairly or unjustly treated.
- Discuss how this ethnic group reacted, and what, if any, action, it or the international community took to end the treatment.

Suggestions:
You may use any ethnic group from your study of global history that was unfairly or unjustly treated. Some groups you might wish to consider include: Armenians in the Ottoman Empire (20th century), Ukrainians in the Soviet Union (1930s), Jews in Germany (1933-1945), Indians in British India (1900-1945). **You are not limited to these suggestions**.

[Note: You may **not** use any ethnic group from the U.S.]

DOCUMENT BASED QUESTION

Directions:
The following question is based on the accompanying documents (1-8). Some of these documents have been edited for the purposes of this exercise. This question is designed to test your ability to work with historical documents. As you analyze the documents, take into account both the source of the document and the author's point of view.

- Write a well-organized essay that includes an introduction with a thesis statement, several paragraphs explaining the thesis, and a conclusion.
- Analyze the documents.
- Use all the documents.
- Use evidence from the documents to support your position.
- Do not simply repeat the contents of the documents.
- Include specific related outside information.

Historical Context:
The issue of which country was to blame of causing World War I (1914-1918) is very controversial. The documents below express different opinions on this question.

Task:
Discuss which nation or nations was most responsible for starting World War I and support your opinion with the documents below and your knowledge of global history.

Part A - Short Answer
The documents below relate to the question of which country caused World War I. Examine each document carefully, and then answer the question that follows it.

Document 1:

GERMANY

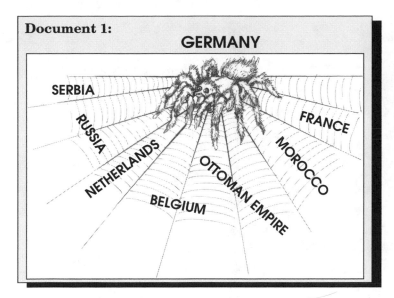

SERBIA

RUSSIA

NETHERLANDS

BELGIUM

OTTOMAN EMPIRE

MOROCCO

FRANCE

Document 1 Question:

What does the cartoon indicate about the expansionist goals of Germany?

Document 2:

"[The British Foreign Minister] could probably have prevented war if he had done either of two things. If, he had given in to the urging of France and Russia and given a strong warning to Germany that...England would take the side of the Franco-Russian Alliance... Or if [he]... warned France and Russia early in the crisis, that if they became involved in war, England would remain neutral..."

– Origins of the World War, 1930

Document 2 Question:

What does the author indicate that the British could have done to avoid war?

Document 3:

"Germany pursued no aim either in Europe or elsewhere which could only be achieved by means of war...France aimed at recovering Alsace Lorraine...whilst Russia wished to possess Constantinople and the Straits, both powers knowing well that these aims could not be achieved without a European war."

– The Case for the Central Powers, 1925

Document 3 Question:

According to the author what aims of France and Russia may have contributed to the outbreak of war?

Document 4:

Document 4 Question:

Why might the position of Germany lead to an early declaration of war?

Document 5:

"...[Kaiser William II] is not blind to the danger which threatens Austria-Hungary and thus the Triple Alliance as a result of the Russian and Serbian Panslavic agitation. ....His Majesty will faithfully stand by Austria-Hungary as is required by the obligation of his alliance and of his ancient friendship."

– Chancellor of Germany to the German Ambassador at Vienna, July 6, 1914

Document 5 Question:

How does this document help to explain Austro-Hungarian willingness to send Serbia an ultimatum?

Document 6:

"...I am struck by the way the [French] Minister of Justice and his colleagues correctly understand the situation and how firm and calm is their decision to give us the most complete support and to avoid the least appearance of difference of view between us."

– Russian Ambassador at Paris to Russian Foreign Secretary, July 14, 1914

Document 6 Question:

How does this document help to explain Russia's willingness to back Serbia?

Document 7:

Document 7 Question:

Why did this event, depicted in the drawing, contribute to the outbreak of war?

Document 8:

"The Royal Serbian Government will furthermore pledge itself:

1   to suppress every publication which encourages hate and contempt for Austria-Hungary...

2   to agree to allow Austrian-Hungarian officials to act in Serbia to end the movement directed against Austria-Hungary...."

–Excerpt of Austrian demands given to Serbs, July 23, 1914.
[Demanded reply by July 25, 1914.]

Document 8 Question:

In what way might agreeing to these demands infringe on Serbia's sovereignty?

Part B - Essay Response

Discuss which country caused World War I.

Your essay should be well organized with an introductory paragraph that states your thesis as to which country started World War I. Develop and support the reasons for your thesis in the next paragraphs and then write a conclusion. In your essay, include specific historical details and refer to the specific documents you analyzed in Part A. You may include additional information from your knowledge of global history.

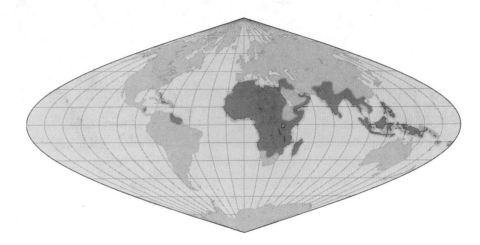

THE WORLD SINCE 1945

AD	
1945–	India and Pakistan independent (1947)
	U.N. Declaration of Human Rights (1948)
1955–	Hungarian Revolution (1956)
	Cuban Missile Crisis (1962)
1965–	European Community established (1967)
	global oil crisis (1973)
1975–	Iranian Revolution (1979)
1985–	Tiananmen Square Massacre (1989)
	destruction of the Berlin Wall (1990)
	U.S.S.R. collapses (1991)
1995–	
	India and Pakistan nuclear tests (1998)
2000–	

Soviets build part of the Iron Curtain – the Berlin Wall.

PEOPLE	PLACES	THINGS
Boris Yeltsin	"Asian Tigers"	Barrios
Deng Xiaoping	Chechnya	Cold War
Jawaharlal Nehru	Dardanelles & Bosporus	Cultural Revolution
Jiang Zemin	Dien Bien Phu	Détente
Mikhail Gorbachev	Kampuchea	European Union
Nelson Mandela	LDCs	Marshall Plan
Nikita Khrushchev	Persian Gulf	NATO
Saddam Hussein	Rwanda	Perestroika
	Tiananmen Square	World Bank

INTRODUCTION

Global changes began when World War II ended in 1945. Tensions between the United States and the Union of Soviet Socialist Republics led to a generation of Cold War confrontations. The early spread – and later retreat – of communism and command economies sparked major shifts in governmental policies. As imperialism declined, the attempts of the **superpowers**[1] to influence the new nations aroused concern in the international community as the emerging nations struggled to stabilize their governments and make economic progress.

The force of nationalism remained strong. It motivated ethnic groups to demand independence. They often achieved that independence by violence against other groups. Yet, this period also saw some solutions to global issues. The progress toward economic union in Europe and elsewhere, the end to **apartheid**[2], the decline in the arms race, and the willingness of the United Nations and other international groups to act to end aggression and promote peace, all these provided hope for the future.

COLD WAR BALANCE OF POWER

GERMANY AND JAPAN: THE LESSONS OF WAR

In the aftermath of World War II, the economies of Western European nations were aided by the U.S. financed Marshall Plan. This program required the European countries to plan together and stimulated their cooperation. They quickly realized that increased coordination and unity promised better economic progress. This led to a series to steps taken by Belgium, the Netherlands, Luxemburg, France, and West Germany that resulted in the European Union of today:

- 1952 – **European Coal and Steel Community** (E.C.S.C.) – removed barriers to free movement of iron, coal, and steel across their borders

- 1958 – **Euratom** – promoted cooperation in nuclear research and development of peaceful uses of atomic energy

- 1958 – **European Economic Community** (E.E.C. – the "Common Market") – removed trade barriers among members, established uniform trade policies against outsiders, and increased competition and movement of capital and labor among members

In 1967, these three agencies were joined to form the **European Community** (E.C.). The 1991 Maastricht Treaty called for the establishment of a central bank, a common currency, and movement toward a closer political union. In 1995, the name was changed to the **European Union** (E.U.). New members gradually added included: Denmark, United Kingdom, Ireland, Spain, Portugal, United Germany, Austria, Finland, and Sweden. The common currency (**euro**) was scheduled to begin circulation on 1 January 1999 in all but four of the fifteen members. The members of this economic union had a combined economy almost as large as that of the U.S. and larger than that of Japan.

In the years after World War II, West Germany emerged as an economic powerhouse with the assistance of U.S. aid. By quickly

---

1 superpower (powerful and influential nation, especially a nuclear power that dominates its allies or client states in an international power block)
2 apartheid (official policy of racial segregation practiced in the Republic of South Africa, involving political, legal, and economic discrimination against nonwhites)

rebuilding industries destroyed by World War II with the newest technology, West Germany gained a large share of the world's market. Low labor costs, high savings rates, large private investment, and the high quality of West German products helped this resurgence. Credit went to the chemical, iron, steel, and engineering sectors. This so-called "economic miracle" also owed much to the "guest workers" from less developed European countries. Their labor was a necessary part of the rebuilding because of German war losses.

Germany

The post-war West German government was democratic and had a bicameral (two-house) legislature: the Bundestag (lower house) elected by the people and the Bundesrat (upper house) represented the states. The president represented the country internationally, but the effective head of government was the chancellor who was advised by the Cabinet of Ministers. The first elected chancellor was **Konrad Adenauer** (1876-1967). He quickly became a highly respected international leader. However, controversy over the election and appointments of former Nazis continued to be a problem on the German political scene.

Economic success also came to Japan after the World War II. The U.S. occupation, under the leadership of General **Douglas MacArthur**, helped to lay the groundwork for an industrial economy based on importation of raw materials and exportation of manufactured products. As in the case of Germany, the rebuilding included the most modern technology. This enabled the Japanese, in a very

short time, to compete with the U.S., especially in the production of electronic goods. The Japanese work ethnic, high education levels, high savings rate, and lifetime employment philosophy aided the recovery. Low defense costs, aided by constitutional limitations and U.S. protection, allowed the government to channel revenues to private industry. Also, Japan invested in Asia and Southeast Asia to take advantage of low labor costs and other economic incentives. At times, these investments encountered resistance from other nations because of resentment over wartime experiences.

Some problems did develop in the Japanese economy. Government protection of home industries and restrictions placed on foreign imports caused resentment and protests, most notably from the United States. The close ties between the government and the **keiretsu**[1] led to accusations of corruption and government resignations. Beginning in the early 1990s, a recession in Japan's overvalued real estate and stock markets affected the world economy. Some companies gave up their lifetime employment policies and began to **downsize**[2]. Bankruptcies increased, and the government seemed unable to make the necessary changes to restore confidence among the Japanese and the international community.

The occupation by the U.S. armed forces also led to a major change in Japanese government. The 1946 constitution established a democratic

---

1 keiretsu (large, diverse, but networked companies and banking houses)
2 downsize (reduce operations or scope of enterprise)

WARTIME "BIG THREE" CONFERENCES

Conference	Significant Decisions
Teheran – 1943	Agreed to open a second front against Germany on the continent of Europe and attack from all directions.
Yalta – 1945	Divided Germany into occupation zones and pushed democratization and due punishment for war criminals. Guaranteed the Poles a broader based democratic government and free and fair elections. Russia promised to enter war against Japan in exchange for territory in the Far East.
Potsdam – 1945	Confirmed Yalta agreements and virtually gave the Soviet Union control of Eastern Europe.

basis for the government. The emperor became a constitutional monarch, the **Diet**[1] (parliament) was elected, women gained the right to vote, and local governments received increased powers. Also, the government made provisions for the guarantee of basic rights.

EMERGENCE OF THE SUPERPOWERS

Two superpowers emerged at the end of World War II – the United States and Soviet Union. Europe and Japan were devastated and faced massive post war rebuilding efforts. The European nations could not reestablish control of many of their colonies. Many were either granted independence or rebelled to achieve it. The **Cold War**[2] quickly developed between the United States and Soviet Union. The Soviets sought to extend their areas of influence in Europe and the developing nations. The United States met this expansion attempt with a policy of **containment** designed to limit the spread of communism. The two countries also became rivals in science, technology, culture, sports, and military and economic development. The "Iron Curtain" (a term popularized by Winston Churchill) descended on Europe. Cold War tensions began to ease in the 1970s and with the emergence of **Mikhail Gorbachev** (1931-) and his 1985 reform policies. Confrontation began to turn toward East–West cooperation.

COLD WAR CONFRONTATIONS

Toward the end of World War II, as Soviet troops pushed the Germans back across Eastern Europe, the Soviets established **satellite governments**[3] in the newly liberated countries.

Despite the efforts of the Western powers at the Allies' wartime conferences, Stalin would not allow the free elections he had promised. In an effort to contain the spread of communism, U.S. Secretary of State George C. Marshall proposed the European Recovery Program in 1947. In what later became known as the **Marshall Plan**, approximately $12.5 billion was offered to all nations in Europe. The Soviets put pressure on their satellites to reject the offer. They offered a less ambitious program, **COMECON** (Council of Mutual Economic Assistance). The Marshall Plan was very successful. In 1947, President Truman proposed a program later known as the **Truman Doctrine** to aid Greece and Turkey against communist threats. This program also achieved its objectives.

GOALS OF THE MARSHALL PLAN

- Promote European economic recovery
- Stop the spread of communism
- Aid the U.S. economy by rebuilding European trade and markets

A DIVIDED GERMANY

The Allies' wartime conferences had resulted in a decision to divide Germany into occupation zones controlled by the U.S., the U.S.S.R., and Britain (later the U.S. and Britain redivided their zones to provide one for France). Even though the city of Berlin was completely within the Soviet Zone, it was divided into occupation

---

1 Diet (national or local legislative assembly in certain countries, such as Japan)
2 Cold War (state of political tension and military rivalry between nations; war fought by all means except direct confrontation among those involved)
3 satellite governments (nation dominated politically and economically by another nation)

zones. Surrounded by a communist state, the British, French, and American sectors of West Berlin became showcases for the achievements of capitalism.

In 1948, the Soviets launched the **Berlin Blockade** in response to the Allies' decision to unify their three occupation zones. The Soviets closed land and water access routes to the city. The Allies responded with the **Berlin Airlift**. For 11 months, Britain and the United States flew more than 2 million tons of supplies to Berlin before the Soviets lifted the blockade. However, there were periodic closures after that time. The Soviets refused to allow free elections in their zone. The Allies combined their zones to form the **Federal Republic of Germany** (West Germany) in 1949. The Soviets responded by establishing the **German Democratic Republic** (East Germany) in their zone in the same year.

RIVAL MILITARY ALLIANCES

Having learned the value of united effort during World War II, the Allies decided to establish a postwar military alliance. **NATO** (North Atlantic Treaty Organization) was organized in 1949. The original members were: United States, Canada, Britain, France, Belgium, Netherlands, Luxemburg, Italy, Portugal, Norway, Denmark, and Iceland. Each pledged to come to the aid of any other member who was attacked. Other nations joined later. It also provided for a unified command and integration of military units from different nations. (Traditionally, an American has been the Supreme Allied Commander of NATO).

From its creation, NATO faced a variety of problems including a Greek/Turkish dispute over Cyprus, withdrawal of French forces from the united command, and the issue of basing nuclear weapons in Germany. In the 1990s NATO faced the crisis in Bosnia, and the issue of membership for countries of Eastern Europe. In 1997, the Czech Republic, Hungary, and Poland became members of NATO.

The Soviets countered NATO with the formation of the Warsaw Pact in 1955. The military forces of the satellite countries were under Soviet control until the Pact ended in 1991.

After World War II, the Soviet Union built a "buffer zone" of satellite countries between the Russian people and Western Europe. Throughout the Cold War, the U.S.S.R. secured its boundaries with a "bear-like" grasp of these countries and the building of the Iron Curtain.

However, Soviet control of the satellites was challenged at various times. During World War II, Yugoslav guerrilla forces fighting against Germany were led by **Tito** (Josip Broz, 1892-1980). At the end of the War, a communist dictatorship was established with Tito as leader. At first there was cooperation between Tito and Stalin, but in 1948, a series of disagreements led to a rupture in the relationship. The Soviets did not send in military forces to end the independence of communist Yugoslavia because of distance and lack of common boundary.

REVOLTS IN THE SOVIET SATELLITES

After Stalin's death in 1953, problems erupted in the satellite nations. At a Party Congress in 1956, Soviet First Secretary **Nikita Khrushchev** (1894-1971) denounced Stalin's actions and policies as "crimes." This caused many in the satellites to question Soviet domination. Poles and Hungarians moved quickly to demand increased freedom. In Poland, the Soviet Union proved willing to cooperate with **Wladyslaw Gomulka** (1905-1982) as head of the government. He pledged to remain in the Warsaw Pact and keep Poland a Communist state.

In Hungary, the new government of **Imre Nagy** (1896-1958) pursued a more independent course. The Soviets sent troops with modern weapons against the Hungarian Freedom Fighters who were equipped with little more than **Molotov cocktails**[1]. The 1956 Hungarian Revolution was suppressed, Nagy was executed, and many Freedom Fighters fled abroad.

In Czechoslovakia, **Alexander Dubcek** (1921-1992) began the movement in 1968 called the Prague Spring. He hoped to combine the best features of democracy with socialism. Soviet leader **Leonid Brezhnev** (1906-1982) sent in Warsaw Pact troops. Although condemned by many Communists, Brezhnev ousted Dubcek and installed an "acceptable" communist regime. Brezhnev's actions resulted in the **Brezhnev Doctrine**. It asserted the U.S.S.R.'s right to intervene against "anti-socialist degeneration" within the Soviet bloc (satellite countries of Eastern Europe).

GLOBAL SCOPE OF THE COLD WAR

The superpowers were also rivals in developing areas of the world. Each wished to extend the area of its influence, control vital resources and strategic locations, and limit the impact of the other. Often the "weapon of choice" was foreign aid, and the less developed countries (**LDCs**[2]) quickly learned to "play" the superpow-

1 Molotov cocktail (makeshift bomb made of a breakable container filled with flammable liquid and provided with a usually rag wick that is lighted just before being hurled; named after Vyacheslav Mikhailovich Molotov, WWII Soviet Defense Minister)
2 LDCs (Less Developed Countries of the world, referred to as "third world" or the "have nots," generally with poor economies, poor health and education, and little industrialization)

A SAMPLING OF SUPERPOWER RIVALRIES

Country	Key Events
Vietnam	1946-1954 - war against France for independence 1954 - international conference, led to division into North Vietnam (communist under Ho Chi Minh) and South Vietnam (non-communist under Ngo Dinh Diem) 1959-1975 - Communist Viet Cong attacked South to reunite country, U.S. aid to South included troops, Soviets and Chinese aided North 1973 - cease-fire negotiated and withdrawal of U.S. troops began 1975 - Saigon fell, country reunited under communist regime
Egypt	1956 - Britain and U.S. dropped financial support for construction of High Aswan Dam. Egyptian leader Gamal Abdel Nassar nationalized Suez Canal to obtain money for Dam's construction; Britain and France threatened invasion of Egypt in alliance with Israel but withdrew after U.N. resolved to send an emergency force 1960 - Dam construction began with Soviets helping with cost and 400 technicians
Congo (Zaire)	1960 - Belgium granted independence; with little preparation or warning; the Congo split by ethnic rivalries and threatened secession of mineral rich province; civil war broke out among groups supporting Joseph Kasavubu (non-communist) and Patrice Lumumba (communist) 1963 - U.N. peacekeepers restored some order 1965 - General Mobutu (Sese Seko) seized power, established dictatorship, U.S. supported initially
Chile	1970 - Socialist Salvador Allende elected President, 1st President elected on a Marxist-Leninist program in non-communist country in Western Hemisphere 1972-1973 - increasing opposition and economic problems led to violence 1973 - military coup with U.S. support overthrew Allende who committed suicide, U.S. continued aid against leftist guerrillas

ers against each other to their advantage. In some cases, internal fighting was involved, but there were no direct confrontations between the superpowers.

Indirect confrontations occurred in surrogate (substitute) countries as diverse as Angola, Iran, Iraq, and Guatemala. Well into the 1980s, the superpowers operated "behind the scenes" giving covert support to rival groups in civil wars. The end of the Cold War brought some relief from these competition problems.

NUCLEAR RIVALRY

The nuclear weapons and space race between the U.S. and the U.S.S.R. began with the race to develop the first atomic bomb. The Soviet Union detonated its first nuclear weapon in 1949, four years after the U.S. Then, Britain, France, and China quickly joined the nuclear club. A number of other nations such as India, Pakistan, Israel, Iraq, and Libya acquired some nuclear capability. The threat of radiation fallout from tests and potential nuclear destruction led to control attempts.

- 1963 - **Limited Nuclear Test Ban Treaty** – prohibited testing in the atmosphere, later space and underground tests forbidden

- 1968 - **Nuclear Non-Proliferation Treaty** – nations willing to forego nuclear weapons promised aid in case of attack and help in development of peaceful uses of atomic energy

- 1972, 1979 - **SALT** (Strategic Arms Limitation Talks) – decreased some missiles and numbers of some warheads

- 1991, 1993 - **START** (Strategic Arms Reduction Talks) – continued process of limiting nuclear weapons and missile delivery systems

THE UNITED NATIONS' ROLE

At the San Francisco Conference in 1945, fifty nations signed the charter creating the **United Nations**. The goals of the U.N. are to promote international peace and security, settle disputes among nations, develop friendly relations among nations, and establish respect for human rights. Soon after it was organized, The U.N. approved the **Universal Declaration of Human Rights** (1948). It provided the basis for modern ideas on human rights. It includes statements on the right of human beings to basic personal, civil, political, social, and economic rights. Included among those rights are the right to life, liberty, and security of person; freedom of movement and residence; and freedom of thought, religion, and opinion. Although the United Nations supports numerous organizations and humanitarian activities, its peacekeeping mission has three main organs:

Flag of the United Nations

- **Security Council** – primary responsibility for world peace; 5 permanent members each with veto power (U.S., Russia, China, Britain, France) plus 10 non-permanent members from various areas of world elected for 2-year terms

- **General Assembly** – includes all U.N. members with 1 vote each; discusses and makes recommendations on world problems, can act if the Security Council is blocked by the veto of a permanent member

- **Secretariat** – administers daily operations under the Secretary General who calls attention to world peace threats, heads U.N. Emergency Forces, and carries out special missions

Like the League of Nations, most of the U.N. successes are in the economic and social fields. Specialized agencies such as the Food and Agriculture Organization (famines, improvement of food production) and the World Health Organization (vaccinations against smallpox, polio, aids epidemic, etc.) improve the quality of life of countless people.

Mini Assessment

MINI-ASSESSMENT

1 The Cold War between the United States and the Soviet Union was characterized by
   1 war between the superpowers
   2 a spirit of cooperation and disarmament
   3 competition to influence newly independent nations
   4 an exchange of technological developments

2 The formation of the Coal and Steel Community (1952) was an initial step toward European
   1 containment   3 military alliance
   2 economic unity   4 disarmament

3 In the years since 1945, United Nations has been most successful in
   1 solving disputes between the superpowers
   2 solving its budget problems
   3 ending the crises in the Middle East
   4 improving the global standard of living

Constructed Response:

Use the quotation below and your knowledge of global history to answer the following questions.

"Civilized people of the world: The Soviet Army is attempting to crush our troubled hearts. Their tasks and guns are roaring over Hungarian soil. Our women...are sitting in dread. Listen to our cry. Extend to us brotherly hands..."

– A broadcast from Hungarian freedom fighters as reported in the *Daily Mail*, 5 Nov. 1956

1 How did the Soviet Union react to the revolt of the Hungarian freedom fighters?

2 In 1956, there was considerable dissatisfaction in the Soviet Eastern European satellites. Why?

KEY DIFFERENCES BETWEEN MARKET AND COMMAND SYSTEMS		
Characteristic	**Market**	**Command**
Maker of economic decisions	Market forces	Government
Ownership of businesses and means of production	Private ownership	Government ownership
Profit recipient	Private owner	Mostly to government
Determination of prices	Market forces of supply and demand	Mostly by government

However, the U.N. Security Council experiences problems with big power veto. Its resolutions are ignored at times as was the case of the Indian annexation of Goa (1961), Soviet intervention in Hungary (1956), and South African apartheid (until 1994). The U.N. Army preserved the independence of the Republic of South Korea (1950-1953).U.N. peacekeeping forces have been helpful in places such as the Congo, Cyprus, and Somalia. Budget problems and the power of small nations in the General Assembly continue to be issues (see Unit 9 for additional U.N. information).

ECONOMIC ISSUES IN THE COLD WAR AND POST-COLD WAR ERAS

Cold War rivalries led to intense economic competition between communist-dominated U.S.S.R. / Eastern Europe and the market-oriented U.S. / Western Europe. The modern free market system owes its origins to the writings of Adam Smith; the modern command system originated with Josef Stalin's first Five Year Plan. The two economic systems differ in important respects (see chart above).

DEMOCRATIC SOCIALISM DEVELOPS

After World War II, many countries combined a free market system with aspects of socialism and developed a type of mixed economic system called **democratic socialism**[1]. This allowed them to use market forces in conjunction with extensive social welfare programs and some government ownership of industries.

For example, after independence, India adopted a mixed economy and the government implemented a five-year plan in 1951. Foreign aid from the United States, the Soviet Union, and international groups such as the World Bank helped the capital-starved country. The infrastructure left by the British provided a base from which to build. Initially, the government supported small industries, and there was a resurgence in handicrafts. However, textiles, jute, iron, and steel quickly became important industries. The Indian government-owned Tata Iron and Steel Company (founded 1907) led the way. However, in 1956, the government decided to nationalize major economic sectors and increase its control over others, as well.

The Green Revolution played a major role in Indian economic development. The increased use of fertilizers, irrigation, and newly developed seeds increased production where the program was implemented. Rice and wheat accounted for about 33% of the **gross domestic product**[2] (**GDP**). Production increased faster than the population and reduced the famine threat. This also made possible the development of more commercial farming including cotton, jute, coffee, and tea.

Along with most areas in the developing world, India began a movement toward the free market system and **privatization**[3] in the early 1990s. A more positive atmosphere toward foreign investment emerged. By the mid-1990s, decreased inflation and increased exports created positive economic conditions. India is among the ten largest industrial nations today.

Government willingness to accept increased responsibility for citizens' welfare goes back to the 19th century. In countries such as Britain,

---

1 democratic socialism (mixed economic system with government controls and the means of production and distribution owned and managed by both government agencies and private investment)
2 gross domestic product (GDP; value of all the goods and services produced in a country in a given year)
3 privatization (to change [an industry or a business, for example] from governmental or public ownership or control to private enterprise)

the government passed legislation governing working conditions and provided for public education and unemployment insurance. The British **Beveridge Report**, issued during World War II, called for a comprehensive program of social welfare benefits.

After the Labor Party victory in 1945, the British Parliament passed the **National Insurance Act** and the **National Health Service Act**. The first act provided for sickness, accident, disability, and old age protection. The second act made provision for free medical and dental care. Later, the high taxes necessary to pay for these programs caused many in Britain to question their continuance.

The British Labor Party Government took the additional step of nationalizing major industries such as transportation, communication, coal, and steel. Small industries remained in private hands. When the Conservative Party was in office, it privatized some of the government-owned industries and tried to limit the **welfare program**[1]. Inflation problems and labor discontent marked the mid 1960s and most of the 1970s. Conservative Prime Minister **Margaret Thatcher** (in office 1979-1990) used high interest rates and budget cuts to deal with inflation. From 1982-1988, Britain experienced an economic boom – along with most of the rest of the industrialized world. The standard of living increased, unemployment decreased, and industrial efficiency improved. However, a revival of unemployment problems and an unpopular tax policy eventually cost Thatcher her party leadership.

United Kingdom

COMMAND SYSTEMS: THE SOVIET MODEL

The command economies of Eastern Europe also had extensive welfare programs, but the governments paid little attention to the demand for consumer goods. Under Soviet dominance, the main emphasis was on heavy industry. Citizens were expected to sacrifice for the good of future generations. The satellite countries were required to put the needs of the Soviet economy before theirs. Successes were achieved in the heavy industry sector, but agriculture and consumer industry lagged.

In these command systems, central planners established production quotas. Managers who exceeded quotas were awarded bonuses and promotions. However, the quotas resulted in poor workmanship and an unwillingness to innovate. For example, the quotas for a particular type of pipe were set in tons. The factories refused to switch from metal to plastic pipe because the lighter plastic made it difficult to reach their tonnage quotas.

The traditional emphasis on military and heavy industry caused consumer industries to fail in meeting demand. The government approved production of radios and TVs, because they could be used for propaganda purposes. But, other products suffered because political planners deemed them less important.

U.S.S.R.

---

1   welfare program (Financial or other aid provided, especially by the government, to people in need; welfare state (social system whereby the state assumes primary responsibility for the welfare of its citizens, as in matters of health care, education, employment, and social security)

Consumers wanted clothes and shoes, but their poor quality kept sales low. To purchase a car, an order had to be placed with full payment in advance, but delivery could take five or six years. Car owners routinely removed windshield wipers, hub caps, and any other easily stolen parts before parking. It was almost impossible to get replacement parts.

Nikita Khrushchev Soviet Government Photo

When Nikita Khrushchev came to power in the Soviet Union in 1953, he wanted to improve the standard of living. He decreased the power of the central planners, increased production of consumer goods, and tried to increase agricultural output. His "Virgin Lands Program" opened new areas for agricultural production, but the central planners ordered the planting of crops unsuitable for the Central Asian climate. This shows the flaw in any centralized command system. Planners thousands of miles away in Moscow were not able to make decisions accurately and quickly.

STRUGGLES OF DEVELOPING NATIONS

After World War II, newly independent developing nations wished to modernize quickly. To focus on the task, they looked for models. Some nations adopted the Soviet approach. Historically, the Soviet Union was not associated with the hated imperialist powers. Its economic development had been rapid, and strong centralized control appealed to many leaders of developing countries.

Other lesser developed countries (LDCs) opted for mixed economies blending capitalism with some form of socialism. Foreign capital investment was needed by those countries without vital resources to sell in the global market. Sometimes capital could be obtained from the U.S. or the Soviet Union as they competed against each other to buy influence in the new countries. However, the superpowers often attached unwanted conditions to this aid. Economic nationalists in the new countries rejected such foreign interference. They leaned toward more neutral international financial institutions such as the U.N.'s **World Bank** and the **International Monetary Fund (IMF)** which financed projects with few "political strings."

The oil crisis of 1973 resulted in large increases in the price of petroleum. LDCs did not have the necessary financial reserves to meet the higher prices. As a result, many LDCs took on heavy debts and were close to bankruptcy. Their inability to meet the terms of the loans forced the international community to decrease interest rates and restructure loans. One condition attached to these loans was a promise to move toward a free market economy. As a consequence, the number of free market economies rose substantially, but their success rate varied considerably.

EMERGENCE OF THE PACIFIC RIM COUNTRIES

In the 1980s, the "Pacific Rim" became a popular name for countries bordering the Pacific Ocean. Nations along the Asian edge of the Rim had experienced tremendous economic growth beginning in the 1970s. Low pay work forces and a large Asian market for low priced goods fueled the expansion. Most of these Pacific Rim countries started out producing inexpensive consumer products, processing local natural

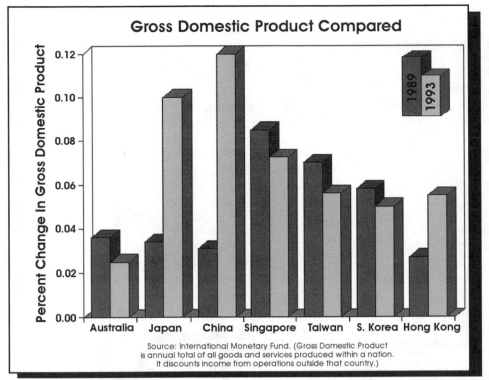

Gross Domestic Product Compared

Percent Change In Gross Domestic Product

0.12
0.10
0.08
0.06
0.04
0.02
0.00

Australia Japan China Singapore Taiwan S. Korea Hong Kong

1989
1993

Source: International Monetary Fund. (Gross Domestic Product
is annual total of all goods and services produced within a nation.
It discounts income from operations outside that country.)

South Korea is one of the more successful of the Asian Tigers. In the last forty years, it has gone from a relatively poor country with few natural resources and subsistence agriculture to rapid industrialization.

By the 1970s, heavy industry emerged with automobiles, electronics, and shipbuilding leading the development. The Gross Domestic Product increased by over 9 percent yearly between the 1960s and early 1990s. Government policies (e.g., tax breaks and low interest financing) encouraged resources, and assembling imported parts for foreign manufacturers in Japan, the United States, and West Germany.

exports and rapid development, combined with low labor wages, fueled the expansion.

South Korea, Hong Kong, Singapore, and Taiwan became known as the "Asian Tigers." (also known as the "Four Little Dragons.") The Pacific Rim's development rested on the rapid growth of the Tigers' economies. In the late 1980s and early 1990s, other Pacific Rim countries such as Thailand, Vietnam, Indonesia, China, and the Philippines began to prosper.

However, the **chaebol**[1] dominated. These economic groupings developed close ties with banks and the government. These ties led to charges of corruption and favoritism. By 1997, inability to reform placed the South Korean economy in difficulty. The country sought economic aid from the international financial com-

1 chaebol (large conglomerates with holdings in many fields)

However, in 1997, the "economic bubble" burst. Many of the Asian countries faced economic crises. Banks, often influenced by close ties with business, made unwise loans. A lack of faith in governments' ability to bring about necessary reforms and open the economies to competition undermined international confidence. These factors caused stock market declines and shrank currency values. This made international transactions difficult and sent the region into a recession.

City of Singapore and harbor: With its high per capita income, Singapore has the leading economy of the South and Southeast Asian region. Due to its strict laws, the city is virtually crime free, very clean, and has no slums and no unemployment. © PhotoDisc, 1994

Mini Assessment

1 The government owns the means of production, makes economic decisions, and receives much of the profit. These are characteristics of a
   1 traditional economy
   2 mixed economy
   3 free market economy
   4 command economy

2 The economic crisis beginning in 1997 in the Pacific Rim countries was primarily caused by
   1 high debt levels and governmental corruption
   2 withdrawal of foreign capital and technological aid
   3 failures in agricultural and consumer industries
   4 declines in tourism and development funds

3 West Germany and Japan became economic powerhouses in the aftermath of World War II because
   1 they had large supplies of coal and iron
   2 their rebuilt industries provided a technological edge
   3 their governments nationalized all major industries
   4 they used immigrant "guest workers" from other countries

Constructed Response:

Use the cartoon below to answer the following questions:

1 Why is the guillotine's blade labeled "loans"?

2 What conditions led LCDs to be in this position?

munity. The World Bank imposed conditions involving an opening of the Korean market to foreign interests, more disclosure of financial information, and a restructuring of the economy.

Thailand is another growing Pacific Rim economy. The rich alluvial soil from the Chao Phraya River made rice the traditional cash crop. After World War II, the government started programs to diversify the economy. By the 1980s, Japanese and other foreign investments in textiles, electronics, and rubber production decreased Thailand's reliance on one crop. Tourism remained the key earner of foreign capital, but manufacturing increased 9.4 percent annually in the 1980s and early 1990s. However, rapid growth and high debt levels led to a loss of confidence in the **baht** (Thai currency) in the summer of 1997. This triggered an economic crisis that spread throughout Asia.

After World War II, communist rebels took control of Northern Vietnam from French colonial forces. In 1954, a treaty partitioned former French Indochina. North Vietnam adopted a command economy, but South Vietnam chose a free market system. North Vietnam began a long war to reunite the two countries. South Vietnam fell to the communists in 1975, and the countries were reunified under a communist command system. Beginning in 1986, government reforms edged the country toward the market system. Rapid growth of over 8 percent per year in the early 1990s was fueled by the paper, cement, textile, and tourist industries.

CHINESE COMMUNIST REVOLUTION

China is the world's third largest country by area and the largest by population. Difficult terrain in the western part of China results in most people living in the eastern third of China. Mountains compose about 43 percent of China, plateaus are about 26 percent, and only about 10 percent of the land is arable. The early isolation of China led to a largely homogenous population. About 95 percent of the population is Han. Most of the minority groups reside on the fringes of the country.

In China, manual labor is the cheapest factor in production. ©PhotoDisc Inc 1994

As was true throughout Chinese history, rivers play a major role in modern China. The Huang He (Yellow) River is known as "China's Sorrow" because it frequently floods its banks, often causing wide spread destruction. The Xi (West) River is a major trade artery. It is navigable to Guangzhou (Canton) making the city a major port. The Yangtze River is currently the subject of controversy. The government's $3 billion Three Gorges hydroelectric program is designed to increase power, but the dam – now under construction – will cost thousands of acres of farmland and force many families to move.

Modern transportation reduced isolation resulting from physical features such as the Gobi Desert, the Himalayas, and the plateaus of Mongolia and Tibet. However, areas in western China have limited contact with the east and with outside nations. Away from major population centers, the roads are often unpaved and impassable during inclement weather. Bicycles remain the most popular form of transportation. Frequent bicycle traffic jams are visible in cities such as Shanghai. New train connections are being established, but the service is not yet up to western standards. Airplane safety and technology have undergone rapid updating. Most of the planes currently in service are Western-made. However, in 1998, the U.S. government had approved "high tech" manufacturing contracts (including airplane assembly) between U.S. and Chinese corporations.

Climate and geography affects crop selection. Northern parts of China produce wheat and **millet**[1] as major food sources; the south relies on rice. Natural disasters cause major problems. Agriculture remains a weak economic sector despite government efforts to increase crop yield.

Terraced[2] Millet Fields in China ©PhotoDisc Inc 1994

---

1 millet (annual grass, cultivated in Eurasia for its white grains)
2 terraced (raised bank of earth having vertical or sloping sides and a flat top, turning a hillside into a series of ascending terraces for farming in rugged terrain)

MONGOLIA

CHINA

KOREA

Mao Zedong's Communist Forces flee Jiang Jieshi's Kuomintang Army

THE LONG MARCH
1934 - 1935

COMMUNIST RISE TO POWER

Marxist communism attracted the interest of some leaders during the Revolution of 1911-1912. In the 1920s in a gesture of friendship, the Soviet communists returned some Chinese territory taken earlier by the tsars. Its aid to the government of Sun Yixian increased friendship between the two nations.

The Chinese Communist Party (CCP) was founded in 1921. In 1923, it allied with the Guomindang to fight the warlords and foreign influence. However in 1927, Jiang Jieshi (Chiang Kai-shek) expelled communists from the Guomindang and began a purge against them.

To escape the armies of Jiang, **Mao Zedong** (1893-1976) led about 100,000 communist guerrillas on a trek of 6,000 miles to Shaanxi in northwestern China. Only about 20,000 completed the **Long March** (1934). In Mao's view, the Chinese peasants were the revolutionary group, critical to the success of his communist movement. He focused on gaining their support. Throughout the March, the communists paid peasants for food and treated them fairly. The Long March enabled Mao to forge the leadership

of a revolution that eventually changed China.

The Japanese invasions of Manchuria in 1931 and the main part of China in 1937 brought about an uneasy union between the communists and the Guomindang. The two armies used different approaches. The communists used **guerrilla**[1] **tactics** and often operated behind Japanese lines. They implemented land reform programs in territories they controlled. They increased their support among the peasants, and many joined their army. The Guomindang employed conventional military tactics and had limited success against the Japanese. They retreated from coastal areas and established inland bases. The morale of their forces dropped, and their leadership employed harsh authoritarian methods in the areas they controlled.

At the end of World War II, Mao's communists controlled much of the north, and the Guomindang occupied the south. The Guomindang maintained power with aid received from the United States. In 1949, the communists established the **People's Republic of China**. For the first time in many years, a central government provided stability for China. Jiang Jieshi and the Guomindang fled to Taiwan and established the Republic of China.

In the 1930s, Japan began seizing territory from China to gain vital raw materials for its manufacturing interests.

---

1 guerrilla or guerilla (member of an irregular, usually indigenous military or paramilitary unit operating in small bands in occupied territory to harass and undermine the enemy, as by surprise raids)

Mao's Communist Revolution

- Centralized economic planning
- **Collectivized**[1] most land and property
- Destroyed the landlord class
- Weakened the urban bourgeoisie
- Raised the status of peasants and industrial workers
- Harsh, totalitarian government abused individual rights

COMMUNISTS ACHIEVE POWER UNDER MAO

As leader, Mao Zedong (the "Great Helmsman") followed the Russian communist model in some respects. He created a totalitarian government which had little respect for basic human rights. Censorship, repression, imprisonment of opposition, propaganda, and restrictions on religious freedom, and the right of assembly became commonplace. However, the government also made progress in some fields. Literacy increased from 20 percent in 1949 to 78 percent

Housing in Shanghai built during the "Great Leap Forward" with Soviet assistance. ©Sue Kime Inc 1997

in 1990. Crime and corruption decreased. Improved health care increased life expectancy from 45 years in 1949 to 68 years for men and 74 years for women in the mid-1990s.

However, China's economy presented enormous problems. In 1953, Mao implemented his first Five Year Plan. Its primary goal, the development of heavy industry, was largely successful. By 1960, China was among the top ten industrial powers. However, agricultural production lagged.

Mao called the Second Five Year Plan the **Great Leap Forward**. It continued the development of heavy industry, but also proposed the mobilization of peasants to increase agricultural production. The Plan established **"People's Communes**[2]**"** of thousands of acres staffed with over 20,000 people. China's central planners established production quotas and attempted to mechanize farming. Each commune was designed as a self-sufficient community with local industries, schools, housing, and child care for working mothers.

By 1960, peasant opposition to this extreme regimentation undermined production. Combined with natural disasters, opposition led to famine. The government finally responded. Peasants were still required to sell set amounts of produce to the government, but they could sell surpluses for personal gain.

Still, the problems in the agricultural sector led to divisions within the Chinese Communist Party. Mao felt that the communist revolution was under attack from reactionaries in the Party. He launched the **Great Proletarian Cultural Revolution** (1966-1969) under the direction of his wife, **Jiang Qing**. She fashioned a fanatical ideological movement in which young teens were organized into the **Red Guard**. Often citing **Quotations of Chairman Mao** (the "Little Red Book"), the Red Guard attacked "counterrevolutionary elements" – those thought to have a bourgeois outlook.

The Red Guard's victims were educated party leaders and factory managers. These targets were subjected to humiliation, beatings,

1 collectivized (to make the means of production owned jointly by all the people of a region or country)
2 commune (community whose members share common interests, work, and income and often own property collectively)

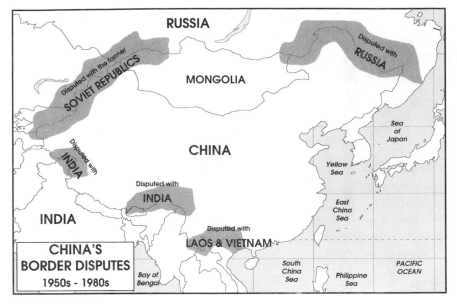

CHINA'S BORDER DISPUTES 1950s - 1980s

infringements, and market accessibility continue to be controversial. Despite these issues, President **Jiang Zemin** (1926-) visited the U.S. in 1997.

During the early years of the communist government in China, the Soviets gave considerable technological and economic aid. However, a number of areas of disagreement developed and the assistance was withdrawn in 1960. After Mao's death relations remained cool, but in the 1980s, the more moderate leaders worked with Soviet leader Mikhail Gorbachev to develop closer ties between the two communist powers.

and in some cases, execution. They were s nt to rural areas to work as farm laborers. About three million people were sent to labor camps. Educational institutions were closed and economic disruption occurred.

In 1969, the army finally acted to end the disturbances. Many Red Guard members were sent to communes, and moderates in the Politburo asserted their power. However, after Mao's death in 1976, the "Gang of Four," a radical group in the Politburo led by Jiang Qing tried to rekindle the Cultural Revolution. They were arrested, tried, and found guilty of actions against the Party and the government. In the next decade, China's more moderate leaders praised some aspects of Mao's policies, but slowly acknowledged his failures.

There were foreign relations problems during Mao's rule. For twenty-six years (1949-1974), the United States refused to recognize the communist government of the People's Republic of China. It supported the Guomindang government in Taiwan. The U.S. led the debate to keep the People's Republic of China out of the U.N., using China's involvement in the Korean War as one of the main reasons. However, in 1971, the U.S. began to shift its policies. It ceased to block U.N. membership for Communist China. U.S. President Richard Nixon visited Beijing in 1972, and tensions eased between the two countries. The U.S. formally recognized the communist government in 1974. Since that time, relations between the two countries have fluctuated. Chinese human rights policies, copyright

SINO-SOVIET AREAS OF DISAGREEMENT

- role of peasantry in revolution
- rivalry for influence in developing areas
- border disputes
- accommodations to capitalists

MODERATION UNDER DENG XIAOPING

After Mao's death in 1976, **Deng Xiaoping** (1904-1997) emerged as foremost leader in the communist oligarchy. Deng's main concerns were modernization and economic progress. He vowed to quadruple agricultural and industrial output by the millennium. He believed that economic reform, not class struggle, was the key to progress. Deng opened China to new ideas by allowing many Chinese to study in the West and by easing restrictions on foreign investment.

Agriculture remained a problem area. Deng instituted the **Responsibility System**. Each

DENG'S FOUR MODERNIZATION PROGRAMS

- modernizing agriculture
- improving the military
- increasing industrialization
- developing technology and science

China's Trade Policy of the 1990s – "Swinging Doors"

Problems with crime and corruption multiplied. Many people felt that relatives of leaders received unfair favors and advantages. Ties between banks and government businesses resulted in unwise lending practices which threatened the financial structure. In 1998, President Jiang Zemin proposed a new program of reform to increase private ownership of business, decrease central planning, and reform financial practices.

Concern over human rights in China continues to be a major issue. Beijing's Tiananmen Square became a focal point in 1989. Deng's reforms helped China's economy, but they were conservative. They unleashed demands for greater freedom among groups of students and workers. In May of 1989, these groups occupied Tiananmen Square, erected a "Goddess of Democracy" statue, and refused to leave.

family was responsible for its own livelihood. Part of its produce had to be sold to the government, but the rest could be sold privately on the open market. Capitalist incentives were used to increase production. Light or consumer industry was partially freed from state control. Deng's rules gave factory managers more decision-making power. Special "Economic Zones" were set up in southeast China. In these areas, foreign companies were allowed to own and operate businesses. Large amounts of foreign investment came from Japan, Hong Kong, Taiwan, and the countries of the West.

CHINA TODAY

By the early 1990s, China's Gross Domestic Product (GDP) was growing at 12 percent – Asia's fastest growth. The standard of living improved, but class differences also increased. Those in urban areas fared better. In 1997, rural per capita income was less that 50 percent of that of urban dwellers. This led to a migration from rural to urban areas despite government attempts to limit access to cities. As a consequence, living conditions in cities deteriorated, homelessness increased, and beggars could be seen on the streets.

The protest movement spread to other major cities. The participants used faxes to keep in contact because of government control of the media. On June 3rd and 4th, People's Liberation Army troops and tanks opened fire. In the **Tiananmen Square Massacre**, 800 to 1000 people were killed, and countless others were wounded. Later, the government imprisoned or executed many protest leaders. These actions were carried out on Deng Xiaoping's orders. The imprisonment of dissidents and the use of forced labor in factories producing goods for export continue to concern the international community.

In 1989, a Chinese student defies the government's power during pro-democracy demonstrations in T'iananmen Square – "*Gate of Heavenly Peace*", Beijing.

Visitors to China today are impressed by the amount of small entrepreneurship. Small shops are everywhere. Barber shops and bicycle repair shops operate on the sidewalk. Open air markets for virtually anything can be found in every city. Hawkers present their wares to foreign visitors at tourist destinations. Small children dress in costumes of various types to pose for tourist cameras. Almost everyone seems to have a small business in addition to a regular job.

©Sue Kime Inc 1997

This concern for freedom was reflected in anxiety over the return of Hong Kong to China on 1 July 1997. The city had become a colony of Britain as a result of the First Opium War. Hong Kong had become a trade, light industry, and financial center for East Asia. Prior to its return to China, it was the major link between the People's Republic and the outside world.

In the **Joint Declaration of 1984**, Britain and People's Republic of China promised to keep the existing social and economic system for 50 years. They also pledged self-government for the former colony. However, events after the signing of the Declaration made clear that Beijing intended to exercise final control. Many Chinese in Hong Kong became apprehensive about the future, but they were also proud of China's achievements. Concerned that conditions would worsen caused as many as one million individuals to try for one of the 350,000 passports offered by the British. Nationalism in China made the return of Hong Kong a major event. Major cities had clocks which counted down the years, months, days, minutes, and seconds until the colony's return.

In the area of women's rights prior to 1949, women were regarded as inferior to men and often secluded in the home. Few received an education, and most were not allowed to own property under the communists. Mao and other communist leaders altered women's status, and women made considerable progress.

COLLAPSE OF EUROPEAN IMPERIALISM

In the aftermath of World War II, the European countries were seriously weakened and unable to maintain their control. During the War, promises of independence or increased self-government were made to colonies to gain their cooperation.

After the War, nationalism exploded in many colonies. The independence of India and Pakistan became role models. Colonial powers granted some colonies freedom (Nigeria) without much disruption; others fought long wars to gain it (Kenya). Despite independence, many of the former colonies continued to have close ties to their former mother countries. Economic and military aid as well as long-standing trade ties made it difficult to end the relationship.

WOMEN IN COMMUNIST CHINA

Progress	Drawbacks
• Equal under the law • Can own property • Can receive at least an elementary education	• Expected to work alongside men on farms and in factories • Must do most of household work • Face discrimination: promotions, pay, higher education

Mini Assessment

MINI-
ASSESSMENT

1 The success of Mao Zedong and the communists in gaining power in China is explained in part by
1 aid obtained from Japan
2 assistance of large landowners
3 land reform promises to the peasants
4 use of standard military tactics

2 Deng Xiaoping's policies stressed the
1 need for economic reform
2 importance of the class struggle
3 necessity of central planning
4 nationalizing of foreign-owned industry

3 The events in Tiananmen Square in 1989 indicated that the Chinese government was willing to
1 use force to keep control
2 relinquish media control
3 allow peaceful demonstrations
4 accept student and worker demands

Constructed Response:

Use the two photos below and your knowledge of global history to answer the following questions.

1 Which picture (photo A or photo B) represents life in traditional China?

2 What do the two pictures reveal about change in modern China?

Photo A

Photo B

Many former colonies experienced problems related to their colonial era. The British policy of "divide and rule" continued to damage Hindu-Muslim relationships in India. Boundaries established by the Europeans often separated ethnic and religious groups. This led to civil wars in nations such as Nigeria and Rwanda. Europeans often encouraged the production of cash crops for export at the expense of agricultural products needed locally.

They also exploited the colony's natural resources. After receiving independence, countries found it difficult to break these patterns and diversify their economies. Developing the local expertise and capital necessary to modernize without foreign help was nearly impossible.

INDEPENDENCE FOR INDIA

Great Britain granted independence to India on 15 August 1947. The agreement established two separate nations, Hindu India and Muslim Pakistan.

The Indian independence movement dated back to the 1800s, but the pressure for a separate Muslim state came from the Muslim

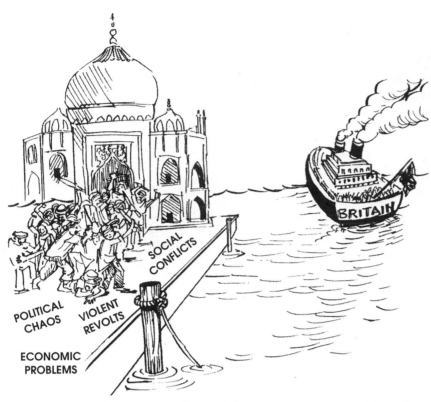

The boundary lines drawn by the British left large minority populations in areas controlled by another religion. This triggered a mass migration of some 10 million **refugees**[1]. Independence leader Mohandas Gandhi opposed the partition. In January 1948, a disillusioned Hindu fanatic assassinated the "Great Soul." Despite the migrations and the 200,000 plus deaths they caused, about 100 million Muslims reside in India.

Perhaps the most troubling problem in India was the **caste**[2] **system**. Gandhi strongly opposed discrimination against the **harijans** (untouchables). India's 1947 constitution forbid discrimination, and the government tried to provide this group with opportunities. Nevertheless, discrimination remained strong in rural areas.

The Europeans left South & Southeast Asia many unresolved problems. The newly independent countries were ill-prepared to govern themselves. Many of these LDCs still view the former imperial powers with suspicion and blame them for many of their current problems.

League under the leadership of **Mohammed Ali Jinnah**. Muslims feared discrimination and persecution in a Hindu-dominated nation.

1 refugee (One who flees in search of refuge, as in times of war, political oppression, or religious persecution)
2 caste (any of four classes, comprised of numerous subclasses, constituting traditional Hindu society)

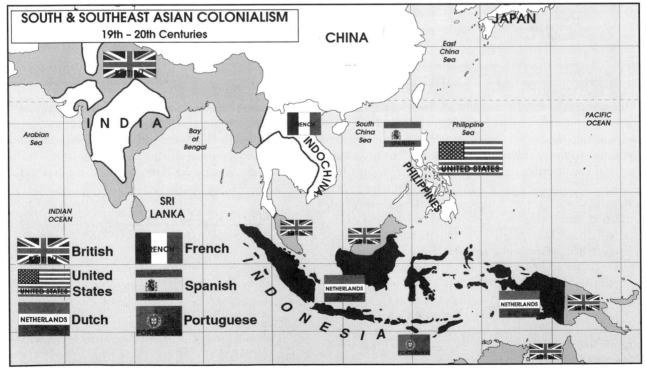

SOUTH & SOUTHEAST ASIAN COLONIALISM
19th – 20th Centuries

British
United States
Dutch
French
Spanish
Portuguese

POST-INDEPENDENCE PROBLEMS FACING INDIA AND PAKISTAN

- Religious differences (Hindu v. Muslim plus Sikhs, Buddhists, Christians)
- Poverty
- Overpopulation
- Border disputes
- Women's rights
- Language differences
- Princely states within their borders
- Cold War foreign policy issues
- Caste System

Increasing modernization and population growth in urban areas led to some improvement for the harijans. In the 1990s, the government tried to increase the number of jobs for them, but high caste opposition was strong, and the plan was dropped.

Foreign policy differences developed between India and Pakistan as each sought to insure its future. The Indians, under the leadership of **Jawaharlal Nehru** (1889-1964), adopted a policy of **non-alignment**[1]. The Indians refused to join the **SEATO** (Southeast Asian Treaty Organization, 1954-1977), a regional **multilateral**[2] defense alliance sponsored by the United States. They accepted aid from both the Soviet Union and the U.S. The Indians were concerned about Pakistani-U.S. ties.

Pakistan joined SEATO and the British-led **Baghdad Pact** (later called CENTO – the Central Treaty Organization). CENTO was an alliance among Turkey, Iran, Pakistan, and Great Britain for mutual defense (1955-1979). As a consequence, Pakistan received considerable Western aid and assistance in the development of peaceful uses of atomic energy. Later, India and Pakistan developed nuclear weapons. The continuing tensions between the two nations makes their possession of atomic weapons a threat to world peace (see pg. 271).

Within India, two separatist groups have threatened stability – the Sikhs and the Tamils. The **Sikhs**[3] combine elements of Hinduism and Islam and are a majority in the state of Punjab. They gained a reputation as fierce warriors prepared to defend their religion. Sikhs feel that they are not obtaining a fair share of central government revenue and have demanded a separate state.

In 1984, Sikhs occupied the Golden Temple in Amritsar, sacred in their religious beliefs. **Indira Gandhi** (1917-1984), the Indian prime minister, ordered Indian troops to retake the Temple. Thousands died. Shortly after, Sikh bodyguards assassinated her in retaliation. The Sikh problems are not solved, and outbursts of terrorism still occur.

The **Tamils**[4] are an ethnic group of about 45 million who live in southern India and Sri Lanka. They played a major role in government and business under the British, but post-independence laws in Sri Lanka gave preferences to the majority Sinhalese. The Tamils have demanded an independent state. The most radical Tamil group, the Liberation Tigers of Tamil Eelam, continue terrorist activities and a guerrilla war in India and Sri Lanka. By 1997, approximately 50,000 had died in the 25-year dispute. One of the victims was the assassinated Indian Prime Minister **Rajiv Gandhi** (1944-1990), son of Indira and grandson of Nehru.

1 non-alignment (refusing the take the same side on all issues)
2 multilateral (involving more than two nations or parties)
3 Sikhism (doctrines and practices of a monotheistic religion founded in northern India in the 16th century and combining elements of Hinduism and Islam)
4 Tamil or Tamils (member of a Dravidian people of southern India and northern Sri Lanka)

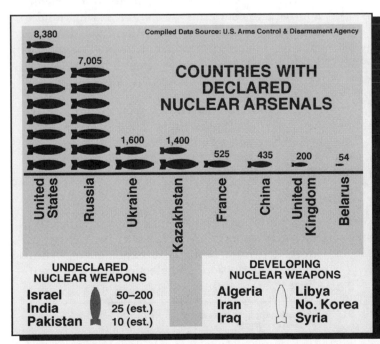

COUNTRIES WITH DECLARED NUCLEAR ARSENALS

Compiled Data Source: U.S. Arms Control & Disarmament Agency

United States	Russia	Ukraine	Kazakhstan	France	China	United Kingdom	Belarus
8,380	7,005	1,600	1,400	525	435	200	54

UNDECLARED NUCLEAR WEAPONS

Israel	50–200
India	25 (est.)
Pakistan	10 (est.)

DEVELOPING NUCLEAR WEAPONS

Algeria	Libya
Iran	No. Korea
Iraq	Syria

AFRICAN INDEPENDENCE AND POST-COLONIAL MOVEMENTS

African people also sought independence after World War II. Using the Indian and Pakistani models, they demanded "Uhuru!" – "Freedom Now" – in the post-war period. The major colonial powers – Britain, France, Portugal, and Belgium – took differing approaches. Sometimes, Britain provided training for self-government and granted home-rule; in others, long wars resulted. Belgium provided virtually no training and few secondary education opportunities for the people in the Belgian Congo. France has tried to maintain its ties with former colonies through currency linkage, aid programs, and in some instances, military intervention. Portugal simply tried to hold on to its colonies as long as possible.

Ghana (Gold Coast) was the first African colony to gain independence in 1957. Nationalist leader **Kwame Nkrumah** established a political party and employed strikes, **boycotts**[1], and riots to achieve his goal. He was arrested by the British, but after his release and the achievement of independence, he became prime minister of the new country.

In **Nigeria**, Britain did some training for self-government, but the hostility among ethnic groups was hard to overcome. The Muslim Hausa and Fulani peoples lived in the north, the Yoruba in the southwest, and the Ibo in the southeast. Initially, anti-British nationalism helped to unite these groups, but after independence was achieved in 1960, problems developed among them. The Ibo seceded in 1967 and established the state of **Biafra**.

Biafrans feared Muslim domination and wanted to keep control of the resources in the southeast. Over a million died as a result of starvation and the civil war which followed. By 1970, Biafra was united with the rest of the country, but religious and ethnic loyalties remain strong.

Although **Nigeria** had a large oil income in the 1970s, its leaders spent money on wasteful projects. During the 1980s, the country faced hard economic times. Since achieving independence, the country has alternated between military and civilian governments.

After declaring a 1993 election void, **Sani Abacha**'s repressive military government postponed numerous promises to hold new democratic elections and restore civilian rule. The powerful dictator died from a heart attack in mid-1998. His place was filled by General Adulsalam Abubakar. In 1999, **Olusegun Obasanjo** was elected president in the first free elections in sixteen years.

In **Kenya**, the drive for independence was complicated by the large number of European settlers remaining in its highland areas. They refused to give up power. **Jomo Kenyatta** (1891-1978), a Kikuyu leader, tried a non-violent approach to changing laws and restoring land to the native people. However, the Mau Mau – an anti-European guerrilla movement among the Kikuyu people – used a campaign of violence and terrorism (1952-1959) to achieve its goals.

By 1956, the Mau Mau movement killed nearly 100 Europeans and 2,000 Kikuyu "loyalists." Kenyatta was jailed and many of the Kikuyu were sent to concentration camps. Ultimately, Kenyatta was freed and like Nkrumah of Ghana, became prime minister of the independent country. Kenyatta set up a one-party state and limited individual rights. After Kenyatta's death in 1978, **Daniel arap Moi** succeeded him. Moi's rule experienced ethnic violence, corruption, and election and civil rights abuses.

---

1 boycotts (group action in abstaining from using, buying, or dealing with as an expression of protest)

Kenya has experienced economic difficulties. The period from 1991-1993 was the worst economic performance since 1963. This led to reforms with the aid of the International Monetary Fund (IMF) and the World Bank. Economic restrictions were loosened and some industry was privatized. Recently, the two international organizations expressed satisfaction with the progress to date, but indicated continued effort was crucial.

Apartheid[1] was the issue which plagued **South Africa**. After the Boer War, Britain granted the area independence (1910). The White-controlled government instituted apartheid. The 1913 **Native Land Act** provided that the Bantus (native people) could own land only on reservations which usually contained poor soil. Bantus were required to carry passes. Later, Bantus found themselves barred from the best mine jobs.

Prior to the constitutional reforms of the 1990s, apartheid policies supported white dominance and racial injustice.

In 1912, middle class, urban-based professionals and chiefs organized the **African National Congress** (ANC), the foremost South African nonviolent civil rights organization. The ANC tried to use legal means to bring about change but without success. Two major leaders of this organization were Bishop **Desmond Tutu** (1931-) and **Nelson Mandela** (1918-). The 1950 **Group Areas Act** created ten homelands for Blacks, but they contained only 20 percent of the land for the Blacks who were 80 percent of the population.

This restrictive legislation led to the Sharpeville Massacres in 1960. Peaceful demonstrators were fired upon and over sixty died. In response, Mandela formed the "Spear of the Nation" movement, an underground military command. It campaigned against the symbols of apartheid. In 1964, the government sentenced

Nelson Mandela

Mandela to life imprisonment. He became the symbolic leader of the nationalist movement. A 1976 protest in Soweto over the required use of **Afrikaans**[2] in schools touched off months of racial violence which drew international attention to the apartheid issue.

The international community opposed apartheid. The United Nations passed resolutions against South Africa and placed an arms embargo on it. The International Olympic Committee barred South African athletes from participation. International corporations, under pressure from civil rights groups in their home bases, left the country. Many large pension funds, insurance companies, and mutual funds **divested**[3] their financial interests and holdings in South Africa.

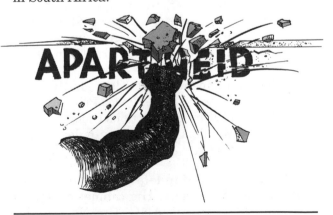

1 Apartheid (official policy of racial segregation practiced until the 1990s in the Republic of South Africa, involving political, legal, and economic discrimination against nonwhites)
2 Afrikaans (language of the Afrikaaners)
3 divested (to sell off or otherwise dispose of financial interests and investments)

The Wolof people, Keur Mibarick Village, Senegal
© David Johnson, 1993

number of riots in Johannesburg by **Coloureds**[1] who claimed discrimination from the **Blacks**[2]. In 1999, **Thabo Mbeki** of the ANC was elected president, replacing Mandela, who retired.

Politically, movements to unite people of African descent began in the 1920s. The first Pan-African Congress met in 1919. Its hope of persuading the participants in the Paris Peace Conference after World War I to recognize African rights was not realized. In 1963, as African nations became independent, the **Organization of African Unity** (OAU) was established. It hoped to eliminate colonialism, defend the independence of African nations, and establish a basis for cooperation and solution of problems among African nations.

Despite the desire of Africans to stand on their own, they continue to have close ties with their former colonial powers. Many former French colonies link their currencies to the French franc and continue to trade mainly with France.

Major French companies have virtual monopolies in former colonies. At different times, the French government has sent in troops to quell disturbances or help preserve independence. Often the former colonial power is a source of economic and military aid. A number of former British colonies continue membership in the Commonwealth of Nations. Regular meetings discuss matters of mutual concern, and members receive preferential trade treatment with Britain as well as aid of various types.

Kenya and Tanzania lead in the effort to decrease foreign influence. Both are trying to move from reliance on one crop or resource and to diversify their economies. Tanzania is shifting from exports to the production of domestic goods and services. In 1960, when Senegal became independent, 83 percent of its exports were peanuts and 75 percent of its exports went to France, Senegal's former colonial power. By 1990, only 25 percent of its exports were peanuts and only one-third went to France.

Change began in the late 1980s with the legalization of the ANC. This was followed by the release of Nelson Mandela from prison by President **F.W. de Klerk** (1936-). Mandela and de Klerk began a series of negotiations that led to change:

- 1990s – Pass Laws lifted, opposition leaders freed
- 1992 – 68 percent of whites voted to end apartheid in a referendum
- 1993 – a new constitution granted political equality for all
- 1993 – Mandela and de Klerk jointly awarded Nobel Peace Prize
- 1994 – Multiracial elections choose Mandela president with de Klerk deputy

As president, Mandela has tried to work with people of all races. His cabinet contained representatives from ANC, the Nationalist Party, and the Zulu Nationalist **Inkatha Freedom Party**. However, tensions continue among the various groups. In 1997, there were a

Despite progress toward economic independence, almost all mines and petroleum operations are foreign owned. Some are joint ventures (foreign and African owners), with the African nations trying to increase their shares.

1 Coloureds (group of racially mixed South Africans, are largely the descendants of European settlers, Khoikhoi, and slaves from Madagascar and Asia)
2 Blacks (racial group with brown to black skin, being of African origin, for example, the Zulu – Bantu people inhabiting northeast Natal province in South Africa)

SOUTHEAST ASIAN INDEPENDENCE MOVEMENTS

Southeast Asian countries faced many of the same problems in achieving independence as the African nations. **Vietnam's** effort was led by **Ho Chi Minh** (1890-1969). He was present at the Paris Peace Conference after World War I when France denied Vietnam independence. During the 1920s and 1930s, he turned to communism and received training in the Soviet Union and China. During World War II, he organized the Viet Minh with other nationalists. They harassed the Japanese occupiers with guerrilla tactics. At the end of the War, his forces occupied parts of North Vietnam, and he declared the Democratic Republic of Vietnam an independent nation. France refused to recognize the new nation and began a war to regain control.

Ho Chi Minh

The first phase of the Vietnam War might be called "the French phase" (1946-1954). The United States gave aid to France because of its belief in the **domino theory**[1]. However, the French campaigns against communist **insurgents**[2] floundered. The surrender of French forces at the Battle of **Dien Bien Phu** led to peace talks in Switzerland. The **Geneva Agreement** (1954) divided Vietnam at the 17th parallel with elections to be held within two years to unite the country.

Ho Chi Minh and his communist followers established a totalitarian government in North Vietnam, copying the examples of Soviet and Eastern European regimes. Ho carried out land reform and won the support of many peasants. South Vietnam came under the control of a non-communist government led by **Ngo Dinh Diem** (1901-1963). However, Diem refused to hold the scheduled elections, because he feared losing to the communists.

The second phase of the war might be called "the American phase" (1959-1975). At first, the United States sent only military advisers to help Diem resist the Viet Cong (communist insurgents). The Viet Cong guerrillas received aid from North Vietnam and harassed the South Vietnamese government. Diem's dictatorial policies, corruption, lack of land reform, and pro-Catholic policies made his government unpopular. A 1963 military coup resulted in Diem's assassination. As North Vietnam sent troops to aid the Viet Cong, the war intensified. In 1964, North Vietnamese attack on U.S. warships prompted action. The U.S. Congress passed the **Gulf of Tonkin Resolution** giving President Lyndon Johnson the power to use force if necessary. Johnson sent U.S. combat forces to Vietnam. The War became unpopular in the U.S. and led to Johnson's decision not to run for reelection in 1968. He was followed by Richard Nixon who promised to end the War.

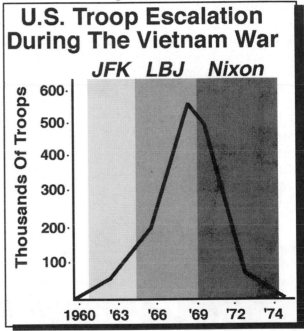

U.S. Troop Escalation During The Vietnam War

JFK   LBJ   Nixon

Thousands Of Troops: 600, 500, 400, 300, 200, 100

1960 '63 '66 '69 '72 '74

STEPS ENDING U.S. INVOLVEMENT IN VIETNAM
1972 – began withdrawal of U.S. troops, "**Vietnamizing**[3]" the war
1973 – secret talks led to a cease-fire and withdrawal of U.S. troops
1975 – Saigon fell and North and South united under communist government

1 domino theory (often cited belief for U.S. troop involvement in Vietnam, if one nation fell to communism, others would follow like dominos)
2 insurgents (rising in revolt against civil or governmental authority)
3 vietnamizing (turning over responsibility for their own future and defense – military operations, for example – to the South Vietnamese)

The effects of bombing, chemical warfare, and unexploded mines and munitions devastated Vietnam. Many Vietnamese fled communism and the problems at home. These "boat people" sought refuge in Thailand, Hong Kong, and other neighboring countries. Some eventually immigrated to the U.S. It was not until 1997 that the U.S. sent an ambassador to Vietnam and reestablished full diplomatic ties.

At first, Vietnam adopted a series of 5-Year Plans similar to those of the U.S.S.R. and its satellites. However, in the late 1970s, it began a move from heavy industry to agriculture and light industry in an attempt to improve the standard of living. The lack of foreign aid and its large defense budget limited its progress. In 1988, Vietnam changed economic policy. The government decreased central planning, increased local decision making, and actively sought foreign investment. The impressive progress led to speculation that Vietnam might be the next "Asian Tiger."

Cambodia was also a victim of the Vietnam War. Viet Cong bases in Cambodia were bombed, and U.S. and Vietnamese troops entered the country. The the Chinese-backed **Khmer Rouge** supported their fellow communists. At the end of the Vietnam War, Khmer Rouge leader **Pol Pot** seized power.

In 1975, he ordered the population of the national capital, Phnom Penh, into the countryside. In his plan to develop an agrarian-based (farming) economy, almost all were assigned work as peasants. Between one and two million Cambodians died in this relocation. Many were executed as enemies of the state, others died from disease, overwork, or starvation. It is estimated that about one-third of the population died in the genocidal "Killing Fields" of Cambodia.

In 1979, Soviet-backed Vietnamese troops invaded Cambodia, unseated Pol Pot, and installed a pro-Soviet communist regime under the leadership of **Heng Samrin**. The government changed the name of the country to **Kampuchea**. Civil war ensued between the forces of Vietnam-backed Heng Samrin and Khmer Rouge factions. In 1989, a new constitution restored the right to private property.

The United Nations arranged a cease-fire, secured the withdrawal of the Vietnamese forces and the agreement of China and the United States to cease aiding warring factions. In 1990, the U.N. Security Council drew up a comprehensive peace plan and supervised an interim government. The U.N. conducted elections in 1993 resulted in Prince **Norodom Sihanouk's** selection as king. However, fighting with the Khmer Rouge continued.

As the decade of the 1990's closed, the UN forces withdrew, and the Khmer Rouge retreated into the hills. Its leadership split, with some defecting to the government. In 1998, Pol Pot was captured by a rival Khmer Rouge faction and died in captivity.

CONFLICTS AND CHANGE IN THE MIDDLE EAST

PHYSICAL SETTING

The Middle East remains a crossroads in the global setting of the late 20th century and is likely to remain so in the 21st century. This meeting ground of Africa, Asia, and Europe is also the location of major waterways important to world trade and international relationships. The **Straits of the Dardanelles and Bosporus**, under Turkish control, command the approach to the Aegean and Mediterranean Seas from the Black

Khmer Refugee Camp at Khao I Dang, Thailand, September 1991
© David Johnson, 1991

Mini Assessment

Answer question 1 based on the outline below and your knowledge of global history.

I._____
    A. Pass Laws enforced
    B. Group Areas Act
    C. Afrikaans only

1 Which heading is the most appropriate for the partial outline above?
    1 Salt March   3 Holocaust
    2 Apartheid   4 October Manifesto

2 The Vietnam and Boer Wars are similar because in both cases
    1 war quickly ended with few casualties
    2 authoritarian, communist regimes emerged
    3 colonial people established independent democracies
    4 a major power suffered embarrassing losses

3 The current status of the harijans (untouchables) in India might best be described as
    1 rapidly improving because of government jobs programs
    2 little changed in rural areas, but with some improvement in cities
    3 basically unchanged from pre-independence India
    4 declining because modernization has cost them jobs

Constructed Response:

Base your answer to the following questions on the two speaker statements below and your knowledge of global history.

Speaker A
"The Hindus and Muslims belong to two different religions, philosophies, social customs, literatures. They neither intermarry nor interdine together and, indeed, they belong to two different civilizations which are based mainly on conflicting ideas and conceptions."

Speaker B
"Pakistan is… impracticable. Such a Pakistan would comprise two main areas, one in the north-west and one in the north-east. Yet the north-west areas would have a non-Moslem minority of 37.93 per cent and the north-east a non-Moslem minority of 48.31 per cent."

1 Which Speaker would support the establishment of separate nations, India and Pakistan?

2 Although the Speakers do not agree, each indirectly predicted problems that would face the Indian subcontinent. Select **one** of the two Speakers and explain why this statement is true.

Sea. Russia still needs access to the seas for warm water ports. The **Suez Canal** links the Mediterranean with the Red Sea and the Indian Ocean. Although the largest oil tankers no longer fit through the Canal, a considerable amount of the world's shipping passes through the Canal. Also in the region, the **Persian Gulf** and the **Strait of Hormuz**, at the Gulf's mouth, are the routes for much of Middle Eastern oil.

Oil is also responsible for much of the global focus on the Middle East. Petroleum resources first assumed importance during World War I.

European countries established the mandate system for this area at the Paris Peace Conference, in part, to maintain control over this vital resource. After World War II, the superpowers struggled to influence the area as colonialism declined. With the increased demand for petroleum in developed Western countries, the Middle East became increasingly important.

The Middle East is an area of cultural diversity and diffusion. Over thirty different languages are spoken. Borders drawn by colonial

**MIDDLE EAST
CONTEMPORARY NATIONS
1990s**

within Israel, different approaches to Judaism range from Reformed to Orthodox and influence everything from politics to culture. Differences among and within the three major religions influence the affairs of the region.

CREATION OF
THE STATE OF ISRAEL

Although the Middle East has seen historic clashes of culture, modern Israel's creation as a homeland for Jews in the post-World War II era destabilized the region. Both the Arabs and Jews have early historic claims to the area. The Hebrew people lived on this land about 4,000 years ago. In the World War I period, Britain gave both groups promises of nationhood. Jewish migration to Palestine, which began in the late 19th century, intensified with the rise of Hitler and anti-Semitism in the 1930s, and further increased in the post World War II period. Arab opposition increased because of concern over becoming a minority in what they regarded as their homeland.

powers often placed different ethnic and religious groups within one country. For example, the hostility of Kurds and Arabs in Iraq continues to plague world affairs today. Islam is the dominant religion. Most Arabs follow Islam, but so do many Iranians, Turks, and Kurds. The major sects of Islam are Sunni and Shi'ite. Different sects are apparent in the Christian communities also. There are Eastern Orthodox, Roman Catholic, and Coptic Christians. Even

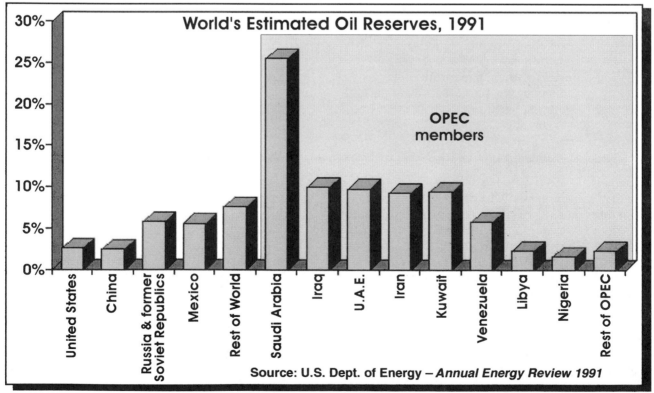

WARS AND TERRORISM

War / Terrorist Campaign	Causes	Results
Suez Canal Crisis 1956	President Nassar of Egypt nationalized the Suez Canal and denied Israel access	Britain, France, and Israel attacked Egypt. U.N. arranged truce and sent peacekeepers
Six Day War 1967	Egypt demanded withdrawal of U.N. peacekeepers, terrorist attacks on Israel, closure of Gulf of Aqaba to Israel	Israel won control of and occupied West Bank, Golan Heights, Gaza Strip, Sinai Peninsula, and all of Jerusalem
Yom Kippur War 1973	Desire of Arabs to regain lost territories led to attack on Israeli troops in Gaza and Golan. U.S. aided Israel; U.S.S.R. aided Syria	U.N. arranged a cease fire
Intifada 1987	Young Palestinians protested Israeli rule of occupied areas with attacks on troops and selected targets	Israeli retaliated by arrests, imprisonment, destruction of homes of Arabs involved, and closure of access to Israeli controlled areas to Arab employees

After World War I, Britain and France ruled areas of the former Ottoman Empire as **mandates**[1]. They created several independent Arab states. Iraq became a nation in 1932, and Jordan, Syria, and Lebanon reached the same status after World War II. However, Britain was too weak to deal with the crisis in Palestine. As a consequence, it turned the problem over to the United Nations. The U.N. came up with a plan to partition the area between Arabs and Jews in 1947. The plan also called for making Jerusalem an international zone under U.N. supervision.

In May 1948, Britain withdrew from Palestine. Israel declared its independence and was immediately recognized by the United States. In what became known as the War for Independence, Arab forces from Syria,

Transjordan, Egypt, Iraq, and Lebanon attacked. Israel won the war and doubled its territory gaining about one-half of Jerusalem in the process. About 700,000 Palestinian Arabs fled to neighboring states. Many of them ended up in refugee camps under U.N. protection and support. Generations of Arabs grew up in these camps, and they became fertile recruitment ground for radical Arab **terrorist**[2] groups.

Since the U.N. arranged truce in 1949, a number of other wars or terrorist campaigns have marred Middle East peace. There have also been numerous attempts to stabilize the area and preserve the peace.

Israel

ATTEMPTS TO PRESERVE MIDDLE EAST PEACE

1967 - *U.N. Resolution 242* – recognized sovereignty, territorial integrity, and political independence of all states in area; Israel to withdraw from territories gained in Six Day War

1978 - *Camp David Accords* – negotiated by U.S. President Jimmy Carter, President Anwar al-Sadat of Egypt, and Prime Minister Menachem Begin of Israel - called for Israeli withdrawal from Sinai, return of U.N. peacekeepers, restoration of economic and diplomatic relations, and discussions on self-rule for Palestine

1993 - *Declaration of Principles for Palestinian Self-Rule* – Prime Minister Begin and Palestinian leader Yasir Arafat agreed to give Palestinians in Gaza and Jericho self-rule in 1994; extended to include West Bank in 1995 by Arafat and Israeli Prime Minister Yitzhak Rabin

1 mandates (commissions from the League of Nations authorizing a member nation to administer a territory as colonies)
2 terrorism (unlawful use or threatened use of force or violence by a person or an organized group against people or property with the intention of intimidating or coercing societies or governments, often for ideological or political reasons)

March 1970 Camp David Accords signed by (left to right) Egypt's Anwar Sadat, U.S.'s Jimmy Carter, and Israel's Menachem Begin.

In 1964, a coalition of groups pressing for a sovereign Palestinian Arab state forged the **Palestine Liberation Organization** (PLO). Although the PLO renounced terrorism in 1988, groups such as Hezbollah, Hamas, and Islamic Jihad continue to pursue their goals through the use of violence. When **Benjamin Netanyahu** (1946-) became prime minister of Israel in 1996, the peace process has slowed. He opposed the agreements negotiated by his assassinated predecessor Yitzhak Rabin and other Israeli leaders. The 1999 election of **Ehud Barak** as prime minister rekindled hope for the peace process.

Economic development is a key issue in the Middle East. Most of the governments have mixed economies. Problems of population growth, irrigation needs, role of foreign investment, large defense budgets, and modernization continue to limit progress.

Israel has a mixed economy with government and private ownership of business. Much of the development capital has come from the U.S. government and Jews living outside of the country. Important industries include processed foods, electrical machinery, precision instruments, and diamond cutting. During the 1970s and 1980s, high **inflation**[1], provisions for a large number of immigrants, a large defense budget, and an unfavorable balance of trade limited progress. However, through the use of science, technology, land reclamation, and irrigation, Israel is close to being self-sufficient in agriculture. Various forms of organization are evident in the agricultural sector:

- **kibbutz** – farmers share work and profits

- **moshav** – farmers work individually, but the settlement markets products

- **moshava** – individual farmers work as private entrepreneurs

KEY MIDDLE EAST STATES

EGYPT

Egypt's greatest economic challenge is feeding its growing population. After **Gamal Abdel Nasser** (1918-1970) emerged from the coup that overthrew King Farouk in 1952, he moved the country toward a mixed economy. Nasser nationalized the Suez Canal, alienating Britain, France, and the U.S. In 1958, he entered a federation with Syria (United Arab Republic, 1958-1961). Land reform and increased irrigation became important goals, but they did not remove

---

1   inflation (persistent increase in the level of consumer prices or a persistent decline in the purchasing power of money, caused by an increase in available currency and credit beyond the proportion of available goods and services)

the differences between middle class farmers and the fellahin (peasants). However, construction of the Aswan High Dam (completed in 1970 with Soviet funding), did provide for more irrigation, opened additional land for farming, controlled Nile flooding, and increased hydroelectric power. In 1961, Nasser began the nationalization of business and began the use of plans to encourage economic development. He tried to resign after Egypt's defeat in the 1967 Six-Day War, but his popularity kept him in office until his death in 1970.

Nasser

Egypt

Nasser's successor, **Anwar al-Sadat** (1918-1981) broke with the Soviets and encouraged an "open door" regarding foreign investment – especially from the U.S. – and some businesses were privatized. Egypt's economic problems may have motivated Sadat's peace efforts, but he was assassinated before seeing their results.

Mohammed Hosni Mubarak (1928-) replaced Sadat as president. In the early 1990s, Mubarak undertook a program of economic reforms advocated by the International Monetary Fund and the World Bank. He decreased price controls and government subsidies and moved to liberalize trade and investment. Key industries include food processing, textile production, and refined petroleum. Serious problems involving population growth, foreign debts, and terrorism of Islamic fundamentalists continue to hurt economic development.

Egypt contends with a weak economy unable to feed an increasing population. The economic problems create fertile ground for discord. Islamic fundamentalists constantly criticize the modernist govenment's policies. To further destabilize Mubarak's government, the fundamentalists have carried out several attacks on tourists, a major source of income for the government.

Turkey

TURKEY

Turkey's economy continues to have strong government influence. Manufacturing has increased considerably since the 1950s. Key products are textiles, processed food, and petroleum products. However, in the early 1990s, agriculture remained a key component of the economy. About 50 percent of the labor force was involved in farming, and the country was self-sufficient in the production of basic foods. By the mid-1990s, increasing budget problems were evident, and annual inflation reached as high as 150 per cent. This led the government to privatize some of the industries and reduce the price of some goods produced by government-owned industry.

In the period after World War II, countries of the region sought to modernize. To many leaders, this meant Westernization. Many aspects of Western culture were adopted as cultural diffusion occurred. This movement was particularly strong among the young. However, the high expectations of improvement were not met, and many became disillusioned. During the 1970s, there were calls for a return to Islam and the *Shari'a*. Some factions blamed problems on Western ways. In many countries, a struggle ensued between secularism and Westernization on one side and Islam and tradition on the other. **Islamic fundamentalism**[1] appeared in both Shi'ite and Sunni Muslim countries. In some instances, fundamentalists gained control of the government; in others, they used terrorism to bring about change. When fundamentalists gained governmental control, major restrictions were placed on the rights of women, but the movement also tried to ease the problems of the poor.

IRAN

The fundamentalist movement first attracted global attention in Iran. The Shah of Iran, **Mohammed Reza Pahlavi** (1910-1980), wished to modernize his country with the oil wealth and aid from the West. However, he tried to separate religion and the state and did not consult the Muslim clerics (clergymen) about his changes. He also used the Savak (secret police) and army to deal strictly with opposition. When a parliamentary leader, **Muhammad Mossadegh** (1880-1967) led the fight to nationalize the foreign owned petroleum in 1953, he was ousted by the Shah with U.S. help.

REFORM GOALS OF THE SHAH
• Improvement of education, medical care, and the infrastructure
• Increase women's rights
• Implement a land reform program

Opposition to the dictatorial government of the Shah increased. Its focal point was a Shi'ite religious leader Ayatollah **Ruhollah Khomeini** (1900-1989), who lived in exile. In 1979, Shah Pahlavi was forced to flee Iran and his government was overthrown. Khomeini established an Islamic Republic, made religion the dominant force in life for all, repealed Westernized aspects of culture, and revoked women's rights legislation. After the Shah was granted entry to the United States for health reasons, the U.S. embassy was seized and fifty-

three hostages were taken. After a 444 days of captivity and a failed U.S. military rescue attempt, negotiations secured their release.

Iran

Khomeini died in 1989, and new leaders pursued slightly more moderate policies. Attempts were made to improve the economy and relations with some Western nations. The 1997 election of President **Mohammed Khatami** brought some promise of a lessening of tensions in U.S.-Iranian relations. Khatami defeated his conservative opponent by a vote of 3 to 1. His support came from women, the educated, the poor, and the young. It sent a message to the conservative parliament. However, high unemployment and a 24 percent inflation rate presented barriers to progress.

FUNDAMENTALISM IN OTHER MIDDLE EAST NATIONS

Other nations are also coping with Islamic fundamentalist groups. In Algeria, there is an ongoing civil war between the Islamic Salvation Front and the military. The 1991 elections which promised an Islamic party victory were canceled by the army. The civil war began in 1992, and it is estimated that there are approximately 30,000 guerrillas operating in the country.

Each year, the Muslim month of Ramadan brings major violence. On the average, over 600 people have been killed during this month in each year of the war. In 1997-1998, entire villages were wiped out. The government blames the Islamic fundamentalists; they blame the government. Given limited access to the areas involved by foreign observers, it is difficult to determine responsibility.

Khomeini

1 Islamic fundamentalism (adherence to basic principles of Islamic Law and observance in public affairs)

LIBYA

Muammar al Qaddafi (1942-) and his followers seized power from the monarchy in 1969. In 1972, he was given the position of head of state. Government policies are derived from his "Green Book," which proclaims Islamic socialism to be the goal. Petroleum revenue is used to build housing, roads, and educational and communications systems. However, much of the wealth is used for the military and terrorism activities. Libyans are believed responsible for a bombing attack on a West Berlin nightclub used by American servicemen. They are also blamed for the sabotage on Pan Am Flight 102 on which all 259 people were killed over Scotland in 1988. Initially, the Libyan government was unwilling to surrender the two men accused in the Pan Am attack. This led to a U.N. ban on arms sales and airline flights to Libya in 1992. Yielding to international pressure, Libya later agreed to turn over the suspects for trial in a neutral country.

Qaddafi

TURKEY

Terrorism is also used by Islamic fundamentalists in Turkey. In 1996, an Islamic-led coalition government ended the secular rule of Turkey that had lasted 70 years. The government strengthened ties to Iran and Libya and carried out some minor pro-Islamic reforms. In 1997, the **Islamic Welfare Party** gave up control of the government when threatened by a military coup. In early 1998, the highest court in Turkey banned the Party saying that it violated the constitutional separation of religion and state. Terrorist incidents increased and appeared to be related to the fundamentalist movement. Islamic Party leadership vowed to return for future elections.

AFGHANISTAN

The Taliban fighters in Afghanistan combine the ideas of Sunni Muslims with those of Mao Zedong. The movement started in the 1980s in refugee camps in Pakistan where people fled the fighting during the Soviet occupation of Afghanistan. The brutal Soviet-backed communist government established in Kabul in 1978 turned the youth against Marxist-Leninist ideas. They turned instead to the ideas of Mao and stated that their goal was to serve the people. After the U.S.S.R. withdrew its troops in 1989, the various resistance groups began to fight among themselves for control. This enabled the Taliban to seize Kabul in 1996, but fighting continued in other areas of the country.

Afghanistan

The Taliban imposed severe restrictions on women. Initially, they were not allowed to work outside the home, leave home without an escort by a male relative, and forced to wear the *burqa*[2]. Later, the order was altered to allow women doctors and nurses to work but under very restrictive conditions. War widows often found themselves with no means of support. Men were given 45 days to grow a Muslim beard (untrimmed) and to wear traditional clothing. Special religious police enforced these orders.

Economic problems continue throughout the Middle East. Frequently, Islamic fundamentalist groups provide food, housing, health care, and education to the population. The takeover of normal governmental services by these religious groups explains the support they enjoy in many countries of the region.

LEBANON

Tensions in the Middle East between religious groups have also led to wars. In post-World War II Lebanon, the Christians were the majority with Muslims sects (Sunni, Shi'ites, Druze) and others forming minority groups. The government was balanced with a Christian president and a Muslim prime minister. However, during the Arab/Israeli wars, floods of Muslim

---

1 burqa (body covering garment with a mesh opening to see and breath)

refugees entered Lebanon. The Muslims then became a majority. The PLO and other more radical groups were active in the refugee camps. They used them as bases to attack Israel, and this led to Israeli attacks on Lebanon. Militia groups fought each other, and Syria and Israel intervened to protect their differing interests.

The U.N. sent in a peacekeeping force in an attempt to stop the bloodshed. In 1983, a car bomb attack took the lives of 241 U.S. Marine peacekeepers and led to the U.N. withdrawal in 1984. By 1990, the fighting lessened, and in 1992, a truce was signed. Beirut, the capital of Lebanon, began to revive economically. However, both Syria and Israel continue their involvement and outbursts of violence occur.

IRAQ

During the 1980s when there was turmoil in Iran, **Saddam Hussein**, president of Iraq, took the opportunity to seize a disputed, oil-rich border area. Khomeini rallied the Shi'ite minority in Iraq against Saddam and his Sunni majority. However, the Iraqi tanks, planes, and poison gas proved to be too much for Iran and its Shi'ite supporters. About 500,000 people died, and both sides lost important oil facilities. In 1988, the U.N. arranged a truce.

Dangerous conditions in the Persian Gulf during the Iran Revolution and the Iran–Iraq War, led President Reagan to reflag (reregister the ships as U.S. property) oil tankers of Kuwait in 1987. These ships were given U.S. naval protection.

Saddam Hussein

In 1990, Hussein turned his attention to Kuwait, another oil-rich neighbor, with which he claimed a border area. In "Operation Desert Shield," a United Nations-approved, U.S.-led coalition of 28 nations won the 4-day ground **Persian Gulf War** against Iraq. After the War, "no fly zones" were established in parts of Iraq to protect the Shi'ite and Kurd minorities from further brutality at the hands of Hussein. The United Nations also levied economic sanctions against Iraq, but later modified them for humanitarian reasons to allow some oil to be sold to purchase medicine and food.

Problems continued. In 1998, Hussein started another crisis when he denied access to buildings which an international team of inspectors wished to enter to search for forbidden nuclear, biological, and chemical weapons.

After a U.S. military buildup in the area, he allowed the inspectors to enter the areas previously denied. However, suspicions remained that the Iraqi government moved its weapons production facilities in advance of U.N. inspectors' arrivals.

Mini Assessment

MINI-ASSESSMENT

1 The Israeli War for Independence (1948) resulted in
1 Israeli control of vast petroleum reserves
2 a loss of Israeli territory to Arab nations
3 an embargo on U.S. military sales to Israel
4 the establishment of U.N. refugee camps for Palestinian Arabs

2 U.S. President Jimmy Carter, Egyptian President Anwar Sadat, and Israeli Prime Minister Menachem Begin cooperated to
1 reopen the Suez Canal to commercial vessels
2 end nuclear weapons research in the Middle East
3 complete Palestinian self-rule
4 negotiate the Camp David Accords

3 Which do Turkey, Egypt, and Algeria have in common?
1 nuclear weaponry
2 NATO membership
3 Islamic Fundamentalist opposition
4 large petroleum reserves

Constructed Response:

Use the sketch below and your knowledge of global history to answer the following questions.

1 What struggle do the right and left hand sides of the sketch represent?

2 Why is this struggle particularly intense in Islamic areas?

COLLAPSE OF COMMUNISM AND BREAKUP OF THE SOVIET UNION

Cold War tensions between the Soviet Union and the Western powers fluctuated during the period that **Nikita Khrushchev** (1894-1971) was the Soviet leader. His denunciation of Stalin led to considerable divisions in the communist world. His attempts to improve the standard of living by shifting production from heavy industry to consumer goods and agriculture appeared to be an acknowledgment of weaknesses in the command system. Internationally, his policy of "peaceful co-existence" promised to decelerate the arms race. On the other hand, his suppression of the **Hungarian Revolution** of 1956, his demand for construction of the **Berlin Wall**, and the **Cuban Missile Crisis** (1962) heightened tensions. Economic failures and foreign policy problems forced Khrushchev from office in 1964. His monument in the Novodevichy Convent cemetery is half black and half white stone, acknowledging his mixed record.

DÉTENTE: EASING TENSIONS IN THE 1970'S

Khrushchev's successor, **Leonid Brezhnev** (1906-1982), also had a variable record. His attempts to increase production of consumer goods resulted in quality improvement, but insufficient quantity. During the 1980s, production shifted back to an emphasis on heavy industry. He followed a harsh policy against **dissidents** (government critics). Some, like the renowned physicist, Andrei Sakarov, were sentenced to internal exile. Others were imprisoned or sent to mental institutions.

Brezhnev's foreign policy was called **détente**[1] (a period of more cordial relations). In the 1970s, it led to the signing of the **SALT** (Strategic Arms Limitation Treaty) and the **Helsinki Accords** in 1975. However, it was Brezhnev's government that ordered the 1968 invasion of Czechoslovakia. He also announced the **Brezhnev Doctrine**, stating that the Soviets had the right to intervene in any communist country whose actions threatened the international communist movement. In 1979, he unleashed an invasion of Afghanistan. The war

On May Day 1980, Soviet Premier Leonid Brezhnev waves a salute to troops from the Kremlin balcony overlooking Red Square.   Soviet Government Photo

was costly in terms of lives and expenditures, and it aroused much opposition within the U.S.S.R. After Brezhnev's death in 1982, his elderly successors – Konstantin Chernenko and Yuri Andropov – had little effect on domestic or foreign policies because they each died shortly after taking office.

SOVIET SETBACK IN AFGHANISTAN

Brezhnev's decision to invade Afghanistan came after a group of leftist military officers overthrew the Afghan government in 1978. They attempted to carry out a land reform program, fight illiteracy, and increase women's rights. Islamic leaders and conservatives opposed these actions and led a revolt against the government. The Soviets feared a spread of the revolution to the large Muslim populations of their Central Asia republics.

The "Bird of Peace" found détente to be a precarious nesting place, at best.

---

1 détente (a period of more cordial relations)

The Soviets began to aid the communist government against the **Mujahadin** rebels. Initially, the rebels received aid from the U.S. and some Muslim nations. The aid was filtered through Pakistan where the Mujahadin had bases. The Soviets used conventional military forces against the guerrilla tactics of the rebels with little success. In many ways, the Afghan invasion for the Soviets was similar to the U.S. experience in Vietnam. The war was unpopular in the Soviet Union. After protests, the government negotiated a truce in 1988, and Soviet troops began withdrawing in 1989. It is estimated that combat deaths totaled 700,000. Civil war continued after the Soviet withdrawal as various Mujahadin groups competed for power.

GORBACHEV'S REFORMS

While Soviet leader **Mikhail Gorbachev's** (1931-) decision to withdraw from Afghanistan was popular at home, some of his other changes led to dissension. His policy of *glasnost* (openness) resulted in an increase in freedom to criticize the government. The government moved in a more democratic direction – some dissidents were allowed to leave the country, more Jews were allowed to emigrate to Israel, and some political prisoners were freed.

Politically, reforms increased the power of the national legislature, the Congress of the People's Deputies, and the power of the president. Rival groups were allowed to form opposition political parties. Many in the Soviet Union interpreted these changes as a sign of weakness. *Perestroika* – Gorbachev's policy of economic

GORBACHEV'S ECONOMIC REFORMS

- power of central planners was decreased
- private enterprise for small businesses was encouraged
- quality and quantity of consumer goods was increased
- agricultural land devoted to free market production was increased

reform – sought movement toward a free market while keeping the basic elements of communism.

Gorbachev had his greatest impact in the area of foreign policy. He repealed the Brezhnev Doctrine, indicating that the Soviets would not intervene in the internal affairs of Eastern Europe satellites. This signaled the development of **pro-democracy movements**. Communist regimes were overturned and, in many cases, replaced by freely elected non-communist governments.

The Warsaw Pact disintegrated in 1991. Gorbachev also signed agreements to decrease missiles and Soviet troops stationed outside national boundaries. For his efforts, he was awarded the Nobel Peace Prize in 1990.

1 glasnost (official policy of the Soviet government emphasizing candor with regard to discussion of social problems and shortcomings)
2 perestroika (organizational restructuring of the Soviet economy and bureaucracy that was begun in the mid 1980's)

Gorbachev

The world supported Gorbachev's reforms and gave him the 1990 Nobel Peace Prize.

At home in Russia, reforms brought frustration to Gorbachev and social pain to the Russians. His popularity and power diminished, and he resigned.

Gorbachev was very popular abroad, but not at home. His policies caused economic dislocation and confusion. Gorbachev agreed to the Treaty of Union which gave considerable power to the republics. Fearing the disintegration of the nation, conservative politboro members captured Gorbachev and launched an unsuccessful coup in mid-1991. Russian Federation President **Boris Yeltsin** (1931-) rallied resistance to the plotters, and the Red Army refused to fire on his supporters. After the coup, the republics declared independence. The U.S.S.R. declared an to end its existence in 1991, and Gorbachev resigned as President.

Boris Yeltsin

shared power with Yeltsin. Today, the Communist Party remains strong in Russia and the former Soviet republics. It controls the lower house of the **Duma** (Russian Parliament) and a number of local governments. Party members or former members often remain at the top of the newly independent republics. A loose union of some of the former Soviet republics, called the **Commonwealth of Independent States** was formed in 1991. However, strong nationalism and fear of Russian domination limit the amount of cooperation among the former Soviet republics.

RUSSIA IN TRANSITION

Boris Yeltsin was Gorbachev's protégé and became the first popularly-elected President of Russia. He resigned from the Communist Party in 1987 because of its resistance to reform and was then elected President of the Russian Federation on a reform platform. After the coup attempt, Gorbachev also resigned from the Party and briefly

Economic problems threaten to overwhelm Yeltsin's government. Reforms to establish a free market economy started in 1991. Privatization of industry faced the opposition of industry managers and conservatives. By 1995 however, 14,000 state and municipally-owned factories were privatized. The speed of the priva-

EASTERN EUROPE, RUSSIA, AND CENTRAL ASIA
CONTEMPORARY NATIONS
1990s

Private enterprise, as observed at the Farmers' Market in Khabarousk, gives evidence of the economic reforms of perestroika.   © Sue Ann Kime, 1993

The Gross Domestic Product reflected the chaos of the early 1990s. In 1994, the GDP was about half of what it was in 1991. Between 1990 and 1993, agricultural output decreased by an average 5 percent per year. Industrial production decreased by 16 percent in 1993 alone. Inflation reached as high as 2600 percent annually in the early years of reform. **Pensioners**[1] and others on fixed incomes experienced serious difficulty. Many people, including government workers, found themselves working for no pay. However, by the mid-1990s, signs indicated that the economic decline had slowed. The Central Bank became more cautious in its loans to former state enterprises, and production of consumer goods increased. Russians sent less capital to foreign banks and the young, professional class was prospering.

tization movement varied. Unfortunately, in many instances, small groups called "the oligarchs" obtained control of many factories. They became influential in the energy, mineral, and media industries. This concentration of wealth in a few hands aroused resentment among the general population.

Urban dwellers were allowed to own their apartments. The limited housing in major cities provided a ready market for those willing to sell. Agricultural land remained in the hands of former collective and state farms. The process of auctioning off agricultural land to private owners began in early 1998.

Corruption and crime became serious in Russia. The people sensed the free market reforms were not improving their quality of life. Many yearned for the return of communism and the "safety net" of welfare programs and benefits. This was particularly true of the older generation. Boris Yeltsin's health was also a concern. His heart problems and withdrawals from public view posed questions about the future. His frequent cabinet changes led to concerns about policy continuity.

Some of the former republics of the U.S.S.R. experienced ethnic violence. The Abkhazia and South Ossetia areas of **Georgia** revolted. The government of **Eduard Shevardnadze**, former Soviet foreign minister, was unable to halt the violence. In 1994, a cease-fire was negotiated. In early 1998, there was no active fighting, but a final solution was elusive.

Armenia and **Azerbaijan** resorted to war over Nagarno-Karabakh, an Armenian-inhabited area located within Azerbaijan. Having experienced the Turkish Massacres of 1915, Armenians were determined to protect their fel-

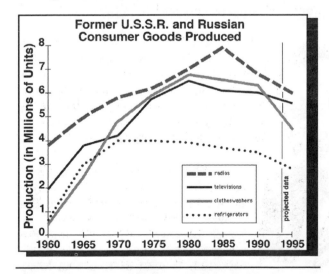

Former U.S.S.R. and Russian Consumer Goods Produced

Production (in Millions of Units)

- ▬ ▬ radios
- ——— televisions
- ▨▨▨ clotheswashers
- • • • • refrigerators

projected data

1   pensioners (those who live on fixed state retirement allowances)

Glasnost, "a new openness," was like opening a window, bringing in a era of "freshness."

1995 brought former communist **Alexander Kwasiniewski** to power largely because of the economic problems caused by the change to a free market economy. However, the communist government simply slowed the pace of reform, rather than reversing it.

One of the most dramatic pro-democracy incidents involved the dismantling of the Berlin Wall in 1990. Originally constructed in 1961 to prevent the flow of educated East Germans to the West, the Wall was a symbol of the division between the democratic, free market of the West and the totalitarian, command systems of the East.

After the opening of the East German border, about 2,000 people per day moved to West Germany. The immigrants created housing and employment problems in West Germany. After reunification was official in 1990, Germany moved to improve conditions in the eastern half. About $70 billion was spent to help the economy, but despite the aid, a period of hardship occurred during the transition to the free market economy. About 50 percent of the population of the east was unemployed and 75 percent of the businesses failed by the end of 1991. Germany also helped to pay for the withdrawal of Soviet troops from the east and provided new housing for them on their return home. By the late 1990s, conditions were slowly improving in the former East Germany. However, the costs created problems for the economy of the former West Germany, and many West Germans resented the higher tax burden created by the need to help.

low nationals in Azerbaijan. Armenia appears to have won with Russian aid; however, its deteriorating economic and political situation lead to questions of continuing control. Azerbaijan, with its considerable oil wealth, may be able to regain control in the long run. A 1994 cease fire was enforced by Russian peacekeepers, but incidents of violence still occur.

SOVIET SATELLITES BREAK FREE

In the late 1980s, a pro-democracy movement swept through the Soviet Eastern European satellites triggered by Gorbachev's policies of *glasnost* and nonintervention. People in many of these countries moved to free themselves of communist control. Poland made a successful transition to democracy under the leadership of the **Solidarity** union and **Lech Walesa** (1943-).

Solidarity won 99 of 100 seats in the Senate in 1989 elections, and Walesa was elected President in 1991. Democratic elections in

Lech Walesa

Ethnic conflicts also broke out in the former satellites and republics of the U.S.S.R. Authoritarian communist governments stifled the nationalism of various ethnic minorities, but with increased political freedom, many of these groups demanded independence.

In Czechoslovakia, the 1948 constitution recognized two major ethnic groups, the Czechs and the Slovaks. However, the western or Czech part was industrial, and the eastern or Slovak part was agricultural. It was difficult to have

economic policies that benefitted both equally. In 1992, the **"Velvet Revolution"** occurred. Czechoslovakia divided peacefully into the Czech Republic and the Slovak Republic. The Czech Republic made considerable economic and political progress under the leadership of President **Vaclav Havel** (1936-), but the agrarian Slovak Republic maintained a slower pace of development.

In Yugoslavia, change was violent. This Balkan federation ruled an area torn by ethnic strife for centuries. After World War II the forceful presence of independent communist leader, Marshal Tito held it together. After his death in 1980, the country experimented with collective leadership. Top positions rotated among the major ethnic groups: Serbs (Orthodox religion), Croats (Roman Catholics), and Muslims. In May, 1991, the Serbs blocked the Croat candidate from assuming the presidency, and a civil war erupted.

The parliaments of Croatia and Slovenia declared independence, followed by Bosnia and Herzegovina. In 1992, Serbia and Montenegro united as a new Yugoslavia. The Civil War was marked by **"ethnic cleansing[1]"**. The atrocities horrified the world. Between 1992 and 1995, U.N. and European Union diplomats' attempts to end the violence met with little success. In 1995, a truce was negotiated which called for NATO troops to act as peacekeepers until stability could be restored. The 1996 elections provided no solution to the problem, and the peacekeeping troops remained. Attempts by the United Nations' International War Crimes Tribunal to bring those accused of committing atrocities met with limited success.

CONTEMPORARY BALKAN STATES
Violent Ethnic Disintegration

---

1 ethnic cleansing (attempt to eliminate a racial, religious, tribal or cultural group)

Mini Assessment

1 Khrushchev and Brezhnev both tried to decrease economic dissatisfaction in the Soviet Union by
1 increasing the production of consumer goods
2 abandoning collective farms for private ownership of land
3 stopping economic aid to the satellites and Cuba
4 ending the role of central planners in setting quotas

2 The destructive force of nationalism can best be seen in the
1 "Velvet Revolution" in Czechoslovakia
2 breakup of Yugoslavia
3 union of East and West Germany
4 establishment of the Commonwealth of Independent States

3 Long term results of the reforms of Mikhail Gorbachev led to
1 an improvement in his popularity at home, but a decline in foreign respect
2 more privatization of agriculture, but increased nationalization of industry
3 more Russian control of the satellites, but a smaller military force in Eastern Europe
4 increase in democracy, but many serious economic problems

Constructed Response:

Base your answer to the following questions on the cartoon below and your knowledge of global history.

1 What does the sinking ship symbolize?

2 How did the sinking of the ship change global politics?

New problems developed in 1998. The Kosovo area, with a 90 percent Albanian population, exploded into violence against its Serb government. The Kosovo Liberation Army resorted to attacks on the Serb military which retaliated with massacres of ethnic Albanian villagers. The international community feared a spread of violence into other areas of the Balkans. U.N. peacekeepers were on alert and hoped to preserve the peace.

POLITICAL UNREST IN LATIN AMERICA
PHYSICAL SETTING

Latin America experienced considerable unrest in the post-World War II period. It is composed of 33 independent nations and 3 colonies. Generally, geographers divide it into South America, Central America, Mexico, and the Caribbean. Geographic features such as the

Andes Mountains and the coastal Sierras in Central America, along with the great Amazon, Rio de la Plata, and Orinoco River systems make regional unity difficult. Resources such as the petroleum and natural gas of Mexico,

Venezuela, and Ecuador along with minerals such as iron, tin, copper, and silver provide natural wealth. However, many make their living agriculturally. Products such as coffee, bananas, sugar cane, and livestock account for much of the national income.

Despite the importance of farming, many countries of the region import food. Technology is good for export crops, but many of the subsistence farmers still use traditional methods. Frequently, land is in the hands of an elite few, and large, multinational corporations often gain most of the profit. Attempted land reforms fail when insufficient funds and training are made available to the **campesinos** (peasants) who become new landowners.

The major Latin American population groups are the Indians, Europeans, and Africans. However, intermarriage among the groups diminishes differences. **Mestizos** (Indian-European mix) make up about one-third of the population. In many areas, racial discrimination is less important than economic differences.

Mezquital District Slum (barrios) – Guatemala City, Guatemala.
© David Johnson, July 1993

The gaps between rich and poor are most evident in urban areas. The wealthy live in large homes or expensive apartments while the poor live in **barrios** (shanty towns). The barrios often lack the basics – electricity, inside plumbing, and sewage disposal. The widespread movement from rural to urban areas increases the problems. It is estimated that 70 per cent of the population is urban and over 20 cities have populations in excess of 1 million. The migration to urban areas is fueled by the hope of jobs, better education for children, and a higher standard of living. Similar hopes lead many to leave Central America for Mexico and Mexico for the United States.

MIGRATION PATTERNS	
From:	**To:**
Mexico & Central America	United States
Central America	Mexico
Colombia	Venezuela
Paraguay	Bolivia, Brazil, Argentina
Caribbean	U.S. and Great Britain

The middle class and the city workers increase in numbers. Both groups are more sympathetic to the urban poor than the wealthy landowners and the military. As a consequence, a shift in the political balance of power is occurring in some areas.

CHANGE IN ARGENTINA

During the early 20th century, Argentina made good economic progress. Its development was aided by relative political stability and beef and wheat exports. However, a wealthy elite was in control of the country. The Great Depression of the 1930s ended the period of relative prosperity and led to a military coup.

In 1946, Colonel **Juan D. Peron** (1895-1974) was elected President. He instituted 5-Year Plans with a goal of making the country self-sufficient industrially. He won the support of poor workers (**descamisados**, "shirtless ones"), and nationalists.

PERON'S ECONOMIC PROGRAM
• nationalization of many industries
• improved wages and benefits for workers
• financing of public works programs
• restrictions on foreign influence in the economy

Peron's wife, **Eva Duarte Peron** (1919-1952), was a valuable political asset. "Evita's" origins were humble, yet she rose to enjoy an extravagant lifestyle. Her beautiful clothes and jewels seemed to say to the poor, "you can do it too." She also helped women to gain the right to vote and sponsored various education and welfare programs. Her death in 1952 deprived Peron of a shrewd political partner.

In 1955, Peron was overthrown by a military coup. The authoritarian nature of his government, the high national debt, inflation problems, and challenges to the Roman Catholic Church increased opposition. Military and civilian governments alternated in power until Peron was restored in 1973. He was then elected President with his third wife, Isabel, as Vice President. He died the next year, and his wife briefly succeeded him until she was deposed by a military coup in 1976.

The military regime faced an ongoing battle with **leftist**[1] guerrillas. In an attempt to control the situation, the military embarked on the "Dirty War." The military kidnapped, arrested, tortured, and murdered opponents or imagined opponents. The victims – the *desaparecidos* ("disappeared ones") – may number 20-30,000, in addition to an estimated 2300 other political murders and 10,000 political arrests.

A group of Argentine mothers whose children disappeared organized the **Mothers of Plaza De Maya**. This group met every Thursday in the Plaza De Maya to demand information about the children's fate. Many victims were thrown from planes or helicopters into the Atlantic Ocean. Eventually, the military admitted responsibility for the murders. Despite strong criticism, in 1989, President Menem pardoned the 277 military and civilians thought to be involved.

Carlos Saul Menem (1930-) was elected President in 1989 after the Argentine loss to Britain in the Falklands / Malvinas Islands War and the development of a severe economic crisis. By the 1990s, the economy was growing with increasing privatization. However, the gulf between the rich and poor remained. Mexican economic problems and the 1997 problems in Asia adversely affected the Argentine economic progress. By 1997, unemployment reached 20 percent and protests occurred in major cities.

1 leftist (people who advocate liberal, often socially radical, measures to change government to achieve equality and freedom sometimes at the expense of order)

FALTERING COMMUNISM IN CUBA

Cuba also faced serious economic problems in the 1990s. The causes can be found in its earlier history. As a result of the United States defeating Spain in the Spanish American War (1898), Cuba received independence in 1902. However, the **Platt Amendment** to Cuba's constitution gave the U.S. the right to intervene in Cuban affairs, if necessary, and rights to maintain a naval base in Guantanamo Bay.

After independence, Cuba fell under the control of a series of dictators who accomplished little. However in 1953, **Fulgencio Batista** (1901-1973) seized power. The Batista regime had close ties to U.S. investors who dominated the sugar cane and tobacco industries. U.S. government influence was also strong. However, little was done to bridge the gap between the rich and the poor, and disenchantment with the Batista government increased.

Fidel Castro

In 1956, **Fidel Castro** (1926-) started a leftist revolution and promised to improve conditions for the poor. By 1959, Batista fled and Castro established the first communist state in the Western Hemisphere. After announcing the Marxist-Leninist state, Castro embarked on a reform program.

Many Cubans refused to live under a communist regime and fled the country. Many came to the U.S. and formed large Cuban communities in major cities. Some of these people became

---

CASTRO'S REFORMS

- nationalization of foreign-owned businesses and plantations
- agrarian reform
- education improvement
- equality for women
- improved medical care

---

involved in plans to overthrow the Castro government. The **Bay of Pigs Invasion** in 1961 was one result. The U.S. covertly aided the plotters, but the plan was betrayed. Cuba's military easily defeated the landing parties. This victory against the "Colossus of the North" increased Castro's popularity at home.

U.S. concerns about its communist neighbor were heightened when it discovered that the Soviet Union was placing missiles with nuclear capability in Cuba. The **Cuban Missile Crisis** (1962) was resolved when President Kennedy ordered a naval blockade of Cuba to force their removal. Soviet Premier Khrushchev agreed to remove the missiles in exchange for Kennedy's promise that the U.S. would not invade Cuba.

Cuba was economically isolated by a U.S. trade **embargo**[1] adhered to by most other nations of the Western Hemisphere. Yet, Castro received considerable trade benefits and aid from the Soviet Union and its Eastern European satellites. This aid enabled him to carry out domestic reforms and spread the communist revolution abroad. Cuban troops were sent to Angola, and aid was given to leftist guerrillas in El Salvador and Nicaragua.

Beginning in the 1980s, Soviet aid decreased, and Castro ceased his assistance to others. As the Cuban economy deteriorated, Castro began to allow some aspects of the free market and encouraged foreign investment. By 1994, Cuba was experiencing an economic crisis. Boatloads of refugees tried to escape to the U.S., often dying before reaching their destination. The Cuban government agreed to curtail the exodus after the U.S. promised to accept 20,000 immigrants annually. In 1996, the U.S. tightened an existing embargo against Cuba after two private

---

1 embargo (government order prohibiting the movement of merchant ships into or out of its ports)

planes piloted by Cuban refugees were shot down by the Cuban Air Force over international waters. However, in 1998 after Pope John Paul II denounced the embargo, President Clinton announced plans to ease restrictions for humanitarian reasons.

INSTABILITY IN CENTRAL AMERICA

Between 1936 and 1979, the Somoza family controlled Nicaragua. Conditions were similar to those found in Cuba. The family was anti-communist and had the support of the military, large landowners, and the United States. However, by the 1970s, the leftist **Sandinista** movement began to use guerrilla tactics to harass the Somoza government.

In 1979, **Anastasio Somoza** (1925-1980) was overthrown by the Sandin-istas. In 1984, the Sandinista candidate, **Daniel Ortega** (1945-) was elected President. The Sandinistas also won the Vice Presidency and control of the National Assembly and began a land reform program.

The new government received assistance from Cuba and the Soviet Union. However, the United States extended aid to the Contras, the opponents of the Sandinistas. This resulted in a civil war and economic disaster.

Several Central American countries were able to work out a compromise between the Sandinistas and the Contras and new elections were held in 1990. **Violeta Charmorro** (1929-), a moderate, unseated Ortega and the Sandinistas. The 1996 elections were also won by a moderate, **Arnold Aleman**, but the Sandinistas continue to be an important political force.

Mini Assessment

1 Argentinian President Juan Peron won support from many of the people because he
 1 decreased the influence of the military
 2 kept inflation and national debt under control
 3 helped the poorest groups in the population
 4 had the support of the Roman Catholic Church

2 Initially, the Cuban regime of Fidel Castro was able to
 1 promote democratic reform
 2 modernize without foreign assistance
 3 win support from the Roman Catholic Church
 4 bring about social and economic progress

3 Leftists and communists have been able to win support in Central America because they
 1 have backing of religious interests
 2 promise land reform for the poor
 3 receive aid from multinational corporations
 4 oppose the interests of Native Americans

Constructed Response:

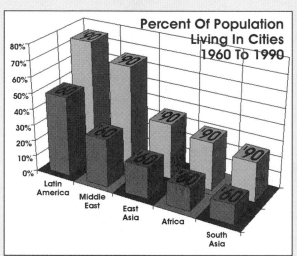

Percent Of Population Living In Cities 1960 To 1990

Base your answer to the following questions on the graph above and your knowledge of global history.

1 Which area had the largest per cent of its population in urban areas in 1990?

2 Identify at least two possible solutions to the problem of increasing urbanization in LDCs.

Guatemala also experienced instability. With U.S. assistance, Col. Carlos Castillo Armas overthrew a left-leaning government with strong ties to the Guatemalan Communist Party in 1954. The military and landowners assumed control. Leftist guerrilla groups formed to harass the government. This led to government use of the military and **rightist**[1] death squads to deal with opposition.

The group most affected were the **native Indians**. It is estimated that 30,000 of them were killed. By the mid-1980s, civilian government was restored, but the military held much of the power. The 1990s saw a decrease in fighting, and by 1994, the revolutionaries and the government agreed to end the 30-year civil war. Later, they agreed to change the constitution to protect Indian rights. The 1996 elections brought **Alvaro Arzu Irigoyen** to power. He moved quickly to rid the military of its most corrupt members and announced privatization plans.

The continuing differences between the rich and the poor in Latin America are likely to lead to additional outbreaks of violence. Going back to colonial days, the large landowners, the military, and often the leaders of the Roman Catholic Church – "the iron triangle" – have come from the same families. The three groups have supported each other and often refused to take steps to alleviate conditions for the poorest groups in the population. The growth of the middle class and the urban workers may lead to the changes that the "iron triangle" of the old elite resisted.

POST-COLD WAR "HOT SPOTS"

As previously mentioned, "hot spots" flared all over the globe since the end of World War II. In many cases, violence and civil war have led to international intervention by the U.N. or concerned countries. In many instances, the treatment of ethnic minorities by the majority was the root cause of the problem. Friction among such groups went back centuries and was manipulated by foreign powers or authoritarian governments in order to maintain control.

In stark contrast in the quality of life, the barrio falls in the shadow of the modern middle-class apartments in Caracas, Venezuela.   © David Johnson, July 1993

The problem among Serbs, Croats, and Muslims in the former Yugoslavia fit such a pattern. Developments in Kosovo province threatened a further expansion of ethnic violence in the Balkans. Middle East volatility arises from conflicting claims by the Jews and the Palestinians. Sikhs and Tamils have long felt discrimination in South Asia and respond with violence and terrorism. In Northern Ireland, Russia, Mexico, Rwanda, and Congo violence erupts over ethnic and religious differences. Many countries have serious economic problems which limit their ability to successfully cope with ethnic difficulties.

NORTHERN IRELAND

The history of the "Troubles" in Northern Ireland goes back centuries – to the early 1600s. At that time, England gave land in Ireland to the Protestant Scots and English in hopes that they would help to secure the area. They forced Irish Catholics off the land to become tenant

1 rightist (people or groups that advocate conservative or reactionary measurers in government or politics)

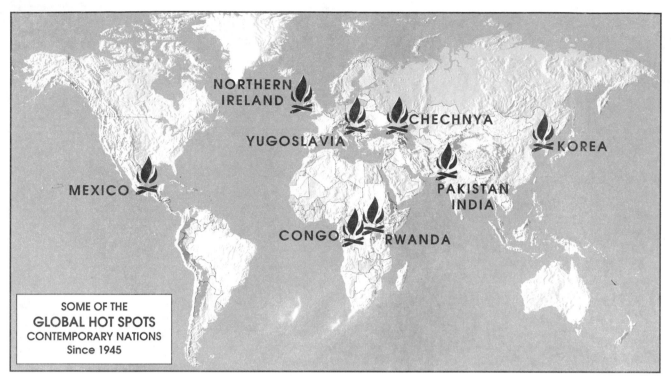

SOME OF THE
GLOBAL HOT SPOTS
CONTEMPORARY NATIONS
Since 1945

farmers. By the 19th and 20th centuries, the Irish Catholics were demanding independence and the Irish Protestants wished to remain with the United Kingdom to ensure their continued dominance. In 1921, Britain established the Irish Free State in the Catholic South while Ulster, the Protestant North, remained part of the U.K.

Northern Ireland

In Northern Ireland, approximately 50 percent of the population is Protestant, 38.4 percent is Catholic, and 11 percent claims no religious affiliation. However, higher Catholic birth rates made Protestants fearful of losing their majority. The Catholics felt that the Protestant-dominated government was responsible for their poor standard of living. Housing, job, and education opportunities were limited for the Catholics.

In 1968, Catholic civil rights demonstrators resorted to violence. In 1969, Britain sent in troops to stop the violence of the **Irish Republican Army** (**IRA**) and the **Protestant Defense League** (**PDL**). Despite numerous cease-fires and promises to end the conflict, the violence persisted.

In June 1996, a new round of peace talks started under the leadership of former U.S. Senator George Mitchell. The British and Republic of Ireland governments want Protestants and Catholics to rule Northern Ireland jointly and to establish a joint cross-border council with the Republic of Ireland. Negotiators promised a bill of rights, justice and equality for all, and police reforms in the North. Outbursts of violence continued during the talks.

However in May 1998, an agreement for proposed union of the two parts of Ireland was approved by a referendum on both sides of the border. Voters in the Republic of Ireland approved by over 90%; voters in Northern Ireland approved by over 70%. The vote in Northern Ireland indicated that a significant number of Protestants voted in favor of the agreement, and this reinforced hopes for a peaceful end to "The Troubles." However, in mid-1999, the proposed union appeared in jeopardy due to protests from moderates about the admission of the radical **Sinn Fein** arm of the IRA into the political-elective process.

CHECHNYA

After the breakup of the Soviet Union, the Russian Federation consisted of 21 autonomous republics and regions. These areas were inhabited by many different ethnic groups. In Chechnya, a province in the Caucusus Mountains, the largely Muslim population resented control by the Great Russians. Chechnya declared its independence in 1991, but Russia refused to recognize its new status. In 1994, Russian military forces were sent to restore control. Twenty months of bitter fighting followed. In 1996, with the increasing unpopularity of the action in Russia, a peace agreement was signed. Russian troops began their withdrawal. However, clashes between Chechen and Russian forces still occur in southern Russia.

With the large number of minorities within Russia and the long history of domination by the Great Russians, the possibility of more Chechen-type actions is strong. The continuation of economic problems in Russia, the high unemployment, the lack of capital for improvements, and the general disintegration of the economy and social welfare safety net may lead other minorities to conclude that their best hope for a more prosperous future may involve independence.

MEXICO

Mexico also has a problem with its largest (29 percent) ethnic minority, the Native Americans. The southern most state of Chiapas has been the site of a peasant revolt against the central government. The Zapatista National Liberation Army began the revolt in 1994. They demanded improved living conditions and greater rights of autonomy for poor Indian communities. Clashes between the Zapatistas and paramilitary groups linked to the government have cost many lives.

Mexico

In 1998, President Zedillo's government proposed to change the constitution to recognize the existence of Native Americans and allow them to appoint some of their village leaders. In a country which often ignored Native American rights, this represented a step forward. However, it did not go far enough for the Zapatistas, and the government refused to grant total autonomy, saying it would hurt national unity. Outbreaks of violence continue.

Again, economic conditions played a role in the crisis. The wealthy landowners view the peasant revolt as a threat to their status. With their influence in the military and the government, the landowners continue to oppose major change. The economic crisis in Mexico which began in 1994 limits the ability of the government to aid the Native Americans without slighting others in the population who also need assistance.

RWANDA

Rwanda, a small country in east-central Africa, has seen some of the worse ethnic violence of modern history. Prior to the colonial period, Rwanda was governed by a Tutsi king and an elite who controlled the Hutu farmer majority.

Rwanda

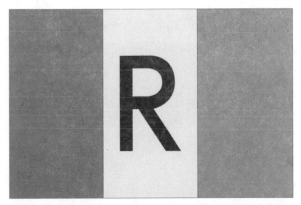

The Tutsis remained in power under German and Belgian control. After the death of the moderate Tutsi king in 1959, Hutu violence increased. Finally in 1961, the Hutus seized control and declared independence. Many Tutsis fled and ethnic violence increased.

In 1990, Tutsi troops invaded Rwanda from bases outside the country. They waged a guerrilla war against the government and occupied parts of north Rwanda. Hutus labeled all Tutsis traitors and killed upwards of 50,000. The shooting down of a plane carrying the President of Rwanda in 1994 led to a massacre of Tutsis and moderate Hutus. The resulting civil war led to Tutsi control of the country, genocide of one million people, and the flight of one and a half to two million Hutu to Zaire and Tanzania – the greatest mass flight of refugees in recent history. In 1996, the Hutu refugees were forced out of Zaire and their return to Rwanda led to thousands more deaths in rebel attacks and army reprisals. U.N. attempts to end the violence have not been completely successful.

CONGO

Congo, the largest nation in central Africa, received its independence from Belgium in 1960 only to face a period of violence and civil war. In 1965 an army general, Joseph Mobutu, established a dictatorship that lasted until 1997. Changing his name to **Mobutu Sese Seko**, the President changed the name of the country to **Zaire** in 1971. The problems of the early independence period combined with Mobutu's decision to nationalize the vast mineral resources led to an economic crisis in the early 1970s. To distract attention from the economy, Mobutu used ethnic violence to divide his opposition. Promises to hold elections were broken and inflation skyrocketed out of control in 1994.

Democratic Republic Of Congo

In 1996, Rwandan Hutus in Zaire refugee camps attacked Tutsis. The Zairian Tutsis and the Rwandan Army defeated the Zairian Army and took over parts of eastern Zaire, driving the Hutus out. While Mobutu was in Europe for cancer treatment, the combined Zairian Tutsi / Rwandan Army seized control of more of Zaire. In 1997, **Laurent Kabila**, the leader of the seven-month rebellion, ousted Mobutu and established himself as the new president and changed the country's name to **Democratic Republic of Congo**. In 1998, he restricted opposition groups and demanded the withdrawal of U.N. investigators examining Tutsi graves for evidence of genocide. Later, army groups originally supporting Kabila, joined with Rwandan army elements trying to drive Kabila from power.

KOREA

North Korea is a "hot spot" for different reasons. The country is one of the few remaining Marxist-Leninist countries in the world. In the 1990s, South Korea, Japan, the U.S., and other nations became very concerned about the development of nuclear capability and a missile delivery system under the leadership of President **Kim Il Sung**. Initially, the government denied entrance to U.N. inspectors. However, former U.S. President Jimmy Carter negotiated a freeze on nuclear weapons development in 1994.

North Korea

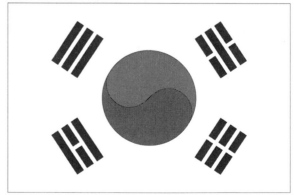

South Korea

In 1994, **Kim Jong Il** succeeded his father as president. He immediately faced an economic crisis. After the Korean War (1950-1953), North Korea tried to establish "self-reliance." Although the country has a good resource base, the war, the nationalization of industry, and the collectivization of agriculture led to economic problems.

Mini Assessment

1 Problems in Chechnya, Georgia, Azerbaijan, and Armenia are primarily caused by
   1 privatization of industry and agriculture
   2 nationalism and ethnic strife
   3 price inflation from the 1973 oil crisis
   4 loss of the Soviet nuclear umbrella

2 The crisis in the Mexican state of Chiapas can be viewed as part of the long term Latin American problem of
   1 a lack of mineral resources and the wealth they provide
   2 geographic factors which hinder development of unity
   3 wealthy, upper class opposition to reform benefitting the poor
   4 division between Native Americans and the Roman Catholic Church

3 In the late 1990s, conditions in North Korea might best be described as
   1 demonstrating the positive results of a command economy
   2 at near starvation levels caused by floods and drought
   3 meeting the people's need for consumer products
   4 positive with little need to enter negotiations with South Korea

Constructed Response:

"In Derry, Northern Ireland in 1966, the heads of all City Council departments were Protestant. Of 177 salaried employees, 145 - earning £124,424 - were Protestant, and only thirty-two - earning £20, 420 - were Catholic."

"There are several ways in which Protestant Councils have discriminated against Catholics. One has been to put Protestants in better houses than Catholics, but charge the same rent. ... Another way has simply been to house more Protestants than Catholics."
– *Sunday Times*, Insight Team, Ulster

1 What do the quotations indicate about some of the causes of "The Troubles" in Northern Ireland?

2 Why are economic and social issues often to blame for "Hot Spots" in global affairs?

To distract the people, Kim sent troops into the demilitarized zone between the two Koreas. He also dispatched a submarine into South Korean waters for a commando raid. Both attempts were checked.

By early 1998, famine threatened the North. Floods and drought conditions limited agricultural production; food stocks were almost gone. The Food and Agriculture Organization of the U.N. urged countries to participate in an international relief program. However, some were suspicious that the food might be diverted to the military rather than aiding the civilian population. Faced with impending crisis and under international pressure, the North Koreans re-entered peace talks with the South. With U.S.

and Chinese diplomats in attendance, the goal was a peace treaty to replace the 45-year-old armistice which ended the Korean War.

SOUTH ASIA NUCLEAR DUEL

In the spring of 1998, both India and Pakistan jolted the world by exploding nuclear devices. This confirmed the long-standing suspicion of their nuclear capability. The Indian explosions occurred first, and despite pleas from the leaders of the major nations and the U.N, Pakistan quickly followed with its own. Within a week, both nations proclaimed a moratorium on testing and announced plans to reactivate peaceful negotiations concerning their problems.

This development was considered a real threat to world peace since both countries have also tested medium range missiles, although it was not clear whether they can carry

India

nuclear warheads. The countries share a common border. In addition, there are years of Hindu-Muslim hatreds that have resulted in three wars since 1947. The state of Kashmir has been a constant source of dispute between the two nations, and increased tensions were immediately apparent in the region. A 1992 study by the U.S. Air Force predicted the possibility of 100 million dead in a full-scale nuclear war between the two nations. The explosions ended the fragile global hope for nuclear non-proliferation.

Pakistan

TIME CAPSULE

In the generations since the end of World War II, political and social change swept the globe. Desires of ethnic groups for equality, justice, and in some cases, autonomy lead to many crises in international affairs. Few of these problems are easily resolved, and some threaten regional peace. Historically, small splinter countries often have difficulty surviving after independence. Large, powerful countries seek to expand their areas of control, and the smaller countries fall victim to dominance. The Russian Empire in the 19th century and the German Empire in the 19th and 20th centuries are examples of this type of expansion.

The period since 1945 witnessed the emergence of two superpowers, the U.S. and the U.S.S.R. Their competition for power, influence, and economic, technological, scientific, cultural, and athletic success did much to shape the postwar world. However, the late 1980s saw the beginning of the decline of the communist system, and countries increasingly turned to the free market approach. It has also seen the rise of Asian countries as economic powerhouses. Despite the economic downturn which began in 1997, most economists expect not only recovery, but further advances in Asia.

This time period also noted a change in imperialism – from political to economic. Country after country acquired independence either because it was granted by the colonial power or because violence and war forced the relinquishment of foreign control. Many of the new countries struggled to establish stable governments and often resulted in authoritarian regimes. The desire to modernize quickly and improve the standard of living for their people led many of the new governments to adopt mixed economies with considerable government control. However, large government bureaucracies staffed by poorly prepared officials led to corruption. Economic crises became common as governments struggled to diversify and reduce their reliance on a single crop or mineral resource.

Recently, ethnic violence has shaken global peace. Countries as far apart as Rwanda, Northern Ireland, India, Mexico, and Russia faced the demands of minority groups. Thousands have been killed in these struggles and more are likely to die before they end. Concern over human rights violations and threats to peace have frequently led to international intervention to curb the crises.

As the 21st century dawned, signs of optimism appeared. Long-standing problems in the Koreas and Northern Ireland showed promise of solution. International cooperation expanded, and agencies such as the U.N. worked to keep the peace in numerous areas and in different ways. However, there are reasons for pessimism. Low standards of living for much of the world's population, ethnic disturbances, the drug traffic, and the spread of diseases such as AIDS are but a few of the issues which will trouble the peace of the 21st century.

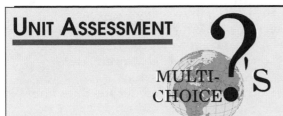

MULTI-CHOICE QUESTIONS

1   A shared goal of the Marshall Plan, Truman Doctrine, and COMECON was to
1   prevent the spread of communism
2   aid newly independent colonies
3   improve the U.S. economy
4   promote World War II recovery

2   The Hungarian Revolution (1956) and the Prague Spring (1968) indicated that the U.S.S.R. was willing to
1   use force to control its satellites
2   permit contested satellite elections
3   encourage satellite economic independence
4   disarm Warsaw Pact nations

3   Since the early 1970s, U.S.-Chinese relations could best be described as
1   hostile with few governmental contacts
2   fluctuating with economic and human rights disagreements
3   cordial with adoption of a joint position toward the U.S.S.R./Russia
4   cooperative, especially in the exchange of military technology

4   Jomo Kenyatta and Kwame Nkrumah are similar in that both were
1   investors in heavy industry and agriculture
2   leaders of independence movements and new nations
3   followers of Gandhi and supporters of non-violence
4   believers in free trade and open competition

5   The Gobi Desert, the Himalayas, and the plateaus of Mongolia and Tibet help to explain the
1   extensive cultural diffusion from China to Russia
2   relatively homogenous Chinese population
3   separation of China from Korea
4   lack of Chinese influence in S.E.Asia

6   After the Great Proletarian Cultural Revolution, China's government
1   tried high ranking Red Army Officers
2   adopted more moderate policies
3   closed all institutions of higher learning
4   refused to consider economic changes

7   During the 1990s, which economic trend was emerging in LDCs (Less Developed Countries)?
1   increased reliance on U.S. foreign aid
2   more dependence on one crop
3   movement toward a free market system
4   lessened interest in industrialization

8   The Hausa and Ibo of Nigeria and the Hutus and Tutsis of Rwanda are similar in that
1   their differences led to disastrous civil wars
2   they failed to unite to oust their colonial masters
3   their economic wealth led to declarations of independence
4   they quickly developed a common culture

9   The newly independent African nations south of the Sahara differed from most Western European nations of the 20th century because the African nations
1   have more industrial development
2   are more vulnerable to outside influence
3   possess more common cultural characteristics
4   are less dependent on subsistence agriculture

10 Which statement about "The Troubles" in Northern Ireland is most accurate?
1   The problems originated in events of the 20th century.
2   Only the IRA has been guilty of terrorist tactics.
3   Britain made no attempt to end the violence.
4   Economic discrimination against Catholics was a key cause.

11 Low defense costs, aided by the protection of the U.S. nuclear umbrella, help to explain the economic success of
1 France   3 India
2 Japan   4 North Korea

12 The position of women in Communist China could best be described as
1 improved compared with pre-1949 period
2 one of complete equality with men
3 equal with men outside of the home
4 providing equal pay for equal work

13 A major cause of problems in the command economy of the Soviet Union was
1 an inability to increase heavy industry output
2 unwillingness of workers to meet quotas
3 central planners out of touch with production realities
4 the drain of satellite economic demands

14 On a global scale, when did the most European colonies achieve independence?
1 before 1900
2 between 1900 and World War I
3 between the World Wars
4 after World War II

Base your answer to question 15 on the cartoon below and your knowledge of global history.

15 Which is a correct conclusion based on the cartoon above and your knowledge of global history?
1 During the 1970s, control in South Africa alternated between Blacks and Whites.
2 Apartheid policies in South Africa pulled down the position of Whites.
3 A White minority dominated a Black majority through the use of apartheid.
4 Apartheid played little or no role in South Africa during the 1970s.

16 In the late 1990s, a major Egyptian economic problem was
1 feeding its growing population
2 completing the High Aswan Dam
3 controlling Nile flooding
4 increasing usage fees for the Suez Canal

17 Which is true of countries controlled by Islamic Fundamentalists?
1 Secular forces dominate daily life.
2 Western culture is widespread.
3 Women's rights are very limited.
4 Close ties with the U.S. exist.

Base your answer to question 18 on the graph below and your knowledge of global history.

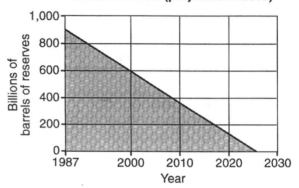

18 Which action will help slow the trend indicated in the graph?
1 expanding food production
2 increasing industrialization in LCDs
3 using alternative energy sources
4 lowering worldwide oil prices

19 In the late 1990s, the position of the Communist Party in Russia might best be described as
1 a party with support only from young voters
2 in control of the executive branch of the government
3 very weak with little chance of resurgence
4 dominant in the lower house of the Duma

20 The Mothers of Plaza De Maya were concerned about
1 cost of Eva Peron's jewels and clothes
2 fate of their children in the "dirty war"
3 violent opposition to President Peron
4 loss of the Falkland-Malvinas War to Britain

THEMATIC ESSAY

Theme: Change

In the period after World War II, economic changes played a major role in global events.

Task:
- Identify one economic change that has affected the course of global history.
- Explain the nature of the change by including information about conditions before and after the change.
- Discuss the impact of the change on global history.

Suggestions:
You may use any economic change that occurred after the end of World War II (1945) that has had a major impact on global history. Some of the changes you may wish to consider include: the postwar resurgence of Japan and West Germany, the oil crisis of the 1970s, the development of regional economic unity, the decline of command economies, the rise of the Asian Tigers, the trend toward free market economies in the 1990s. **You are not limited to these suggestions**.

DOCUMENT BASED QUESTION

Directions:
The following question is based on the accompanying documents (1-8). Some of these documents have been edited for the purposes of this exercise. This question is designed to test your ability to work with historical documents. As you analyze the documents, take into account both the source of the document and the author's point of view.

- Write a well-organized essay that includes an introduction with a thesis statement, several paragraphs explaining the thesis, and a conclusion.
- Analyze the documents.
- Use all the documents.
- Use evidence from the documents to support your position.
- Do not simply repeat the contents of the documents.
- Include specific related outside information.

Historical Context:
The end of the Soviet Union (U.S.S.R.) had a profound effect on the lives of the people in Russia. Some benefitted and some suffered because of the change.

Task:
To what extent was the end of the Soviet Union (U.S.S.R.) a positive or negative factor in the lives of the Russian people? You may wish to include in your analysis the results of the change in relation to groups of people in the population. Support your opinion with the documents below and your knowledge of history.

Part A - Short Answer
The documents below relate to the question of positive and negative effects of the end of the Soviet Union (U.S.S.R.) on the Russian people. Examine each document carefully, and then answer the question which follows it.

Document 1:

"...The younger people are adapting far more readily to the chaos - and opportunities - of the emerging market system...[Valeriy] Savitsky, 33, earns up to $1,000 a month working for a company that imports spare parts for foreign cars, a booming business...His salary...allows them [members of his family] to buy good food, clothes, and luxuries such as a VCR."

– *National Geographic*, June 1998

Document 1 Question:

What advantages has the end of the U.S.S.R. brought to Savitsky and his family?

Document 2:

"Up to 40 million Russians — nearly a third of the population — require humanitarian help because of poverty as their vast country shifts to a market economy, a Red Cross official said....It [the figure of up to 40 million Russians] largely comprised the homeless and the disabled."

– Reuters, 23 October 1996

Document 2 Question:

Why is the Red Cross involved in Russia?

Document 3:

"...The World Bank estimates that one-third of Russia's...people live below the minimum means necessary for (a decent standard of living) compared to 10% in the Soviet era, when a patriarchal state lived up to its promise to provide jobs and enough to eat."

– Los Angeles *Times*, 21 July 1996

Document 3 Question:

How has the number of people below the poverty level changed since the Soviet period?

Document 4:

Russian Government Statistics - 1996

Minimum income necessary for subsistence living – 363,000 rubles

Average monthly income – 773,000 rubles

Average monthly pension – 311,000 rubles

Document 4 Question:

According to the chart at the left and your knowledge of global history, which group of people is having difficulty obtaining even a subsistence standard of living?

Document 5:

FIRST ROUND NATIONAL ELECTION RESULTS - 1996*	
Candidate	**Percent of votes**
Yeltsin	35.28
Zyuganov	32.03
Lebed	14.52
Yavlinsky	07.34

*Chart shows the five candidates with the highest per cent of vote. Actual candidate field numbered nine.

Document 5 Question:

In what way do these election results differ from those of the Soviet era?

Document 6:

© Kime, 1997

Document 6 Question:

Why would this scene be less likely to have occurred when the U.S.S.R. existed?

Document 7:

above: typical urban housing of Soviet era for common people
(small 3-room apartment for 3-4 people)

below: vacation home for Soviet era communist official in
Kharbarovsk, Russian Far East

Document 7 Question:

Why were there such differences in housing during the Soviet period?

Document 7:

The Moscow Times

1,000 PHONES DEAD AFTER CABLE THEFT

Some 1,000 phones were cut off this week in Moscow's northwestern Tushino district when vandals cut out sections from eight underground telephone cables. Such thefts of telephone cables occur from time to time and are mostly people hoping to sell the copper cables.

IN BRIEF: MOSENERGO SHARES

MOSCOW – Moscow's heating and power utility, Mosenergo, said Wednesday that shareholders had authorized 3048 billion new shares and approved 1997 dividends of 0.05 new rubles, unchanged from last year.

RUSSIAN TRAFFIC POLICE BEGIN TO POLISH IMAGE

Russia's infamous traffic police, despised by motorists and widely perceived as some of the country's most corrupt officials, are finally taking steps to clean up their image.

KREMLIN VOWS NO FORCE IN DAGESTAN

Moscow learned its lesson in Chechnya and this time around will used the carrot instead of the stick in the restive province of Dagestan, Interior Minister Sergi Stepashin said today.

Document 8 Question:

How would these 1990s news excerpts differ from those likely to be found in a newspaper before the end of the U.S.S.R.?

Part B - Essay Response

Discuss the extent to which the end of the Soviet Union (U.S.S.R.) was a positive or negative factor in the lives of the Russian people.

Your essay should be well organized with an introductory paragraph that states your thesis on the impact of the end of the Soviet Union (U.S.S.R.) on the lives of the Russian people. Develop and explain why you have reached this conclusion in the next paragraphs and then write a conclusion. In your essay, include specific details and refer to the specific documents you analyzed in Part A. You may include additional information from you knowledge of global history.

Unit 9

TOWARD THE APOCALYPSE?

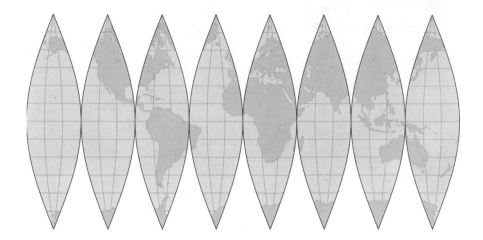

GLOBAL
CONNECTIONS &
INTERACTIONS

AD

1970–

computer processor invented (1971)

1975–

1980–

1985–

Chernobyl nuclear accident (1986)

Exxon *Valdez* oil spill (1989)

1990–

Earth Summit in Rio de Janeiro (1992)

1995–

1st American on Russian Mir Space Station (1995)

Asian Economic Crisis (1997)

2000–

INTRODUCTION

Numerous issues face the global community as it enters the 21st century. Economic decisions involving the selection of a basic system to guide choices on how to use scarce resources, ways to resolve differences between the wealthy and the poor, and modernizing without losing traditional values must be addressed. At the same time, environmental questions, population trends, technological progress, and global migrations are issues that demand study and resolution both in the global context and on a national level.

ECONOMIC TRENDS

NORTH/SOUTH DICHOTOMY

The **North/South Dichotomy**[1] is the division between the "have nations," mostly in the Northern Hemisphere, and the "have-not nations," mostly in the Southern Hemisphere. Most of the northern nations are wealthy compared to those of the south. The "have nations" have higher **literacy**[2] rates, higher per capita incomes, longer life expectancies, and fewer children per family. These are all indicators of high standards of living. Many of the "have nations" have mixed economies, but in recent years their "mixes" have shifted in the direction of capitalism or free market. Most of the have-

Key Terms	
acid rain	hunger
cartels	immigration
desertification	Internet
endangered species	North/South Dichotomy
genetics	nuclear accidents
global warming	terrorism
Green Revolution	urbanization

not nations – the less developed economies, referred to by economists as "LDCs" – struggle with a wide variety of problems. The differences between rich and poor make economic development difficult. They include factors such as: pressures of **urbanization**[3], unstable governments, civil wars, lack of capital for investment and improving the **infrastructure**[4], and ethnic rivalries.

---

1 dichotomy (division into two usually contradictory parts or opinions)
2 literate (able to read and write)
3 urbanization (to make in the nature or character of the city or city life)
4 infrastructure (basic facilities, services, and installations needed for the functioning of a community or society, such as transportation and communications systems, water and power lines, and public institutions including schools, post offices, and prisons)

THE "HAVE" AND "HAVE NOT" COUNTRIES
Based on per capita Gross Domestic Product

This location map shows the per capita Gross Domestic Product in world nations. In general, the lower the per capita GDP, the lower the standard of living and the poorer the country is. In most cases, the low GDP countries are the "have not" or LDCs.

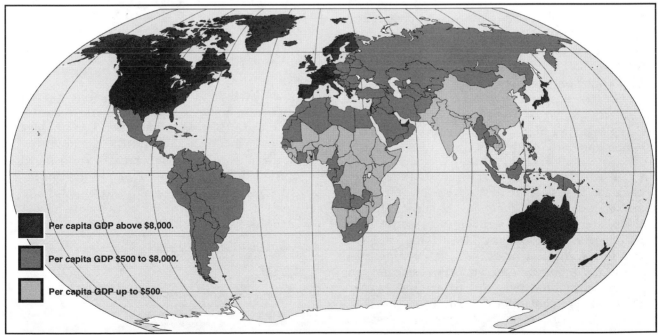

■ Per capita GDP above $8,000.

■ Per capita GDP $500 to $8,000.

■ Per capita GDP up to $500.

NORTH / SOUTH DICHOTOMY: A COMPARISON

"Have" Nations

Country	Per Capita GDP (1995)	Birth Rate per 1000 (1997)	Death Rate per 1000 (1997)	Life Expectancy (1997)
Japan	$21,300	10	8	76.7
United States	$27,607	15	9	76.0
Great Britain	$19,500	13	11	76.0

"Have Not" Nations

Country	Per Capita GDP (1995)	Birth Rate per 1000 (1997)	Death Rate per 1000 (1997)	Life Expectancy (1997)
Ethiopia	$400	46	18	46.6
Rwanda	$400	39	21	39.0
Haiti	$1,000	33	15	49.0

Most LDCs entered their post-colonial periods with a need to **diversify**[1] their economies and decrease reliance on a single crop or natural resource. In many instances, the colonial legacy of intensely developing **cash crops**[2] left them without sufficient food crops. Hunger and famines sapped the strength of the work force.

Even after independence, much of the best farmland was still controlled by large, multinational corporations or foreign investors. LDCs leaders feared that economic dominance by foreigners would replace **political oppression**[3] they had just shed. They adopted a spirit of **economic nationalism**[4] that often led the new countries to refuse extensive aid from the former mother country. During the Cold War, some LDCs solicited aid from the United States or the Soviet Union. In more recent times, they sought aid from the World Bank or prospering nations. Some incurred high debt and interest payments which hampered their growth.

The 1973 global oil crisis created major setback for LDCs. Most LDCs were oil importers, and oil was vital to their development. Many of them sought loans to pay the increased costs of oil imports. With so many LDCs demanding limited funds, interest rates rose. This compounded the LDCs' problems and led to **recessions**[5] that lasted into the 1980s. International lenders required financial reform plans from the LDCs before lending. These "belt-tightening" reforms led to decreased government spending, fewer programs to help the poor, postponement of infrastructure development, and more economic suffering. In the 1990s, some LDCs recovered from these stringent reforms with stronger economies, but others continued to languish in debt.

ECONOMIC DECISION-MAKING IN DEVELOPING ECONOMIES

In the post-colonial era, newly independent countries sought swift modernization and economic development. Some rejected capitalism, because they were bitter from the exploitation of their former colonial masters.

Some leaders admired the brutal, but rapid growth of the Soviet Union in the 1930s and of China in the 1950s. As a consequence, a number of the newly independent countries adopted various forms of socialism. They created centralized command systems. The governments maintained strong oversight and planning for the economy plus control of vital resources. Unfortunately, such far-reaching power led to

1 diversify (to distribute or investment among different companies or securities in order to limit losses in the event of a fall in a particular market or industry)
2 cash crop (agricultural crop, such as tobacco, grown for direct sale rather than for livestock feed)
3 oppression (to keep down by severe and unjust use of force or authority)
4 economic nationalism (belief that nations will benefit from acting independently rather than collectively regarding management of their own resources)
5 recession (extended decline in general business activity for 3 or more consecutive quarters of falling real gross national product)

greater corruption and abuse in the elaborate **bureaucracies**[1] that they created.

After the economic crises of the 1980s, the reforms forced by financial lenders led many LDCs toward **privatization**[2]). Many adopted more free market approaches. The "Asian Tigers" (Hong Kong, Singapore, South Korea, Taiwan) made considerable progress under such **free market initiatives**[3]. Other nations, such as Brazil, Mexico, and Argentina, actually shed their LDC label for a "more developed" status. However, many "have-not nations" continued to struggle with problems remaining from their early years of independence.

WORLD HUNGER

Famine and hunger continue to be global problems. Famine is caused by an insufficient amount of food for a long period of time. It can cause a rise in national death rates. Hunger is the result of an inadequate supply of food which can cause weakness or illness. Hunger exists in every country of the world, but famine is more apparent in LDCs. Famine conditions often bring a global relief response, but ongoing hunger problems rarely gain international attention. There are many causes of famine and hunger (see chart).

Unfortunately, some authoritarian leaders use control of food supplies to further their political ends. In the 1930s, Stalin used starvation to end kulak opposition to his regime in the Ukraine. Pol Pot's determination to have complete control over Cambodia led to a 1970s famine. In the

CAUSES OF FAMINE AND HUNGER

- Drought, especially the failure of monsoon rains
- Pests & epidemics of plant & animal diseases
- Wars and civil disturbances
- Poor or nonexistent infrastructure
- Soil erosion
- Reliance on cash crops at expense of **subsistence agriculture**[4]
- Reliance on traditional farming methods

1990s, Muslim forces in northern Sudan limited relief shipments to the Christian south to gain control of that area. These conditions limit the relief efforts of international organizations such as the U.N.'s FAO.

DRUG CARTELS

For centuries, Native Americans in countries such as Bolivia, Peru, and Colombia grew coca leaves for their own consumption. However, the global increase in illicit narcotic use in the 1970s made cocaine and other drugs important and valuable export crops for poor countries. The elimination of border controls in Western Europe and the collapse of the Soviet Union increased the difficulty of stopping the drug traffic. As the number of disturbances, conflicts, and civil wars broke down order around the globe, more people were willing to participate in the lucrative drug traffic.

Groups of individuals formed organizations or **cartels**[5] to provide the necessary avenues for drugs to move from producers to users. Over the last few decades, drug cartels such as the Medellin Cartel of Colombia, purchased the raw drugs, processed them in its factories, and provided transportation to markets. Pablo Escobar, the Medellin Cartel leader, died in 1993. The Cali Cartel of Colombia emerged as the next major cocaine and heroin supplier to the U.S. market. It is estimated that it supplied 80% of

1 bureaucracies (administrative system in which the need or inclination to follow complex procedures impedes effective action)
2 privatization (to change an industry or a business from governmental or public control to private enterprise)
3 initiative (power or ability to begin or to follow through energetically with a plan or task; enterprise and determination)
4 subsistence agriculture (basic necessity of food for one's own needs)
5 cartels (combinations of dealers who regulate production, pricing, and marketing by others)

the cocaine and 30% of the heroin in the United States in 1995.

International drug enforcement officials claim that groups such as Burma's military **junta**[1], former Haitian and Panamanian military rulers, and Mexican and Colombian civilian and military officials take bribes to protect drug traffic. However, the very high profits lead to violence. Kidnapping and murder of government officials by rival traffickers occurs often.

The U.S. government's war on drugs led to pressure on other countries. However, many believe that the U.S. needs to deal with the demand for drugs among its own citizens first. Drug-producing farmers in other lands were offered U.S. aid if they planted other crops. The U.S. Drug Enforcement Administration (DEA) stepped up border drug inspections. In addition, the Coast Guard began to intercept suspicious ships, and radar was used to track possible drug-carrying planes. Despite all these efforts, drug use in the U.S. remains high.

1   junta (group of military officers ruling a country after seizing power)

URBANIZATION

As countries move from agricultural to industrialized societies, it is normal for the growth rate of urban areas to be twice as great as the overall population increase. Rural population drains into the cities, but this movement has not led to a decrease in rural populations in most areas because the overall population increase has been so great.

In 1950, it was estimated that 29% of the world's population lived in urban areas. In 1990, the figure was 43%. The global urban population is projected to reach 50% by 2000. In Africa and Asia, approximately 33% of the people live in urban areas; while the figure is about 70% for Europe, North America, Latin America, and the Caribbean.

In 1950, only New York had a population over 10 million, and most of the largest cities were in the developed nations. In 1994, eleven of the world's largest urban areas were in LDCs. Authorities estimate that by 2015, thirteen of the largest urban areas will be in LDCs. Bombay, Lagos, Jakarta, Sao Paulo, and Karachi are expected to be the largest.

Mini Assessment

1   Before granting loans to LDCs in the 1990s, foreign bankers and international financial organizations frequently
  1   imposed stringent reform requirements
  2   demanded control of resources as security for loans
  3   required a government to increase its economic control
  4   seized control of the collection of tariffs

2   Governments of LDCs face serious problems resulting from the growth of urban areas because
  1   the decline in rural population leads to food shortages
  2   scarcity of resources limits their ability to provide necessary services
  3   the new migrants lack the ambition necessary for urban success
  4   urban birth rates are higher than those in rural areas

3   Which is an indicator of a high standard of living?
  1   high birth rate
  2   high illiteracy rate
  3   low death rate
  4   low life expectancy

Constructed Response:

Use the North/South Dichotomy chart on page 282 and your knowledge of global history to answer the following questions.

1   Based on the chart statistics, which country would have the highest standard of living?

2   Select one (1) of the three countries listed on the chart for the have-not nations and use your knowledge of global history to explain why it is a "have-not" nation.

The poor of Caracas, Venezuela live in the barrios. These overcrowded houses (several families per one to three room units) are built of cheap materials, often having poor or no sanitation, running water, or electricity.   David Johnson, 1993

The Korean War (1950-1953) was the first use of a U.N. army. Sixteen nations committed troops to fight under U.S. command. Since that time, the Suez Canal, Lebanon, the Congo, Cyprus, Haiti, Angola, Somalia, Rwanda, Georgia, and the former Yugoslavia have seen the blue beret of U.N. forces. However, the U.N. has difficulties securing the necessary troops and funding to supply peacekeepers to all the global trouble spots.

The tremendous growth of urban areas in LDCs presents a challenge to governments. Many of the new urban dwellers live in shanty towns on the outskirts of the cities. Housing is inadequate, and basic services (water, sewers, electricity) are often non-existent. **Unemployment**[1] and **underemployment**[2] are high among people whose expectations for an improved standard of living are also high. This combination presents a dilemma of scarcity. If governments spend scarce resources to improve conditions in the shanty towns, they encourage more migration. On the other hand, if they spend resources to improve the rural quality of life to discourage migration, they will not have resources for the explosive urban situations.

Examples of Rights found in the _Universal Declaration of Human Rights_
• Life, liberty, and security of person
• Freedom from slavery or servitude
• Equality before law
• Freedom from arbitrary arrest, detention, or exile

The U.N. Charter reaffirms "faith in fundamental human rights" and pledges "to promote social progress and better standards of life." As a result of concern about human rights, the _Universal Declaration of Human Rights_ was adopted by the General Assembly in 1948. The document states: "all human beings are born free and equal in dignity and rights." They are entitled to the rights stated in the document regardless of "race, color, sex, language, religion, political or other opinion, national or social origin, property, (or) birth."

ROLE OF THE UNITED NATIONS

PEACEKEEPER

One of the main responsibilities of the U.N. is to work for the preservation of peace. The U.N. has no military forces of its own. However, the Security Council may ask member nations to donate troops needed for peacekeeping missions. The first use of such troops occurred in 1948 after the U.N. agreed to monitor the truce following the first Arab-Israeli War.

The U.N.'s Economic and Social Council studies and recommends ways to increase economic and social cooperation among nations. It coordinates

1 unemployed (not having work; jobless)
2 underemployment (inadequately employed, especially employed at a low-paying job that requires less skill or training than one possesses)

the work of the specialized agencies such as the FAO (Food and Agriculture Organization), WHO (World Health Organization), and UNESCO (United Nations Education, Scientific, and Cultural Organization).

PATTERNS OF GLOBAL MIGRATIONS

TURKISH AND YUGOSLAV IMMIGRATION TO GERMANY

In the post-World War II period, war losses left West Germany with an insufficient labor supply. As a consequence, liberal immigration laws encouraged "guest workers" to come to West Germany. However, the reunification with East Germany has left the country with 4.5 million unemployed (c. late 1997). Approximately, 8% of the total workforce and 15% of the manual workers are immigrants. In 1993, 28% of the immigrants came from Turkey and 18% from the former Yugoslavia. Approximately 9% of the German population is foreign-born compared with 5.7% in France and 3.8% in Britain. The unemployment rate, combined with housing and economic conditions in the former East Germany, led to resentment against foreign workers. Neo-Nazi groups led attacks on foreigners. In 1992, there were reports of 2,300 such attacks.

In 1993, the German government changed the immigration law to limit immigrants. The new law seeks to eliminate those coming for economic reasons and limits those seeking **political asylum**[1]. However, in 1994, the government also increased penalties for racially inspired attacks. Germany faces a moral dilemma. On one hand, it seeks redemption for the World War II genocide by helping people in need now; on the other hand, it faces problems potentially destructive to its social and economic fabric.

NORTH AFRICAN IMMIGRATION TO FRANCE

In 1990, there were an estimated 2.5 million North Africans living in France. High unemployment rates and poverty in immigrant areas led to an increasing resentment against Blacks and Arabs from North Africa. There were a number of attacks on these groups by right-wing

extremists[2] resulting in violent retaliation. As a consequence, stricter immigration laws were passed in 1993. In 1994, government guidelines restricted the wearing of religious symbols in schools. Muslim girls were expelled for wearing head scarves. This led to widespread protests and law modifications. However, in 1995, plane loads of illegal immigrants were expelled as France tried to quell the violence and deal with extremists on both sides of the issue.

LATIN AMERICAN AND ASIAN IMMIGRATION TO THE U.S.

Latin American and Asian immigration to the U.S., legal and illegal, swelled during the 1970s and 1980s. Approximately, three-quarters of a million legal immigrants come to the U.S. yearly. Of that number, over 50% are of Hispanic and Asian **ethnicity**[3]. Many experts view immigrants as essential to avoiding negative population growth by 2030. The decline in birth and **fertility**[4] rates in the U.S. might be offset by immigrants and their higher birth rates. In 1986, a new immigration law made it possible for illegal immigrants already living in the U.S. to begin the citizenship process. Also, U.S. immigration laws have special provisions for those with valuable job skills, countries under-represented in its population, and those with immediate family members in the country.

Many immigrants enter the United States illegally. Estimates place the illegal immigrant total at more than 500,000 per year. Some come across the border illegally; others overstay visitor **visas**[5]. Most of the illegal immigrants come across the border from Mexico aided by "coyotes" who sell their guide services.

Other immigrants come by boats from Caribbean islands such as Haiti and Cuba. Shiploads of illegal Chinese immigrants were discovered off both coasts of the U.S. There is evidence that organized groups bring in Chinese willing to pay high prices. Many illegal aliens

1 political asylum (protection and immunity from extradition granted by a government to a political refugee from another country)
2 extremists (one who advocates or resorts to measures beyond the norm, especially in politics)
3 ethnicity (people sharing a common and distinctive racial, national, religious, linguistic, or cultural heritage)
4 fertility (capable of initiating, sustaining, or supporting reproduction)
5 visa (official authorization appended to a passport, permitting entry into and travel within a particular country or region)

MINI-ASSESSMENT

1 Which UN agency is a country likely to call for assistance when it experiences an outbreak of cholera?

1 FAO   3 Security Council
2 UNESCO   4 WHO

2 Foreign workers face discrimination in Germany and France because both countries
1 lack laws to limit immigration
2 oppose use of workers from Asian countries
3 face unemployment and other economic problems
4 have high native birth rates

3 Immigrants may be important to the U.S. economy in the next century because
1 declining U.S. birth rates may lead to labor shortages
2 unskilled labor will be the greatest economic need
3 technology will replace most migrant farm labor
4 mechanization will decline, creating a demand for labor

Constructed Response:

Use the cartoon below and your knowledge of global history to answer the following questions.

1 What does the cartoon tell you about a U.N. problem?

2 Select **one** (1) of the countries where U.N. forces have been active and explain the problems they faced.

---

disappear into the barrios or ethnic neighborhoods of major cities and obtain illegal work from their fellow nationals. Some disappear into "**sweat shops**[1]" and others become migrant farm workers. As a result of their illegal status, many live in constant fear of discovery and **deportation**[2]. As a consequence, **assimilation**[3] to American life is very difficult.

SCIENCE AND TECHNOLOGY

INFORMATION SOCIETY / COMPUTER REVOLUTION / INTERNET

Many people think that the concept of the "Information Society" began during World War II when University of Pennsylvania scien-

tists created an early computer to do calculations for the Manhattan Project (atomic bomb) and for artillery target estimates. The first computers were large enough to fill a warehouse-sized room, weighed 30 tons and were generally used for business purposes.

In 1953, there were about 100 computers in use world-wide; today that number exceeds 100 million. The key development was the personal computer, made possible by the invention of the **microprocessor**[4] by Intel in 1971. The smaller computers expanded the market to small business-

---

1 sweat shops (shop or factory in which employees work long hours at low wages under poor conditions)
2 deportation (forced departure from a country by official decree, to banish)
3 assimilation (process whereby a minority group gradually adopts the customs and attitudes of the prevailing culture)
4 microprocessor (integrated circuit that contains the entire central processing unit of a computer on a single chip)

Computers, the key factor in the communications highway, have changed the nature of business, government, and life in general. PhotoDisc Inc. 1994

es and homes. The development of word processing software, electronic spreadsheets, and games increased the popularity of computers.

The Internet is a global connection of computer networks which allows the machines to communicate and send information to each other. The World Wide Web Internet is a collection of files with text, graphics, sound, and video information. Computer programs called "browsers" make it possible to retrieve the files.

Businesses use computers to keep track of inventories using bar codes and scanners, to check customers' credit cards, and to transfer funds electronically. Home uses include adjusting indoor temperatures, activating home security systems, and turning appliances on and off. Cars use computers to regulate the flow of gasoline, advise drivers of maintenance needs, and operate on board navigational systems. In addition, there are numerous uses for computers in scientific research, education, and the military.

Despite the wonder of the computer age, many problems are apparent. Computer hackers violate privacy and destroy records. Transmitted viruses cause the loss of information and computer malfunctions. However, the issue of regulation of materials on the Internet is very controversial. Many parents wish to determine what their children view on the Internet. There are instances of crimes committed by people who contact their victims via the Internet. In some cases, this involves children. Yet, it is difficult to write legislation that also protects rights to freedom of speech and press.

IMPACT OF SATELLITES

Satellites[1] circling the Earth provide a wealth of information. The "spy in the sky" or military satellite can provide information from nuclear explosion data to ship and troop movements. Much of the information that is used by U.N. weapons inspectors in Iraq is supplied by U.S. satellites. Weather forecasting is improved through the use of information gained from weather **surveillance**[2] satellites that relay information from outer space. These satellites can provide information on hurricanes, clouds, and wind and temperature data. As a consequence, weather predictions are more accurate, and warning of impending natural disasters is improved.

Television signals, telephone conversations, and digital data can all be transmitted using

United States astronauts work from the cargo bay of the space shuttle during the repair of a satellite. PhotoDisc Inc. 1994

---

1 satellites (objects launched to orbit Earth or another celestial body for the purpose of scientific research, communications, and information gathering)
2 surveillance (close observation from space of activities on the Earth, especially those under suspicion)

orbiting satellites. Communications satellites began operating in the 1960s. Their numbers have increased over a hundred times in twenty years. They make possible long distance communication of TV signals. Therefore, the whole world can view the Olympics held in Japan. It also makes it possible for areas that are poor or have few people to receive TV signals. Transcontinental and other long distance phone service has improved and become less expensive through the use of communications satellites.

SPACE EXPLORATION

Space exploration is regarded as the "new frontier," and it is also an area of international cooperation. Spacecraft without human crews contain radio transmitters to send back information. Scientific data on the solar system and universe is obtained this way. Unmanned vehicles send back information on areas such as Mars, Venus, Mercury, Jupiter, Saturn, and Uranus.

Manned vehicles must make special provision for the air, food, water, and living accommodations for the crew. They also require a special heat shield to protect the crew during reentry into Earth's atmosphere. The high costs of these programs leads to international cooperation.

Russia's *Mir* space station was designed to be permanently staffed. In 1995, the first American, **Norman Thagard**, lived on board for three months. The U.S. space shuttle *Atlantis* docked with *Mir* to bring Thagard back. The old and unreliable *Mir* was taken out of service in 1999, with the promise of a new multinational space-lab station to take its place.

LITERACY AND EDUCATION

Literacy rates and levels of education are often used as economic indicators. In 1971, U.N. studies estimated that over 780 million people over 15 years of age were **illiterate**[1]; the figures for 1989 were 1.3 billion. Most of the illiteracy was concentrated in Latin America, Africa, and Asia. It is more common in rural than urban areas because of differences in the availability of education. Poverty and illiteracy go together. The twenty-five poorest nations have illiteracy rates in excess of 80%. International agencies such as UNESCO, governments, churches and other private groups work to improve literacy rates. Countries such as Cuba, Tanzania, Nicaragua, and China have made considerable progress.

---

1   illiterate (unable to read and write, usually, having little or no formal education)

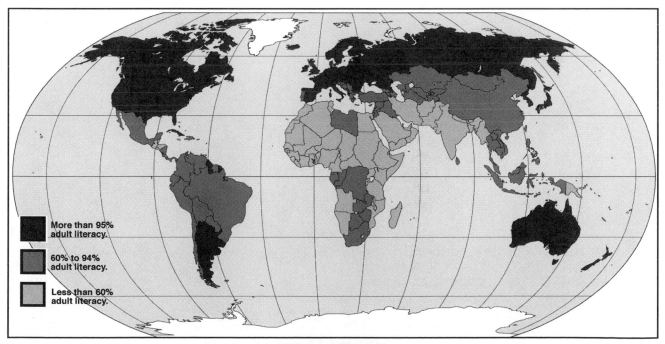

WORLD LITERACY
This location map shows literacy in regions of the world. In general, the highest illiteracy is found in the "have not" or LDCs. These are the poorest nations, often with the highest birthrates and lowest standards of living.

GLOBAL ECONOMY AND EDUCATION

COUNTRY	(GDP) Per Capita Income (1995)	Adult Literacy Rate (1995)
Bangladesh	$1,130	38%
Rwanda	$400	61%
Laos	$1,100	57%
Haiti	$1,000	45%
Mali	$600	31%
Morocco	$3,000	44%
Afghanistan	$600	31%
Germany	$17,900	100%
United States	$27,607	96%

STEPS FOR TRANSFER OF TECHNOLOGY TO LDCS

- Change from traditional plants, animals, and production techniques to a completely new, imported approach is necessary

- Research to change approaches must take into consideration the physical and social environment of target country

- Local governments must support the transfer of knowledge

- Necessary changes in infrastructure (property ownership, transportation, law, etc.) must occur

Developed nations have high basic literacy rates, but there is increasing concern over **functional literacy**. Functional literacy requires meeting the reading and writing demands of a complex society. Studies show that anywhere from 10% to 50% of literate individuals may be functionally illiterate in today's modern societies.

GREEN REVOLUTION

The **Green Revolution**[1] began in the late 1960s with the introduction of new hybrids of vital food crops such as rice, wheat, potatoes, and corn in LDCs. In order for these new types of seeds to be successful, special programs had to be established. These involved large amounts of expensive petrochemical fertilizers, irrigation, and pesticides. In the India states of Punjab and Haryana, where sizable amounts of the new crops are produced, there is considerable progress. In other areas of India where cost factors often limit implementation, producing enough food to feed the population remains a struggle. These same costs limit the use of the new seeds in other LDCs.

---

1 green revolution (significant increase in agricultural productivity resulting from the introduction of high-yield varieties of grains, the use of pesticides, and improved management techniques)

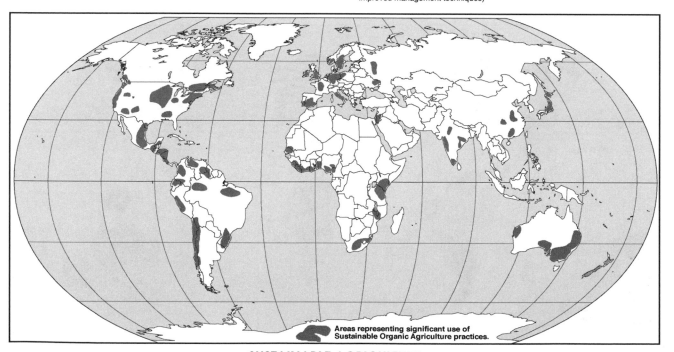

Areas representing significant use of Sustainable Organic Agriculture practices.

SUSTAINABLE AGRICULTURE

This location map shows areas of the world where sustainable organic agriculture is being practiced on a large-scale. Many "green" scientists and environmentalists are encouraged by widespread cooperation among many nations.

American agronomist (agricultural scientist) **Norman E. Borlaug** (1914 -) is sometimes regarded as the father of the Green Revolution. In 1970, he won the **Nobel Prize**[1] for developing wheat strains adapted for the warmer, more arid soils of Mexico and India. Dr. Borlaug developed a program for the transfer of new procedures and programs to developing areas.

The U.N., individual nations, and private organizations took steps to implement the Green Revolution. In those areas where it could be implemented, considerable progress occurred in feeding the population, and in some cases, exporting surplus production. Where opposition to chemical fertilizers and pesticides has arisen, the U.N. and private aid agencies have launched natural, **sustainable agriculture** programs (see map on previous page).

MEDICAL BREAKTHROUGHS - DISEASE CONTROL / LIFE EXPECTANCY / GENETICS

The discovery of penicillin and the subsequent development of antibiotics during World

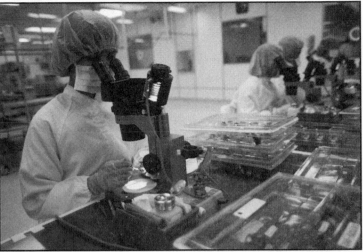

This research lab is working on the development of a vaccine against a potentially deadly strain of Hepatitis.   PhotoDisc Inc. 1994

War II brought about major progress in the treatment of diseases such as pneumonia, tuberculosis, and bacterial meningitis. However, the power of the new "wonder drugs" led to overuse. As a consequence, some types of infections developed a resistance to these drugs. By the 1980s, the market for antibiotics seemed to be saturated. Research for new "wonder drugs" has started, but development, testing, and approval times often cause long delays.

---

1 Nobel Prizes (six international prizes awarded annually by the Nobel Foundation for outstanding achievements in the fields of physics, chemistry, physiology or medicine, literature, and economics and for the promotion of world peace)

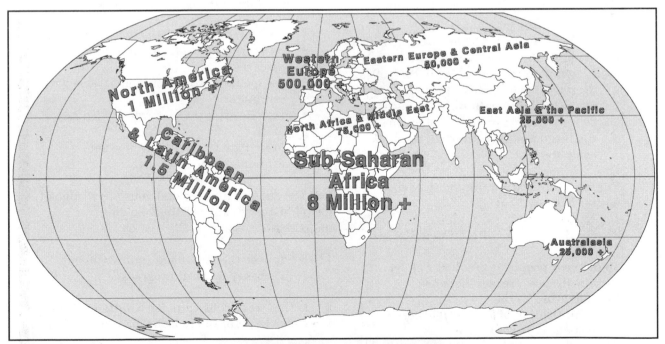

HIV – THE SPREAD ALL OVER THE WORLD

This location map shows the areas of the world where the retrovirus HIV, which causes AIDS, has had the greatest effect. Based on these 1993 statistics, the World Health Organization expresses real concern for the worldwide spread of the disease.

Vaccination programs conducted by governments or the World Health Organization made considerable progress in eliminating diseases such as polio and measles. However, it has been noted that failure to continue **immunization**[1] programs may result in a resurgence of the diseases. This occurred in the case of measles in the early 1990s in the U.S.

LIFE EXPECTANCIES AT BIRTH (YEARS) - SELECTED COUNTRIES		
Country	1977	1993
Angola	37	47
China	59	69
Colombia	59	69
Guatemala	53	65
Haiti	48	57
Ireland	71	75
Rwanda	48	47
United States	71	76

cases, international organizations led the fight to prevent the spread of these diseases.

Medical research is finding genetic markers that help predict which people are at greatest risk for specific diseases. **Genetic markers**[2] have been identified for certain types of breast cancer, a major killer of women. This information combined with new research that the drug **Tamoxifen** may be useful in the prevention of breast cancer as well as in its treatment, provide hope for those at risk. Although still in testing, long-term laboratory work has developed **angiostatin** and **endostatin** drugs with the potential of blocking the growth of cancerous tumor blood vessels.

Other major health risks include the HIV virus (AIDS), Ebola, and Dengue Fever. HIV affects virtually every part of the world. In developed nations, combinations of expensive drugs have extended life expectancy considerably. AZT, a drug useful in combating AIDS, decreases the number of babies born with AIDS if given to pregnant women. However, its cost limits availability in poverty areas. In the mid-1990s, an outbreak of the deadly Ebola virus occurred in Africa, and Dengue Fever resurfaced in parts of Latin America. In both

---

1 immunization (inherited, acquired, or induced resistance to infection by a specific pathogen)
2 genetic marker (known DNA sequence associated with a particular gene or trait that is used to indicate the presence of that gene or trait, associated with certain diseases which can often be detected in the blood serum)

Mini Assessment

1 Computers have revolutionized the way many things are done; however, they have also led to many problems. Which problem is associated with computer use in the 1990s?
   1 decreased availability of information
   2 incompatibility with military needs
   3 concerns about privacy protection
   4 the large space required for most computers

2 Functional literacy would most likely be a matter of concern in
   1 Bangladesh   3 Mali
   2 Haiti   4 United States

3 To discover people at greatest risk for certain diseases, researchers are concentrating on the
   1 identification of genetic markers
   2 increased use of x-rays
   3 development of new surgical methods
   4 discovery of new vaccines

Constructed Response:

"The child of the late 20th century can:

- be viewed before birth with a sonogram
- be vaccinated against childhood diseases
- escape the discomfort of infections with antibiotics
- replace exploratory surgery with an MRI
- anticipate the company of great-grandparents."

Use the quotation above and your knowledge of global history to answer the following questions.

1 What does the statement indicate about 20th century medical progress?

2 Is this statement valid for children world-wide? Explain the reasons for your answer.

Organ transplants, open heart surgery, and less invasive medical techniques, such as laser and laparoscopic surgery, have lengthened life expectancies in developed countries and made surgical procedures less traumatic. New diagnostic tools such as CT scans (computerized images using x-rays) and MRIs (magnetic resonance images) have made earlier, more accurate diagnoses possible.

Life expectancies have increased in most countries as a result of improved health care. Some areas plagued by civil disturbances or breakdowns in delivery of medical care are exceptions.

THE ENVIRONMENT

POLLUTION – AIR, WATER, TOXIC WASTE

Twentieth century increases in population and industrialization caused increases in air, water, and **toxic waste**[1] pollution. Burning coal, oil, and gasoline caused most of the air pollution. Much of it is generated by electric power plants, industrial boilers, home furnaces, and automotive exhausts. It has led to the **greenhouse effect**[2] and global warming. Extreme predictions include the melting of the ice cap,

loose icebergs in shipping lanes, and the flooding of low-lying areas such as the Netherlands, New York City, and Florida. Air pollution also causes **acid rain**[3]. It endangers plant and animal life as well as lakes and forests – the damage often occurs hundreds of miles from the source of the problem. Historic buildings and sculptures exposed to such elements also suffer serious damage.

Sewage, toxic wastes, chemical pesticides, fertilizers, and oil spills cause much of the water pollution. The oil spill in Prince William Sound, Alaska caused by the tanker *Exxon Valdez* (March 1989) endangered fish and wildlife and cost millions to clean up. During the Iran/Iraq War in 1983 and during the Persian Gulf War in 1991, Iraq ordered intentional releases of oil that seriously damaged marine life. Some of that oil threatened desalination plants vital to life in the desert area. In general, water pollutants often include cadmium, mercury, arsenic, and lead. These cause serious health risks and are lethal in large amounts. Governments in developed

1 toxic waste (garbage, trash or other useless or worthless byproduct of manufacturing, capable of causing injury or death, especially by chemical means; poisonous)

2 greenhouse effect (phenomenon whereby the Earth's atmosphere traps solar radiation, caused by the presence in the atmosphere of gases such as carbon dioxide, water vapor, and methane that allow incoming sunlight to pass through but absorb heat radiated back from the earth's surface)

3 acid rain (atmospheric acidic–contaminated precipitation carried by the Earth's winds)

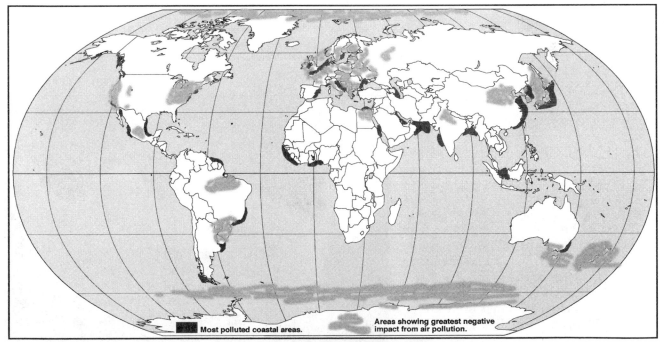

Most polluted coastal areas.

Areas showing greatest negative impact from air pollution.

POLLUTED REGIONS OF THE WORLD
This location map shows the areas of major pollution and areas with the greatest negative impact from air pollution. Note that it is not just the areas near the industrial nations that have major pollution problems, but also around some of the LDCs..

nations pass laws requiring the treatment of household and industrial wastes before their release. However, accidents occur, and there is some evasion of the law.

Toxic wastes pose serious problems globally. The developed nations, well aware of their hazards, are reluctant to provide for the costly, proper treatment and disposal. As a consequence, they are often sent to LDCs where provisions for disposal are not safe.

DEFORESTATION

Some of the dwindling tropical rain forests exist in parts of Indonesia, Thailand, Ghana, and the Ivory Coast. At the current rate of **deforestation**[1], tropical rain forests could disappear by 2030. With their destruction would go hundreds of species of plant and animal life. Some of the plants may contain the cure for deadly diseases such as cancer and AIDS. The destruction of the trees limits the removal of carbon dioxide from the air and increases the likelihood of problems from the greenhouse effect.

The area which attracts the most attention from environmentalists is the Amazon River Valley in Brazil. This rain forest was subjected to large scale development beginning in the 1980s. **Slash-and-burn**[2] agriculture destroyed large areas of the rain forest as poor Brazilians tried to establish farms and ranches. Under international pressure, the Brazilian government tried to limit development and protect the resources of the rain forest. However, it is a difficult balancing act.

Economic development demands and heavy population pressure in northeast Brazil weigh heavily in favor of exploitation of the resources by domestic and foreign companies.

The world's **1992 Earth Summit** in Rio de Janeiro, Brazil called for a decrease in the emission of gases to limit global warming. It also included a **biodiversity**[3] agreement which called on signatory nations to develop plans to protect endangered species and their habitats. The 1997 Kyoto Protocol called for a decrease in carbon dioxide and other greenhouse gases from the 1990 levels. European Union members were to decrease their emissions by 8%, the U.S. by 7%, and Japan by 6%. LDCs were asked to set voluntary targets. The ratification process is not complete and sanctions are not established. International agreement on these issues is not easy. Frequently, LDCs accuse developed nations of using environmental limitations to hinder their development.

---

1   deforestation (to cut down and clear away the trees or forests)
2   Slash-and-burn (systematic, mechanical method of felling and clearing large tracts of forested land)
3   biodiversity (the millions of species of plants and animals sustaining a harmonious relationship in the environment)

"Slash & Burn" – Deforestation of the Amazon Rain Forest in order to gain grazing land for cattle, Brazil, South America.   PhotoDisc Inc. 1994

With little or no green vegetation and water, the devastating effects of desertification are evident in the appearance of the emaciated Sahel cattle around Keur Mibarick, Senegal, Africa. © David Johnson 1993

DESERTIFICATION

Desertification, the transformation of arable or habitable land to desert, may be caused by a variety of factors. Some causes are natural, such as insufficient rainfall and strong winds. However, much of the desertification is caused by too many people, too much livestock, and over-cultivation of the fragile environment. Overgrazing on the edges of deserts damages the plants that hold the moisture and soil - the result is a spread of the desert. In a 1984 U.N. report, it was stated that 35% of the Earth's land surface was at risk for desertification. The most serious problem developed in the **Sahel**[1] area of Africa between the late 1960s and the early 1980s. A drought depleted the minimal water supply, and economic conditions limited the ability of governments to decrease human and livestock use of the area. The result was a famine which required an international relief effort. Recent reports indicate a return to more normal rainfall and an easing of the famine conditions.

ENDANGERED SPECIES

Endangered species[2] disappear at a rate of a minimum of 4,000 every year, and the figure may be as high as 50,000. Most of this loss is caused by a destruction of **habitats**[3], especially tropical rain forests and coral reefs. The giant pandas of China are threatened because their habitat and main food supply, bamboo, are being reduced by development. In addition, **poachers**[4] kill members of those species with high economic value. For example, rhinoceros' horns have a medicinal value in China. Despite laws protecting these animals, they are frequently killed, the horns removed, and the bodies left for scavengers. The 1973 ***Convention of International Trade in Endangered Species*** prohibited trade in plants and animals in danger of becoming extinct, but enforcement is difficult.

---

1 Sahel (semiarid region of north-central Africa south of the Sahara Desert. Since the 1960's it has been afflicted by prolonged periods of extensive drought)
2 endangered species (plant or animal threatened with extinction)
3 habitat (native environment of a plant or animal)
4 poacher (one who hunts or fishes illegally on the property of another)

CLOSE LOOK

ENDANGERED BY HUMANS

Plastic is a large problem in our ocean. We (Marine Mammal Stranding Center) have found that dolphins, whales, sea turtles, and seals all have suffered from plastic, not to mention the countless sea birds and fish that have died as a result of plastic, either through ingestion or by their being entangled in it. Helium filled latex balloons, released into the air, often end up in the sea, where they may be eaten by some sea creature. Plastic ribbons from

beer and soda six-packs as well as general litter also injure marine life. Please consider this before discarding these materials.

adapted from a flyer of the
Marine Mammal Stranding Center

NUCLEAR SAFETY - CHERNOBYL

In 1986, the accident at the Chernobyl nuclear reactor in the western region of the former U.S.S.R. (now Ukraine) brought world attention to dangers from nuclear plants. Radioactive contamination spread over much of Europe, and over 135,000 people were evacuated from the area around Chernobyl. In a 1995 report, WHO stated that there was an "explosive increase" in childhood thyroid cancer in Belarus, Ukraine, and Russia. The report attributed the increase to the radioactive exposure from Chernobyl's fallout. In the aftermath of the accident, the international community made plans for inspections, renovations, and closings of dangerous nuclear plants.

Plants similar in design to the one at Chernobyl were built throughout the Soviet Union and in the satellite countries. Many are near large population centers such as St. Petersburg, Russia. However, relatively little has been done to improve their safety or close them down. The cost of renovation is very high, and most of the countries involved cannot afford the expensive, high tech upgrades.

In addition, these countries depend on the nuclear plants for much of their electricity and do not have alternate sources of supply. Economic considerations have kept most of these plants in operation. Finally, in 1994, Western nations suggested an aid package to completely close the Chernobyl site, and Ukraine agreed to do so by the year 2000.

CLOSE LOOK

GLOBAL FALLOUT – THE SPREAD OF RADIATION
AFTERMATH OF THE EXPLOSION AT REACTOR #4,
26 APRIL 1986 – CHERNOBYL, UKRAINE (FORMER U.S.S.R.)

Source: Compilation of Satellite Data and Computer Models, Apr/May 1986

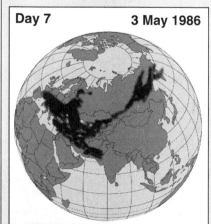

Day 2   **28 April 1986**

Day 4   **30 April 1986**

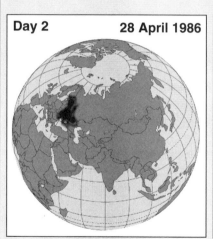

Day 7   **3 May 1986**

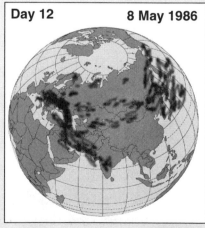

Day 12   **8 May 1986**

On 26 April 1986 after two years of operation and during a test "experiment" to improve the safety of Reactor #4, V.I. Lenin Nuclear Power Plant, Chernobyl, Ukraine (in 1986 part of the U.S.S.R.) overheated. Steam exploded blowing the 1000 ton roof off the reactor. Fires started, and the radioactive inventory of the reactor was thrust into the atmosphere. Radiation spread northward covering much of Eastern Europe by April 28; by the 30th, the radiation cloud spread further north, into Western Europe and Western Asia. By May 3rd the radiation had spread throughout most of Western Europe and Central and Southern Asia. By May 8th, radiation covered Europe, Asia, and into the Pacific Ocean. In three weeks, radiation had spread over much of the Northern Hemisphere.

The United States suffered a near disaster in 1979 at the Three Mile Island plant near Harrisburg, PA. The Nuclear Regulatory Commission moved to strictly regulate nuclear power plants. After this accident, power companies placed no new orders for plants, and the NRC denied certification (licensing) to many of those scheduled to open. However, countries such as France (obtains about 75% of its electricity from nuclear plants) continue to operate them and defend their safety.

BIRTH RATES – SELECTED COUNTRIES

COUNTRY	Birth rate per 1,000 (1993)	Percent urban (1995)	Fertility Rate per woman (1995)
Afghanistan	51	20	6.9
Bangladesh	36	18	3.1
China	18	30	1.8
Chad	44	21	5.5
Kenya	44	28	4.9
Argentina	20	88	2.6
El Salvador	33	45	3.1
United States	16	76	2.0
France	13	73	1.6
Russia	11	76	1.4

POPULATION PRESSURES AND POVERTY

After thirty years of worry, it appears that population pressures are diminishing in the world as a whole. The global average replacement rate is 2.1 children per woman. In the 1950-1955 period the birth rate was 5 children per woman; in 1975-1990, it was 4; in 1995, it was 3; and in 1998, it was estimated at 2.8 and decreasing. The LDC birth rate was 6 children per woman between 1965 and 1970; it is now 3 and decreasing rapidly. However, with the exception of areas such as China, Cuba, and Thailand, the LDC birth rate remains above the global replacement rate. Although the rates are decreasing in sub-Saharan Africa, experts expect the area to have the highest population growth rate in the 21st century. The European rates are estimated at 1.4 per woman (see chart above).)

Experts attribute the decline in the population growth rate to a number of factors. As societies move from rural to urban, the concern is

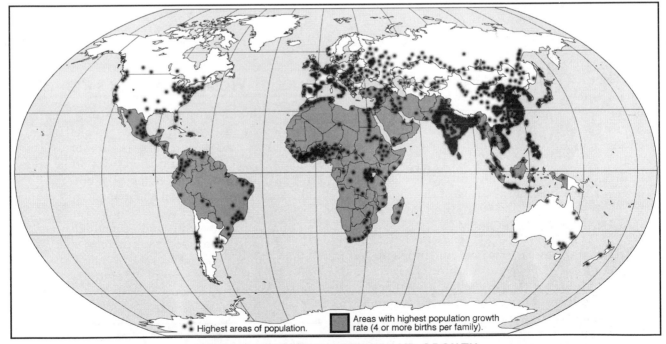

Highest areas of population.

Areas with highest population growth rate (4 or more births per family).

WORLD POPULATION CENTERS AND GROWTH

This location map shows the regions of the world with the fastest population growth rates are also the poorest regions of the world, already having the greatest population. For the most part, these regions consist of the "have not" or LDCs.

another mouth to feed in the city as opposed to another worker on the farm. Later marriages, lower **infant mortality rates**[1], improved **contraception**[2], and women's rights and higher education for women figure in the decline. Also, economics is a growing consideration. However, religious pressures often work in the opposite direction. Heavily Roman Catholic countries and fundamentalist Islamic cultures often have higher birth rates.

Government policies and pressures also affect child bearing decisions. China's "one family, one child policy" in the 1980s and 1990s had built-in penalties for more children. While the government allowed exceptions for minorities and families in rural areas, the program is bringing down the birth rate in the world's most populous country. Later, China employed U.N. help to experiment with lifting this policy in certain areas of the country. The hope is that some of the social and medical factors mentioned above will take the place of government pressures.

There are close ties between population growth and poverty. Poverty areas with high infant mortality rates often have high birth rates. Parents are afraid that babies will not survive the rigors of growing up and tend to have additional children to insure that some survive to adulthood. For example, Afghanistan has an infant mortality rate of 154 per 1,000 live births; the figure for Chad is 115. The comparable rate for the U.S. and France is 7.

Concerns about population pressures continue for some of the LDCs. However, many of the developed countries are more concerned about declines in birth rates. The **demographic**[3] changes in Europe, Japan, and North America indicate an increasing number of elderly. The aging of the existing population leads to concerns about who will take care of the them.

INTERNATIONAL TERRORISM

International terrorism continues to be a threat to world peace and stability. Terrorism seems to be the weapon of choice for those who wish to call world attention to their demands. It is a frequently used tool by groups who desire to establish their own independent nations. Although the PLO (Palestine Liberation Organization) renounced the use of terrorism to gain Palestinian autonomy, other radical Islamic fundamentalist groups such as **Hamas**, **Hezbollah**, and the **Islamic Jihad** movement commit acts of terrorism not only against Israel, but also against any who are considered supporters of the Jewish State. The Irish Republican Army frequently used violence in its struggle to unify Northern Ireland with the Republic of Ireland. Most of its violence occurred in Northern Ireland or against English targets. In August 1998, brutal attacks on U.S. Embassies in Kenya and Tanzania were attributed to groups engineered and financed by international terrorist **Osama bin Laden**. Most nations supported the unilateral bombing destruction by the United States of terrorist training camps in Afghanistan and a chemical factory in Sudan.

While older terrorist groups seem to be moderating, newer groups have intensified activities. The **Zapatista National Liberation Army** struggles against the government of Mexico to gain reforms to benefit the Native American population. The **Kosovo Liberation Army** demands freedom from Yugoslav rule, and the **Liberation Tigers of Tamil Eelam** want an independent nation in Southeast Asia. Sometimes, as in the case of the **Islamic Salvation Front of Algeria** and some groups in Turkey, the goal is control of the government. Many of the newer groups have confined their terrorism to a narrow geographic area and have not yet attempted global targets.

STATUS OF WOMEN / WOMEN'S RIGHTS

Traditionally, women's education was primarily in the area of domestic skills and obtained at home. Marriage was important for support and children, and there was often pressure to have children, especially males. The Industrial Revolution and the global wars of the 20th century accelerated change. Gains were made in political, social, and economic equality. Women gained the right to control property, to equal opportunity, and to vote in many areas of the world. However, complete equality proved elusive, and many traditional areas of the world fell behind on these issues.

---

1 infant mortality rate (number of deaths among children under one year of age per thousand births)
2 contraception (intentional prevention of conception or impregnation through the use of various devices, agents, drugs, sexual practices, or surgical procedures)
3 demography (study of the characteristics of human populations, such as size, growth, density, distribution, and vital statistics)

By the mid-1960s, improved contraception had become available in developed areas. This decreased child bearing and child rearing tasks. The global inflation in the early 1980s made two incomes a necessity for many families. By the mid-1980s, approximately 50% of the workers in England, France, Germany, and the U.S. were women. However, women found themselves in low paying jobs such as teaching, nursing, and clerical positions. Gradually, women began to break through the "glass ceiling" barrier to high paying corporate leadership positions. They made considerable progress in professions in the United States. Women lawyers and judges went from 7.1% in 1975 to 29% in 1996. The comparable figures for physicians were 13% and 26.4%.

Traditionally, communist regimes espoused the rights of women and proclaimed them equal. In reality, few women occupied high positions. In many of these countries, they received less pay than their male counterparts. Social expectations required them to shoulder the full responsibility of running the home, but they were expected to work outside the home.

In LDCs, many problems remain. Often industrialization in non-Western areas results in the end of some traditional economic arrangements which benefit women. This results in women becoming dependent on low paid factory labor, if they can get a job at all. Countries which embrace Islamic Fundamentalism often return to traditional values and limit educational and work opportunities for women.

Mini Assessment

1 Destruction of rain forests is difficult to stop because
   1 international agreements are impossible to obtain
   2 their fertile lands produce high yields for many years
   3 developing nations want to exploit their resources
   4 few political leaders realize their importance

2 It is difficult to carry out the changes necessary to avoid another Chernobyl disaster because the
   1 economic costs of renovation or closing nuclear plants is high
   2 nuclear energy is the least expensive source of power
   3 nuclear plants have had no other operational problems
   4 available capital is spent to build new nuclear plants

3 Which statement is most accurate regarding the position of women in traditional countries?
   1 They are 50% of the work force.
   2 They face limited education and work opportunities.
   3 They have made considerable progress in the professions.
   4 They have achieved equal pay with men for equal work.

Constructed Response:

Use the *U.S.News* covers on page 294 and your knowledge of global history to answer the following questions.

1 What types of pollution are identified on the covers?

2 Select **one** (1) of the pollution types shown on the covers and explain why it is dangerous.

The less equal position of women still concerns the international community. The U.N. announced the "Decade for Women" in 1975 and tried to turn attention to women's issues, their contributions, and their rights. World conferences dealing with international women's issues continue to be held every five years under U.N. sponsorship.

CONCLUSION

Globalization is a reality as the world approaches the 21st century. Technology has brought the world closer together. Air travel and new methods of communication lead to quick transmission of ideas and products. They also mean that it is difficult for societies to maintain their identities in the face of global commonalities.

Countries no longer live in isolation. Outbreaks of violence frequently lead to international responses designed to restore stability and peace and prevent the spread of fighting to other areas. International groups also struggle to deal with the economic and social problems of the world such as hunger and disease.

Mass movement of people occurs frequently. In some cases, this is caused by the desire to escape from persecution or violence. In others, the motivation is economic and social betterment. With these movements come reactions against the newcomers, sometimes caused by economic fears, but often by dislike of someone who is different.

The impact of environmental changes and disasters affect not just the area where they occur, but potentially the entire world. Air currents carry pollutants hundreds of miles from their source, and deforestation and desertification affect the quality of life globally.

One of the best indications of the global community in which we live is the sizable number of international organizations which have developed in recent years. It is both necessary and possible to deal with many of the problems which we face, but only through international cooperation.

MULTI-CHOICE QUESTIONS

1 A negative result of the use of chemical pesticides and fertilizers is that they
1 lower crop yields
2 increase income per capita
3 may contaminate the soil
4 destroy some crops

2 Since the end of World War II, means of communication have
1 heightened the possibility of global war
2 increased cultural diffusion
3 limited the spread of technology
4 decreased internationalism

3 The *Universal Declaration of Human Rights* is most similar to the
1 Pass Laws
2 French *Declaration of the Rights of Man*
3 *Petition of Right*
4 Nuremberg Laws

4 • **Weather predictions**
 • **Long distance phone calls**
 • **International TV broadcasts**

All of these are improved or made possible by
1 satellites   3 CT scans
2 fiber optic cables   4 X-rays

Base your answer to question 5 on the graph below and your knowledge of global history.

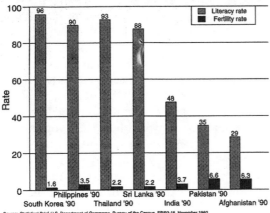

Selected Asian Countries: Fertility vs. Literacy

Literacy rate
Fertility rate

South Korea '90 — 96, 1.6
Philippines '90 — 90, 3.5
Thailand '90 — 93, 2.2
Sri Lanka '90 — 88, 2.2
India '90 — 48, 3.7
Pakistan '90 — 35, 6.6
Afghanistan '90 — 29, 6.3

Source: *Statistical Brief*, U.S. Department of Commerce, Bureau of the Census, SB/93-18, November 1993

5 What is a valid conclusion based on the information provided in the graph?
1 The Philippines had a higher fertility rate than Afghanistan did.
2 In most instances, nations with higher literacy rates tend to have lower fertility rates.
3 The literacy rates for South Asian nations are higher than rates for Southeast Asian nations.
4 Southeast Asian nations have a higher rate of population growth than any other region in the world.

6 A major drawback of the Green Revolution is
1 lack of farmland suitable for implementation
2 government opposition to "hi tech" approaches
3 high cost of necessary seeds, fertilizers, and irrigation
4 reluctance of the U.N. to back the program

7 The increasing global pollution is causing concern among scientists because
1 LDCs are responsible for most pollution
2 health effects are more evident
3 developed nations refuse to respond to the threat
4 corrective technology is unavailable

8 Which statement about population pressures is most correct in the late 1990s?
1 LDC birth rates continue to climb.
2 Sub-Saharan Africa has the lowest growth rate.
3 European birth rates are below the average replacement rate.
4 Catholics and Muslims support birth control efforts.

9 Hamas, the Irish Republican Army, and the Liberation Tigers of Tamil are similar in their
1 use of terrorism to gain attention for their demands
2 employment of U.S. Army advisors
3 support of humane rules of warfare
4 goal to establish a theocracy

10 Which statement is most accurate regarding the Chinese government's birth control policy in the late 1990s?
1 The one child, one family policy remains in control throughout China.
2 Only minorities and farm families may exceed the one child limit.
3 All penalties for exceeding the one child limit were removed.
4 The government is lifting the one child, one family policy experimentally in some areas.

THEMATIC ESSAY

Theme: Science and Technology

Medical science has made tremendous strides in the 20th century, but new developments have led to controversy and moral dilemmas.

Task:

- Select **one** (1) area in which medical science has led to new developments, and identify the resulting controversy or moral dilemmas.

- Using factual information, explain **both** sides of the controversy or dilemma involving the development selected.

Suggestions:

You may use any example of a new development in medical science which occurred in the 20th century, but you must present facts for both sides of the controversy or dilemma surrounding the development. Some of the examples of medical developments you might wish to consider include: genetic engineering, cloning, use of life support systems, infertility treatments, and birth control. **You are not limited to these suggestions**.

DOCUMENT BASED QUESTION

Directions

The following question is based on the accompanying documents (1-6). Some of these documents have been edited for the purposes of this exercise. This question is designed to test your ability to work with historical documents. As you analyze the documents, take into account both the source of the document and the author's point of view.

- Write a well-organized essay that includes an introduction with a thesis statement, several paragraphs explaining the thesis, and a conclusion.
- Analyze the documents.
- Use all the documents.
- Use evidence from the documents to support your position.
- Do not simply repeat the contents of the documents.
- Include specific related outside information.

Historical Context:

Environmentalists are very concerned about development of the Amazon rain forest area.

Task:

Why is development of the Amazon rain forest of great concern to environmentalists? Answer this question using the documents below and your knowledge of global history.

Part A - Short Answer

The documents below relate to development of the Amazon rain forest. Examine each document carefully, and then answer the question which follows it.

Document 1:

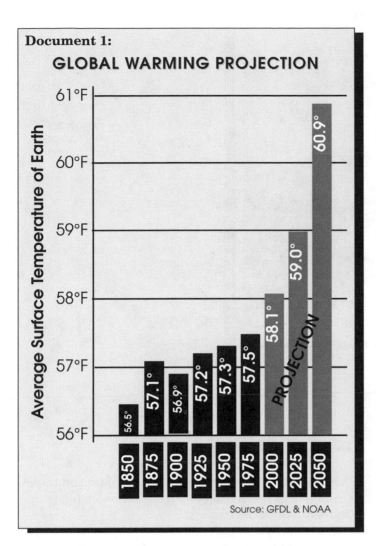

GLOBAL WARMING PROJECTION

Average Surface Temperature of Earth

- 61°F
- 60°F
- 59°F
- 58°F
- 57°F
- 56°F

1850	1875	1900	1925	1950	1975	2000	2025	2050
56.5°	57.1°	56.9°	57.2°	57.3°	57.5°	58.1°	59.0°	60.9°

PROJECTION

Source: GFDL & NOAA

Document 1 Question:

If the data in the graph is accurate, what will be the effect on the environment in the year 2050?

Document 2:

"Because rain forests contain the Earth's greatest diversity of plants and animals, they also represent giant gene banks that can provide new drugs, foods, and other products."

– Michael Goulding

Document 2 Question:

If rain forests disappear, what would humanity lose?

Document 3:

"In the early 1970s the country (Brazil) built the Trans-Amazon Highway, a system of roads that ran west...toward the Peruvian border. The idea was to prompt a land rush similar to the...American West."

– *Time*, 1989

Document 3 Question:

What danger is involved in the construction of the Trans-Amazon Highway?

Document 4:

New Look of the Amazon Rain Forest Following Deforestation - ©PhotoDisc 1994

Document 4 Question:

What effect does "slash and burn" agriculture have on a rain forest?

Document 5:

"Nearly half the world's 233 primate species are threatened, largely because of their dependence on large expanses of tropical forest. ...In hotspots of forest loss, ...such as the Atlantic rainforest of eastern Brazil ... roughly 70 percent of primate species face extinction."

– Worldwatch

Document 5 Question:

What effect has the forest loss in Brazil had on the primate population, some of which are endangered species?

Document 6:

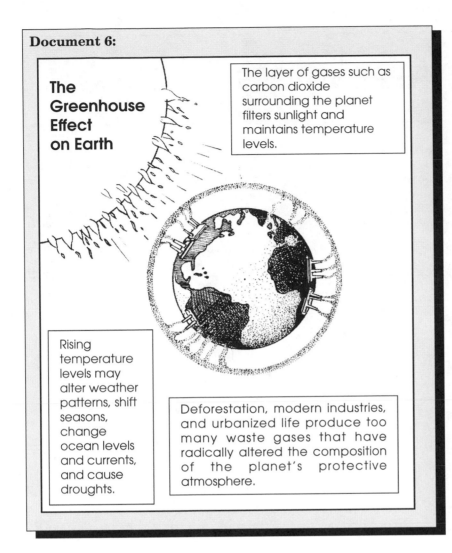

The Greenhouse Effect on Earth

The layer of gases such as carbon dioxide surrounding the planet filters sunlight and maintains temperature levels.

Rising temperature levels may alter weather patterns, shift seasons, change ocean levels and currents, and cause droughts.

Deforestation, modern industries, and urbanized life produce too many waste gases that have radically altered the composition of the planet's protective atmosphere.

Document 6 Question:

What effect does deforestation have on the Earth's atmosphere? Why is this dangerous?

Part B - Essay Response

Why is the development of the Amazon rain forest of great concern to environmentalists?

Your essay should be well organized with an introductory paragraph that states your thesis about why development of the Amazon rain forest is of great concern to environmentalists. Develop and explain why you have arrived at this answer in the next paragraphs and the write a conclusion. In your essay, include specific details and refer to the specific documents you analyzed in Part A. You may include additional information from your knowledge of global history.

APPENDICES

EXAM STRATEGIES

Columbus was a focused person with a plan. To succeed on any examination you need to have a plan. There are a few basic steps you can take that will help you succeed.

TAKE THE FULL AMOUNT OF TIME

You have studied hard. You may be tense or nervous about the exam, but do not rush. Take a few minutes to calm yourself and make up your mind that you will not be rushed. A little extra time spent looking over your paper at the end can be very helpful in spotting an error or an omission.

SKIM OVER THE ENTIRE EXAMINATION

In light pencil, answer any Part One question of which you are absolutely sure. On a piece of scrap paper, jot down ideas as you read quickly through the Part Two. Put down names, laws, events, and dates that you think will fit. Do not try to fashion any organized answers yet, this is just a way of calmly adjusting to your task (becoming focused).

ATTACK THE MULTIPLE CHOICE QUESTIONS

Answer as many questions as you can, but don't linger too long on the harder ones. Leave them blank and go back to them later. Many times, an answer will seem more obvious after you have been working for a while. Also, remember that Part One is an overview of the whole global history course. There is quite a bit of material covered. Look to see if there are any ideas on Part I that can help you on the Part Two written responses. If so, make note of them on your scrap paper.

WORK ON THE CONSTRUCTED RESPONSE QUESTIONS

The questions are in sets. The first question flows <u>directly</u> from the quotation or the graphic and is usually quite obvious. Generally, the second question requires you to add background knowledge connected to the quotation or the graphic. Remember, there are not many points involved here, so the answers should be brief. A sentence or two incorporating a key fact or idea is usually enough.

WORK ON THE DOCUMENT-BASED QUESTION

1 Look at the main theme and scan the documents before beginning. Usually, you have to take a position on an issue (e.g., did an event have a positive or negative effect?). Decide what your position will be. That becomes the basis of your essay. It is your *thesis* – what you want to prove. Look at the documents with your thesis in mind. How can you use them to prove your thesis?

2   Answer the questions that accompany each document. Be brief and concise.

3   Look at the documents again with your thesis in mind and review your brief responses. Determine how to connect the responses to your thesis. Jot down connecting phrases.

4   Outline your essay in a simple, straightforward fashion:

- *Introduction* – based on your thesis

- *Body* – arrangement of ideas incorporating the documents and their meaning, extra information on the subject – besides the documents – that relates to your thesis

- *Conclusion* – that restates your thesis

WORK ON THE THEMATIC ESSAY QUESTIONS

Outline the "task" components on scrap paper, so that what you have to do is clear. Select one of the topic "suggestions" listed at the bottom of the question. They are usually good "triggers" for ideas to incorporate in the body of your essay. (You can use another idea if you wish, but the ones they provide are the most obvious approaches.) On your scrap paper outline, fill in facts connected to the topic suggestion you selected – names, laws, events, documents, and dates. Restate the "Theme" statement as your introduction. Then, respond to each of the points in the task, incorporating factual information as you write.

Words of Wisdom: In writing your essay, avoid using phrases like, "I feel that ..." or "It's my opinion that ..." or "I think that..." Instead, when you state your thesis (which may very well be your <u>best</u> <u>guess</u>), support it with data in the body of your essay. Use "quotes" from documents; include historical dates, places, and people; use specific events to back up your thesis; and, when you write your conclusion, show the reader that you have supported your introductory thesis.

REVIEW YOUR TEST PAPER

Be sure there are no blanks on Part One. If you are not sure, a guess is better than a blank. Check your written responses. Be sure there are no parts missing on any fill-ins. Proofread your essay responses. Check that they make sense. Review your grammar. Finally, make sure that you have included all the parts that are required to be there.

PART ONE
(ANSWER ALL QUESTIONS - 55 PTS.)

1 If it is true that economics is the study of how societies cope with scarcity, then the universal economic problem is the
 1 value of currency
 2 limitation on resources
 3 generation of tax revenue
 4 extent of consumer demand

2 Which combination occurred as humans turned to agriculture during the Neolithic Era?
 1 improved diet, longer life spans, and longer reproductive periods
 2 overpopulation, desertification, and air pollution
 3 economic depression, absolutism, and industrialization
 4 nationalism, assimilation, and socialism

3 Which factor affected life in early societies on the subcontinent of India?
 1 constant flooding of river valleys
 2 a strong centralized government
 3 monsoons influencing the climate
 4 profitable trade with China

4 In comparing the two leading poleis (city-states) of ancient Greece, the culture of Athens revolved about a democratic structure, while that of Sparta was a(n)
 1 socialist state
 2 absolute monarchy
 3 military aristocracy
 4 closed theocracy

5 In the 7th century AD, the T'ang rulers of China consolidated their rule by
 1 making tribute payments to the Shoguns
 2 redistributing land among the peasants
 3 making Buddhism the state religion
 4 abolishing civil service examinations

6 Among the Romans' cultural contributions are that they
 1 unified all of Europe and Asia
 2 relieved citizens of military duty by using mercenaries
 3 persecuted all major religions equally
 4 preserved and adapted Hellenistic culture

Base your answers to questions 7 and 8 on the following passage and on your knowledge of global history.

"Ramses ordered all farmers and artisans to work on the great temple at Karnak for three months, interrupting the normal flow of their commerce."

7 Which interpretation of the quotation would indicate that Egypt had reached the status of a civilization?
 1 the indication that the ruler had absolute control
 2 the idea that farmers and artisans could work together
 3 the concept that a complex job took only three months
 4 the reference to "normal flow of their commerce"

8 In which economic system would Ramses' action be most commonly found?
 1 tradition
 2 market
 3 command
 4 mixed

9 In the Middle Ages in Europe, manorialism referred to the relationship between those who held the land and the
 1 peasants who worked on the land
 2 merchants who supplied goods
 3 clergy who controlled spiritual matters
 4 emperors and kings who protected the land

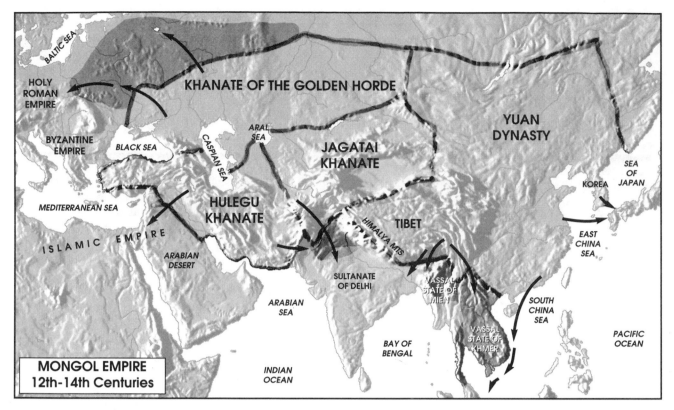

**MONGOL EMPIRE
12th-14th Centuries**

Labels on map: BALTIC SEA, HOLY ROMAN EMPIRE, BYZANTINE EMPIRE, BLACK SEA, KHANATE OF THE GOLDEN HORDE, ARAL SEA, CASPIAN SEA, JAGATAI KHANATE, YUAN DYNASTY, SEA OF JAPAN, KOREA, MEDITERRANEAN SEA, HULEGU KHANATE, ISLAMIC EMPIRE, HIMALYA MTS, TIBET, EAST CHINA SEA, ARABIAN DESERT, SULTANATE OF DELHI, VASSAL STATE OF MIEN, SOUTH CHINA SEA, PACIFIC OCEAN, ARABIAN SEA, VASSAL STATE OF KHMER, BAY OF BENGAL, INDIAN OCEAN

Base your answer to question 10 on the map above and your knowledge of global history.

10 One result of the vast extent of Mongol rule in Eurasia was
1   unity of religion and language throughout the Mongol Khanates
2   increased trade and travel among many cultures
3   driving the Christian Crusaders from Jerusalem
4   the need for Europeans to seek ocean routes to East Asia

11 In the 13th century, Chinese and Portuguese maritime expeditions resulted in
1   reopening the Silk Route
2   commerce along the coasts of Africa
3   the conquest of Islamic civilizations
4   opposing military alliances

12 Which idea was shared by the ancient Maya, Aztec, and Inca civilizations?
1   practicing rituals to please the gods
2   equality among social classes
3   direct democracy
4   monotheism

13 Which is an example of cultural diffusion?
1   Diocletian split the Roman Empire into Eastern and Western Provinces (286 AD).
2   In the 7th century AD, a schism divided followers of Islam into Sunn'ites and Shi'ites.
3   In the 6th century AD, Chinese monks introduced Buddhism to Japan.
4   Justinian appointed of a commission to organize Roman law (528 AD).

14 Which was one of the Byzantine Empire's greatest contributions?
1   preservation of classical Greco-Roman culture
2   creating a rigid class structure that bound peasants to the land
3   raising taxes on merchants' activities
4   overseeing a schism between the Roman and Orthodox branches of Christianity

15 In the Medieval period, Japanese culture and European culture had similar
1   seclusion policies
2   revolutionary movements
3   state-directed education systems
4   feudal power structures

Base your answer to question 16 on the following passage and your knowledge of global history.

> "It is essential, therefore, that a prince who would maintain his position, to have learned how not to be good, and use or not use his goodness as necessity requires."
>
> – Niccolo Machiavelli, *The Prince*, c. 1530

16 To which event would Machiavelli's observations apply?
1   the invention of moveable type
2   authors writing in the vernacular
3   the rise of nation-states in Europe
4   publication of the *Ninety-five Theses*

17 The concept of humanism followed by Renaissance intellectuals reflected a
1   desire to enrich their mother country
2   growing confidence in individual spirit and ability
3   glorifying of the Church's power
4   code of courtesy, honor, and gallantry toward women

18 "[Gold] ... overcomes all impossibilities, for it is the master ... without it all is weak and without movement." The speaker reflects the opinions of
1   Cavaliers
2   Puritans
3   Machiavellians
4   Mercantilists

19 Much of the Russian expansion during the 19th and 20th centuries can be explained in terms of Russian's
1   need for warm water ports
2   lack of natural resources
3   desire to control Scandinavia
4   wish to spread communism

20 Which item describes the difference between absolute monarchy and constitutional monarchy?
1   Absolute monarchs dominate the nobility.
2   Constitutional monarchs abolish citizen rights.
3   Constitutional monarchs' powers are limited by a legislature.
4   Absolute monarchs have sole control of taxation and spending.

Base your answer to question 21 on the map below and your knowledge of global history.

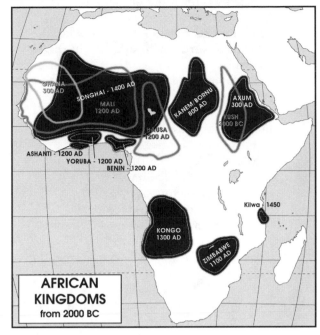

AFRICAN KINGDOMS from 2000 BC

21 One result of the lively trade that developed between 300 – 1500 AD between the African Kingdoms and Mediterranean Arabs was
1   commercial development of the Niger and Congo Rivers
2   development of a universal language in Africa
3   conversion of many Africans to Islam
4   the isolation of Western Europeans from East Asia

22 A common theme anthropologists detect in the art and architecture of Mesoamerican civilizations and early African empires is
1   prominence of religious values and practices
2   peaceful relationships with nearby cultures
3   significance of democratic values
4   isolation and absence of trade relations with neighboring peoples

23 Jethro Tull, Charles Townshend, and Robert Bakewell made inventions that
1   raised cotton textile production
2   improved land transportation
3   changed steel production methods
4   increased agricultural production

24 Which caused an increase in the trans-Atlantic slave trade?
  1 restriction of Western trade in China's ports by later Ming emperors
  2 establishment of cross-Saharan commercial routes by Arab traders
  3 desire to spread Christianity in the New World
  4 development of encomiendas in the Spanish Empire in America

25 Simón Bolívar found it difficult to unite South America because
  1 Protestants and Catholics could not agree on a state religion
  2 the U.S. government opposed independence for South America
  3 troops from France were sent to help Spain keep control
  4 physical barriers made communication difficult

26 The Congress of Vienna and the Paris Peace Conference are similar in that both
  1 based decisions on the principles of nationalism and democracy
  2 were dominated by leaders of powerful nations
  3 resulted in freeing Europe from major wars for close to 100 years
  4 established effective international forces to carry out decisions

27 The patterns of the French, Russian, Chinese, and Iranian Revolutions indicate that
  1 revolutions often end with the emergence of a strong ruler
  2 violence is not necessary for a successful revolution
  3 revolutions lead to the immediate establishment of a free market system
  4 religious ideas provide the basis for a successful revolution

28 "Any society in which the guaranty of rights is not assured or the separation of powers is not determined does not have a constitution." This quotation would most likely be found in
  1 Locke's *Second Treatise of Civil Government*
  2 Rousseau's *Social Contract*
  3 Montesquieu's *The Spirit of Laws*
  4 Voltaire's *Letters on the English*

Base your answer to question 29 on the map below and your knowledge of global history.

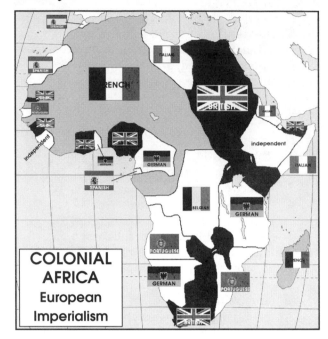

COLONIAL AFRICA
European Imperialism

29 Which conclusion is correct based on the map above and your knowledge of global history?
  1 No African countries were independent prior to World War I.
  2 Belgium controlled the most territory in Africa.
  3 Germany kept Britain from realizing its Cape to Cairo goal.
  4 France controlled most of the sub-Saharan area.

30 "The receptivity of the masses is very limited, their intelligence is small, but their power of forgetting is enormous ... All effective propaganda must be limited to a very few points and must harp on these slogans until the last member of the public understands..." Which statement most accurately reflects the main idea of the quotation?
  1 If you show people you are reasonable, they will believe you.
  2 The purpose of propaganda is to weigh all sides of an issue.
  3 Successful propaganda stresses a few ideas and keeps repeating them.
  4 People easily see through false propaganda claims.

Base your answers to questions 31 and 32 on the cartoon below and your knowledge of global history.

31 The cartoon is primarily concerned with determining responsibility for which situation?
   1 the holocaust in Europe during the 1930s and 1940s
   2 slave labor camps in the Soviet Union during the Stalin Era
   3 use of poison gas during World War I
   4 apartheid practices in the Republic of South Africa

32 The trial symbolized in the cartoon is significant because it was the first time that
   1 the United Nations International Court of Justice worked effectively
   2 individuals were prosecuted for crimes against humanity
   3 war guilt was applied to a whole nation
   4 international law was enforced

33 The *Atlantic Charter* of Roosevelt and Churchill resembled the *14 Points* of Wilson because both documents
   1 outlined details for military preparedness
   2 promised to end threats of communism and fascism
   3 provided for postwar occupation of defeated nations
   4 stressed the need to eliminate the causes of war

34 Karl Marx and Adam Smith disagreed most strongly in their views on the
   1 nature of wealth
   2 role of government in the economy
   3 need to improve workers' standard of living
   4 importance of raw materials for development

35 Under the 5-Year Plans instituted by Stalin in the Soviet Union
   1 decisions regarding quotas were made solely by each factory manager
   2 land was privatized to improve conditions for the small farmer
   3 the greatest successes were achieved in consumer industry production
   4 agricultural production increases were needed to pay for industrial development

36 Which of these statements correctly associates imperialism with World War I?
   1 Imperialist struggles between mother countries and colonies led directly to war.
   2 Most colonies became independent immediately after World War I.
   3 The Paris Peace Conference failed to address the issue of German colonies.
   4 Imperialist rivalries between major powers were a major cause of World War I.

37 Which is the most valid conclusion about European affairs from 1930 through 1939?
   1 The need to solve economic problems encouraged international cooperation.
   2 Disarmament conferences greatly reduced the threat of war.
   3 International organizations were effectively used to avoid war.
   4 Economic problems affected the ability of democracies to resist fascist demands.

38 A likely long-term result of the formation of the European Union is
   1 a large decrease in industrial production within Union borders
   2 an increased standard of living for people in member nations
   3 an increase in the number of currencies in circulation among members
   4 an end to competition among nations in international trade

Base your answer to question 39 on the cartoon above and your knowledge of global history.

39 "For 28 years it had stood as the symbol of the division of Europe and the world... That hideous, 28-mile-long scar through the heart of a once proud European capital..." The quotation refers to the
1 Berlin Wall
2 Great Wall of China
3 Rhine Barrier
4 Danube River

40 The *Treaty of Versailles* (1919) violated the spirit of Wilson's *14 Points* in that it
1 reestablished Poland as an independent country
2 returned Alsace and Lorraine to France
3 created a League of Nations
4 blamed Germany and its allies for causing the war

41 The actions of Marshall Tito of Yugoslavia in 1948, the Hungarian Freedom Fighters in 1956, and the Czech supporters of Alexander Dubcek in 1968 indicated that
1 *glasnost* and *perestroika* had no support among satellite nations
2 opposition to Soviet domination existed in communist countries
3 communists expected to achieve the goals of Karl Marx
4 the economies of Eastern Europe were rapidly improving

42 In 1998, the actions of India and Pakistan warned the global community of the
1 impending disasters of the monsoon season
2 increasing failures of the Green Revolution
3 expanding number of nations with nuclear weapons
4 threatening steps taken by Russia on their borders

43 Since the death of Mao Zedong, the leadership of China has
1 ended human rights abuses
2 encouraged development of some free enterprise
3 abolished all birth control regulations
4 stopped claiming rights to Taiwan

44 Nigeria in the 1960s is similar to Yugoslavia in the 1990s because in both cases
1 the inability of ethnic groups to live together led to civil war
2 serious droughts led to major international relief efforts
3 the Soviet Union intervened to protect a communist government
4 NATO forces were used to stop foreign invaders

45 Supporters of Islamic fundamentalism wish to
1 increase the role in women in the work force
2 separate the powers of church and state
3 modernize the teachings of the *Qur'an*
4 return to traditional Muslim values

Base your answer to question 46 on the graph below and your knowledge of global history.

ON-LINE SALES

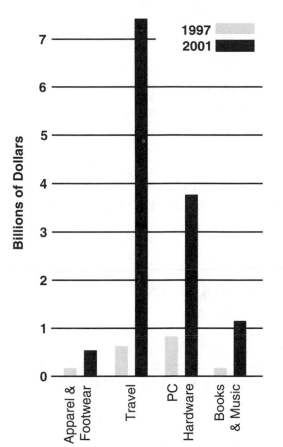

Source: Forrester Research, 1998

46 The graph above indicates that
   1 online sales are expected to decline between 1997 and 2001
   2 in 2001, estimates indicate that Travel will have the largest dollar sales online
   3 in 1997, Travel had the smallest dollar sales online
   4 the number of people shopping online will decline between 1997 and 2001

47 Apartheid in South Africa was based primarily on the concept of
   1 protection of human rights
   2 equality of humankind
   3 division of labor
   4 segregation by race

48 The Soviet invasion of Afghanistan was similar to United States involvement in the Vietnam War because
   1 both wars were unpopular and sparked protests
   2 the superpowers primarily used guerrilla tactics
   3 their victories increased their international prestige
   4 the UN Security Council supported their actions

49 The UN agency with primary responsibility for fighting the international aids epidemic is the
   1 FAO
   2 General Assembly
   3 WHO
   4 Security Council

50 The 1992 Earth Summit and the 1997 Kyoto Protocol are international attempts to
   1 protect the environment
   2 limit proliferation of nuclear weapons
   3 ease Japanese trade restrictions
   4 solve the problem of desertification

Part Two continues on the next page

Part Two:
Thematic Essay
(15 Pts.)

Theme:

Individual Influence on Human Progress

In Less Developed Countries (LDCs), past and present leaders have impacted progress in both negative and positive ways.

Task:

- Select three (3) past and/or present leaders of Less Developed Countries (LDCs).
- Discuss a significant action or program the leader initiated.
- Explain how the action or program affected the country.

Suggestions:

You may use any leader of any LDC whose actions have had significant impact on the progress of the country. Some leaders you might wish to include: Fidel Castro / Cuba; Suharto / Indonesia; Pol Pot / Cambodia, Daniel Moi / Kenya, Nasser / Egypt. You are not limited to these suggestions.

Document-Based Question
(Answer All Parts – 30 Pts.)

Directions:

The following question is based on the accompanying documents (1-7). Some of the documents have been edited for purposes of this exercise. The question is designed to test your ability to work with historical documents. As you analyze the documents, take into account both the source of the document and the author's point of view.

- Write a well-organized essay that includes an introduction with a thesis statement, several paragraphs explaining the thesis, and a conclusion.
- Analyze the documents
- Use all the documents
- Use evidence from the documents to support your thesis position
- Do not simply repeat the contents of the documents
- Include specific related outside information

Historical Context:

The development of modern nationalism is often dated to the French Revolution Era. Since that time, nationalism has had both positive and negative impacts on the development of global history.

Task:

Evaluate the positive and negative impacts of nationalism on global history and support your position with the documents below and your knowledge of global history.

Part A – Short Answer [15 points]

The documents below relate to the impact of nationalism on global history. Examine each document carefully, then answer the question that follows it.

Document 1:

"From the late eighteenth century, governments of western nation states ... consciously began to make good citizens. ... Through the establishment of school systems they fostered national patriotism. Laws, courts, taxes became increasingly national rather than local or provincial. Citizens were thus conditioned to be interested in their nation, their nation-state, their common national needs and aspirations, and they often responded enthusiastically.."

— Boyd Shafer, *Nationalism: Interpretations and Interpreters*

Document 1 Question:

How did nationalism and the development of nation-states help to unify people?

Document 2:

"During my lifetime I have dedicated myself to this struggle of the African people. I have fought against White domination, I have fought against Black domination. I have cherished the ideal of a democratic and free society in which all persons live together in harmony and with equal opportunities. It is an ideal which I hope to live for and to achieve. But if needs be, it is an ideal for which I am prepared to die."

— Nelson Mandela

Document 2 Question:

In what way does Nelson Mandela unite the ideas of nationalism and democracy?

Document 3:

"...The gratitude of every home in our Island, in our Empire, and indeed throughout the world, ... goes out to the British airmen who ... unwearied in their constant challenge and mortal danger, are turning the tide of world war by their prowess and their devotion. Never in the field of human conflict was so much owed by so many to so few."

— Winston Churchill, "So Much Owed by so Many to so Few," (A Tribute to the Royal Air Force during the Battle of Britain), 20 August, 1940

Document 3 Question:

How could Churchill's speech strengthen the national pride and Britons' determination to defend their country against German attack?

Document 4 continues on the next page

Document 4A: *Pre-World War II*

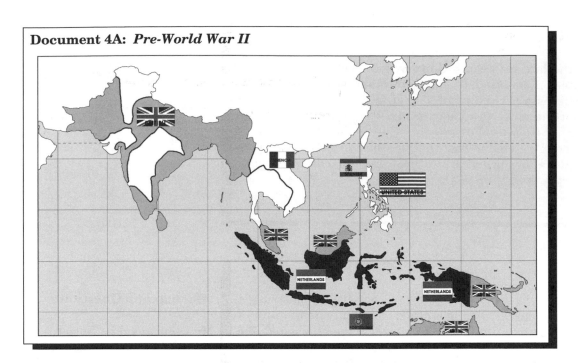

Document 4B: *Post-World War II*

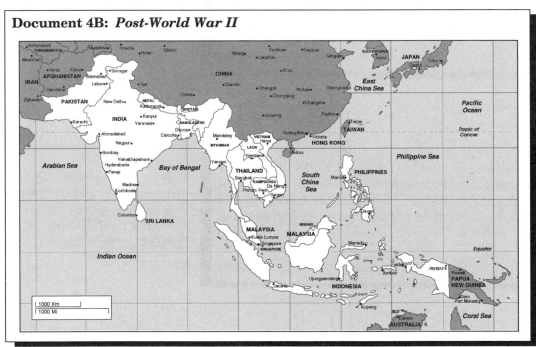

Document 4 Question:

In what way is nationalism, at least in part, responsible for the differences between the two maps of Southeast Asia?

Document 5:

"Palestine is our country,
Our aim is to return,
Death does not frighten us,
Palestine is ours,
We shall never forget her.
Another homeland we shall never accept!
Our Palestine, witness, O God and History
We Promise to shed our blood for you!"

– Oath taken by Palestinian children as their school day begins

Document 5 Question:

What does this document indicate about the impact of nationalism on children?

Document 6:

"Orthodoxy, Autocracy, and Nationality" was the slogan of the czars until the Romanov regime fell in 1917. ... Autocracy was the will of the czar that held the nation together. [Czar Nicholas II] demanded enforcement of an earlier rule that compelled all Great Russians, Byelorussians, and Ukrainians to be members of the Russian Orthodox Church. ... {Nicholas II] used the term [nationalism] to justify the imposition of Russian culture on non-Russian minorities in the Russian Empire:

– Michael and Hyman Kublin, *Russia*

Document 6 Question:

How did nationalism lead to the violation of the rights of minorities in Russia?

Document 7:

THE LOGICAL END RESULT OF EAST EUROPEAN NATIONALISM...

Document 7 Question:

What does this cartoon suggest about the danger of East European Nationalism?

Part B - Essay Response [15 points]

Evaluate the positive and negative impacts of nationalism on the development of global history. Your essay should be well organized with an introductory paragraph that states your thesis as to the impact of nationalism. Develop and support the reasons for your thesis in the next paragraphs and then write a conclusion. In your essay, include specific historical details and refer to the specific documents you analyzed in Part A. You may include additional information from your knowledge of global history.

MAP LIST

WITH TITLE, DESCRIPTION, & PAGE REFERENCE

GLOSSARY OF TERMS AND INDEX

WITH PAGE REFERENCES

Treaty Organization), 241

baht (Thai currency), 232

Bakewell, Robert (1725-1795, agrarian inovator, scientific breading), 162

Balboa (1513, Spanish explorer of Cen. Am., Pacific), 128 [chart]

balance of power (distribution of power; single nation is able to dominate or interfere with others), 151, 221

Baldwin of Flanders (Crusades leader), 82

Balfour Declaration (1917, WWI promise of nationhood to gain Jewish support for British war effort), 189

Balkan Empires 19th C., 160 [map]

Balkan Wars (1912-1913, Ottoman Empire against Serbia, Bulgaria, Montenegro, and Greece), 186

Balkans (mountain range in southern Europe; Yugoslavia and group of small countries often torn by nationalist /ethnic strife), 19, 261 [+map]

Balseros (1990s, Cuban refugees escaping communism by makeshift rafts and boats), 265

Baltic Sea (northeastern Europe), 99 [chart]; 83, [maps 68, 103, 133, 153 187, 210]

Bangladesh (East Pakistan declared indep. country, 1971)

Bantu (South African people), 243

Baptism (Christian rite), 54, 104

Barak, Ehud (1942– , moderate, military hero, Labor Party leader, elected prime minister of Israel 1999), 250

Barbarian Kingdoms 5th-8th Centuries, 75 [map]

barrios [los] (Latin American urban slums), 263

barter / barter economy (direct exchange of goods and services of equal value without use of money), 23, 79, 98

Bartolomé de Las Casas (colonial Lat. Am. priest led protest over the mistreatment of Indians and African slaves), 130

Batista, Fulgencio (1901-1973, Cuban dictator deposed by Castro in 1958), 265

Bataan (1942, with Corregidor, "death march" to Japanese prison camps), 211

Battle of Britain (1940, German Luftwaffe's attempt to destroy British defences failed), 210 [chart]

Battle of Lepanto (1571, Ottoman Empire's westward expansion blocked by Italian states and Spain), 126

Battle of Nations (1814, Leipzig, Napoleon's defeat), 148

Battle of the Bulge (December 1944-January 1945, Allied forces advance into Germany), 210

Battle of the Coral Sea and Midway (1942, naval defeat discouraged Japan from invading Australia, Midway, and Hawaii), 211 [chart]

Battle of Trafalgar (1805, Napoleon defeated by Admiral Nelson), 147 [illus]

Battle of Verdun (WWI: 6-month battle in which each side had 330,000-350,000 casualties), 187

Battle of Waterloo (1815, near Brussels, Belgium, Napoleon defeat by Duke of Wellington), 148

Bavaria (state in southern Germany), 157 [map]

Bay of Bengal (body of water off S.E. coast of India), 10

Bay of Pigs Invasion (1961, from U.S., Cubans try to overthow Castro in Cuba, fail), 265

Bayeux Tapestry (11th C., 230 foot long linen and wool embroidery depicting Norman conquest of England by William the Conqueror), 80

Beer Hall Putsch (1923 uprising began Hitler's rise to fame), 207 [chart]

Belarus (also Byelrus, Byelorussia, or White Russia; independent nation [1991]; formerly one of the 15 republics of the Soviet Union), 258

Belgium, 105, 152

"belt tightening" reforms (changes in national policy usually resulting in cuts in gov't programs), 282

Benedictine Rule (rule of Saint Benedict of Nursia governing monks), 80

Benin (13th C. African kingdom), 122 [+ map], 123 [+ illus]

Begin, Menachem (Israeli Prime Minister, Camp David Accord, 1977), 250 [illustration], 249

Beirut Terrorist Attack (1983, 241 U.S. Marine peacekeepers killed in car bomb attack), 254

Berlin Blockade (1948, Soviets cut off West Berlin), 224

Berlin Airlift (Allied attempt to supply German city cut off by Soviets in 1948), 224

Berlin Conference (1884-1885; African territorial claims partially worked out by Europeans), 171

Berlin Wall (built by Soviets in 1960s to deter escapes from communist zone of the city), 25; (dismantled in pro-democracy incident in 1990), 260

berm (mound or bank of earth placed against the wall of a building to provide protection or insulation), 77

Beveridge Report (British post-WWII plan for expansion of socialist programs), 229

Bhagavad Gita (poem from Mahabharata, most widely studied sacred writings of Hinduism), 31, 55 [chart]

Bill of Rights [British] (limited power of monarchs in England, 1689), 136 [chart]

Bill of Rights [U.S.] (first 10 amendments to *U.S. Constitution*, outlines basic individual rights), 144

Biafra (Republic of; breakaway province of Nigeria, civil war 1967-1970), 242

Bible (sacred scriptures of Judeo-Christian religions), 36, 54 [chart] bicameral (two house legislature), 40, 107

"Big Three" (1919-1920, United States, Britain, France at Paris Peace Conference), 197

bin Laden, Osama (Saudi-born millionaire, sponsor of jihad against the U.S.; financer of multinational network of Islamic fundamentalist terrorist operations; heads the Advice and Reformation Committee in Afghanistan; called "most dangerous man in world" by Clinton), 298

biodiversity (millions of plant / animal species sustaining a harmonious relationship in the environment), 294

Biodiversity Convention, The (1992 U.N. Earth Summit document; protects marine, animal and plants), 294

birth control (see World Issues - Population), 298

birth rates (selected countries, 1993, 1995), 297 [chart]

Bismarck, Otto von ("Iron Chancellor" unified modern German state in late 19th C.), 158 [chart], 171, 185

Black Death (bubonic plague, wiped out nearly one-third of Europe's population in late Middle Ages), 97 [graph]

Black Friday (stock market crash in October 1929), 201

Black Hand, the (c. 1914, Bosnian Serb radical group assassinated Archduke Franz Ferdinand), 186

Black Sea, 68, [maps: 10, 12, 34, 37 44, 48, 51, 56, 57, 66, 68, 72, 92, 96, 103, 125, 133, 153, 160, 184, 187, 188, 210, 224, 248, 258]

Blackshirts (Italian fascist paramilitary group), 200

blitzkrieg ("lightning war" tactic used by Nazis), 209

Bloody Sunday (period of violence during the Russian Revolution of 1905), 191

Boccaccio, Giovanni (Renaissance literature - 100 tradition-al tales of medieval life in vernacular Italian), 101 [chart]

Boer War (1899-1902, war between British and Boers of Transvaal and Orange Free State), 172

Boers (Dutch settlers of South Africa), 171

Bolívar, Simón (Creole leader of So. American independence movement; founder of Gran Colombia), 149, 154

Bolshevik Revolution (November 1917 phase of Russian revolution led by Lenin), 192

Bolsheviks (Russian Marxist political group leadership of Lenin), 191, 192

Bonaparte, Joseph (established as King of Spain by his brother), 148

Bonaparte, Napoleon (see Napoleon), 146, 148

Book of Songs, The (c. 500 BC, ancient oral myths), 32

Book of the Dead (Egyption collection of prayers and advice on achieving the afterlife), 25

Books of Knowledge (holy book from Sanskrit collected by priests and warriors), 30

Borlaug, Norman (1914- , Agronomist, founded Green Revolution, Nobel Peace Prize in 1970), 291

Bosnia (west central Balkan nation broke from Yugoslavia 1991), 261 [+map]

Bourgeois Monarch (France's Louis Philippe, Duke of Orleans in 1830), 152

bourgeoisie (French member of the mercantile class of a medieval European city, see also burgher [German] and burgesses [England]), 97

Boxer Rebellion (1899, attacks on Chinese Christians and foreigners), 173

Boycott (economic sanction: customers refuse to purchase goods or services), 242

Brahman Nerugna (Hindu Deity, the creator), 30, 55 [chart]

Bramaputra (Brahmaputra - major river system in India), 29

Brahmins (Hindu priests), 30, 55 [chart]

Brewers' Guild (famous main door, London, England), 97 [illus]

Brezhnev Doctrine (Soviet pledge to intervene in any nation whose actions endangered communism), 225, 256

Brezhnev, Leonid (1906-1982, Soviet leader 1965-1983), 225, 256

Britain, Battle of (Hitler's relentless air attacks on British), 210

British Commonwealth of Nations (Economic and political association of former British colonies), 244

British East India Co. (trading co. became base for British imperialism in India), 170

British Labor Party (1945 victory led to socialistic programs in Britain), 228

Buddhism (major religion of eastern & central Asia, 6th C. BC), 34, 53, 55 [chart], 56, 90

Buddha (6th C. BC, India, Siddhartha [Siddarta] Gautama, founder of Buddhism), 55 [chart]

Bulgaria, 184 [+ map], 186, 187, 188 [map]

Bulgars (an invading group from Central Asia), 68 [+map]

bulwark (wall or embankment raised as a defensive fortification; a rampart), 77

bureaucracy (a core of administrators, clerks, and officials that carry out the laws, policies, programs of a gov't), 23, 38, 282

burgesses (England - members of the mercantile class of a medieval European city, see also bourgeoisie (French and burgher [German]), 97

burgher (German - member of the mercantile class of a medieval European city, see also bourgeoisie (French and burgesses [England]), 97

bushido (traditional code of the Japanese samurai, stressing honor, self-discipline, bravery, and simple living), 91

Buttuta, Ibn (visitor to Yuan Dynasty of Kublai Khan), 94

Byzantine Emperor Michael III (c. 832), 68

Byzantine Eastern Roman Empire and Barbarian Invasions (5th-12th Centuries), 84 [map]

Byzantine Empire (East. Roman Empire 4th-15th C. AD), 49, 65, and Barbarian Invasions 5th-12th Centuries 66 [map]

Byzantium (see also Megara, provincial trading town on Bosporus Strait), 39, 65

Cabinet of Ministers (gov't advisors / heads of depts.)

Cabot, John (1497, explorer, English claims to Canada), 128 [map + chart]

Caesar Augustus (c. 27 BC, first Roman Emperor), 47

Caesar, Julius (d. 44 BC, military dictator of Rome), 47

caliph (also calif or khalifa; title for successor to Muhammad as leader of Islam), 54 [chart], 57, 70, 125

calligraphy (artful writing), 32

Caligula (37-41 AD, Roman emperor), 47

Calvin, John (1509-1531, Swiss theologian, Eur. Protestant Reformation, *Institutes of the Christian Religion*), 54 [chart], 104

Cambodia (S.E. Asia mainland nation), 246

Camp David Accords (1979 Middle East peace agreements), 249

Campesinos (paid laborers, tenant farmers, or peasants of Lat. America), 263

Canaan (eastern Mediterranean shore settled by founders of ancient civilization of the Hebrews), 36

Cape Colony (Dutch colony of South Africa, 1652-1806), 170

Cape to Cairo (British desire for colonization of Africa), 171

Cape-to-Cairo Railroad (Cecil Rhodes project for linking British territories in E. Africa), 171 [Close Look]

Cape Town (British South Africa aquisition,1815), 171

capital (sums of money), 99

capitalism (economic system in which the means of production and distribution are privately or corporately owned), 99, 127, 165, 281, 283

capitalist (member of economic group that supports a "free marketplace"), 165, 228, 283

capitulations (terms of surrender giving special privileges to the conquerer), 159

caravel (Spanish ship), 127 [illus]

Cardinal Armand Richelieu (1585-1642, chief minister to, and given full authority by, Louis XIII), 107

Cardinal Mazarin (chief minister who dominated the gov't during reign of Louis XIV), 132

Caribbean, 149

Carolingian Dynasty (732 AD, founded by Charles Martel), 76

Carranza, Venustiano (1859-1920, Mexican statesman, elected president 1917), 156

carte blanche (unqualified support), 187

Cartel (combination of economic units to limit competition), 283

Carter, Jimmy (U.S. Pres.; 1970s: Panama Canal and Mid-East Camp David peace agreements, Haiti crisis negotiator), 249

Carthage/Carthaginian, 34, 46

Cartier, Jaques (1534-1535 explorer, made France's claims to St. Lawrence in Canada), 128 [chart]

cartographers (mapmakers), 11

Cartwright, Edmund, (1743-1823, invented the power loom), 162 [chart]

cash crop (agricultural crop, such as tobacco, grown for direct sale), 282

caste system, 48, 240 [India]

castes (rigid Hindu system of hereditary social groupings dictating one's rank and occupation), 30

Castro, Fidel (1926- , Cuban communist leader), 265

censorship (examination of books, films, or other material and removal or suppression of what is considered morally, politically, or otherwise objectionable), 189

Central Treaty Organization (1955-1979, Baghdad Pact, CENTO), 241

centralized command systems (such as in the Soviet Union in the 1930s and China in the 1950s), 282

centralized decision-making, 15, 282 [chart]

centuries (forces of 100 men), 46

Cervantes, Miguel de (Spanish Renaissance writer: *Don Quixote*), 101 [chart], 132

chaebol (Asian large corporate conglomerates with holding

in Latin American affairs), 265

Columbus, Christopher (1451-1506, explorer in pay of Spanish Crown credited with beginning the Age of Colonization in Latin America), 127, 128 [chart]

COMECON (Soviet-sponsored common market for Eastern European nations), 223

command economic system (economic decisions controlled by gov't, also authoritarian socialism), 13, 15 [chart], 23, 188, 228, 229, 281, 282

command systems: Soviet model (gov't quotas and 5-year plans, no private ownership), 229

Commercial Revival (economic movement which opened Europe to world wide trade enterprises [11th-18th C.]), 98

Common Market (Western European trade assoc.; see European Union, formerly European Community), 221

commonweal (ideal Christian community as described by St. Augustine, 5th C. theologian), 79

Commonwealth of Independent States (CIS; loose military and economic confederation of former Soviet republics formed after U.S.S.R. collapsed in 1991), 258

Commonwealth of Nations (see British Commonwealth of Nations), 244

communism: (system of gov't and economics in which the state plans and controls the economy and a single, often authoritarian party holds power, claiming to make progress toward a higher social order in which all goods are equally shared by the people; Marxist-Leninist version of Communist doctrine that advocates the overthrow of capitalism by the revolution of the proletariat), 193, 234

Communist Manifesto (1848, Marx and Engels' work: socialist doctrine), 165

Communist Party (China - CCP founded in 1921), 234

Communist Party (Russia), 193

computers (as key to technological and economic advancement), 287, 288 [+photo]

computer hackers (individuals who invade and violate privacy and destroy records on the Internet; "technology terrorists"), 288

concentration camps (reference the Jews WWII, where prisoners of war, enemy aliens, and political prisoners are detained and confined, typically under harsh conditions), 208

Concordat of 1801 (established friendly relations with the Catholic Church on Napoleon's terms), 146

Concordat of Worms (compromise by the Holy Roman Emperor with agreement to the selection of bishops and abbots by the clergy), 80

confederation (group of confederates, especially of states or nations, united for a common purpose), 16

Confucianism (basic social philosophy of China from ancient), 32, 36, 55 [chart]

Confucius (c. 551-479 BC, also Kongzi, ancient China teacher/political advisor), 54 [chart]

Congo (river basin of cent. Africa; also Zaire Basin, former Belgian colony; called Zaire in 1971, called Republic of Congo in 1997), 226, 270

Congo Free State (1885, African colony given to Leopold II of Belgium), 171

Congress Party (India's Hindu-dominated nationalist movement & most powerful political faction), 203-204

Congress of the People's Deputies (Soviet Union's national legislative body under Gorbachev; chose President and Supreme Soviet; dissolved nation in 1991), 195

Congress of Vienna (1814-1815, organized the restoration of political power in Europe after the defeat of Napoleon), 148, 150, 169

conquistadores (Spanish conquerors of Latin American Indian lands, set up colonial rule), 119 [illus]

contraception (intentional prevention of conception or impregnation through the use of various devices, agents, drugs, sexual practices, or surgical procedures), 298

Corcyra (see Corinth), 39 [chart]

conscription (draft, compulsory enrollment in the armed forces), 186

consent of the governed (power is granted by the group being ruled), 16

Conservatism (political philosophy or attitude emphasizing respect for traditional institutions, distrust of gov't activism, and opposition to sudden change in the established order), 164 [chart]

Conservative Party (Great Britain), 229

Constantine the Great (r. 306-337 AD, Roman emperor; issued the Edict of Milan in 313 AD), 48, 49

Constantinople (Turkey's capital; earlier called Byzantium, central city of Eastern Roman Empire; center of Ottoman Empire), 49, 65

constitution (system of fundamental laws and principles that prescribes the nature, functions, and limits of a gov't or another institution, Cromwell's the Instrument of Gov't), 135

constitutional law (body of rules by which the powers of gov't are exercised), 16

constitutional monarchy (Britain's monarchy limited by Parliamentary rule), 136

Consulate (1799-1804, an oligarchy of three rulers dominated by Bonaparte), 146

containment (U.S. policy attemped to limit the spread of communism during the Cold War), 223

continents (principal land masses of the Earth, usually regarded as including Africa, Antarctica, Asia, Australia, Europe, North America, and South America), 10

Continental System (Napoleonic trade regulations of 1806; hurt British trade and gave France economic supremacy on European Continent), 147

continuum (continuous extent, succession, or whole, no part of which can be distinguished from neighboring parts except by arbitrary division), 15

Contras (rebel group seeking to overthrow communist rule in Nicaragua), 266

Convention of International Trade in Endangered Species (1973, prohibited trade in plants or animals in danger of becoming extinct), 295

Copernicus, Nicolaus (1473-1543, Polish astronomer), 141

cordillera (extensive chain of mountains or mountain ranges, Andes of South America), 115

Corinth (Greek mother city-state; colony Epidamnus, Corcyra, Syracuse), 39 [chart]

Corn Laws (a series of British laws in force before 1846 regulating the grain trade and restricting imports of grain), 166

Corpus Juris Civilis (Justinian Code), 69

Corregidor (1942, with Bataan, "death march" to Japanese prison camps), 211

Cortes, Hernán (1485-1547, Spanish explorer, overthrew Aztec rule in Mexico and established New Spain), 119

cosmopolitan (wordly sophistication, awareness of many spheres of interest), 99

Cossack (member of a people of southern European Russia, noted as cavalrymen during czarist times), 153

Cottage industries (Gandhi's 1930s campaign to make Indians independent of British goods), 204

Council of 400 (594 BC, aristocrats in Solon's bicameral legislature), 40

Council of 500 (510 BC, bureaucracy in Cleisthenes'

expanded democracy), 40

council of ministers (see cabinet; executive arm of parliamentary gov't; can also mean a junta or oligarchy in non-democratic forms)

Council of Mutual Economic Assistance (see COMECON)

Council of Trent (16th C. reorganization of the Catholic Church in response to the Protestant Reformation), 104

Count de Saint Simon (1760-1825, Claude Henri de Rouvroy - favored planned societies with public ownership of the means of production), 164

Counter Reformation (offensive drive by Roman Catholic Church in the 15th C. against the Protestant Reformation), 104

coup d'état (sudden overthrow of a gov't by a usually small group of persons in or previously in positions of authority), 141

craftsmen (highly skilled workers such as blacksmiths, weavers, armorers), 97

Crassus, Marcus (c. 70 BC, Roman consul, one of triumvirate), 47

Creoles (see also criollos, Spanish subjects born in the American colonies), 149

Crete (see Knossos), 37

Crimean War (1854-56 cost Russia much Balkan territory), 153, 159

criminal law (imposes penalties for anti-social behavior), 17

criollos (American-born sons of Spanish nobles [peninsulares]), 130, 154

Croatia (N.W. Balkan nation broke from Yugoslavia 1991), 261 [+map]

Cro-Magnon (c. 26,000 BC, earliest modern people to inhabit Europe), 21

Crompton, Samuel (1753-1827, invented the spinning mule), 162 [chart]

Cromwell, Oliver (British Puritan dictator, declared Lord Protector 1653), 135 [illus]

crop rotation (research by Charles "Turnip" Townshend), 162 [chart], 162 [chart]

Crusades (attempts by various Medieval Christian nobles to win back Jerusalem and its surrounding regions from Muslims), 19

Crusades: Causes and Results, The; 83 [chart]

Crusade of the Teutonic Knights; 1198-1411 AD; 82 [illus]

Cuauhtemoc (Aztec ruler or tlatoani), 119

Cuba, 256, 265

Cuban advisors in Africa (aid for communist insurgents), 265

Cuban Missile Crisis (1962, Cold War crisis), 256, 265

Culture (a people's whole way of living: language, traditions, customs, institutions, religions, and folkways), 18-19

cultural diffusion (cultural patterns spreading from one people to another), 18, 22

Cultural Revolution (internal power struggle in Maoist China in the mid-1960s), 235

cuneiform (ancient Sumerian system of writing using wedge-style ideographs on wet clay tablets), 27

Curie, Marie (1867-1934, French physicist - proved [with Pierre] that atoms could be split), 183

Curie, Pierre (1859-1906, French physicist -proved [with Marie] that atoms could be split), 183

Cynics (Diogenes, Antisthenes-philosophical sect believed happiness is achieved by cultivating virtue and self-control), 43

Cyrene (see Thera), 39 [chart]

Cyril (laid basis for Slavic alphabet-cyrillic), 68

cyrillic alphabet (modified form of the Greek alphabet basis for Russian and some Slavic languages), 68

Cyrus the Great (c. 539 BC, Persian king conquered Lydia near Ionian coast), 27, 34, 37, 40

Czar (see "tsar")

Czechoslovakia, 260

Czech Republic (western half of former Czechoslovakia, independent 1992), 260

D-Day (6 June 1944, Invasion of Normandy began Allied counter-offensive against Germany in WWII), 210

Dachau (German concentration camp), 208

DaGama, Vasco (Portuguese explorer reached India by rounding the Cape of Good Hope in 1497), 96, 128 [chart], 170

Dali, Salvador (surrealism artist - *The Persistence of Memory* about WWI), 190

da Gama, Vasco (15th C. Portuguese explorer; reached India via Cape Horn in Africa in 1498), 96, 128 [map + chart]

Daimler, Gottlieb (1834-1900, German Inventor - gasoline engines), 163

daimyo also daimio ("Great Lords" of Japan's feudal era, 1300-1600), 128

Damacus Gate (Jerusalem c. 1200; A major objective of the Crusaders); 82 [illus]

Danelaw (large parts of eastern & northern England controled by Danish Vikings), 77

Dante Alighieri (Italian Renaissance writer: *Divine Comedy*), 101 [chart]

Daode Jing (sacred text of Daoism), 55 [chart]

Daoism (Chinese philosophy), 55 [chart]

Darius I (522-480 BC, Persian king), 27, 34, 40

Dark Ages (Early European Medieval period; 500 to 1000 AD), 75

"Dark Continent" (name popular in 19th C. Europe for Africa because its vast interior sections were unknown to European colonial powers)

Das Kapital (1867, Marx's elaboration of communist philosophy), 165

da Vinci, Leonardo (central figure of Italian Renaissance art, *Mona Lisa, Last Supper*), 101 [+chart]

David (c.1000 BC, united tribes of Israelites into a Kingdom of Israel), 36, 54 [chart]

Dawes Plan (1923, U.S. lowered WWI reparation payments and provided loans to Germany), 200

Dead Sea (salt lake, about 397 m [1,300 ft] below sea level, between Israel and Jordan), 37

"Decade for Women" (U.N. announcement in 1975 to turn attention to women's issues worldwide), 300

Deccan Plateau (occupies most of the peninsula area of India and holds much mineral wealth), 29 [map]

Decembrist Revololution (a palace coup d'état against the Tsar in 1825), 152

decison-making (making of decisions, especially by persons in positions of authority or power), 282

Declaration of Independence (U.S. revolutionary document by Thomas Jefferson reflected ideas of John Locke), 144

Declaration of Rights of Man and of the Citizen (1789 Thomas Paine's French Revolution document justified overthrow of monarchy with Enlightenment ideas), 144

Declaration of Palestinian Self-Rule (1993-1995 between Prime Ministers Begin and Rabin and Palestinian leader Yasir Araafat), 249

deficit spending (spending of public funds obtained by borrowing rather than by taxation), 201

Deforestation (over-cutting of timber resources), 294

de Klerk, F.W. (Prime Minister of Republic of South Africa, 1989-1994), 244

Delian League (naval alliance with Athens as central polis), 41

Delphi (sacred city with temple of the god Apollo), 38

demand (amount of a resource or service people are ready and willing to consume), 13, 99

demesne (manorial land retained for the private use of a feudal lord), 77

democracy (power in the hands of many; gov't by the people, exercised either directly or through elected representatives), 16, 41

Democratic socialism (mixed economic systems in European nations with extensive welfare systems), 228

Democritus (460-370 BC, Greek philosopher/thinker who expounded elementary ideas about the basic composition of matter, the atom), 42

demographics, changes in (characteristics of human populations and population segments, especially when used to identify consumer markets), 298

demotic (common language), 25

Deng Xiaoping, (1904-1997, reformist Chinese leader after Mao), 236

Deng Xiaoping's Modernization Program (1976 plan), 236 [chart]

Dengue fever (sporadically infectious disease of warmer climates, lthough painful, dengue fever usually ends in complete recovery within a few week, fever has caused numerous deaths in children in recent years), 292

der Fuher (German, "for the leader," Hitler), 206

Descartes, Rene (French philosopher-mathematician, 1596-1650, held the belief that science could have practical application), 141 [chart], 142

desert (Koppen-type Bw), 70

desertification (transformation of arable or habitable land to desert, as by a change in climate or destructive land use), 120, 295

Desert Dwellers, 11

Desert Shield / Desert Storm, Operation (see Persian Gulf conflict), 255

deportation (non-voluntary expulsion of an undesirable illegal immigrant or individual from a country), 287

desaparecidos ("disappeared ones"), 264

détente (lessened diplomatic tension), 256

developing economies (LDCs making improvements in standard of living, industrialization, and per capita income), 282

Development of Islamic Law and Its Impact, 71 [chart]

devshirme system (under this system, Christians who converted to Islam were offered positions in the military and bureaucracy), 126

dharma (sacred duty one owes to family and caste), 30, 50, 55 [chart]

Dias, Bartolomeu (Portuguese explorer reached Africa's Cape of Good Hope in later 1480s), 96, 128 [chart]

Diaspora (c. 70 AD, dispersion of the Jews from Palestine into world from the sixth C. BC,), 37

Diaz, Porfirio (Mexico dictator, 1876-1911), 155

Dictatorship of the Proletariat (Marxist dogma that indicates working classes will eventually rule society for the benefit of all), 165

Dien Bien Phu (final defeat of French colonialism in Vietnam, 1954), 245

diet (assembly, two-house legislature of Japan), 168, 223

Diesel, Rudolf (1858-1913, German inventor - diesel engine), 163

Diocletian (r. 284-305 AD, Roman emperor who divided Roman Empire into eastern & western regions), 48

Dionysus (god of fertility, ritual dance, mysticism; supposedly invented wine making & considered patron of poetry, song, & drama), 38 [chart]

Directory (oligarchy), 146

"Dirty War" (Argentina 1979, military resorted to kidnapping, torture, and murder of dissenters), 264

Disraeli (1804-1881, British Prime Minister), 198

Dissenters see dissidents)

Dissidents (those who disagree with institutional authority), 256

divan (council of religious adviisors), 125

diversify (to distribute or investment among different companies or securities in order to limit losses in the event of a fall in a particular market or industry), 282

Divesting (termination of investments in South Africa enterprises as an economic protest against apartheid policy), 244

"divide and rule" (British policy to damage Hindu-Muslim relations), 239

divine right (absolute power coming from God with no responsibility to those ruled), 16, 24, 106, 130

Dneiper River (river system in western Russia and Ukraine), 68

dogma (doctrine relating to matters such as morality and faith, set forth in an authoritative manner by a church), 67

Dome of the Rock Mosque (Islamic shrine in Jerusalem), 72 [photo]

domestic system (commercial production done in homes and coordinated by an entrepreneur), 100, 163

"Domino Theory" (communist victory in one small, weak state would lead to other nations falling), 245

Dorians (1100 BC, northern Greek warlike people), 38

downsizing (gov't - cutting of programs for economic consideration; corporation that downsized its personnel in response to a poor economy), 222

Draco (621 BC, Athens dictator, encoded laws), 40

draft (conscription, compulsory enrollment in the armed forces), 186

Drake, Sir Francis (1541-1596, Elizabeth I's sea dog), 108

Drakensberg Mountains (Southern Africa), 120

drawbridge (used in castles, bridge that can be raised or drawn aside either to prevent access), 77

drug cartels (groups of individuals organized for purpose of growing, sale, and distribution of illegal substances often violent, such as the Medellin Cartel of Colombia), 283

Drug Enforcement Administration (U.S. DEA), 284

Du Fu (c. 750, T'ang poet), 64

Dubcek, Alexander (1921-1992, leader of the Communist Party of Czechoslovakia, c. 1968), 225

duhkha (Buddhism belief of Four Noble Truths), 55 [chart]

Duke of Wellington (1769-1852, defeated Napoleon at Battle of Waterloo, 1815), 148 [illus]

Duma (national legislative body under tsars in 19th and 20th C.), 191

Dunant, Jean Henri (1828-1910, founded the Red Cross, cowinner of the first Nobel Peace Prize in 1901), 7

Dutch (United Provinces of the Netherlands), 129

dynasties (family of hereditary rulers), 24

Earth Summit (1992 U.N. sponsored global meeting on environmental issues), 294

East Europe: Physical Features, 68 [map]

Easter Rebellion (1916 uprising against British, leading to independence for Ireland), 268

Eastern and Russian Orthodox (Catholic) Church, 67 [+photo]

Eastern Europe: physical features, 68 [map]; satellites in the Cold War, 223-225

Eastern Hemisphere (continents of Africa, Europe, Asia, and Australia), 10-11 [map]

Eastern Mediterranean Civilizations; 1500-500 BC, 37 [map]

Ebert, Friedrich Ebert (1871-1925, first president of the Weimar Republic established after WWI), 200, 201

ebola (ebola virus causes ebola fever, highly virulent, 90% death rate, discovered in 1976 in the Ebola River, area in northern Zaire), 292

economic decision-making Continuum, 15 [chart]

economic nationalism (stimulation of internal development using gov't policies to eliminate outside competition), 282

ecomomics, 13, 281

Edict of Milan (granted freedom of worship to all Christians in Roman Empire, 313 AD), 65

Edict of Nantes (1598, Henry IV granted religious tolerance to communities where Protestants were in majority), 105, 107

Edo (center of Japan's Tokugawa gov't, later called Tokyo), 91

education (program of instruction to reduce illiteracy from primary through higher-learning), 289

Education, Global (illiteracy rates v. schooling), 290 [chart]

Edward I (during his reign, Model Parliament established the concept of the power of the purse in 1295), 107

Egypt (called "Gift of the Nile"), 226

Egyptians (ancients), 34

Eight Crusades, The; "Holy Christian Wars"; 11th-13th Centuries, 82 [map]

Eightfold Path (Buddhism's basic concepts), 54 [chart]

Einstein, Albert (1879-1955, German, expressed Curies' concept - formula, E=MC^2 - *Theory of Relativity*), 183

El Greco (1541-1614, Spanish painter), 132

Elders, Council of (formed the judiciary and counseled the Assembly and the Ephors-Sparta), 40

Elea (see Miletus), 39 [chart]

Elizabeth I (r. 1558-1603, absolute monarch of England, established the nation as a power in Europe), 107, 108 [illus]

Elliot, T.S. (wrote *The Hollow Men* about WWI experiences), 189

Emancipation Edict (1861, Tsar Alexander II abolished Russian serfdom), 153

Embargo (refusal to sell or trade), 265 [Cuban]

emirs (Muslim rulers), 73

émirgré (one who has left a native country, especially for political reasons), 146

Emmanuel III, King Victor (1922, named Mussolini premier of Italy), 200

Emperor Justinian (r. 527-565 rebuilt Constantinople after great fire of 532), 66, 69

Emperor Michael III (Byzantine c. 832), 68

enclaves (small armed settlements), 76

Enclosure Acts (British farm lands fenced for pasture purposes), 161

encomiendas (feida;-type land grants), 129, 130

endangered species (plant or animal threatened with extinction), 295 [+close look]

endostatin (drugs with the potential of blocking the growth of caner in blood vessels), 292

England (see Great Britain, or United Kingdom)

Engels, Frederick (collaborator with Karl Marx on *Communist Manifesto*, 1848), 165

enlightened despot (tyrant who uses autocratic power for the benefit of the people), 143

enlightenment (also called Age of Reason or the Intellectual Revolution, intellectual movement in 17th-18th C. Europe), 142 [chart], 143 [chart], 144

entrepreneurial system (individuals organize, operate, and assume the risk from business ventures), 163

Environment (the habitat or setting in which people live), 293

Environmental concerns (problems over deterioration of the natural ecology), 293

Epicureans (Epicurus-philosophical sect believed knowledge is based on sense perception, 43

Epidamnus (see Corinth), 39 [chart]

Ephors, Council of 5 (veto power over actions of the Spartan Assembly), 16, 40

Erasmus, Desiderius (Netherlands Renaissance writer, *In Praise of Folly*), 101 [chart]

Erechtheum, Porch of (columns on the Athens' Acropolis near the Parthenon), 42 [photo]

Escobar, Pablo (head of Colombian Medellin Cartel until 1993), 283

Essay on the Principles of Population, (1798, Malthus, Thomas - argues that population tends to increase faster than food supply, with inevitably disastrous results, unless the increase in population is checked by moral restraints or by war, famine, and disease), 166

estates (social position or rank, especially of high order: 1st estate - major social class, such as the nobility, the commons, or the clergy, formerly possing distinct political rights), 144

Estates General (French Parliament, or national assembly, under Bourbon monarchs), 107. 145

Ethiopia, 171

ethnic (people sharing a common and distinctive racial, national, religious, linguistic, or cultural heritage), 184, 261, 286

ethnic cleansing (policy in war-torn Yugoslavia between Christians and Muslims - attempt to eliminate a racial, religious, tribal or cultural group), 261

ethnocentrism (belief in the superiority of one's own ethnic group and an over-riding concern with race), 124

Euclid (c. 300 BC, most famous mathematician of all time despite the fact that little is known of his life, save that he taught at Alexandria, Egypt), 45

Euphrates River, 27 [+ map]

Eurasia (includes continents of Europe and Asia), 51

Euratom (European Atomic Energy Community; post-WWII consortium of Western European nations to deal with nuclear power management), 221

Euripides (Greek dramatist), 43 [chart]

euro (common currency of the European Union to be put into circulation 1999), 221

Europe (1914-1918, during WWI - major battles and offensives), 187 [map]

Europe(1918-1922, post-WWI - showing new countries and borders), 188 [map]

Europe (Climatic Features), 75 [map]

Europe (Physical Features), 75 [map]

Europe (WWI), 184 [map]

European Age of Exploration and Discovery (c. 15th C.), 169

European Coal and Steel Community (1951 co-op plan [R. Schuman, Fr.] by 5 W. European nations; forerunner of "Common Market"/European Union), 221

European Community (EC; see renamed European Union [1994]; originally "Common Market"), 221

European imperialism (post-WWII), 238

European Trade (13th C.), 96 [map]

European Union (originally the "Common Market," then the European Community; ongoing attempt to unify European nations' trade and commerce), 17

excommunication (depriving of the right of church membership by ecclesiastical authority), 103, 221

exodus (1200 BC, Hebrews, led by Moses leave Egypt and move into the Sinai Desert), 36

Expansion In Medieval Europe (9th-13th C), 76 [map]

Expansion of Islamic Empire (622-c. 740), 72 [map]

Explorers (Age of Discovery 15th-16th C.), 127-128 [+chart, map]

Extraterritoriality (foreigners not subject to a host country's laws), 168

extremists (right wing or leftist groups who advocate or resorts to measures beyond the norm, especially in politics, including violent retaliation), 286

Exxon Valdez (March 1989, ran aground in Prince William Sound, Alaska, spilling oil, endangering plant and animal life, costing millions of dollars to clean-up), 293

Factory Act (1833, protection for British workers), 165

factory system (coordinates a large number of laborers and power-driven machines in a centralized place), 163

Falklands/Malvinas Islands War (Argentina v. Britain, Britain won with U.S. spy satellite help), 264

fallow (plowed but left unseeded during a growing season), 78

Family Responsibility System (see Responsibility System)

famine (drastic, wide-reaching food shortage resulting in severe hunger and starvation), 282

FAO (Food and Agricultural Organization, U.N. agency fighting hunger), 227, 271, 286

Farouk, King (Egypt, overthrown in 1958 by Nasser), 50

fascism (system of gov't marked by centralization of authority under a dictator, stringent socioeconomic controls, suppression of the opposition through terror and censorship, and typically a policy of belligerent nationalism and racism), 199, 200

Fascism (rise of in Europe), 189

Fashoda Crisis (1898, dispute between Russia and Britian over spheres of influence in Iran), 174, 186

fealty (allegiance, loyalty, faithfulness to obligations, duties), 78

Federal Republic of Germany (official name for West Germany before reunification in 1989; official name of unified Germany, 1990), 224, 260

federal system (centralized system of gov't), 16

Ferdinand, Archduke Franz (d. 28 June 1914, with wife, Sophie, assassinated in Sarajevo by the Serbian rebel roup, "the Black Hand" - blamed for immediate "cause" of WWI), 187

Ferdinand VII of Aragon (1784-1833, ruled Spain with Isabellaof Castile), 127

Fertile Crescent (Middle East region between the Tigris and Euphrates Rivers considered to be the Cradle of Civilization), 9, 27, 36

fertility rates (birthrate of a population), 286

feud also called fief (self-sufficient feudal manor granted by a lord to a vassal on condition of homage & service), 78

feudalism (landholding-based lord / vassal economic-political-social system), 32, 78

Fichte, Johann Gottlieb (1762-1814, early theorist on German nationalism), 158

fief also called feud (self-sufficient feudal manor granted by a lord to a vassal on condition of homage & service), 78

"Final Solution" (1941 Hitler plan for the systematic elimination of the Jewish people), 208

finance (monetary resources; funds, especially those of a gov't or corporate body), 16

fiqh (human effort to translate the will of God into specific rules or Islamic jurisprudence), 71

First-Consul-for-Life (Napoleon Bonaparte staged a plebiscite to establish this title), 146

First Estate (French Roman Catholic Church, high gov't officials), 145

First Punic War (264-241 BC), 46

Five Pillars (basic beliefs and duties of Muslim faith), 54

[chart]

Five Power Naval Armaments Treaty (1922, Britain, France, U.S. Japan, Italy agreement to control production of war ships), 203

Five Year Plans (gov't command in socialist economies) Soviet Union, 193, 228; China, 235; Vietnam, 246

Florence, Italy (Center of Renaissance Art), 102 [illus]

flying shuttle (invented by John Kay), 162 [chart]

For Whom the Bell Tolls (Ernest Hemingways' work about the Spanish Civil War, 212

"Four Little Dragons of the Pacific Rim" (also called the "Asian Tigers" nickname for powerful economies of Singapore, Hong Kong, Taiwan, and South Korea), 231

"Four Modernizations" (revision of China's economic priorities under Deng Xiaoping), 236

Four Noble Truths (basic beliefs of Buddhism), 55 [chart]

Four Power Treaty (1921, Britain, France, U.S., Japan agreement to respect possession in E. Asia), 203

Fourier, Charles (1772-1837, favored ideal communities where all shared in the work and received the benefits of joint labor according to need), 164

Fourteen Points, The (WWI peace plan for Europe drawn up by U.S. President Wilson, 1918), 196, 197 [chart]

France: 76 [map], 82, 102,132-133, 144-148, 149, 151, 152, 157, 158, 159, 161, 162, 163, 170, 172, 185, 186, 197, 198, 200, 202, 203, 210, 221, 223, 224, 242, 244, 245, 249

Franchise (right to vote; see Chartist Movement), 166

Franco-Prussian War (1871; Bismarck used conflict enhance prestige of new German state), 158 [illus], 185

Frankish Empire (referred to by early historians as "The Dark Ages," 75 [map]

Franklin, Benjamin (1706-1790, American revolutionary leader, *Albany Plan of Union*, 1754), 144

Franks (5th C. AD, people of the central and western sections of Gaul [France]), 75

Franz Ferdinand, Archduke (heir to Austrian throne; 1914 assassination fomented WWI), 187

Frederick II (German king [1212-1220], king of Sicily [1197-1250], and Holy Roman emperor (1220-1250, Crusades leader), 82

Frederick the Great of Prussia (1740-1786, enlightened despot), 143

free market systems (economy that operates according to the relationship of supply and demand), 281

free market initiatives (gov't offer of individual capitalism inorder to improve the overall national economy, such as in Hong Kong, Singapore, South Korea, Taiwan, Brazil, Mexico), 283

French Community; (also French Union; retained ties with former colonies; similar to British Commonwealth)

French Empire (1904-1814, ruled by Napoleon Bonapart as emperor by plebiscite), 146

French Revolution (rebellion against Bourbon monarchy c. 1789 transformed the country into a republic), 144

frescoes (murals done in wet plaster), 69

Freud, Sigmund (1856-1939, founded the field of psychoanalysis), 183

Fronde, The (1648-1653, series of major revolts by merchants, peasants, and nobles in the reign of Louis IV), 132

FSLN (Sandinistas national liberation front - Nicaraguan communists), 266

Fuehrer, der (German title for leader used by Hitler), 206

Fujiwara family (ruled Japan from the 10th-12th C.), 90

Fulani (Muslim people in north of Nigeria), 242

Funan Kingdom (kingdom was established on the lower Mekong River), 63

functional literacy (meeting the reading and writing

demands and standards of a complex society), 290

Gaius Graccus (Roman tribune), 46

Gaius Marius (r. 104-100 BC, Roman consul), 46

Galileo Galilei (1632, used telescope to prove planets revolved around sun), 141 [chart]

Gandhi, Indira (Indian Prime Minister: 1966-1984), 198, 241

Gandhi, Mohandas K. (1869-1948, non-violent Indian independence movement leader, assassinated 1948), 204, 240

Gandhi, Rajiv (Indian Prime Minister 1984-1991), 241

Gang of Four (power struggle in China after Mao's death), 236

Ganges (major river system in India), 29, 34, 50

Gapon, Father (Russian Orthodox priest staged a peaceful march fomenting Bloody Sunday massacre in 1905), 191

Garibaldi, Guiseppe (1807-1882, Unification leader provided military leadership, Red Shirt campaigns), 159 [chart]

GATT (General Agreement on Trade and Tariffs– U.N.-sponsored multilateral treaty on global commerce; 1 January 1995: World Trade Organization [WTO] moderates trade disputes among its 116 member states.)

Gautama, Siddhartha [Siddarta] (6th C. BC, founder of Buddhist faith), 55

Gaza Strip (Mediterranean coastal territory taken from Egypt by Israel in 1967 War), 249 [chart]

GDP (Gross Domestic Product; total value of goods and services produced annually within [even by foreign owned firms] a particular nation; excludes income from foreign business operations by firms owned by that nation), 228, 231 [chart]

Gela (see Thera), 39 [chart]

Gellert, Leon (*Songs of a Campaign* - poems about his experiences during the Gallipoli Campaign in WWI), 189

General Assembly (U.N. made up of all member nations with equal vote), 227

General Secretary of the Party (head of the Secretariat and most powerful person in U.S.S.R.), 195

genetic markers (known DNA sequence associated with a particular gene or trait that is used to indicate the presence of that gene or trait, associated with certain diseases which can often be detected in the blood serum), 292

genetics (biological research to improve life), 292

Geneva Agreements (after French defeat at Dien Bien Phu in 1954, provided for an independent and neutral Indochinese states at 17th parallel), 245

Genocide (deliberate elimination of a racial or cultural group), 188 [chart], 208

George, David Lloyd (1863-1945, British Prime Minister at Paris Peace Conference), 197 [chart]

Georgia (former Soviet Republic where revolution took place, 1994), 259

German Democratic Republic (official name of East Germany, 1949-1990), 224

Germanic tribes (overran Europe in the 5th-7th C.), 48

Germany, Federal Republic of (official name after *Treaty of Final Settlement* 12 Sept. 1990 reunified E. & W. Germany, also German Empire, and Third Reich), 221

Germany divided (East - under control of U.S.S.R. and West - under control of U.S., France, & Britain), 223

Germany post-WWII (British, French, American, and Soviet Zones), 224 [map]

German surrender (8 May 1945, WWII), 210

Gestapo (German, Hitler's secret police), 206

Ghana (West African empire 7th-11th C. AD), 123, 242

ghettoes (ethnic or cultural area or neighborhood; section or

quarter imposed or evolving because of social, economic, or legal pressure; also see *barrios*), 106

Gilgamesh (Sumerian literature epic tale of heroic king), 27

Gladstone, William (1809-1898 British Prime Minister), 198

glasnost ("openness"- Gorbachev's political reform policies), 223, 257

Global Connections and Interactions (today toward the future), 280

global economy (taking into account developed and LDCs), 201

Global Positioning System (GPS, satellite navigation and guidance system giving precise [within 1 meter] latitude, longitude, and elevation), 11

Global Trading Centers; 94 [chart]

global warming (indication that the average Earth temperature is increasing due in part to human pollution of the atmosphere), 293

Glorious Revolution (Catholic James II deposed; placed Protestant William III [of Orange] & Mary II on English throne in 1688), 135

GNP (Gross National Product – total value of goods and services produced annually by a nation at home and abroad; replaced in international finance by GDP, see Gross Domestic Product)

Gnaeus Pompey (c. 70 BC, Roman consul - one of a triumvirate), 47

"Goddess of Democracy" (statue representing freedom, erected by the demonstrating students in Tiananmen Square, 1989), 237

Godfrey of Bouillon (1060-1100, 1st Crusades leader), 82

Goebbels, Joseph (1897-1945, Hitler's minister of propaganda), 206

golden age (period of intellectual and crative achievement), 32, 34 [China]

Golden Age of Chinese culture (Zhou kings after 770 BC), 32

Golden Age of Islamic culture (Abbasid Dynasty, 750–1258 AD), 72

Golden Horde, Khanate of (1223, name given to the Mongol state established in south Russia), 69

Golden Temple in Amritsar (1984, site of Sikh struggle against Indira Gandhi's forces), 241

Gomulka, Wladyslaw (1905-1982, communist, Polish head of gov't), 225

Gorazde (central Bosnian town, site of Serbian massacres of Muslims in 1994 civil war), 261

Gorbachev, Mikhail (1931- , Soviet reform president 1985-1991), 223, 257

GOSPLAN (Soviet Union's central economic decision-making agency sets production goals), 193

Gothic style (lighter, refined, architectural style found in the cathedrals and castles of later Medieval Period), 80

Goths (barbarian tribes occupied Italy and Spain 5th C.), 75

government (agency that exercises control and administration of a political unit), 14

GPS (Global Positioning System), 11

Graccus, Gaius (see Gaius Graccus), 46

Gran Colombia (short-lived union of Venezuela, Colombia, Peru, and Ecuador c. 1820), 150

grass roots rebellion (uprising from the lowest level of society, not from the gov't down), 103

Great Britain (island nation off the NW coast of Europe; nation formed by 1707 union of England, Wales, and Scotland; built world empire from 16th to 20th C.; also England and United Kingdom), 82, 97, 98, 99, 101, 104, 107-108, 129, 131, 134-136, 142, 147, 148, 151, 159, 161, 162-164, 165-167, 169-172, 185, 186, 187, 188, 189, 197, 198, 201, 202, 203, 204, 209, 210, 212, 221, 223, 224, 225, 226, 228, 229, 238, 239, 240, 241, 242, 243, 244, 248, 249,

of travelers; conductor of souls to the underworld; messenger of Zeus), 38 [chart]

Heroditus (Greek father of history), 43

Herzegovina (former part of Yugoslavia, joined with Bonia in 1991 civil war), 261

Herzl, Theodor (1860-1904, Zionist leader), 159

Hezbollah (Palestinian group commits acts of terrorism against Israel and supporters of the Jewish State), 298

Hidalgo, Miguel (1753-1811, Catholic priest began Mexican independence movement), 155

Hierarchy (ascending order of leaders)

hieroglyphics (ancient system of picture writing), 25, 118

Himalaya (Asia, world's highest mountains), 50

Hindenburgh, Paul Ludwig Hans Anton von Beneckendorff und von (1847-1934, served as a German field marshal in WWI, president of Weimar Republic), 201

Hindu Congress Party (India), 203

Hindu / Hinduism (believers of / major religion of India), 30, 34, 53, 55 [chart], 239

Hindu Influence & Spread of Buddhism to 500 AD, 56 [map]

Hindi (widely spoken native language of India)

Hindu Kush (western Himalayas, in Tajikistan to northwestern Afghanistan), 29

Hippocrates (Greek father of medicine), 42

Hippodrome (amphitheater), 65

Hiroshima (U.S. atom bomb target at end of WWII), 211 [chart]

Hitler, Adolf (chancellor, Nazi dictator of Germany 1933-1945), 206, 207 [Close Look]

Hittite Empire (E. Mediterranean; skilled crafts were widely diffused in Africa after its fall, c. 1200 BC), 27, 28, 34, 37 [map]

HIV virus (known cause of AIDS disease), 291 [+map]

Hobbes, Thomas (1588-1679, English political theorist, defended absolutism as part of natural law), 131

Ho Chi Minh (1890-1969, communist Viet Minh leader), 245

Hokkaido (Northernmost major Japanese island), 89 [map]

Hollow Men, The (written by Elliot, T.S. about WWI experiences), 189

Holocaust, Jewish (Nazi genocide against Jews, estimated 6 million killed), 207, 208

Holy Roman Empire (ruled by Charlemagne who was crowned by Pope Leo in 800 AD), 76

homage (publicly showing obeisance, honor, and respect), 78

Homer (c. 850 BC, Greek epic poet. Iliad and Odyssey), 38

homo or hominid (human-like creatures), 21

homo erectus (extinct species of human beings, regarded as an ancestor of Homo sapiens), 21

homo habilis (man earliest human remains in Africa), 21

homo sapiens (Neanderthals, early remains found in Germany's Neander Valley), 21

Homogeneous (same or similar in kind), 185

Hong Kong, 231, 238

Hong Wu (formerly Zhu Yuanzhang 1328-98, overthrew Mongol authority and launched the Ming Dynasty), 124

Honshu (largest and most developed island of Japanese group), 65

Horace (65-8 BC, Roman lyric poet, Odes and Satires have exerted a major influence on English poetry), 49

Horus (Eqyptian god of light; son of Amon-Re), 25

Huang He River Valley (see Yellow River Valley), 31, 32 [map], 34, 233

Hudson, Henry (d. 1611, English navigator and explorer who discovered (1609) the Hudson River on an expedition for the East India Company, Netherlands), 128 [chart]

Huehueteotl (Aztec fire deity, identified with the renewal of time itself), 119

Huguenots (French Calvinists), 105, 107

Huitzilopochtli (Aztec warrior-hero god), 119

Hulegu Khanate (Persia - one of four kingdoms resulting from division of Genghis Kahn's Mongol Empire), 93 [chart]

hunter-gatherer (early man, lived off the land, both meat and farming), 21

human culture (total of human knowledge and acquired behavior of humankind), 18

human geography, 12

Humanism (cultural and intellectual movement of the Renaissance that emphasized secular concerns), 100, 102

Hundred Years' War (1337-1453, France and England battled sporadically over dynastic claims in France), 98, 107

Hungarian Freedom Fighters (headed by Imre Nagy, fought Soviet troops during 1956 Hungarian Revolution), 225, 256

Hungarian Revolution (1956), 225, 256

Hungary, 225, 256

hunger (lack of sufficient nutrition for quality of life functions - good health, life expectancy), 282

Husayn ibn Ali (1854-1931, established an Arab Kingdom, angering the Zionists), 189

Hussein, Saddam (President of military council of Iraq;), 254

Hutu and Tutsis Violence (1994 flight of 2 million Hutus to Zaire, forced from Zaire in 1996, thousands died in reprisals), 270

Hyksos (foreign people of Southwest Asia), 25

hypothesis (tentative explanation that accounts for a set of facts and can be tested by further investigation, a theory), 5

I Ching (The Book of Changes [Yijing] is one of the central texts of Confucianism), 32

Iberian Peninsula (Spain and Portugal)

Ibn Buttuta (visitor to Yuan Dynasty of Kublai Khan), 94

Ibn Rushd (Islamic philosopher known in the West as Averroes, 1126-1198), 73

Ibn Sina (Islamic chemist known in the West as Avicenna, wrote Canon of Medicine c. 900 AD), 73

Iceland, 242

icons (sacred paintings), 69

ideographs (pictures used for concepts or ideas), 32

Ignatius Loyola (1491-1556, founded Jesuit missionaries), 104

ijma (Islamic law - consensus of the community - judicial precedents), 71

illegal immigrants (those that enter a country without that county's authorization), 286

Iliad (Homer's epic poem of life in the Dorian era), 38, 42

illiteracy (being unable to read and write), 289

illumination (decorating text pages with ornamental designs or lettering), 80

IMF (see International Monetary Fund), 230, 243, 251

Immigrants (settlers moving from one country to another), 167

Immigration (enter and settle in a country or region to which one is not native), 167 [Irish], 286 [to Germany]

immunization (produce immunity in, as by inoculation), 292

Imperator Caesar Agustus (r.27 BC-14 AD, "exalted" Roman emperor), 47

Imperial Eagle (Russia), 190

imperialism (policy of extending a nation's authority by territorial acquisition or by the establishment of economic and political hegemony over other people), 129, 169, 186, 221

imperialism (types of: economic, social, political), 169 [chart]

Man's Burden" - and "The Man Who Would Be King" [1889], 169 [chart]

Klee, Paul (brooding and gloomy subject artist "Death and Fire" 1940), 212

knight (medieval gentleman-soldier-tenant giving service as a mounted man-at-arms to a feudal landholder), 78

Knossos (Crete), 37

Knox, John (1514-1572, Scotland, used Calvin's ideas to found Presbyterian Church), 104

Koch, Robert (1843-1910, German medical researcher - bacteriology and diagnosing diseases), 184 [chart]

Kongo (African kingdom), 122 [chart + map]

Kongzi (also Confucius, ancient China teacher/political advisor, c. 551-479 BC), 55 [chart]

Koppen, Wladimir (1846-1940 Austrian geographer, created a system of classification of climates), 11.

Koran (also *Qur'an*, Islam's sacred text), 54 [chart], 57, 71

Korea: 18, 34, 270, 285

Korean War (1950-1953, under U.S. command; first use of U.N. army "peacekeepers"), 285

Kosovo Liberation Army (Yugoslavia 1998, Albanian province revolted against Serb gov't), 262, 298

Krishna (Hindu god of love), 30 [illus]

Kristallnacht (Night of Broken Glass, November 1938, attack on Jews by the German state), 207

kshatriyas (Hindu warrior caste), 30

Kublai Khan (13th C. Mongol-Yuan emperor of China), 64, 94

Kulaks (Russia– wealthier peasants and landowners; resisted the Bolsheviks and Stalin), 191

Kuomintang (see Guomindang)

Kurds (in Northern Iraq, people persecuted by Hussein), 255

Kush (ancient African kingdom), 122 [chart + map]

Kuwait, 255

Kwasiniewski, Alexander (communist elected in 1995 to head Poland's gov't), 260

Kyto Protocol (December 1997 Earth Summit on Global Warming, agreement [not ratified] to reduce carbon dioxide and other greenhouse gases down from the 1990 levels), 294

"La Nuit" (1958, Wiesel, Elie - Jewish writer of Auschwitz concentration camp experiences), 212

Labor Party (British; favors socialist programs), 229

laissez-faire (opposes gov'tal regulation or interference in commerce beyond the minimum), 164 [+chart]

lakes, 10

Landed aristocracy (see oligarchy; governing power of elite group)

Las Siete Partidas, Spanish code of laws that barred Jews from holding public office), 105

Lascaux (cave site near Montignac in Dordogne, France, prehistoric art on walls), 21

Latin America: 262 [+map]

Latin America immigration (to U.S.), 286

Latins (c. 1500 BC, European people who founded Rome), 45

latitude, [+map] 10

law (system of standards of conduct, obligations, and rights), 16

Lawrence of Arabia (1888-1935, T.E. Lawrence, guerrilla organizer in the Arab Revolt of 1916-1918), 189

Laws of the Twelve Tablets (c. 450 BC, basis for the Roman legal system), 46

lbadat (Islamic law, duty to god), 71

ld al-Adha (Islamic festival), 54 [chart]

ld al-Fitr (Islamic festival), 54 [chart]

LDCs (Less Developed Countries of the world, the "have nots," generally with poor economies, poor health and education, and little industrialization), 9, 225, 230, 281, 289

League of Nations (1920, world peace organization established after WWI), 17, 197, 203, 208, 227

Lebanon, 253

Lebensraum (Hitler's expansionist policy of "living space"), 208

Legalism (3rd C. BC, Chinese philosophy - punishment should be very severe for even minor offenses), 32

Legion of Honor (award established by Napoleon for those who performed important services for France), 146

Lenin (Vladimir Ilyich Ulyanov, 1870-1924; a.k.a. "Nikoli" Lenin; Marxist leader of Bosheviks in 1917 Russian Revolution), 190, 191

Leopold II (King of Belgium; established Belgian Congo colony; began the imperialist "Scramble for Africa," c. 1880s), 171

Lepidus, Marcus (d. 13 BC, consul with Julius Caesar in 46), 47

levee en masse (drafting civilians into the military), 146

li (rules of social etiquette and personal deportment), 33

Li Bo (c. 750 AD, T'ang Dynasty poet), 64

Li Peng (Chinese Premier unleashed troops on T'iananmen Square student demonstrators, 1989)

Li Si (chief minister of Shi Huangdi), 35

Li Yuan (r. 618-626, founded T'ang Dynasty), 64

Liberal (favoring proposals for reform, open to new ideas for progress, and tolerant of the ideas and behavior of others; broad-minded), 190

Liberation Tigers of Tamil Eelam (1990, Indian-Sir Lanka, separatist responsible for thousands of deaths), 298

Liberia (West Africa), 171

Libya (North Africa), 253

life expectancy (number of years that an individual is expected to live as determined by statistics), 281, 292 [chart]

Limited Nuclear Test Ban Treaty (1963; outlawed tests in the atmosphere), 226

Lipari (see Thera), 39 [chart]

Lister, Joseph (1827-1912, British medical researcher - discovered use of antiseptics to destroy bacteria), 184 [chart]

Literacy, World (condition or quality of being literate, especially the ability to read and write), 281 [+map], 289 [+map]

"Little Red Book, The" (*"Quotations of Chairman Mao"*), 235

Liu Bang (r. 210-195 BC, Liu Qi, founded Han Dynasty, 36

Liu Chi (Liu Chi, see Wudi), 36

Liu Qi (see Liu Bang, r. 210-195 BC; see also Wudi r. 141-87 BC), 36

Livy (Roman historian), 49

Locarno Pacts (1926, helped establish European boundaries after WWI), 200

Locke, John (1632-1704, English Enlightenment philosopher, *Two Treatises of Gov't,* 1690), 142 [chart], 144

Lombards (replaced Goths in Italy 6th C.), 75

L'Ouverture, Toussaint (led 1791 insurrection established Dominican Republic), 149

Long March (1934-1935, general retreat of Mao's communist forces in which 45,000 died), 205, 234 [+map]

longitude (lines of meridians dividing the Earth into 24 segments, each representing 1-hour of time), 10

Lord Castlereagh (1769-1822, English player in Congress of Vienna), 151

Louis XIII (r. 1610-1643, weak son of Henry IV), 107

Louis XIV of France (17th C. French devine right ruler), 16

[chart], 132 [illus]

Louis XVI of France (18th C. French ruler, executed by the French Revolutionaries), 145

Low Countires (Netherlands, Denmark, Holland), 163

Loyola, Ignatius (1491-1556, founded Jesuit missionaries), 104

Lucius Sulla, (c. 88 BC, Roman civil war general), 46

Lumumba, Patrice (Marxist leader in Congo [Zaire] civil war, c. 1960s), 226 [chart]

Lusitania (1917, British passanger ship sunk by German submarine, brought U.S. into WWI), 188

Luther, Martin (1483-1546, German cleric began Protestant Reformation), 54 [chart], 103

Lydians (ancient civilization of Western Turkey, seafaring traders), 34

Lytton Commission (1931, League of Nations investigation of Manchurian railroad explosion), 203, 234

MacAdam, John (1756-1836, with Thomas Telford, invented hard surfaced roads), 162 [chart]

MacArthur, Douglas General (American commander, WWII & Korea; post-war occupation of Japan), 211, 222

Macaulay, Thomas Babington (1800-1859, British historian), 159

Maccabees (139-63 BC, village priests from near Jerusalem who, in 168 BC, instigated an uprising to defend Judaism), 37

Macedonia (3rd C. BC Balkan kingdom of Philip & Alexander the Great; independent nation broke from Yugoslavia in 1991), 41, 44

Machiavelli, Nicolo (wrote *The Prince, Discourses* 1469-1527; advice on how to increase and hold power), 101 [chart], 131

Machu Picchu (Incas' famed fortress city in the Peruvian Andes), 118

magistrate (minor official, such as a justice of the peace, having administrative and limited judicial authority), 29

Magna Carta, (guarantee of rights signed in 1215 by English King John), 136 [chart]

Magellan, Ferdinand (1519-1522, Spanish explorer; expedition circumnavigated globe, claimed many Pacific Islands), 128 [chart]

magnetic compasses (instrument that uses a magnetized steel bar to indicate direction relative to the Earth's magnetic poles), 96

Mahabharata (100,000 verse epic from Sanskrit contains teaching of the Hindu god Krishna), 30, 31, 55 [chart], 64

Mahan, Alfred (American naval strategist), 186

Mahayana (Buddhism sect), 55 [chart]

Mbeki, Thabo (1942– , ANC candidate elected president of So. Africa in 1999, British education, Soviet Union military training, promarket economics, "politics before fighting"), 244

Meir, Golda (1898-1978, prime minister of Israel from 1969 to 1974), 198

Major Deities in Ancient Greece's Olympian Pantheon, 38 [chart]

Mali (ancient African state), 123

Mansa Kankan Musa (most famous of the Muslim rulers of Mali, 14th C. AD), 123

Mali (West African Islamic kingdom, c. 1200 AD), 122 [chart + map], 123

Malthus, Thomas (1766-1834, economist, philospher, writer, *Essay on the Principles of Population*, 1798), 166

Manchukuo (Chinese state "puppet" gov't of Japanese), 203

Manchuria , 203

Mandate (right or command,League of Nations authorized rule of former territories of Central Powers by Allies, to prep. for independence in post-WWI Era), 203

mandate of heaven (China, modified divine right system), 32, 36

Mandela, Nelson (1918- , So. African anti-apartheid leader; elected President, 1994), 243

Manhattan Project (U.S. scientific project to build the atomic bomb), 287

manor (district over which a lord had domain and could exercise certain rights and privileges in medieval western Europe), 77

manor house (European noble's feudal walled compound [castle]; on high ground for protection of estate's people), 77

Manorial Relationships, 78 [chart]

manorialism (relationship between lords and serfs), 77

mansa (African emperor), 123

Mansa Musa (legendary 14th C. Mali emperor in central Africa), 126

Mao Zedong (1893-1976, "the Great Helmsman," Chinese leader, established communist regime), 205, 234

Mao's Communist Revolution (plan), 235 [chart]

Marco Polo (Italian visitor to the court of Kublai Khan, 13th C.), 94

Marcos, Ferdinand (Philippine dictator, 1965-1986), 77

Marduk (chief god of Babylon, important in the reign [18th C. BC] of Hammurabi), 27

Mare Nostrum (Mussolini's expansionist program, c. 1930s), 208

Maria Theresa of Austria (1740-1780, enlightened despot), 143

Marie Antoinette (wife of King Louis XVI), 145 [illus]

Marius, Gaius (see Gaius Marius), 46

Market System (economic decisions based on free interaction of consumers and producers, minimal gov't regulation; also capitalism), 13, 15 [chart], 228

Marlowe, Christopher (Elizabethan England, poet, dramatist), 108

Marshall Plan (U.S. European Recovery Act gave assistance in rebuilding Europe after WWII;), 221, 223 [+ chart]

Martel, Charles (founded the Carolingian Dynasty, Franks' chief, turned back Muslim invaders at Battle of Tours, 8th C. AD), 76

Mary of Orange (with William, took over throne of England after the Glorious Revloution 1688), 135

Marx, Karl (1818-1883, see Marxism, author *Communist Manifesto, Das Kapital*), 165

Marx and Lenin (Key Ideas of), 192 [chart]

Marxism (socialist interpretation of history as class struggle [workers v. capitalists]), 165 [+chart], 191

"master race" (Hitler belief in Aryan racial superiority), 207

Mau Mau (Kenyan terrorist group in 1950s), 242

Maurya, Chandragupta (r. 321-297 BC, king of Magadha), 50

Mauryas (ancient civilization of India, 3rd C. BC), 34, 50 [map]

Maximillan (Austrian archduke set up by the French as emperor of Mexico, 1863), 155

Mayan Ceremonial Headdress, Mexico, 117 [photo]

Mayan Empire (50 BC - 1400 AD, Southern Mexico, Yucatan, Guatemala, Central America), 118 [chart]

Mazarin, Cardinal (chief minister who dominated the gov't during reigh of Louis XIV), 132

Mazzini, Giuseppe (1805-1872, organizer of 19th C. nationalists in Italy), 158

McCrae, John (wrote *In Flanders Fields* poem about WWI and the Callipoli Campaign), 189

Mecca (Islamic holy city, Saudi Arabia), 54 [chart]

Medellin Cartel (Colombia drug lords, led until 1993 by Pablo Escobar), 283

Medical Advances (chart of contributors), 184

Medieval Era (500-1500 AD, Europe, also considered the Feudal Era, or Middle Ages), 74

Medieval Manor (10th C. AD), 77 [illus]

Mediterranean Sea, 38

Megara (Greek mother city-state; colony Byzantium, Megara Hyblaea), 39 [chart], 65

Megara Hyblaea (see Megara)

Meghaduta (c. 400 AD, ancient sanskrit work by Kalidasa), 64

Mehmed I (Ottoman sultan), 125

Mehmed II, (Ottoman sultan who conquered Constantinople in 1453), 125

Meiji (1867-1912, transformation of feudal Japan into a modern constitutional state), 168

Mein Kampf (Hitler book, "My Struggle"), 206, 207 [close look]

Mekong (Southeast Asian river system), 22

Menem, Carlos Saul (1930- , elected Argentine president in 1989 after loss in Falklands/Malvinas Islands War with Britain), 264

mercantilism (theory and system of political economy based on national policies of accumulating bullion, establishing colonies and a merchant marine, and developing industry and mining to attain a favorable balance of trade), 129, 163 [chart]

meridian of longitude, 10 [+map]

Mesoamerica (cultural region occupied by the native people extending south and east from central Mexico to include parts of Guatemala, Belize, Honduras, and Nicaragua), 119

Mesopotamia, 22, 27, 28

Mesopotamian Civilizations (3000-144 BC), 27 [map]

Methone (see Chalcis) 39 [chart]

Metternich (1773-1859; Austrian statesman; worked to restore the pre-French Revolution European status quo and limit Prussian power), 151

mestizos (racial mixture: European colonizers of Latin America intermarried with Indians), 130, 154, 263

Mexico, and Latin America, 269

Mexican Revolution (1910-1930, begun in the 1810 struggle for independence against Spain), 155

Michael III (c. 832, Byzantine emperor), 68

Michelangelo Buonarotti (Italian Renaissance artist: *Sistine Chapel, Pieta, Moses,* and *David*), 101 [chart]

microprocessor (computer component, integrated circuit that contains the entire central processing unit of a computer on a single chip invented by Intel in 1971), 287

Middle Ages (Europe, see Medieval Period)

Middle East (Traditional name used by Western scholars for region where South west Asia and North Africa meet), 10 [map], 246, 248 [contemporary map]

Midway, Battle of (1942 sea battle considered to be turning point for U.S. in Pacific Theater of WWII), 211 [+map], 211 [chart]

Migration Patterns (current Latin American immigration), 264

Miletus, 39 [chart]

Militarism (a policy in which military preparedness is of primary importance to a state), 186, 208

millennium (thousand year period of time), 63

millet fields in China (terraced to make use of mountainous region for agriculture), 233 [photo]

Minamoto Yoritomo (r. 1192-1199 - Shogun), 91

minaret (slender tower), 73

Mines Act of 1842 (English worker safety), 165

Ming Dynasty (China, 1368-1644; restorers of traditional Chinese society), 123

Minoans (seafaring traders), 34

mir (Tsarist Russia: village community council), 153

Mir (Russian space station, launched 1986, still in service 1998),

missi dominici (Charlemagne's traveling investigators), 76

Mitchell, Senator George (former U.S. senator assisted in the June 1966 Irish peace talks between the Catholics and Protestants), 268

mixed economic system (combines elements of market and command), 13, [chart] 15, 228, 281

mixed decision-making, [chart] 15

Mobutu, Joseph (Mobutu Sese Seko, leader of Zaire, 1964-1997), 226 [chart], 270

moat (deep, wide ditch, usually filled with water, typically surrounding a fortified medieval town, fortress, or castle as a protection against assault), 77

Model Parliament (English legislative prototype, established the concept of the power of the purse in 1295), 107

Mogul (also Mughal, Mongol rulers of India, 16th-19th C. AD), 131

Mogul Rule Over India, 16th-18th Centuries, 131 [map]

Mohenjo-daro (c. 3000 BC, India's earliest civilization), 29

Moi, Daniel (2nd president of Kenya after Jomo Kenyatta), 242

moksa [moksha] (liberation from the world and union with Brahman Nerugna), 30, 55 [chart]

Molaca (see Miletus), 39 [chart]

Moltke, Helmuth von (1800-1891, German Unification leader), 158 [chart]

Molotov cocktails (makeshift bomb made of a breakable container filled with flammable liquid lighted just before being hurled), 225

Mombasa (historic East African trading city with Islamic influence),123 [photo]

monarchy (power in the hands of one), 16, 41

monastery (religious comunities bound by vows and often living in partial or complete seclusion), 80

money (exchangeable equivalent of all other commodities used as a measure of their comparative values), 23, 98

Mongol Empire; 12th-14th Centuries; 92 [map]

Mongol Impact; 93 [chart]

Mongol Golden Horde (1223, name given to the Mongol state established in Central Asia & south Russia), 69

Mongols (Central Asian nomads, extensive conquests & empires, 12th-14th centuries), 64, 92

monotheistic religion (belief in one god), 36, 53

Monroe Doctrine (U.S. 1823 policy warned European nations against re-establishing colonies in Latin America), 150

monsoons (prevailing winds in East, South, and Southeast Asia; reverses direction in summer and winter), 11, 29

Montesquieu, Baron de la Brede de (1689-1755, French Enlightenment writer), 142 [chart]

Montezuma II (Aztec ruler or tlatoani), 119

Montgomery, General Bernard L. (WWII British army commander; defeated Rommel at El-Alamein allowing Allied invasion), 210

Montenegro (S.W. Balkan nation joined with Serbia in new Yugoslavian state in 1991), 379 [+map], 261 [+map]

Moors (Christian name for Muslims), 73

More, Thomas (statesman and author Renaissance England; *Utopia*), 101 [chart]

Moroccan Crises (1905, 1911, disputes between Russia and Britian over spheres of influence in Iran), 174, 186

Morton, William (1819-1868, American medical researcher - discovered use of ether as anesthetic), 184 [chart]

Mosaddeq, Muhammad (1880-1967, also Mossadegh, Iranian nationalist leader in 1950s), 252

mosque (Islamic house of worship), 54 [chart], 73; of Sultan Selim II, 16th C., 126 [photo]

Moses (law-giver, leader of ancient Hebrew civilization), 36, 54 [chart]

moshav (Israeli gov't agricultural organization), 250

moshava (Israeli farmers working as private entrepreneurs), 250

Mothers of Plaza De Maya (Argentine mothers whose children disappeared in the "Dirty War"), 264

Mt. Fuji (a massive dormant volcano, a symbol of Japanese cultures's respect for the forces of nature), 90 [photo]

mountains, 10

Muawiyah, [Muawiya] Caliph (c. 632 AD, Sunni leader established the Umayyad Dynasty), 57, 70

muamalat (Islamic law, duty to people), 71

Mubarak, Mohammed Hosni (1928- , replaced al-Sadat as president of Egypt), 251

Mughal (Mongol rulers of India, 16th-19th C. AD), 93, 131

Muhammad (originator and major prophet of Islamic faith), 54 [chart], 57

Mujahadin (Afghan Muslim insurgents who challenged the Soviets, 1970s and 1980s), 257

mulattos (African-Caucasian intermarriage in Latin America), 130, 154

multinational corporations (MNCs; major business enterprises involved in many nations - Unilever, Mitsubishi, ITT, General Motors, Exxon,)

multinational empires (Eastern Europe autocratic empires - Russian, German, and Austro-Hungarian), 184

mummified (dead body of a human being or an animal that has been embalmed and prepared for burial, as according to the practices of the ancient Egyptians), 26

Munich "Beer Hall" Putsch (Hitler plan to take over state gov't of Bavaria), 207

Munich Conference (1938 summit meeting at which Britain and France appeased Hitler, yielding Czech territory), 209

Murad II, (Ottoman sulton), 125

Murasaki Shikibu (c. 978-1026, wrote Tale of Genji, an early novel of life among the court nobles in Japan), 90

Muslim League (agitated for partitioning of India into Hindu and Muslim sectors), 203, 239

Mussolini, Benito (1883-1945, Italian Fascist leader, 1922-1940s), 200

Mutsuhito (1867-1912, Emperor of Japan, see Meiji), 168

Mycenae (c. 1600-1100 BC, important center of Aegean civilization on the Greek mainland in the Late Bronze Age), 37

Mycenaeans (first Greek speaking people), 37, 40

Myron (Greek sculptor, 5th C. BC), 42

NAFTA (North American Free Trade Association; Canada, Mexico, U.S. trade treaty and zone)

Nagasaki (site of 2nd atomic bomb dropped by U.S. in 1945), 211 [chart]

Nagy, Imre (1896-1958, Hungarian head of gov't, attempted to become independent of U.S.S.R.), 225

Nahuatl, (Aztec language of learning that accompanied hieroglyphic writing system), 118

Napoleon Bonaparte (1769-1821, ruler of France), 146 [illus], 148 [illus]

Napoleonic Code of Laws ([Code Civil] legal system for 19th C. French Empire), 146

Napoleonic Wars (periodic warfare in Europe c. 1802-1815 Britain, Austria, Russia v. France), 147-149

Nasser, Gamal Abdel (1918-1970, nationalist leader of Egypt in 1950s), 226 [chart], 250

nation (relatively large group of people who share common customs, origins, history, and frequently language, organized under a single, usually independent gov't), 106

nation-states (political unit consisting of an autonomous state inhabited especially by a predominantly homogeneous people), 16

National Assembly (declared by the Third Estate at the beginning of the French Revolution), 146

National Congress Party (see Congress Party)

National Convention (also National Assembly; legislature in midst of French Revolution), 146

National Health Service Act (1945, British - provided free medical services), 229

National Insurance Service and National Health Service (British welfare system), 229

National Socialist German Workers Party (NSDAP, Nazi Party), 201, 206, 207 [close look]

National Unification Leaders - Italy - Germany; 158 [chart]

nationalism (belief that nations will benefit from acting independently rather than collectively, emphasizing national rather than international goals), 151, 169 [Japan], 186 [Britain, France, Germany], 221

Nationalist Party (see Guomindang; also called Kuomintang Party in 20th C. Chinese Civil War), 173

Nationalization (gov't. takeover of private enterprises), 193

Native Land Act (1913 apartheid rule forbade black South Africans to own land off reservations), 243

NATO (see North Atlantic Treaty Organization), 224 [+map]

natural law (a body of moral principles common to all humankind; Enlightenment philosophical theories), 142

natural rights of man (basic human rights theories growing out of Enlightenment Era), 142

Naxus (see Chalcis, colony associated with Greek mother city-state; colony), 39 [chart]

Nazi Germany (1920s-1940s), 205

Nazi persecution of Jews), 207-208

Nazi-Soviet Non-Aggression Pact (1939, Stalin and Hitler agree to avoid war), 208

Nazi Storm Troopers (Hitler's elite military), 206

Nazi Youth Movement (German young people, their education stressed physical fitness and obedience to state), 206

Neanderthals or Homo sapiens (early remains found in Germany's Neander Valley), 21

Nebuchadnezzar, King (c. 612 BC, built the Hanging Gardens), 27

Nehru, Jawaharlal (1889-1964, disciple of Gandhi in the Congress Party, became the 1st Prime Minister), 241

Nelson, Admiral Horatio (1758-1805; defeated Napoleon in Battle of Trafalgar), 147 [illus]

Neolithic Revolution (life began centering on agriculture), 7, 21

Nero (r. 54-68 AD, Roman emperor), 47

Netanyahu, Benjamin (1946- , Prime Minister of Israel in 1996), 250

Netherlands (includes references to Dutch colonialism), 105, 128, 132, 133,

New Deal (FDR plan for recovery from the Great Depression), 201

New Economic Policy (1921-1927, NEP; Lenin's socialist economic structure for the U.S.S.R.), 193

New Harmony (utopian living experiment by English socialist Robert Owens in Indiana, U.S.A., 19th C.), 164

New Imperialsim (c. 1870-1945, types of: economic, social, political), 169 [chart]

New Lanark, Scotland (utopian living experiment by English socialist Robert Owens, 19th C.), 164

New Spain (northern sector of Spain's American/ Caribbean empire 15th to 19th C.), 130 [+map]

New Testament (Christian scripture – the Gospels of Matthew, Mark, Luke, and John), 54

New York Stock Exchange, 201

Newton, Sir Isaac (1643-1727, universal law of gravitation), 141 [chart], 142

Ngo Dinh Diem (1901-1963, president of the Rep. of South Vietnam, 1955-62), 245

Nicaea (see Miletus), 39 [chart]

Nicaragua, 266

Nicholas I (repressive Russian Tsar 1825-1855), 152

Nicholas II (1894-1917, last Romanov Tsar during Revolutions & WWI, abdicated, killed w/family by Bolsheviks), 185, 191

Nietzsche, Friedrich Wilhelm (1844-German philosopher "Germans are best and the race must be kept pure"), 207

Nigeria (Federal Republic of), 242

Nightingale, Florence (1820-1910, British nurse - founder of modern nursing), 184 [chart]

Nile River Basin (Egypt), 251

Nine Power Treaty (pledged respect for the independence and territory of China, Open Door Policy), 203

Ninety-Five Theses (Martin Luther and reformation), 103

nirvana (Hindu cycle of reincarnation broken when one achieves a perfect state of mind), 55 [chart]

Nixon, Richard (U.S. president 1969-1973, involvement in Vietnam, reopen relations with Red China), 245

Nkrumah, Kwame (nationalist leader and first President of Ghana), 242

"no fly zones" (over Iraq, U.S. imposed areas to keep Hussein from attacking minorities), 255

"no mans land" (WWI term for the area between the systems of trenches), 187

Noh (plays of 14th C., Japanese myths and history), 92

Non Nok Tha (Thailand), 22

nomadic (life-style of constant migration, seeking food), 11, 21

non-alignment (refuse to always be on same side in all issues), 241

non-renewable resource (material, such as coal and oil, that once used can not be recycled for additional product or energy), 13

North African immigration (to France), 286

North Africa Offensive (1940-1943, WWII in Africa), 210 [chart]

North Atlantic Treaty Organization (see NATO)

North German Confederation (1866, union of German states established by Prussia after the Austro-Prussian War), 158

North/South Dicotomy (division between the "have and have-not,"), 281, 282 [chart]

Northern Hemisphere, 11 [map]

Northern Ireland (northeastern part of Ireland, majority of Protestants), 268

November Revolution (see Bolshevik Revolution

Novgorod (important trading center for the Slavs who settled along the rivers in early Russia), 68

Nubia / Nubian, 51

Nuclear Arsenals (declared and undeclared nuclear weapons), 241 [chart]

Nuclear Nonproliferation Treaty (1968; attempted to stop spread of nuclear weapons to countries not already having them), 226

Nuclear Regulatory Commission (inspects, certifies, and licenses nuclear power plants), 297

nuclear safety (question of the safety records and maintenance of nuclear power plants), 296

Nuclear Test Ban Treaty (1963), 226

Nuclear weapons, 241 [chart]

Nuremberg Laws (1935, against Jews, loss of German citizenship), 207

Nuremberg Trials (Nazi leaders tried for war crimes), 212

Oaxaco - Pre-Columbian Figure South Mexico, 117 [photo]

Obasanjo, Olusegun (1937– , freely elected president of Nigeria in 1999, People's Democratic Party, Biafra war hero, devout Baptist, religious author), 242

occupation (military guarding of conquered places by conquerors; of Japan & Germany by U.S., 1945-1952), 144, 221-223

ocean (body of salt water that covers more than 70 percent of the Earth's surface; any of the principal divisions of the ocean, including the Atlantic, Pacific, and Indian oceans), 10

Oceania (Southwest Pacific region)

Octavian (63-14 BC, 1st Roman emperor), 47

October Manifesto (issued by Tsar Nicholas II, promised more power for the national legislature [Duma], and granted basic civil liberties, 1905), 191

Odesseus (see Miletus), 39 [chart]

Odyssey (8th C. BC, Homer's epic poem of life in Dorian era), 38, 42

O'Higgins, Bernardo (Creole leader, liberated Chile, 1810-1823), 149, 150

oil crisis of 1973 (reduced supply of world raw petroleum caused big increase in oil prices), 230, 282

oil reserves (control of large oil fields and independence in Egypt [1922], Saudi Arabia [1927], Iraq [1930]), 205, 248 [graph]

Olbia (see Miletus), 39 [chart]

old regime (ancien régime, allowed the king to wield absolute power over a tight-knit social hierarchy), 145

Old Testament (of the Bible; Jewish teachings and law on moral behavior), 54 [chart]

Olduvai Gorge (Tanzania, East Africa, one of the most famous finds in modern anthropology), 21

Oleg (c. 862 AD, Varangian chief took over Kiev), 68

oligarchy (power in the hands of a small group), 16, 40, 41, 258

Omar Khayyam (c. 1000 AD, author of the Rubaiyat, Islamic poetry), 73

Olmec Empire (1200 BC-400 BC, Southern Mexico, El Salvador), 118 [chart]

One-crop economies (Latin America: coffee, bananas, or sugar), 115

"one family, one child" (China policy since the 1980s to reduce the population growth rate), 298

OPEC (Organization of Petroleum Exporting Countries; cartel of oil producing states), 248 [chart]

Open Door Policy (China open for trade), 203

Opium Wars (1839-1841, Anglo-Chinese power struggle), 172

oracle (an authoritative counselor), 38

oracle bones (c. 1600-1027 BC, inscribed animal bones on which are preserved the earliest examples of Chinese writing), 33

Orange Free State (Boer settlement after Dutch South African Cape Colony fell to British, c. 1830s), 172

ordeal (accused had to endure physically painful or dangerous tests, the result being regarded as a divine judgment of guilt or innocence), 78

Orders in Council (1807, British response to trade restrictions of Napoleonic Continental System), 147

Organization for African Unity (OAU settles disputes, promotes causes), 244

Orinoco River (northern South America), 263

Orkney Islands (Scottish islands, first inhabited by Neolithic people), 22

Ortega, Daniel (Nicaraguan President), 266

Orthodox Christian Church (also Eastern, Greek Orthodox or Orthodox Catholic Church), 67

Osiris (Egyptian god of the afterlife), 25
Ottoman Empire (major Muslim / Turk political structure from 13th-20th C.), 125 [map]
Over There (song written by George M. Cohan about WWI), 189
overproduction (to produce in excess of need or demand), 201
Ovid (Roman poet; *Metamorphoses*, c. 8 AD), 49
Owen, Robert (1771-1858, English utopian socialist, founded New Lanark, Scotland, and New Harmony, Indiana, U.S.), 164

Pacific Rim (broad term for countries surrounding the Pacific Ocean), 8, 230
Pacific Theatre in WWII, 211 [map]
pagodas (religious building of the Far East, especially a many-storied Buddhist tower, erected as a memorial or shrine), 65
Pahlavi, Muhammad Reza Shah (1910-1980, pro-Western monarch overthrown in 1978 Iranian Revolution), 252
Paine, Thomas (1737-1809, revolutionary writer, *Common Sense* [1776]), 144
Pakistan, 271
Pakistan - India Nuclear Duel (1998, India conducted nuclear bomb testing, Pakistan responded with their own tests), 271
paleontology (study of life in prehistoric or geologic times through fossil remains), 21
Paleolithic Era (Old Stone Age - 2 million to 12,000 BC), 21
Palestine (historical region of southwest Asia between the eastern Mediterranean shore and the Jordan River roughly coextensive with modern Israel and the West Bank), 45
Palestine Liberation Organization (PLO; seeks separate Palestinian Arab state in areas occupied by Israel; involved in terrorist activities), 249, 250, 254, 298
Palestinian refugee camps (700,000 Palestinians fled from Israel to neighboring states and special U.N. camps after 1948 War of Independence), 249
Pan-Africanism (movement to provide for African unity in global issues; see OAU), 244
Pan Am Flight 102 (terrorist bombing incident killed 259 passengers over Scotland, 1988), 253
Pan-Arabism (movement to provide for Arab unity in world political and economic issues), 205
Pan-Slavism (movement to provide for Slavic unity in world political and economic issues, pre-WWI), 186
Pancho Villa (1877-1923, Mexican revolutionary), 156
Pankhurst, Emmeline (1858-1928, leader of the woman's movement in Britain), 198
panna (Buddhism practice of Eightfold Path), 55 [chart]
pantheon (all the gods of a people), 38, 119
papyrus (paper-like plant leaves, used for writing), 25
parallel of latitude, 10 [+map]
parapet (earthen or stone embankment protecting soldiers from enemy fire), 77
pariahs (Hindu outcasts, slaves, later called untouchables), 30
Paris Peace Conference of 1919 (*Treaty of Versailles*), 189, 197, 202, 208
parliament (national representative body having supreme legislative powers within a state), 107
Parthenon (ancient Athenian temple), 41 [photo]
Patricians (aristroctats) rich and powerful nobles of ancient Rome), 46
Pass Laws (So. African apartheid laws made all non-whites over 16 carry passbooks restricting where they could travel and work; repealed 1984), 244

Passover (in Judaism, holiday commemorating the exodus of the Jews from Egypt), 54 [chart]
Pasteur, Louis (1822-1895, French medical researcher), 184 [chart]
Pax Mongolia (brief era of peaceful Mongol rule), 93
Pax Romana (200 year domination of ancient Mediterranean world by the Romans, golden age of Roman civilization), 47, 48
Peace of Augsburg (1555, ended twenty years of fighting between the Catholic Holy Roman Emperor Charles V and German Lutheran princes), 105
Peace of Westphalia (1648, ended the Thirty Years' War), 105
Peaceful coexistence (Khrushchev's foreign policy of minimizing confrontations with Western powers), 230, 256
Pearl Harbor (U.S. naval base in Hawaii), 211 [chart + map]
Pearl Harbor Attack (7 December 1941, Japanese surprise attack on U.S. naval base), 211 [chart]
peasant (poor tenant farmer), 77
Peasant discontent (basis for Mao Zedong's success in Chinese civil war), 234
Peasants' War (1524-1526, German peasants, small-town artisans, and laborers sacked castles and monasteries), 105
Peisistratus (c. 605-527 BC, became tyrant of Athens in 561 BC, reformer who redistributed land), 40
Peking (older spelling of Beijing; China's capital)
Peloponnesian League (of ancient Greek city-states; a military alliance formed by Sparta), 17, 40
Peloponnesian War, 41
Peloponnesus (see Mycenae), 37
Peninsula, 10
peninsulares (Iberian-born nobles who acted as crown-appointed rulers in colonial Latin America), 130, 154
peons (laborers heavily in debt to landowners), 156
Peony Pavilion, The (Ming Dynasty literary work), 125
Pepin III (c. 714-68, first Carolingian king of the Franks, father of Charlemagne, 752), 76
People's Communes (Mao's "Great Leap Forward" plan for agricultural expansion), 235
People's Republic of China (Communist regime came to power in 1949), 234
Per capita income (total national income ÷ population = share per person), 281
perestroika (Gorbachev's proposals for restructuring U.S.S.R.'s economy), 223, 257
Pergamum (ancient city founded by Greek colonists on the Aegean coast of Anatolia), 45
Pericles (ancient Greek statesman, 461-429 BC), 41 [+photo]
Peron, Juan (1895-1974 Argentine ruler), 264
Peron, Eva (1919-1952, "Evita"), 264
Perry, Commodore Matthew (c. 1853, U.S. naval commander negotiated reopening of Japan to international trade), 168
persecution (act or practice of persecuting on the basis of race, religion, sexual orientation, or beliefs that differ from those of the persecutor), 190 [chart]
Persia (see present day Iran, vast empire of southwest Asia founded by Cyrus II after 546 BC and brought to the height of its power and glory by Darius I and his son Xerxes), 37
Persian Gulf (center of oil production in Middle East), 247, 255
Persian Gulf War (1990-1991, Iraq invaded Kuwait, U.S. led coalition forces drove Hussein out), 255, 293
Persistence of Memory, The (surrealism artist Salvador Dali about WWI), 190

Peru, 118, 119

Peter the Great (Tsar, 1682-1725, Westernized Russian culture and economy), 133, 134

Petition of Right (1628 act strengthened British Parliament), 136 [chart]

Petrarch, Francesco (Renaissance literature, sonnets and love songs in Italian), 101 [chart]

petrochemical (chemical products derived from oil, plastics, fertilizers, pesticides), 290

Petrograd Soviet of Workers' and Soldiers' Deputies (1917, rival Bolshevik gov't set up against provisional gov't), 192

phalanx (blocks of infantry carrying overlapping shields and long spears), 45

pharaohs (rulers), 23

pharmacology (science of drugs, including their composition, uses, and effects), 26

Phidias (c. 490-430 BC, greatest of the ancient Greek sculptors, Phidias, renowned for the majesty of his figures), 42

Philip II of Macedonia (359-336 BC; ruler of Hellenes; father of Alexander the Great), 44

Philip II of France (1165-1223, Crusades leader), 82

Philip II of Spain (defeated by Elizabeth I of England in famous English Channel battle 1588), 132

philosophers (scholars who analyze processes of reason), 42

philosopher-kings (an educated elite group of citizens), 43

Phnom Penh (capital of Cambodia), 246

Phocaea (Greek mother city-states), 39 [chart]

Phoenicia (small group of city-states - Eastern Mediterranean Sidon, Tyre, Ugarit, beginning in 3000 BC), 50

Phoenicians (Mediterranean traders; developed an alphabet code in which each letter stood for only one distinct sound), 9, 34, 50

physical power (strongest, or best armed, holds power and offers protection to the weaker), 16

Picasso, Pablo (1937 painting of "Guernica" – outrage at German bombing of Spanish town), 212

The Pillow-Book (c. 966-1013, a diary describing court life in Japan), 90

Pindar (c. 518-438 BC, lyric poet of ancient Greece,), 43

pinnacle (small turret or spire on a roof or buttress), 26

Pizarro, Francisco (1475-1541, Spanish conquistador, conquerered Incas), 119

plain (extensive, level, usually treeless area of land), 19

plateau (elevated, comparatively level expanse of land; a tableland), 10

Platt Amendment (1902, Cuba's constitution, gave U.S. right to intervene in Cuban affairs), 265

Plato (philosopher of Ancient Greece, c. 428-347 BC), 43, 81

plebians (common people- farmers, merchants, artisans - of ancient Rome), 46

plebiscites (voters express their will on an issue directly at the polls), 146

PLO (see Palestine Liberation Organization), 249, 254, 298

poachers (those who hunt or fish illegally on the property of another or on protected lands), 295

pogroms (organized, often officially encouraged massacre or persecution of a minority group), 159, 190 [chart]

Pol Pot (d. 1998, Cambodian Premier ,violent purges, "killing fields" of 1970s), 246, 283

poleis (plural of polis) / polis (city-state), 38

Politburo (part of the Communist Party that determined policies in the U.S.S.R. and China), 195, 236

political asylum (protection and immunity from extradition granted by a gov't to a political refugee from another country), 286

political philosophers (17th-18th C. European Enlightenment: Locke, Voltaire, Montesquieu, Smith, Paine), 142

political science (study of structures, activities, and behavior of gov't), 14

pollution (contamination of soil, water, or the atmosphere by the discharge of harmful substances), 293 [+map]

polygamy (having more than one wife), 71

polytheism (belief in multiplicity of gods), 22, 55 [chart]

Pompey, Gnaeus (c. 70 BC, Roman consul, one of a triumvirate), 47

Pope (bishop of Rome and head of the Roman Catholic Church), 54 [chart]

Pope Leo (crowned Charlemagne as Holy Roman Emperor 800 AD), 76

Pope Urban II (called for a crusade to regain control of the Holy Land from the Muslim Turks in 1095), 82

Population density (number of people per square mile), 297 [+map]

Population and poverty (relationship), 297

portcullis (armored gate), 77

Portugal, 95-96 [+map], 124, 127-129, 130 [map], 147 [map], Poseidon (producer of thunder; also the earth-shaker), 38 [chart]

postwar conversion depression (1919, early 1920s period after WWI of drastic decline in the international economy), 201

posterity (future generations), 42

Potato Famine (see Great Hunger, The), 166

Potsdam Conference (1945, disagreements among WWII Allies), 212, 223 [chart]

Pottery Figures; Shi Huangdi Grave, Xi'an, China, 36 [photo]

poverty (poor, lack of the means of providing material needs or comforts), 297

power of the purse (financial control of gov't revenues), 107

power loom (invented by Edmund Cartwright), 162 [chart]

pragmatist (practical, matter-of-fact way of approaching or assessing situations or of solving problems), 107

"Prague Spring" (1968, Czechoslovakian movement to combine democracy and socialism under Alexander Dubcek's leadership), 225

pratity asamut pada (Buddhism belief suffering itself has a cause), 55 [chart]

Praxiteles (370-330 BC, Greek sculptor), 42

Pre-Columbian (ancient cultural groups included the Aztec, Maya, Mixtec, Olmec, Toltec, and Zapotec), 119

precedent (act, legal decision, or instance used as an example or standard in dealing with subsequent similar instances), 107

Presbyterian Church (Scots Calvinist sect), 104

Precedents (past actions and decisions that act as models), 71 [chart]

prehistoric (before writing), 21

PRI (Institutional Revolutionary Party established in 1929 Mexico), 156

priest-warriors, 27

primary sources, 5

Prime Meridian (zero meridian [0°], used as a reference line from which longitude east and west is measured. It passes through Greenwich, England), 10

"prime the pump" (economist Keynes plan of deficit spending to overcome economic depression), 201

Prince Henry (see Henry the Navigator)

Prince William Sound (1989, costly Alaskan oil spill), 293

princeps (first citizen), 47

principle of legitimacy (Congress of Vienna's reason for restoring the pre-1789 rulers or their heirs to power), 151

private or civil law (applies rules when one person claims that another has injured his or her person, property, or reputation), 17

Privatization (turn gov't-operated facilities into private businesses; opposite of nationalization), 228, 258, 283

pro-democracy movements (in U.S.S.R., E. Europe, 1980s under Gorbachev), 257

proletariat (poorest class composed of industrial wage earners who, possessing neither capital nor production means, must earn their living by selling their labor), 144, 165, 190

Pugachev (Russian serf rebel), 144

propaganda (use of media to promote or oppose a cause), 189

Protestant (member of a Western Christian church adhering to the theologies of Luther, Calvin, or Zwingli), 103

Protestant Defense League (PDL, Northern Ireland's protestant counter-parts to the IRA), 268

Protestant Reformation (16th-18th C. Europe religious reform), 7, 54 [chart], 102

Provisional Government (set up when Russian Tsar Nicholas II abdicated), 191

psychoanalysis (method of psychiatric therapy originated by Sigmund Freud), 183

Purge (eliminated any opposition; ex. Stalin brutally purged Soviet Communist Party in 1930s - 20 million est. dead), 195

Puritan Revolution (1642; overthrow of British monarchy), 135

Puritans (Calvinist Anglican reformers, C. 16th-17th C.), 135

Pythagoras of Samos (ancient Greek mathematician; principles of geometry, d. 500 BC), 42, 45

Q'in (Ch'in) Dynasty (221-210 BC, unified China), 19, 34, 35

Q'ing Dynasty (1644-1912, last of the "Mandate of Heaven" dynasties), 172

qiyas (cautious use of analytical reasoning in Islamic law), 71

Qaddafi, Muammar al- (1942- , Libyan leader, overthrew monarchy, 1969; involved in terrorism), 253

Quechua (spoken language of Inca), 118 [chart]

Quetzalcoatl (Aztec feather serpent, symbolic of the earth), 119

Quipu (Inca civilization; official records by knot-cord), 118 [chart]

quota (proportional share, as of goods, assigned to a group or to each member of a group; an allotment), 229

Quotations of Chairman Mao (Mao's communist philosophy), 235

Qur'an (*Koran* – Islam's sacred text), 54 [chart], 57, 71

Ra Horakhty (Egyptian sun god, later Amon-Re), 25

rabbis (Jewish religious teachers), 54 [chart]

Rabelais, Francois (French Renaissance writer: *Gargantua and Pantagruel*), 101 [chart]

Rabin, Yitzhak (Israeli Prime Minister in 1993), 249

radar (WWII invention, method of detecting distant objects and determining their position, and velocity by analysis of very high frequency radio waves reflected from their surfaces), 209

radiometric dating (measuring the age of materials by their radioactive contents), 21

raison d'état (reason of state or national security), 107

rajahs (warrior chiefs), 29

Rama (Hindu god of conquest), 30 [photo]

Ramadan (ninth month of the year in the Moslem calendar often associated with violence against Jews and Westerners), 252

Ramayana (3rd C. BC, 24,000 verse epic from Sanskrit), 30, 31, 55 [chart], 64

rampart (fortification consisting of an embankment, often with a parapet built on top), 77

Ramses II (r. 1304-1237 BC, Egyptian king [pharaoh] of the 19th Dynasty), 25

Rape of Nanking (1937, Japanese assault on Nanking, atrocities), 203

Raphael (Rafaello Sanzio, Renaissance painter, *Disputa, Sistine Madonna*), 101 [chart]

Rasputin, Gigory (1865-1916, dissolute monk, consultant to Tsarina Alexandra), 191

ratification (nations requirement to approve and give formal sanction to certain international agreements), 294

Reagan, Ronald (U.S. President 1981-1989), 254 [illus]

real cost (economic concept of looking at total cost of a decision, also "opportunity cost"), 13

recession (general business decline [falling real GDP] for 3 consecutive quarters), 282

reclamation (restoration), 26

Reconquista (13th C., Spanish European kingdoms driving out Moors), 74, 127

Red Army (secured Russia for the Bolsheviks 1917-1921, under Leon Trotsky), 192

Red Guards (Chinese students mobilized in 1960s Cultural Revolution), 235

Reds (Bolsheviks), 192

Re-flagging (registering other nation's ships as U.S. vessels to insure the safe transportation of vital supplies), 254 [illust.]

Refugee camps, 246 [photo]

regency (person or group selected to govern in place of a monarch or other ruler who is absent, disabled, or still in minority), 132

region (areas with common physical, political, economic, and / or cultural traits), 8, 10

Reign of Terror (1790s: French Revolution, the execution of between 15-45,000 opponents), 145 [chart], (1930s: U.S.S.R.), 195-196

Reich Culture Chambers (Nazi agencies established to control the work of artists), 206

Reichstag (lower house of the German parliament c. 1930s), 306

reincarnation (Hindu belief in rebirth of the soul in another form of life), 30

Reinsurance Treaty (1887, German secret agreement with Russia), 185

Remarque, Erich (*All Quiet on the Western Front* written about WWI), 189, 212

Renaissance (13th-17th Centuries European revival of classical culture), 7, 100, 102

reparations (ompensation or remuneration required from a defeated nation as indemnity for damage or injury during a WWII), 212

republic (form of gov't, representative democracy, people elect representatives to make decisions), 45

Republic, The (most famous of Plato's *Dialogues*), 43

Republic of China (Taiwan gov't) 234

Republic of Ireland (southern portion of Ireland, 92% Catholic), 268

Republic of South Africa, 172, 243

Republic of South Vietnam, 232

Republic of Singapore, 231

res publica ("the people's thing" - Roman state, republic, or commonwealth), 45

Responsibility System (instituted by Deng Xiaoping, each family was to be responsible for itself), 236

Restoration Period (rule of Charles II in 1660s after the English Puritan Revolution), 135

revenue (income, gov't income from taxes, fees), 23, 66, 107

Revisionist (one who attempted to change an accepted view of Marxism), 192

Revolutions of 1848 (throughout Europe, key revolutions in France, Austria, Germany), 152 [chart]

Rhodes, Cecil (1853-1902, British imperialist in Africa), 171 [Close Look]

Rhodes, Thera, & Samos, (Greek mother city-states), 39 [chart]

Ricci, Matteo (1552-1610, Italian Jesuit missionary involved in expansion of astronomy under Ming scholars in Beijing), 125

Richard the Lion Hearted (1157-1199, English monarch - Crusades leader), 82

Richelieu, Cardinal Armand (1585-1642, chief minister to and given full authority by, Louis XIII), 107

Rightly Guided Caliphs (a kind of Islamic "mandate of heaven"), 54 [chart]

Rio de la Plata (River of Silver in South America), 263

Rival City-States - Athens and Sparta, 40 [chart]

river, 10

Roman Catholic Church, 54 [chart]

Roman Colosseum, 47 [photo]

Roman Empire, 34, 44, 48 [map], 52 [chart]

Roman republic (res publica - "the people's thing"), 45

Romanesque and Gothic style (11th-12th C., European architecture containing both Roman and Byzantine elements, characterized by thick walls, barrel vaults, and relatively unrefined ornamentation), 69, 80

Rome, 45

Rome-Berlin-Tokyo Axis (1939; pre-WWII alliance of Italy, Germany, and Japan), 203, 208

Rommel, Field Marshall Erwin (German tank division commander in North Africa), 210 [chart]

Roosevelt, Franklin D. (1882-1945, U.S. President, 1933-45), 201

Roosevelt, Theodore (U.S. President, 1901-09), 168

rotten boroughs (19th C., places with little or no population, but represented in the British Parliament), 166

Rosh Hashana (Jewish New Year), 54 [chart]

rotation-in-service (trained soldiers returned to civilian workforce as new groups took their place), 186

Rotten boroughs (Britain - districts with little or no population and representation, 19th C.), 166

Roundheads (see Puritan Revolution in England), 135

Rousseau, Jean-Jacques (1712-1778, French Enlightenment writer), 142

Rubaiyat (c. 1000 AD, Islamic poetry by Omar Khayyam), 73

Ruhr Crisis (1923; highlighted Weimar Republic's economic problems), 200, 205

Rurik (Varangian leader, first family to rule Russia), 68

Rushd, Ibn (1126-1198, Islamic philosopher known in the west as Averroes, 1126-1198), 73

Russia (ancient civilization of easternmost Europe; spread into Central Asia under Tsars; overthrown by Bolshevik Revolution, 1917; also see U.S.S.R. and Russian Federation), 133, 258 [map]

Russian civil war (1917-1921, Bolshevik Reds v. anti-communist Whites), 192

Russian dancers (Anna Pavlova, Vaslav Nijinsky), 389

Russian Expansion; From the Late 15th C.; 133 [map], 153 [map]

Russian Federation (independent nation [1991] in E. Europe and Asia; formerly largest of the 15 republics of the Soviet Union and its center; one of the original members of the Commonwealth of Independent States [CIS]; Moscow [cap.]), 258,

Russian Orthodox Church, 67-68, 134, 152, 193

Russian Revolution of 1905 (revolt against Tsar Nicholas II in Russia), 191

Russian Revolutions of 1917, 191 [March], 192 [November]

Russification (conquered people forced to adopt Russian language, culture and religion to increase unity), 190 [chart], 196

Russo-Japanese War (1904-1905), 168

Russo-Turkish War (1877-1878), 160

Rwanda, 269

Rwanda and Tutsis violence (1959-1996, continues), 269

sabbath (seventh day of the week, Saturday, observed as the day of rest and worship by the Jews and some Christian sects), 54 [chart]

sacraments (Christian rites; Baptism, Eucharist, Mass), 54 [chart]

Sadat, Muhammad Anwar al- (1918-1981, Egyptian President, Camp David Accords, assassinated 1981), 249, 251

Sadler Report (1832, British industrialization, factory conditions), 165

Sahara (N. Africa, world's largest desert), 121-123, 295

Sahel (a drought-stricken area of West Central Africa), 295

Saint Augustine (5th C. theologian wrote The City of God), 79

Saint Benedict of Nursia (followed the Benedictine Rule which governed monks after 6th C.), 80

Saint Petersburg (Peter the Great's westernized imperial Russian capital on Baltic; also called Leningrad under communists), 134

Sakarov, Andrei (Soviet dissident and physicist sentenced to internal exile), 256

salat (Islamic ritual prescribed prayers performed five times each day), 54 [chart]

SALT agreements (U.S.-U.S.S.R. arms limitation treaties, 1970s), 226, 256

Salt March (Gandhi's non-violent protest of British tax system), 204

Samarkand (important commercial center along Silk Route), 51

Samos, Miletus & Phocaea (Greek mother city-states; colony Side, Appolonia, Istros, Odesseus, Olbia, Theodosia, Sinope, Siris, Elea, Nicaea, Agatha, Hemeroscorpian, Molaca, 39 [chart]

Samos, Thera, & Rhodes (Greek mother city-states; colony Gela, Lipari, founded kingdom of Cyrene in northeast Libya), 39 [chart]

samsara (Buddhism belief of rebirth), 55 [chart]

samurai (Japanese feudal military - professional warrior belonging to the aristocracy), 91, 168

sanctions (coercive measure adopted usually by several nations acting together against a nation violating international law), 294

Sandinistas (Nicaraguan communist guerrilla movement, ruled 1979-1990), 266

San Martín, Jose de (19th C. Creole leader - South American liberator), 149, 150

sanskrit (ancient language of India), 30

Santa Anna, Antonio Lopez de (1795-1876, four-time Mexican president/dictator), 155

Sappho (c. 630 BC, most famous woman poet of all time, known for her lyrics, born at Eressos on the Greek island of Lesbos), 43

Sarajevo (capital of Bosnia and Hercegovina, large Muslim population), 186

Sargon the Great (c. 2300 BC, Akkad leader), 27

Sassanid Empire (Persian), 63, 70

Satellite (nation and gov't dominated by an outside power;

Eastern Europe under Soviets 1945-1990), 223, 229

satellites ("spies in the skies" - instruments that orbit the Earth providing communications and data information), 288

Savak (Iran: Shah's secret police), 252

savanna (tropical or subtropical grassland [Bs]), 21, 120

sawm (Islamic fasting), 54

schism (a serious split or formal break – usually applies in religious matters), 67

scholasticism (reconciling the classical works with the teaching of the church), 81

scientific breading (researcher Robert Bakewell), 162 [chart]

Scientific socialism (see Marxism),165

Scione (see Chalcis), 39 [chart]

scorched earth policy (Russians' destroy and retreat tactics defeated Napoleon, Hitler), 148

Scramble for Africa (European imperialism in 19th C.), 171

S.E.A.T.O. (see Southeast Asia Treaty Organization)

Sea Dogs (privateers encouraged by England's Elizabeth I), 108 [illus]

seclusion policy (isolating a country from the outside world as in Japan under the Tokugawa Shoguns), 91

Second Estate (nobility), 145

Second Punic War (218-201 BC), 46

Secretariat (part of the Communist Party in the U.S.S.R. that made appointments to gov't and kept records), 195

Secretariat (U.N. - responsible for daily operations under the Secretary General), 227

sects (groups), 104

secularization (to draw away from religious orientation and to transfer from ecclesiastical or religious to civil or lay use or ownership), 198, 251

Security Council (U.N. - 5 permanent members - U.S. Russia, China, Britain, France and 10 non-permanent members), 227

seed drill (invented by Jethro Tull), 162 [chart]

Sei Shonagon (c. 966-1013, poet produced *The Pillow-Book*, a diary describing court life in Japan), 90

Seko, Mobutu Sese (a.k.a. Joseph Mobutu; leader of Zaire), 270

Seljuk Turks (11th C. conquerers of Asia Minor [Turkey]), 82

Senate, (Roman advisory body to the Etruscan kings), 45, 48

Senegal (1960 independence), 244

Sepoys (regular soldier in some Middle Eastern countries, especially an Indian soldier formerly serving under British command), 170

Sepoy Mutiny (1858, see Sepoy Rebellion, India:Hindu and Moslem mercenaries v. British), 170

Serbia (central Balkan nation in 1990s, part of Yugoslavia), 261 [+map]

Serbs (dominant ethnic group in central Balkans), 160 [map], 186-187, 261

serfs (peasants, member of a servile, feudal class of people in Europe, legally bound to the land and owned by a lord), 77

Seven Years' War (worldwide Anglo-French colonial struggle, 1757-1763), 170

Shah Jahan (1627-1658; Mughal Indian ruler, continued golden age begun by Akbar), 93

shahada (Islamic profession of faith in god), 54 [chart]

Shakti (Hindu deity), 55 [chart]

Shakuntala (ancient sanskrit work by Kalidasa c. 400 AD), 64

Shang Dynasty (first documented Chinese civilization, 1700 BC), 32 [+map]

Shang-Di (supreme deity in China), 33

Shanghai (major port of the Yangtze, China), 233, 235 [photo]

Shari'a ("the way" - Islamic moral rules are incorporated into a code of law), 54 [chart], 251

Sharpeville Massacres (1960, apartheid led to sixty peaceful demonstrators killed), 243

Shevardnadze, Eduard President of Republic of Georgia), 259

Shi Huangdi (first emperor of China), 35

Shi Ji (Records of the Historian, c. 100 BC written by Sima Qian), 36

Sieyes, Abbe (author *What is the Third Estate?*), 145

Shaka (Zulu leader in 19th C.), 171

Shikoku (major island of Japan group), 89 [map]

Shinto (religion native to Japan, characterized by veneration of nature spirits and ancetors and by a lack of formal dogma), 89

Shintoism (Japan: trad. religion), 168

Shi'ites (member of the branch of Islam that regards Ali and his decendants as the legitimate successors to Mohammed; Muslim fundamentalist sect), 54 [chart], 57, 70, 252, 254,

Shiva (Hindu deity), 55 [chart]

shogun (hereditary commander of the Japanese army who until 1867 exercised absolute rule), 91

Shotoku Taishi (573-621, created a central authority based on laws related to China's Confucian social order), 90

Si River Valley, 34

Siberia (Northern part of Asiatic region of Russia), 133 [+map], 153 [+map], 195

Siddarta [Siddartha] Gautama (Buddha, the Enlightened One), 55 [chart]

Side (see Miletus), 39 [chart]

Sidon (Phoenicia city-state), 50

Sierra Madre (cordillera in Mexico and Central America), 115, 116 [map]

Sihanouk, Prince Norodom (Cambodian ruler 1942-1963), 246

Sikhs (Hindu sect founded in the 15th C.), 241

Silk Route [Road] (merchant route through deserts and mountains of Central Asia toward Persia), 34, 51 {map]

Sima Qian (wrote *Shi Ji* [*Records of the Historian*, c. 100 BC] first major history of China), 36

Sima Xiangru (poet of Han Dynasty), 36

simony (buying or selling of ecclesiastical pardons, offices, or emoluments), 103

Sinai Desert (triangular desert peninsula that forms a land bridge between Africa and Asia in northeast Egypt), 36, (conquered by Israel in 1967 War; returned to Egypt by Camp David agreement), 249

Sinbad (ledgendary Islamic literary character), 73

Singapore, Republic of, 231 [photo]

Sinn Fein, ("We Ourselves"; Irish Nationalist Movement begun in 1905; now active as political extension of the Irish Republican Army in Northern Ireland), 268

Sino-Japanese War (First: 1894-1895), 168, 173

Sino-Soviet Relations (Red China / U.S.S.R.), 236 [map + chart]

Sinope (see Miletus), 39 [chart]

Sir Francis Drake (1541-1596, Elizabeth I's sea dog), 108

Siris (see Greek colony), 39 [chart]

Six-Day War (1967 Arab-Israeli War), 249 [chart], 251

Six Principles (Kemalism or Ataturkism), 198

Skara Brae (c. 3000 BC, Neolithic settlement located on the west coast of Mainland Island), 22

slash and burn (systematic, mechanical method of felling and clearing large tracts of forested land), 294

Slavs (occupied Balkan region 6th C., dominant E. European tribal group; ancestors of Poles, Slovaks, Czechs, Slovenes, Croats, Serbs), 75

slavery (a social system in which one individual is owned and exploited by another), 71

Sumerians (c. 3000 BC, ancient civilization in Mid East's Fertile Crescent), 29

Summa Theologiae (Thomas Aquinas [1224-1274], reconciled Christian teachings with Aristotelian philosophy), 81

Sun King (reference to France's Louis XIV's absolute power; monarch as center of all existence), 132

Sun Yixian, also Sun Yat-sen (1866-1925, early 20th C. Chinese nationalist leader; established the Republic of China), 173, 204, 205

Sundiata (13th C., Africa, Mali epic tale), 122

Sung Dynasty (see Song Dynasty)

sunna (also sunnah; way of life prescribed as normative in Islam), 57, 71

Sunnis (major Islamic sect), 54 [chart], 57

Sunn'ites (members of Islamic majority), 70

superpowers (powerful political states - U.S. and former U.S.S.R.), 221, 223, 225

Superpower Rivalries (including Vietnam, Egypt, Congo, Chile), 226 [chart]

supply (amount of resource or service available for meeting a demand), 13, 99

supranational government (gov't that extends beyond or transcends established borders or spheres of influence held by separate nations), 17

Supreme Allied Commander (title of military head of NATO), 224

Supreme Soviet (legislature of the Soviet Union), 195

surrealism (20th C. literary and artistic movement), 190

sustainable agriculture (environmentally safe farming avoids harmful pesticides and fertilizers), 290 [+map]

sustainable development (environmentalist principle allowing growth to improve life with conscious care to preserve ecology), 290

sutras (Buddha's teaching), 55 [chart]

"sweat shops" (shop or factory in which employees work long hours at low wages under poor conditions), 287

Sweden, 134

synagogue (house of worship or congregation of Jews for the purpose of worship or religious study), 54 [chart]

Syracuse (greatest Greek city in west; see Corinth), 39 [chart]

Tacitus (Roman historian), 49

Taiping Rebellion (1850-1864, Chinese national reformers against the Q'ing Dynasty), 173

Taiwan (Republic of China; stronghold of Chinese nationalists), 231

T'aizong (r. 627-649, son of Li Yuan expanded into Tibetand Central Asia), 64

Taj Mahal (magnificent Indian building of Shah Jahan's reign), 93

Tale of Genji (early novel of life among the court nobles in Japan, c. 1026), 90

Taliban Fighters (1980s movement with refugees fighting in Afghanistan supporting Sunni Muslims and Mao Zedong ideas), 253

Talleyrand, (1754-1838, French Foreign Minister who skillfully negotiated to protect France after the French Revolution), 151

Talmud (holy book of Judaic faith, knowledge, and ethics), 54 [chart]

Tamerlane (1336-1405, Timur Lenk, a Turk-Mongol who revitalized the Persian and Turkestan khanates in the 14th C.), 93

Tamils (member of a Dravidian people of southern India and northern Sir Lanka), 241

Tannenberg, Battle of (Russia v. Austria in WWI), 187 [map]

Tamozifen (drug maybe useful in prevention or treatment of breast cancer), 292

T'ang Dynasty (China; revived Confucianism, 618-907 AD), 64

T'ang Empire - [616-902 AD] & Song Empire [960-1279 AD], 64 [chart]

Tanzania, 244

Taoism (also Daoism, ancient Chinese philosophy), 32, 55 [chart]

tariffs (import taxes one country charges a duty or tax to another country to sell goods inside the first), 201

Tashkent (important commercial center along Silk Route), 51

Tata Iron and Steel Company (founded 1909, Indian-owned), 228

technological base (machines and methods of production), 185

Technology Transfer (steps to improve technology in LDCs), 290 [chart]

Teheran Conference of 1943 (WWII Allied meeting), 210, 223 [chart]

Telford, Thomas (1757-1783, with John MacAdam, invented hard surfaced roads), 162 [chart]

Ten Commandments (Judaism, basic laws), 36, 54 [chart]

Ten Hours Act (1847, British law limits work: women, children), 165

Tennis Court Oath (1789, French Revolution, pledge of delegates to the Estates General), 145 [chart]

Tenochtitlan (Aztec city-state; present site of Mexico City), 118

Teotihuacan Aztec Figure, Mexico, 117 [phjoto]

terrorism (systematic use of violence to force a group to do something), 249, 298

Teutonic invaders (1190, Germanic tribes; Vandals, Goths, Saxons, Alemanni, Franks), 48, 65

Tezcatlipoca (Aztec most powerful, supreme deity, associated with destiny), 119

Thagard, Norman (1995, first U.S. astronaut to live on board the Russian space station, *Mir*), 289

Thailand, 232

Thatcher, Margaret (British Prime Minister, 1979-1990), 229

theocracy (community, state, or gov't ruled by religious principles), 104

Theodosia (see Miletus), 39 [chart]

Theory of Relativity (Albert Einstein - time, space, and motion relative), 183

Theravada (Buddhism sect), 55 [chart]

Thermidorian Reaction (1794, French Revolution - reaction against excesses of Reign of Terror), 145 [chart]

Third Estate (the common people - bourgeoisie, proletariat, and peasantry), 144

Third Punic War, 46

Third World (economically underdeveloped nations, also LDCs), 9, 225, 230, 281

Thirty Years' War (1618-1648, last major religious struggle in Europe), 105

Three Georges Hydroelectric Program ($3 billion Chinese project to obtain energy), 233

Three Mile Island (1979 nuclear incident at Harrisburg, PA nuclear power plant), 297

Three Principles of the People, The (political beliefs of Sun Yixian), 173

Thucydides (Greek writer), 43

T'iananmen Square Massacre (by order of Deng Xiaoping's orders, Beijing, 1989), 237

Tiber River, 45

Tiberius (r. 14-37 AD, Roman emperor), 46, 47

Tighris-Euphrates (S.W. Asia cradle of civilization), 9, 27 [+map]

Timbuktu (ancient West Africa Islamic trading city), 122

Timur Lenk (see Tamerlane)

tithe (tenth part of one's annual income contributed voluntarily or due as a tax, especially for the support of the clergy or church), 80

Tito, Marshall (Josip Broz, 1892-1980, led Yugoslav guerrilla forces against Germany in WWII, became dictator after WWII), 225

Tlaloc (Aztec rain deity, identified with life-giving rain), 119

tlatoani (Aztec ruler-emperor), 118

"toilers" (1922, U.S.S.R. "workers"), 193

Tokugawa, Shogunate (1603-1867, began the seclusion policy in Japan), 91, 168

Tokugawa Ieyasu (appointed emperor in 1603, first from who the Tokugawa shoguns were descended, c. 1603-1867), 91

Tokyo (capital city of Japan), 203

Tonantzin (Aztec female earth deity), 119

Tonatiuh (Aztec sun deity), 119

Torah (Hebrew holy scripture), 36, 54 [chart]

Totalitarian government (absolutist gov't), 188, 195

Tours, Battle of (Franks stopped Muslim invasion, 8th C. AD), 76

Townshend,Viscount Charles "Turnip" (1674-1738, prominent agricultural innovator), 162 [chart]

Toxic materials and waste (dangerous poisons, chemicals, and materials), 293

traditional economic system (economic system based on past experience, custom, and religion), 13, 23

Trajan (r. 98-117 AD, Roman emperor), 48

Transvaal (one of the inland colonies established by Dutch Boers in South Africa, c. 1830), 171

Trans-Siberian Railroad (opened Russia's Siberian region to development in 20th C.), 153 [map] 154

Treaty of Brest-Litovsk (removed Russia from WWI), 192

Treaty of Kanagawa (1854, Japan-U.S. agreement, opened trade), 168

Treaty of Nanking (1842, China ceded the island of Hong Kong to Britain and opened five treaty ports to foreigners), 172

Treaty of Portsmouth (ended Russo-Japanese war, 1905), 168

Treaty of Saragossa (1529, divided Eastern Hemisphere colonial regions of Spain and Portugal), 128

Treaty of Sevres (1920, Ottoman Empire lost control of the Straits of the Dardanelles and Bosporus), 198,

Treaty of Tientsin (ended 2nd Opium War), 172

Treaty of Torsedillias (set up by Pope in 1494 to divide Western Hemisphere colonial regions of Spain and Portugal), 128

Treaty of the Union (Gorbachev agreed to give considerable self-power to the republics), 258

Treaty of Versailles (1919, ended WWI), 17, 197 [+chart], 200

Thera, Samos, & Rhodes (Greek mother city-states;), 39 [chart]

tribunes (Ancient Roman representatives of plebeians), 46

tributary arrangements (protection payments in lieu of conquest), 125

tribute (payment in money or other valuables made by a feudal vassal to an overlord to show submission or as the price of protection or security), 76, 93

Trinity (Christian belief of one god in three personifications; creator-Father, redeemer-Son, sustainer-Holy Spirit), 54 [chart]

Tripitaka (scriptural text Buddha's teaching, sutras), 55

[chart]

Triple Alliance (pre-WWI: Germany, Austria-Hungary [1879], and Italy [1882]), 185

Triple Entente (1907, pre-WWI understanding of France, Russia, and Britain), 185

triumvirate (3 person oligarchy), 47

Trojan War (c. 1300 BC, Greek principalities against Troy), 38

Tull, Jethro (1674-1741, agrarian innovator, seed drill), 162

Trotsky, Leon (major figure of Bolshevik Revolution), 192, 193

Truman, Harry S (1884-1972, U.S. President, 1945-1953; dropped atomic bombs; set up Marshall Plan), 209, 223

Truman Doctrine (1947; designed by U.S. to help Greece and Turkey resist the threats of communism), 223

tsar (title of Russian Emperor, also commonly spelled as czar and tzar), 133

tsunami (very large ocean wave caused by an underwater earthquake, underwater landslide, or volcanic eruption), 89

Tsurezure Gusa (*Idle Jottings*, 1320 kabuki theater), 92

Tudors (English dynasty, 1485-1603), 107

Turkey, 251, 253

Turkish immigration (to Germany), 286

Turks (dominant Mid East group 1450-1915 AD), 125-127; (see Ottoman Empire),

Tutsis (1990 invasion of Rwanda), 270

Tutu, Bishop Desmond (1931- , S. African anti-apartheid leader), 243

Twenty One Demands (Japanese attempt to subjugate China in the pre-WWI period), 202

Twelve Tables (c. 450 BC, codified laws of the ancient Romans), 48

tyrant (Greece, benevolent dictator supported by the Assembly), 40

Tyre (Phoenician city-state), 50

U-boats (German submarines), 209

Ugarit (Phoenician city-state), 50

Uhuru (rallying cry for African independence movement), 242

uji (ancient Japanese clan), 90

Ukraine (independent nation [1991] in E.Europe; a former republic under U.S.S.R.), 194, 296; (Stalin's ruthless suppression of peasant resistance), 195

ultimatum (a threatening final statement of terms), 187

Umayyad (also Omayyad; Muslim dynasty, 632 AD), 57, 70, 73

ummah (religious community living in accordance with the *Shari'a*), 71

underemployment (inadequately employed), 285

unemployment (not having work; jobless), 285

Unification of the German and Italina States 19th C.; 157 [map]

Unified Field Theory (Albert Einstein - explains subatomic behavior, gravitation, and electromagnetism), 183

Union of South Africa (semi-autonomous British dependency unified Cape Colony, Transvaal, and Orange Free State, c. 1910; independent Republic of South Africa, 1961), 172, 243

Union of Soviet Socialist Republics (1917-1991, U.S.S.R., or Soviet Union; also see Russia)

United Arab Republic (1958-1961, Egypt and Syria federation), 250

United Kingdom (union of England, Scotland, Wales, and Northern Ireland; see Great Britain)

United Nations 17, 226 [+chart]

United Nations Economic and Social Council (studies ways to increase cooperation among nations), 285

United Nations Education, Scientific, and Cultural Organization (UNESCO), 286, 289

United Nations International War Crimes Tribunal (brought into action in the Bosnian - Serbian civil war in the former Yugoslavia for crimes of "ethnic cleansing" and brutality), 261

United Nations peacekeepers (U.N. military actions), 226 [chart], 249, 254, 285

United Nations Resolution 242 (1967, recognized sovereignty of all states around Palestine after the Six-Day War), 249

United States Constitution, (1789, incudes the ideas of Montesquieu on the separation of powers and a check and balance system), 144

Universal Declaration of Human Rights (1948, U.N. approved basis for modern ideas on human rights), 227, 285 [+chart]

University of France (1802, established by Napoleon as a national system of education in France), 146

Upanishads (900-600 BC, latest portions of the Vedas, the sacred texts of Hinduism), 30, 64

urbanization (relocating to the cities from the country; from farm to factory, from family homes to apartments, etc.), 281, 284

usul al-fiqh (sources of Islamic law), 71

usury (in Medieval times, lending money at interest - in modern times, charging interest at an exorbitant or illegally high rate), 80

utopian socialist (Robert Owen, others in 19th C. attempted to set up ideal societies run by workers), 164

utopian society (ideal society in which the state functions for the good and happiness of all), 101 [chart], 164

V-1 and V-2 (jet-propelled bombs developed by Nazis in WWII), 209

vaisyas (Hindu herders, farmers, merchants, artisans), 30

Varangian (Scandinavian-Norse Vikings), 68, 77

varnas (social classes), 30

vassals (subordinates, knights swearing oaths of loyalty to the more powerful nobles in Medieval European feudal system), 32, 78

Vedas (holy book from Sanskrit), 30, 55 [chart]

Velvet Revolution (quiet, voluntary 1992 separation of Czechoslovakia into the Czech Republic and Slovak Republic), 260

vernacular (everyday language spoken by a people), 103

Versailles (Louis XIV's Palace outside Paris, Fr.), 132 [photo], 197; (see also Treaty of Versailles)

Vespasian (r. 69-79 AD, Roman emperor, built Colosseum), 48

viceroys (governor of a region or people, ruling as the representative of a king), 130

Victoria, Queen (r. 1837-1909, British), 198

Vietnam, Socialist Republic of, 226 [chart], 232, 245

Vietnam War, 232, 245; ("the American Phase" 1959-1975), 245; ("the French Phase" 1946-1954), 245; Troop Escalation (U.S. troops under JFK, LBJ, Nixon), 245 [graph]; U.S. Ends Involvement (1972-1975), 245 [chart]

Vietnamese "boat people," 246

Vikings (Norsemen; 8th-12th C. invading groups overran Europe), 76

Villa, Pancho (early 20th C. Mexican revolutionary), 156

Vindication of the Rights of Women, A (1792, written by Mary Wollstonecraft, British leader in the women's suffrage), 198

Virgil (Roman poet; *Aeneid*, c. 19 BC), 49

Virgin Lands Plan (1960s U.S.S.R. plan by Khrushchev for vast new state farms), 230

visas (official authorization appended to a passport, permitting entry into and travel within a particular country or region), 286

Vishnu (Hindu deity), 55 [chart]

viziers ancient (prime ministers), 24

Vladimir I (956-1015, GrandDuke of Kiev), 68

Voltaire, Francois Marie Arouet (1694-1778, French Enlightenment writer), 142 [chart]

Voting Rights, Reform Bill of: 1832, 1867, 1884, 1918, 1928, 1969 (British laws), 166 [chart]

Voyages of Exploration; 1487-1609; 128 [map]

Wagner, Richard (1813-1883, German nationlist music composer), 212

Walesa, Lech (1943- , led Polish Solidarity labor movement President of Poland 1991-1995), 260

War Communism (1917-1921, Bolsheviks' initial command economic policy in Russia during the civil war), 193

war crimes (crimes committed "in the name of war" but are atrocities beyond military action), 261

war debts (WWI German debt in excess of $47 billion), 200

War of Religion (1562-1598, involved Calvinist Huguenots), 105, 107

"war on drugs" (U.S. policy of stiff anti-drug enforcement, initiated by President Reagan), 284

Warsaw Pact (Soviet alliance of Eastern European nations), 224 [+map], 257 {dissolved, 1991]

Washington Naval Arms Conference (1921-1922, limited Japanese naval power in comparison to that of Britain, France, and the U.S.), 202 [+chart], 203

water frame (invented by Richard Arkwright), 162 [chart]

Waterloo, Battle of (final defeat of Napoleon, 1815),148

Watt, James (1736-1819, invented the steaam engine), 162 [chart]

Wealth of Nations, The (1776, Adam Smith - doctrine of laissez-faire), 164

Weimar Republic (1919-1933, weak German gov't), 200

welfare program (financial or other aid provided, especially by the gov't, to people in need), 229

welfare state (system whereby the state assumes primary responsibility for the welfare of its citizens, as in matters of health care, education, employment, and social security), 229

West Bank of Jordan (Israeli-controlled Palestinian area), 287 [+map], 249

West Germany (Allied portion of Germany post-WWII until the reunification, 3 October 1990), 222, 260

Western Hemisphere; Climatic Features; 118 [map]

Western Hemisphere (North and South America and surrounding ocean areas), 11 [map]

Western Hemisphere; Physical Features; 116 [map]

westernization (Peter the Great's attempts to emulate Europe and modernize 17th C. Russian society), 133, 134,

westernization of Turkey (centuries of attempting to incorporate Western modernization), 197, 251

White Paper of 1939 (British limited Jewish immigration to Palestine), 205

Whites (anti-Bolshevik opposition to after 1917 Rev.), 192

WHO (U.N. - World Health Organization), 227, 286, 296

Wiesel, Elie (Jewish writer of Auschwitz concentration camp experiences, "La Nuit" 1958), 212

William II (r. 1888-1918, German Kaiser succeeded Bismarck), 185, 196

William III (of Orange) and Mary II (17th C. English monarchs installed after Glorious Revolution ousted King James II), 135

Wilson, Woodrow (1856-1924, U.S. President, WWI), 196, 197 [chart]